STILL DANGEROUS!

STILL DANGEROUS!

The Harmony Hammond Reader

HARMONY HAMMOND

Edited by
Tirza True Latimer

with a Foreword by
Julia Bryan-Wilson

Duke University Press *Durham and London* 2026

Printed in the United States of America on acid-free paper ∞
Project Editor: Liz Smith
Designed by Courtney Leigh Richardson
Typeset in Garamond Premier Pro by Westchester Publishing Services

Library of Congress Cataloging-in-Publication Data
Names: Hammond, Harmony author | Latimer, Tirza True editor
Title: Still dangerous! : the Harmony Hammond reader / Harmony Hammond ; edited by Tirza True Latimer.
Other titles: Harmony Hammond reader
Description: Durham : Duke University Press, 2026. | Includes index.
Identifiers: LCCN 2026004185 (print)
LCCN 2026004186 (ebook)
ISBN 9781478038863 paperback
ISBN 9781478034001 hardcover
ISBN 9781478062479 ebook
Subjects: LCSH: Hammond, Harmony—Criticism and interpretation | Feminism and art—United States | Lesbian artists—United States | Artists—United States | Feminism in art | LCGFT: Autobiographies
Classification: LCC N6537.H345 A2 2026 (print) | LCC N6537.H345 (ebook) | DDC 709.2/52—dc23/eng/20260401
LC record available at https://lccn.loc.gov/2026004185
LC ebook record available at https://lccn.loc.gov/2026004186

Cover art: Harmony Hammond, 2019. © Clayton Porter, Santa Fe, NM.

Publication of this book has been aided by a grant from the Wyeth Foundation for American Art Publication Fund of CAA.

Contents

2. 1980s

3. 1990s

4. 2000s

5. 2010s

6. 2020–2023

Captions to Color Plates

PLATE 1 *Hair Bags*, 1972–73. Mixed media. *Top, L to R: Jenny Snider*, 8 × 8.5 in. (20.32 × 21.59 cm); *Harmony Hammond*, 3 × 7 in. (7.62 × 17.78 cm). *Middle, L to R: Sarah Draney*, 6 × 8.5 in. (15.24 × 21.59 cm); *Elizabeth Weatherford*, 5 × 10 in. (12.70 × 25.40 cm). *Bottom, L to R: Louise Fishman*, 7 × 9 in. (17.78 × 22.86 cm); *Patsy Norvell*, 7.5 × 7 in. (19.05 × 17.78 cm). Getty Research Institute, Los Angeles (2016.M.3). Photo: James Gott and John Kiffe.

PLATE 2 *Presences*, 1972. Mixed media. Dimensions variable. Installation *Harmony Hammond: Material Witness, Five Decades of Art*, Sarasota Art Museum of Ringling College of Art and Design (2020). Photo: Ryan Gamma. Harmony Hammond Core Collection.

PLATE 3 *Presence VI*, 1972. Mixed media. 80 × 33 in. (203.2 × 83.82 cm). Harmony Hammond Core Collection.

PLATE 4 *Floorpieces*, 1973. Acrylic and cloth. Dimensions variable. Installation *Harmony Hammond: Material Witness, Five Decades of Art*, The Aldrich Contemporary Art Museum, Ridgefield, Connecticut (2019). Photo: Jason Mandella. Harmony Hammond Core Collection.

PLATE 5 *Rosetta*, 1977. Oil and Dorland's Wax on canvas. 14 × 45.5 in. (35.56 × 115.57 cm). Harmony Hammond Core Collection.

PLATE 6 *Rosetta* (detail), 1977.

PLATE 7 *Collection of Fragments*, 1974–75. Mixed media. Dimensions variable. Installation, *Becoming/Unbecoming Monochrome*, RedLine Contemporary Art Center, Denver, Colorado (2014). Tia Collection.

PLATE 8 *Collection of Fragments*, 1974–75. Installation shot (close up), RedLine Contemporary Art Center, Denver, Colorado (2014). Tia Collection.

PLATE 9 *Swaddles* (detail), 1979.

PLATE 10 *Swaddles*, 1979. Cloth, gesso, Rhoplex, wood, foam rubber, and latex. 80 × 90 in. (203.20 × 228.60 cm). Denver Art Museum. Gift of Chris Connal and Kathy Hardigan (1982.246).

PLATE 11 *Hunkertime*, 1979–80. Cloth, gesso, acrylic, Rhoplex, wood, metal, and latex rubber. 81 × 192 in. (205.7 × 487.7 cm). Brooklyn Museum. Gift of Elizabeth A. Sackler in honor of Catherine Morris, Sackler Senior Curator of the Elizabeth A. Sackler Center for Feminist Art (2019.23a-i).

PLATE 12 *Farm Ghosts*, 1990. Mixed-media installational painting. 97 × 189 in. (246.38 × 480.06 cm).

PLATE 13 *Untitled (buckets)*, 1995. Oil on canvas with metal. 96 × 96 in. (243.84 × 243.84 cm). Harmony Hammond Core Collection.

PLATE 14 *Untitled*, 1995. Mixed media on canvas. In two parts: 74 × 41 in. (187.96 × 104.14 cm) each, 74 × 82 in. (187.96 × 208.28 cm) overall.

PLATE 15 *Chicken Lady*, 1989. Mixed media. 96 × 127.5 in. (243.84 × 323.85 cm). Minneapolis Institute of Art. Gift of Mary and Bob Mersky (2022.98.19A-C).

PLATE 16 *Inappropriate Longings*, 1992. Mixed-media installational painting with metal water trough and dried leaves. Left panel: 92 × 73.25 in. (233.68 × 185.42 cm). Center panel: 92h × 73 in. (233.68 × 18.78 cm). Right panel: 93 × 74.5 in. (236.22 × 187.96 cm). Tia Collection.

PLATE 17 *Suture*, 2002. Oil on canvas with metal. 90 × 149 in. (228.60 × 378.46 cm). Harmony Hammond Core Collection.

PLATE 18 *Rupture*, 2002/2016. Oil on canvas with metal. 93 × 149.5 in. (236.22 × 379.73 cm). Harmony Hammond Core Collection.

PLATE 19 *Muffle*, 2009. Oil and mixed media on canvas. 98.125 × 79.5 in. (249.24 × 201.93 cm). Harmony Hammond Core Collection.

PLATE 20 *Red Bed*, 2011. Oil and mixed media on canvas. 80.5 × 50.5 in. (204.47 × 128.27 cm). Harmony Hammond Core Collection.

PLATE 21 *Rib*, 2013. Oil and mixed media on canvas. 90.25 × 72.25 in. (229.2 × 184.2 cm). Harmony Hammond Core Collection.

PLATE 22 *Bandaged Quilt #1* (detail), 2018–19. Oil and mixed media on canvas. 72.125 × 63.375 in. (183.04 × 163.35 cm). Private collection.

PLATE 23 *Bandaged Grid #1*, 2015. Oil and mixed media on canvas. 44.125 × 76.5 in. (112.39 × 194.31 cm). Collection of Diana Bowes.

PLATE 24 *Black Cross II*, 2020–21. Oil and mixed media on canvas. 90.375 × 72.25 in. (229.6 × 183.5 cm). Collection of Catherine Montgomery.

PLATE 25 *Red Cross*, 2019–20. Oil and mixed media on canvas. 92.75 × 76.5 in. (235.6 × 194.3 cm). Tia Collection.

PLATE 26 *Patched*, 2022. Acrylic, oil, and mixed media on canvas. 84.5 × 78.25 in. (214.6 × 198.8 cm).

PLATE 27 *Chenille #7*, 2018. Oil and mixed media on canvas. 58.25 × 118.25 in. (148 × 300.4 cm). Private collection.

PLATE 28 *Chenille #7* (detail), 2018.

Editor's Note

I first became aware of Harmony's work in the 1970s, when I was a student at Sarah Lawrence College in New York. Gravitating to New York City, to the Village, I sought out lesbian-friendly sites of sociability, artistic experimentation, and political activism (like La MaMa Theatre, Judson Poets' Theater, Daughters Inc., and more than a few lesbian bars). I met people who knew people who knew Harmony, or at least knew who she was. She was already a bit of a legend within New York's lesbian feminist milieu. In the 1980s, in Berkeley, California, I bought a signed copy of her book *Wrappings* at Mama Bears, a women's bookstore up the street from where I lived. The book helped me see how lesbian feminist activism and artistic practice, including art history and criticism, could work powerfully together. In the 1990s, as a middle-aged graduate student in art history, this lesson served me well. In 2000, I taught my first real class, Lesbian Art and Theory, at the invitation of Moira Roth, then chair of the art history department at Mills College. Moira recommended Harmony's book *Lesbian Art in America* as the textbook. Around 2010 I finally met Harmony in person, and we had our first impassioned conversation about lesbian art at Kim Anno's dinner table. We haven't really stopped talking since. This anthology of Harmony's writings brings her conversations with figures across the spectrum of cultural production back to mind and back to life. Which is where they belong. Thank you, Harmony, for your writings and for the profound love of women radiating from these pages.

—TIRZA TRUE LATIMER

Foreword
Reading Harmony Hammond

JULIA BRYAN-WILSON

How do you read a legendary artist like Harmony Hammond? There are many answers to this question. In the first place: You savor the way that her artworks propose multiple meanings across the false binary of abstraction and figuration. You grapple with them as visual texts in which materiality and process hold great significance. In Hammond's capable hands, her paintings, prints, and sculptures generate an abundance of signification as she wields texture, surface incident, color, thread, grommets, braiding, fabric, scale, and pigment, just to name a few of the tools in her ample artistic toolbox. You read them as all-over propositions, in which relations are painstakingly built within a single canvas, where a tear in cloth here catalyzes your reaction to a drip of paint there.

You can also read her as a crafter of words, for Hammond is a prolific, witty, and intelligent writer whose influential exhibition catalogue texts, essays, reviews, and interviews have been at the forefront of queer feminist theory for the last five decades. Hammond's name is frequently invoked alongside the phrase "the first"—she curated the first show dedicated to lesbian art in 1978; she was an originating member of A.I.R., the first major women's cooperative gallery raised by the tide of second-wave feminism in 1972; and she wrote the first history of contemporary lesbian art in America, published in 2000, to name but a few of her firsts. Along the way, she has been a barrier-breaking advocate for trans and nonbinary folks and for those who live outside the centers of the art world, insisting on a capacious understanding of queerness that thrives everywhere, as in exhibitions such as *¿Y QUÉ? Queer Art Made in Texas* (1999). In her writing from the 1970s and '80s, she grappled with issues such as motherhood, women's form, and lesbian sexuality in alternative publications (including *Heresies*, which she helped found) and was bravely ahead of her time in terms of thinking about the intersections of class, sexuality, region, and gender. In fact, her essay "Class

Notes" (1977), in which she articulates a pointed analysis of the way privilege functions in the art world and how it compounds straight and masculinist bias, is now considered a fundamental text in queer theory.

One of her earliest pieces, "My Daughter Is Finally Napping. . . . ," appeared in 1972 in the defiantly noncommercial feminist homesteading newsletter *Country Women* alongside other texts about the importance of women's health and self-care, the joys of raising sheep, and hand-drawn diagrams about spinning.[1] In Hammond's cri de coeur, she narrates snatching a moment to theorize her own artistic practice while her child sleeps. The essay is short but full of fiery feminist anger, invoking her desire to "breakdown the distinctions between art and 'women's work,' between painting and sculpture, between art and craft." In retrospect, it functions like a road map for the artist Hammond was already in the process of becoming. She also writes that she is "not interested in art history, for its relationship to me never becomes clear." Indeed: Art history in 1972 centered Western white male artists. Why would she imagine there would ever be a place for an artist like her, a poor dyke who scavenged rags? It is only because of Hammond's activism, alongside that of her feminist colleagues, that this has changed.

Attempting to create a more expansive art history that did not yet exist for her, Hammond wrote well-researched, historically inflected essays that span topics from architecture to petroglyphs to women's tin-smithing traditions. Her art criticism, much of which was published in local publications in her chosen home of New Mexico, celebrated artists of color and Indigenous artists long before they were embraced by more mainstream venues. Bridging her status as a maker and an astute witness to others' artistic practices, she is most fascinated by the haptic and the pleasurable, penning essays on women's touch and paying close attention to material choices in her criticism and curation. She has also emphasized the damages wrought by what she identifies as cultural amnesia witnessed in her long engagement with erasure, marginalization, vandalism, and censorship.

Last, you can read Hammond; that is, you can approach her words queerly, as a "read," to use the parlance familiar to drag communities and their aficionados. Reading, which originated with queens of color, is a practice of creative critique in which cutting remarks are exchanged, with the recipient usually in on the joke. To read Hammond's early writings in this way might be to critically situate them as products of their own time, with some of the blind spots that entails. You can break down her texts in order to reevaluate them, for they hold up under scrutiny. Her prose is tough and uncompromising, yet always generous and often infused with a sly sense of humor. She herself keeps expanding her vision of the art world she wants to change, keeps revising her words, keeps making art that broadens our understanding of what and how matter means. *Still Dangerous!* is finally bringing together her world-changing writings so that we can read them, learn from them, and keep building on them.

NOTE

1. Harmony Hammond, "My Daughter Is Finally Napping. . . . ," *Country Women/ Women and Art* 1, no. 3 (1972): 10.

Introduction

Dangerous

TIRZA TRUE LATIMER

Harmony Hammond found a pink postcard in her loft mailbox in January 1976. It read:

> If you consider yourself a feminist, would
> you respond by using one 8½ × 11″ page
> to share your ideas about what feminist art
> is or could be. . . .
>
> In sisterhood,
> Ruth Iskin, Lucy Lippard, Arlene Raven[1]

Hammond dashed off her response across a sheet of graph paper.[2] The text reads like a draft of a manifesto, or notes from a workshop:

> There is no one feminist art—it can be any material, color, form, size, subject, or technique—it's a matter of consciousness
> Feminist art is by women, for women—not just about women's experience—that is sensibility that comes through in spite of—
> Feminism implies consciousness and feminist art implies a political awareness and intent expressed in the work.
> Feminist art is the form
> becoming real
> *Dangerous*[3]

This was not Hammond's first attempt to address the question. Nor would it be her last. Her interrogation reverberates within a studio practice of over fifty years and unfolds apace in writings, curatorial initiatives, interviews, and talks.

The texts by Harmony Hammond (b. 1944) selected for this volume—organized, for the most part, chronologically—enable us to appreciate how grappling with "what feminist art is or could be" remains urgent within shifting political contexts. This and related questions—such as, "What is lesbian art?" "What is queer art?" "How can abstraction carry political content?"—provide a framework for analyzing and revalorizing diverse forms of cultural expression that have been marginalized, censored, erased, or deformed by appropriation.

For feminists responding to the 1976 survey, feminist art, like feminism, meant many different things. Ruth Iskin, who directed the gallery at the Women's Building in Los Angeles, organized an exhibition of the two-hundred-some-odd responses. These included collages, prints, drawings, poems, manifestos, statements, and everything in between. "All we can know of feminist consciousness," Martha Rosler responded, "is that it is a product of one's time and place and particular position in the socioeconomically defined world."[4] According to Arlene Raven, "What feminist art is or could be is a question which remains open as long as the women's movement lives, and permits women's experience to unfold in the public arena."[5] Both Rosler and Raven took the long view and evoked feminism's evolution within changing sociopolitical conditions. This volume provides access, through Hammond's writings, to that evolution. Because the artistic, social, political, and economic environment is constantly changing, layers of meaning accrue to Hammond's writings as well as to her artworks over the decades.

Certain underlying values, the grounds of feminism, hold fast. Feminism refuses to be silenced. It challenges the values and hierarchies imposed by and perpetuating patriarchy: the subjugation of women, the denial of women's agency as producers of culture, the negation of women's sovereignty as autonomous bodies and social subjects. Women's oppression (male supremacy) rehearses all hierarchizing discourses of dominance. Speaking out against subjugation is, indeed, *Dangerous*. Dangerous for patriarchy. And dangerous for women, too, as campaigns for dominance, played out in domestic settings or on a global scale, effectively demonstrate. Feminism is a calculated—and an essential—risk. Forty-five years after receiving that pink postcard signed by three high-profile feminist art activists, and forty-four years after the display of responses at the Women's Building, Hammond received a follow-up query. Mary Savig, then curator of manuscripts at the Smithsonian's Archives of American Art (where the Women's Building papers are conserved), was restaging the 1976 pink postcard exhibition. She invited the survey's original respondents, along with some new voices, to address the same question—what is or could be feminist art?—in 2019. This time around, Hammond responded with just two words, written in bold letters, diagonally across the page: STILL DANGEROUS.[6]

Hence the title of this volume: *Still Dangerous! The Harmony Hammond Reader*. The other component of the title appears, at first, self-evident. A reader presents a selection of texts—texts, in this case, by the artist and writer Harmony Hammond. The word *reader*, though, has another denotation: It may refer to a person who reads. Or has read. Or will read.

Who reads Harmony Hammond? These texts speak to, and speak of, members of historical activist communities and their allies in the arts. Feminists. Lesbians. Queers. Artists. Critics. Curators. Because the writings are *Still Dangerous!*, they interpolate new readers (activists, teachers, students . . .). The texts contest linear master narratives of art history—and history, for that matter. They reject myths of universality and monolithic aesthetic discourse. They resist co-optation, domestication, appropriation, and relegation to the past. They resist. Period. They gesture toward readers of the future—and will do so not only "as long as the women's movement lives" but as long as "women" remain a class defined by patriarchy.

Harmony Hammond has always had multiple practices. In a conversation organized by the art historian Richard Meyer under the rubric of "Double Duty," Hammond quipped, "'Double Duty' sounds like a vacation!"[7] She is, at the very least, an artist; writer; professor emerita, University of Arizona; fifth-degree black belt in the martial art of aikido; volunteer firefighter for ten years (now retired); and a seasoned curator.[8] In each and every context, she is an activist. The writings published here attest to her centrality to both feminist art and queer art's histories.[9]

A native of suburban Chicago, Illinois, Hammond got her BFA at the University of Minnesota in 1967 and was active in the Minneapolis art scene until migrating to New York City in 1969. She became an influential figure in the nascent feminist art movement as one of the cofounders of A.I.R. (Artists in Residence), which, in 1972, broke new ground to become the first women's cooperative art gallery in New York City of the women's liberation movement era (see fig. I.1).[10] She came out as a lesbian in 1973 and walked from Christopher Street to Central Park with her three-year-old daughter on her shoulders in the Gay Pride March of June 1974.

Already a recognized artist and activist, Hammond first tried her hand as a writer in 1975 at Sagaris—an institute for radical feminist thought that convened for two five-week sessions that summer on a mountainside in Lyndonville, Vermont. At Sagaris, "a faculty of well-known lesbian, radical, cultural, and socialist feminist leaders" came together with a diverse "student body of grassroots activists and organizers from across the United States" to brainstorm about leadership, power, and feminist organizing strategies.[11] Hammond was invited to teach T'ai-chi Ch'uan during the very first session and, in exchange, could participate in all the classes. "We were given problems to solve about community organizing and leadership issues," she recalls. "I came back from that summer politicized and with organizing skills."[12] At Sagaris, Hammond also began writing "some horrible poetry" and letters to editors of art magazines.[13]

Back in New York, she brought both her newly acquired organizing skills and her evolving writing skills to the table as a cofounder, in 1976, of *Heresies: A Feminist Publication on Art and Politics* (see fig. 1.3). Her first article appeared in the inaugural issue. "It was about content in feminist abstract art, an aspect of feminist art that until recently few historians or curators have addressed."[14] Throughout the journal's first decade, Hammond regularly contributed essays "about feminist art in and from the voice of an artist activist."[15] She served as office manager for a year and coedited issues 1, 3, and 9. The third issue, "Lesbian Art and Artists" (1977, see figs. 1.4 and 1.5), stood out as a milestone in the literature of lesbian culture.

The relationships Hammond formed during this decade included a deepening friendship with the writer and independent curator Lucy Lippard. She vividly recalls their first meeting in 1970: "Word was out that there was this art historian/critic named Lucy Lippard who was going up and down stairs in loft buildings, making studio visits. She was the only one who was looking at art made by women. She eventually came to my studio."[16] And she purchased *Bag IX* (1971). This was Hammond's first sale in New York.

Hammond's artwork exemplified a category that Lippard had recently invented to describe work that deviated irreverently from the formalist rigors of minimalism.[17] What Lippard called "eccentric abstraction" was, she wrote in 1966, "allied to the nonformal tradition devoted to opening up new areas of materials, shape, color, and sensuous experience" and adhered closely to the "nature of materials and physical phenomena."[18]

The formulation perfectly describes Hammond's practice. After moving to New York, she began to explore what she calls "a third, or queer space" between painting and sculpture.[19] Her encounters with the arts of non-European cultures in the late 1960s and early 1970s opened this space. She responded on a deep level to the materials, forms, and patterns of the objects she saw displayed in European museum collections, on travels to North Africa, and in the Museum of the American Indian on Manhattan's Upper West Side. She turned away from the geometric hard-edge abstraction of the "big boys in NY," her references as an art student in the 1960s, and took painting "out of the rectangle and off the wall."[20] In the early 1970s, she began to lay the foundations for a feminist art practice that carried political content into the field of abstract painting. This practice emerged through a deep engagement with materials to participate in the narrative of modernist painting while "at the same time interrupting and revising that narrative to include voices of difference—those on the fringes, those who have been marginalized or silenced, to make work about agency."[21] Voices of difference resound not only in Hammond's studio but also in her writing, curating, and other sites of cultural activism.

Making work out of whatever materials came to hand, "making something out of nothing," Hammond built aesthetic forms through additive and repetitive processes—layering, wrapping, twining, weaving, crocheting, knitting, braiding, plaiting, needlework, all manner of traditional handiwork.[22] Renouncing the immaculate surfaces of minimalism, which bear no trace of the maker's hand, she adopted materials historically associated with women's work: repurposed scraps of fabric; curtains, blankets, bedspreads, quilts, and other domestic linens; human hair; natural fibers; and clay, referencing women's traditional creative practices such as sewing, weaving, crocheting, quilting, basket weaving, and pottery making. She initiated, in this way, the "survivor aesthetic" that continues to inform her work to this day.[23] At the same time, she began to theorize her aesthetic choices and to theorize feminist art in her writings.

In the statement written for her first solo exhibition in New York, at A.I.R. Gallery in 1973, Hammond acknowledged the stakes of her woman-centered engagement studio practice. Unlike the legendary formal leaps made by male modernists in the interests of imbuing their artworks with the potency of non-Western objects, Hammond's debt to ethnological collections was based on identification rather than usurpation:

> It is the connection to my female ancestors that provides an ethnographic content to my work, but extending this, it is also a desire to break down the distinctions between painting and sculpture, between art and "women's work," and between art in craft and craft in art. It is like trying to find a place for myself. I want to move freely between them all as if they are one, just as I want to grasp my total whole. To give form to my female feelings to give form to myself, it seems necessary to work with women's materials—cloth, thread, hair, etc.—trying to combine a sort of figurative representation with abstraction.[24]

Looking back on this period from the vantage point of the early 2000s, she reflected on the implications of the work in the historical context of its production and on how its meanings unfold over time. She identified the evolving installation piece *Collection of Fragments*, first presented at Carlo Lamagna Gallery in New York City in 1976, as a touchstone of her practice, "central to all my work."[25] The installation *Collection of Fragments* (1976; figs. I.1 and I.2; see plate 7) incorporated a vitrine, simulating those used by ethnographic museums, containing baskets and sandals woven by Hammond, clay shards Hammond made and

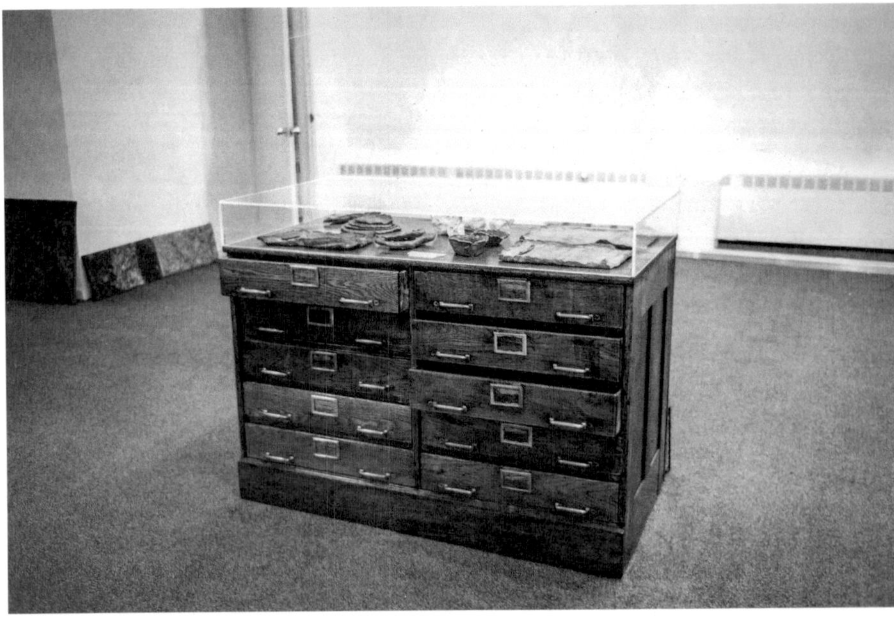

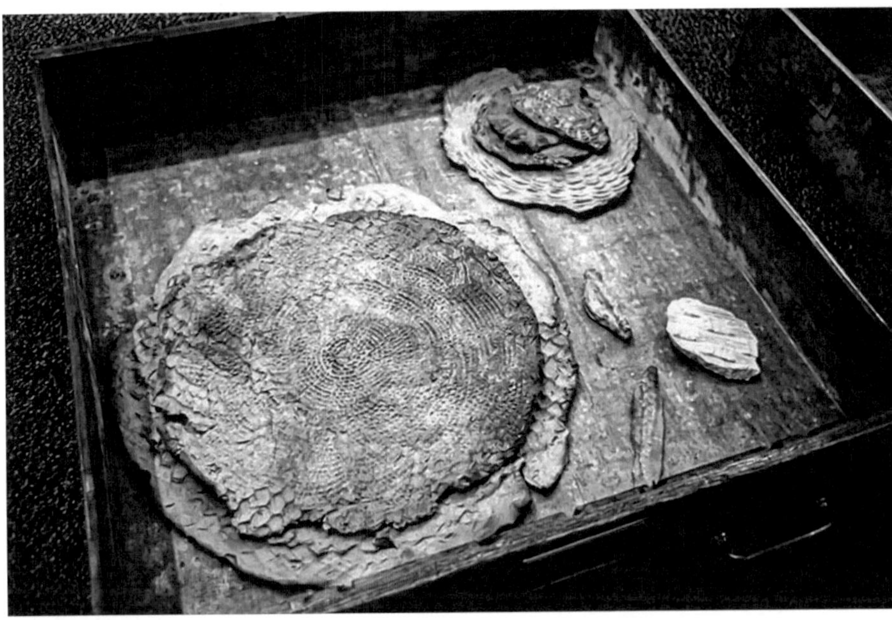

FIGURE I.1. Harmony Hammond, *Collection of Fragments*, 1975/2014. Dimensions variable. Original installation at Carlo Lamagna Gallery solo exhibition, 1976. Tia Collection.

FIGURE I.2. Harmony Hammond, *Collection of Fragments* (detail), 1975.

imprinted with basket and sandal weaves, and a captioned postcard (ca. 1910) picturing a "Moki woman making pottery." Museum-style labels identifying the artist as the maker accompanied these "fragments" along with a text: "Baskets are the Indian Woman's poems, the shaping of them her sculpture. They wove into them the story of their life and love."[26] Nearby, Hammond placed a few of her thickly textured *Weave Paintings* (see plates 5 and 7) in dialogue with the installation. Over time, these paintings from the 1970s became part of the installation, not displayed-along-with but integral to it. The paintings merge formal abstraction with political content arising out of marginalized creative histories.[27]

The Lamagna Gallery artist's statement (fig. I.3), an amalgam of citations and affirmations, reads like a poem itself. Or a belief statement. It speaks to and about the "fragments" on display. It is an ode to the fragment, "A piece of a whole. A record and impression of a creative moment" and the process by which one innovation leads to another, work builds out of work, and a generative core survives.[28] The statement opens and closes with this epigraph: "Women made the first basketry and pottery. They smeared the outside of their baskets with clay or pitch so the baskets would hold water and keep it cool. Later when the baskets grew old, they were discarded in the fire and the women saw that the clay (pot) remained."[29] Hammond's statement—indeed, her writing generally—is as recursive as weaving, basketmaking, and pot making. It affirms both transformation and an indestructible core.

Collection of Fragments pieces together a narrative of women's creative practices and positions Hammond's work within that narrative. At the same time, with the conceit of ethnographic museum display, Hammond crossed fine arts and craft divides to interrogate the museum's implication—through its collection, labeling, documentation, and display conventions—in the creation and validation of dominant cultural histories and artistic hierarchies. In multiple ways, this installation serves as a metaphor for Hammond's practice; its material and written components concurrently participate in, and engage critically with, her cultural heritage. All of it.

In 1978, Hammond organized *A Lesbian Show* (see figs. 1.6–1.9), the first exhibition in New York City devoted exclusively to art by artists courageous enough to show their work under the heading "Lesbian." If they experienced threats and professional backlash, they also reaped significant rewards (building solidarity and community, breaching isolation and silence, affirming and celebrating). For a few weeks, the show transformed 112 Greene Street, an alternative art space in SoHo, into a lesbian cultural epicenter. *A Lesbian Show* included performances, poetry readings, film, video, and discussions on lesbian art and politics. Events included an evening open house for *Heresies: A Feminist Publication on Art and Politics* and an open slideshow of work by lesbian artists in the

WOMEN MADE THE FIRST BASKETRY AND POTTERY. THEY SMEARED THE OUTSIDE OF THEIR BASKETS WITH CLAY OR PITCH SO THE BASKETS COULD HOLD WATER AND KEEP IT COOL. LATER WHEN THE BASKETS GREW OLD, THEY WERE DISCARDED IN THE FIRE AND THE WOMEN SAW THAT THE CLAY (POT) REMAINED.

THE RITUAL SITUATION GIVES IMPORTANCE TO THE MATERIAL.

THE FRAGMENT - A PIECE OF THE WHOLE. A RECORD AND IMPRESSION OF A CREATIVE MOMENT. AN OBJECT THAT NOW TAKES A SPACE BUT RECORDS A TIME AND SPACE OF AN UNKNOWN CREATOR. THE OBJECT THAT TAKES THAT SPACE IS SEPARATE FROM THE MOMENT YET EMBODIES THE RITUAL AND A NEW RITUAL EVOLVES OUT OF THE REMAINS OF THE OLD. THE REMAINING FRAGMENT OF A CREATIVE MOMENT THAT ONCE EXISTED.

FRAGMENT/WHOLE
MOVING THROUGH THE WHOLE

A LINE IS NOT FLAT. THINK OF EDGE NOT ONLY AS A LINE ON A PLANE DIVIDING TWO SPACES, BUT ALSO AS A LINE MOVING THROUGH SPACE, CONNECTING NOT DIVIDING. THE PAINTING SURFACE AS EDGE. EDGE AS FORM, CARRIER OF MEANING.

FRAGMENT/WHOLE
THE FORM BECOMING REAL

THE SHAMAN IN ECSTATIC TRANCE IS CAPABLE OF DESCENDING INTO THE UNDERWORLD OR ASCENDING TO THE SKY BY THE SACRED TREE GROWING AT THE MIDPOINT OF THE EARTH. THE CENTER IS A POINT NOT ON, BUT IN. THE PSYCHIC AND METAPHYSICAL BALANCE OF THE SHAMAN GIVES HIM THE ABILITY TO CROSS OVER FROM ONE WORLD INTO ANOTHER. HE MUST NOT HESITATE, MUST NOT FOCUS ON THE EDGE. HE DEMONSTRATES THIS CONCEPT OF "HAVING BALANCE" BY FLYING FROM ROCK TO ROCK AT THE EDGE OF A HIGH WATERFALL. BEGINNING "...A SERIES OF SPECTACULAR AND VERY DANGEROUS RAPIDFIRE LEAPS...FROM ONE ROCK TO ANOTHER, WITH ARMS OUTSTRETCHED, OFTEN LANDING INCHES FROM THE SLIPPERY EDGE... HE WOULD SUDDENLY MAKE A GREAT LEAP TO THE OTHER SIDE OF THE RUSHING WATER NEVER BETRAYING THE SLIGHTEST CONCERN THAT HE MIGHT LOSE HIS BALANCE AND FALL INTO SPACE." THE CONCEPT OF METAPHYSICAL EQUILIBRIUM.

THE SHAMAN - FORM BECOMING REAL

WOMEN MADE THE FIRST BASKETRY AND POTTERY. THEY SMEARED THE OUTSIDE OF THEIR BASKETS WITH CLAY OR PITCH SO THE BASKETS COULD HOLD WATER AND KEEP IT COOL. LATER WHEN THE BASKETS GREW OLD, THEY WERE DISCARDED IN THE FIRE AND THE WOMEN SAW THAT THE CLAY (POT) REMAINED.

Statement by Harmony Hammond, January, 1976 for exhibition at the Lamagna Gallery. Source material: Indian Basketry, George Wharton James, Dover. 1972, and "The Roots and Continuities of Shamanism," Peter T. Furst. Arts Canada. December, 1973.

FIGURE I.3. Harmony Hammond, statement for solo exhibition at Carlo Lamagna Gallery, New York, 1976.

interest of constructing a lesbian art archive. Hammond's press release made the show's ambitions clear: "In order to validate lesbian experiences, it is important that lesbian artists become visible to each other as well as to the women's community, the art world, and people outside the art world. Until we have visibility, we cannot begin to explore [. . .] the role and implications of lesbian culture in a larger social and political context."[30]

Hammond's book *Wrappings: Essays on Feminism, Art and the Martial Arts* (see fig. 2.2), published by Time and Space Limited (TSL) in 1984, furthered this mission. A collection of texts by Hammond on feminist art, *Wrappings* presents unpublished essays, pieces previously published in *Heresies*, select artist's statements, examples of her earliest exhibition and book reviews, drawings, and photographs of artworks (hers as well as those of other artists).[31] *Wrappings* became a foundational reference, and many of its essays have been repeatedly anthologized. With its ever-expanding web of connections to other publications and other readerships, *Wrappings* established Hammond as a writer.

The year 1984 proved pivotal for another reason as well: Hammond left the New York scene for northern New Mexico. "I liked the landscape, the wide-open space. I like the cultural mix. I like the toughness and the outlaw sensibility."[32] Although she originally intended to stay for a year, she has now lived in New Mexico for over four decades: "There's something about this big space that gives everybody room to be who they think they are. Historically that's been true for women. If they didn't fit into the social structures on the East Coast, and they didn't have money to go to Europe, they went west. So there's this history of women, especially writers, anthropologists, and photographers who came west. They could smoke cigarettes. They could wear pants. They could swear. They could do whatever. Many were bisexual or lesbian. The West—it's outlaw territory. I'm just assuming that's one reason I feel quite comfortable."[33]

The juxtaposition of different creative traditions, long generative for Hammond as an artist, characterizes the Southwest, crossroads of Native, Hispanic, and Euro-American peoples. Intercultural dynamics animate her critical writings and curation as well as her art making at this time.[34] In the studio, she staged "uneasy juxtapositions" that increasingly questioned "artistic appropriation and cultural gentrification, my part in it as well as others" and opened spaces for dialogue and negotiation.[35]

In 1989, Hammond settled in the Galisteo Basin, territory east of Santa Fe that still bears traces of its Tano/Tewa heritage and Spanish colonial occupation.[36] She made her home in an old stone barn used by generations of sheep ranchers for the storage of wool. She constructed a studio on the land where she could make large-scale paintings, store artworks, and stock materials. The character of the materials she scavenged and incorporated in her paintings changed with the surroundings and with the increased storage capacity her home, studio, and acreage provided. Mexican and New Mexican tin lighting fixtures, candlesticks, and frames lined up on her mantel and windowsills. Rescued corrugated metal roofing, buckets, gutters, and bits of rusted farm equipment accumulated outside the studio awaiting transformation. Hammond's hallmark "near-monochromes" owe much to the Southwestern environment as well. They are as monochromatic as the desert—that is to say, not at all. The longer you look, the more color, texture, and life you see.

In Galisteo, Hammond began conducting research for *Lesbian Art in America: A Contemporary History* (see fig. 4.1).[37] She described it as "the book that was missing," a book about lesbians, lesbian artists, and their history, which "wasn't written down anywhere."[38] The first version began with a chapter devoted to the long history of women loving women in the arts, but Hammond ultimately chose to focus on contemporary artists, post-Stonewall, who embraced the term *lesbian* and addressed sexual politics in their work. Drawing on her personal archives and networks expanded in the course of curatorial initiatives, artist talks, workshops, residencies, conferences, and her tenure as cochair of the College Art Association's Queer Caucus for Art in the mid-1990s, she visited the studios of at least a hundred self-identified lesbian artists over a ten-year period. *Lesbian Art in America* earned a Lambda Literary Award the year it was published and remains a primary text on the subject.

Lesbian Art in America and other writings from the 1990s and early 2000s elaborate a number of recurrent themes, all highly political: identity politics in relation to cultural production; visual and material strategies for imbuing artworks with historical and political content; forms of resistance to censorship and silencing; the political agency of art (whether abstract or figurative—or some combination of both).

At the turn of the new millennium, Hammond responded vigorously to the censorship campaigns that characterized the culture wars (orchestrated right-wing fundamentalist attacks on federal funding for the arts that inspired acts of violence against feminist artists, queer artists, border artists, artists of color, and their works). She produced overtly political work such as *Speaking Braids* (2001–2; see figs. 4.4 and 4.5) and *A Queer Reader* (2003; see fig. 5.7) that intentionally dealt with queer and feminist issues such as voice/voicelessness, censorship, and historical erasure. At the same time, she strove to redress the prevailing "cultural amnesia" (within queer communities as well as the mainstream) about feminism's generative legacy.[39]

As she approached the age of seventy, in the 2010s, a new preoccupation came to the fore in Hammond's writings and public presentations: archival preservation. She urged women artists to take responsibility for indexing and archiving their work and for writing their histories.[40] Her own experience as a lesbian feminist cultural historian made her keenly aware of the challenges of conducting research on marginalized subjects when no secondary sources exist and primary materials are not conserved in public archives. She became a persuasive advocate for archiving and preserving one's life work and actively participating in the creation of historical memory.

Over decades rife with feminist struggles for visibility and cultural recognition, Hammond has consistently affirmed her commitment to making art "that is FOR something and not a reaction against" and to "creating a continuous female presence" in the arts and in the world.[41] The same is true of her writing.

While each text in this volume has its own impact and historical resonance, the cumulative effect reveals the trajectory of ideas forming, evolving, and contributing, over time, to cultural change. The complex interrelationships among Hammond's multiple practices come into focus. We see how her writing practice lays the ethical and theoretical foundations for her studio practice, creates the conditions of possibility for her work's reception, and opens pathways for the future of feminism. Her studio work, in turn, materially grounds the writings. In this back and forth, we see feminist consciousness "becoming real," as predicted by Hammond in her response to the 1976 questionnaire about what feminist art is or could become. The reader illuminates all stages of Hammond's development as an artist, writer, activist, and curator. Selected texts are presented chronologically under the decades of Hammond's output: 1970s, 1980s, 1990s, 2000–2009, 2010–19, 2020–23 (the date we finalized the table of contents). This chronological structure renders period debates vivid while fully contextualizing Hammond's artistic production and reception during these decades. These texts, like Hammond's artworks, "participate in multiple narratives," to use a phrase oft repeated by the artist, who sees her work "as contributing to both dominant and oppositional discourses." They trace the development of career through lines: the impact of martial arts on Hammond's art and philosophy; the materialization of female bodies and histories in works of abstraction; the different forms of antipurism that shape Hammond's "survivor aesthetic"; the valorization of the cast-off, the cast out, the fugitive, the fleeting; the staging of "uneasy juxtapositions"; the affirmation of female creative practices; social abstraction in theory and practice; acts of resistance to the censorship/silencing of queer, two-spirit, nonbinary, and trans artists as well as women; the importance of "organizing and participating in local and regional queer exhibitions with emerging and upcoming artists, to occupy space, to continue being visible!"[42]

Many of these texts have not been previously published. Some are composed from drafts or notes for oral presentations, or transcripts of recorded interviews.

A number of the previously published texts have been reprinted elsewhere (some more than once); we chose in most cases to present the original, first-published version. Certain texts have been abridged or excerpted to reduce repetition across the volume, and many of these have been edited to enhance flow, clarity, and continuity.

Hammond insists that she is neither an art historian nor a theorist—despite her contributions in these areas. She identifies, rather, as "a thinking, writing, visual artist whose approach to talking about content in visual art—whose critical thinking and visual analysis—were heavily influenced by feminisms and feminist process."[43] While historical context and theory are hugely important, "it all starts with the artwork itself."

This volume "presences" Hammond's artworks by incorporating a generous insert of color plates and a range of black-and-white images reproducing page art, facsimiles of statements, documentary photographs, and photographs of artworks. In most cases, the images do not illustrate the texts but rather provide a visual thread that runs alongside, and sometimes intertwines with, the writings, decade by decade. While Hammond's visual practice and writing practice are intimately interrelated and impossible to discuss responsibly in isolation, this volume is the first since the publication of *Wrappings* in 1984 to prioritize her written and spoken words—which are *Still Dangerous!*

NOTES

1. Lucy R. Lippard, invitation to Ruth Iskin, January 23, 1976, Woman's Building records, 1970–92, Archives of American Art, Smithsonian Institution, https://www.aaa.si.edu/collections/items/detail/lucy-r-lippard-invitation-to-ruth-iskin-22468.

2. "Harmony Hammond Response to 'What Is Feminist Art?,'" ca. 1976–77, Woman's Building records, 1970–92, Archives of American Art, Smithsonian Institution, https://www.aaa.si.edu/collections/items/detail/harmony-hammond-response-to-what-feminist-art-12891.

3. Emphasis here and throughout the volume is that of the author.

4. Martha Rosler, quoted by Mary Savig, "What Is Feminist Art?," *Archives of American Art Journal* 60, no. 1 (2021): 64.

5. Arlene Raven, quoted by Savig, "What Is Feminist Art?," 64.

6. What Is Feminist Art? questionnaire responses, 2019, box 1, folder 19, Archives of American Art, Smithsonian Institution, https://www.aaa.si.edu/collections/what-feminist-art-questionnaire-responses-21690.

7. "Double Duty," panel presentation, roundtable organized by Richard Meyer, University of Southern California, Los Angeles, 2012.

8. Hammond curated or cocurated eleven exhibitions from 1968 to 2012. She organized *Contemporary Graphics Published by Universal Limited Art Editions*, Dayton's Gallery 12, Minneapolis, 1968; *A Lesbian Show*, 112 Greene Street Workshop, New York,

1978; *Home Work: The Domestic Environment as Reflected in the Work of Women Artists*, sponsored by the New York State Council of the Arts (NYSCA) and the Women's Hall of Fame, Seneca Falls, New York, 1981; cocurated, with Jaune Quick-to-See Smith, *Women of Sweetgrass, Cedar and Sage* at the American Indian Community House Gallery, New York, 1985, Wheelwright Museum, Santa Fe, New Mexico, and other venues; cocurated, with Catherine Lord, *Gender, Fucked: An Exhibition Made by Lesbians About Gender*, Center on Contemporary Art, Seattle, 1996; curated *Material Girls: Gender, Process and Abstract Art Since 1970*, Gallery 128, New York, 1997; curated *Queer Video Screening*, VOID, NYC, sponsored by the Center for Lesbian and Gay Studies of City University of New York and the Gay and Lesbian Caucus of the College Art Association, 1997; with the Curatorial Committee of Queer Caucus for Art, College Art Association, organized *Troubling Customs* at Ontario College of Art and the Design and School of Boston Museum of Fine Arts, 1998; curated the exhibition *Out West* and *Out West Queer Video*, a program of single-channel videos that accompanied the exhibition at Plan B Evolving Arts, Santa Fe, 1999; curated *¿Y QUE? Queer Art Made in Texas*, Landmark Arts, Texas Tech University, Lubbock, 2007; cocurated the solo exhibition *Erasing Censorship*, in collaboration with three different cocurators at three different venues—the first with Christopher Reed at Lake Forest College, Lake Forest, Illinois, 2007; the second with Simon Taylor at Left Coast Books, Goleta, California, 2011; the third with Eve Fowler at Artist Curated Projects, Los Angeles, California, 2018; she also curated *Material Engagements*, RedLine Contemporary Art Center, Denver, in 2012.

9. Hammond's studio practice participates hand in glove with her writing practice in the development of these fields; her artworks were featured in groundbreaking feminist and queer exhibitions, such as *The Great American Lesbian Art Show* (Woman's Building, Los Angeles, 1980), *Extended Sensibilities: Homosexual Presence in Contemporary Art* (New Museum, New York, 1982), *In a Different Light* (University of California Berkeley Art Museum, 1995), *Sexual Politics* (Hammer Museum, Los Angeles, 1996), and *Wack! Art and the Feminist Revolution* (MOCA, Los Angeles, 2007–9).

10. Gallery 15, founded in New York City in 1958, preceded A.I.R. as a cooperative art gallery featuring work by women. Harking even further back, to the first-wave feminist movement, Argent Gallery opened in New York City under the aegis of the National Association of Women Painters and Sculptors in 1889 and remained active in the first four decades of the twentieth century.

11. Harmony Hammond, interview by Julia Bryan-Wilson (excerpts), September 14, 2008, Archives of American Art, Smithsonian Oral History Program; audio recording and full transcript, accessed May 30, 2024, https://www.aaa.si.edu/collections/interviews/oral-history-interview-harmony-hammond-15635.

12. Hammond, interview by Bryan-Wilson.

13. Hammond, interview by Bryan Wilson.

14. Hammond, interview by Bryan-Wilson.

15. Hammond, interview by Bryan-Wilson.

16. Hammond, interview by Bryan-Wilson.

17. *Eccentric Abstraction*, Lucy Lippard's groundbreaking 1966 exhibition of postminimalist works at the Fischbach Gallery in New York City, brought together artists who were trained as painters and then moved into three dimensions.

18. Lucy Lippard, "Eccentric Abstraction" (1966), in *Changing: Essays in Art Criticism* (New York: Dutton, 1971), 98–99.

19. Harmony Hammond, "Harmony Hammond's Ongoing Revolution," interview by Nancy Zastudil, *Hyperallergic*, June 9, 2024, https://hyperallergic.com/924019/harmony-hammond-ongoing-revolution/.

20. Harmony Hammond, statement for the exhibition *How American Women Artists Invented Post-Modernism*, curated by Judith Brodsky and Ferris Olin, Mason Gross School of Art Galleries, Rutgers University, December 2005–January 2006; Harmony Hammond, "Writings on the Seventies, Arrival in New York, Blankets, Bags, Presences, Floorpieces, Weave Paintings, and Fragments," unpublished statement, 2006.

21. Hammond, "Harmony Hammond's Ongoing Revolution."

22. Harmony Hammond, email message to author, March 19, 2022.

23. Hammond, "Writings on the Seventies."

24. Harmony Hammond, unpublished statement dated 1972, written for Hammond's first solo exhibition in New York, at A.I.R. gallery in 1973.

25. Harmony Hammond, email to author dated September 3, 2023. Due to a typographical error, the name *Lamagna* is misspelled in the original statement, reproduced along with *Collection of Fragments* in the volume introduction (see fig. I.3). *Collection of Fragments* (see figs. I.1 and I.2) has evolved over the years from its first presentation in 1976 at Lamagna Gallery in New York City to its display in *Becoming/UnBecoming Monochrome* at RedLine Contemporary Art Center, Denver, 2014. The configuration displayed at RedLine included weave paintings on the wall. Which weave paintings and their placement in relation to the vitrine is flexible, as is the exact selection of woven and clay fragments. The labeling, too, has varied slightly from installation to installation. The piece was recently acquired by Tia Collection in Santa Fe.

26. The Navajo School of Indian Basketry, *Indian Basket Weaving* (1903; reprint, New York: Dover, 1971), was a reference for this text, but the wording is Hammond's.

27. Hammond, "Writings on the Seventies."

28. Harmony Hammond, statement, Lamagna Gallery, New York City, 1976.

29. Hammond, statement, Lamagna Gallery. Hammond reproduced this statement in her book *Wrappings: Essays on Feminism, Art, and the Martial Arts* (New York: TSL Press, 1984).

30. Harmony Hammond, press release for *A Lesbian Show*, 1978.

31. One review reproduced, first published in 1977 in *Women Artists Newsletter*, discusses Lucy Lippard's book *From the Center: Feminist Essays on Women's Art* (1976).

32. Hammond, interview by Bryan-Wilson.

33. Hammond, interview by Bryan-Wilson.

34. In this volume, see Harmony Hammond, book review, "*The Arts of the North American Indian: Native Traditions in Evolution*, [edited] by Edwin L. Wade," *Southwest Contemporary Arts* 11, no. 2 (1987): 57–59; and Harmony Hammond, book review, "*Frida: A Biography of Frida Kahlo* by Hayden Herrera," *13th Moon* 8, nos. 1 and 2 (1984): 218–26. In 1985, Hammond cocurated, with Jaune Quick-to-See Smith, the first national survey of contemporary Native American women artists, *Women of Sweetgrass, Cedar and Sage*, at the gallery of the American Indian Community House, New York. The exhibition traveled to eight additional venues across the country by the end of 1986.

35. Harmony Hammond, interview with Neery Melkonian, *THE Magazine*, October 1992, 12.

36. See Lucy Lippard, *Down Country: The Tano of the Galisteo Basin, 1250–1782* (Santa Fe: Museum of New Mexico Press, 2010).

37. Harmony Hammond, *Lesbian Art in America: A Contemporary History* (New York: Rizzoli, 2000).

38. Hammond, interview by Bryan-Wilson.

39. See, in this volume, Harmony Hammond, "Against Cultural Amnesia," *Art Papers*, November 1994, 9–11.

40. In 2016, the Getty Research Institute announced the acquisition of Hammond's archive.

41. Harmony Hammond, "Affirming the Existence of the World of Images," in *Wrappings: Essays on Feminism, Art, and the Martial Arts* (New York: TSL Press, 1984), 109–10.

42. Hammond, "Harmony Hammond's Ongoing Revolution."

43. Harmony Hammond, email message to author, November 1, 2023.

Preamble

Art History

Art Journal (1996)

It all has to do with her work. The specificity is important. This is part of her story. The '60s. Minnesota. Two young artists. Married. He's gay and knows it. She's gay and doesn't know it. They remain married for seven years. She can't understand what's wrong. They are victims of pre-Stonewall and pre-feminist isolation. How to convey the intensity and desperation of the period in which her art was made? She painted larger-than-life-sized hermaphrodites. No one talked about the content. She writes:

> The last few years in Minneapolis, I hung out with fags, diesel dykes, and transvestites at their bars, dinners, and parties, and shopped for clothes at gay male stores (leather and faux leather pants and jackets, Jimmy Dean T-shirts with rolled up sleeves). Of course, the dykes thought that if he was, she was . . . and she was, only she didn't know it. All I knew was that this camp world was much more fun than anything else in those days and a

lot safer. In identifying with [Jean] Genet's *Our Lady of the Flowers*, I was a sexual being of sorts—perverse, a martyr, fascinated, and turned on by it all. In the meantime, while sharing (rarely sexually) my husband—who thought that he was "sick"—with his boyfriends, I thought if I could just be a better wife, he would no longer have "this problem," and we could have better sex and a better marriage. He drank. I tailored his shirts and learned to cook French and Indonesian. Nothing helped. Neither one of us got *it*. And there was no one, no context to help us *get it*. Thank God, I had my art, the one thing I could trust and count on. The one thing that didn't go away.

When we moved to New York in 1969, he went into therapy. Then we did. Then I did. Then we found that I was pregnant with our child and we parted ways. I had my daughter Tanya and continued making art. I went to a CR [consciousness-raising] group and had a fit at the first meeting when Louise [Fishman] and Esther [Newton], the one couple in the group, thought they deserved special attention because they were gay. I circled around the Firehouse (just doors from A.I.R.) and hung out at Bonnie and Clyde's (the Duchess was older, more middle-class, and decidedly more boring), identifying myself as a lesbian years before I had actually made love with a woman. Louise, Esther, and the women I met through them were a big influence. Judith [Friedlander] and I finally got it together, rather pleasurably I might add, in 1973. I was, to use [the words of] Bertha [Harris], in love with the "lesbian brain"—not to mention lesbian bodies. So, to simply say that I was married and then came out in the WLM [women's liberation movement] just doesn't tell the story.

ED. NOTE

"Art History" was first published in the "We're Here: Gay and Lesbian Presence in Art and Art History" issue, *Art Journal* 55, no. 4 (Winter 1996): 78–79.

Art Journal 55, guest edited by Flavia Rando and Jonathan Weinberg, was the first College Art Association (CAA) publication devoted entirely to lesbian and gay themes. The thematic issue grew out of a session at the CAA annual conference, "Who's Building the Closet? Visual Culture and Art Historical Suppressions," sponsored by the then newly formed Gay and Lesbian Caucus of CAA. Hammond's piece, a coming-out story that factors in art making, told in the third and first person, past and present tense, complexifies the conventions of two genres: the coming-out narrative and the artist biography. A detail from Hammond's piece *Burden* (1995) accompanied the text.

1

1970s

Editor's Introduction

In 1969, a couple of months after the Stonewall rebellion, Hammond migrated from Minneapolis to New York City. Her studio practice and her activism advanced in tandem. She and nineteen other feminists founded A.I.R. (Artists in Residence) Gallery in 1972 (fig. I.1) to provide a permanent exhibition space for women artists in an era when commercial galleries predominantly showed men. Her first solo show in New York opened at A.I.R. Gallery in 1973 (fig. I.2). The statement for this launch sets the agenda for feminist art practice.

Hammond's writings, activism, and exhibitions of the 1970s established interrelated formal and feminist agendas: valorizing traditional female crafts and exploring abstraction's feminist potential. Her text-based page art, textile-based *Bags*, *Presences* (see plate 2), and *Floorpieces* (see plate 4) body forth interrogations of genre and gender incubated within her consciousness-raising group. In parallel, her writings both perform and theorize modes of genre crossing.

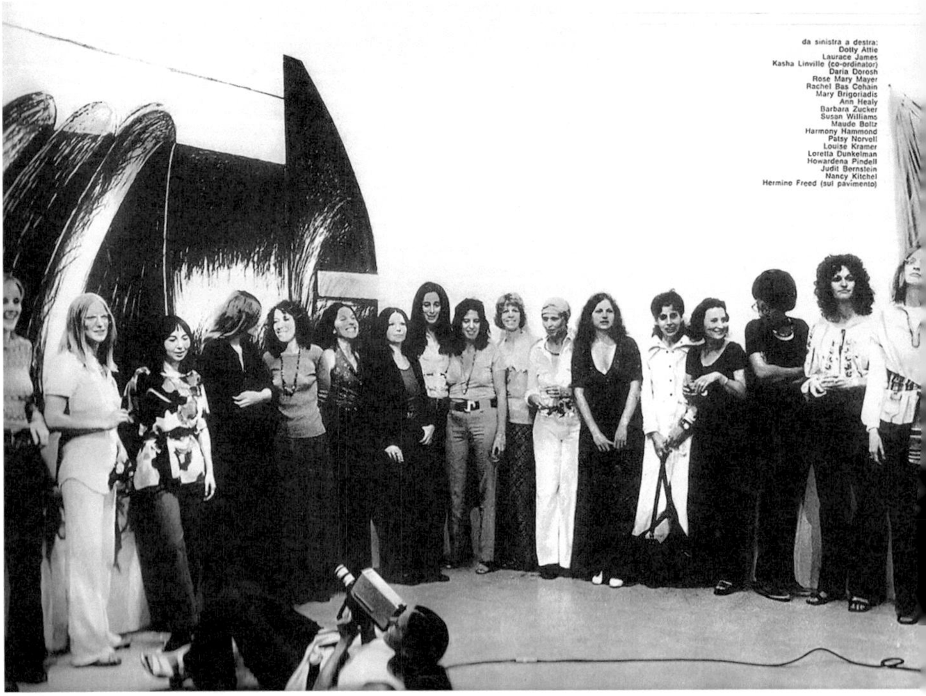

FIGURE 1.1. A.I.R. members at the opening of A.I.R. Gallery at 97 Wooster Street, New York, September 16, 1972. *L to R:* Laurace James, Kasha Linville (gallery coordinator), Daria Dorosh, Rosemary Mayer, Rachel bas-Cohain, Mary Grigoriadis, Ann Healy, Barbara Zucker, Susan Williams, Maude Boltz, Harmony Hammond, Patsy Norvell, Louise Kramer, Loretta Dunkelman, Howardena Pindell, Judith Bernstein, Nancy Kitchel. Hermine Freed, videographer, prone. Four founding members of A.I.R. do not appear in this version of the photograph: Dotty Attie, Blyth Bohnen, Agnes Denes, Nancy Spero. The artists' names listed in the upper right-hand corner of the picture include some misspellings, corrected above. A.I.R. is now located in DUMBO (acronym for the area in Brooklyn "Down Under the Manhattan Bridge Overpass"—on the East River between the Brooklyn and Manhattan bridges). It is the longest-running alternative space for women artists in the United States. Photo: Linda J. Gustas.

The decade saw the publication of Hammond's earliest exhibition reviews and critical writings. In 1977, she became a member of the mother collective for *Heresies: A Feminist Publication on Art and Politics* (fig. 1.3), and her written contributions to the journal brought an artist's perspective to bear on the development of feminist criticism and lesbian art (figs. 1.4 and 1.5).

In 1978, her pathbreaking curatorial initiative *A Lesbian Show* at 112 Greene Street Workshop in New York City (figs. 1.6–1.9) brought lesbians together

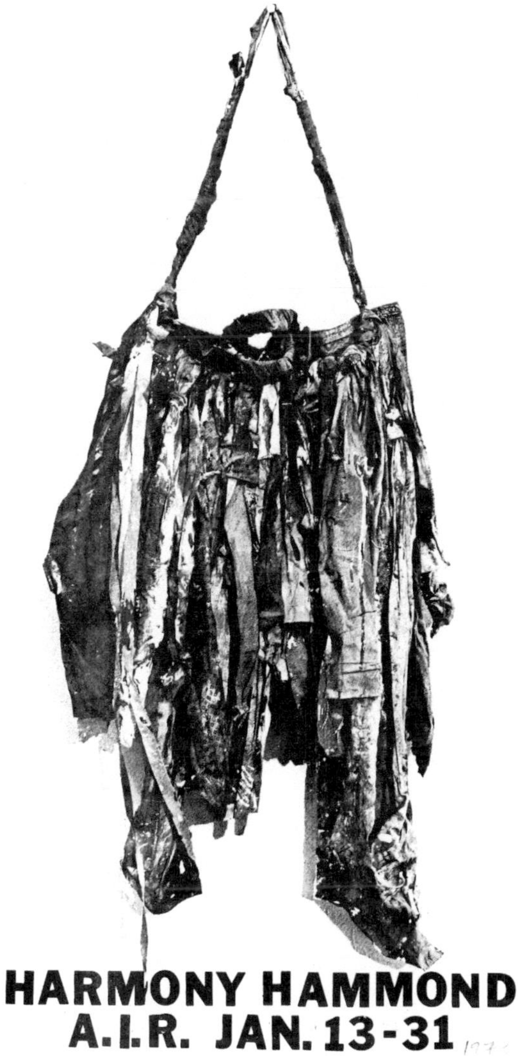

FIGURE 1.2. Exhibition announcement, depicting *Bag VI*, for Harmony Hammond's first solo show in New York, at A.I.R. Gallery, January 13–31, 1973.

as a visible cultural community and demonstrated the vigor and diversity of their creative practices. From the start, Hammond's writings about lesbian and feminist art rejected sexuality-based essentialism as a viable interpretative lens, arguing that even works by lesbian feminist artists exploring the erotic imagination do so strategically, with politically expressive aims.

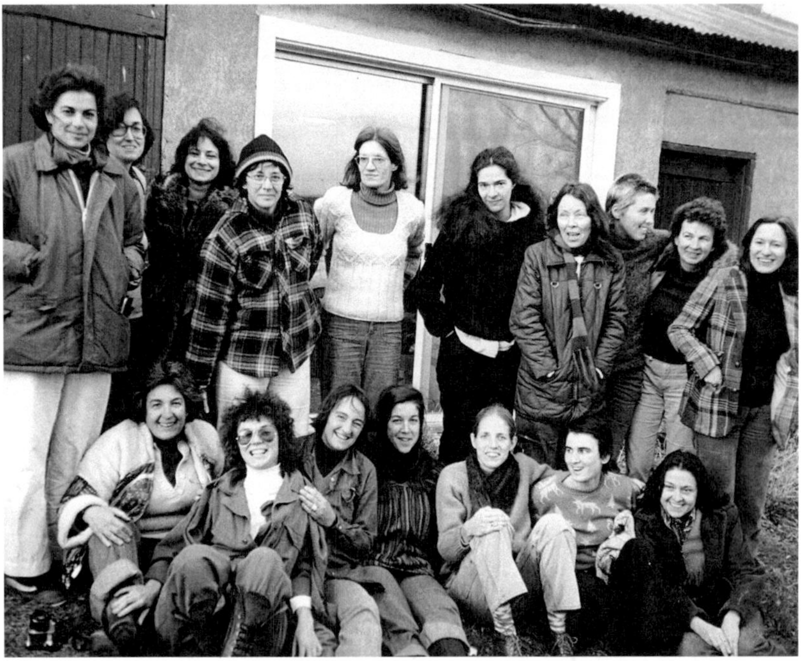

FIGURE I.3. *Heresies* founding collective members (referred to as the "mother collective") at Joan Snyder's Pennsylvania farm, 1976. *Front, L to R:* Miriam Schapiro, Mary Beth Edelson, Lucy Lippard, Joan Braderman, Elizabeth Weatherford, Mary Pottenger, Michelle Stuart. *Back, L to R:* Mary Miss, Joyce Kozloff, Arlene Ladden, Joan Snyder, Patsy Beckert, Elizabeth Hess, May Stevens, Harmony Hammond, Sally Webster, Susana Torre. Cofounders not pictured in this informal group portrait: Elke Solomon, Pat Steir, Nina Yankowitz. Photo: © Mary Beth Edelson. Courtesy Estate of Mary Beth Edelson and Accola Griefen Fine Art.

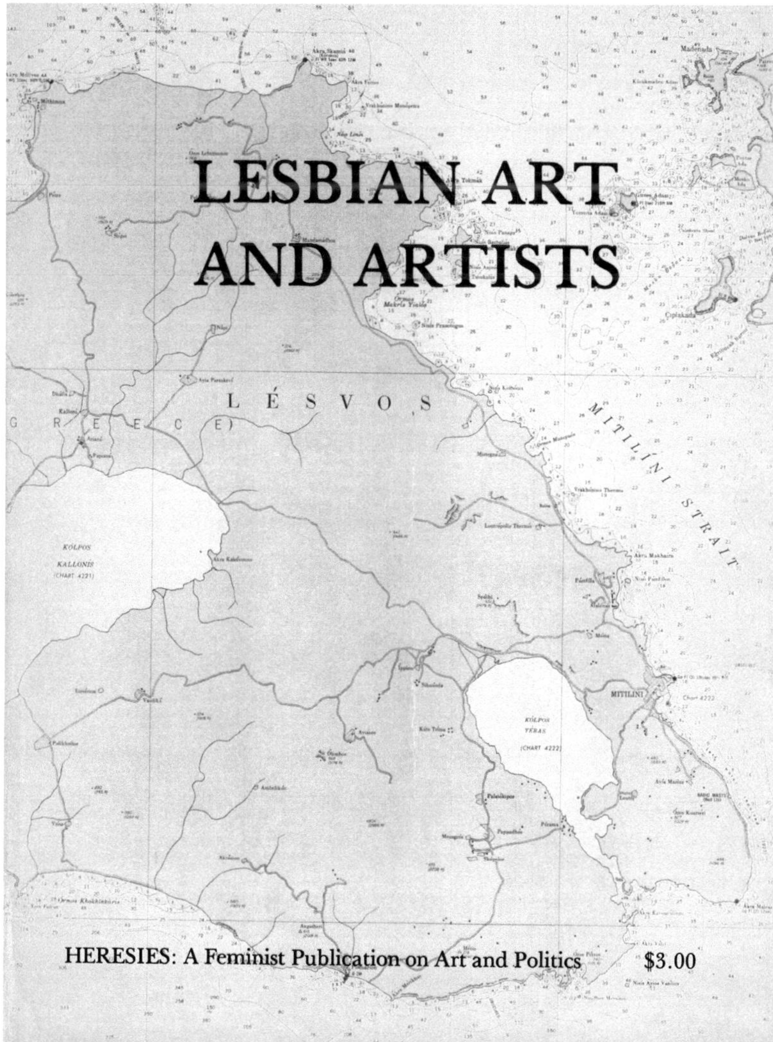

FIGURE 1.4. "Lesbian Art and Artists," *Heresies: A Feminist Publication on Art and Politics*, no. 3 (Fall 1977). Cover designed collaboratively by the issue's editorial collective. They chose to use a map of the Greek island Lesbos (Lesvos) for this issue devoted to lesbian culture and lesbian culture makers. The archaic lyric poet Sappho, a native of Lesbos, has been an important reference and inspiration within lesbian culture historically. The map of Lesbos on the cover of the "Lesbian Art and Artists" issue graphically locates the origin of terms for women-loving women: "sapphists" and "lesbians."

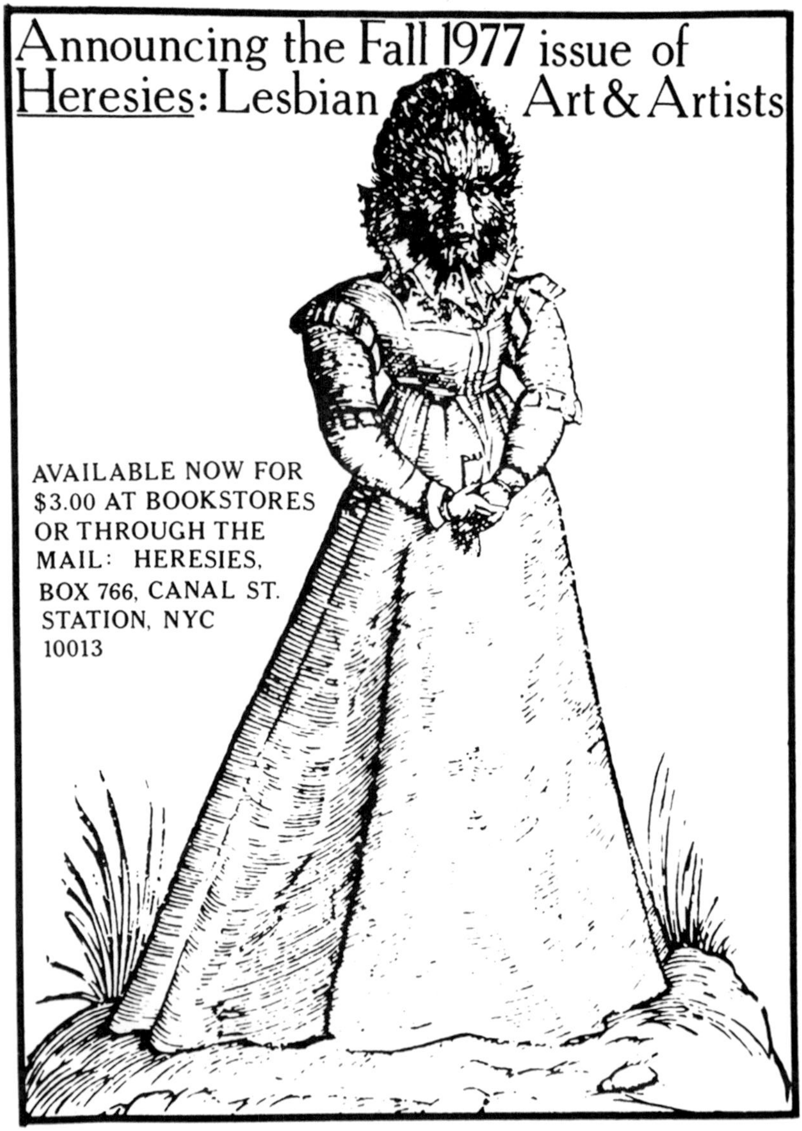

The lion-headed Barbara Urselin, born in 1641 in Augsburg, from Aldrovandus' *Opera Omnia Monstrum Historia*, 1668.

FIGURE 1.5. Collaboratively designed announcement for "Lesbian Art and Artists," *Heresies: A Feminist Publication of Art and Politics*, no. 3 (Fall 1977). The announcement features an image that embodies difference. The engraving from 1668 portrays Barbara Urselin, a woman who was considered a monster and put on display because of the golden hair that grew all over her body.

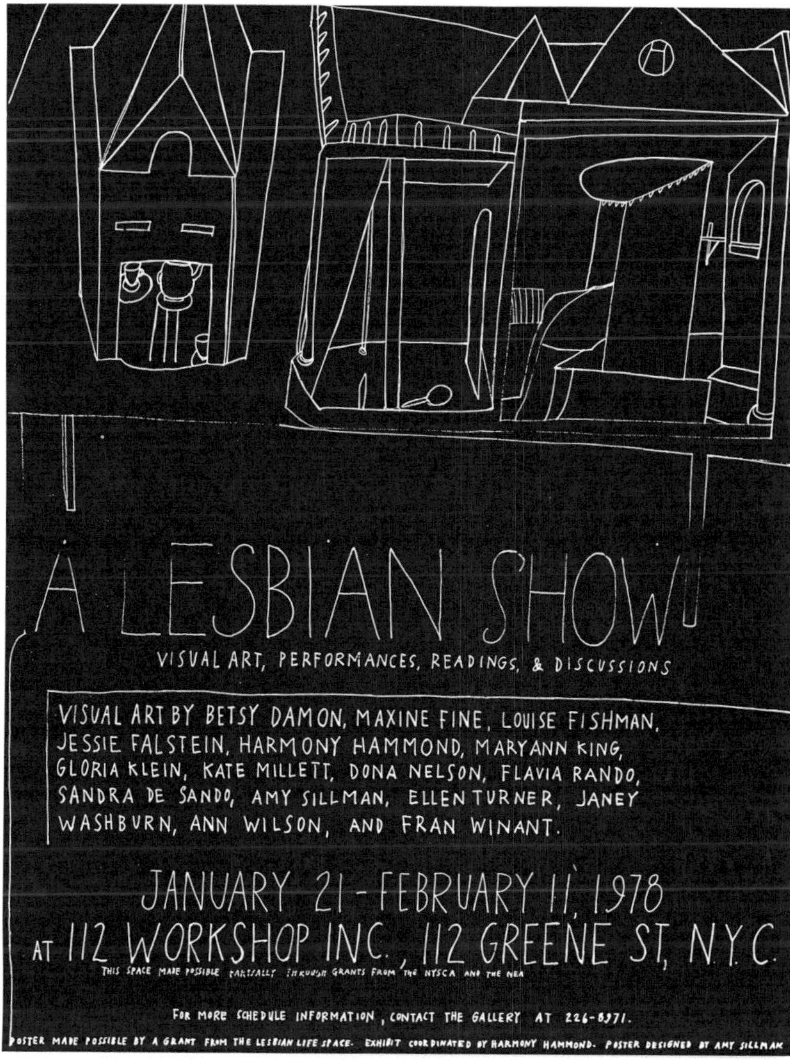

FIGURE 1.6. Poster for *A Lesbian Show*, 112 Greene Street Workshop, New York, 1978. This poster, publicizing the exhibition Hammond organized featuring works by lesbians, was continuously torn down or defaced during the run of the show, even though the poster's design featured no sexual content. The show's title alone sufficed to provoke acts of suppression. Design: Amy Sillman. Courtesy of the artist.

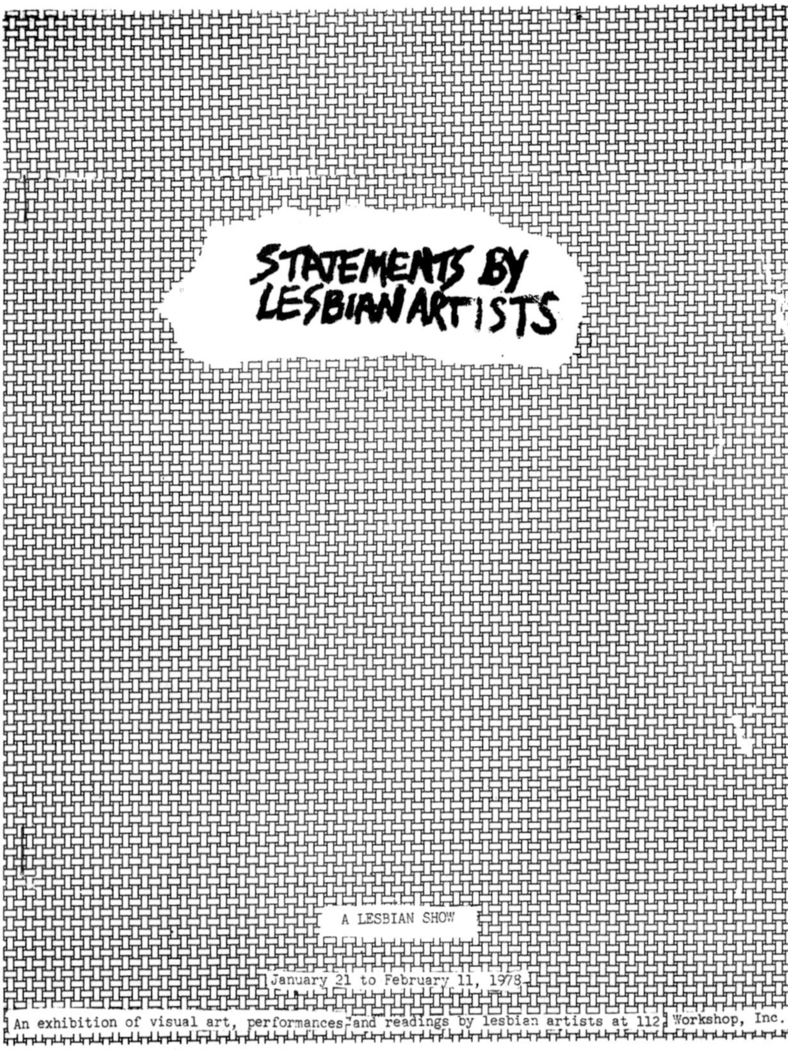

FIGURE I.7. Cover, *Statements by Lesbian Artists*, xeroxed catalogue for *A Lesbian Show*, curated by Harmony Hammond at 112 Greene Street Workshop, New York, 1978. Hammond compiled and assembled statements by the show's eighteen participating artists, bringing together their voices to preserve a record of the event presenting their artworks. Design: Harmony Hammond.

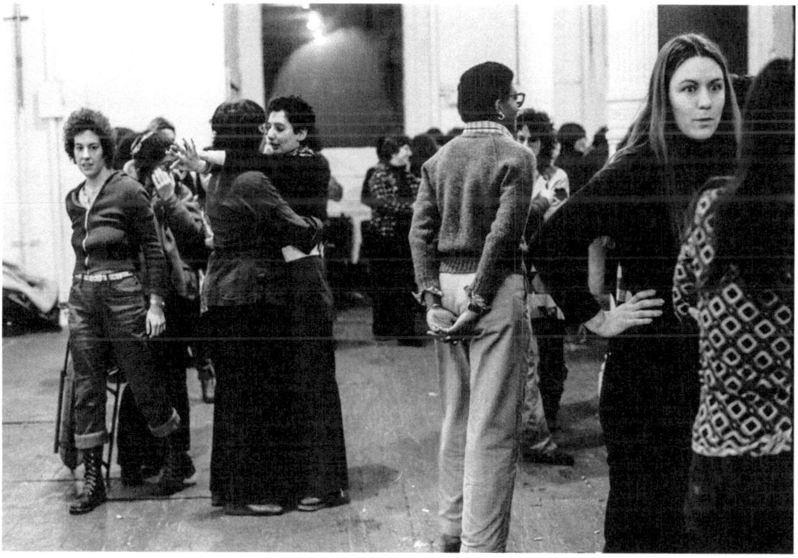

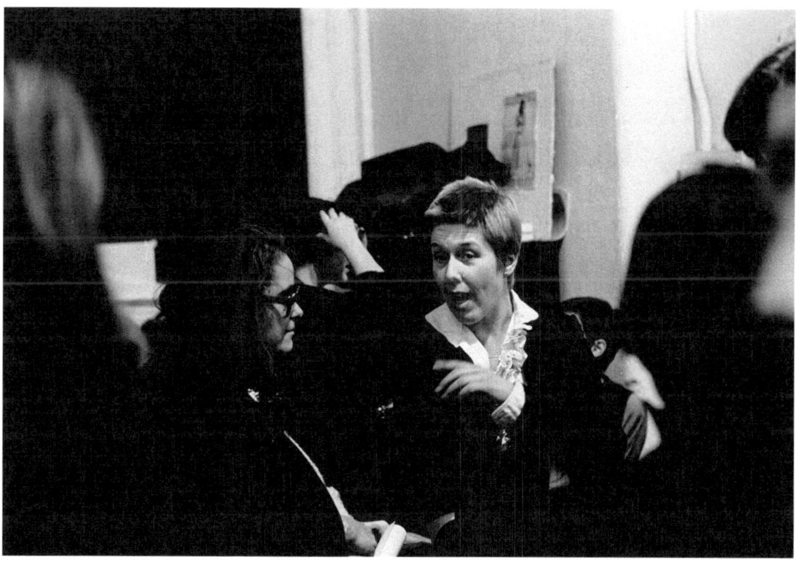

FIGURE 1.8. Opening of *A Lesbian Show* at 112 Greene Street, New York, 1978. Photo: Susanne Kaufman.

FIGURE 1.9. Writer and artist Kate Millett (*left*) and Harmony Hammond (*right*) at the opening of *A Lesbian Show*, 112 Greene Street, New York, 1978. Photo: Susanne Kaufman.

Statement, A.I.R. Gallery

New York (1973)

> Baskets are the Indian Woman's poems;
> the shaping of them her sculpture. They
> wove into them the story of their life
> and love.[1]

My work is for and about women. I want to develop a personally based feminine art. I am not interested in art history, for its relationship to me is never clear; rather I am interested in developing an imagery and way of working that directly express my anxiety as a woman artist (the tension being between the "woman" and the "artist" in me, for surely they are mutually exclusive). I want my emotions and experiences to be the basis of my art, and thus to contact a whole tradition of women's feelings. I am one woman. I am all women. All women are me. The rags and hair come from women and add their personal power to my pieces. It is the connection to my female ancestors that provides an ethnographic content to my work, but extending this, it is also a desire to break down the distinctions between painting and sculpture, between art and "women's work," and between art in craft and craft in art. It is like trying to find a place for myself. I want to move freely between them all as if they are one, just as I want to grasp my total whole. To give form to my female feelings to give form to myself, it seems necessary to work with women's materials—cloth, thread, hair, etc.—trying to combine a sort of figurative representation with abstraction. *Bags*, rugs, baskets, even the *Presences* [see plate 2], are essentially vessels or containers for feelings. They define an inner and outer space or territory. They are empty, filled, covered, layered, spilling out. The pieces are defensive, protective, manipulative. Contacting my insides, the insides come out. I like them and I hate them. I want my work to demand your attention because I can get it no other way. Is this not part of my woman's madness?

ED. NOTES

Unpublished artist statement for solo exhibition at A.I.R. Gallery, New York, January 1973.

1. These are Hammond's words, reformulating a statement in the introduction to Navajo School of Indian Basketry, *Indian Basket Weaving* (1903; reprint, New York: Dover, 1971).

More on Women's Art

An Exchange

Art in America (1976)

The history of the patriarchal art world is and always has been the history of definitions and boundaries. The artist is special and in "his" own unique space. As the audience, or as a certain kind of artist, you are on the outside, for boundaries put people either in or out, and those who have not been into making white Western male art were and are out. Women are out. And now we are questioning if we even want in. Questioning the art world is only one part of questioning the patriarchy. We are acknowledging, exploring, and developing women's creativity, and we see that our art has powerful political implications.

I'm bored with men's needs to define feminism and feminist art or insisting that we must define it for them—right now. What is so outrageous is that they can't keep their hands off. Yes, I'm talking about Alloway's patronizing "progress report" informing us how we are doing, how we are coming along. How does he know? Is he a woman? Is he a feminist? If at least, like some men, he understood feminism (to be feminist implies a political analysis of being a woman in a male-dominated society), he would see that it is important for women to develop our own definitions and processes. But he hasn't really grasped this basic feminist concept, and since he is a man with certain art world credentials and power, I am concerned about the women reading his article and other such articles, reviews, and catalogue introductions that may come along. Some of you may say, but after all he IS writing about women, women who need visibility and publicity. That's more than most men and some women do. I say to you, as I say to myself, BEWARE. It is easy to be wooed, for the knife is hidden among the laurels. Let's not be dazzled. We must pay attention and listen to what he is saying, for they are dangerous words. In the name of publicity, he is shaping our art and politics and getting paid for doing so.

An analysis of the report makes clear his intentions. Hidden underneath many compliments he attempts to moralize, criticize, and invalidate the impact of the feminist movement. By attacking the movement, he attacks our art. He pretends to offer objective observations that are really negative criticisms in disguise. It is implied that feminist questioning of group structure and dynamics in the areas of leadership and power, the individual and the collective, task and process, have failed to meet the male ideal of organizational structure. Further, we should aspire to those male ideals in order to function more efficiently. The fact that efficiency is not the only concern of feminist groups is not acknowledged.

While unable to deny the cultural impact of feminism, Alloway tries to discount the political impact by saying that it was an accidental phenomenon because of the general discontent of the late '60s and early '70s, a convergence of causes that is now outdated and irrelevant. By calling us the "new avant-garde" it is implied that we are merely passing through some phase and there will be a new avant-garde tomorrow—that we will outgrow feminism. He even goes so far as to call the *Women Choose Women* exhibition at the New York Cultural Center in 1973 the culminating show of women's art. This implies that a peak has been reached and it is downhill all the rest of the way. If that was the culmination, where does he place all the work that was not included in that show, and all the work since then? In reality, *Women Choose Women* was one of many continuing excellent shows of women's art.

In his report, the richness of diverse feminist philosophies (as well as the diversity of feminist art) is seen as divisionary rather than forming the basis of feminism itself. We are told that opposing ideologies imply conflict and are therefore bad and destructive. When speaking of the United Nations World Conference of Women in Mexico last summer, he attempts to separate women of different cultures (as did the Mexican/male government) by pushing women to focus on differences rather than shared conditions and problems. "The process of differentiation has begun," and he implies that it will only continue to the destruction of an already dying movement. Actually, the experience of women attending the conference was one of acknowledging not only our differences, but also the worldwide oppression of women as a class, recognizing that feminist issues did not relate only to white middle-class American women, as well as doing consciousness-raising around economic, racial, geographic, sexual, and cultural issues.

Alloway then takes it upon himself to pinpoint our critical problems. Apparently, he still doesn't think women are capable of doing it for themselves. The main problem in his eyes is the discrepancy between work and theory in feminist art (though I would ask how they can be separated). We are criticized for not having one comprehensive theory of feminist art in a manifesto like the Surrealists and Futurists stating our theory. When will it be realized that feminism is not a lifestyle or an art movement but a political condition? The fact that we are exploring not one but many areas of feminist artmaking seems to give the man great discomfort. One by one, he refutes ideas about central imagery, women's self-imagery, women's sexual imagery, feminist herstory as resource material and a source of iconography, craft techniques and materials, primitivism, and decoration on the basis that they are not the one central theory out of which all feminist art must come, or that men too could work with these concerns. One could argue that it was feminism that made it acceptable for men to work in these areas; however, the real point is that these ideas do recur over and over again in women's art, and consciously in feminist art, and for this reason alone they are of interest to us. We are not interested in imposing definitions or boundaries on other women. We have been excluded too long to be interested in excluding our sisters. Feminist art is art that does not oppress other women. Our theories will evolve as our art evolves for the two are connected, not separated.

Next, Alloway tries to affect the nature of our art and politics—tries to change and redirect the focus of feminist art and artists. Based on his analysis and criticism, he states what issues and problems feminism must deal with. By forcing us to focus where he wants, he keeps us from dealing with the more relevant (and to him more threatening) issues—issues important to our art, such as: Can we develop feminist art forms as well as work with feminist content? How are feminist concepts and goals embedded in our art? What is the function of our art? How can we make art accessible to women of different class backgrounds? What are the political implications of our art? How and can we cause social and cultural change through our art? What image of women do we portray in our art? Do we see our art in relationship to a larger movement? To whom should our art be accountable?

Alloway looks upon group exhibitions as temporary coalitions providing personal contact and support as well as visibility for women artists. It's assumed that the next step is to move on to individual exhibitions. Alloway misses the point that group exhibitions are not necessarily second best but can be statements about connections, influences, and shared concerns among women. Feminist artists are saying yes, we do influence and affect each other. Our personal lives are part of our art. We are breaking down the myth of artists as alienated and misunderstood genius. This in fact was the point of *A Women's Group*, an exhibition at the Nancy Hoffman Gallery in January 1974. It was an exhibition of work by five women artists who had been meeting (along with a woman anthropologist) for four years and discussing their work and work issues in relationship to feminism.

While Alloway credits women with organizing their own shows and co-ops, he seems to feel that this was only a necessary step in order to enter the male art world. So, while validating shows and co-ops that have enabled women's art to become visible, he criticizes them and decides that they are limited and it is time to move on, for co-ops "have not demonstrated that they can develop careers in terms of reviews, collections, and out of town galleries and museums." This is only a half-truth, for I can say that as a member of A.I.R. [Artists in Residence] I did get reviews and shows in other galleries, and most certainly expanded my career. But he continues and tells us that the next step we must take is to fulfill requirements of "distribution in terms of information and marketing." So, it seems that his theory of feminist art has a definite economic base rooted in the capitalist gallery system. While some artists in co-ops probably feel the same as he does, most co-ops are established as alternatives to the gallery system. They do not want to be commercial galleries. In fact, women's co-ops have been quite successful in fulfilling their goals of making women's art visible and in providing a supportive environment for women making art. Perhaps co-ops are not stepping stones to private galleries but stepping stones to get out of the system. It is time for co-ops to question and re-evaluate, to define future goals, but I would not agree that we should be taking a new art and fitting it into an old system. Feminist art is one aspect of a larger concept of feminism which also includes developing new economic systems.

Attempts such as this report to foster competition among women are highly suspicious. The fact that *Art in America* publishes such a report where a man writes about feminist art and spends almost every chance he gets attacking specific women who have been vocal about their politics, does us all a disservice. We need to develop systems of accountability between artists and audience, and to develop new forms of art criticism. To be an artist may take on a new feminist meaning. It is our art that contains the possibilities of cutting across class, race, and cultural lines. All good criticism must deal with art in the terms that the art itself sets up. If men can't deal with feminist art, they shouldn't write about it.

ED. NOTE

"More on Women's Art: An Exchange" was first published in "Issues and Commentary," *Art in America*, September–October 1976, 13, 15, 17. Copyright 1976. Penske Media Corporation. Hammond's response was one of several by women speaking back to Lawrence Alloway's article "Women's Art in the '70s" in *Art in America*, May–June 1976. Her quotes of Alloway are from the article. Emphasis in this text, and all others in the volume, is that of the author.

Feminist Abstract Art—a Political Viewpoint

Heresies: A Feminist Publication on Art and Politics (1977)

There are many articles written on feminist art that try to pinpoint and define a feminist sensibility. Few of these articles go beyond the recognition that feminist art is based on the personal experiences of women by beginning to question its larger political implications and the role it plays in feminist revolution. Most articles originating from the art world tend to be formal descriptive attempts at documenting what women are doing and do not attempt a feminist analysis of function and meaning.

In a reactionary escape from formalist criticism, most movement writing on feminist art deals with political issues but lacks any real understanding of the creative process, how it functions for the artist, and how it affects form and content. Without such an understanding it is impossible to evaluate the work as art. While feminist poets and writers comment on each other's work and write of their own processes, we visual artists tend to remain silent and let others do the writing for us. Our silence contributes to a lack of dialogue between artist and audience, to the lack of criticism from a feminist perspective, and ultimately to the misinterpretation of our work.

In this article I wish to focus on abstract art and show that it can have a feminist basis and therefore be political. Feminists are not the only people to attempt political or revolutionary art, but because certain ideas and issues occur over and over, they are of interest to us and worth exploring. I will focus on one area of abstract art by discussing concepts of marking and language in feminist drawing and painting—to show its origin, meaning, and political potential.

In "Prime Time: Art and Politics," Alexa Freeman and Jackie MacMillan look at how art is viewed in this capitalist, patriarchal society and criticize activists for reacting too quickly and overlooking the revolutionary potential of art.[1] However, they in turn react to male establishment myths about abstract (nonrepresentational) art and exclude it from feminist and political potential. They view abstract art as private expression that is not understandable or analyzable to the audience, and therefore irrelevant to feminist political goals. Thus, they incorrectly see elitism as a precondition of abstract art, rather than realizing that this is how abstract art has been used by men as a defense mechanism against the alienation of their own capitalist system; that as well as furthering the myth of artist as alienated and isolated genius, abstract art has offered an illusion of objectivity. Such notions suggest that the content of one's work can be separated from one's political beliefs. By sponsoring international exhibitions showing apolitical abstract paintings by former Communist Party members, the CIA (via the Museum of Modern Art) has sought to impress other nations with the cultural freedom of the U.S.A. The way in which abstract expressionist art was defined and developed by the artists and then used by others to further cold war politics in the '50s is only one example of the manipulation of abstract art to create the illusory separation of art and politics.[2] Thus when women continue to respond to abstract art as "apolitical," they are reinforcing and maintaining myths established by men.

The Freeman/MacMillan article is typical in its analysis of art and politics. Abstract art has become taboo for most artists who consider themselves political feminists. Because of the history outlined above, it is difficult to determine abstract painting's relationship to feminist ideology. There are radical feminists who are making abstract art. Radical feminism operates from the belief that women as a class are oppressed, and that a mass political women's movement is necessary to overthrow male supremacy.[3] Therefore, we might ask, how are the visions of radical feminists analyzed and portrayed in this art?

It is necessary to break down the myths and fears surrounding abstract art and make it understandable. Women—artists and nonartists—need to talk about art, and talking about abstract art need not be more difficult than discussing portraits, nudes, vaginas, or whatever. Every work of art is understandable on many different levels. It is by talking about our work and work processes that we will not only begin to develop a new language for interpreting abstract art but also to integrate this work with society. This language, which I see evolving from consciousness-raising techniques, will be able to be shared with any woman, regardless of class background. For artists, such a dialogue with the audience is essential, as it offers valuable feedback for the development of our art.

I want to reclaim abstract art for women and transform it on our own terms. It is interesting to note that much of women's past creativity, as well as the art by women of non-Western cultures, has been abstract. I'm thinking of the incredible baskets, pottery, quilts, afghans, lace, and needlework women have created. Many of the motifs used were based on "the stitch" itself. The repetition and continuity of the stitch or weaver formed the individual shape and also the pattern resulting from its repetition. Usually, these motifs and patterns were abstract and geometric. Patricia Mainardi points out that they had specific meaning for the women who made them, and in a sense formed a visual language in themselves:

> In designing their quilts, women not only made beautiful and functional objects, but expressed their own convictions on a wide variety of subjects in a language for the most part comprehensible only to other women. In a sense, this was a secret language among women, for as the story goes, there was more than one man of Tory political persuasion who slept unknowingly under his wife's "Whig Rose" quilt. Women named quilts for their religious beliefs . . . or their politics—at a time when women were not allowed to vote. The "Radical Rose" design, which women made during the Civil War, had a black center for each rose and was an expression of sympathy with the slaves.[4]

As we examine some contemporary abstract art by women, it is important to develop a sense of identity and connection with our own past creativity rather than that of the oppressor who has claimed "fine art" and "abstract art" for himself. In fact, the patriarchal put-down of "decorative" traditional art and "craft" has outright racist, classist, and sexist overtones. Elizabeth Weatherford states: "Art history assigns creative products to two categories—fine arts and crafts—and then certifies as legitimate only the fine arts, thereby excluding those creative traditions of primitive peoples, peasants, women, and many other groups outside the mainstream of Western history."[5]

Until recently, decorative art, or craft techniques and materials, have been valid only as sources for contemporary male artists. While women working with these ideas, techniques, and materials have been ignored (Ann Wilson first painted on quilts in 1958) or put down for doing "women's work," men like [Alan] Shields, [Claes] Oldenburg, [Frank] Stella, and [Kenneth] Noland are hailed as innovative. But times have changed. Today many female artists are connecting to a long line of creativity by proudly referring to women's traditional arts in their own work. They are recording the ritual of women's artmaking both in the past and the present, thereby reflecting a feminist concern not only with the end product but with the daily process and function of making art. Sewing techniques and materials as both process and content are used in a variety of ways in the abstract works of Sarah Draney, Pat Lasch, Nina Yankowitz, Paula Tavins, Patsy Norvell, Rosemary Mayer, and many other women. Barbara Kruger says that she first learned to crochet and sew when she decided that these techniques could be used to make art.[6] For women, the meaning of sewing and knotting is "connecting"—connecting the parts of one's life, and connecting to other women—creating a sense of community and wholeness. Other women, drawing on women's traditional arts, make specific painterly reference to decoration and craft. Miriam Schapiro utilizes remnants of fabric, lace, and ribbon along with handkerchiefs and aprons in large collages, thus making the very material of women's lives the subject of her art. Joyce Kozloff and Mary Grigoriadis explore decoration as fine art, basing their paintings on the abstract patterning of Islamic architecture and tiles, Tantric art, Caucasian rugs, and Navajo weaving.

The way many women *talk* about their work is revealing, in that it often denies formal art rhetoric. Women tend to talk first about their personal associations with the piece, and then about how these are implemented through visual means; in other words, how successful the piece is in its *own* terms. This approach to art and to discussing art has developed from the consciousness-raising experience. It deals primarily with the work itself, what it says and how it says it—rather than with an imposed set of esthetic beliefs.

In her excellent catalogue introduction to *Changes*, an exhibition by Betsy Damon and Carole Fisher, Kathryn C. Johnson comments that "intent" is most important when defining feminist art. She states that it is "a powerful oneness of subject and content" that makes certain work feminist: "Their work both *is* and tells *about* the pain of their life experiences. It is about pain and is painful, but does not present woman as passive victim. The pain is presented with deep understanding of its sources and effects, and the anger which follows confrontation with the hurt."[7] Fisher writes: "Betsy looked at the work and recognized the fact that I worked to survive, to keep from growing crazy, and to keep the pain from becoming too great. She recognized the pain in my work instantly! This was something I had only come to recently recognize and acknowledge in my work. Like many women in our culture, I had become adept at hiding and covering my pain. I had gotten all the messages that to be vulnerable in our culture is to be weak and despised."[8]

It is this "oneness of subject and content" that carries their work through feminist consciousness beyond the personal to the political. It is also present in abstract paintings that seem superficially more related to the male modernist tradition than to women's creativity in that they involve the physically expressive manipulation of paint on a two-dimensional surface.

In much of this work the recurring stitch of women's traditional artmaking becomes the repetitive mark, taking on a new form as a "visual diary." Such works are daily records of thoughts and are used as such by the artists. Just as the weaver continues from day to day, from one physical and psychic location to another, materials and dyes changing slightly, irregularities and tension showing, the painted marks also reveal daily emotional changes and tensions. They are a record of present feeling, a ritual giving in to the repetitive gesture, a language to reveal self—a woman's mantra.

Jenny Snider's nervous lines recall ancient Chinese calligraphy, which has both a letter/character reference and a body/figure reference. Her drawings are made with and are about her nervousness and vulnerability. She "is" the mark, the line. As the marks are repeated and contained in different spaces (usually grids or rectangles suggesting fabric, rooms, and houses), the quality and feeling of the line changes and she becomes more comfortable in some spaces than in others. She explores her self-image and feelings about her body in relationship to other people and spaces. Snider describes these works as "figurative." To me, it is the mark and its repetition that is most important. Her works are figurative in the sense that Chinese calligraphy is figurative—in having a direct body reference. Words are sometimes combined or used interchangeably with the markings, reinforcing Snider's commitment to the diaristic mode. As she says, "The words and lines come from the same psychological place and gesture and are not intended to describe or explain what the drawings are in terms of images—but rather express the fact that they come from a nervous hand and a yakking heart."[9] Phrases such as "little sounds arose (and it showed)"; "Well, for one thing, never step on broken glass"; and "Remember when we saw the ocean? It was just like this, wasn't it?" tell where the drawing is coming from and what the drawing is about.

Louise Fishman's paintings also function as a place for personal confrontation and as a statement directed toward other women. Fishman ripped up her old paintings and reconnected them by sewing and knotting them together with fragile thread. Her past was used to make a statement about her present. The strips and connecting thread formed loose grids, transformed in later work to a series of strokes or marks repeated across the page or canvas or within the confines of a particular shape (a circle or a piece of irregularly cut masonite). The marks of paint, layered on top of each other, lead eventually to a rich sensuous surface. The top layer usually consists of strong marks holding the partially revealed undermarks to the painting surface—feelings revealed and hidden. Fishman has always talked about her work in terms of hiding, guilt, vulnerability, anger, and personal individuation.

In a seven-panel reversible painting on unstretched canvas, Fishman deals with her feelings about her mother, also an artist. One side of each canvas is painted with calm strokes, while on the other side the marks explode into intensely scrawled letters reading "A letter to my mother about painting." Another canvas has the Star of David and the words "I am a Jewish working-class dyke" scratched into the surface. Just as consciousness-raising leads to political awareness, this work moves from the personal into the political. [Her *Angry Paintings* from 1973], titled *Angry Jill, Angry Djuna, Angry Paula, Angry Sarah*, and so on [. . .] seem to be painted *with* the anger. When she made these "angry paintings," Fishman said that all she could feel was her rage. When she looked around at other women, she saw that they were crippled by their anger too. These paintings were made to force women to confront it rather than letting it turn inward and become self-destructive. Grouped together as a wall of women's anger, the paintings show a tremendous amount of energy that can now be redirected toward feminist creativity and revolution.

These women as well as others (Joan Snyder, Carla Tardi, and Pat Steir, to name a few) have used words and marks fairly interchangeably as abstract gestures with concrete feminist meanings. Words are marks and marks are words; their repetition becomes not only an interior monologue but also a dialogue with other women. Like Damon and Fisher, these artists make individual feeling and experience the subject of their work, while the content deals with the difficulties and ambiguities of being a feminist artist in a patriarchal society. Their painting surfaces are often violated or mutilated; cut, gouged, ripped, scratched, or torn. The reversal of the usual additive process of painting refers to the violation of the traditional painting surface and also to the physical and psychic violation of women. The thick paint applied with a palette knife in Fishman's work, for instance, acts both as poultice for wounds and cement for holding self together. In Joan Snyder's recent work, the marks, cuts, and burning combine with words and color to make a passionate statement about sexuality.

This work is certainly political. Yet Freeman and MacMillan, in their attempt to distinguish protest from political art, to show that specific forms are more conducive to one or another, still ignore the political potential of abstraction.[10] They accept male definitions of what art is and do not deal with the evolution of a feminist creative process or feminist art forms. Theirs is a reformist approach to a revolutionary endeavor.

I am reminded of Andrea Dworkin's "afterword," "The Great Punctuation Typography Struggle," in her book *Woman Hating*, where she explains how the text was altered against her will by the publisher's insistence on uppercase letters and standard punctuation. She had wanted the book to be as empty of convention as possible, to create a new form that would merge with the content:

> reading a text which violates standard form forces one to change mental sets in order to read. there is no distance. the new form, which is in some ways unfamiliar, forces one to read differently—not to read *about* different things, but to read in different ways.
>
> to permit writers to use forms which violate convention just might permit writers to develop forms which would teach people to think differently: not to think about different things, but to think in different ways. that work is not permitted.[11]

The fact that innovative form is so feared by the male establishment shows that, like content, it has a power of its own. If our lives and our art are connected, and if "the personal is political" in the radical sense, then we cannot separate the content of our work from the form it takes. As abstract artists, we need to develop new abstract forms for revolutionary art.

The women's work I've discussed here, and I include my own, is moving in this direction. We are not yet there. Hopefully, as we create art within the context of other women's art, and within the context of evolving feminist theory, we will develop a new visual language. Art in transition is political, for it is both our development and describes our development. In a sense we are coming out through our art and the work itself is a record of the ongoing process of developing a feminist esthetic ideology.

ED. NOTE

"Feminist Abstract Art—a Political Viewpoint" was first published in the "Feminism, Art, Politics" issue, *Heresies: A Feminist Publication on Art and Politics* 1, no. 1 (1977): 66–70. All issues of *Heresies* are preserved in the Heresies Collection, Special Collections and University Archives, Rutgers University Archives, New Brunswick, New Jersey.

The numbered endnotes for this essay, below, are by the author.

NOTES

1. See Alexa Freeman and Jackie MacMillan, "Prime Time: Art and Politics," *Quest: A Feminist Quarterly*, Summer 1975, 27–39.

2. See Eva Cockcroft, "Abstract Expressionism, Weapon of the Cold War," *Artforum*, June 1974, 39–41.

3. See Brooke, "The Retreat to Cultural Feminism," in *Feminist Revolution*, ed. Redstockings (New York, 1975), 79–83.

4. Patricia Mainardi, "Quilts: The Great American Art," *Feminist Art Journal* 2, no. 1 (Winter 1973): 19.

5. Elizabeth Weatherford, "Craft for Art's Sake," *Ms. Magazine*, May 1973, 29.

6. Weatherford, "Craft for Art's Sake."

7. Kathryn C. Johnson, catalogue introduction to *Changes*, exhibition by Betsy Damon and Carole Fisher at the College of St. Catherine (St. Paul, Minnesota, 1976), n.p.

8. Carole Fisher, in Johnson, catalogue introduction.

9. Attributed to Jenny Snider, source unidentified.

10. Freeman and MacMillan, "Prime Time."

11. Andrea Dworkin, *Woman Hating* (New York: E. P. Dutton, 1974), 202.

Class Notes

Heresies: A Feminist Publication on Art and Politics (1977)

Class hierarchies and heterosexuality are patriarchal institutions that divide women, give some women power over others, and destroy our strength. As a lesbian feminist artist, I am interested in examining the assumption of class and heterosexuality in art, and the role of lesbian art as a potential catalyst for social change. This article will focus on the myth of art as classless, and how this myth functions to separate us from the reality of our lives and affects the way in which we see ourselves. Specifically, I want to discuss how we as lesbian artists need to defy this myth by developing class consciousness and incorporating it in the development of lesbian art and culture.

The Myth

Fine art is a reflection of upper-class interests, values, tastes, and patterns of thinking. The images found in art reflect and serve the needs of a small group of "corporate-government elite" (upper-class white men) who define culture in America and elsewhere if they can profit from it. They found, fund, and run art museums, set standards of taste, and have a vested interest in creating, validating, and supporting art whose form and content justifies and furthers a patriarchal social order.[1] Jackie St. Joan has defined this social order as: "[. . .] that system—intellectual, political, social, sexual, psychological—which requires in the name of human progress that one group (in the history of the world, rich, white men) controls and exploits the energies of another, and in which women are particularly despised. It includes patriarchal institutions (heterosexuality, the nuclear family, private property, etc.) which are the tools of oppression as well as the patriarchal mind-constructs which, like capitalist mind-constructs, limit even our ability to think beyond what is."[2]

Rarely does fine art include images of workers, the workplace, or daily survival. Rarely does it depict the experiences of Blacks, Native Americans, women, or lesbians. When these images do appear, they seem outside the experience of those portrayed because they are romanticized or stereotyped, rather than real. For instance, lesbian sexuality is rarely portrayed in visual art and when it is, say in film, lesbians are presented in butch/femme roles, as sick, masochistic, and sadistic, and as though sexuality was the only important thing in their lives. This limited male view hardly relates to my experience as a lesbian. Nor do I feel that my identity as an artist is realistically portrayed. The artist's life is romanticized as a chosen struggle of economic hardship necessary to produce art rather than as a product of the alienation of artists from society.

If art provides a way for us to perceive ourselves and the world around us, it seems necessary that we examine what is validated as art. An excellent example of an attempt to write social history through art was the exhibition *American Art*, a collection belonging to John D. Rockefeller III, which was shown last fall at the Whitney Museum as our bicentennial survey exhibition of American art. This collection contains one work by a woman artist, one work by a Black artist, and no work by Hispanic or Native American artists. The absence of work by women and Third World artists in this and most other collections and exhibitions denies the experiences of most Americans. Not to see their experiences reflected in culture is to say that they don't exist. Because art both creates and reflects social realities, their absence becomes a political issue. As the artists writing in *an anti-catalogue* state: "Omission is one of the mechanisms by which fine art reinforces the values and beliefs of the powerful and suppresses the experiences of others."[3]

Another mechanism reinforcing upper-class values is the myth of art as classless and universal. By creating the myth of universal art, those in power teach us to identify with images and the experiences these images represent, which have nothing to do with our own class position. We are told that art, and therefore the artist, is classless, and that our experiences are immaterial and should be ignored.

All classes accept this myth, for to question it would be to reveal the oppressive political structures and social institutions underlying patriarchal capitalist society. Rita Mae Brown writes that "America is a country reluctant to recognize class differences. The American myth crystallized is: This is the land of equal opportunity; work hard, stay in line, you'll get ahead. (Getting ahead always means money.)"[4] Identification with this myth of classlessness redirects us from dealing with our own particular oppression as working class, as women, as lesbians, etc. The artists in *an anti-catalogue* state: "The mystification of art depends upon two things—upon our surrendering our capacity to judge and upon unquestioning acceptance of authority in place of the printed word and the authority of scholarly titles and distinctions. The mystification of art takes our passivity for granted. It encourages us to look upon art as if art had no bearing on experience."[5]

Accepting the myth is accepting our invisibility and powerlessness. To question cultural attitudes is to question social conditions. Passivity smooths the pain of powerlessness and helps us to survive these conditions. We need to see that behavioral patterns affect who becomes an artist, what artists create, what art is validated as "quality," and how art in turn reinforces those patterns.

How I Bought the Myth

Thinking back to junior high school in the fifties, I see that one reason I chose to be an artist was to escape the daily pain of lower middle-class life in Hometown—of living in a duplex, taking a bus to school, and wearing hand-me-downs until I got a job at Lerner's and could buy my own clothes. The guy I went with turned me on to [Gerry] Mulligan, Coleman [Hawkins], [Stan] Getz, and all that jazz and the beat writers [Jack] Kerouac, [Allen] Ginsberg, and [Jacques] Prévert. They were "artists" and intellectuals, without money (like me), and romanticized. I thumbed my nose and fantasized riding naked down the highway. We fucked. I got a scholarship to the Saturday School of the Art Institute of Chicago. I wanted to be a dress designer or fashion illustrator because it sounded "classy" and "sophisticated." If all else failed, I could be an art teacher.

In the museum I saw "real" painting and sculpture. I remember sitting in front of the Pollock, the Rothko, and the Still, thinking that I could do those paintings, but not realizing that I was a woman and that it didn't matter what I did. In the studios I saw art being made by grubby students and I took note that the artist could wear anything, say anything, and didn't have to socialize. The artist seemed special and not bound by class behavior. I would be an artist. Accepting fine art meant renouncing my class background and stepping out of the lower middle-class life of Hometown into the universal world of the muses. Safe and protected at last. Who ever heard of a middle-class muse?

The Myth Shattered: Class Is How You See the World. Art Is How You See the World.

It has taken me a long time to begin to understand and accept my lower middle-class background, and to realize that the art world I entered wasn't an alternative to middle-class society but that women, Blacks, and the poor are also oppressed within the alternate "world of culture." As long as society allowed me to be a "starving artist" I did not question my own experiences, or how they affected my work and work attitudes. Acting out a romanticized art life was my option to upward mobility.

Heterosexual women get their privilege from the same patriarchal systems that give privilege to middle- and upper-class women. Coming out as a lesbian with a feminist consciousness forced me to realize what class privilege I did and did not have, and what I would now lose. Even the fact that I first came out to myself through my art and not in bed is in itself a reflection of my class position. As a feminist artist I had learned to use my work as a place to confront fears and other feelings privately in my studio. A woman working as a maid, a waitress, or a seamstress does not have this option.

Analysis—Reintegration

Ultimately it is a question of the function of art beyond the personal. It is not merely a matter of doing work that doesn't oppress others, but also of doing work that pushes further toward a redefinition and transformation of culture. For me, coming out as a lesbian has a lot to do with developing a class consciousness, and that consciousness brought to my art raises questions of imagery, permanence, scale, ways of working, and concepts of art education. It raises questions of money and power, who sees my work, and what effect I want it to have on others.

This does not mean that we as class-conscious lesbian artists must make paintings with recognizable figurative imagery, that we must be downwardly mobile, give up making art for "real political struggle," or involve ourselves in the rhetorical circles of the artistic left. What it does mean is not making or accepting class assumptions about art such as what is allowable as art, who makes it, who sees it, and what its function is to be. By removing esthetic hierarchies and the need to pretend that we all share the same experiences, meaning can become accessible and available.

Talk about "bringing art to the people" only reinforces class distinctions. Class consciousness can be reflected through our art by demystifying and de-privatizing the creative process. Presently it is difficult for a working-class woman who likes to write, paint, or dance even to consider being a professional artist. When making art as well as owning art ceases to be a privilege, and the artmaking process itself is available to women of different classes, races, and geographic backgrounds, we can begin to understand the political potential of creative expression.

As lesbians, we need our experience validated culturally. To refuse art that denies our existence and to deny that art is apolitical and universal is to actively challenge the wealthy few and their supporters who have been defining and controlling social order through the manipulation of fine art. Demanding group and self-identity in art is one means of resisting oppression. The artmaking process is a tool for making these demands and changes.

Art is essentially work. Simone Weil writes that art is a surplus commodity in this culture because it does not have immediate consumption and is not shared and used by the people. That artists are not part of the paid workforce further separates the productive from the consumptive classes. The work process (and the purpose of work) has always been external to the worker. Just as she writes that our main task is to discover how it is possible for the work to be free and to integrate it, we must free the artmaking process so it is accessible and understandable to everyone. The process should be as available as the product.[6]

As a lesbian, however, I was forced to confront and give up illusions I had about being accepted and rewarded by the male art world where they treated art "seriously." To be public about being a lesbian means that your work may not be taken seriously, or may be squeezed into a category of "camp" or "erotic art." Because you do not hang out with the right men or the right women (those who hang out with the men) at the right bars, and since the lesbian feminist community doesn't yet support its visual artists, you are less likely to make your work visible, to have professional dialogue, and to support yourself through your work either directly (sales) or indirectly (teaching). For women, the economic class system is largely determined by their relationship to men. The higher up the man she relates to, the more she benefits from the system. The lesbian, by not relating to men, does not benefit economically and has no privilege unless she is independently wealthy. Most of us do not have that kind of support and opportunity, and without support, it is very difficult to continue making art. Historically, known lesbian visual artists (Rosa Bonheur, Romaine Brooks, etc.) were wealthy. Only they had the privilege to continue making art despite their public lesbian lifestyle.

If we examine the relationship of lesbians to the class system, and to patriarchy, we can get an idea of the active role art can play in developing a culture that does not make women powerless and invisible. In "Lesbians and the Class Position of Women," Margaret Small writes:

> At this point in history, the primary role that lesbians have to play in the development of revolutionary consciousness is ideological. Lesbians are objectively outside of the reality which heterosexual ideology explains. Therefore, they have the potential for developing an alternative ideology, not limited by heterosexuality. [. . .] Lesbians stand in a different relation to the three conditions that determine the class position of women: reproduction, production (domestic labor), and sexuality. The lesbian does not have a domestic base that is defined by the production of new labor power and maintenance of her husband's labor power. Her primary relationship to class society is in proletarian terms. That element of slave consciousness which is integral to heterosexual women is missing.[7]

I am interested in how we can do this [develop a class consciousness] through art. Developing a class consciousness does not mean that each work of art by a woman would have to directly relate to women of all classes, but rather that the form and content of the work, be it figurative or abstract, would somehow illuminate experience in such a way that it is shared with and includes rather than excludes women from different backgrounds. Instead of presenting one universal experience that is supposed to represent ALL of us yet represents few, art should reflect and give information—facts, emotional response, visual accounting, ways of seeing into and understanding different experiences and feelings. We must acknowledge our differences in order to learn about, support, and work with each other. Thus I feel that to make art as a lesbian with class consciousness has far-reaching creative and political potential for connecting women through work. This means actively rejecting cultural dictates, taking responsibility for our work, and questioning the concept of apolitical art. Artmaking is where consciousness is formed.

Acknowledging the existence of class structures, and how through art they can affect cultural attitudes, is just a beginning—a necessary step one. In the long run, we should not focus merely on the relationship of one class to another, or on the relationship of art and class, but on defining a future classless society. The integration of art into the lives of all people and not just the upper class contributes to that vision. "Revolution presupposes not simply an economic and political transformation but also a technical and cultural transformation."[8]

ED. NOTE

"Class Notes" was first published in the "Lesbian Art and Artists" issue, *Heresies: A Feminist Publication on Art and Politics* 3 (1977): 34–36. All issues of *Heresies* are preserved in the Heresies Collection, Special Collections and University Archives, Rutgers University Archives, New Brunswick, New Jersey.

The numbered endnotes for this essay, below, are by the author.

NOTES

1. The Catalogue Committee of Artists Meeting for Cultural Change, *an anti-catalogue*, 1977. The catalogue was written as a protest to the Whitney exhibition *American Art*, 1976. I have included a condensed version of a more detailed discussion of "how art is mystified, how art exhibitions influence our views of history, and how collectors such as John D. Rockefeller III benefit from cultural philanthropy" [*an anti-catalogue*, n.p.].

2. "A Lesbian Feminist: Jackie St. Joan," interview, in *Big Mama Rag* 5, no. 1 (January–February 1977): 11.

3. Catalogue Committee of Artists Meeting for Cultural Change, *an anti-catalogue*, n.p.

4. Rita Mae Brown, "The Last Straw," in *Class and Feminism: A Collection of Essays from the Furies*, ed. Charlotte Bunch and Nancy Myron (Baltimore, MD: Diana Press, 1974), 14.

5. Catalogue Committee of Artists Meeting for Cultural Change, *an anti-catalogue*, n.p.

6. See Simone Weil, *First and Last Notebooks*, trans. Richard Rees (London: Oxford University Press, 1970).

7. Margaret Small, "Lesbians and the Class Position of Women," in *Lesbianism and the Women's Movement*, ed. Nancy Myron and Charlotte Bunch (Baltimore, MD: Diana Press, 1975), 59, 60.

8. Weil, *First and Last Notebooks*, 60.

Lesbian Artists

Our Right to Love: A Lesbian Resource Book (1978)

What can I tell you except the truth? We do not have a history. We are not even visible to each other. Many well-known women artists of the twentieth century have been lesbians, but if they are famous as artists, it is never mentioned that they are lesbians or how that might have affected the way they live, their work, or work processes. The best we have is Romaine Brooks, but she was rich and ensconced in villas, surrounded by monocled countesses. As wonderful as this sounds, it is unrealistic on my $360 a month. Rosa Bonheur lived with her Natalie for forty years and dressed in pants, but she didn't think that other women should.

In my search for contemporary lesbian artists, I spend much energy wondering and fantasizing about women who rejected passive female roles and committed themselves to art. After all, they did have young women as assistants and companions. But there is a space between us—time . . . , a silence, as large as the desert, because history has ignored lesbian visual artists. The patriarchy has taken them.

The silences, the words omitted from the biographies of lesbian artists, have denied us role models and the possibility of developing work that acknowledges lesbian experience as a creative source for artmaking and a context in which to explore it. I refuse to let them dispose of me in this way—to obliterate my existence as a lesbian and as an artist. I refuse to be quiet; I want lesbian artists to be visible.

Art not only reflects but creates and transforms cultural reality. Cultural reality is a whole made up of individual realities. I first came out as a lesbian through my work. I knew and identified myself as a lesbian before ever sleeping with a woman. My work is the place where I confronted myself, gave form to my thoughts, fears, fantasies, and ideas. I had been drawing on a tradition of women's creativity in my work, so it was only natural to acknowledge my feelings and desires for women. My work is a lover, a connection between creativity and sexuality. Since I came out as a lesbian through my work, I came out as a lesbian artist, meaning the two are connected and affect each other. This was relatively easy, perhaps as a matter of evolution. As lesbians we have the possibility of the utmost creative freedom to make the strongest, most sensitive statements. Passion gives substance.

I believe that there is something as yet indefinable in my work, and other work that we might call "lesbian sensibility," but for the most part it is hidden. As our work becomes more visible, public recurring themes and approaches will emerge and we can examine and develop them. How can lesbian sensibility exist in the context of patriarchal art? In some works lesbian imagery is overt, at least to other lesbians; in others it is hidden or perhaps less important. That is okay; it's there and will come out. We do not need to define or limit it.

I feel that we are at a very important time, with new creative energy coming from political consciousness in our work. To be a lesbian artist is not a limitation or a box any more than being a feminist is, unless you make it so. It is a statement of commitment, energy, interest, and priority. As a feminist, and as a lesbian, I can express myself in any media, and I can use any technique or approach to artmaking. But, whatever I do, be it overt lesbian imagery or a more covert statement, it will come from a consciousness of myself as a lesbian and an artist. It is a question of where you get your support and whom you give your energy to, and not just a matter of whom you sleep with, nor your lifestyle. Where I put my creative energy is a political decision. It is important that we identify ourselves as lesbians as well as artists. No one is going to give us space or visibility. We must take it.

Since we have no history, we can begin to paint, draw, weave, and write our own. In sisterhood . . .

ED. NOTE

"Lesbian Artists" was originally published in *Our Right to Love: A Lesbian Resource Book*, ed. Virginia Vida, National Gay Task Force (Hoboken, NJ: Prentice-Hall, 1978), 261.

Statement, Lerner-Heller Gallery

New York (1979)

Rags (scraps, leftovers, hand-me-downs) wrapped around a wooden frame (skeleton). Not stuffed. But layers wrapped around. Literally held together by the paint. A skin of paint. A metaphor for the function of my art in my life holding me together. The process showing but not intellectualized. The physicality of making the pieces is part of their physical presence in the end. The paint surface as skin.

The shapes are intuitive. They resemble body parts yet feel whole in themselves. The shapes or the frames were found on the streets. A sense of personage calling out. Surface grows out of a painterly process that is additive. Surface activated by wrapping rather than brush strokes. Density and weight is important. Here. Solid. Presence. I am interested in the notion of presence—not merely the physical space of something. *Presence as essence made visible. A felt imagery rather than seen.* Like a body, my body, solid but not hard. Full of chi. Not mummifying anything inside but rather layers building out—creating out of self. Outsides touching. They come from a female world and allude to a female sensuality. A felt not a seen content.

They are the sculptural counterparts to the *Crying Bead* and *Fan Lady*. Developed out of the *Crying Bead* when I needed to get away from the control and compulsiveness of the paintings.

Poetic prose. Abstract fiction. The work has become an extended novel with the characters leaving the stage of the painting surface and edges. Nonlinear. They appear, disappear, and reappear at different times in different situations. On the floor, against the wall, on the wall. In books, in drawers, in closets, in pockets. On the street. Poetic metaphors. Personages. Staring at survival. Something swollen and vulnerable coming from personal hurt. Moving toward the humorous. The *Crying Bead* [see fig. 2.3] disappeared on the mesa and *Fan Lady*, as inscrutable as she is, emerged out of the piñon. And *Ruffled Waters* joined from the Yucatan. They have a life of their own, so you have to keep an eye on them.

The density. The space around them too is full. Organic and active but not aggressive. Never empty, not really negative space. They are not about push/pull space. They fill space. Because they are created out of the accumulated. Sometimes reaching out, almost touching or touching themselves or others. The language of relationships. They say internal energy or chi can be stored in the marrow of the bones. The drawings have more space, are less insistent. A clarity from the center. In New Mexico, the horizontal space expanse brings you back into yourself. A sense of humor is a necessity.

Fans. A woman's iconography. Fan Painting. An image found in the art of many women. The iron fan—a weapon, a martial art form. Fans are like combs for hair and combs on top of Mayan architecture where buildings are faces/personages. The decorative element.

The *Crying Spirits*. Edges of torn paper, hurt. Tear, tear. The words as both descriptive of a state and a command to act/feel. Touch, ouch, touché.

ED. NOTE

This unpublished artist statement accompanied Hammond's exhibition *New Work* at Lerner-Heller Gallery, New York, March 31–April 26, 1979. The exhibition and written statement followed a one-semester teaching residency at the University of New Mexico, Albuquerque, fall 1978, and a trip that same fall to the Yucatan with the artist Ann Wilson.

A Sense of Touch

New Art Examiner (1979)

I was asked to write about "lesbian imagery in art" or "sexuality in art by women" as though these were the same thing. While I am willing to conjecture that perhaps all woman-focused sexuality (and the ways in which it is expressed in art) contains some lesbian feeling, regardless of whether the artist is straight or lesbian, all art by lesbians is not sexual in nature. So it seems there are at least two different articles here.

Lesbians, like other artists, create art about many different subjects. But people are constantly defining lesbians only in terms of their sexuality, as if compulsive uncontrollable sex were the one preoccupation of their lives, which is like saying that Gertrude Stein and Virginia Woolf never wrote, or that Romaine Brooks never painted. Visual art by lesbians is not always overtly lesbian in character. Also, at this time it is impossible to determine whether there is a lesbian aesthetic or imagery, sexual or otherwise. It is my hope that we never limit ourselves to one, for stylistic labels and definitions are oppressive and keep us from true creative expression. While sexual imagery has played a role in the art of many cultures, until recently very little of it reflected sexuality from a woman's point of view. However, in the last ten years, within the context of the feminist movement, women, both lesbian and heterosexual, have been getting in touch with and reclaiming their bodies and their sexual feelings, and have been expressing these feelings in their art. While we can find some early examples—such as the shells, flowers, and landscapes of Georgia O'Keeffe; the abstract sculptural references to women's bodies by Louise Bourgeois; the portraits of female friends and lovers by Romaine Brooks; and the depictions of working women spending intimate time together by Isabel Bishop—there is now a new and abundant range of visual art dealing explicitly with women's sexuality as experienced by women. This is the work I will focus on in this article.

Since a woman's sexual experience is not the same as a man's, only women can express women's sexuality. Any art that is really about women's sexuality as experienced by women is woman-centered. (This differs from sexual imagery by women that is male-centered, which I am not discussing here.) If we begin to look at woman-centered work, we can begin to see recurring characteristics as well as themes and approaches.

In this work, women are not shown as weak, sick, or passive. They are not objectified or exploited. Instead, they appear strong, healthy, active, and comfortable with their bodies. This is in contrast to the misogynistic attitudes toward women's bodies and bodily functions, such as reproduction, masturbation, and menstruation, that we observe throughout the history of art.

In her article "The Esthetics of Power in Modern Erotic Art" (*Heresies: A Feminist Publication on Art and Politics*, January 1977), Carol Duncan points out ". . . that the subjugation of the female . . . appear[s] to be one of the primary motives of modern (male) erotic art."[1] To achieve this power and dominance, the artist turns the model into the ideal universal and unreal nude or the female vampire she-bitch (the femme fatale) who deserves to be and must be restrained or destroyed through specific imagery or through the more sophisticated and subtle but no less dangerous means of fragmentation and abstraction. Woman must be separated from herself, and it must be made clear that she owes her existence to the male artist, rather than his owing his existence to her. As Duncan says, for the male artist, creation seems to equal possession.

This is not true of sexual imagery in woman-centered art. First of all, women are no longer being defined in relationship to men. The male presence is gone. Women do not depict each other as sex objects, or for that matter as objects of any kind. Niki de Saint Phalle's *Nanas* [1960s] and Kate Millett's gigantic *Naked Ladies* [1970s] are powerful women who take up space. Hardly the ideal of the classical contained nude, these women are big—often ten feet tall—and out of proportion, have lumps and bumps, and seem to be totally here and in touch with their physical selves. They are not passive but active, full of energy and exuberance.

Portraying women in this manner is a break with history and is disturbing to many people. Allan Kaprow ("Female Art: No Games," *Village Voice*, April 28th, 1966) wrote in response to an exhibition of Martha Edelheit's work in 1966:

> Female art in general plays no games as men's art does. No one wins; there are no victims or protagonists. It is thoughtful, but not intellectual insofar as intellectuality is a game. It is not editorial either, insofar as discriminations between degrees of moral good and bad are also a game. Female fantasy is pervasive, boundless, unconcerned with definitions and measure. When sex is its primary involvement the involvement is total and therefore shameless. It is for this reason terrifying to men, not because it implies the loss of their status, but because it implies the loss of the game (which is their life).[2]

In Nancy Fried's salt, flour, and water plaques, reminiscent of cloisonné enamels, women are shown together, usually undressed, relaxing at home—lying around, getting something out of the refrigerator, or perhaps snuggling in each other's arms in front of the TV. Fried takes delight in all the little details of women's bodies—a hairdo, a tattoo, pubic and underarm hair, the pattern of the wallpaper, the crewelwork of a pillow, or the cat curled up in the corner. These women are comfortable with each other and with us, which shouldn't seem unusual except that it is exactly the kind of image that has been missing in art for centuries.

In her series of drawings entitled *The Lesbian Body* [1970s], Kate Millett combines words with gestural drawings of breasts. The visual effect is one of a relaxed, chummy conversation between two breasts about life and love with political overtones. Millett draws on Eastern art for sources in her work but combines these sources with the reality of daily living as a lesbian. Her calligraphic drawings of women in erotic poses relate not only to Japanese brush painting but also to a tradition of explicitly erotic art. Only her drawings are meant for a female audience.

Women artists are creating images of women making love together or just openly showing affection for each other in a way that is not voyeuristic. Often shown on posters or reproduced in feminist magazines—that is, consciously directed toward a female audience—these images are easily accessible and understandable to nonartists. While they are especially popular with lesbians, they fill a great need for all women to see images of women relating to each other.

In our art we are depicting women's bodies as they really are—in different shapes, sizes, and colors. We are painting women of different ages, so that all the freckles, wrinkles, and stretch marks show. In her paintings, Joan Semmel shows close-up landscape examinations of her own body, the body of a middle-aged woman stretching, folding, falling where it will, warm and sensuous. It is not the firm, glossy body replica on record album covers, or the thin asexual thread we find in fashion magazines (the slick media versions of the twentieth-century paintings Duncan was talking about). In Semmel's paintings the feeling is one of a woman's body as directly connected to a cycle of nature, as nature itself. The image is focused downward, the view of what the eye can see is framed by the canvas edge, as if to show us an intimate secret shared—not viewed from the outside, but examined up close. Again, the body fills the space.

Semmel's paintings point to an important aspect of woman-centered sexual work. We, the viewers, see and feel the meaning of the pictures simultaneously. We feel the touch on our own body. This is quite different from the manner in which women have been sexually portrayed in male work, where the way visually into the painting was to identify with the male artist, creating and controlling the depicted woman. As women viewers we could not identify with the woman but had to distance ourselves in order to even look at the work at all. In female-centered work like Semmel's, we identify with the woman. The body in the painting is the artist's body (literally or metaphorically) and becomes our body, and we identify through this connection and feeling. Unlike in viewing the work of men, we become the female in the picture, in this case the artist, looking at and feeling herself. The sense of touching oneself is extended.

In Marisol's drawings and lithographs, hands or fingers appear carrying pocketbooks, forming suggestive shapes, or just floating in from the edges of the paper. The hands are simultaneously used to refer to another part of the body and also remain hands, the touching organs. The gesture is uncompleted but implies a sexuality of touching, allowing us to feel out or complete our own fantasy.

For many women a strong body sense is indicated through their choice of materials and the physical manipulation of those materials. Like many male artists, women have played with the sensuousness of thick paint, but for the women this has been done most often with an awareness of the paint's being a "skin" of paint, and therefore a body/skin metaphor. I immediately think of Louise Kramer's giant inflated latex balls with their organic skin surfaces or of Louise Fishman's work in which layers of oil paint and wax are applied and then scraped off with a palette knife, leaving a surface sometimes thick, gooey, and sensuous, and sometimes painful as if layers of skin had been scratched and were peeling away, revealing what lies underneath.

When Joan Snyder slashes one of her paintings and squishes paint, gauze, glue, or papier-mâché into the wound, it is not only a violation of the traditional painting surface but also speaks of the sexual violence to women's bodies. Her conscious use of different materials, and their accompanying associations, is part of her attempt to deal with sexual violence to women through the act of painting.

Likewise, a skin of paint literally holds my recent wrapped rag sculptures together, becoming a metaphor for how my artmaking functions for me—holding me and my life together. Also, wrapping the fabric is in itself a very physical activity, involving the whole body and ultimately contributing to the abstract sensual body sense of the finished piece. I find that materials that suggest direct hand manipulation (such as clay, plaster, papier-mâché, latex, fabric, and paint used to suggest "finger painting"), as well as materials actually taken from bodies (such as hair, nail clippings, teeth, and leather), seem to convey sexual references.

Helène Aylon's *Pouring Formations* [1977] implies a flowing earth connection to sexuality. They are made by soaking horizontal sheets of paper-backed masonite with brown oil. As the oil lies dormant for several weeks, it creates oval pockets of oil covered with a thin skin. When Aylon tips the masonite up vertically, the oil breaks the skin and oozes down from the pocket, leaving a painting in its wake. April Kingsley recently described Aylon's process as "midwifing the birth of the images."[3]

For many women artists, this material and process reference to sensuality is combined with an abstract imagery referring to parts of the body, yet simultaneously to the entire body, thus creating a sense of wholeness. The latex, plastic, and marble sculptures by Louise Bourgeois; the hydrocal *Huts* by Barbara Zucker; the carved wood receptacles by Debbie Jones; the latex, foam, wax, and knot pieces by Lynda Benglis; the wedges and pubic mounds by Sandy de Sando; the early latex flowers and the eraser and chewing gum pieces by Hannah Wilke; and my own wrapped sculptures are just a few of many examples.

In Lynda Benglis's early work, the orgasmic sexuality seemed very self-focused and women-centered, masturbatory. The sexuality was the orgasmic feeling caught in action in the latex and foam pieces, or the definite labia imagery of the wax pieces. Benglis herself has stated: "All my art is erotic, suggestive. It is about female sexuality, about being a woman."[4] I find it ironic that most people did not listen to what she was saying until in later work she changed the focus to a primarily male art audience—outside herself. Women talk about getting in touch with themselves as they make work, and about that process becoming part of the meaning of the pieces. Many young lesbians have told me that they came out simultaneously as lesbians and as artists. They say that getting in touch with their physical/sexual selves was tapping their creative selves, and that this allowed them to work from their whole being.

Debbie Jones draws distinctions between the visual art created by heterosexual women and the visual art created by lesbian women.[5] She says that straight women depict female forms from the outside at a distance, while lesbians depict the same forms as they are physically felt inside or experienced as a whole. This sounded right to me at first, but now I am not sure whether I totally agree. The boundaries aren't all that clear. What Jones points out certainly seems true of art created by lesbians working with sexual imagery, but it also seems true of any woman-centered sexual imagery. The work is felt, not just viewed from a distance; and the sexuality comes from a sense of wholeness, the whole self. While some of us feel that it is lesbian in that sense, this woman-centered work is made both by women who define themselves as lesbian and by women who define themselves as heterosexual.

Women working with sexual symbolism often use vaginal imagery. Shells, flowers, fruit, caves, containers, bags, houses, boxes, eggs, and landscape are frequently used. In fact, so many women have been working with this kind of symbolism, as a stand-in for the female form, that it would be difficult to discuss them all. Let me mention just a few who came immediately to mind: Judy Chicago, Buffie Johnson, Carla Tardi, Mary Beth Edelson, Hannah Wilke, Ellen Lanyon, Lee Bontecou, Shirley Bernstein, and Jane Abrams. Shirley Bernstein's pastel *Shells* fill the space of the page. They are depicted not at a distance, but close-up. As we follow the contours of the shell around to its insides, the feeling is not so much about a reference to female genitals, although that is there, but about an intimacy, openness, and vulnerability, a warmth and sexuality.

Jane Abrams's work is interesting because it combines the image of a hand with a body symbol. She uses the image of a rose (the female body) and within it another more detailed close-up of a rose (genitalia) being touched lightly but deliberately in its center by a female hand, whether hers or another's we do not know. Often this pastel triple-layered image (the layers of a fantasy or dream state) is placed on a page that is covered with a feminine pattern reminiscent of bedroom or bathroom wallpaper. The fact that her process is complex and time consuming, combining photography, intaglio, silk screen, and drawing, gives the pieces a relaxed, extended sense of time and heightens the erotic sense. I feel her images as if the hand in one of her pieces were touching me.

This is only a beginning discussion of feminist art which deals with woman-centered sexuality. I have focused almost entirely on painting, drawing, and sculpture, but it should be mentioned that this theme is also very frequent in performances and photography by women. In fact, Carolee Schneemann was insisting on sexual and erotic female images in her performances and happenings in the early '60s, and still continues to use them.

As women we are exploring our erotic imaginations, and to do so is political, for it challenges the basis of male supremacy. Or, as Joan Semmel, as editor, has written in her introduction to *The New Eros*, an unpublished anthology about sexual imagery and art which includes articles by Semmel, Lucy Lippard, Carol Duncan, Elizabeth Weatherford, Eunice Lipton, Rosalind Schneider, and April Kingsley, ". . . it touches on the raw nerves of a system whose most basic structure is being questioned."[6] For a long time, and in varying degrees, women have denied the sexual imagery in their work. As if it were too threatening to take seriously, woman-centered art that is overtly sexual is still trivialized, ridiculed, or ignored by the professional art world. However, the consciousness and claiming of oneself, physical and psychological, opens a powerful creative source for women. I think we are just beginning to see it reflected in our art.

ED. NOTES

"A Sense of Touch" was first published in *New Art Examiner*, Summer 1979, 4, 10.

1. Carol Duncan, "The Esthetics of Power in Modern Erotic Art," *Heresies: A Feminist Publication on Art and Politics* 1, no. 1 (1977): 46.

2. Allan Kaprow, "Female Art: No Games," *Village Voice*, April 28, 1966, 12.

3. April Kingsley, "Art: Nature Takes Its Course," *Village Voice*, April 2, 1979, 79.

4. Lynda Benglis, cited by Dorothy Seiberling, "The New Sexual Frankness: Good-Bye to Hearts and Flowers," *New York Magazine*, February 17, 1975, 42.

5. Debbie Jones, "What Does Being a Lesbian Artist Mean to You?," *Heresies: A Feminist Publication on Art and Politics* 3 (Fall 1977): 46.

6. From 1973 to 1976, Semmel worked on (edited and wrote the introduction for) *A New Eros: Sexual Imagery in Women's Art* (originally titled *Through the Object's Eye*), with contributions by Lucy Lippard, Carol Duncan, Eunice Lipton, April Kingsley, Roz Schneider, and Elizabeth Weatherford. The book was scheduled to be published by Hacker Art Books but did not ultimately come to fruition.

2

1980s

Editor's Introduction

Hammond, in her 1984 essay "Affirming the Existence of the World of Images," commits to "creating a continuous female presence" in the arts, including the realm of criticism.[1] Like many feminists of her generation, she developed agility, stamina, strength, and self-confidence through the practice of martial arts; she studied and taught the Japanese art of aikido for thirty-six years (1973–2009), eventually earning a fifth-degree black belt. (fig. 2.1). The title of her book *Wrappings: Essays on Feminism, Art, and the Martial Arts* (1984; fig. 2.2) aligns *feminisms* and *art* with this empowering third term. This groundbreaking publication brings the martial arts, visual arts, personal life (fig. 2.3), poetry, political theory, criticism, and activism together as intertwining elements of feminist practice.

Hammond's writings throughout the 1980s contribute to the restoration of women to histories of culture making and to the revalorization of women's

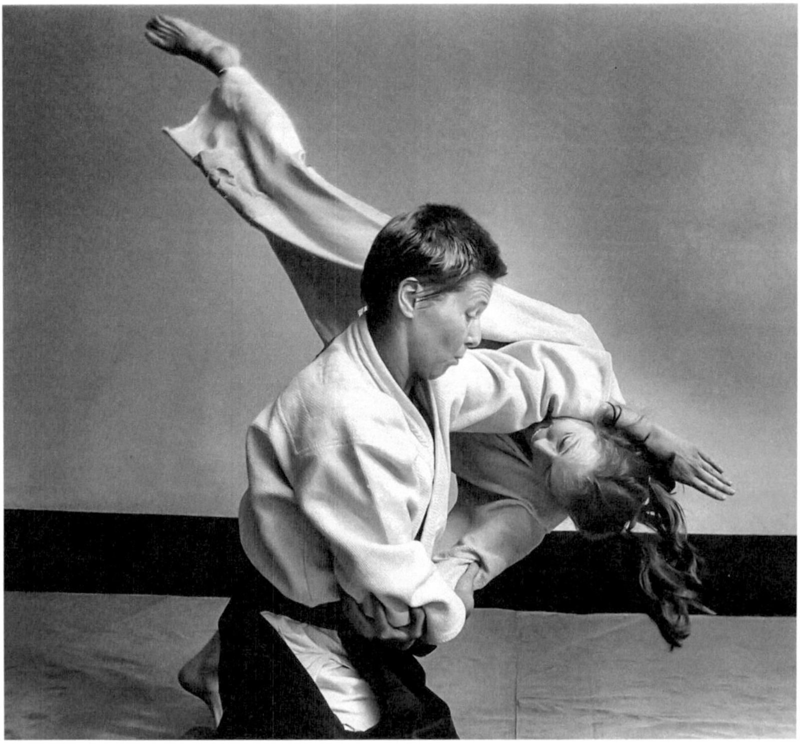

FIGURE 2.1. *Harmony Hammond Practicing Aikido*, 1982. Photo: Ellen Jaffe.

labor—including activism and artmaking (fig. 2.4). She contests dominant cultural criteria of artistic evaluation, including traditional conventions of beauty. She affirms feminism's power, through creative practice, to foster radically different social and artistic values. Emphasizing the diversity of feminist communities and feminist artistic strategies, she rebuffs attempts by the art establishment to define feminist art in narrowly formal terms.

Beginning in the mid-1980s, when she moved from New York City to northern New Mexico, Hammond's ideas about abstraction register the impact of the Southwest's open horizons and complex cultural histories. In the late 1980s (traveling back and forth from Galisteo to Tucson, where she began teaching one semester a year at the University of Arizona) she salvages materials from abandoned farms, such as roofing tin, gutters, burned wood, linoleum, buckets, and water troughs. She incorporates these remnants of rural life into paintings and installations that suggest narratives of territorial occupation and survival, as

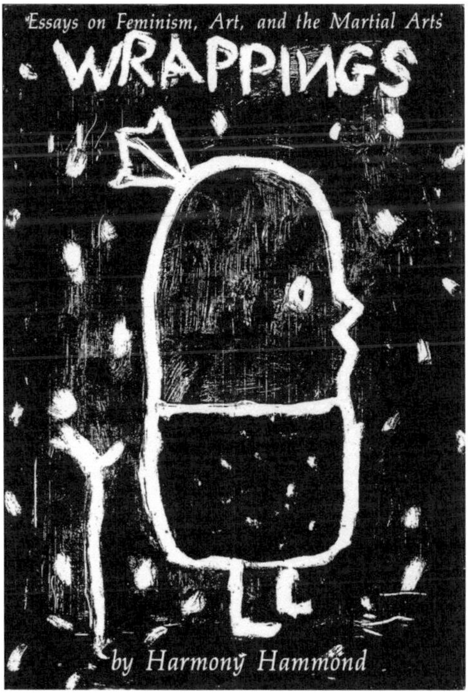

FIGURE 2.2. Cover with drawing by Harmony Hammond, *Wrappings: Essays on Feminism, Art, and the Martial Arts*, 1984. Courtesy Time and Space Limited Press.

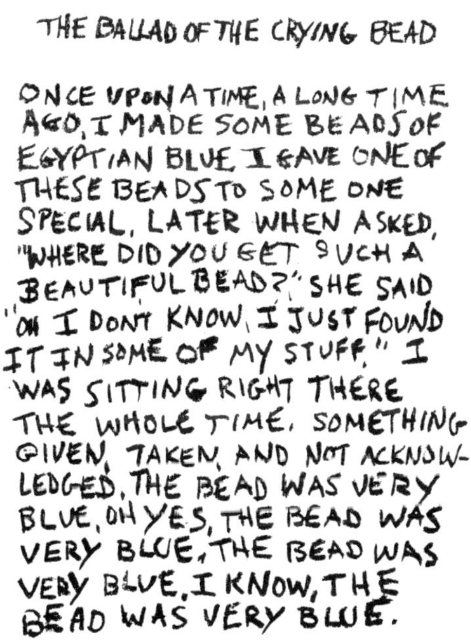

FIGURE 2.3. Harmony Hammond, *Ballad of the Crying Bead*, 1978, hand printed as page art for *Wrappings*, 1984.

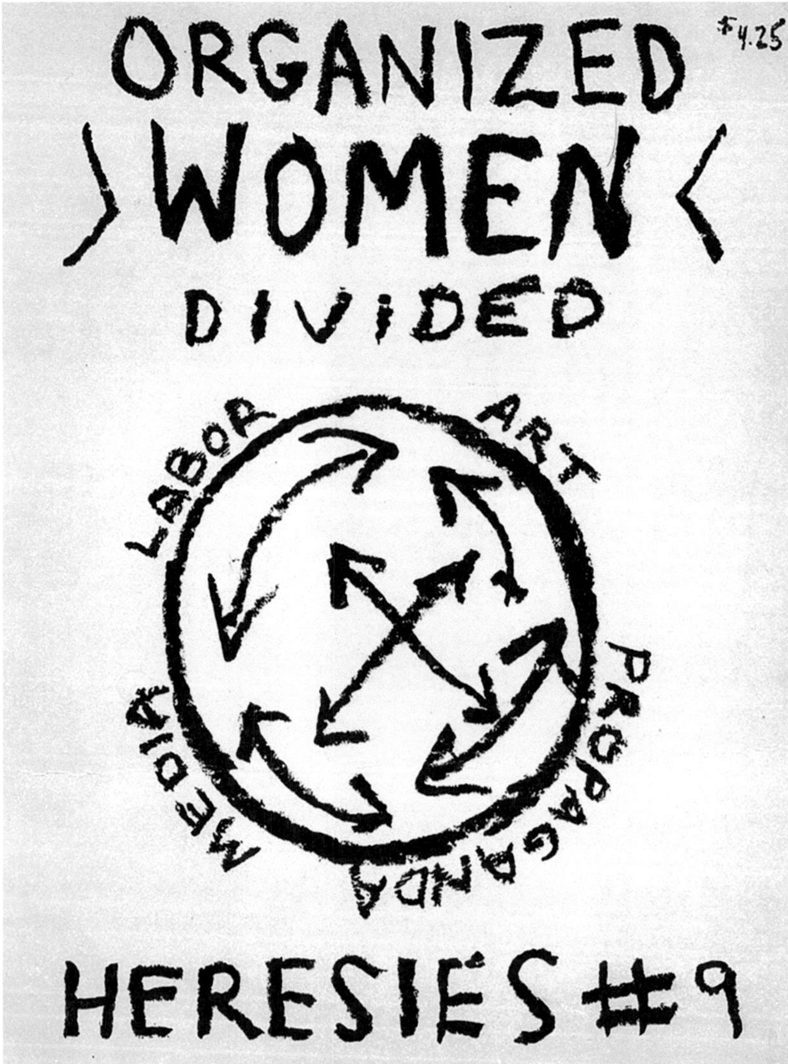

FIGURE 2.4. "Women Organized/Women Divided: Power, Propaganda and Backlash," *Heresies: A Feminist Publication of Art and Politics*, no. 9 (1980). Cover designed collaboratively by the issue's editorial collective.

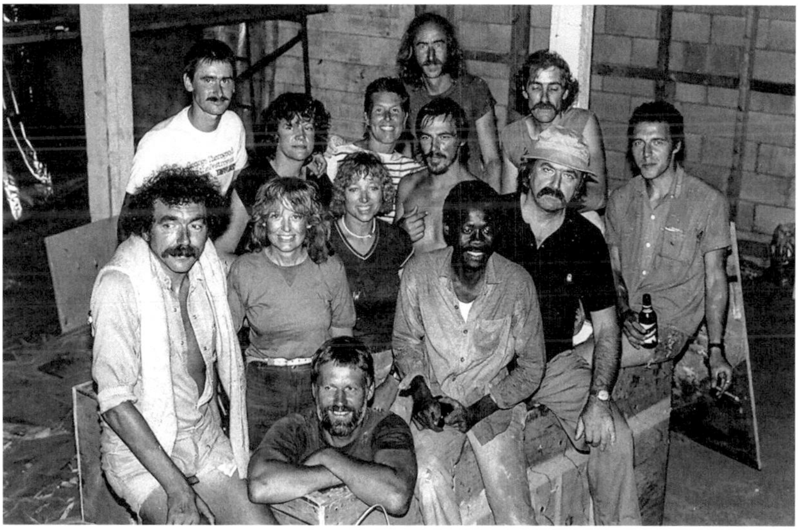

FIGURE 2.5. Artists in residence, Rendez-vous International de Sculpture '84, Saint-Jean-Port-Joli, Quebec, 1984. *Front, L to R:* Peter Gnass, Aly Traore Diop, Michelangelo Pistoletto, Julien Opie. *Middle, L to R:* Daniel Couvreur, Tatiana Démidorf-Séguin, Brigitte Radecki, Guy Nadeau, Pier Cloutier. *Back, L to R:* Gary John Williams, Nina Goerres, Harmony Hammond, Michel Goulet. The first international sculpture biennial, sponsored by the Saint-Jean-Port-Joli Artisan's Association, invited fourteen Canadian and international artists and artisans to realize out-of-doors site-specific sculptures that would remain on site in Saint-Jean-Port-Joli. Photographer unknown. Photo: Collection Harmony Hammond. Courtesy Jean-Pierre Pelletier, La Biennale de Sculpture de Saint-Jean-Port-Joli.

well as processes of gentrification. By the end of the decade, her writings, while still centrally concerned with gender politics, evidence a deepening engagement with the problematics of colonization, migration, cross-cultural appropriation, and cross-cultural influence (figs. 2.5 and 2.6).

NOTE

1. Harmony Hammond, "Affirming the Existence of the World of Images," in *Wrappings: Essays on Feminism, Art, and the Martial Arts* (New York: TSL Press, 1984), 110.

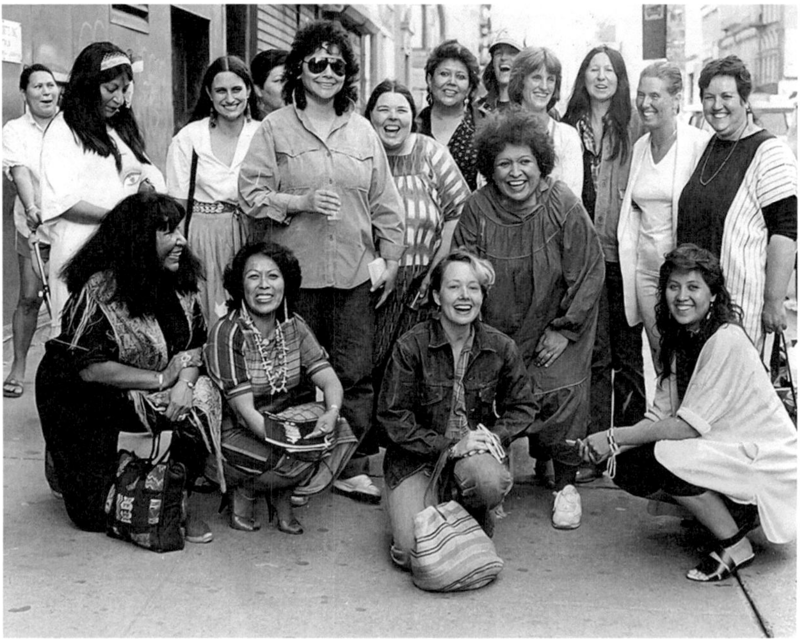

FIGURE 2.6. Artists, organizers, and attendees outside the Gallery of the American Indian Community House, New York, 1985, at the opening of the exhibition *Women of Sweetgrass, Cedar and Sage: Contemporary Art by Native American Women*, cocurated by Harmony Hammond and Jaune Quick-to-See Smith. *Front, L to R:* Gloria Miguel, Dorothea Romero, Donna Couteau, and Jolene Rickard. *Back, L to R:* Vickie Tarrant, Vera Colorado, Charleen Touchette, Lillian Pitt, Marta Carlson, Gail Trembly, Lisa Mayo, Muriel Miguel, unknown, Erin Younger, Jaune Quick-to-See Smith, Harmony Hammond, and Kay Miller. This was one of the first traveling exhibitions to present a wide range of work by contemporary Native American women, including paintings, weavings, ceramic work, jewelry, beadwork, photography, quilts, and basketry. After opening in New York, the exhibition toured North America for over two years, traveling to eight additional venues across the country. Photo: Jesse Cooday, Tlingit. Courtesy American Indian Community House.

Horseblinders

Heresies: A Feminist Publication on Art and Politics (1980)

In 1980 there is still pressure to answer the question, "What *exactly* is feminist art?" This does not reflect an interest in the function and concerns of art by feminists, or in what issues feminist art might address, but rather an obsessive need for a rigid definition of what a "politically correct" feminist art *should* look like. Curators, dealers, critics, and artists—male and female (who come from the male-centered art world), as well as, unfortunately, many feminist artists and/or political activists—all have an investment in such a stylistic definition of feminist art. No matter where this fixation comes from, I find it equally disturbing in its narrow and dogmatic attitudes, its focus on the object-ness of art, its distraction from the creative process, and its avoidance of true critical discussion.

The main problem is that both the art establishment and the feminist community approach feminism as an aesthetic or a style. But feminism is not an aesthetic. It is the political analysis of the experience of being a woman in patriarchal culture. This analysis becomes a state of mind, a way of being and thinking when it is reflected in one's life. It can be articulated in art, and the art itself can in turn contribute to the process of analysis and consciousness. If art and life are connected, and if one is a feminist, then one must be a feminist artist—that is, one must make art that reflects a political consciousness of what it means to be a woman in patriarchal culture. The visual form this consciousness takes varies from artist to artist.

Thus, art and feminism are not totally separate, nor are they the same thing. If this is not understood, if we view feminist art as an aesthetic represented by one correct style, then anything unexpected or unfamiliar is excluded. Art not derived from the white middle class is excluded. Radical new forms are excluded. The history of the patriarchal art world is and always has been the history of definitions and boundaries—the history of who has been excluded. To continue defining art according to this tradition affects the creative freedom and possibilities of those feminists making art and affects the possible roles of the art itself. Isn't this part of what we hope to change?

The male-dominated art establishment has a need to qualify feminist art as just another style. I heard one well-meaning male critic, Carter Ratcliff, refer to it as "the avant-garde of the modernist tradition."[1] While I believe he was referring to the power and innovative energy of feminist art, he reduced it to the latest development in a linear progression of inner art dialogue, where styles are bought, copied, and subverted, resold and dismissed as "past art movements." This attitude also implies that those women who are "good artists" will outgrow their feminist phase.

In 1976, Lawrence Alloway made a similar statement in his patronizing progress report on feminist art, where he informed us how we were doing, where our critical problems lie (in having no comprehensive theory of feminist art and no manifesto to state this theory), and what we now had to work for.[2] At the same time that he criticized feminist artists for the discrepancy between their work and his theory, he attacked those very women who were out there actively creating work and developing theory. Since in his eyes no one woman's ideas were comprehensive enough to stand for the whole movement, he discredited them all. In fact, he saw the richness of diverse philosophies and aesthetics as divisionary rather than as the basis of feminism itself. In the end, Alloway's report was an attempt to foster competition among women artists (as they strove for his critical approval).

The newest updated version of this patronizing intellectualization of women's experience reflected in art is by Donald Kuspit, who, like Alloway, claims to speak for feminists since he apparently doesn't think that we are yet capable of speaking for ourselves.[3] He states that the "aggressive," "revolutionary" feminist "critical intention" (the critical relationship to the existing order?

to the masculine?) has nearly been lost because of "authoritarian," "cosmetic," "transcendental" feminism, epitomized at its worst by those women artists dealing with pattern and decoration in their work. This "authoritarian feminist art" arises from a "willful exercise of power—an attempt to achieve dominance, or at least prominence in the art world." Kuspit makes no mention of the many hundreds of male and female artists all across the United States who are also working with these issues, nor does he mention the role the art market has played in the visibility of these works. I agree that no one style should dictate what other feminist artists should do. That is what I am writing about. But that is hardly what feminist pattern painters are attempting. Kuspit superimposes his own authoritarian position onto feminist art and then turns around and tells us that "authoritarian feminism in fact signals a split in the feminist camp."

I say he is trying to split and divert us. Just what is the "old," "revolutionary" feminist critical intention? Transcendental feminism? Authoritarian feminism? I have been a part of the feminist art movement since its beginnings, and have been around the national and international feminist communities quite a bit more than Mr. Kuspit, and I have never heard either of such a split or of these feminist categories. They do not exist merely because he says so. He assumes they do because he cannot imagine a feminist art that is not authoritarian, or part of a linear progression.

Women do not think about feminist art this way. Such short-sighted thinking and language do not encompass the most unique and powerful aspects of feminist art. While obviously influenced by modernism, feminist art in its very diversity of content, style, form, media, and technique proves that it is outside of and separate from that linear tradition.

However, the patriarchy has directly and indirectly affected feminist artists by defining, institutionalizing, and marketing feminism. The pressure to weave a definable feminist art can only be exerted with capitalist threads attached. There is recognition and money to be made by men and women off of the commodity status of a standardized feminist art object. While women don't seem to need or want such a thing, many are invested in spreading or popularizing a look that approaches their own. Unfortunately, this too encourages distractions and competition: who did what first, who is a feminist artist and who isn't (who is and who isn't "politically correct"), and a subtle but important shift of focus from the work to the person. In some instances, the artist herself is marketed or markets herself within the male art world or the feminist community. This feminist art community, which is a loose network of many communities, galleries, organizations, support groups, and individuals across the country, competes within itself as a marketplace for feminist art, artists, art schools, and art magazines.

Additional pressure on feminist artists with a political consciousness to define a feminist art style comes from within the movement, from feminist activists who have bought the old belief that art is across the board apolitical and elitist. Unfortunately, many women (frequently Marxists, lesbian separatists, and anarchists) still feel that to be nonelitist, art must be overtly political in imagery. Here they fall into the reactionary anti-art trap, espousing simplistic notions about what is "political" and politically correct—only posters, buttons, murals, guerrilla theater, graffiti, media art, and representational painting, sculpture, film, and photography—certainly nothing abstract.

Such narrow definitions only provide new limitations in place of the old. Political limitations instead of aesthetic ones. Instead of bringing their political consciousness to art and examining the ways art can have political impact, many women take the easy way out. As a result, those feminist artists who are struggling to integrate their art and their politics are supported neither by the art world nor by their own social and political communities. For instance, in our desire to dissolve hierarchies, we have been quick to develop the unspoken belief that collective means better, and many women fail to validate individual expression. But I think it is important to see that even collective art comes in many forms: a performance piece conceived and directed with input from all the participants, a community mural conceived and painted by neighborhood residents, the "benevolent hierarchy" of Judy Chicago's *The Dinner Party* [1979], or an individual artist collaging materials given to her by her friends or her grandmother.

It is ironic that in consciousness-raising we validate the individual experience as representative of all women's experiences, and then at other times we turn around and criticize an individual if she does anything on her own, as if that would somehow threaten the cohesiveness of the group. Because collectives are made up of individuals, and individuals are nourished by the collective spirit, we need to validate all these ways of working. One way is not more correct than another. The group and the individual experience can be supported and connected. However, when this does not happen, we find ourselves pressured to choose between the two. We end up guilt-tripping individuals who are trying to do both rather than creating a place where the two can coexist. Women are forced to choose when they shouldn't have to.

We do need to develop a social conscience about art—and its effect on people, especially on women. But to do this we must go deeper than the surface. We must examine the potentials of different mediums and contexts, rejecting all pressures to limit our forms and ways of working so that they fit preconceived notions of "good art" or "politically correct art." I want feminist art to fit both of these categories, but I also want it to go far beyond them.

I have met many women who—perhaps because they are desperate from longtime exclusion, perhaps because they have been trained by art schools to imitate successful art world styles, or perhaps in response to criticism that they are not political enough, or perhaps because they need to attach themselves to something powerful—are copying some preconceived notion of feminist art. This is different from working with common concerns, being genuinely influenced by other women's work, or finding similarities because they come from shared female experience. That is not what I am talking about. But we should question where these notions come from. Any piece of fabric push-pinned to the wall doesn't make it as art. The materials have to be transformed. Too much women's work looks like what we think feminist art should look like. The essence of the creative process, the why and how we make art, is bypassed in the attempt to make acceptable or politically correct feminist art. Too often the result is an empty copy. A shell. And looks it. One of the essential lessons of feminism as applied to artmaking has been missed—that is, how the artmaking process functions for us as we make art and how this becomes part of the communicative sense of the piece. If you merely copy the "look" of an art object, whether it is feminist or not, you sidestep the importance of making art.

A feminist visual rhetoric can be as dogmatic and dangerous as any political rhetoric. It is not politically correct nor necessarily good art to paint fruit, flowers, goddesses, or women showing physical affection for each other, or to use the color pink, or to work with fabric and sewing techniques merely because they have been used traditionally by women. Rather, it is our right and our choice to draw on these subjects, sources, materials, and techniques if we wish to, if they aid expression, give layers of meaning to our work, and create a context for communication. But if we set out to make something that fits a predetermined concept of feminist art, we are only making something without substance, without passion, without presence. Likewise, if we as artists and viewers dismiss work by others because it does not fit into narrow definitions, we are just repeating what the boys have been doing for centuries, and we are likely to miss some real and moving statements about women's lives and experiences that are different from our own.

I want us to push ourselves. There was a time in the late '60s and early '70s when we needed to support any work done by a woman. But that time is past. It is no longer enough. We deserve better, and we owe it to each other to make the best possible work and to develop and offer each other criticism—political and aesthetic (not that they are separate). Anything is not okay in the name of feminism, just as it is not okay in the name of art. Honest criticism goes further than dishonest support.

As feminists, we can participate in the development of a criticism aimed at helping each other make art with meaning. Energy need not be wasted in defending the very right to content. We can help each other to say what we want to say in the clearest, most effective way. That done, we can then hold ourselves accountable for the work—for what it is about and how it affects women.

An honest criticism would bring art and politics together, helping us to understand their relationship, and furthering their mutual development. We need to develop criteria through a critical practice of our own, to hold each other accountable without censoring our creative imagination. Criticism must be integrated into the artmaking process, and vice versa. Feminist art criticism evolves as our art evolves, where women have the passion and honesty to articulate what we believe and know, to admit what we do not know, to question each other and ourselves, and to hear the answers we offer.

ED. NOTE

"Horseblinders" was originally published in "Women Organized/Women Divided: Power, Propaganda and Backlash" issue, *Heresies: A Feminist Publication on Art and Politics* 3, no. 9 (1980): 45–47. All issues of *Heresies* are preserved in the Heresies Collection, Special Collections and University Archives, Rutgers University Archives, New Brunswick, New Jersey.

The numbered endnotes for this essay, below, are by the author.

NOTES

1. Carter Ratcliff, "The Personal and the Public in Women's Art," panel discussion, Brooklyn Museum, 1977.
2. See Lawrence Alloway, "Women's Art in the 70s," *Art in America*, May–June 1976.
3. See Donald B. Kuspit, "Betraying the Feminist Intention: The Case Against Feminist Decorative Art," *Arts Magazine*, November 1979.

Curatorial Statement, *Home Work* Exhibition

Women's Hall of Fame, Seneca Falls, New York (1981)

In the last ten years, a large and growing body of work by women has appeared that contains images, materials, or processes (activities or techniques) that are associated with the domestic environment. This is the visual reflection of an examination of women's roles and experiences in this culture that has been taking place within the feminist movement. Until very recently these experiences have been absent from mainstream art. In the past, creative work that was done in the home (and which was therefore usually by women) was ignored or put down as "craft." Since women in their experiences were not considered important, any work that was reflective of the home, the place where "women's work" was done, was considered unimportant or minor.

Today, women are responding to the home as a powerful source for their art-making. In doing so, they are reclaiming and affirming women's lives and daily experiences as important and interesting. Others, through their art, critique these culturally imposed roles.

Obviously household images have been and are used by male artists. But, when we look at how they are used, when we look at what the concerns are, and what the particular statement or feeling of the piece is, they usually appear quite different than work by women. For instance, it is interesting to note that most Pop artists (and certainly the most popular of them) were men, and while they chose the commonplace object as their subject matter, the work generally was about the media and marketing of these objects. They were presented in a detached way, objects in the world at large rather than in the privacy of the home. It is as if the home was pillaged to make a statement about culture out there as opposed to the home, which was not considered to be part of the culture. As Lucy Lippard points out, if the first Pop artists had been women, chances are that Pop Art as a movement would probably never have gotten off the ground or out of the closet since it would have been dismissed as too personal, or merely genre.

When we begin to examine the work being done today by women that deals with the domestic environment, we begin to see several recurring approaches to the subject matter. As Lippard writes, "women seem to be taking off from, rather than getting off on, the implications of floors, brooms, and dirty laundry."[1]

The main way that domestic imagery appears is in a renewed interest in the still life, a form that can be simultaneously personal, intimate, and political. Women have been redefining the traditional still life in a number of ways. Instead of the classical arrangement of fruit and wine bottle (usually arranged in a studio), we are presented with the reality of what surrounds women in their daily lives—sinks full of dirty dishes, unmade beds, laundry, appliances to be used or polished, food cooked and put up in canning jars, or cellophane wrapped from the grocery store. Sometimes these still lives are presented neatly put away on shelves or in drawers, but usually the objects take over, multiply, as if to say a woman's work is never done. The images fill the canvas as the chores fill the day. The artist's perspective, and therefore our perspective as we view the work, is directly over the sink looking down, the edge of the canvas framing and limiting our range of vision, or objects viewed from the floor as if we were down there scrubbing away. Even what would seem to be traditional drapery studies have the added content of unmade beds, folded clothes, and dirty laundry.

Other still lives are like visual scrapbooks, with fragments of women's lives coming together. These are often autobiographical and intimate in nature, including grandmother's china or needlework, a photograph, textiles, favorite jewelry, other special mementos, or objects from collections. They are arranged like knickknacks on a coffee table or altars on our dresser top. Many women are collectors, and their collections seem to find their way into their art.

Sometimes, but rarely, women are actually pictured within the domestic scene. More often we, the viewers, are left to project ourselves into this private world. When women are depicted, they are usually alone having a quiet cup of coffee, isolated, or perhaps looking out a window. Always a private world is alluded to—sometimes hope, escape, transformation, or connection.

Perhaps it is women's use of the grid that most implies connections and ties. Women have used the grid as a means of organizing and controlling their art much in the same way that lists organize their lives. When combined with marking, the grid is transformed from its reference to weaving to design, decoration, and patterning.

Even the materials that women use to make their art often reflect activities that normally take place in the home. In addition to traditional art materials such as paint, pencil, chalk, and clay, women are using such materials as cloth, thread, sequins, beads, ribbons, rickrack, and yarn, which refer to women's traditional needle arts. Or, they are utilizing lint, shopping lists, newspaper and magazine clippings, coupons, kitchen shelving paper, patterns, tiles, linoleum, wallpaper, aprons, napkins, food itself, and all sorts of leftovers, odds and ends, and hand-me-downs. Indeed, it seems that their ability to make use of everything extends to their art.

Both materials and techniques have been used with a consciousness that contributes to the meaning of the works. For instance, the tools used to do cooking and housework are often used to apply paint or manipulate other materials used in the art. Activities that are associated with women's work are utilized in a creative way. Gardening, ironing, cleaning, nesting, sewing, weaving, knitting, quilting, crocheting, interior decorating, cooking, keeping family histories, polishing, china painting, and cake decorating techniques, are all ways of giving reference to domestic roles. Creative possibilities are expanded. Repetitive acts reflect the tediousness or take on a new dignity. All three of these—images, materials, and processes—are combined in various ways by each woman. While there is a common denominator of shared experience as women in this society, the work is as varied as each individual woman and her experiences and feelings. While the work takes on different forms, there is a literal as well as metaphorical and political level.

All the work in this exhibition has been chosen from slides by artists who are on file at the visual arts referral service at CAPS [Creative Artists Public Service Program]. As such they represent a sampling of an even larger body of work existing by women dealing with these issues.[2] Finally we are seeing art that reflects the reality of our lives as women. Domestic imagery and references are one way that this reality is given form.

ED. NOTES

Originally published as the curatorial statement in the exhibition catalogue for *Home Work: The Domestic Environment as Reflected in the Work of Women Artists*, National Women's Hall of Fame, Seneca Falls, New York, 1981, n.p.

1. Lucy R. Lippard, *From the Center: Feminist Essays on Women's Art* (New York: Dutton, 1976), 57.

2. The Creative Artists Public Service Program (CAPS) was funded by the New York State Council on the Arts to support individual artists' work in a variety of disciplines. The Visual Arts Referral Service was a slide and information registry conceived to promote the work of CAPS Fellowship recipients and semifinalists. Established in 1970, CAPS awarded fellowships ranging from $3,500 to $10,000 to artists for over a decade.

Monstrous Beauty

The Woman Gone Wild

Beauty and Critique (1982)

> Art and artists are made on earth, in history, in organized society. And in the modern era, as in the past, what has been sanctified as high art and called True, Good, and Beautiful is born of the aspirations of those who are empowered to shape culture.[1]

Beauty and notions of beauty have been mostly male-defined. Universal beauty as a basis of a belief system called aesthetics is a concept of rich white men. Those in power. Those who have a vested interest in themselves and their kind—in validating that which reflects and benefits their lives. Art which reflects this interest they call universal. It is based on institutionalized beauty, that is beauty as one more patriarchal construct.

> Institutionalized beauty is what white Western men decide is good to look at.
> Institutionalized beauty is a container.

Institutionalized beauty is not truth.
Institutionalized beauty is not real.
Institutionalized beauty lies.
Institutionalized beauty smooths over differences (class, sex, race, age, cultures).
Institutionalized beauty is passive, not active.
Institutionalized beauty reinforces power via aesthetics.

When we talk about beauty or its philosophical extension, aesthetics, we are talking about a belief system that has been used to subjugate certain peoples. Images of beauty that are woman-centered or created by Third World people are examples of images that are either ignored or ridiculed, although occasionally they are temporarily adopted by mainstream culture (the marketing of "the exotic" or "the taboo"—afros, "ethnic" looks, hints of lesbianism in fashion magazines).

According to patriarchal concepts, images of women in art and media, and therefore women themselves, must fit certain male descriptions/limitations in order to be considered beautiful to look at. However, in these images, women are unhealthy, passive, and powerless. The patriarchal concept of female beauty is a passive one—the female being acted upon rather than acting on, or even acting at all.

As Carol Duncan points out in her article "The Esthetics of Power in Modern Erotic Art," Western art history is full of images depicting male domination and power over women.[2] From Delacroix's *Death of Sardanapalus* (1827), Ingres's *Roger Freeing Angelica* (1819), and Hiram Powers's *The Greek Slave* (1843), to Edvard Munch's *Madonna* (1893–94) and *Vampire* (1894), Picasso's *Les Demoiselles d'Avignon* (1907), and Willem de Kooning's *Woman* series (c. 1950s), to the currently popular and marketable new expressionist sex violent painting from Germany and media images such as record album covers of the Rolling Stones, Ohio Players, and the Plasmatics, women are portrayed as victims. And this victimization is meant to be part of their sexual appeal. "So often do such works invite fantasies of male conquest (or fantasies that justify male domination) that the subjugation of the female will appear to be one of the primary motives of modern erotic art."[3]

To achieve power and dominance, the male artist turns woman into the ideal universal and unreal nude or vampire she-bitch (the femme fatale) who deserves to be and must be destroyed or restrained through specific imagery (Delacroix, Ingres, Munch, Klimt, Kirchner, etc.) or through the more sophisticated and subtle but no less dangerous means of fragmentation and abstraction (Picasso and de Kooning, etc.). Woman must be separated from herself and it must be made clear that she owes her existence to the male artist and not he to her.[4] As Duncan says, for men, "to create is to possess, to dominate, and to be quintessentially male."[5]

Art promotes the relationships it portrays.

Images, objects, or persons outside these descriptions are not considered beautiful, that is, not good to look at. Art that is not considered beautiful is considered bad. Raw. Undeveloped. Unrefined. And while folk art, [so-called] primitive art, or "outsider art" may momentarily be in favor, they ultimately are not considered equal to or part of the great white male aesthetic.

The traditional concept of beauty is one that is bestowed and institutionalized by patriarchy in its own interests. Women who are outside of this concept—that is, women who are healthy, active, and powerful—become threatening and are made into monsters like the women in de Kooning's and Picasso's paintings. The woman who is herself with power, passion, and direction must not be considered beautiful. Render her ugly and gross. When beauty and power combine, the result is called a monster, a vampire, a witch, a lesbian, a mad woman, Medusa, a woman gone wild.

A Male Description
Webster's New World Dictionary

The Medusa—*one of three Gorgons slain by Perseus—like a jellyfish with tentacles.* Gorgon—*from gorgos—terrible, firm, Greek myth—any of the three sisters with snakes for hair—so horrible that the beholder was turned to stone—any ugly, terrible, repulsive, terrifying woman.* To gorgonize—*to petrify or stupefy with a look.* Gore—*the filth, and blood shed from a wound, clotted blood.* Gorge—*the throat or gullet place to swallow up—stomach of a voracious animal—a feeling of resentment or anger.* Gorgeous—*from gorges—is beautiful, wonderful, delightful.*[6]

A Female Description
Lesbian Peoples: Material for a Dictionary, *Wittig and Zeig*

Medusa. *Celebrated as Medusa the Ferocious. Queen of the Gorgon Amazons who lived in Libya during the Bronze Age. Medusa had an abundant and curly head of hair, into which she immingled black snakes. When Medusa galloped the snakes moved around her head, and some coiled around her neck. But when she joined in battle on her mare, all the snakes would rise at once, hissing, furious, agitated with movement, sowing panic among her enemies. Medusa could petrify all those who rose up against her by the look in her eyes. [. . .] The Gorgons under Medusa, and the Libyans under Athena, were led to fight during the most terrifying battle known within Amazon memory. [. . .] Medusa was killed by Athena, Queen of the Libyans. Later on, even when she was celebrated as a goddess, Athena kept on her chest the head of the terrible Gorgon whom she secretly loved, it is said. Gorgons [. . .] as of other Amazons [. . .] had an Amazonian structure without compromise [. . .] Long after their splendor has "paled" however, something of their indestructible nature simmers on and from time to time, breaks out of its obscurity.*[7]

In the first description, Medusa is found to be ugly, terrible, and repulsive. A connection is suggested between beauty, power, and the woman as monster. But in Wittig and Zeig's description, Medusa is a powerful and active agent—she can turn you to stone with her looks *if she so chooses*—it doesn't just happen because of the way she looks. Medusa is a woman of power, a fighter, and that fighting spirit of hers and the other Gorgons still appears in women today.

In going out of control, she takes control and becomes more than a representation of that fear of the powerful female. She becomes powerful.

The Medusa. My first etching as an art student was a head of Medusa. I was always fascinated by her, even though I didn't know who she was exactly, mythologically speaking. But somehow, that image of the woman—slightly mad, passionate, with her hair swirling out from her head and tangled, was a powerful image for me—daring, and strong. She seemed intense, right here, focused—exactly who she was, in her own self—a truth and in that sense beautiful.

In art history classes I was always attracted to the femme fatale from the turn of the century. I didn't understand that like the vampire or monster, the femme fatale is a man-made phenomenon created in order to match and control the awesome power of the female who bleeds but does not die. I loved who she was and simultaneously thought I was her. I didn't understand how she was both temptress and victim, how she was a male fantasy created to validate the subjugation of female power. I did not understand that she was supposed to be a monster.

It was her madness. I identified with madness as power repressed/expressed. Madness giving me room outside the stereotypical female role. A woman could be powerful and affect others if she was a bit mad, I thought. Or her powers came out of her madness. Out of control. Am I too powerful? If a woman is mad, you can dismiss her seriousness (but not her danger), unlike a mad man who, of course, is a genius. But then women are dismissed anyway, I intuited, so at least with madness—they just call creative women mad—at least with this you could go ahead and do what you wanted to do—to be your total self.

Later, when I was making sculpture by accumulating and recycling old rags that women gave me into female *Bags* and *Presences* [see plate 2], I wanted my work to be so beautiful that it demanded your attention. A beauty out of the raw fragments of women's lives. A wholeness of survival. In a statement accompanying my first New York exhibition in 1973, I wrote: "I want to demand your attention because I can get it no other way. Is this not part of my women's madness?"[8] While I meant this ironically, I think it reflects how, even then, making work that reflected women's experience in this culture, work that connected me to a line of female creativity before me, work that was about women taking personal and political space—even then I was uncomfortable with actively taking that space. There was still a part of me, as with many women artists, which did not feel I had the right to make art, to create new and powerful images of women. And so it was easier to associate myself with that disease—women's madness.

> When [. . .] one reads of a witch being ducked, of a woman possessed by devils, of a wise woman selling herbs [. . .] then I think we are on the track of a lost novelist, a suppressed poet, of some mute and inglorious Jane Austen, some Emily Bronte who dashed her brains out on the moor or mopped and mowed about the highways crazed with the torture that her gift had put her to.[9]

And so, like the kudzu vine imported into the South by the patriarchs to control nature (soil erosion) and hide their government research plants and their nuclear reactors . . . like the kudzu, which has now gotten out of control and which wildly wraps around, covers, and feeds off anything it so chooses, the monster (the mad/creative woman) is out of control (actively creating art in her own image). In going out of control, she takes control and becomes more than a representation of that fear of the powerful female. She becomes powerful.

Bertha Harris, in her article "What We Mean to Say: Notes Towards Defining the Nature of Lesbian Literature," has examined the image of the monster in literature and film and developed the idea that "Monsters are, and have always been, invented to express what ordinary people cannot: feeling [. . .] the quintessence of all that is female; and female enraged."[10] The monster represents patriarchy's most extreme fear—the woman-identified woman, the lesbian. For like all monsters, the lesbian is powerful in her difference, and is capable of seducing and converting others to her ways. Harris looks to film classics such as Frankenstein and Dracula and to contemporary monster films such as *Jaws* and *King Kong* as examples of the lesbian in mainstream art—the monster representing the extreme of patriarchal fear, the woman loving women, the woman of power, the woman whose power is part of her beauty, the lesbian.

Keep the ugly edge. The edge is the place of truth and the truth is beauty.

Just as men perceive power in men as beautiful, feminists perceive power in women as beautiful. Only it is a different kind of power. It is a transformative power, a creative power, changing one form of energy into another, rather than power over something or someone. Feminists see this sense of self emanating from within women, this strength, as beautiful, not threatening, but beautiful and good to look at and be. In woman-centered art, women are not shown as weak, sick, or passive. They are not objectified, exploited, or victimized. Nor are they shown in conflict with each other. Instead, they appear strong, healthy, active, and comfortable with their bodies and their sexuality. This is in direct contrast to the misogynist attitudes inherent in patriarchal concepts of institutionalized beauty, that is, in contrast to images of women throughout the history of Western art.

In our art we are depicting women's bodies as they really are—in different shapes, sizes, and colors. We are painting women of different ages so that all the freckles, wrinkles, and stretch marks show. Joan Semmel paints close-up landscape examinations of her own body—the body of a middle-aged woman stretching, folding, and falling where it will, filling the space of the canvas, warm and sensuous. It is not the firm, glossy body replica on record album covers or the thin asexual threads we find in fashion magazines (the slick media version of the twentieth-century paintings Duncan was talking about). In Semmel's work, and the work of many other women, the feeling is one of a woman's body following a natural cycle, the body as nature itself. Changing, and beautiful in its change.

Women do not depict each other as sex objects to be dominated or possessed, or as objects of any kind. Niki de Saint Phalle's *Nana*, Kate Millett's *Naked Ladies*, Betsy Damon's *7000 Year Old Woman*, and Mary Beth Edelson's Goddess figures are powerful women who take up and fill space. Hardly the ideal of the classical contained nude, these women are big—often ten feet tall—out of proportion (out of control?), have lumps and bumps, and seem to be totally here and in touch with their physical selves. They are not passive, but active, full of energy and exuberance, and in this sense both beautiful and erotic.

For many women, a strong female body sense is indicated through their use of materials and the physical manipulation of those materials. I think immediately of Eva Hesse's work, of Lynda Benglis's orgasmic latex and foam pieces, the definite labia imagery of her delicately colored wax pieces, Hannah Wilke's early fragile latex flowers, Amy Hamouda's fiber sculptures, and my own recent wrapped sculptures. In this work, abstract female body references are presented in direct powerful ways. All this work shows how in the last ten years, within the context of the feminist movement, women, both lesbian and heterosexual, have been getting in touch with and reclaiming their bodies and are expressing these feelings in their art.[11]

Getting back to my own work, what do I think about when I make art? Do I think about making something beautiful? Something powerful? No, I think more (when I think at all) about getting an essence, a presence into the work—an honesty and a truth that to me is beauty. Giving form to something that does not exist in the physical sense. Like I said, a presence, which I would define as an essence made visible. A female presence in all its power. Somehow I always imagine that essence will be somewhat crude and raw, certainly with energy—active. Not existing in previous categories of beauty or non-beauty. Something other, of itself. But no, already that implies too much conscious thinking. All this is more what I know, not what I think.

ED. NOTE

Originally published in Richard Milazzo, ed., *Beauty and Critique* (New York: Time and Space Limited, 1982), 97–103.

The numbered endnotes for this essay, below, are by the author.

NOTES

1. Carol Duncan, "The Esthetics of Power in Modern Erotic Art," *Heresies* 1, no. 1 (1977): 50.
2. See Duncan's article for a full discussion of these works.
3. Duncan, "The Esthetics of Power in Modern Erotic Art," 46.
4. See Harmony Hammond, "A Sense of Touch," *Heresies* 3, no. 4 (1981).
5. Duncan, "The Esthetics of Power in Modern Erotic Art," 47.
6. *Webster's New World Dictionary*, Second College Edition (Glasgow: Collins and World, 1974).
7. Monique Wittig and Sande Zeig, *Lesbian Peoples: Material for a Dictionary* (New York: Avon, 1979), 106, 28.
8. Harmony Hammond, statement for exhibition at A.I.R. Gallery, New York, January 1973. [Ed.: This was Hammond's first solo exhibition in New York City.]
9. Virginia Woolf, *A Room of One's Own* (London: Grafton, 1977), 55.
10. Bertha Harris, "What We Mean to Say: Notes Towards Defining the Nature of Lesbian Literature," *Heresies* 1, no. 3 (1977): 6–7.
11. Harmony Hammond, restatement of a related discussion in "A Sense of Touch," *New Art Examiner*, Summer 1979; revised version in "Sex Issue," *Heresies* 3, no. 4 (1981): 43–46.

Affirming the Existence of the World of Images

Wrappings: Essays on Feminism, Art, and the Martial Arts (1984)

Trying to walk to Lake Salagou we got lost. It happened little by little. Everyone said you couldn't walk there but we had a map. The path gradually disappeared as we went over hills, down through brush and trees. Perhaps we were following animal tracks, weeds faintly beaten down, or where wind brushed the tips of the grasses. We could see the lake for it was very large, but hills off and unreachable during the remaining sun. We made it as far as the bories *but after that lost the yellow markers among ochre lichen. Stone walls. Fragments of a maze we could not comprehend but had to walk around. Trying to retrace our steps there was no way. The grasses had closed after us. The sun shone from a different angle. Not being able to see the path, or seeing paths where there were none, we had to admit that we were lost, really lost without a sense of which direction to go. No immediate markers. Useless references. She kept looking back at Lacoste, the small medieval village we left behind but it was now hills and valleys away. Unreachable. I kept looking to the lake. But where was I when I first saw the lake? Our sense of direction was different. We circled many hours looking for the path. Try to go back to the one standing* borie *I thought. Shelter for the night without fire and only bodies to warm each other until the next full day. But she did not want to spend the night there and frankly, neither did I. We were foolish not to have left markers, to think we knew the way. But then, looking forward seeing something different than what we were looking for. Vineyards visible in the distance. And seemingly walkable in the time left. If there is a vineyard there is a path and a path leads to somewhere. A path leads to another path or a road. . . .*

Working on *Wrappings*. Affirming the existence of the world of images. A discovery. A risk. A stepping out of history. A stepping into the world of abstract imagery. Journey. Planes of nature. Forms of desire. Systems of belief. A new world.

Wrappings is history. A history that needs to be known, needs to be taught and included. But the spiral turning back on itself leads to another plane. Younger women say their issues are not the same as ours. They are right and they are wrong. Feminist history can fill the silence, can teach us who we are and what we have done. Provide paths where we might choose to walk. As my friend Claudia B. says, women must not forget the struggles of the past for many are still the struggles of the present; but women must also be willing to pull away from those struggles and LEAD.[1] To move in new directions. To not stand still. To not repeat. Change.

By now, almost everyone has acknowledged the contribution of feminism to the art of the '70s, and in one way or another, most major critics have stated (what we artists knew all along) that the most innovative work was either done or influenced by women. An emphasis on content and insistence on nonhierarchical pluralism. An interest in intimacy, autobiography, traditional arts, and art of non-Western cultures. The decorative. The functional. A renewal of interest in watercolor, political and performance art, collective and collaborative work, and the use of alternative art spaces. Feminism has not provided a stylistic movement but a personalization and political consciousness of materials, process, and imagery. Lucy L. has stated, "Feminism's greatest contribution to the future of art has probably been precisely its *lack* of contribution to modernism."[2] Without feminism, there would not have been the rich pluralism of the '70s.

Of course, not everyone has liked this pluralism, or as Jeff P. has pointed out, in the '70s, pluralism meant "women," and that meant "no news," at least until absorbed and renamed postmodernism.[3] But backlash is "news." The macho stance of the artist was reborn with the Picasso exhibit [*Pablo Picasso: A Retrospective*] at MoMA in 1980, and nurtured by the media. Since then, more dealers and curators seem to be showing less work by women. And to date, there still has not been a major museum-scale exhibition documenting the range and influence of feminist art.

The commercial marketing of the neo-expressionist movement has raised the anger of women artists to a height not seen since the early '70s. The exclusion of women artists who have been visibly working in an expressionist mode throughout the last decade is a constant topic of panel discussions and personal conversations. If she is lucky, the forty-five-year-old woman artist is in the same place in her career as the twenty-eight-year-old male artist. And, beyond the brush strokes, much of the work which does get exhibited these days is overtly sexist in content. Many women artists wonder, are we really back to the limitations of the '60s? Carrie R. observes that whenever the male international art warfare escalates, the boys are sent to the front.[4]

Anger. Disillusionment. Bitterness. A discontent that is distracting. Separating us from our work. I am not surprised by this backlash because I never felt that the art world "gave" women anything. For the most part, the visibility we have today is because of our activism. We insisted on the right to make and show work. We created art groups, workshops, slide registries, art education programs, co-op galleries, and alternative spaces. We created art journals, books, and films. In spite of the recent slip in percentage of women represented in commercial galleries, the fact remains that more women's work IS VISIBLE than ever before. This is why our history, even our recent history, is important. Or we forget what we've done and it gets difficult to move on. If we, for one moment, believe that the art world gave us space and permission to make art, then it seems like they can take it away. But if we realize that they never gave us anything, then we have no expectations. While I think we should protest discrimination, the real danger is shifting our focus away from our work. That is the real danger of backlash. Work can only grow out of work.

I am surprised by how much attention and creative energy this backlash is sapping from women artists. Yes, I, too, want to be visible, want to make a living as the artist I am, and I will fight against being excluded, but how diversionary is it? Given a choice between fighting and working, I choose working. But that isn't a decision we have to make. The ultimate passivity is not working. The situation today is different than in the early '70s. We work with a sense of self, a focus, and the knowledge that we are not isolated. A loose network of individuals and groups connects women artists of the past to women artists of today, and artists of today to each other and to women who are not artists. And we have an awareness of the contradictions of being artists in this society—knowing that at its best art has nothing to do with the art world. The problem is how to make demands without putting too much energy into it. And how to make work relevant to the '80s and '90s. To not compromise but to move on in spite of the distractions.

I, too, get drawn into it sometimes. I do not even notice. Writing this last piece for *Wrappings* based on the moment, and trying to see my way through to a vision that I am not able to communicate, I, too, sound tired and angry. Linda M. tells me, "You sound like Mother Courage pulling her burden of art and politics through SoHo looking for a break."[5] She is right. Ugh. She says that the '80s offer no time for anger or tiredness. That is why cocaine has become important. You have to be fast and have good reflexes (video games) like [David] Salle, [Julian] Schnabel, et al. Theirs is a reflex art—art that is against. Reactionary. Modernism. The history of art that is against.

It is easy to lose the vision. To refuse product orientation is difficult in a society where the only way artists are supported is through products. How to feed the spirit. The stones know. The question is how to make art that is FOR something and not a reaction against. Art that is INSPIRATIONAL, a positive force in the face of sexist backlash and the threat of nuclear and environmental disaster. Art that goes beyond critique. Creating a continuous positive female presence. I envision a feminist work of outrageous quality. Complex. Deep. Rich in associations. Full of content and meaning. Committed. Responsible. Passionate. Not stereotyped or compromised by market success, mainstream backlash, or political correctness. It is a continuance of the best of our work. Developed and refined. Affirming the existence of the world of images. The ancient role of artist as shaman.

ED. NOTE

"Affirming the Existence of the World of Images" was originally published in Harmony Hammond, *Wrappings: Essays on Feminism, Art, and the Martial Arts* (New York: Time and Space Limited, 1984), 107–10.

The numbered endnotes for this essay, below, are by the author.

NOTES

1. Claudia Bruce, personal dialogue.
2. Lucy Lippard, "Sweeping Exchanges: The Contribution of Feminism to the Art of the 1970s," *Art Journal*, Fall/Winter 1980, 362.
3. Jeff Perrone, "No News," *Art*, February 1983, page unknown.
4. Carrie Rickey, "Put the Blame on the Boys, Mame," *Village Voice*, November 2, 1982, 7.
5. Linda Mussmann, personal dialogue.

Statement, *Chicken Lady*

A.I.R. Gallery, New York (1984)

Chicken Lady is in each of us. We enter into the painting with her. Gradually, her little legs move out, sometimes aggressively, where she meets other characters floating about in the world. Tree of life/spine. Ribs. The primitive beginnings of *Chicken Lady*, her primordial beginnings, her history, where she comes from, is her backbone. We see inside her and see her insides projected outside. It is an expressionist metaphysical world of female characters implying growth and organic development. Spiral spirits come out of her mouth. Life breath, energy, going in and/or coming out of her. The visualization of sound. Internal voices. Tongue. Words. Intestines. The symbol of migration. Seeing the life energy. Auras. To activate the paint as air around a person is activated. The painting as an energy field.

The depicted space is visually simple—a tension existing between the depth or illusionistic space and the flat space which is the here and now, the present. The rectangle frequently in the corner is the unfinished part, the space left open, the window to space beyond. Windows are the eyes in Pueblo architectural ruins. The sipapu is the navel of the earth by which the spirit enters to our world. Windows let us enter the painting.

Frequently, two "Chicken Ladies" merge. A relationship between parts of self, two individuals, or groups. Are they merging or separating? Do they know? Lover and I, mother and daughter. One becoming two. Two becoming one. One inside the other as lover or child. Or the spirit inside. Here creation, development, exploration, and identification are the same. Forms of Desire are intellectual and spiritual as well as sexual. Planes of Nature. Systems of Belief.

ED. NOTE

Hammond wrote this statement for her solo exhibition at A.I.R. Gallery, New York, 1984.

Book Review, "*Frida: A Biography of Frida Kahlo* by Hayden Herrera"

13th Moon (1984)

Frida Kahlo was a painter few North Americans knew of until ten years ago. Seeing her work for the first time, women, in particular, responded to its strong personal vision and overt female content. However, unless we had been fortunate enough to visit the Frida Kahlo Museum on the edge of Mexico City (in the artist's home), we knew little about Kahlo other than the myth that accompanied her when, in the 1930s and '40s, she traveled to the United States as the beautiful costumed wife of the famous communist muralist Diego Rivera.

One of the focuses of the feminist art movement has been to research the lives and work of women artists of the past, and to rewrite ourselves back into the history of art. Gradually, through the research and writing of art historian and critic Hayden Herrera, who spent much of her childhood in Mexico, we began to learn more about Kahlo and her work, and have been awaiting Herrera's full-scale biography.

In *Frida: A Biography of Frida Kahlo*, Herrera combines art, life, and politics in postrevolutionary Mexico as she presents informational and narrative accountings, alternated throughout with substantial quotes from personal diaries and letters. This is generously supplemented with many color and black-and-white reproductions of Kahlo's paintings. While I felt that there were too many letters to Kahlo's young sweetheart Alejandro Gomez Arias, in general, the combination of material that Herrera presents makes the 440-page biography informative and interesting. The details behind the self-portraits begin to fill in and take form. Kahlo's unconventional life and personality led to unconventional work.

Frida Kahlo was born in 1907 in Coyoacán on the residential periphery of Mexico City. (Later she decided that she and modern Mexico had been born together so she changed her birthdate to coincide with the beginning of the Mexican Revolution in 1910.) Her mother, Matilde Calderon, was Mestiza (of Spanish-Indian heritage) and her father was a Hungarian Jew. Like the fathers of so many women painters, Guillermo Kahlo was an artist—a professional photographer and amateur painter; he taught Frida how to develop, touch up, and hand-color photographs. This detailed work, as well as the stiff poses of his portraits, appears years later in the tiny brush strokes, minute detail, and frontal pose of her paintings.

Frida, who was a tomboy, and her father's favorite daughter, was one of thirty-five girls to be admitted along with 2,000 boys to the [Escuela Nacional] Preparatoria, the best school in Mexico, and considered to be preparation for the university. This meant that Frida took the one-hour bus ride into the city each day and got out beyond the protective walls of her barrio and into a hotbed of revolutionary debate and activism.

But Frida became a "wounded bird," a victim of many physical problems, and eventually had to drop out of school. She had polio when she was six, leaving her with a weak and withered leg. When she was eighteen years old, the bus she was riding smashed into a trolley and impaled her on a handrail, breaking her spine, collarbone, leg, and pelvis, and crushing and dislocating her right foot. They did not know if she would live or ever walk again. While she did miraculously recover, "her life after 1925 was a battle against slow and painful decay." In constant pain throughout her life, she was frequently hospitalized or bedridden, going through thirty operations, a miscarriage, three therapeutic abortions, a series of plaster, leather, or metal corsets to brace her back, and then finally the amputation of her leg, after which she died in 1954.

There is so much myth around Frida Kahlo, which she herself participated in making, that it is sometimes difficult to really know how things happened. Herrera presents the myths as partial reality (for instance Frida's undying devotion to the philandering Diego Rivera) but she also goes beyond it, giving us insights into the often frustrated and lonely person behind the face of *alegría* that Frida presented to those who knew her, and behind the intense non-emotional masks of her self-portraits.

Apparently, Frida began painting during her confinement after the accident or during an early relapse. She asked to use her father's paints, and a special easel was made for her since she couldn't sit up. Her first serious painting was a Botticelli/Modigliani-type self-portrait that was a gift for Alejandro. It was a token to bind him to her. In later years, Frida "often used painting as a gift to hold on to someone or tell them her feelings." Slowly, painting became one of the means by which Frida was able to overcome pain and suffering. A literal depiction of the physical often symbolized personal and political feelings. She painted the world around her: friends, lovers, children, animals, and the many popular folk objects that she collected. A self-taught artist, Frida said, "I paint myself because I am the subject I know best."

It is also part of Frida's myth that she first became fascinated with Diego Rivera when he was painting murals at the Preparatoria while she was a student there. In any case, years later, after meeting him through the Italian-born American photographer Tina Modotti (who also introduced Frida to communism), she showed Diego some of her paintings and demanded his honest response to them. He found both her and her work highly interesting, and after a short courtship they were married when he was forty-one and she was twenty-two. Because he weighed over 300 pounds and she was very petite, people called it a marriage between an elephant and a dove. Celebrated by the Mexican people, Herrera asks, what was the truth of their relationship?

Clearly Frida admired and was obsessed with Diego. She thought him a genius and he likewise had great respect for her painting. But theirs was not a traditional marriage even by bohemian standards of the day. Because Diego was one of Mexico's most famous and infamous painters and politically active, their marriage was very public and constantly followed by the press. For years, Frida, devoting herself to Diego's needs, and, when physically able, accompanying him on his commissions and exhibitions, suffered from being the "wife of the famous male painter." At times she hardly painted. They both had casual and not-so-casual affairs, frequently lived separately, were divorced and later remarried with Frida's stipulation that there be no sex, and gradually evolved a marriage of "mutual independence" while remaining deeply tied to each other. They shared a bohemian lifestyle full of surprise and fantasy, a joy of art and ideas, a belief in Marxist politics and the important role that art played in revolution, and a commitment to the Mexican cultural renaissance.

Before the revolution, Mexicans had looked to Europe for their culture. Now after the revolution, there was a cultural revival—*mexicanidad*—where pre-Columbian and peasant art, handicrafts, food, costume, dance, theater, anything indigenous to Mexico was valued.

At this time, as Herrera puts it, "all but the most retrograde artists incorporated Mexican elements into their work." For Frida, this took several forms: her clothes, her house, and her painting. At first Frida dressed in regional costume to emphasize her Mestiza background, and because Diego liked it, but gradually the costume became her presentation of herself to the world, her communication with it. Her clothes, jewelry, and hair styles were a palette with which each day she went through the elaborate ritual of self-creation. She dressed primarily in the loose blouse and long skirt of the Tehuantepec where "women are famous for being stately, beautiful, sensuous, intelligent, brave, and strong. Folklore has it that theirs is a matriarchal society where women run the markets, handle fiscal matters, and dominate the men." The costume functioned on many levels. The long skirts hid the awkward corsets and braces she was forced to wear; they attracted attention (it was hard to compete with the famous Diego) while masking the real person inside; they represented freedom from bourgeois restrictions; and they were a statement of solidarity with *la raza*.

In a sense, the clothes began to represent the person. Frida dressed up even when she was very sick, or was to have an operation. When she was furious with Diego, she responded by cutting off her hair and wearing men's clothes. (*Self Portrait with Cropped Hair*, 1940, shows her with her hair cut and wearing one of Diego's huge suits.) She painted her empty clothes: in *My Dress Hangs There* (1933), her dress hangs in the middle of the Manhattan skyline as a symbol stating that while her clothes were in New York, her heart and soul were in Mexico.

Frida's house, like her body, was eclectically decorated with folk objects from the markets, Diego's collection of pre-Columbian art, her doll collection, and gifts from friends. Many of these objects appear in her paintings. What looks like very bizarre imagery in *The Dream* (1940), where a skeleton wrapped in dynamite and holding flowers lies on top of the canopy of her bed, and the blanket covering the tiny sleeping Frida is covered with branches, was, in fact, partial reality: Frida had a large Judas figure outside her door, a papier-mâché skeleton on top of her bed, and a coverlet with vines and leaves on it. But reality is transformed in the painting. The bed floats in the air like a dream, the branched vine might easily take over the sleeping Frida, its roots hang down where her feet should be, and the skeleton becomes a companion or guardian.

Herrera sensitively describes and discusses each painting, incorporating Frida's statements about specific works, and her own critical interpretations of a growing personal iconography based on Frida's life and Mexican culture. Frida's central subject was herself. Personal body imagery connected Frida to nature, to the life and death cycle, and to Mexico itself. She painted herself bleeding, weeping, pierced, wounded, and cracked open. The emotional edge in her painting comes from this body/nature metaphor: wounds fertilize the earth, a necklace of thorns pierces her flesh, decorative ribbons become veins, which in turn become roots of blood flowing into the earth. Often, we see her insides projected on the outside of her body, or totally separated from it by a thin thread/vein/vine as if to say that the body and the person are not the same. While some of her paintings were deliberately political—she was working on an unfinished portrait of Stalin when she died and worried whether her work would contribute to the revolution—most of her painting combined reality with dream and myth. She did exhibit with the Surrealists but she did not consider herself a Surrealist painter, because, as she said, she did not paint dreams—she painted "her reality." She disliked the pompous tone of the Surrealists, and André Breton in particular, and referred to them as "the *cacas* of surrealism."

Likewise, Frida was not a "primitive," although Diego liked to refer to her "Indian" heritage. While her work refers to Aztec mythology, Mexican folklore, portraiture, and tin *retablos*, she was also very knowledgeable about European and North American modern art. What might seem macabre to the Protestant Anglo was not at all unusual to Mexican Catholic or Indian culture with its images of body parts, bleeding hearts, tears, skeletons, coffins, and skulls. She consciously chose to work with images and references whose iconography connected her to a Mexican art tradition, but also enabled her to transform her personal pain into art. "To Kahlo, death was a companion—part of life's cycle and she enjoyed flirting with *la pelona* as though it were a companion ever close at hand."

Frida Kahlo is mostly known for her many intense self-portraits but she began, in 1932, a series of *retablo* paintings that outrageously dealt with overt female experience: birth, miscarriage, abortion, mothering, masturbation, and sexual violence. As far as I know, there is no comparable precedent for these paintings in the work of any European artist. [...]

My Birth (1932) is a double self-portrait recording, as Frida put it, "how I imagined I was born." Herrera writes: "We see the infant's large head emerging between the mother's spread legs from the doctor's vantage point. Heavy, joined eyebrows identify the child as Frida. Blood covers the inert, drooping head and skinny neck. The baby looks dead. A sheet covering the woman's head and chest, as if she had died in childbirth, emphasizes the total exposure of delivery. As a substitute for the mother's head, on the wall directly above her is a painting of another grieving mother, the Virgin of Sorrows pierced by swords, bleeding and weeping." This painting refers to the recent death of Frida's unborn child, her own mother's death, childhood memories, and is an image of Frida giving birth to herself. Most of these paintings are small and intimate in the tradition of religious *retablo* paintings, partially because Frida often painted in bed but also because the artist or viewer literally couldn't deal with the intense subject matter if painted larger.

Frida Kahlo was openly bisexual and had lesbian relationships. Considering that Mexican society accepted such relationships between women, it is particularly disturbing that [Herrara devotes] so much detailed discussion [. . .] to Frida's relationships with men—Alejandro [Gomez Arias], Diego [Rivera], [Isamu] Noguchi, [Leon] Trotsky, and others—while there are never any details about her love relationships with specific women. The men are named and the women are nameless. This is a serious omission when one is writing art history from a feminist perspective. I feel a responsibility to talk about those "intimate relationships" among women. Herrera doesn't totally avoid the issue, but she skirts it. While she mentions that Frida had lesbian relationships, that lesbian imagery appears in several paintings, we are once again forced to read between the lines and guess "who." More space is given over to Frida's pet monkeys and the men she didn't like such as André Breton than to women like Jacqueline Breton who was an "intimate friend." Frida wrote a letter (supposedly to Jacqueline) referring to past time shared together in Paris:

> I have not forgotten you . . . the nights are long and difficult . . . Today I would like my sun to touch you . . . But the color of your skin, of your eyes and your hair changes with the wind of Mexico. You also know that everything my eyes see and everything that I touch with my own self, from all the distances is Diego . . . you felt it, for that reason you allowed the boat to carry me from Le Havre, where you never said goodbye to me . . . I will always continue writing to you with my eyes . . .

Now, to me, this is in part, a love letter. Herrera describes it as "wistful." We are told that Frida had her first lesbian relationship when she was eighteen, when a woman employee of the Ministry of Education library seduced her, and that Frida's family ended the affair when they found out about it. Near the end of the biography, Herrera states that in the years before she died, Frida's most intense relationships were with women, that the women were more than just attendants to Frida's death. (The names of Maria Felix, Teresa Proenza, Elena Vasquez Gomez, Machila Armida, and Irene Bohus, along with Diego's, were painted in pink on her bedroom wall.) But the discussion of Frida's lesbianism becomes an account of her aggressiveness as a sick, almost fevered person who seduced other women with her desperate sexual advances; the story is told of a "little lesbian girl" who was so attached to Frida that at one point when Frida was repelled by her, the girl committed suicide at the foot of Frida's bed. I found this particularly outrageous, considering the peculiar lack of discussion of the positive lesbian relationships that Frida clearly had. Lesbianism is presented as part of a sexual aggressiveness, never as a sexual outgrowth of intimacy, trust, and sharing between women.

Who were the women with whom Frida had relationships? How long did they last? What was their nature and intensity? Does the silence make more of her lesbian relationships than they really were? What effect, if any, did these relationships have on Frida's painting? What responsibility is there to the living who may not wish to be mentioned in certain ways? On the other hand, who has the right to censor or silence another's life, to distort the truth? What if mentioning someone's bisexuality or lesbianism would stop publication of a biography? Is it better to omit certain information so that at least the biography is printed? It is a difficult and complex issue.

But the omission of discussion of relationships between women trivializes these relationships, and prevents the discussion of how we affect each other's work. There is only passing mention of the lesbian imagery in Frida's paintings. In *What the Water Gave Me* (1938), two nude women, one darker-skinned, sitting with the head of the lighter-skinned woman on her lap, float on a sponge as part of a complex composition in what seems to be a hallucinatory view of the artist's own bathwater. In *Two Nudes in a Forest* (1939), the pose of the two women is the same, but now they become the subject of the painting. They are in front of a background of vegetation with vines clearly entwined and holding onto each other while a strange powerless figure (Diego?) looks out at them in a manner reminiscent of Rousseau. These are just two specific examples, but they, and the lesbian sensibility in Kahlo's frequent image of two women being one, and one being two, are never really described in the same depth that Herrera discusses other aspects of Frida's paintings.

Gradually Frida became more and more autonomous, and to take herself seriously as an artist. She began to sell work, which facilitated her economic independence from Diego. She had well-received solo exhibitions in New York and Paris and was included in the important Surrealist exhibit at the Museum of Modern Art. Less than a year before she died, she was honored with her first solo exhibit at home in Mexico. Quite ill then, she attended the opening by having her bed brought into the gallery.

Apart from the lack of discussion of Frida's lesbian relationships and lesbian imagery in her work, Herrera's biography presents a sense of a full person, of an artist coming into her own. In its insistence on discussing art in relationship to the artist's life and to the political climate, *Frida* is an excellent example of revisionist feminist art historical writing. Just as Frida Kahlo's painting is an inspiration to many women artists (and I should think especially to Chicana artists), Hayden Herrera's biography, in its strength and shortcoming, should inspire further and much-needed biographies of other women artists.

ED. NOTE

This review first appeared in *13th Moon* 8, nos. 1 and 2 (1984): 218–26. The text has been abridged for inclusion in this volume. All quotes are from Hayden Herrera, *Frida: A Biography of Frida Kahlo* (New York: Harper and Row, 1984).

Book Review, "*The Arts of the North American Indian: Native Traditions in Evolution* by Edwin L. Wade"

Artspace: Southwestern Contemporary Arts Quarterly (1987)

In his introduction to this book, Edwin Wade asks, what is authentic Native art? Are there things that Native art can offer our postindustrial, depersonalized, capitalist, technologically arrogant society? Thus, he sets a tone for the book, a concern with aesthetics as both reflecting change and as a potential vehicle for it. The question of what is Native art is dealt with as a large one, involving whole societies, as well as individuals with their own beliefs, imaginations, and personal creativity. *The Arts of the North American Indian: Native Traditions in Evolution* was initially designed as a catalogue to accompany an exhibition of American Indian masterworks organized by the Philbrook Art Center [now Philbrook Museum of Art] in Tulsa. Actually, it is an anthology of essays by fourteen scholars who met with American Indian artists and consultants at the international convocation on Native American art sponsored by the Philbrook during the early planning stages of the exhibition.

Beautifully illustrated, the catalogue examines objects made by members of over sixty tribes representing the major culture areas and spanning a period of three thousand years. This is not to say that the book is a survey or is comprehensive, but rather that the thoughtfully written and sequenced articles draw on a wide range of art and artifacts for their discussion.

The first chapters are a bit academic, with the authors struggling to restate once again the problems of the Euro-Western mind grappling with interpretation or understanding of meaning in Native art. (Here and throughout the catalogue the imagined reader is assumed to be non-Indian.) But, can the Western mind adequately know such meaning?

Most societies did not differentiate art objects from nonart objects. Indeed, there was no word for "art." In the first essay, William Sturtevant defines an artifact as any tangible object with a style associated and a particular time, place, function or value, and he distinguishes an artistic artifact as one which engenders a strong emotional response in members of the society of origin. External meanings of North American Indian art are qualities recognized in it by the society that has classified it as "art," but the internal meanings (be they intentional or nonintentional) come from within. While internal and external meaning can overlap, they are the same, Sturtevant feels, only if the maker and observer share the same cultural understandings. Since even within tribes the meaning of a particular design element is often attributed by the individual artist, it is very rare for tribal members, much less for members of a different tribe or for the non-Indian mind, to fully understand the symbolic content. Thus, in spite of the best and most sensitive intentions, he acknowledges that there is great difficulty in interpreting and fully appreciating art from a culture other than one's own.

Since all cultural systems exist in a constant state of change, the concept "traditional" is neither simple nor absolute and, as J.C.H. King points out, it is often loaded with semantic associations and value judgments. Traditional can be defined in several ways and need not automatically imply the opposite of non-traditional. "Tradition" defined as lines of traits can be based on techniques, materials, forms, functions, and meanings and is just as valid as any chronological sequence. Like meaning, traditions have been influenced by both internal and external forces such as trade, warfare, early contact with Euro-American culture, the adaptation of European designs and materials, colonization, commercialization, and the influence of white institutions. In fact, King says, the notion of what constitutes traditional Native art is largely based on collections formed from 1860 to 1930, a time of extreme upheaval in North American Indian life as Native peoples were forced to give up their land and nomadic lifestyles for confinement on reservations. It could be argued that collecting itself is either part of, or the byproduct of, colonizing. Since colonizers often collected only what they deemed beautiful in accordance with their European aesthetics, who determines what is "traditional" becomes an important consideration.

In his essay, Norman Feder continues King's discussion and goes on to dispel the stereotype of the changeless "good old days" of true Indian art. Focusing on the alteration of Plains Indian art, he discusses the effects of new European materials such as bright, pigment dyed wool yarns, glass beads, and mirrors. Among the Kiowa, for instance, new materials were usually adapted to old art forms. Women simply substituted the new beads into quillwork patterns. Only later were new patterns adopted from the outside. Trade between tribes, forced migrations and the ensuing migration wars, the unavailability of certain materials, the extinction of some plants and animals, and the tourist trade—all had their effect on what was basically a change resistant culture.

No one system of aesthetics applies to all art, and definitions of beauty differ from culture to culture. "A given culture's idea of beauty is seen as group aesthetics and is usually only fully appreciated by members of the group that evolved it . . . a predicament that has led to frequent misinterpretation and underestimation of primitive art by Euro-Americans," says Wolfgang Haberland in an examination of Navajo and Northwest coast blanket designs. The utilitarian nature of the blankets also raises other issues: art versus craft, discrimination against art made of certain materials, professionalism, and the fact that North American Indian art is rarely seen outside of anthropological contexts and is rarely properly documented with titles and names of the artists, even when this information is known. Like King, Haberland questions the basis of what is considered to be "traditional" when anthropological collections are usually based on the closest appropriation of the cultural "norm" rather than building an art collection based on quality examples both common and uncommon. Finally, he addresses the relationship of the fine arts to the performing arts (something I wish had been discussed further in the anthology).

Bill Holm emphasizes the importance of cultural context to an appreciation of aesthetics in his concise article about the headdresses worn as part of ceremonial masked dancing on the Northwest coast. He states that the issue of aesthetic context goes beyond the object—the carved frontlet cannot be separated from the rest of the headdress, the headdress cannot be separated from the dance, and the dance cannot be separated from a body of stories, origins, and myths. The stories are part of the headdress as much as the wood or fur. Sight, sound, and motion combined to form a complex creative vision.

This larger aesthetic context must also be taken into any consideration of quality. Can a judgment of quality be made cross-culturally? In their essays, Christian Feest and Evan Maurer point out that in Native American cultures, quality was determined by technical perfection. Technical skill was taught and passed on from one generation to another and perfected through years of experience. By tribal standards, technical excellence ranked higher than aesthetic evaluation. Through a consideration of a wide range of sculptural forms including masks, dolls, spoons, pipes, rattles, pottery, baskets, and house pots, Feest emphasizes the ever-changing measures of excellence set up within tribes. Only since the late nineteenth century have the definitions of art and artists changed to emphasize personal expression, hence the modern willingness to consider aesthetic quality separate from technical mastery, which Maurer says is "one symptom of the separation of art from life that exists in our culture, a separation that has . . . led to the estrangement of the artist from his own society."

With the essays on "individuality," the pace picks up and lively and interesting discussions lead directly to the underlying theme of the book—change and the Native American artist today. John Anderson Warner, Marvin Cohodas, Jamake Highwater, Edwin Wade, and Gerhard Hoffman confront the real differences in value and belief systems between Indian and non-Indian art.

Warner examines what he sees as three periods of individualism in Native art: aboriginal, reservation, and modernist. He asks important questions of each, such as: What is the role in society of the individuals who are artistically active? What is the function of art in society? For whom is the art intended? And finally, who are the consumers of the art and what are their needs? The answers to these questions document change.

In discussing the Indigenous precontact period, Warner points out that certain Native groups are more self-oriented while others are more collectively oriented, and that these patterns of culture are reflected in their art forms. For instance, among the Plains Indians, where the cult of the male warrior, heroism, and glory dominate, individuals were given some room for personal expression; using the narrative form of quasi-realistic pictographic images on hides or tipis, men were expected to paint their own achievements. As long as no false stories were told, the individual's story was seen to reflect the tribe's story; this is in direct contrast to collective, female-dominated Pueblo cultures where pottery utilizing abstract design patterns was made for private use, was not attributed to individuals, and did not record individual lives. However, despite the differences, both are examples of Indigenous art, which is basically collectively oriented, and where the artists subordinated their own interests for the benefit of the group.

But, by the end of the nineteenth century, almost all North American Indians had to make a living in a new way. The reservation system completely tore up aboriginal economic systems and political structures and introduced dominant white values: possession of personal property, accumulation of money, competition, the "get ahead" ethic, Christianity, and the postponement of gratification, etc. Hunters were now expected to farm. Those who couldn't adapt found themselves dependent on welfare and charity. For a few, art and craft production began to bring in additional income. Now, for the first time, there was an economic motivation for artistic production and artworks were made specifically for sale. The consumers of this new ethnic art were whites who wanted to buy a romantic and nostalgic image of the Native American and this white patronage initiated a system of virtualizing with a new emphasis on individual attribution, signing works, collecting. *Who* made it became the measure of value and prestige.

Warner uses the examples of Nampeyo, the great Hopi potter who is credited with the revival of Hopi pottery, and Maria Martinez who, along with her husband Julian, developed and redefined the famous blackware of San Ildefonso. These artists were encouraged and supported but also exploited by white middlemen like railroad entrepreneur Fred Harvey. With Harvey's patronage and merchandising of their work, many women created pottery specifically to sell to tourists. While traditional in design, their work was frequently far removed from any original function.

Ledger drawings are another example of ethnic art created during reservation times. Plains Indians incarcerated at Fort Marion in 1875 were given pencils, crayons, and paper from ledger books by the soldiers. With time on their hands and an opportunity to sell the drawings to soldiers for a little pocket money, the prisoners made drawings that were to become the transitional form between earlier hide paintings and the easel painting of the 1920s and '30s. Like all ethnic art, they glorified the old days back home, were created mainly for non-Indian audiences who wanted something "authentic," and were usually signed in some way.

In his essay on Washoe fancy basketry, Cohodas provides an excellent discussion of individuality, its relationship to tribal traditions, and the power of the marketplace. He examines the personal stories of the work of five women (1895–1935) but focuses primarily on Louisa Keyser (Dat So La Lee), the most innovative and influential, who enjoyed the unique patronage of Abe Cohn, a clothing store merchant in the Lake Tahoe area, and his wife Amy. For three decades, the Cohns provided Louisa and her husband Charlie with food, clothing, medical care, and shelter. In exchange, she was to give them all her work and to weave in public to attract store customers.

Economically secure and freed from the degrading effects of commercialism, Keyser could devote full-time to her baskets and perfect her art. Also, being away from other Washoes allowed her the freedom to break with traditions and experiment. In Cohn's store she saw Pomo gift baskets from California. To the Pomo motifs and shapes, she added her own larger scale, fine stitching, red and black color scheme, and illusion of perspective (integrating the design motif with the basket shape), creating her trademark Degikup, an elegantly simple woven sculpture without any utilitarian function or precedent of an early Washoe weaving.

The Cohns documented Keyser's work, made a film on her, and put her on display for tourists as a symbol of the Washoe tribe. They set high, fine art prices for her work. Then, to market her baskets, they began to develop and promote Keyser's public persona, fabricating stories about her birth and tribal background, the development of her baskets, and even false interpretations of the motifs used in her weaving. While Keyser created the baskets, Amy Cohn created the context that was intended to make Keyser and her designs fit an invented romanticized ideal of Washoe culture and precontact time. Here is an early example of merchandising used to create an artist's persona in order to sell the art product. Ironically, Keyser's real artistic originality and inventiveness were obscured in order to make her seem more authentic and more "Indian."

Wade's article studies the controversy of individualism among Pueblo pottery makers and the effect of the arts and crafts market on Native artists, their families, and communities. The underlying controversy is the fundamental difference between mainstream and Native American worldviews. He writes, "Individual artistic success runs counter to Southwestern attitudes concerning man's relationship to the supernatural (which is considered a collective responsibility) and to the egalitarian idea of what constitutes a 'good' man or woman. . . ."

He also discusses the "merchandising of the gods," particularly the problems of making and selling Kachinas and Yei figures. It is a traditional belief that sacred art cannot be individually owned and should not be sold, for each work contains a spirit or life force. The object is an extension of the supernatural being. To sell, trade, or steal such a mask or figure, before properly retiring it with the appropriate ceremony to send the spirits home, is completely unethical. However, because there is a large money market for contraband religious art objects, some Puebloans have sanctioned the making and selling of a variation on the sacred object. But this practice is still highly controversial and even easel paintings that depict ceremonies have been severely criticized.

What seems to be even more controversial than the question of acceptable imagery is the conflict that ensues when artists function as "individuals" in the marketplace. The star image of the celebrated Native American artist (and there are some who can well compete with the public personas of [Andy] Warhol, [Georgia] O'Keeffe, or [Julian] Schnabel) conflicts with the Southwest Indian definition of a good man or woman. If successful as an artist it is hard to succeed as a good tribal member. Wade asks, can the artist be heard simultaneously in two worlds that define goodness and success differently?

Wade uses the career of San Ildefonso potter Maria Martinez as an example of an artist who was able, though not without difficulty, to be successful in two worlds. As Martinez's highly polished blackware came into great demand, her career soared and her pottery sold for much higher prices than the work of other potters. However, while she enjoyed this artistic recognition, Martinez was able to maintain her reputation as a good housekeeper because she employed Spanish-American women to perform the traditional household duties expected of Pueblo women. To keep up with the demand for her work, Martinez trained family members to help make her pottery, and at times she bought unfinished pots from neighbors, finishing and signing them with her own name. Certain employees were even responsible for signing her signature to the bottom of every vessel.

Money and ambition changed artistic behavior and attitudes within the Pueblo. While there was a great deal of competition between Martinez and the other women potters, their financial success introduced more than new pottery forms or new means of pottery production. It gave the women tremendous power. The practice of buying and selling labor, with the wealthier artist hiring the poor of the Pueblo and thus creating two economic classes, was a major and revolutionary change. Artists took on leadership roles. The pot, which was once associated with the earth, was now a symbol of money, power, prestige, and white life.

Yet another type of work began to develop during this period, one that was generated by institutions outside of the tribal context. Easel painting crystallized in the 1920s in the state of Oklahoma where a United States Indian Service field matron named Susan Peters had organized an arts club for young Kiowa students. Some of these students went on to the university where they were introduced to the elements of American Art Deco. The work of the artist known as the Kiowa Five developed a hybrid style of painting with strong ties to traditional hide painting and ledger book drawing but took a modern approach to expression. Likewise, the artists attending Dorothy Sunn Studio School in Santa Fe in the '30s created a similar style of painting, emphasizing flat colors, clear outlines, and sinuous curves. This design-conscious style of work came to be known as "traditional Indian painting." However, while new in format, it, like the earlier hide paintings and ledger drawings, depicted nostalgic themes.

Modern individualism has existed since World War II in an atmosphere of stylistic pluralism. While some contemporary artists continue to make work that elaborates on reservation art traditions, many are now exploring new content and form and diverse media, and are making art that is pretty much assimilated into the mainstream. Working abstractly and figuratively, with up-to-date aesthetic concerns, these artists create a sort of reference to the past in the present, a mythmaking based on North American Indian culture, the land, nature, and spirituality. Their work speaks not only to Indian people but to the world at large.

North American Indian arts had declined somewhat in the 1940s and '50s as work was made primarily for the tourist market. It had grown far from its original roots and function without yet acquiring a modern vocabulary. The paintings of Oscar Howe were important transitional works during this period. After returning from the Second World War, he integrated the cubism that he had seen in Europe with traditional American Indian artistic values. His work provided a kind of role model for much that was to follow.

A major new change was initiated in 1962 when the Institute of American Indian Arts opened in Santa Fe, with the progressive new attitude toward art education. The paintings of Fritz Scholder who taught there (he had been a student of Howe's) and other work coming out of the school were considered highly controversial in that they were [instigating] a counter movement to traditional approaches and to the regional art world.

Highwater continues where Warner and Wade leave off by commenting on current controversies in Native American art. In general, North American Indian artists are becoming more individualistic than tribal in their creativity and this gradual change toward individualism within the context of tradition has proved to be an area of great struggle and friction. Highwater feels that the art itself reflects the struggle for identity.

Contemporary Native American artists confront the difficulty of several audiences for their work, and a marketplace still based on nostalgia and ready to provide big money for stereotyped notions of what Indian, albeit contemporary Indian, art should look like. The fact is that today there is still a very special art market available to any American Indian artist whose work "looks Indian." Economic success supports artists but at the same time ghettoizes them, and few have been able to cross boundaries and go back and forth from the American Indian art world to the larger New York–dominated art world. Artists like Emmi Whitehorse, George Longfish, Jaune Quick-to-See Smith, Randy Lee White, Peter Jemison, Harry Fonseca, Fritz Scholder, George Morrison, Kay Walkingstick, James Harvard, and Kay Miller walk a narrow tightrope not because of the intentions of their art, which is simply to make quality art that in some way reflects who they are in the world, but because they still remain somewhat sheltered from the reality of being individual artists in the larger art world without the backup of the Indian market, or even American Indian museums, galleries, and collectors of contemporary Indian art to support them.

A question for the future that Warner raises is: Will American Indian art and the American Indian individual continue to need such a special market for survival? These artists hope that the answer is no. While most wish to speak to an audience of Indian people in North America as well as to a world-sophisticated art audience, they are very clear about not catering to the curio mentality of collectors of contemporary ethnic work as it abounds in Santa Fe and Scottsdale. Indeed, this scenario is enacted and discussed in Strickland's humorous play "of memory and imagination," also included in the catalogue. Strickland's characters are based on well-known stereotypes from the Indian art world. Like the authors of the essays in this book, they gathered to discuss the past, present, and future of North American Indian art.

As with all artists, danger comes with success, but these new North American Indian artists face many special problems. All too often the galleries handling their work do not encourage change and frequently they are asked if they couldn't add a few shells or feathers to make the work look more "Indian." At the same time, the mainstream art world has not taken their work seriously (nor the work of women or other ethnic minorities). Native artists were not presented in the Museum of Modern Art's *"Primitivism" in 20th Century Art* exhibition, nor the more recent exhibition *The Spiritual in Art: Abstract Painting 1890–1985* at the Los Angeles County Museum of Art—both exhibits with themes that relate to contemporary Native American concerns. Ironically many Native American artists have drawn heavily on European and American artists who themselves drew on the art of primitive cultures ([Paul] Klee, [Wassily] Kandinsky, [Pablo] Picasso, [Jean] Dubuffet, the Cobra artists, or even current work by artists like [A. R.] Penck, [Morris] Graves, and [Jean-Michel] Basquiat).

Central to this issue is the ongoing question of what is authentic American Indian imagery? The North American Indian artist today faces the same aesthetic challenges as any artist of minority or ethnic background: how to hold on to what is distinctive about their art and yet fit into the 1980s? What images, but even more, what emotional attitudes are appropriate in contemporary Native painting and sculpture?

Highwater insists that images and feelings of any kind are the sole province of the artist and that the right to define Indian art belongs to Indian artists. But the freedom of self-definition does not come easy. Some Indian people will label such work "assimilated" and the white mainstream will call it "derivative."

However, like all artists, Native American artists should have the personal freedom of expression to choose their sources of inspiration.

In discussing contemporary Native American art within the context of modernism and postmodernism, Gerhard Hoffman insists that any discussion of American Indian art must include the concept of the "Fourth World," a term first introduced by Nelson Graburn to refer to "native peoples whose lands fall within the national boundaries and techno bureaucratic administrations of countries of the First, Second, or Third Worlds." Graburn points out that the art of Fourth World people "must take into account more than one symbolic aesthetic system and the fact that the arts may be produced by one group for consumption by another." He calls the study of the Fourth World arts the study of "changing arts—emerging ethnicities, modifying identities, commercial and colonial stimuli and repressive actions."

Hoffman shows how contemporary Native American artists are drawing not only on their traditions but on images and traditions from other cultures around the world and from Western art history. However, he feels that in drawing on modernism, these artists must somehow translate it and change it if they are to truly reflect their experiences (however diverse they may be) as Indians in the world today—that is if they are to be truly authentic. To do this they will need to purify clichés and to find forms, images, and materials that together can concentrate and intensify experience and feeling.

There is a false notion that traditional art can preserve a culture. But static cultures are dying cultures and static art is dying art. Right now, Native American art is very much alive. As Hoffman insists, only if we view Indian art as a changing art can we see that to be modern, the North American Indian need not lose his or her authenticity.

The Arts of the North American Indian: Native Traditions in Evolution is a full-bodied anthology, an honest and knowledgeable attempt to break down stereotypes, to connect art and life, and to openly discuss the issues raised in any critical discussion of Native American art. Individually and collectively, the authors have created a living picture of the art of Native Americans as a changing art.

ED. NOTE

This review originally appeared in "Ethnic and Folk Art: Tradition and Transition," special issue, *Artspace: Southwestern Contemporary Arts Quarterly* 11, no. 2 (Spring 1987): 57–59. Permission: Artspace, Spring 1987. All quotes are from Edwin L. Wade, ed., *The Arts of the North American Indian: Native Traditions in Evolution* (New York: Hudson Hill Press in association with Philbrook Art Center, Tulsa, OK, 1986).

Interview with MaLin Wilson[-Powell]

Jonson Gallery, University Art Museum,
University of New Mexico, Albuquerque (1988)

MALIN WILSON: When you first came to the gallery in 1985 a major focus of your interest was the work by Agnes Pelton and Florence Pierce, members of the Transcendental Painting Group, and their relationship to the "thought-forms" illustrated in the Theosophical texts of Annie Besant and C. W. Leadbeater . . .

HARMONY HAMMOND: Yes, years ago in the early '70s, Rosemary Mayer, an artist friend of mine, introduced me to the book *Thought-forms* [1905]. The color plates in the book (paintings of actual seen thought-forms) made a strong impression on me. They were like outrageous Kandinsky paintings. Almost tantric. I immediately thought of doing paintings lifted directly from the color plates because they were so beautiful in and of themselves. But then I realized that I didn't just want to copy them, nor was I ultimately interested in their literal translation of specific forms or colors as having specific meanings. What excited me was the notion of abstract visual forms recording emotional states. Abstraction could have meaning. Language. So, the book remained a reference that I looked at from time to time, and frequently provided titles for my work.

When I moved to New Mexico in 1984, Karolyn Wayman, who was then the director of the Jonson Gallery, showed me some of the work of Raymond Jonson. I had never even heard of the Transcendental Painting Group before. Later Tiska Blankenship, the assistant curator, specifically mentioned that two of the Transcendentalist painters were women, and she invited me to come to the gallery to see their work. That's when I met you. When I did see their work, I was very excited because I felt an immediate connection. We were doing something very similar. Like the Transcendentalists, I was involved with issues of abstract painting and the world of the spirit. Also, I immediately knew that Agnes Pelton had been looking at the same color plates of the thought-forms. It was right there in her painting.

I am interested in the issue of how one develops an abstract iconography. How can one bring content into abstract art? There are numerous ways. In the early '70s, notions of marking, visual diaries, and women's traditional needle arts informed my work. Later, references to pictographs and petroglyphs—also preexisting visual manifestations or ideas—and more recently, references to thought-forms or other representations of the world of the spirit. Also, there have always been a lot of cross-cultural references in my work.

It seems to me that artists deal with abstraction basically in two different ways. References and associations always appear, crop up in the work as the artist is working. Some artists fight this, try to paint out any references or associations, and a certain visual tension comes out of this. Others choose to heighten or utilize suggestive associations. But in the ambiguity, there is also a tension. I am one of those artists. I take great pleasure in making references multilayered, ambiguous, or even contradictory. That's why I loved the exhibition at the Los Angeles County Museum of Art, *The Spiritual in Art: Abstract Painting 1890–1985*, which was so controversial in some circles—it went against the Greenbergian notion of abstract art as only being self-referential. It was a statement about the potential of abstract art to embody content. So I am dealing with concepts about "representing," which are somewhat different than current postmodernist ideas of representation or deconstruction.

WILSON: When selecting pieces for this show, there was one piece that was very different. *Grasping Nature* is almost floral—open, awkward, and strange.[1]

HAMMOND: Right. I can tell you exactly how that piece was made. It came out of several things. On the one hand, the imagery grew out of abstract forms I was working with in New Mexico. I don't draw directly from nature but rather think of nature as condensed energy. I had been working with many of the forms that are actually in the works of this exhibit when I went off to Vermont to teach for three weeks. Several of the pieces, including *Grasping Nature*, were actually made there. Often I set up arbitrary situations just to force change in my work. I had taken a lot of odds and ends of half-used tubes of acrylic paint with me and had decided that I had to use whatever colors were in these tubes. I was not going to carry them back on the plane. At first I was working on *Radiant Spirit*. Because the paint would dry, I would take any leftovers and use it up as I started other pieces including *Grasping Nature*. Because I assumed I would paint over these initial markings, I worked very loosely. Also, in *Grasping Nature* I actually reworked an Arthur Dove form, not something I usually do. I had brought the Dove catalogue raisonné with me to Vermont and was spending a lot of time not only looking at the reproductions but even reading the text. I am interested in the simplicity and outrageous abstraction in his work. I'm very drawn to it because the forms are so suggestive. I think they are uniquely his own. Anyway, I worked from a tendril-like, reaching form of Dove's that related to what I called "grasping forms" that I had used in various ways for several years in both my painting and sculpture. The central finger-type projections gave me so many compositional areas to work around in the painting. It was very easy to respond to the space around the form, and to fill in or activate the space. I felt like I learned a lot of what Dove was doing. How he made decisions. And it was amazing because it was so easy! That's not the way I usually work. I start working on a painting by having this huge empty white space and putting in a few of my forms, which are fairly self-contained and separate from each other. Although that is changing. It fascinated me doing this piece because it came together out of all these things. It was so easy, and I liked it. I left it very open. I felt that I could leave all that whiteness there and still fill the space.

It also helped me to understand how difficult what I'm usually doing is. How do I fill all that space when there's nothing there to respond to? There's really nothing there. How do I paint energized space? I'm not painting something that exists in the concrete sense, nor am I taking painting space and dividing it up into an abstract composition. I am painting something less tangible than that. The unusual situation of working from the Dove form helped me to focus on the issues in my own work. All these little understandings—that's what I got from doing *Grasping Nature*, liking that openness—seeing how I tend to fill up the spaces. Can I keep a feeling of activated and energized space without filling it all in? That becomes an interesting problem for me.

WILSON: In this body of work, the prints also have this open, lighter quality.

HAMMOND: Yes, that comes from the nature of monoprints. I always think of monoprinting as a sort of collaboration between myself and the press. I paint an image on the plate but never really know how it will print when run through the press. The press does its own thing. I try to create wonderful accidents where forms bleed, merge, print, or don't print. It's what I call working in a state of peripheral control. Also, the print or ink is literally pressed into the surface of the paper rather than sitting like a blanket on top. I too love the spirit of lightness that is in the monoprints and am working to get it into my large canvases. I can do it with watercolor on paper, but how to do it with thick oil paint is a different problem. How can I get lightness of spirit into the paintings when the very physicality and materiality of the thick oil paint is a contradiction? That's exactly the thing that interests me. It's very easy to open up in the prints. They've taken me to a new place, and I feel like they are probably a very good indication of the way the paintings will go. But I don't know how the canvases will get there because they have to find their own path. Even in these paper paintings I am trying to not compulsively fill all the space. Somehow my response to New Mexico and the space out here is to try and open up my paint surfaces.

WILSON: Every artist I have ever seen who moved here had to grapple with the landscape.

HAMMOND: Yes, it's hard to know in my case exactly how the landscape affects me because I don't seem to respond to it visually in stereotyped ways. It seems to have more to do with opening up the picture surface. It is full and energized, it is not empty space out here to me at all. On the other hand, it has to do with the quality of my life out here. In New York, I have these tendencies to fill up every minute of my time, every inch of my life doing something . . . because you are bouncing off all these other people and I have all these ideas, and there is so much to do. And so to leave open spaces is very difficult for me, and yet very important. That's how the outside world enters in; it's also how you hear yourself internally. I know all that but sometimes I have great difficulty doing it. I think my decision to come out here, and then my decision to stay, have to do with leaving some open space in my life.

WILSON: As a curator I've always been interested in the presentation of artists' work. I was very unhappy when I went to MOCA and the AE [abstract expressionist] works were hung in large galleries, when they were meant to be huge paintings in small rooms.

HAMMOND: And they became small, little, like reproductions. . . .

WILSON: Right! These really wonderful paintings were reduced to being illustrations of the chronology of art history. Viewers were given no idea of their original impact.

HAMMOND: Obviously I care a lot about presentation, and when I can control it, I do. Especially the first time work is shown. But the fact is the work eventually goes out of your hands and out of control . . . it's disturbing. Sometimes, installing outside of your studio you learn things about your own work. Taking your example of the space in which we make the work—the ceiling height, the wall height, how much other stuff is in the room—all of that affects the work. When I install an exhibit, I have very strong feelings about pieces finding their place, and the total exhibit becomes very installational to me even though I'm not doing an installation piece. I like to create a quality of feeling. Subtly direct people how to look at the work. The fact is how you put the work out there originally affects how people see it, how it's written about and so forth.

WILSON: In *The Sketchbooks of Picasso* catalogue [*Je Suis le Cahier: The Sketchbooks of Picasso*, Pace Gallery, New York, 1986] Rosalind Krauss reminded me how backward the artist biography approach is, and how inadequate. For example, we have been treated to endless descriptions of Picasso living in such and such a house, and married to his wife, and therefore he did this kind of work. Krauss reminds us that Picasso had that house and that wife because his work . . .

HAMMOND: Took him in these directions?

WILSON: In *Wrappings: Essays on Feminism, Art, and the Martial Arts* [1984], the book of your collected writings, you clearly state that your life has always been directed by your art.

HAMMOND: It's true. I don't separate them. In other words, art is a big part of my life. . . . It's not everything but it's not separate from the other things in my life. So it's very difficult to talk about whether the art is affected by where I'm living, whom I'm involved with, what projects I'm working on, or what other art I'm seeing . . . or am I living somewhere, doing something, etc., because of the needs of my art. It's all connected. I know that and I feel very comfortable with it.

WILSON: Do you feel that you've relinquished something by coming to New Mexico? You did leave a mark on art history. I'm interested in your view of the idea that once you've separated yourself from a place like New York, it's "out of sight out of mind." . . .

HAMMOND: What do you mean?

WILSON: Well, you've been an important role model for women artists through your art, your organizing, your teaching, and your writing.

HAMMOND: But you're implying that leaving something is a loss. . . . Well, I do think about it. I make art quite well in New Mexico. But I worry about not being as professionally visible as in New York. But one always has to leave things and go on. I'm going to make an analogy. When you develop a way of working, like the wrapped sculptures I worked on for many years, the first ones were very crude, and didn't make it as whole pieces, but there was something that interested me. I knew I was onto something, whatever that thing was. So I worked at it until I got very skilled. The making, the process, the materials, everything leads you, and you make decisions, and the works grow, and you learn about them while you're doing them and you get to a point where you really know what you're doing—you even control the uncontrollable. That's a very exciting point because that's the point where the work is really developed and pushed. But you can't stay there. We say that this work is a good example of a particular body of work because you've pushed everything and it all comes together, and there's magic on top of it. But if you stay there, the magic is lost and the work becomes dead, OK? Well, I believe that's true in life also. And so that's why we move on, that's why we make changes. Besides, obviously the world around us changes. Feminism of the '70s must change and move on. In terms of leaving New York, I do think about my decision to move. I am still a very committed feminist, but recent work does not overtly deal with feminist issues. Feminism, like art, is one important but integrated part of my life. Right now, I am involved in other issues in my art. Although there is still the problem of getting the work out. My political work seems to be teaching, writing, lecturing, and sometimes curating exhibitions. Here I am constantly raising issues of feminism, class, and race. I am interested in the politics of culture. But mostly I'm very involved with being in the studio and painting. . . . For the first time in my life I am in the studio every day.

WILSON: It's the nature of this kind of place, being solitary. . . .

HAMMOND: It's also a part of the times. In terms of the feminist art movement, there's a lot of activity and then there's a lull. Cycles. There were a lot of activities in the early '70s when women were discovering each other and organizing and taking on an activist role instead of passively waiting to be recognized by the patriarchal art world, which had discriminated against women for centuries. We set up our own galleries, slide registries, exhibitions, magazines, presses, etc.

And through this organizing effort, more women's art became visible than ever before in history.

Around 1975 there was another huge burst of activity. There were a lot of big movement events that happened in the summer of '75. *Heresies Magazine*, and *Chrysalis Magazine*. Lucy Lippard's book [*From the Center: Feminist Essays on Women's Art* (1976)] came out right around then. Also, the large exhibition *Women Artists 1550–1950*, curated by Linda Nochlin and Ann Sutherland Harris, happened around this time.

Now there is a whole new dialogue around essentialist versus deconstructive feminist art and feminist art criticism. Feminist art of the '80s has been different. Because it has tended to question the concept of woman through the deconstruction of the representation of woman, many feminist artists have not tended to be involved with other women on activist group projects. I find all this very interesting even though my art is not involved with some of these issues. No, that's not entirely true. Since my work has often had cross-cultural references and since I am interested in writing about art of cultures other than my own, I'm very interested in issues of cross-cultural appropriation and think that must be a necessary part of the formulation of any feminist art criticism.

WILSON: Well, when I came to your studio in 1985, I was very surprised because I had always thought of your work as sculptural. It coincided with some admittedly primitive questions in my own mind about how painting was, perhaps, a more intrinsically male arena.

HAMMOND: I don't understand your thought. Why painting versus sculpture, which has always in modern art history been a male-dominated territory?

WILSON: Well, women's work always struck me as more structural, and textural, and taking a place in the world in that way. And, so, I walk into this feminist artist's studio who I've always thought of as a sculptor, and it took me longer to see your painting.

HAMMOND: I have two immediate connections to that. Actually, in recent art history both painting and sculpture have been dominated by men. All artmaking has seemed to be their territory. The experience of women's lives was excluded from fine art. Thus, one of the ways for women to get female content into their work in the early '70s comes out of the handling and manipulation of materials. Some of the most radical and exciting work grew out of using nonart materials. It was coming out of Eva Hesse and women's bodies and materials related to the home and traditional arts. A lot of early feminist work did have to do with three-dimensional things.

In sculpture, women changed not only content but the very form of sculpture itself. In painting, I think it was different. Changes were in content and not form. I've always moved back and forth in terms of my working process. I shift between painting and sculpture because the ideas lead me back and forth. Sometimes I'm doing both, sometimes there's an emphasis more on one than the other. What I'm really interested in is the notion of "presence," which I define as "essence made visible." Felt but not illustrated. In recent years I've felt that it's much more difficult to do that in painting. I find it much easier to get a sense of presence in sculpture where you have the actual object occupying space. How to get the same physicality and felt presence out of the two dimensional really interests me. And it interests me in other painters' work. Dove has it. So does [Willem] de Kooning, [Philip] Guston, Elizabeth Murray, and Bill Jensen, and they all use paint very differently. It's really magic—all you have is a thin skin of paint. How do you have a spatial presence when it's not literally taking up real space?

WILSON: You do have a sort of horror-vacui approach to the usage of space.

HAMMOND: Really? I don't feel that. I love open space. It's a sense of the physical self in space.

WILSON: Don't you think that you have a tendency to fill up your work with activity?

HAMMOND: There's a lot of spatial contradictions in the work, and there's some level on which I like that. That interests me in our lives: how different ideas or different ways we act out our lives can coexist, and how we find ways of balancing these things or putting them together. And that's what happens in the world of my paintings—not only choices in terms of how forms are depicted, but the space around them. I'm quite likely to combine deep-layered space with flat frontal space. Maybe it's like loving New York and loving New Mexico and all the energy that's in both places. They are both grand landscapes. In New York there is the energy of all those millions of people crowded together on a tiny island, and in New Mexico there is the timeless energy of the land.

ED. NOTES

This interview was first published as "Edited Conversations" in the unpaginated exhibition brochure for *Harmony Hammond: Radiant Spirits*, curated by MaLin Wilson[-Powell] at Jonson Gallery, University Art Museum, University of New Mexico, Albuquerque, November 20, 1987–January 22, 1988. Courtesy of the University of New Mexico Art Museum.

1. Works featured in *Harmony Hammond: Radiant Spirits*: *Emerging*, 1984, acrylic on paper, 30 × 21¾ in.; *Thought Form*, 1985, acrylic on paper, 29½ × 42 in.; *Flaming Spirit*, 1985, acrylic on paper, 62 × 42 in.; *Grasping Nature*, 1985, acrylic on paper, 50 × 38 in.; *Grasping Spirit*, 1985, acrylic on paper, 50 × 38 in.; *Radiant Spirit*, 1985, acrylic on paper, 50 × 38 in.; *Singing Spirit*, 1985, acrylic on paper, 50 × 38 in.; *Embracing Nature*, 1985, acrylic on paper, 41½ × 29⅝ in.; *Spirit with Spine*, 1985, monoprint, 34¾ × 25 in.; *Form I*, 1986, acrylic on paper, 50 × 38 in.; *Form II*, 1987, acrylic on paper, 50 × 38 in.; *Transformation II*, 1987, monoprint, 42 × 29½ in.; *Transformation VIII*, 1987, monoprint, 42 × 29½ in.; *Transformation IX*, 1987, monoprint, 42 × 29½ in.

Artist's Statement

(1989–1990)

I have always been involved with collage or assemblage—either literally or metaphorically. Collage carries the great potential of providing content in abstraction, and I have mostly worked with recycled materials because: 1) I can't throw anything away, 2) recycled materials have a previous history of uses, and 3) because they make references to the lives and creative histories of those who, like myself, have been relegated to the margins of culture. In the past, much of my work dealt with notions of difference and connection—of being a woman and a lesbian in patriarchal culture.

Since 1984, I have lived in Northern New Mexico where I have used the *campo santos*, the *cerquitas*, and the *descansos* as sources of inspiration for highly charged and activated paintings that mark the spots of change and transformation (the last place that the physical body touches the earth before moving into another state). I have tried to paint the world of the spirit, while it is contradicted by the very materiality of the thick oil paint I use.

My recent work has brought together the sculpture of the '70s with the paintings of the early '80s. I am using old, dirty recycled corrugated tin—affixing it to the painting surface, painting directly on the tin, or what is most interesting to me—juxtaposing it to large "beautifully painted" canvases. These problematic juxtapositions create an uneasy tension—much like that of disparate groups of people living together in the same neighborhood. The tin comes from the Barrio Viejo in Tucson where I live and work each fall for four months, or the small villages of Northern New Mexico where I live the rest of the time, or the dirt roads somewhere in between. Tin is a material that speaks to many people. It is urban, it is rural, it is international. It crosses race and class lines. It is even used to decorate yuppie bars where they serve up pink and turquoise margaritas, or to merchandise "third world clothes" at Banana Republic. I am interested in appropriation and context. How the tin varies in value and meaning (like the rags I used to use) according to the cultural context and economic position of the viewer. A material considered disposable and discardable by one group of people is saved, used, and reused, indeed necessary to the survival of others. An esthetic of necessity develops. And then what happens when I bring these materials into the fine arts context?

The painted forms come from tracings of templates used to make corbels, vigas, *latillas*, and other decorative elements of Hispanic architecture. Combined with the painted surface, they call up the history of Western art (cubism) but in fact come from Hispanic craft traditions (think of the Spanish heritage of cubism). The assemblages embody the complexities of gentrification as reflected in architecture—the gentrification of neighborhoods, cultures, art. They are about change. Sometimes there is writing but only if there is a story to tell. Each piece is different. They are about the homeless, abortion, violence, *los muros*, *las fronteras*, censorship, the fights and struggles for freedom, cultural change, and the juxtaposition of different creative traditions.

ED. NOTE

Hammond wrote this statement for her John Simon Guggenheim Memorial Foundation Fellowship application (awarded in 1991).

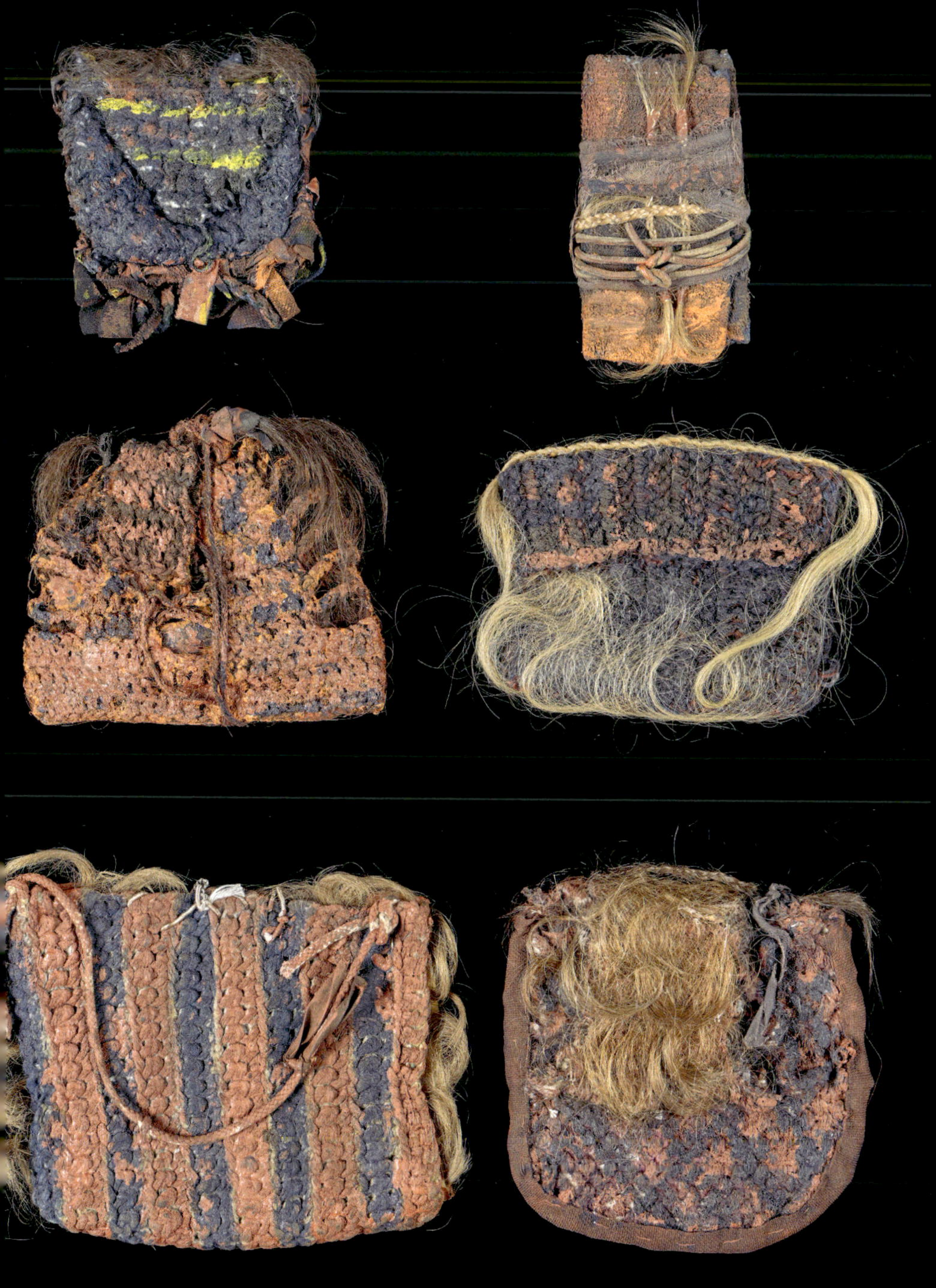

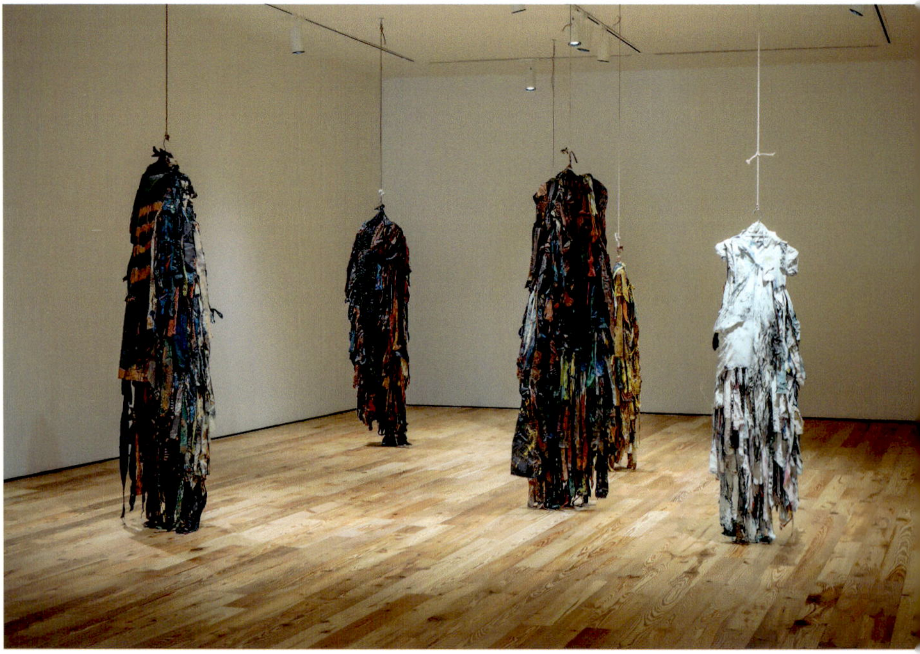

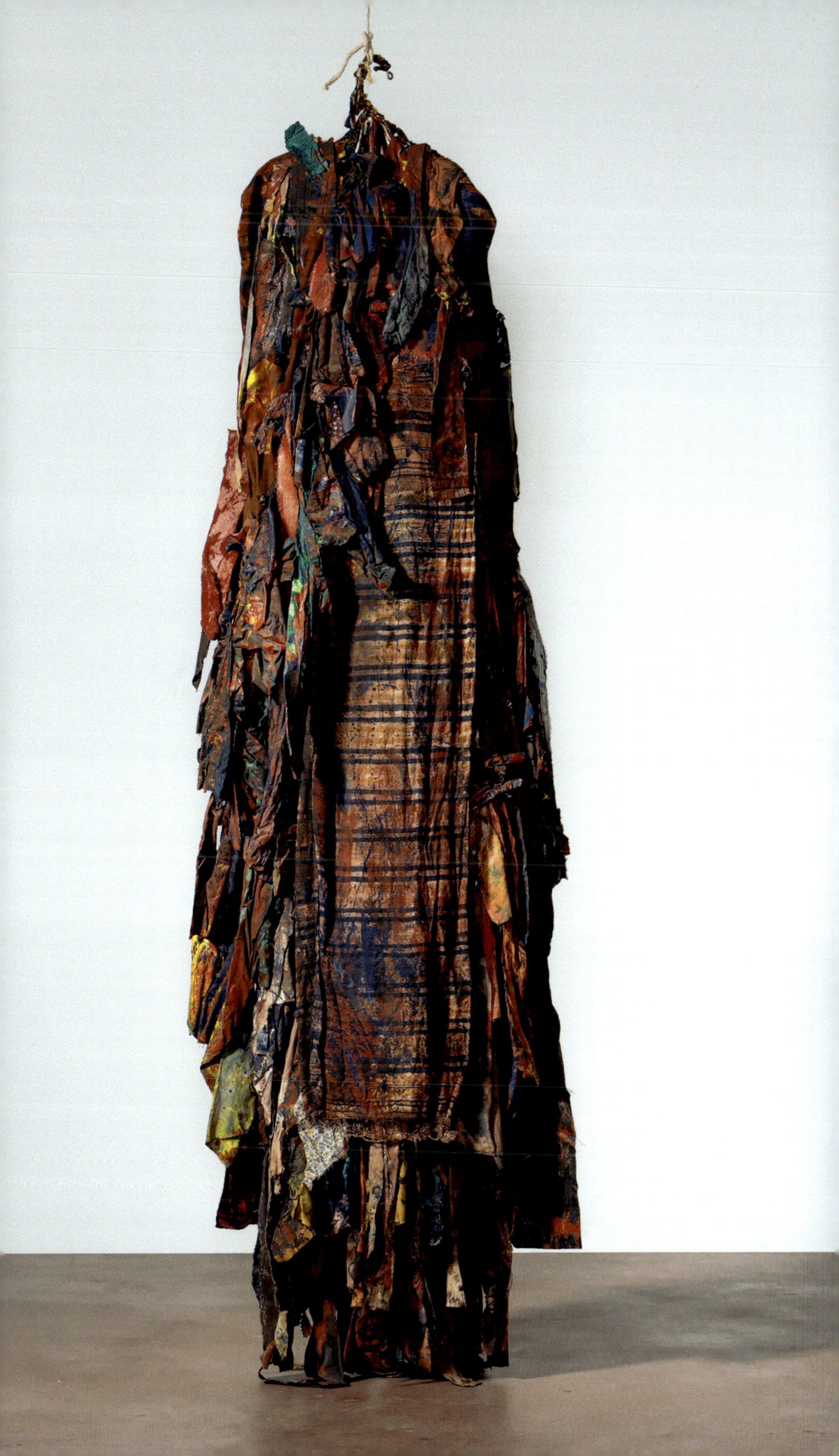

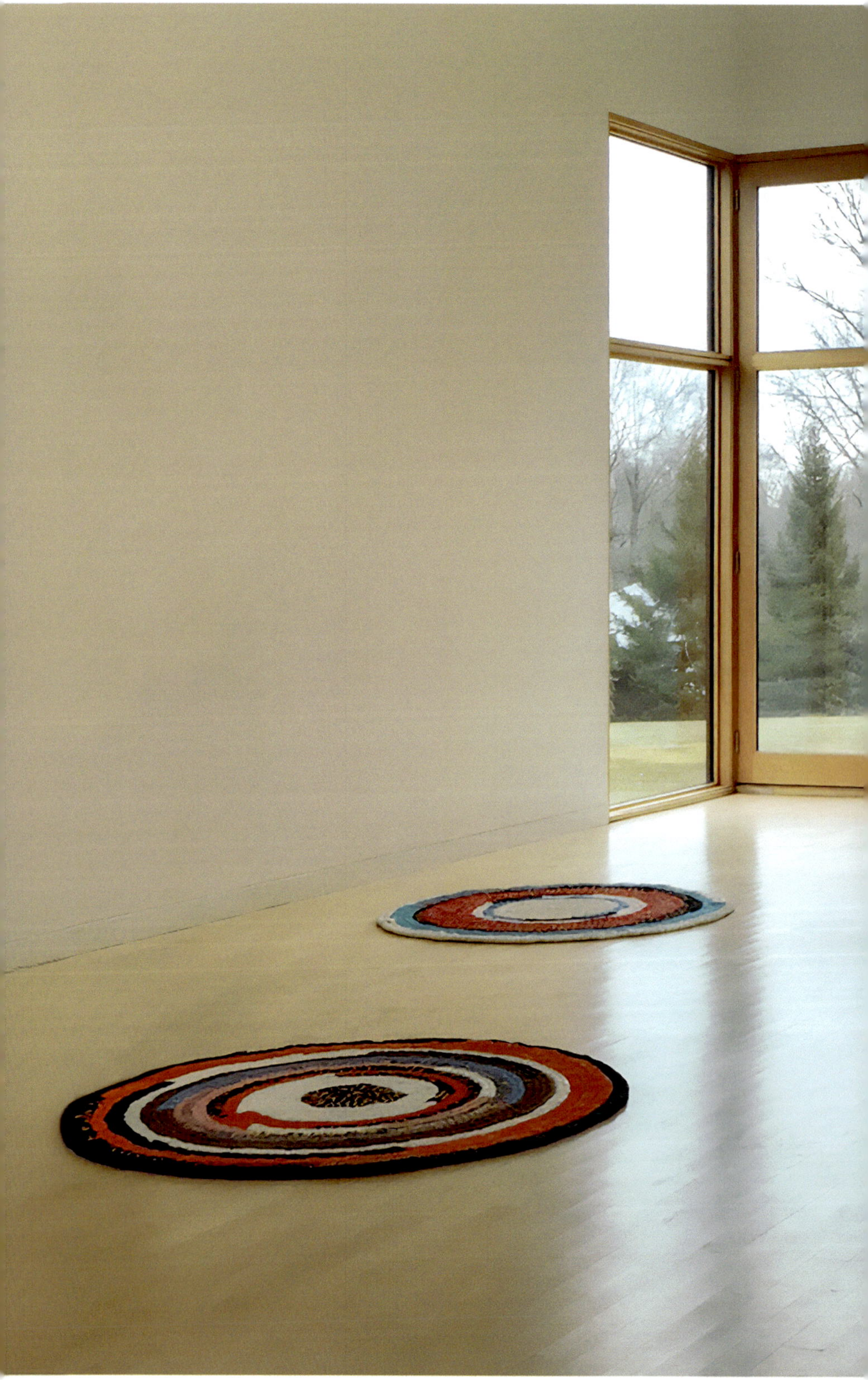

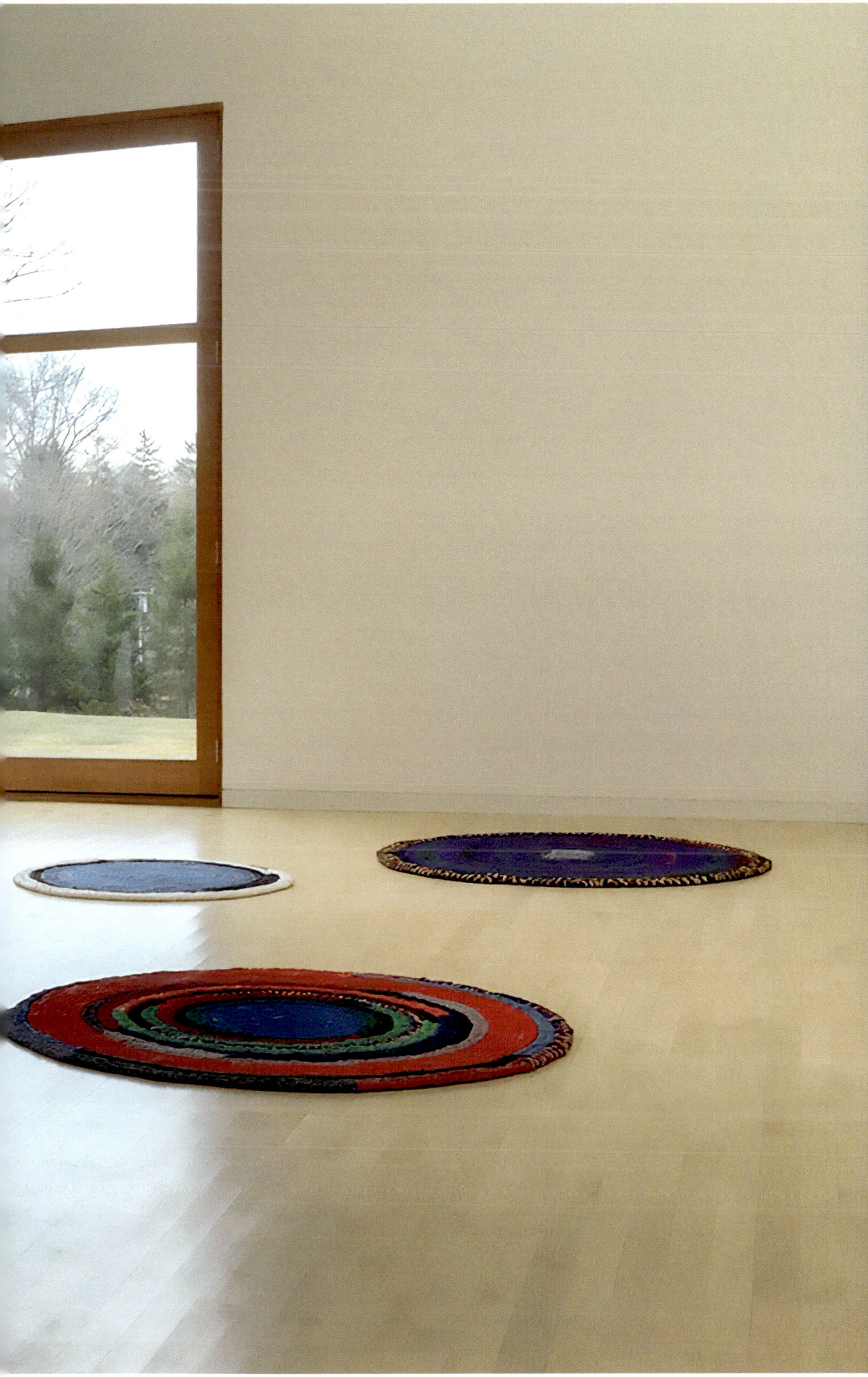

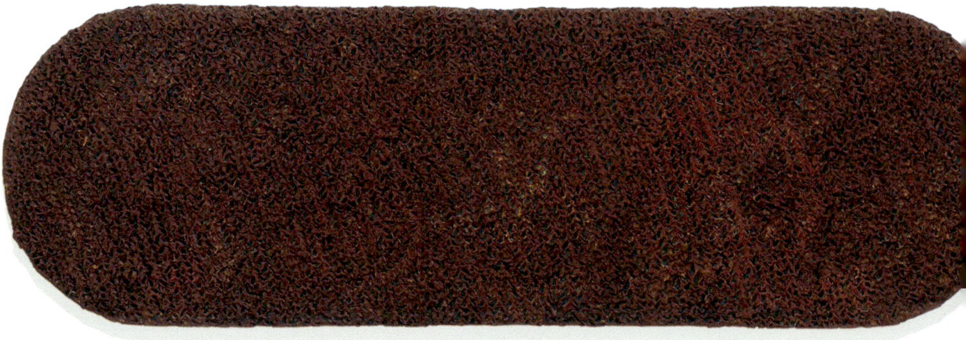

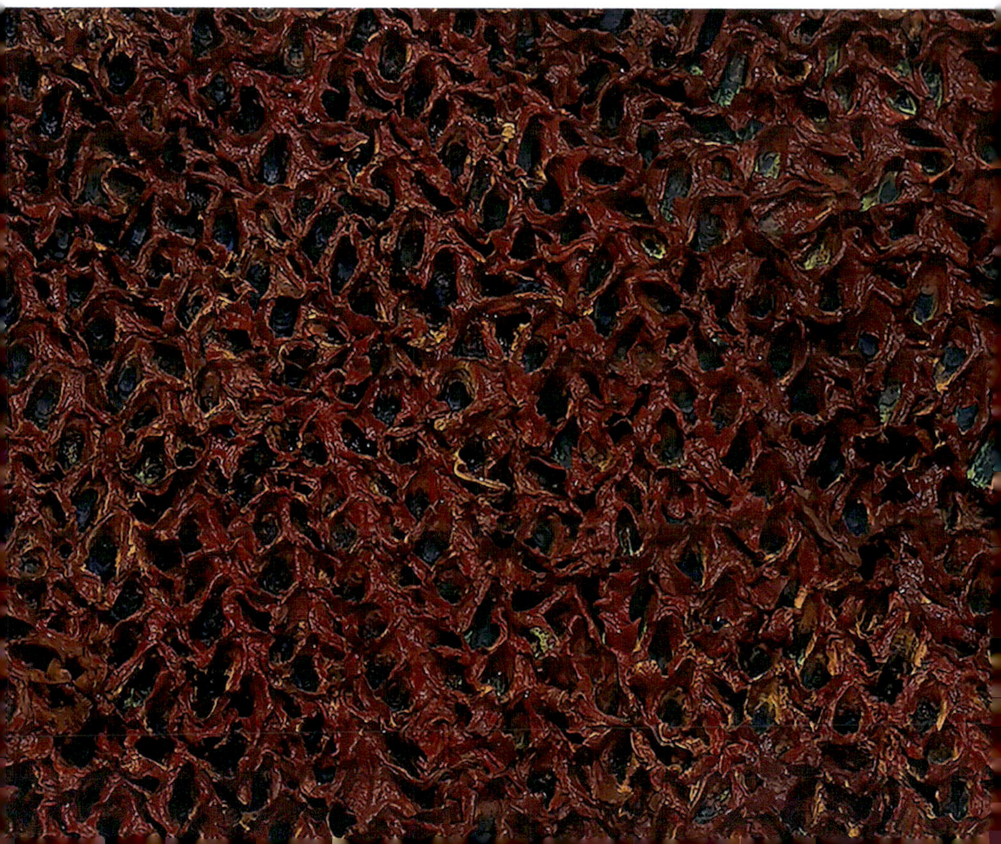

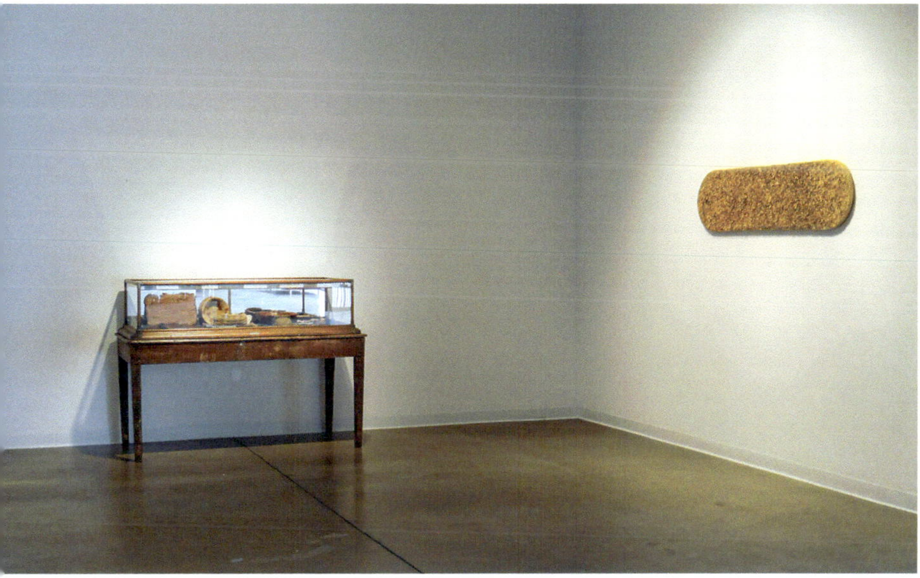

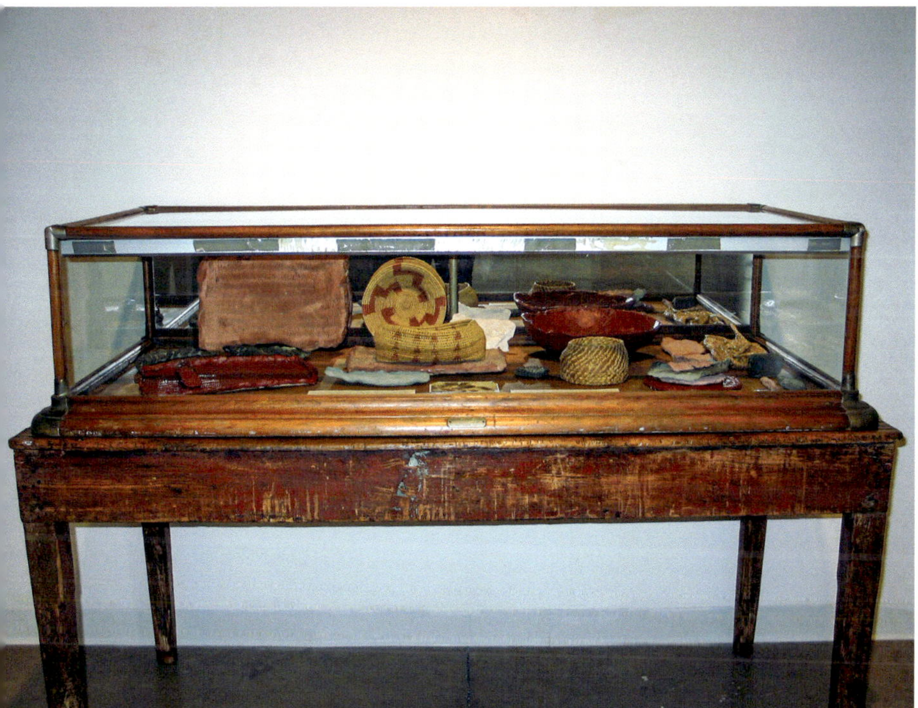

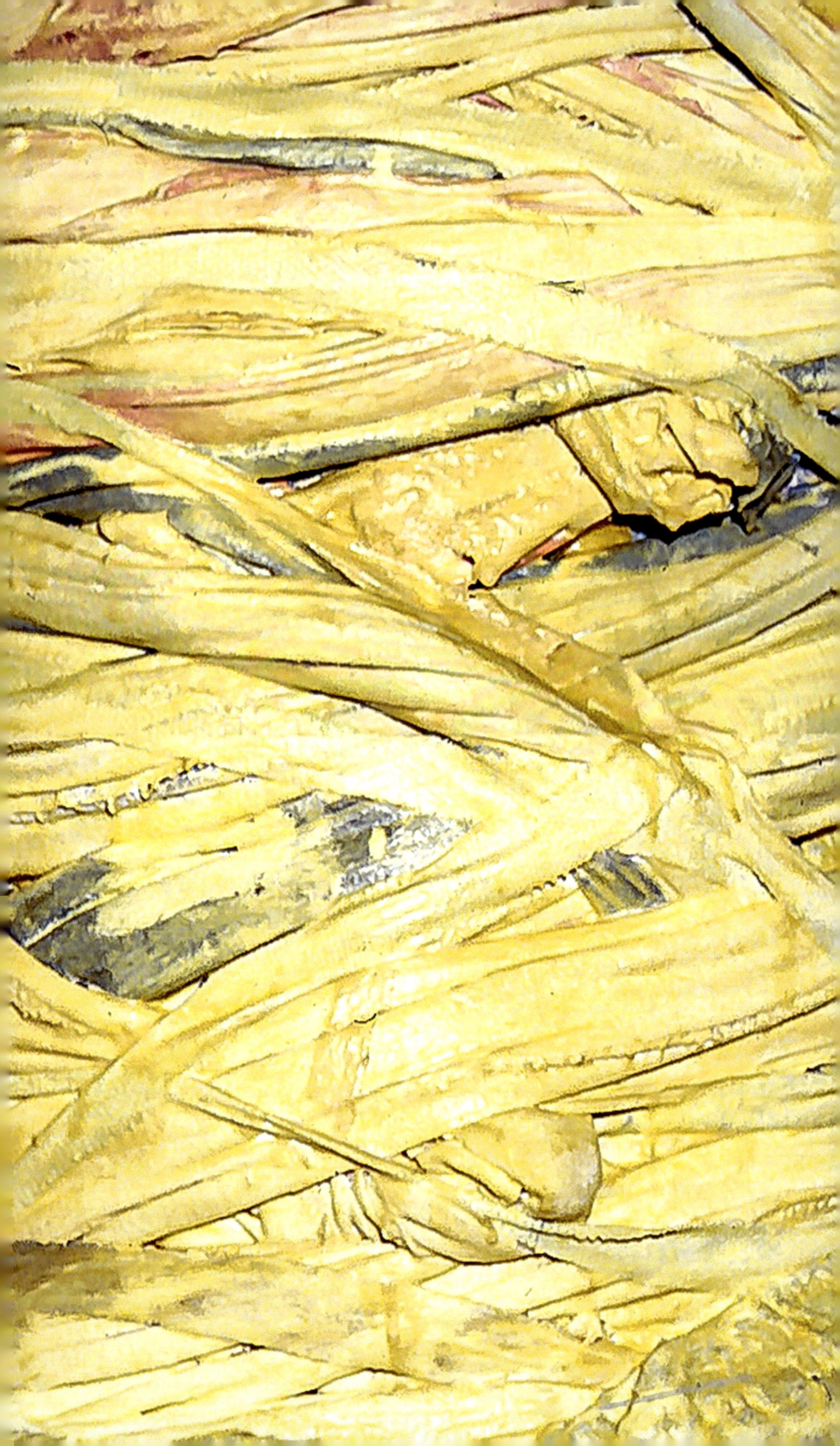

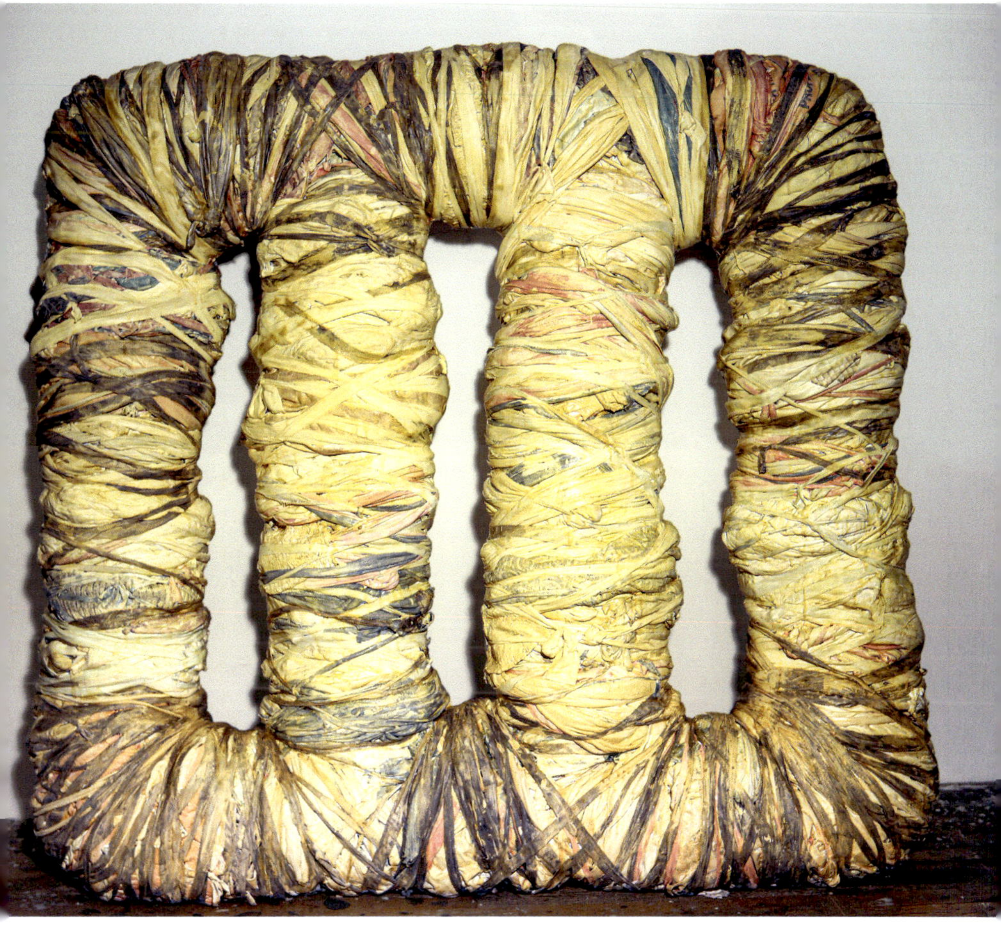

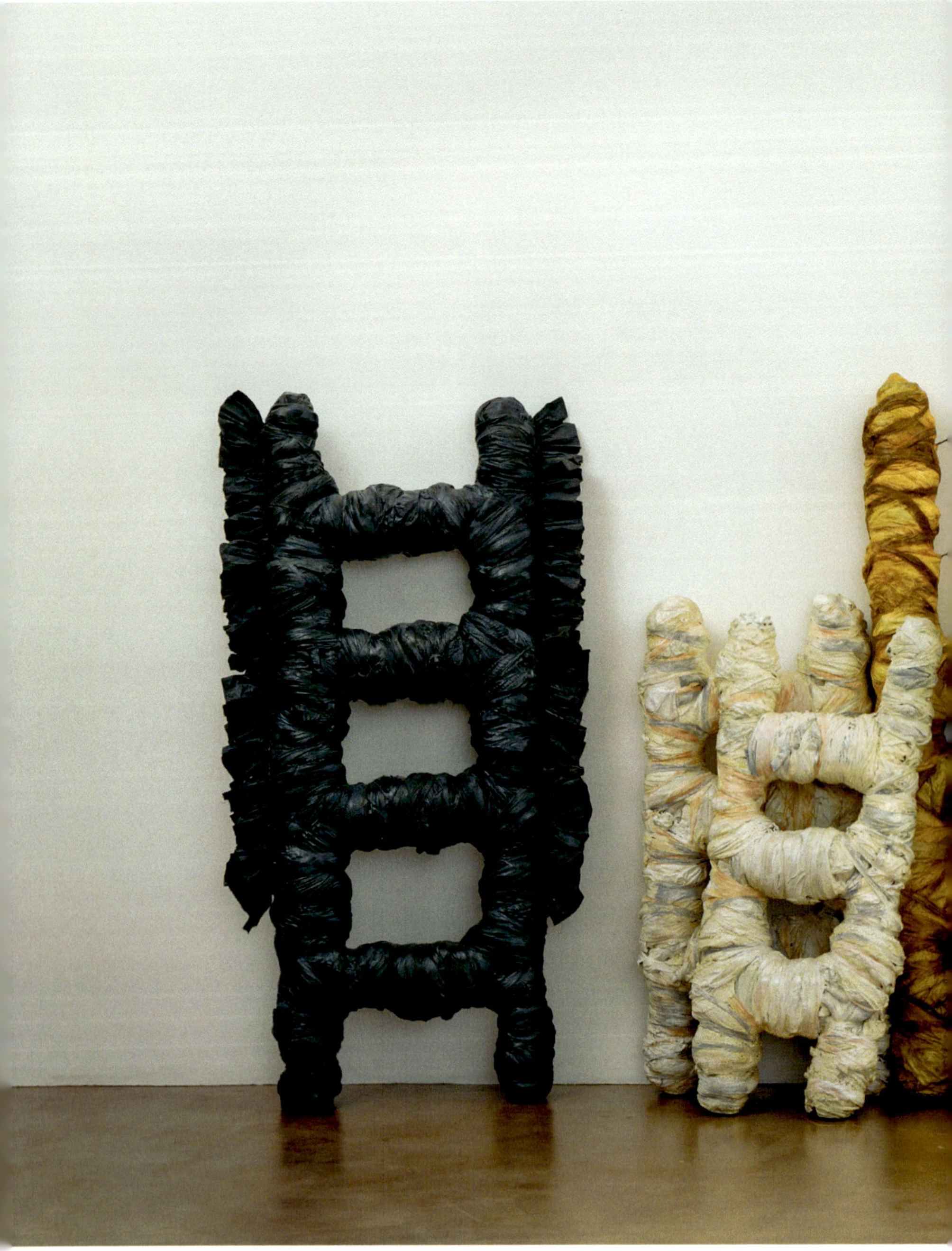

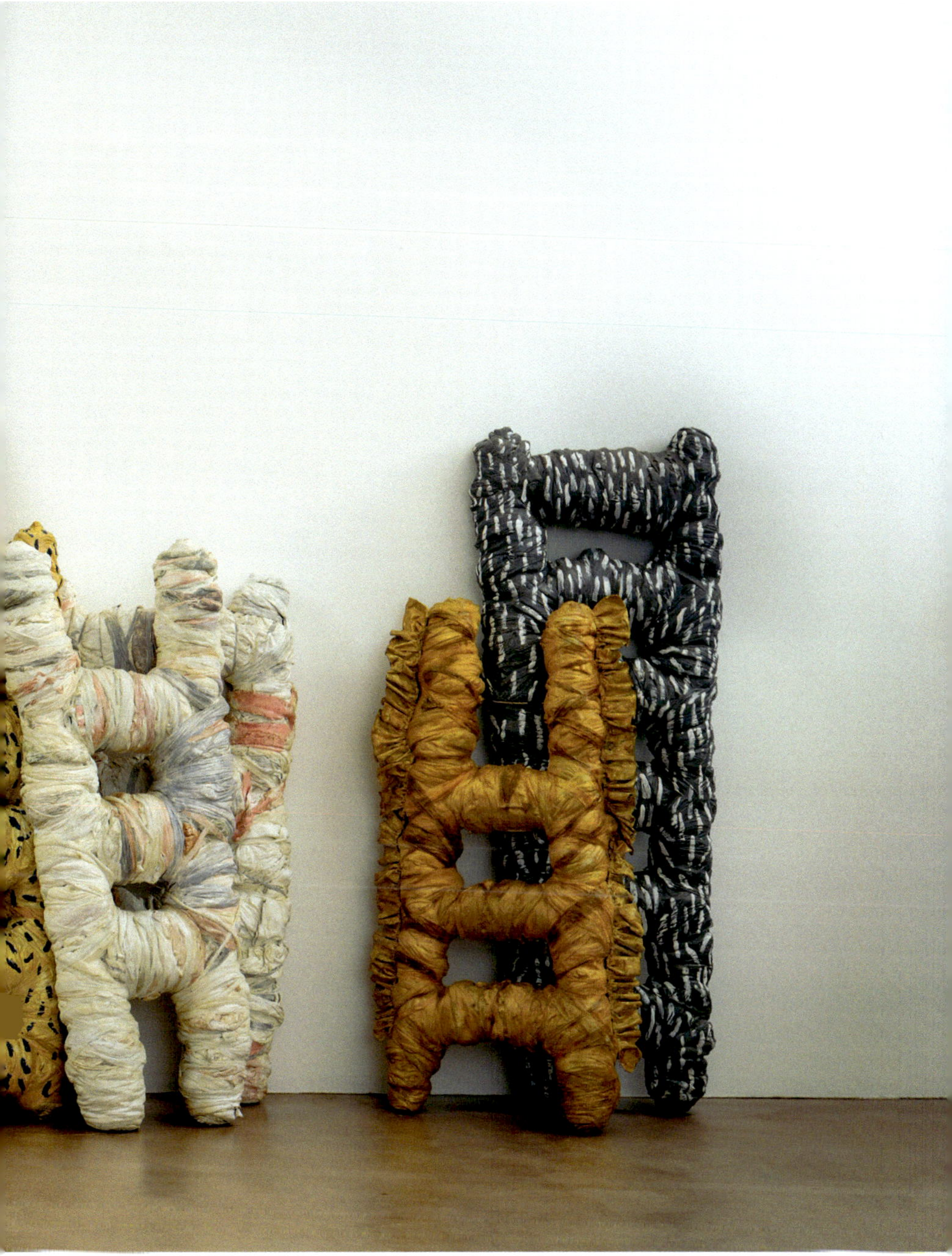

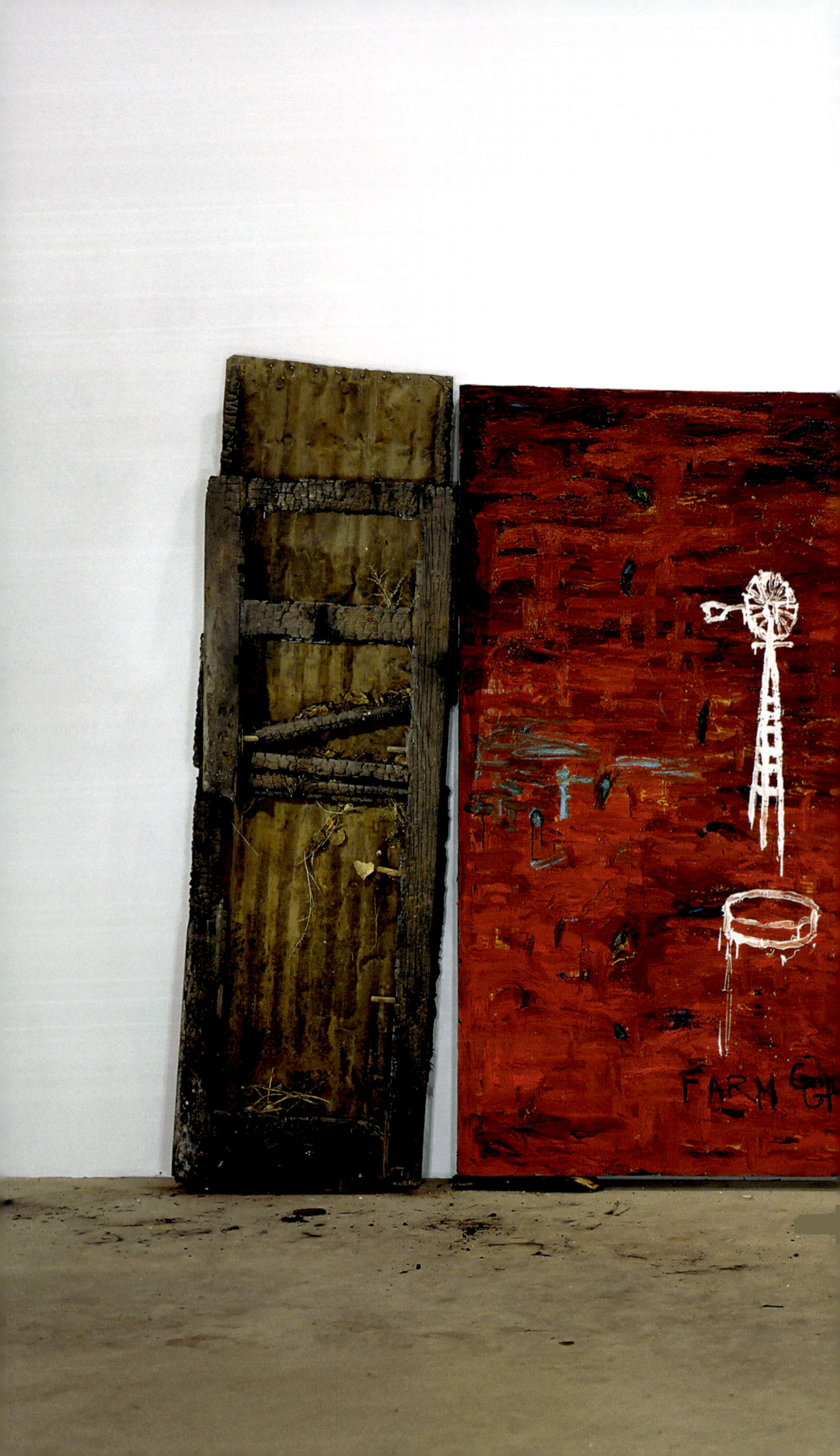
FARM

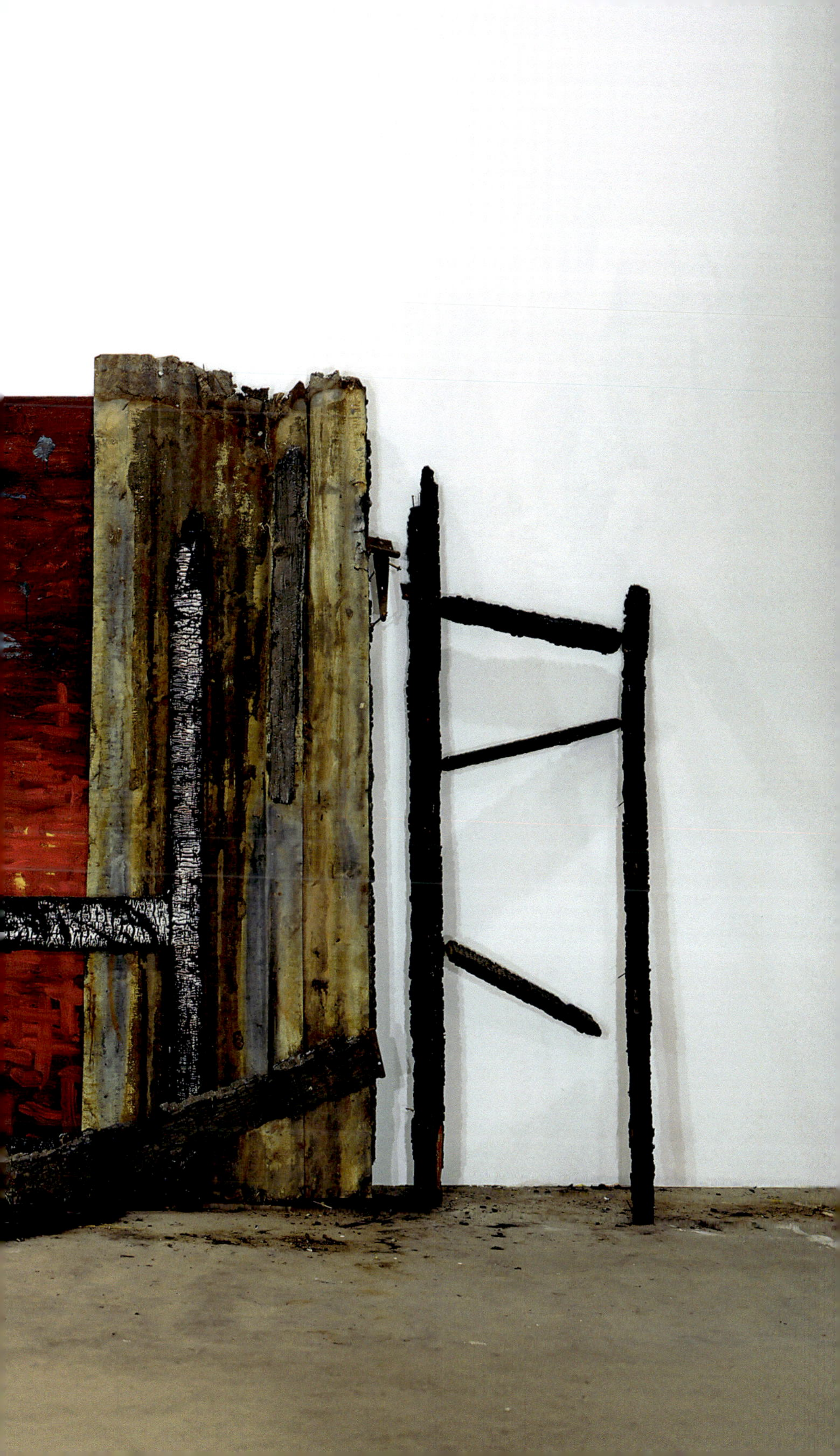

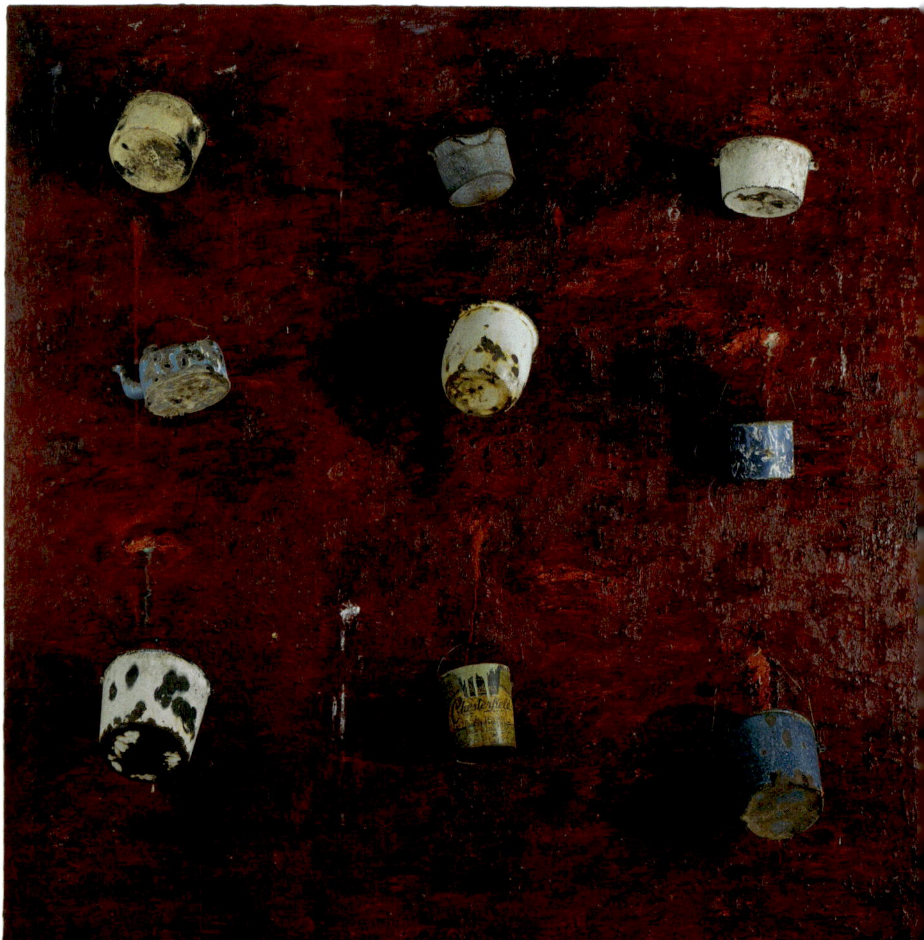

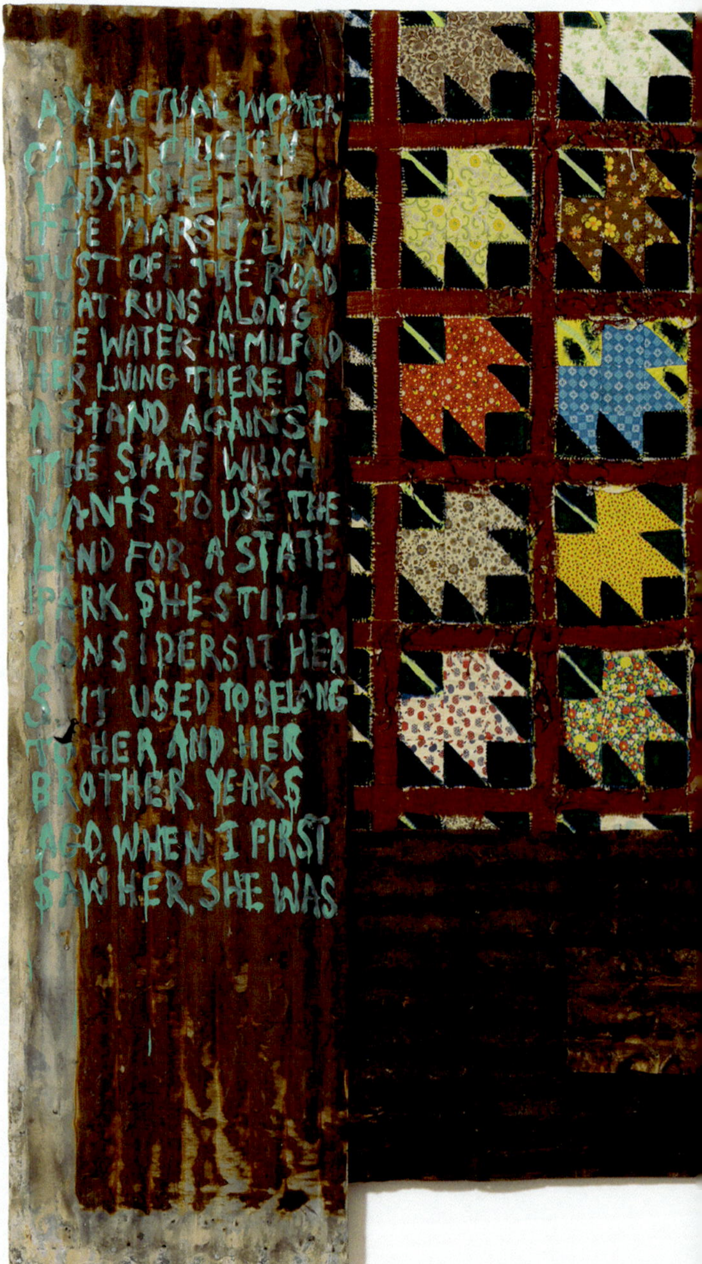
AN ACTUAL WOMEN
CALLED CHICKEN
LADY. SHE LIVES IN
THE MARSHY LAND
JUST OFF THE ROAD
THAT RUNS ALONG
THE WATER IN MILFORD
HER LIVING THERE IS
A STAND AGAINST
THE STATE WHICH
WANTS TO USE THE
LAND FOR A STATE
PARK. SHE STILL
CONSIDERS IT HER
S. IT USED TO BELONG
TO HER AND HER
BROTHER YEARS
AGO. WHEN I FIRST
SAW HER, SHE WAS

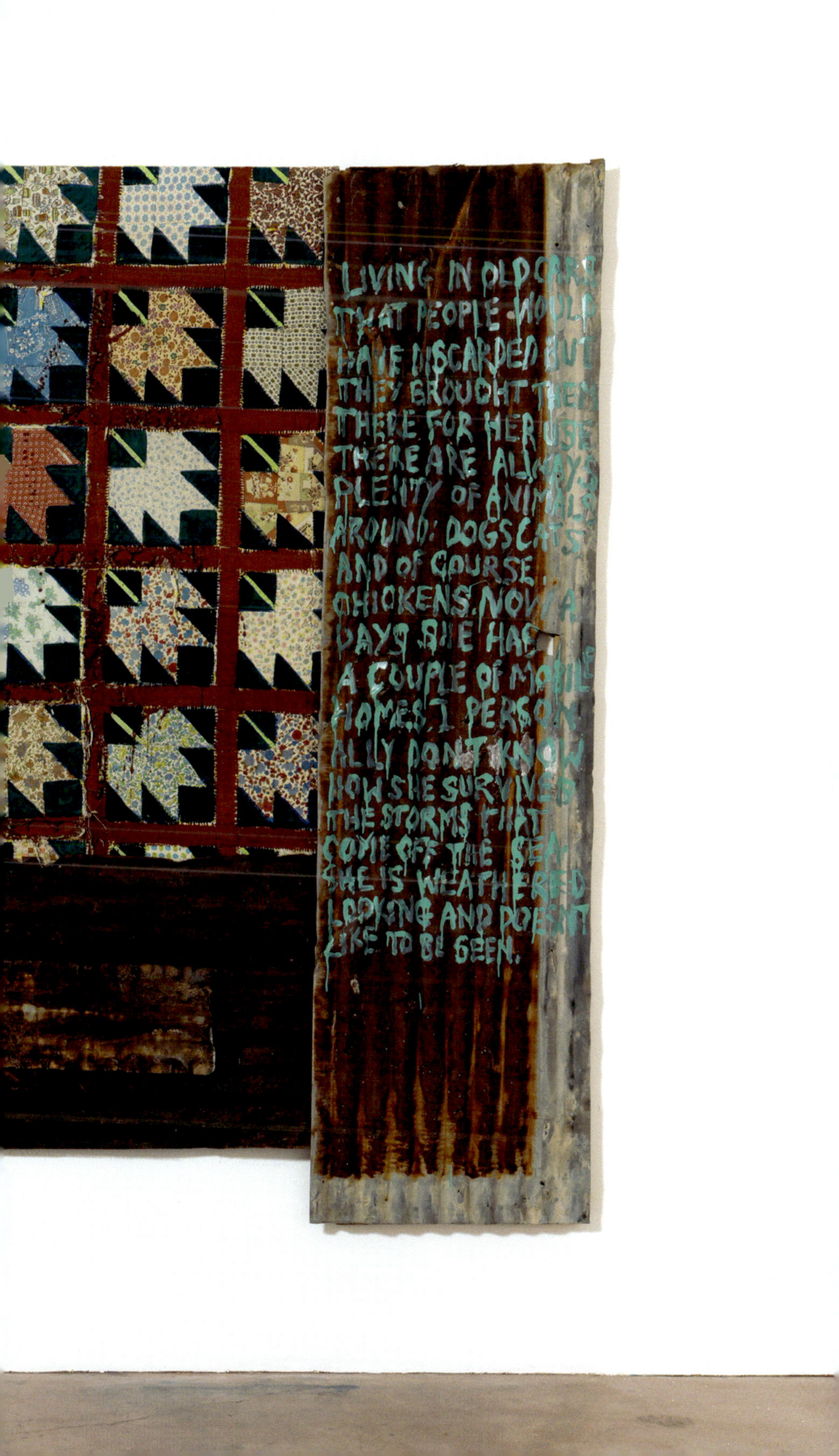
LIVING IN OLD CARS
THAT PEOPLE WOULD
HAVE DISCARDED BUT
THEY BROUGHT THEM
THERE FOR HER USE
THERE ARE ALWAYS
PLENTY OF ANIMALS
AROUND: DOGS CATS
AND OF COURSE,
CHICKENS. NOW A
DAYS SHE HAS
A COUPLE OF MOBILE
HOMES. I PERSON
ALLY DONT KNOW
HOW SHE SURVIVES
THE STORMS THAT
COME OFF THE SEA
SHE IS WEATHERED
LOOKING AND DOESNT
LIKE TO BE SEEN.

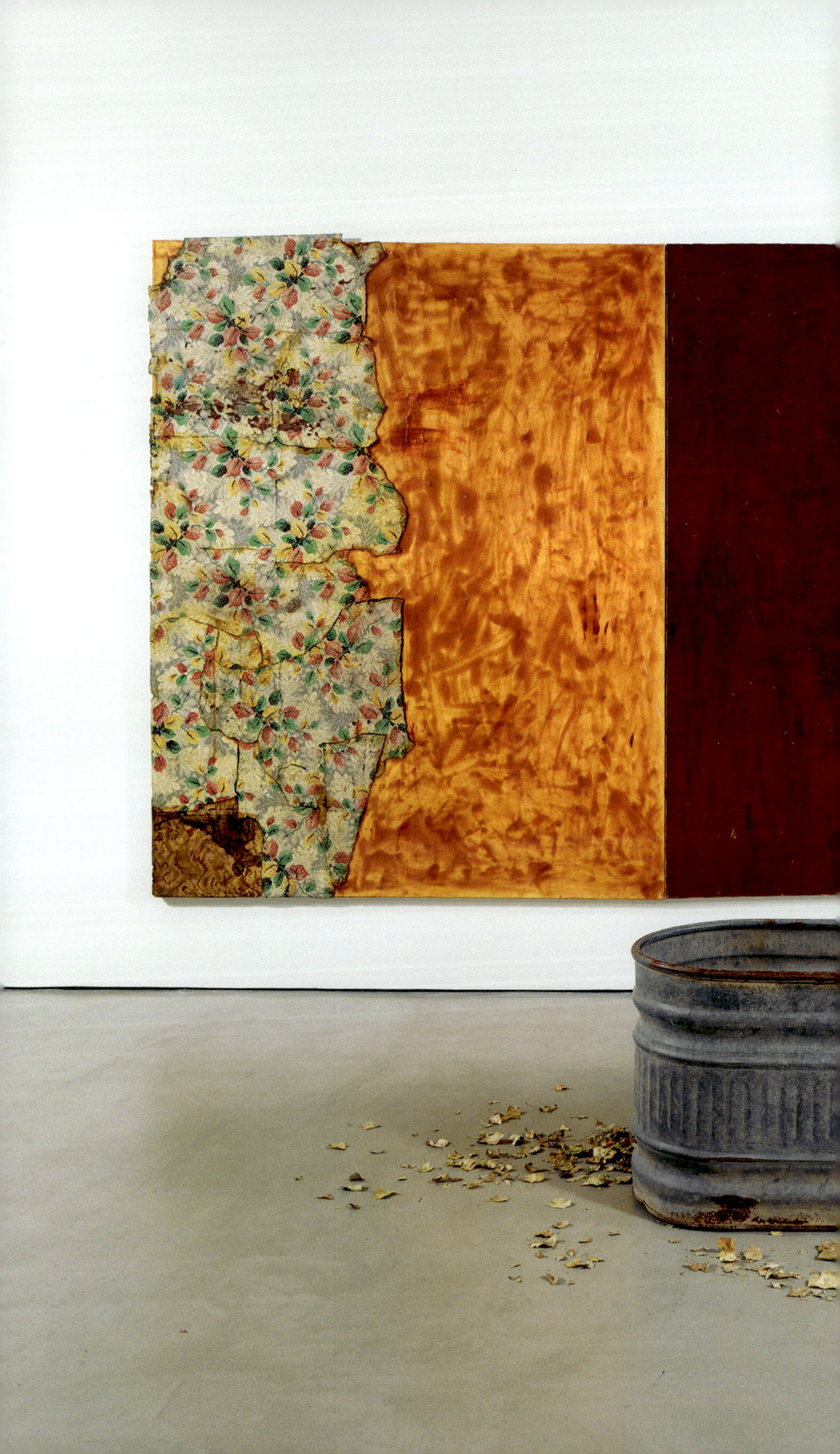

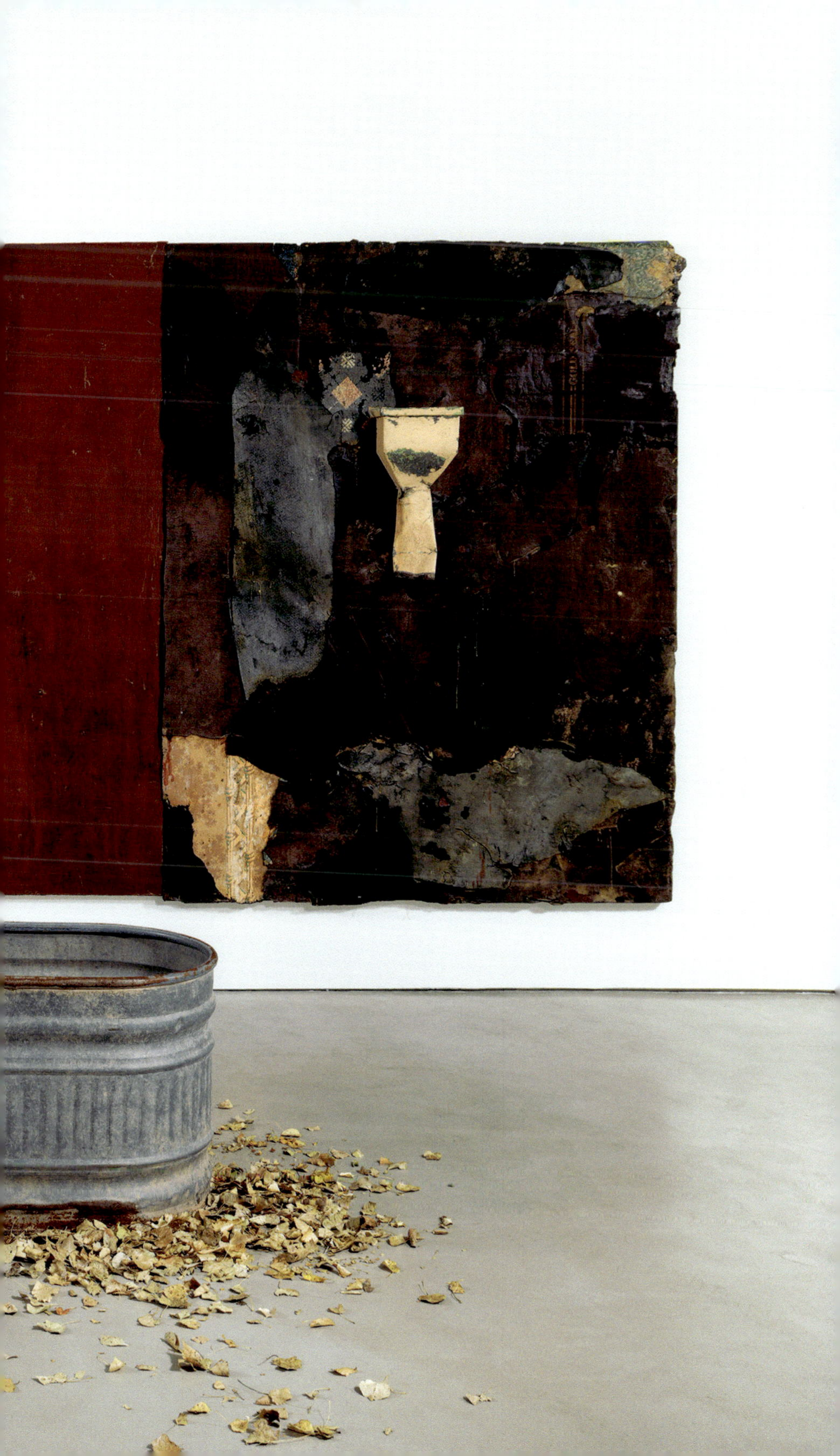

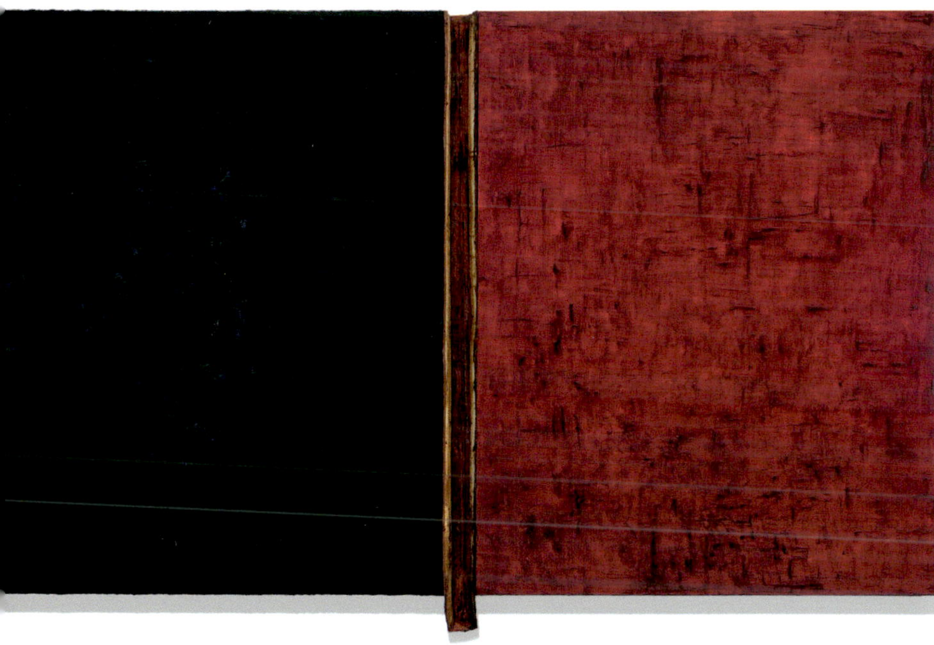

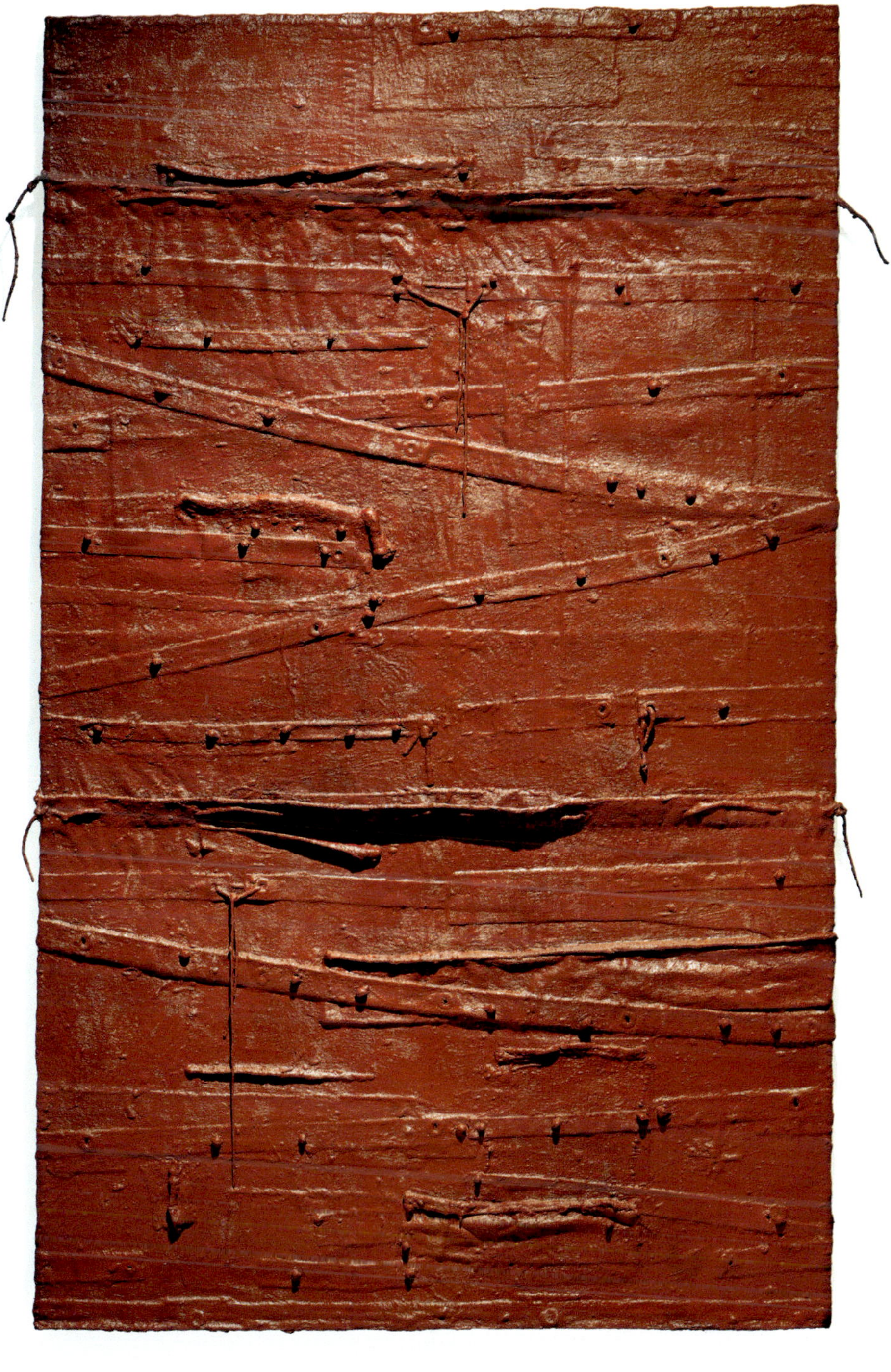

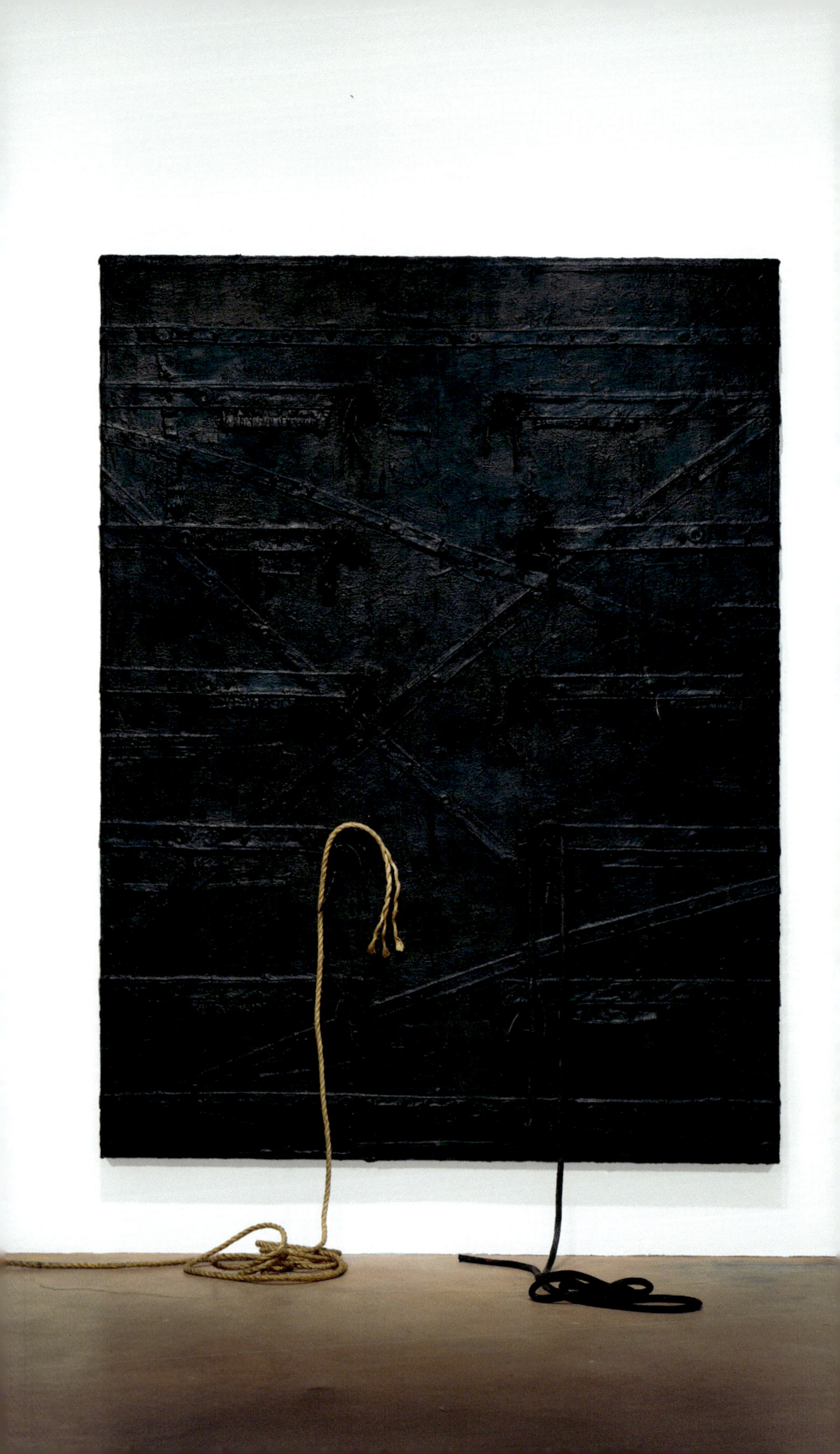

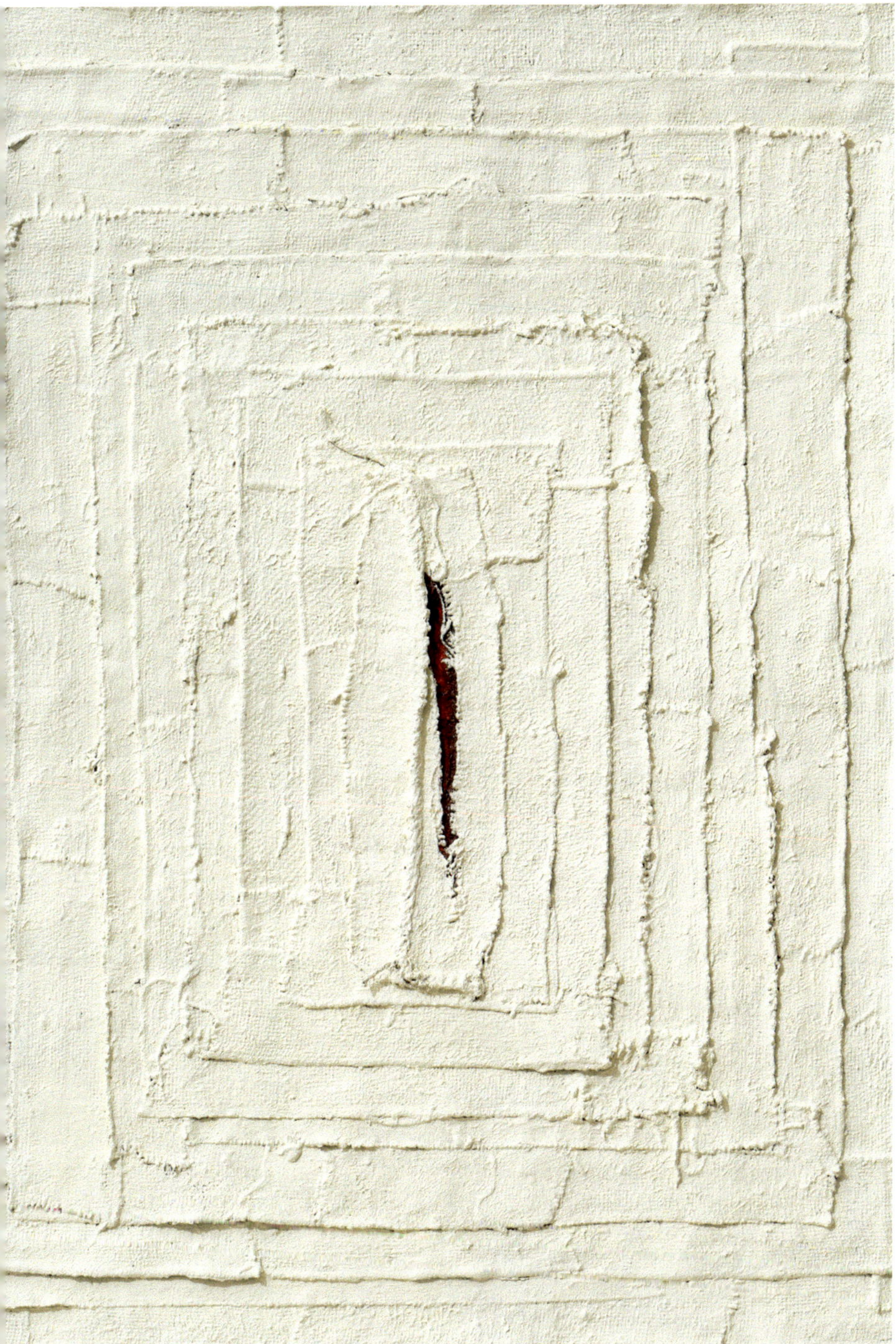

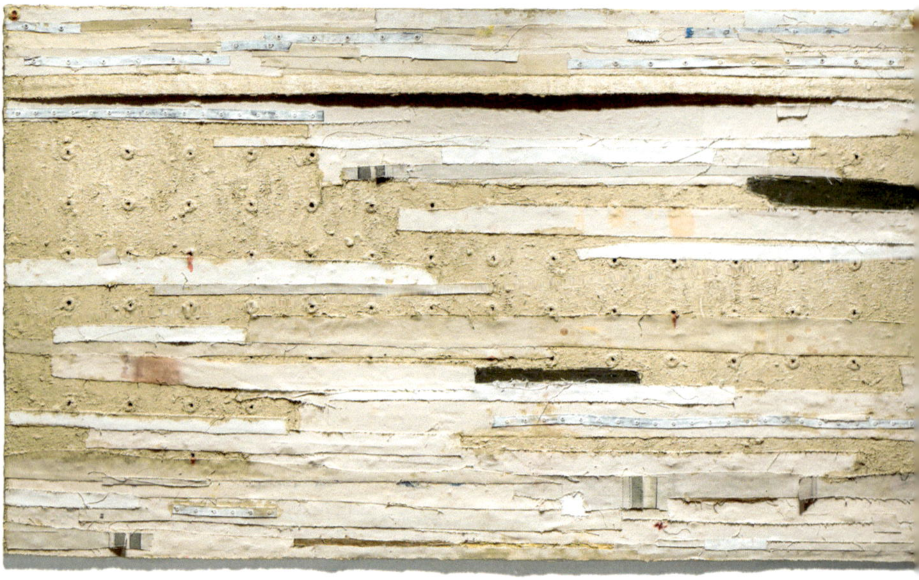

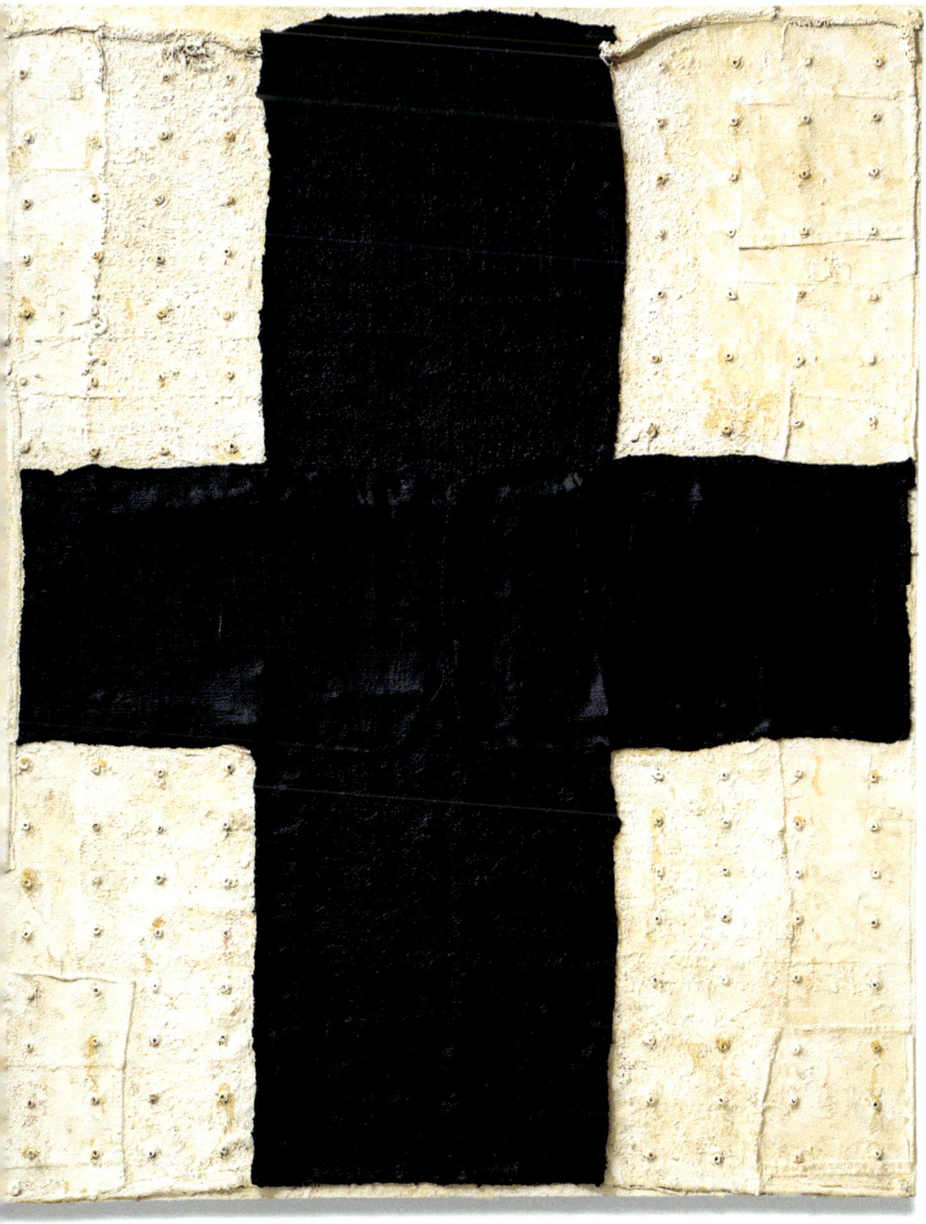

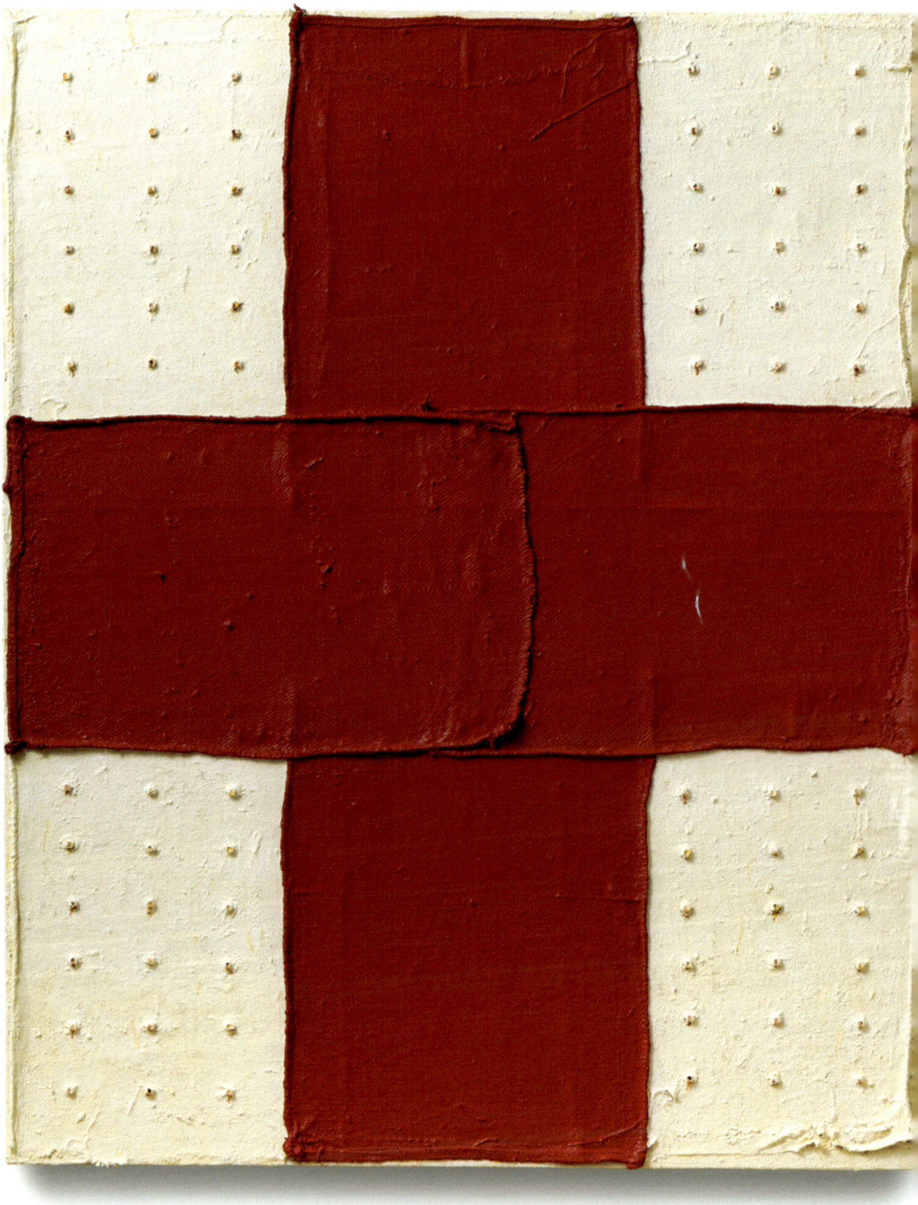

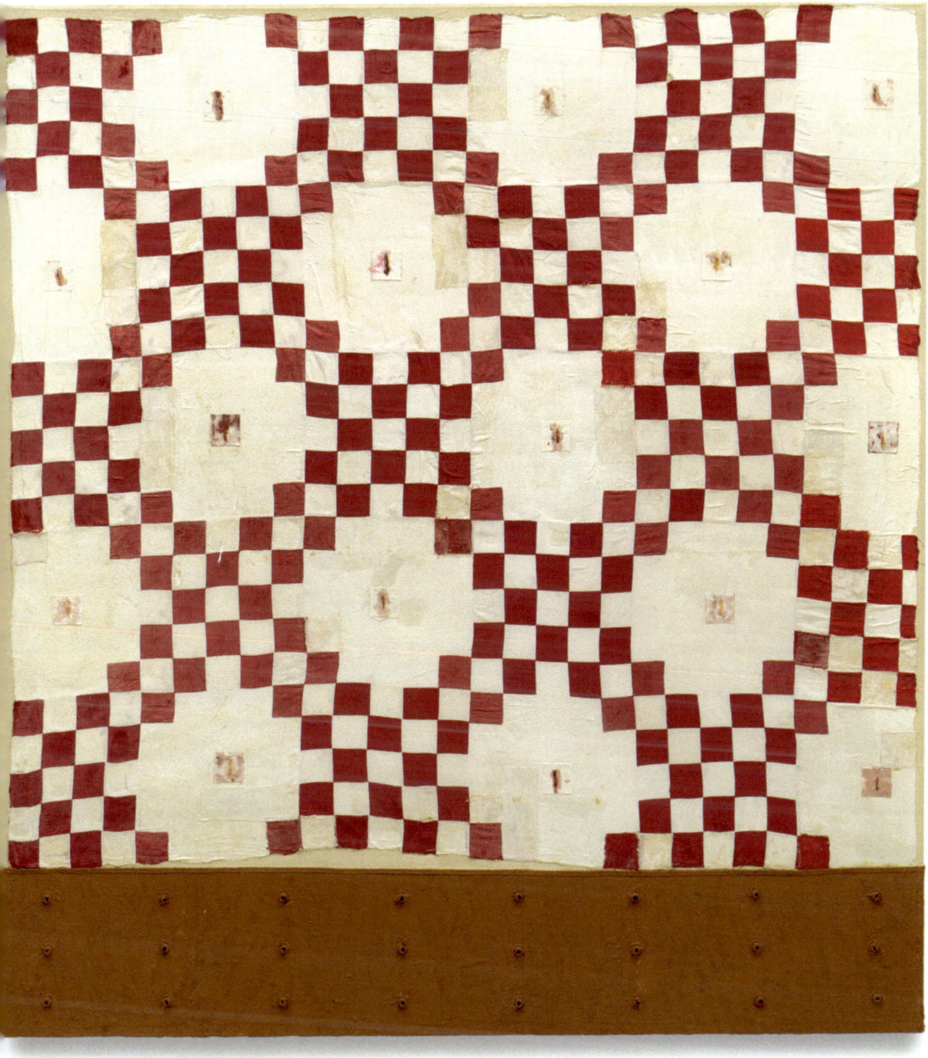

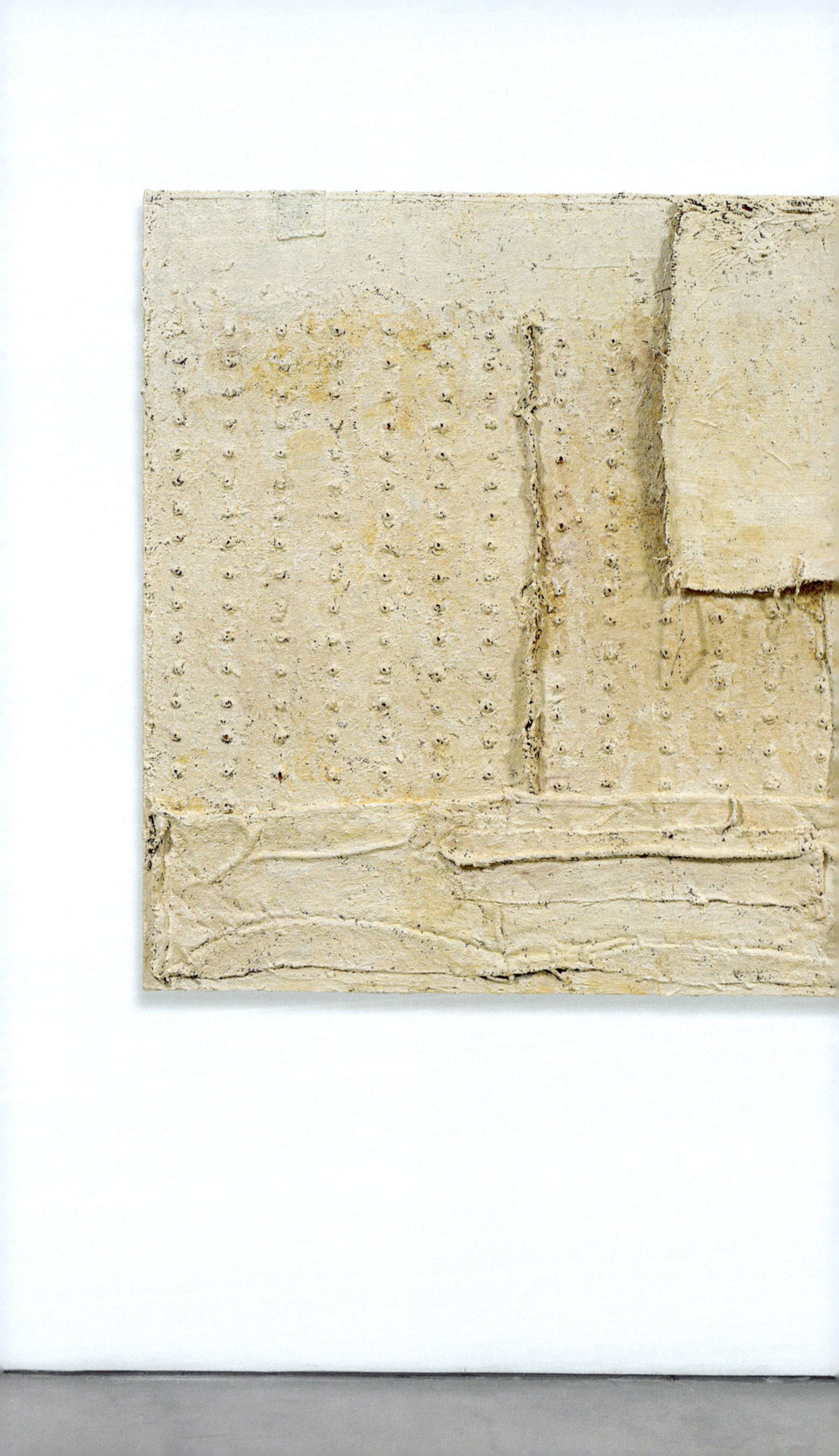

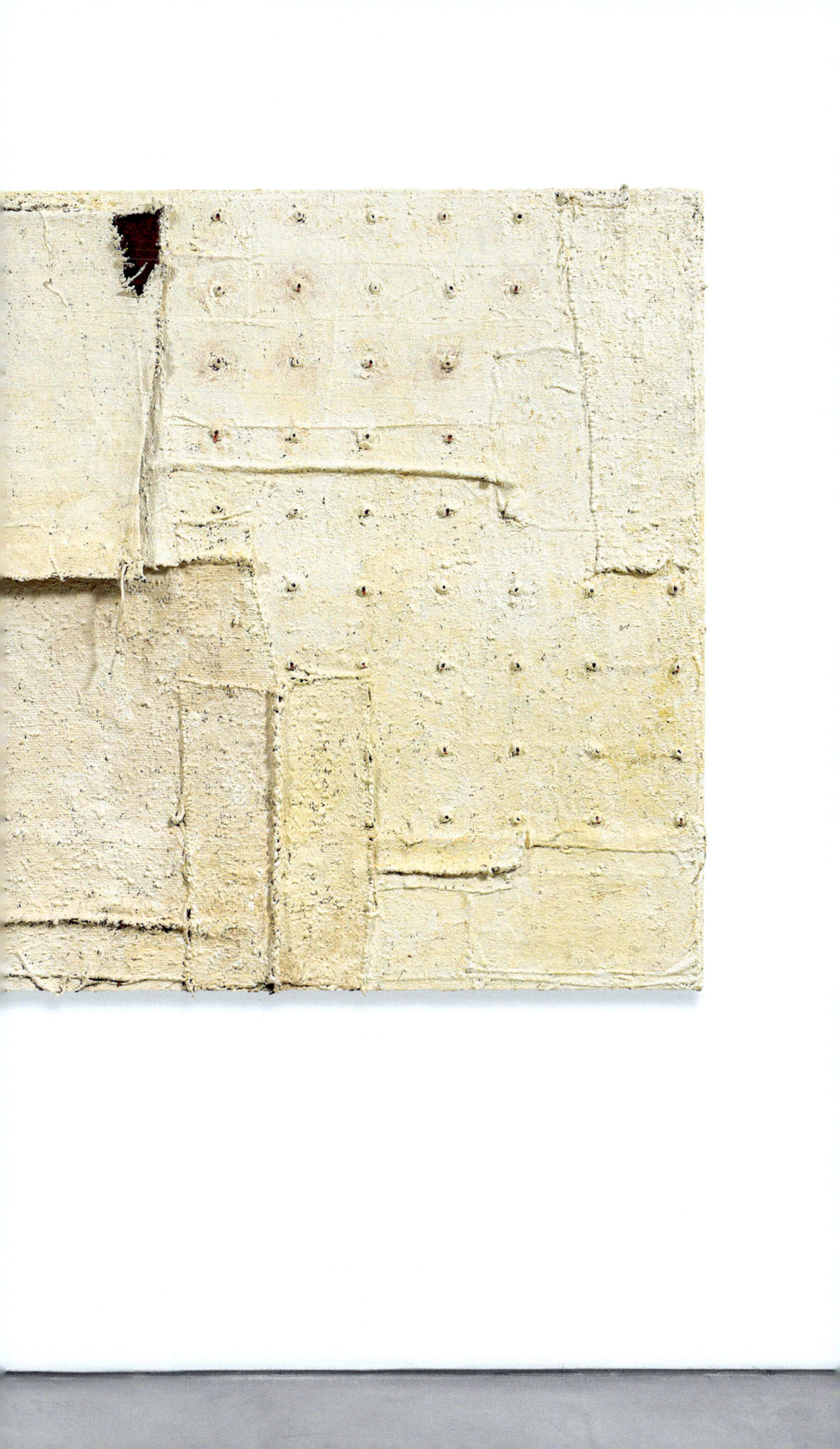

3

1990s

Editor's Introduction

In the 1990s, Hammond's writings engage with shifting political imperatives, especially right-wing attacks on federal funding for artists and the censorship campaigns of the so-called culture wars (campaigns that lay the groundwork for things to come). A nuanced understanding of identity politics in relation to cultural production, hammered out in arenas of lesbian feminist engagement during the 1970s and '80s, undergirds Hammond's defense of art as a site of resistance in the 1990s. She repeatedly addresses the urgent necessity for feminism to encompass a wide range of women's experiences and those of other marginalized people oppressed by the institutional silencing of their voices. Today, as Native Americans, people of color, queers, and women of all categories must once again defend themselves and fight back against state-sponsored violence (including the banning of most of the words in this paragraph) Hammond's work resonates more strongly than ever.

Her written, spoken, and visual practices of the 1990s culture-war era underscore certain signature themes: the problematics of exclusion, marginalization, appropriation, agency, "presencing," (self-)representation, lesbian and queer kinship affiliations, and questions of historical transmission (thus survival). These themes materialize throughout her prolific curatorial career, including in the three exhibitions (figs. 3.1–3.3) she brought to fruition in the 1990s.[1]

She also trains her razor-sharp focus on more insidious forms of censorship, censorship from within. Against the backdrop of events commemorating the thirtieth anniversary of the Stonewall rebellion, she speaks out against the eclipse of lesbian art and lesbian cultural histories in the "Gay '90s."[2] She maintains that the "cultural amnesia" erasing radical feminist initiatives of the 1970s from the gay historical record (i.e., the scarcity of lesbian art and activism in Stonewall anniversary exhibitions) symptomatizes a misunderstanding of early lesbian art and its generative relationship to the "more complex" theories of difference animating activism and dissident art in the postmodern 1990s.[3] In dialogue with foundational discourses of queer feminism, Hammond shows how the queer theories and queer artistic strategies emerging during this decade relate to earlier modes of feminist and lesbian critique and continue to provide models of radical practice.

NOTES

1. *Gender, Fucked: An Exhibition Made by Lesbians About Gender* at the Center on Contemporary Art, Seattle, Washington, cocurated with Catherine Lord, in 1996; *Material Girls: Gender, Process and Abstract Art Since 1970* at Gallery 128, New York, in 1997; *Out West* and *Out West Queer Video* at Plan B Evolving Arts, Santa Fe, New Mexico, in 1999.

2. For example, the exhibition *After Stonewall: Sexual Identity and Politics, 1969–1989*, organized by the Leslie-Lohman Museum of Gay and Lesbian Art (currently Leslie-Lohman Museum of Art) and the Grey Art Gallery, New York, and curated by Jonathan Weinberg, Tyler Cann, and Drew Sawyer. Following its launch in New York (April 20–July 20, 2019), the show traveled to the Frost Museum, Miami, Florida (October 2019), and the Columbus Museum of Art, Columbus, Ohio (February 14–May 17, 2020). Hammond's work appeared in this exhibition, and the catalogue, copublished by the Columbus Museum of Art, includes an interview with her by Tara Burk.

3. Harmony Hammond, "Against Cultural Amnesia," first appeared in *Art Papers*, November 1994, 9–11.

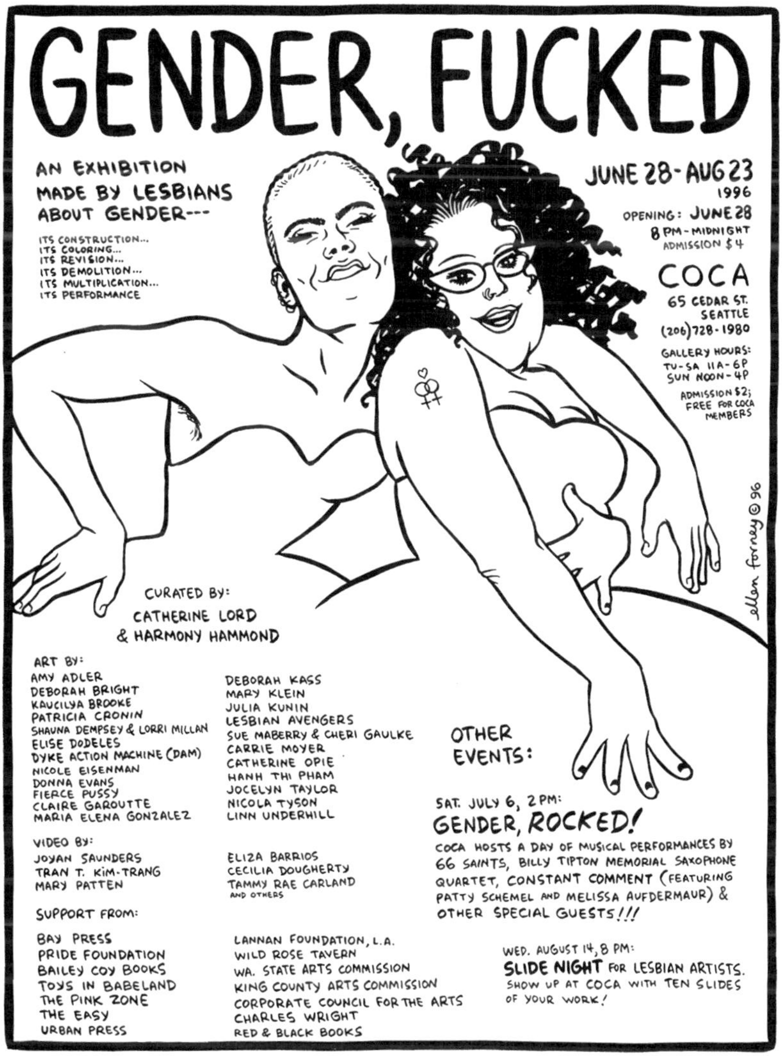

FIGURE 3.1. Poster for *Gender, Fucked: An Exhibition Made by Lesbians About Gender*, cocurated by Harmony Hammond and Catherine Lord, Center on Contemporary Art, Seattle, 1996. Design: Ellen Forney. Courtesy Center on Contemporary Art (CoCA), Seattle, Washington.

MATERIAL GIRLS

GENDER, PROCESS & ABSTRACT ART SINCE 1970
GUEST CURATED BY HARMONY HAMMOND

DIYAN ACHADI KIM ANNO LISA BECK LYNDA BENGLIS SYDNEY BLUM
KATE CHURA SARAH DRANEY ANA FERRER MAXINE FINE MARIA ELENA GONZALEZ
HARMONY HAMMOND CAROL HEPPER ELIZA JACKSON KAZUKO GLORIA KLEIN
JULIA KUNIN LINDA MATALON JOANNE MATTERA ROSEMARY MAYER
MARY MISS PATSY NORVELL HOWARDINA PINDELL SARAH RAPSON
ANDREA REYNOSA KIKI SMITH JOAN SYNDER MICHELLE STUART
CARLA TARDI JACKIE WINSOR CARRIE YAMAOKA NINA YANKOWITZ

OCTOBER 1-NOVEMBER 1, 1997

GALLERY 128

128 RIVINGTON STREET/NEAR ESSEX STREET
NEW YORK CITY 10002
212-674-0244
GALLERY HOURS: WED. TO SAT., 12 NOON-6 PM

OPENING RECEPTION: WEDNESDAY, OCTOBER 1, 6-8 PM

READINGS FROM NEW WORK, SATURDAY, NOVEMBER 1, 7-9 PM
FEATURING WRITERS: BERTHA HARRIS, ANN ROWER, ANA MARIA SIMO
CO-ORDINATED BY AMY SCHOLDER

FIGURE 3.2. Announcement for the exhibition *Material Girls: Gender, Process and Abstract Art Since 1970*, curated by Harmony Hammond, Gallery 128, New York, 1997.

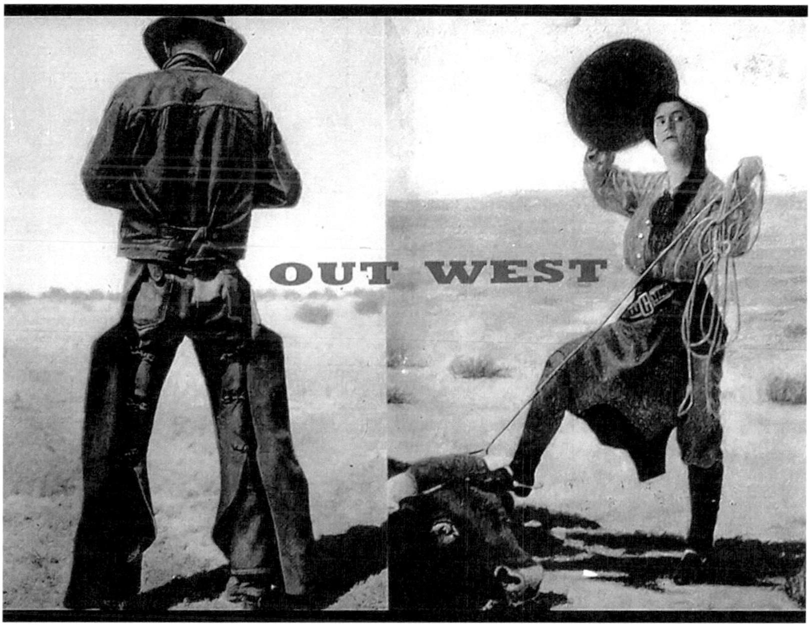

FIGURE 3.3. Announcement for the exhibition *Out West*, curated by Harmony Hammond, Plan B Evolving Arts, Santa Fe, New Mexico, 1999. The show broke new ground by bringing together forty-two lesbian, gay, bisexual, transgender, and two-spirit artists from around the Southwest. Although *Out West* featured very few sexually explicit artworks and its promotional material was not sexually provocative, the local press and the art press shied away from covering the event. Regardless, the show's record-breaking attendance provided leverage for subsequent initiatives, such as, eight years later, Hammond's show *¿Y QUÉ? Queer Art Made in Texas* at Texas Tech University School of Art in Lubbock, Texas. The title *Out West* was recently recycled by the New Mexico Museum of Art, Santa Fe, for a complementary show covering earlier historical terrain, *Out West: Gay and Lesbian Artists in the Southwest 1900 to 1969*, curated by Christian Waguespack. Although Hammond's original exhibition featured contemporary queer artists, the digitally collaged images Hammond chose for her *Out West* announcement—a cowboy and a cowgirl of an earlier era—hinted at this deeper LGBTT historical background.

Interview with Neery Melkonian

THE Magazine (October 1992)

NEERY MELKONIAN: Throughout the '70s and early '80s your work was about being female in this culture—I am referring to your wrapped sculptures and rag pieces with which you made your mark in the art world. Your new body of work [presented in *Harmony Hammond: Uneasy Juxtapositions* at the Center for Contemporary Arts (CCA), Santa Fe, New Mexico] does not necessarily focus on a feminist perspective but deals with broader issues such as censorship, domestic violence, sexual abuse, foreclosed farms, and lesbian identity. What contributed to this change?

HARMONY HAMMOND: A lot of it has to do with the times, for art is made in a sociopolitical climate and in relationship to other art. In the early '70s, it was important for me and a number of other women artists to make work about the experience of being female in this culture and to direct our work toward an audience primarily of women because this had not been done before. Women were strangely absent from the world of fine art. It had to do with a cultural presencing of women. In examining the representation of women in language and visual images, and seeing how this representation is constructed and how it mediates our experience, women in the last decade have begun to understand how other groups of people who are also marginalized have been disempowered by silencing or (mis)representation. Feminism has had to open up and embrace a wide range of diverse experiences among women and other marginalized peoples.

Thus, my work now deals with many different things—some of which are specifically female-focused and some of which aren't. While each work is about something slightly different, they all give voice to those who cannot speak. They are in response to the different forms of institutional silencing of voices from the margins of society. They point to a lack of respect for human life—a condition that unfortunately crosses gender, race, class, and geography.

MELKONIAN: Also, you probably are not interested in the work remaining in the same place . . . ?

HAMMOND: You are right. To stay in the same spot would be rather boring, and it certainly makes for boring art . . . there are no risks. I am interested in what I do not know. What happened with the wrapped sculptures is that I got to a point where I knew exactly what I was doing, which meant that I controlled the pieces to such a degree I was in danger of losing all their awkward life qualities. When I start on a new direction, I seldom know what I am doing. This period is very exciting to me, but doesn't usually produce interesting, finished works that I want to show to anyone else. However, after working with the materials and new ideas, it gradually all comes together. But I cannot stay there, in the same place, or the work will get redundant, dry, without life. There is no choice but to move on. I like working in what I call "a state of peripheral control," meaning I try to create situations for wonderful accidents and revelations. A place for materials, images and text to enter into metaphoric dialogue. I am interested in the problematics of things—the complexities and contradictions that usually coexist. For example, in the CCA exhibit I combine both fine art and nontraditional materials in what I call "uneasy juxtapositions." A large part of the work process in these mixed-media paintings is to move the materials around and see how they begin to talk with each other, and to see what art and nonart experiences and discourses they reference.

MELKONIAN: This shift began around the same time you moved to New Mexico. How else did the move influence your work?

HAMMOND: While the shift from sculpture to painting had begun in New York, I had a different kind of time and space here in New Mexico to work with. I was frustrated in New York because my work time was so fragmented by teaching at six places simultaneously in order to earn a living. It was hard, if not impossible, to make art with any sense of daily continuity. Without realizing it, I had, over the years, developed ways of making sculpture that did not necessitate being in the studio each day. Neither my materials nor my techniques were adversely affected if it took several days to get back to the work. However, working with oil paint the way I do—wet into wet—is a different story. To keep the skin of paint alive you must work on it, into it, each day or the surface simply dries up. The materials have different demands. Moving to New Mexico allowed me to work in the studio every day, and I could push my paint surface, imagery, and scale. While I had been mostly making sculpture for years, the problematics of painting began to engage me more and more. I wanted to use paint as a material equal to rags, latex rubber, human hair, corrugated roofing tin, or burnt wood. It is hard to create a paint surface that can hold its own against the materials. In fact, it has taken me years to get to this point. But, finally, painting and sculpture have come together in a way that pleases me, where both have equal weight, presence, and authority. . . .

MELKONIAN: Your current exhibition comprises two series of work. Could you tell us how they came about?

HAMMOND: The work in this exhibit at CCA deals with two different but related bodies of ideas. *Farm Ghosts* [1990; see plate 12] deals with the abandoned and foreclosed farms that dot rural America. There is no one out there any more—just an economic system that won't support the small farmer. The birds and dry leaves have taken over the gutted houses and rusted farm equipment. There is no water. Only the windmills stand guard over the deserted landscapes, and even they are crumbling. The other pieces suggest narratives that are open to a variety of readings less dependent on image. They utilize various materials to speak of injustice and violence—semiconscious or remembered. Pieced and layered, like memory herself, they name and give voice to that which has been un-nameable or silenced. Many of them suggest an intimacy, a sexuality, a negotiation of desire and pleasure in the age of AIDS, and different kinds of censorship.

MELKONIAN: The juxtaposition of traditional materials such as oil paint and bronze with nontraditional, found, or recycled materials like tin, linoleum, rubber, hair, burnt wood, gutters, leaves, and water troughs certainly reinforce what you are trying to elicit. . . .

HAMMOND: These juxtapositions constantly question artistic appropriation and cultural gentrification, my part in it as well as others'. The material, not just the symbols or iconography, bring[s] part of the meaning to the works. For instance, hair, off the body, always has sexual references. And the latex rubber is clearly the body if not the sexual female body. The old, rusty, roofing tin references abandoned farms, boarded-up houses, sheds and fences in the barrios, and even yuppie bars and stores like Banana Republic that merchandise the "Third World." It is an international material that crosses cultures, classes, and geographic locations. The meaning of pieces that utilize the old tin varies with the economic and cultural position of the viewer. I like the old tin because it is saved and reused. It speaks of survival and construction—what is disposable to one group of people is a necessity for another. I like to use found and recycled materials, not only because they are cheap but because I don't like wasting things that have histories and reference other time, places, and peoples.

The power of collage/assemblage is in its ability to bring content into the world of abstraction. What happens when I take materials from one context and put them in another? How does the meaning shift? This putting together of things that don't normally or easily go together creates uneasy juxtapositions that create dialogues and demand negotiations. It creates a space of unfixed meanings and possibilities. . . .

MELKONIAN: Earlier you described your paintings as being about skin. Could you elaborate on that notion and address some of the formal elements of your work?

HAMMOND: I don't use the painting surface as a ground but rather as a highly charged surface or space that is an active part of the work. It is as important as anything else. The frontal positioning of images, or even the works themselves, create a sort of insistence that I like. I want the viewer to feel the piece, not just see it. I don't want the piece in its unfixedness to hide. I want it to occupy space. Of course, this filling of space and moving from the inside out, from the personal to the political, relates to aikido, a Japanese martial art, that I have been studying for years. I am very aware of paint being a skin of paint, and because of this, the painting surface always has body references for me. I now find myself both painting a skin, and using skin/rubber—a material usually utilized in sculpture—to paint. Both the painting surface and the metal and linoleum surfaces refer simultaneously to body and landscape. The surface is violated. Even the hard metal rusts and becomes fragile. There are wounds and scars. I use paint as a healing agent, as a poultice, to patch up these wounds—thus talking about the function of art itself. Lately, I am working a lot with water troughs and gutters.

They collect and move water like our circulatory system, which moves life body fluids of blood and water. But, in a dysfunctional society or culture where life is not valued, life systems can become clogged. There is a profound loss and sadness somewhere in these pieces that is far deeper than the rage of earlier work from the '70s. My work is not about critiquing but rather about opening up a space of narrative possibilities and about self-construction. It is about acknowledging the complexity and multiplicity of things. In this sense, I think of it as life-affirmative.

MELKONIAN: Some of your new work deals with redefining lesbian identity. What have some of the difficulties been in addressing such concerns? How do present-day concerns differ from older ones? Do they confine or open new arenas in artistic expression? Is there, for example, a lesbian gaze in aesthetics?

HAMMOND: I have dealt with lesbian content in my work on and off over the years. It is one of many things that I make art about. To talk about art by lesbians or gay men, one must talk about identity. For most lesbians and gay men, sexual definitions have proved inadequate, and existing stereotypes (whether deriving from psychoanalysis or pseudo-scientific and pathological texts of the nineteenth century, or from notions of political correctness within gay and lesbian communities) have been limiting and disempowering and have little to do with our lives as lived. I personally don't believe that there is one queer identity or sensibility. [... I believe] we must create ourselves. And one way we do that is through art. For one of the great services of art is to tell us who we really are. There is room for a wide range of diversity and invention. There have always been a lot of lesbian artists and since the '70s many have come out of the closet, although only a few, like myself, in the art world made art with lesbian content. However, this is changing.

Because of right-wing backlash and censorship, many gay and lesbian artists are refusing to be silenced, and in response to censorship are flaunting their sexual preference and utilizing self-representation to reflect and create identities. There is an explosion of art all across the country of work by gay men and lesbians. My concern, of course, is that there be a strong lesbian presence. Because women have always been portrayed for the male gaze, the issue of lesbian self-representation in art becomes very important. What might a lesbian gaze be? Can woman be both subject and object? While visual art by lesbians in the '70s was mostly about being visible and creating a lesbian space, and about looking for a sensibility, the new work is interested in exploring a range of identities and sensibilities that self-identify as lesbian. Much of this work deals with the problematics around the construction and representation of a lesbian erotic art. Thus, the multiple and shifting nature of lesbian identity, as it is reflected and constructed in art, creates a space of infinite and pleasurable possibilities. . . .

ED. NOTE

The interview originally appeared in *THE Magazine*, October 1992, 8–11.

Mechanisms of Exclusion

THE Magazine (April 1993)

"As our government applauds the destruction of walls in Eastern Europe, a new cold war is intensified here against people of color, gays and lesbians, women, the working class, as well as artists in general." Given this statement by the *Artists' Coalition for the Freedom of Expression* in 1989, the recent resistance to President Clinton's attempts to issue an executive order rescinding the ban on gays in the military should not come as a surprise. It follows on the heels of right-wing fundamentalist attacks on federal funding of artists who produce work that is explicitly sexual in nature, and institutions that exhibit, publish, or present this work. Understanding all too well the power of expression and representation, the religious right, according to *Village Voice* critic Elizabeth Hess, "began to develop a new strategy to roll back gay, civil, and reproductive rights by limiting the content of art in this country."[1] After the initial attacks on artists such as [Robert] Mapplethorpe, [Andres] Serrano, [David] Wojnarowicz, [Tim] Miller, [Holly] Hughes, and [Karen] Finley, it became obvious that most of the work being targeted was homoerotic in nature. Soon after, it became clear that it wasn't an issue of sexual imagery in art at all, but simply gay identity and creativity that the right was after.

The language, agendas, and strategies underlying current fundamentalist mobilization throughout the country to prohibit, limit, or eliminate basic civil rights for homosexuals are the same as those utilized during the years of the Bush administration to censor the creative imagination. The outrageous attempt to pass a statewide initiative in Oregon—Measure 9—which would have "prohibited all governments from protecting, encouraging or facilitating homosexuality" and to "recognize that homosexuality, pedophilia, sadism, and masochism as abnormal, wrong, unnatural and perverse behaviors to be discouraged and avoided," was defeated.[2] Sound similar to the compromised version of the Helms Amendment to the NEA reappropriations bill that Congress passed in 1989? You bet! "If it had passed," points out Julian Spaulding in *Man, Alive!*, a local journal of men's wellness, "it would have been the first time in US history that a constitution had been amended to take away rights of its citizens. Measure 9 represented one of the harshest attacks on the basic human rights of a specific group of people ever mounted in the United States."[3]

Recent and ongoing battles around state referendums in Colorado and New Mexico (with similar measures being planned in at least thirteen other states) show how important and necessary these rights are. In Colorado, voters supported Amendment 2, barring local governments from enacting gay rights legislation, thus making illegal previous laws on the books in Denver, Boulder, and Aspen that prohibited discrimination on the basis of sexual orientation. However, while there is a temporary injunction against Amendment 2 taking effect "until further order of the Court," and there is a huge boycott and protest movement gathering force, the fact is that violence against gays and lesbians in Colorado has increased sharply since the amendment passed.

As of this writing, the national extreme right has joined with some local forces to oppose [New Mexico Senate Bill] SB 91, which was passed by a narrow majority in the Senate and now must be approved by the House and Governor Bruce King. "The New Mexico Human Rights Act currently prohibits discrimination based on race, age, religion, color, national origin, ancestry, sex, physical or mental handicap, or medical condition in employment, housing, public accommodations, and credit. The proposed legislation, SB 91, adds 'sexual orientation' to that list." (Sexual orientation includes heterosexuality, homosexuality, and bisexuality.) As reported in *Out!*, New Mexico's gay, lesbian, and bisexual news magazine, this legislation, like all civil rights legislation, "does not provide for special rights. . . . [It] promotes equal rights by decreeing that personal prejudices and private beliefs are not legal grounds to deny employment, housing, public accommodations or credit."[4]

Basic civil rights are linked to the rights of expression and representation, be it the voice or images of a specific sex, class, race, or culture. For art (and I mean fine art, media, and other forms of popular culture) reflects who we are. Without a visible culture, a people do not have an identity, and therefore do not exist. It remains to be seen if President Clinton will support a gay and lesbian civil rights bill that is making its way through Congress and how quickly and to what extent he implements his campaign and anti-censorship promises. Given the current political climate, with the possibility of being denied basic civil rights and the threat of being artistically silenced for being gay and lesbian, we can't afford to be silent and let others define who we are or what kind of art we may or may not make. As Russell Ferguson has written, the question of how to affirm cultural identities in an often repressive society is complex. However, a diversity of voices from the margins disrupts "the unified tone which can so easily become the commanding voice of authority, the voice which subsumes all differences under its cloak."[5]

I see artmaking, especially that which comes from the margins of the mainstream, as a site of resistance, a way of interrupting and intervening in those historical and cultural fields that continually work to exclude me, a sort of gathering of forces on the borders. For the dominant hegemonic stance that has worked to silence and subdue gender and ethnic difference has also silenced difference based on sexual orientation. Just as it is necessary to add "sexual orientation" to the list of civil rights for all citizens, it is essential that as art-concerned peoples, we bring it into the current discourses on difference and representation, along with race and gender, for they are parallel exclusions. Artist David Wojnarowicz wrote about censorship and self-censorship: "The once unspeakable can make the invisible familiar. To speak of ourselves in a climate and country that considers us, our bodies, our thoughts taboo, is to shake the boundaries of the illusion of the ONE TRIBE NATION. To keep silent, even when our individual existence contradicts the illusion of the ONE TRIBE NATION, is to lose our identities and possibly our lives. If people don't say what they think and feel, those ideas and feelings get lost, and if this is the case often enough, they never return."[6]

The Vietnamese-American filmmaker and theoretician Trinh T. Minh-ha has nuanced notions of cultural difference and thought deeply about the challenges of negotiating multiple identities. "Which [identity] comes first?" she asks.[7] Negotiating multiple identities is what filmmaker Marlon Riggs brilliantly addresses in [his 1989 film] *Tongues Untied*, when he discovers that as a gay man he is invisible among black brothers, and that as a black man he doesn't exist in the gay meccas of Christopher and Castro Streets.[8] In questioning the language of cultural representation, identity, and difference, Trinh has called for "distinctions" between the alienating notion of "otherness" (the other of man, the other of the West) and an empowering notion of "difference." But she asks, "How do you inscribe difference without bursting into a series of euphoric, narcissistic accounts of yourself and your own kind? Without indulging in a marketable romanticism or in a naive whining about your condition? In other words, how do you forget without annihilating? Between the twin chasms of navel-gazing and navel-erasing, the ground is narrow and slippery. None of us can pride ourselves on being sure-footed there."[9]

Like Trinh, I believe the answer lies not in accepting or choosing identity, but in creating one. And one way we create identity is through art. As critic Lucy Lippard writes, "Art would not have to speak for everyone if everyone could speak for themselves."[10] But how hard it is to find one's own voice. How difficult it is to affirm cultural identities, to recreate them so that they are not simply a counternarrative to the authoritative center, to what African-American poet Audre Lorde called the "mythical norm," or that which is "white, thin, male, young, heterosexual, christian, and financially secure."[11] How hard it is to get past the privileged authority who doesn't even have to be present to exert his influence. How hard to give form to oneself honestly.

Stuart Hall writes, "[Cultural identity] is not something which already exists, transcending place, time, history and culture. . . . Far from being grounded in a mere 'recovery' of the past, which is waiting to be found, and which, when found, will secure our sense of ourselves into eternity, identities are the names we give to the different ways we are positioned by, and position ourselves within, the narratives of the past."[12] Thus identities can be seen as ever-shifting fields of persons, things, events, ideas, fantasies, and relationships.

French philosopher Michel Foucault insisted, "We have to not only affirm ourselves as an identity, but as a creative force."[13] In their interview with Foucault, Bob Gallagher and Alexander Wilson point out that this declaration raises important issues. "Should gay people embrace a social identity that was largely created from the sexual mores of the late nineteenth century, or pursue relationships of differentiation, or creation, or innovation . . . an identity unique to ourselves?" "If gay people are truly to know themselves," suggests Foucault, "they must examine and rely on their own potential—in short, create themselves—rather than insist on conforming to the socially constructed role of 'the homosexual,' a consciousness that has primarily been defined by others."[14]

Foucault concludes, "We must define who we are, who we can become, what our community consists of, and how we are going to change the world so it will accommodate us . . . we are shaped by our sexual identity, and it, in turn, is shaped by us. It is not a simple matter of accepting or denying our sexual identity; we must continually construct it. Let us hope that it will be an identity strong enough to protect us and flexible enough to liberate us."[15]

David Leavitt writes that what distinguishes gay and lesbian artists is that their difference is located in the realm of sexuality. Therefore, the work they create in a culture that is both sex-phobic and homophobic becomes particularly susceptible to the charge that it is obscene, although we know there is no official or shared definition of obscenity. But then, obscenity is not the real agenda of [Jesse] Helms, [Pat] Buchanan, [George H. W.] Bush, the American Family Association (which orchestrated the first attempts to control art in the NEA's twenty-five-year history), Colorado for Family Values (the Colorado Springs group that launched Amendment 2), or as artist Holly Hughes calls it, "their white, straight, male, Christian country club" (or those who want in it).

As Leavitt explains, the recent and continuing attacks on the NEA have "little to do with the arts at all and everything to do with the extreme right wing's determination to terrorize an already ambivalent American population by manipulating its entrenched fears of anything foreign, unfamiliar, or explicitly sexual," which is most things queer.[16] It is this fear of difference that creates the hatred and tyranny that breeds sexism, racism, and homophobia.

Ironically, because of right-wing attacks on sexually explicit art and gay and lesbian artists, the need to assert sexual identity has intensified, and there is literally a renaissance of overtly queer art and exhibitions. In direct response to xenophobia, censorship, and the war on so-called deviants, gay, lesbian, and queer artists are out, proud, and flaunting it—insisting on the right to produce images that reflect their diverse identities, experiences, and cultures if they so choose. Much of this work directly addresses the social construction of gender, sexuality, and identity politics. An impressive list of artists includes: Adam Rolston, David Wojnarowicz, Zoe Leonard, Lenore Chinn, Ester Hernandez, Millie Wilson, Marcia Salo, Lyle Ashton Harris, Robert Gober, Luis de Jesus, Victoria Lena Manyarrows, Nayland Blake, Kaucyila Brooke, Deborah Bright, Hollis Sigler, Laura Aguilar, Carrie Yamaoka, Janet Cooling, Martin Wong, Ross Bleckner, and groups such as Kiss and Tell, Act Up, and Fierce Pussy, as well as New Mexico artists Herbert Lotz, Ada Medina, Richard Hooker, Maxine Fine, Max Pruneda, David Keating, and myself, to name just a few—the list could go on and on. . . .

Queer identity and its expression have the potential of not only confronting the tyranny of enforced heterosexuality and empowering gays and lesbians, but of critiquing the politics of patriarchy, thus playing a major role in the empowering of all marginalized peoples. It is only by examining this connectedness which doesn't deny difference, thus crossing racial, sexual, and cultural borders, that we will be able to fight the reactionary forces at work today. It is not only about supporting individual artworks or artists as they get attacked (although we must do that too), but rather looking at the underlying issues. In challenging heterosexist assumptions, homosexuals disrupt and destabilize many established codes and institutions of oppression.

To get a sense of our artistic power, I find it helpful to look at border art practices. Emily Hicks, an Anglo member of the ethnically mixed La Taller Frontera (Border Arts Workshop) in San Diego/Tijuana, describes the border as a zone of mergings, confrontations, skirmishes, and healings that constantly changes and replenishes itself. It is a place where we physically act out beliefs and philosophies. Border art practices are based on multiplicity and understanding of both sides. And border art is any art that questions the hegemonic Western discourse. Hicks elaborates that to even read a border text, for example, is to cross over into another "set of referential codes," decentering the text as well as the reader.[17] In crossing (or even getting too close to) a border, the writer and reader are changed. In this way, art has the potential to transform social relations and dematerialize limits and boundaries.

Queer art is border art. For all the talk about multiculturalism and diversity, the fact is that homosexuality is still a border that many do not want to cross. Linda Burnham, writing an editorial in *High Performance*, puts it this way: "As fear stampedes across America, everybody is learning a lot about where they draw the line, and many draw it at the acceptance of homosexuality. If some group has to be the scapegoat in these conservative times, let it be the queers, so the rest of us can go on with business as usual."[18]

Audre Lorde also wrote, "Certainly there are very real differences between us of race, age, and sex. But it is not those differences between us that are separating us. It is rather our refusal to recognize those differences, and to examine the distortions which result from our misnaming them and their effects upon human behavior and expectation."[19] She says we must find new patterns of relating across difference. "For we have, built into all of us, old blueprints of expectations and response, old structures of oppression, and these must be altered at the same time as we alter the living conditions which are a result of those structures. For the master's tools will never dismantle the master's house. [. . .] Change means growth, and growth can be painful. But we sharpen self-definition by exposing the self in work and struggle, together with those whom we define as different from ourselves, although sharing the same goals."[20]

There are all kinds of crossings. Some are noisy, visible, and meant to draw attention. Some are quiet. We do not hear them. Some are secret. We do not see them. Some go unnoticed until it is too late. And some who have gone first have paid the price. Sometimes we are scared. Sometimes we don't think about it. But the crossings go on day and night, in light and shadow. Most of us cross back and forth daily and take others with.

* * *

Author's Note: After heated debate SB 91 passed the House Government and Urban Affairs Committee only to have Governor Bruce King publicly say that the issue was the most sensitive and controversial one he has faced in his three terms as governor and he hoped the bill would die on the House floor and not reach his desk. Governor King had his wish when on March 18th, the Judiciary Committee voted 7 to 5 to table SB 91, allowing the opposition to, in effect, kill the bill without ever going on the record in opposition of civil rights.

ED. NOTES

"Mechanisms of Exclusion" was originally published in *THE Magazine*, April 1993, 41–43.

1. Elizabeth Hess, "Gutter Politics," *Village Voice*, July 3, 1990, 89.

2. Oregon Ballot Measure 9, November 3, 1992, was a citizens' initiative that aimed, by amending the Oregon Constitution, to prohibit antidiscrimination laws regarding sexual orientation and to declare homosexuality to be "abnormal, wrong, unnatural, and perverse."

3. Julian Spaulding, "Old Myths Die Hard or . . . You Think It Can't Happen Here?," *Man, Alive!* 5, no. 4 (Winter 1992/93): 1.

4. "Amending the New Mexico Human Rights Act to Prohibit Discrimination Based on Sexual Orientation," *Out! Magazine: New Mexico's Gay, Lesbian and Bisexual News Magazine* 44 (February 1993): 14.

5. Russell Ferguson, "Introduction: Invisible Center," in *Out There: Marginalization and Contemporary Cultures*, ed. Russell Ferguson, Trinh T. Minh-ha, Martha Gever, and Cornel West (Cambridge, MA: MIT Press, 1990), 10.

6. David Wojnarowicz, *Close to the Knives: A Memoir of Disintegration* (New York: Vintage Books, 1991), 121.

7. Trinh T. Minh-ha, *Woman, Native, Other: Writing Postcoloniality and Feminism* (Bloomington: Indiana University Press, 2009), 6.

8. Marlon T. Riggs, dir., *Tongues Untied* (Frameline, 1989).

9. Trinh, *Woman, Native, Other*, 28.

10. The quote attributed to Lucy Lippard appears in Marty Pottenger's editorial statement, "From the Lesbian Issue Collective," "Lesbian Art and Artists," special issue, *Heresies: A Feminist Publication on Art and Politics* 1, no. 3 (1977): 3.

11. Audre Lorde, "Age, Race, Class, and Sex: Women Redefining Difference," in *Out There: Marginalization and Contemporary Cultures*, ed. Russell Ferguson, Trinh T. Minh-ha, Martha Gever, and Cornel West (Cambridge, MA: MIT Press, 1990), 282. First published in Audre Lorde, *Sister Outsider: Essays and Speeches* (Freedom, CA: Crossing Press, 1984).

12. Stuart Hall, "Cultural Identity and Diaspora," in *Identity: Community, Culture, Difference*, ed. Jonathan Rutherford (London: Lawrence and Wishart, 1990), 225.

13. Michel Foucault, "Sex and the Politics of Identity: An Interview with Michel Foucault," in *Gay Spirit: Myth and Meaning*, ed. Mark Thompson (New York: St. Martin's Press, 1987), 25–26.

14. Foucault, "Sex and the Politics of Identity," 25–26.

15. Foucault, "Sex and the Politics of Identity," 25–26.

16. David Leavitt, "Fears That Haunt a Scrubbed America," *New York Times*, August 19, 1990, section 2, page 1.

17. Emily Hicks, *Border Writing: The Multidimensional Text* (Minneapolis: University of Minnesota Press, 1991), xxvi.

18. Linda Burnham, editorial, *High Performance* 51, no. 13 (Fall 1990): 11.

19. Lorde, "Age, Race, Class, and Sex," 282.

20. Lorde, "Age, Race, Class, and Sex," 287.

Resistances

Cultural Tourism and Native Resistance Through Self-Representation

THE Magazine (June 1993)

Any representation is negotiating some border.—GLORIA ANZALDUA

All photographs of American Indians are photographs of dead people, in that their use assumes ownership of the subject, which is seen as static, completely "understandable." —JIMMIE DURHAM

What if Indians had invented photography?—HULLEAH TSINHNAHJINNIE

During the last few years, Santa Fe has been host to a series of art conferences and symposiums which attempt to examine and reflect upon issues in contemporary art, historical practice, and critical theory. One of these recent symposiums, "Images Across Boundaries: History, Use and Ethics of Photographs of American Indians," turned out to be one of the most interesting I've been to in some time. It was organized by Rick Hill and Willow Powers, and jointly sponsored by the

Institute of American Indian Arts (IAIA) and the Museum of Indian Arts and Culture (MIAC).

At the symposium, held at the Museum of Indian Arts and Culture, Native and non-Native artists, anthropologists, historians, critics, museum directors, and archivists spoke on the history of photography of American Indians by Native and non-Native photographers, the ethics of photography (especially cross-cultural photography), its use, reuse, and abuse in primary and secondary image-making (postcards, posters, books, advertising, museum installations), stereotyping, the economic packaging and marketing of "the exotic other" for political propaganda or to further tourism, the role of photography in the lives of Indian people today, tribal repatriation of photographs of sacred sites and ceremonies, and self-representation by contemporary Native photographers and their development of a critique from within.

Certain issues surfaced over and over again. The camera "stealing souls" and photographers "stealing images" are separate but related, and important, concepts. It is well known that many Native peoples, believing that the camera would steal one's soul or spirit, refused to pose for photographs. If indeed the camera can steal souls, the stealing of images becomes a very serious business. Stealing images can mean a range of things from the simple act of "taking" a photograph, to photographing against tribal or individual will, to taking images of sacred sites or ceremonies not meant to be seen by non-Native eyes, or perhaps not meant to be photographed at all. It could also apply to the expansionist ideology of accreting and appropriating cultures through systematic mapping, documenting, and naming of the colonized culture. Curtis Hinsley's discussion of this kind of cultural colonization and his presentation about the production, consumption, and function of the photographic images of Pueblo Indians collected as objects to be displayed on the Victorian parlor wall remains relevant to collecting art today.

Another major area of concern throughout the symposium was the role of photographers and photography (versus painting, for instance) in the creation and maintenance of Native American stereotypes. Through their use of selective imagery, costuming, and posing of subjects, or even retouching the photographs to make Native people, clothes, and artifacts look "more Indian," many white photographers create the romanticized image of the authentic "noble savage" to symbolize a way of life now lost, and to capitalize on "the exotic other." Curator/photographer Rick Hill (Tuscarora/Mohawk) listed what he calls the 5C's who are responsible for many of the stereotypes that exist today: Christ, Columbus, Caitlin, Custer, and Curtis. The legacy of these men, he says, still affects Indians today ([e.g.,] images of Indians used for logos of sports teams).

As an example, Jim Faris (NTA [no tribal affiliation]) showed how images of Navajos which have changed little over the years are locked into several stereotypes: the depersonalized, fragmented body used as a prop to show off silver and turquoise jewelry, the Navajo "in nature" against the very red rock landscape that they are denied, or the picturesque domestic narrative of a Navajo weaving in front of a hogan with sheep being herded in the background. Even the Navajo Tourism Development Office has absorbed these stereotypes and put them to commercial use—a sign reads "Welcome to Navajo Land . . . Camera Ready . . . Picture Perfect." Images of Indians have become so associated with photography that they are often used to advertise cameras, film, and other photographic equipment.

Stereotypes are insidious and more complicated than might appear at first glance. Because Native people have often been paid to dress up or perform for the camera, many have begun to absorb and become their own stereotypes—what photographer Jolene Rickard (Tuscarora) has referred to as an economic and emotional "space of survival." Thus, the question, what is the role of stereotypes in relationship to the construction of Native self-identity, has a complex and multifaceted answer.

Hulleah Tsinhnahjinnie (Seminole/Creek/Navajo) cautions Native Americans to look carefully at Native stereotypes in art—including their own—to see where they've come from, for it's too easy to absorb questionable ideals of, or to judge work from, the European mindset of the colonizer. As an example, she points to art by many Native men who, instead of portraying Indian women in their own strength and beauty, have accepted Euro-Western body types and standards of female beauty and used them to depict Indian women.

Tsinhnahjinnie feels that the 1990 Indian Arts and Crafts law (Public Law 101–644) which states that tribal enrollment is necessary to be recognized as an authentic Indian artist and to sell work, is an extension of expansionist colonial thinking, the "ultimate example of Natives stereotyping Natives." In *Creative Native* (1990), a series of straightforward black-and-white self-portraits, Tsinhnahjinnie has pressed her tribal enrollment number in large pressure-sensitive letters across her face. The numbering feels violent as it interrupts, competes with, and almost dominates her image. The number, and not her face, represents identity, for as she says, "Identity has become a government issue."

Nobody's Pet Indian, a conceptual installation, is in response to Public Law 101–644, which, despite what its proponents say, is not about art, but about identity. The installation consists of nineteen 30 × 40″ stark black-and-white portraits of artists who oppose the law but are forced to be labeled and categorized by numbers in order to function as artists. Each portrait is accompanied by text, sometimes the artist's response when Tsinhnahjinnie asked for their tribal enrollment number, and sometimes her own commentary. Some artists do not have a visual portrait and are represented only by their number placed in a two-foot-wide black dot on the wall. Tsinhnahjinnie asks, "Will we recognize them by their number?" *Nobody's Pet Indian* is about giving faces to Native American artists and recognizing them as individuals, which is the reverse of Public Law 101–644 which treats identity as a simple, black-and-white matter. What constitutes Indian-ness? Who determines identity? Tsinhnahjinnie asks about Indian people who for various reasons can't prove tribal affiliation or who simply disagree with the principles underlying this law and refuse enrollment. Does this mean that they are not Indians? Are these people who fall between the cracks the price paid for authentic Indian art, an art that is racially pure? Tsinhnahjinnie says, "The focus on numbers and blood quantum turns art into a commodity, as the law becomes a tracking vehicle of our most creative minds."

Larry McNeil (Tlingit/Nishka) addressed the issue of "double standards" in contemporary photo-criticism. A basically positive review of *And the Message Continues*, an exhibition of photography by IAIA students and alumni stated that the work in the show had "gone beyond the usual cultural baggage." McNeil asks, "What did this mean?" Does "cultural baggage" mean traditional? What's wrong with traditional? He cited the example of his own work from 1983, a series of beautiful portraits of clan leaders from the village of Angoon, Alaska, which was criticized for looking too much like the traditional photographs of Edward Curtis (NTA). Actually, his portraits were quite different from Curtis's in that they were commissioned by the village, along with other art, for their new tribal house; and clan leaders chose what they wanted to wear—that is, how they wished to (re)present themselves in this important context. In the images I saw, all chose traditional or ceremonial clothes. For this reason and the sepia-tone of the photographs, the portraits DO have a traditional look—but why is this bad? Why is it okay for non-Natives to do work that looks traditional or that references the traditional arts of other cultures, but receives a negative criticism or put-down when applied to work by Native artists? McNeil asks again, "Just whose cultural baggage is this?"

Jolene Rickard talked about going back to her Tuscarora heritage and drawing on traditions such as the fancy beadwork made by women and sold to tourists near Niagara Falls. The beadwork, she explains, functions as a site of women coming together to share information and pass on traditions, and as an economic stabilizer in the community, thus empowering the women in several ways. Rickard's juxtaposition and layering of images of nature, traditions, and family with her own self-portrait, sometimes combining them with non-photographic materials or objects, allows her to move freely and cross time and space. Focusing on

Native over non-Native audiences, Rickard often chooses to work with symbols that might not be fully understandable to the non-Native viewer. In response to, "But does it transcend?" Rickard replies that this question, often posed by the dominant culture, assumes a white audience and thus represents a kind of hegemonic Western privileging that is essentially racist.

I learned a lot from all of the exceptional presentations, but for me the symposium lingered too long in the archival (and safe) past. While histories ARE important—all the more so if we come from a group of peoples who have been displaced, relocated, and marginalized, whose land, children, traditions, and culture have been stolen, whose history has been denied or (re)written by the colonizer—it is easy to get stuck in the historical past, trying to reconstruct truths amidst webs of questions about authenticity and intent.

Perhaps it is the seduction of photography that it promises "truth" if you just know how to read the image. However, given the lack of information surrounding many early photographs, the range of photographic agendas, and the problems of translation and interpretation that most of the presenters themselves emphasized, I found this fixation, this quest for "truth"—as if it were some stabilized, fixed, monolithic entity with clear contours—to be rather strange.

Time and time again it was pointed out how no photograph is neutral, and how all photography is, in a sense, fiction, and that to try to read the image is at best risky business. Obviously, as Alan Trachtenberg (NTA) pointed out, "Use cannot be separated from production." (I would add intended audience, and as A. D. Coleman (NTA) emphasized, the social implications of phototechnology.) Trachtenberg stated, "We need to be aware not only of the dynamics of the original 'looking' of the photographer, but of our 'relooking,' to continuously reflect on our own critical act of 'looking.'" And he quoted Trinh T. Minh-ha, the Vietnamese-American filmmaker and theoretician who talks about "looking" as a treacherous activity, for who looks at whom and from where keeps shifting. . . . This is brilliantly illustrated by the work of Zig Rising Buffalo Jackson (Mandan, Hidatsa, Arikara), who photographs unaware "real tourists" as they are busy photographing "real Indians."

Since 1985 there has been, as curator/writer Teresa Harlan (Santa Domingo/Laguna) pointed out, a growing interest not only in Native cultures, but in Native self-representation, and especially in photography. However, despite this interest which is resulting in a burst of exhibitions and publications, Harlan says that there is still too little opportunity to hear what Native peoples have to say about Native photography. Lucy Lippard's (NTA) recent book *Partial Recall* (reviewed in this issue) and symposiums like these are steps in the right direction.

However, instead of obsessing on early photographs that are de-contextualized and resist clear reading, why not listen to "living photographers" who are sharing personal, tribal, and cultural contexts for their work, the very missing context of the past we are hunting for. All too often artists are asked to present their work, and then critics and historians are called in to translate, contextualize, authenticate, and bestow value. In a situation like this, it can too easily become the white (and often, male) critic who discusses the work of the Native artist. I wish there had been more Native voices present throughout this symposium—not only artists, but Native curators, historians, critics, and archivists—critical voices like those of Gerald Vizenor, Jimmie Durham, Ravna Green, Suzanne Benally, Gerald McMaster, and Jaune Quick-to-See Smith. The presentations by Harlan, Monty Roessel (Navajo), Linda Poolaw (Delaware), and the video on Tewa art, *Nambi T'oh*, were welcome in this respect, but not enough. Non-Native cultural critics of color, such as bell hooks, Trinh T. Minh-ha, Michelle Wallace, Kobena Mercer, Gloria Anzaldúa, or Coco Fusco might have provided further insights from their own decolonized perspectives, thus creating a true multicultural dialogue.

What is clear from the strong self-presentations of artists at the symposium is that Native Americans are not only becoming both the subjects and objects of art, but major voices in the cultural discourse. As margins shift, centers are destabilized, creating new spaces of understandings, misunderstandings, possibilities, contradictions, questions, dialogues, and much creative energy—a fluid field of many and diverse voices that hopefully continues to resist quick or stereotyped readings.

ED. NOTE

"Resistances: Cultural Tourism and Native Resistance Through Self-Representation," a review of the symposium "Images Across Boundaries: History, Use and Ethics of Photographs of American Indians," co-organized by the Institute of American Indian Arts and the Museum of Indian Arts and Culture in Santa Fe, New Mexico, was originally published in *THE Magazine*, June 1993, 27–29. Symposium presentations were the author's source for all quotes in the review, with the exception of the epigraphs. The author did not identify sources for those quotes.

A Space of Infinite and Pleasurable Possibilities

Lesbian Self-Representation in Visual Art

New Feminist Criticism: Art/Identity/Action (1994)

I am an artist, a feminist, a lesbian, middle-class, white. When I'm good, I'm an artist. When I'm bad, I'm a feminist. And when I'm horrid, I'm a goddamn dyke. I feel like being horrid these days. Given the current political climate around art and the threat of being artistically silenced for being queer and female, I can't afford to be quiet or to let others define who I am and what kind of art I may or may not make.

I see artmaking, especially that which comes from the margins of the mainstream, as a site of resistance, a way of interrupting and intervening in those historical and cultural fields that continually exclude me, a sort of gathering of forces on the borders. For the dominant hegemonic stance that has worked to silence and subdue gender and ethnic difference has also silenced difference based on sexual preference. It is essential that we bring sexual preference into the current discourses on difference and representation, along with race and gender, and that there be a strong lesbian presence in this discourse.[1]

Critic Martha Gever has written that "to *be* a lesbian means engaging in a complex, often treacherous, system of cultural identities, representations and institutions, and a history of sexual regulation."[2] So, then, what does it mean to identify oneself as a lesbian artist? As an artist who is "out" as a lesbian? Who sometimes makes work about the experience of being lesbian? Both "lesbian" and "artist" are problematic identities open to interpretation and self-construction. How do we negotiate multiple identities? The Vietnamese-American intersectional theorist Trinh T. Minh-ha asks, "Which comes first?"[3] Which identity is most important? In questioning the language of cultural representation, identity, and difference, Trinh has called for making the distinction "between the alienating notion of 'otherness,' [. . .] and an empowering notion of 'difference.'"[4] But, she asks, "How do you inscribe difference without bursting into a series of euphoric narcissistic accounts of yourself and your own kind? Without indulging in a marketable romanticism or in a naive whining about your condition? In other words, how do you forget without annihilating? Between the twin chasms of navel-gazing and navel-erasing, the ground is narrow and slippery. None of us can pride ourselves on being sure-footed there."[5]

Like Trinh, I believe that the answer lies not in accepting or choosing identity, but rather creating it, and one way we create identity is through art. The great service of art is to tell us who we really are.[6] To use the words of critic Lucy Lippard, "Art would not have to speak for everyone if everyone could speak for themselves."[7] But how hard it is to find one's own voice. How difficult it is to affirm cultural identities, to recreate them so that they are not simply a counternarrative to the authoritative center, to what African-American poet Audre Lorde called the mythical norm or that which is "white, thin, male, young, heterosexual, christian, and financially secure."[8] How hard it is to get past the privileged authority who does not even have to be present to exert his influence. How hard to give form to oneself honestly.

For most gays and lesbians, sexual definitions have proved inadequate. Existing stereotypes (whether deriving from psychoanalysis, from pathological and pseudo-scientific texts of the nineteenth century, or from notions of political correctness within gay and lesbian communities) have been limiting and disempowering and have little to do with the reality and range of our lives as lived. There is no single homosexual identity or homosexual sensibility (which I see as the expression of that identity), but rather a dialectic between the homosexual's being articulated and articulating her[-] or himself.

On a 1982 panel titled "Extended Sensibilities: The Impact of Homosexual Sensibilities on Contemporary Culture," sponsored by the New Museum, *Village Voice* critic Jeff Weinstein was quoted as saying, "There is no gay sensibility, and it has a tremendous amount of influence."[9] Everyone in the audience and on the panel laughed, for they knew what he meant. Homosexual eroticism and sensibility are marketed to and lavishly consumed by heterosexual culture, thereby rendering it nonexistent, although as writer and sculptor Kate Millett pointed out, "[H]omosexual sensibility as it is generally understood . . . almost includes lesbians but doesn't quite. Really [it] mean[s] gay men." Millett suggested, "What if we were to rephrase this question and were to ask, 'What is the impact of lesbian sensibility on contemporary culture?' I would respond right offhand without even shifting gears, that it's zilch."[10] Again, everyone in the audience and on the panel laughed, for they knew what she, too, meant. Lesbians have no visible presence in the historical mainstream of Euro-Western art, nor in contemporary popular culture. If, as Stuart Hall says, "identities are the names we give to the different ways we are positioned by, and position ourselves within, the narratives of the past," lesbian sensibility, given its invisibility, would have to be created out of nothing.[11] It would establish a lesbian subject full of complexity and contradiction, unfixed, ever-shifting and reinventing itself in order to embrace and reflect an articulation of difference not only from men and straight women, but among lesbians.

Michel Foucault has stated that "we have to not only affirm ourselves as an identity, but as a creative force."[12] In [the preface to] their interview with Foucault, Bob Gallagher and Alexander Wilson point out that this declaration raises important issues. [. . .]

> If gay people are truly to know themselves, suggests Foucault, they must examine and rely on their own potential—in short, create themselves—rather than insist on conforming to the socially constructed role of the "homosexual" a consciousness that has primarily been defined by others. [. . .] We must define who we are, who we can become, what our community consists of, and how we are going to change the world so it will accommodate us. This challenge—and invitation—doesn't come from a naïve or idealistic individualism but from an understanding that we are shaped by our sexual identity, and that it is, in turn, shaped by us. It is not a simple matter of accepting or denying our sexual identity; we must continually construct it. Let us hope, that it will be an identity strong enough to protect us, and flexible enough to liberate us.[13]

[As Gallagher and Wilson affirm, . . .] Foucault, in his late writings, has had a major impact on the development of queer theory. While he addressed himself almost entirely to gay men, his discussion of the social construction of homosexual identity, its relationship to desire, pleasure, and sexual practice, and his openness to exploration and invention in the reconfiguration of relationships is relevant and of interest to the construction of lesbian identities (it is also limited, given his disregard for gender politics). Foucault, who was involved with alternative forms of sexuality within the gay movement, embraced the potential of all segments of what today we would call the continuum of queer society, not just those sectors most politically correct or acceptable to the straight world. Like the leatherman, fag, transvestite or drag queen, the butch, femme, kiki, bull dagger, and lipstick lesbian may be identities "at least partially of their own invention."[14]

It is this quality of "invention" that is apparent in lesbian art being made today and which differentiates it from earlier art by lesbians in the '70s. In a sense the art both reflects and contributes to ever-shifting definitions of lesbian identity, and can be seen to mirror both the desexualization of lesbian feminism in the '70s and early '80s, and the exploration of lesbian fantasy and desire in the late '80s and '90s, which reasserts sexuality as central to lesbian identity.

In her 1992 article "Sisters and Queers: The Decentering of Lesbian Feminism," Arlene Stein reflects back and discusses the emergence of lesbian feminism as a political entity in the late '60s and early '70s.[15] Pre-Stonewall and pre-feminist lesbian culture was semisecret, mostly urban and working class, and [in Stein's words] "formed in relation to the hegemonic belief that heterosexuality was natural and homosexuality an aberration." As author Jill Johnston says of this period, "Identity was presumed to be heterosexual unless proven otherwise. . . . There was no lesbian identity. There was lesbian activity."[16] Stein describes how lesbian feminism emerged out of the radical sectors of the women's movement with lesbians who felt neither at home in the left nor comfortable in mixed gay organizations like the Gay Liberation Front, or in primarily straight-identified organizations like the National Organization for Women (NOW). The many women like myself, primarily middle class, who "came out through feminism" in the early and mid-'70s did not believe that we were failed women, nor that we were necessarily straight or gay from birth, although some of us recognized that for many "primary lesbians" (old dykes), the latter was true. In a sense we became lesbians by choice and our new bonding and connecting to a "class of women" extended quite pleasurably to sexual practice.

As it began to critique patriarchy and its institution of compulsory heterosexuality, lesbian feminism rapidly grew to be a collective identity and a political movement. *The Woman-Identified Woman*, authored by the Radical Lesbians in 1970, was important in broadening the definitions of lesbianism from a medical condition, or even just sexual preference, to a general sense of connectedness with other women based on mutuality and similarity of the experience of being a woman in patriarchal culture. Lesbianism had become a gender issue.

[The year 1974] saw the first of the National Women's Music Festivals, and 1975 was a summer of many national and regional feminist conferences, workshops, and festivals (such as Sagaris: Institute of Radical Feminist Political Thought and the Socialist Feminist Conference). Women were literally coming out all over the place. It was said that if these gatherings were 80 percent lesbian to start with, they were 99.9 percent lesbian when over. [. . .] Never before had so much social space opened up so quickly to middle-class women who dared to defy deeply held social norms about their proper sexual place. As a result, the group of women who called themselves lesbian, became increasingly heterogeneous, at least in terms of sexuality. A popular slogan of the time said that "feminism is the theory, lesbianism is the practice." And Alix Dobkin sang, "Every woman can be a lesbian," on *Lavender Jane Loves Women*, one of the earliest dyke albums. Thus, the definition of "lesbian" broadened at this time from women who are sexually attracted to women exclusively, act on it, and claim an identity based on this attraction, to "biological women who do not sleep with men and who embrace the lesbian label." This broadening of lesbian identification was paralleled in lesbian visual self-representation, which in the '70s moved away from images of subculture outlaws (rooted in sexual identification) to a more general female that was by extension woman-identified or lesbian (rooted in gender).

In her important article "Dykes in Context: Some Problems in Minority Representation," Jan Zita Grover points out that the roots of lesbian self-representation lie in pre-Stonewall and pre-feminist subculture magazines and journals, and personal snapshots passed privately among friends.[17] Old dykes documented their parties, friends, and lovers, and made real (as only a photo can do) an otherwise hidden culture of their own. Some of these photos were erotic, and all had a sense of secrecy as they were not meant for public viewing.

However, as Grover points out, by the early '70s feminist and lesbian feminist journals and publishers were rapidly proliferating and wanted politically correct lesbian images. Soon, visual work by movement photographers such as JEB (Joan E. Biren) and Tee Corinne was visible on the pages and covers of journals such as *The Ladder*, *Amazon Quarterly*, *Sinister Wisdom*, *Conditions*, and *13th Moon*. Art by lesbians was on the walls of women's bookstores, coffee houses, and restaurants, and occasionally the walls of women's co-op art galleries (although because these galleries operated on the peripheries of the art mainstream, with most of the membership straight-identified, they were very sensitive to being put down by the male-dominated art world as a "bunch of dykes" and thus seldom exhibited work that was overtly lesbian).

By the mid-'70s gay men and lesbians began to show together at the Gay Academic Union held annually in New York, and a few mixed gay galleries opened and closed. Most of the work being exhibited by gay men was erotic, worshipped the perfect male body, was without any political consciousness, and was put down by lesbians for being so. Most of the work by lesbians was in keeping with the current politically correct lesbian feminist position of not representing or objectifying women's bodies and downplaying sexuality. While one might have seen abstract images of labia, clits, breasts, and vaginas, or two women being chummy and hugging (the second woman being the lezzie signifier), you certainly never saw them "doing it."

There have always been a lot of lesbian artists. Since the '70s many have come out of the closet, although only a few in the art world made art with lesbian content (although a case could be made for the existence of coded imagery). Many women, especially on the West Coast, where performance was utilized as a consciousness-raising tool, came out simultaneously as lesbians and artists. Because the focus in lesbian feminism at the time was on gender issues, and lesbian definitions were being broadened to include any woman-identified women, female space depicted visually (say through landscape, fruit, and flower imagery) was by extension considered "lesbian." (A large group of lesbian-identified artists continue to work in this tradition.)

Other themes that reoccurred frequently [in works from this era] were anger, concealment, secrecy, guilt, coming out, celebrating the female body, and generally creating a visible lesbian presence. There were humorous pieces relating food and sexuality such as Sharon Deevey's *Choc-clit Bar* (melts in your hand, melts in your mouth), Clsuf's *Hershe Kisses Her* [1977], and Sandy de Sando's plaster whipped cream-and-cookie pubic mounds. Portraits were common but often decontextualized, or avoided representing "deviant and perverted spaces such as bars" in favor of stable "dykes are people too" or "women working together" images. A few artists such as Lili Lakich, who works in neon, referenced historical lesbian writers and artists such as Djuna Barnes, Natalie Clifford Barney, or Romaine Brooks.

Janet Cooling, Hollis Sigler, and Nancy Fried depicted woman-centered domestic environments: a kitchen, a living room, a bedroom as stage for possible lesbian relationships, hinting at sexuality. Sigler, Nicole Ferentz, and Kate Millett (who also made calligraphic drawings of the female body) included diaristic text that referred to female lovers and the nuances and complexities of intimate relationships among women. Sigler's drawing with the words "Loving the Lady Inside Myself" can be read several ways. Janey Washburn and Ellen Turner dealt with anger and guilt. Louise Fishman's wall of *Angry Paintings* [1973] was meant for women, many of them lesbian, so they could confront their anger, which held them back in the world. Fishman, now working totally as an abstract painter, writes that her "early pieces have to do with the anger connected to trying to make art and trying to show that art while remaining identified as a Jew, a woman, and a lesbian."[18] Lesbian artists who wished to be taken seriously and to claim their whole selves and not suffer for it had to negotiate their many positionings—and it wasn't easy, for the art world wasn't welcoming women, much less lesbian, artists.

Jody Pinto and Fran Winant had their alter egos: Pinto's male persona, Henry, who could fly and swim in a sexual dreamscape, or Winant's dog Cindy. In *The Kiss* [1979], Winant depicts what appears to be a woman kissing her dog, with strange calligraphy—a secret language that Winant had devised years earlier for writing poetry that no one else could interpret—in the corner. In another painting, Cindy is surrounded by this secret language. Winant was not only able to illustrate a "different sexuality," a forbidden, or unnatural love, but also to refer to animals in work of earlier lesbian artists such as Rosa Bonheur and Romaine Brooks.

Some of my own work from this period dealt with coming out, homophobia, the difficulties of personal violence and political trust in lesbian relationships, and, later, in the early '80s, the creation of an overtly lesbian sensual-sexual presence and the social and political effect of such a presencing. For example, the wrapped rag sculpture *Sneak* [1978] presented an ever-multiplying army of black, white, and gray female forms insidiously banding together and marching forward. *Kudzu* [1982] referred to the Southern plant that was brought into the United States to control soil erosion and then went out of control, indiscriminately covering and consuming everything in its path. Created in North Carolina, the large, black, aggressive *kudzu*, with its finger or rib-like forms, is a conscious metaphor for xenophobia, racism, and homophobia, PR [public relations] people's fear of difference and being out of control.

Because feminists in the '70s opposed "the sexual exploitation of women and mounted specific critiques of the representation of women as exclusively sexual beings in advertising, media and pornography," there was a widespread reactive move away from representing the female body or female sexual experience.[19] This, combined with the fact that lesbians were trying to combat being defined solely on the basis of sexual practice, meant that the lesbian, with few exceptions, was no longer even self-represented as a sexual being.

Grover talks about this loss, which was especially apparent in photography, the main art form where previously there had been a lesbian erotic presence. The older representations (like those gracing the covers of lesbian pulp novels), in their sex-role stereotyping, had acknowledged the power of lesbian sexuality. Somehow in the '70s, as Grover points out, "in seeking to represent the female sexual outlaw, the dyke, as a whole person, many photographers have ceased imag(in)ing her as a hole person."[20]

While it was important at that time to show that lesbians made all kinds of art, much of the work, while raw and passionate, now sometimes seems simplistic, or "lesbian" only in that we knew that the artists were lesbian and that certain pieces were directed more to a lesbian audience than to the general art world. Often the works tended to romanticize or sentimentalize lesbian experience. It must not be forgotten, though, that just to be in these shows took strength and courage and was a radical and risky gesture not to be underestimated. It made one's personal life public, and artists risked everything, from family disapproval to job discrimination or dismissal to artistic stereotyping. At least one artist was threatened by her gallery: If she exhibited "as a lesbian," she could say goodbye to the gallery's exhibition and representation of her work. (She didn't show.)

On her page in the photocopied catalogue for *A Lesbian Show* at the 112 Greene Street Workshop in 1978, artist Barbara Asch wrote above her delicate cave and germinating-flower forms, "This show frightens me."[21] Many of the participating artists felt this way. This first exhibition of lesbian art in New York grew out of the silence unearthed by the groundbreaking and beautiful "Lesbian Art and Artists" issue of *Heresies: A Feminist Publication on Art and Politics*. Generally speaking, the "Lesbian Issue" of *Heresies* (1977), *A Lesbian Show* at the 112 Greene Street Workshop (1978), *The Great American Lesbian Art Show* (GALAS) at the Women's Building in Los Angeles (1980), and even the New Museum exhibition *Extended Sensibilities: Homosexual Presence in Contemporary Art* (1982) were fairly asexual and safe. While they attempted to discover and define an essential lesbian (or gay) sensibility, they simply presented a wide range of work by artists willing to be public about their sexual preference and willing to show in that context. In doing so, these shows and projects were successful in creating, for the first time, a public lesbian/homosexual presence in the visual arts and stimulating dialogue within the art world, and among lesbian and gay communities.

It was against this backdrop of expanded identities and dissolving boundaries between lesbians and straight feminists that Monique Wittig made her controversial presentation "The Straight Mind" at the Modern Language Association in 1978.[22] In response to the growing destructive focus "on the woman question," Wittig asked, "What is woman? . . . Frankly, it is a problem that lesbians do not have." For she says, "lesbians are not women." Nor are they men. ". . . [I]t would be incorrect to say that lesbians associate, make love, live with women for 'woman' has meaning in heterosexual systems of thought and heterosexual economic systems." Lesbians (who are not women) love lesbians (who are not women). "It is not as 'women' that lesbians are oppressed, but rather in that they are 'not women.'" Wittig views heterosexuality as "a cultural construct designed to justify the whole system of social domination based on the obligatory reproductive function of women and the appropriation of that reproduction." It tries to make the difference between the sexes a natural and not a cultural one, with reproduction as its goal and all else perversion. Since for lesbians, sexual pleasure is for the sake of sexual pleasure alone, lesbians exist outside of the heterosexist field, and might well "ask heterosexual society: 'what have you done with our desire?'" For "if desire could liberate itself, it would have nothing to do with the preliminary marking by sexes." "Lesbianism is the culture through which we can politically question heterosexual society on its sexual categories, on the meaning of its institutions of domination in general, and in particular on the meaning of that institution of personal dependence, marriage, imposed on women."

Lesbians and gay men, Wittig feels, must break through this heterosexist contract by refusing to be "women" or "men" and find a means to "do away with genders, the linguistic indicator of political oppositions." Wittig's presentation at the MLA and her other writings and presentations from around that time, in the extremity of their views regarding the separation of lesbian from straight women, departed from the main flow of lesbian feminist thinking. She was criticized by many as separatist. However, in her shift away from a definition of lesbian identity based on gender to one based on sexual preference, as well as her deconstruction of sex, gender, and the lesbian body in order to (re)member it, Wittig, like Foucault, anticipated and influenced much of today's rich discourse around the body and sexuality.

By the early '80s, as Stein has documented, "a series of structural and ideological shifts conspired to decenter the lesbian feminist model of identity." As "the predominantly white and middle-class women who composed the base of the movement aged" and "changed, women of color, working-class women, and sexual minorities [. . .] asserted" their presence and forced an acknowledgment and reexamination of multiple identities and difference within lesbian communities. In particular, "sexual difference posed a challenge to lesbian-feminist constructions of identity."[23]

Coming out of the '70s activism combating sexual violence against women—Women Against Violence Against Women (WAVAW) and Women Against Violence in Pornography—and the sex debates on pornography and censorship in the '80s, sexuality burst forth as a major feminist issue. More than anything else, pornography (and there are a range of feminist definitions) continues to cause debates and splits within the feminist community. This debate is relevant here, because erotic art, like pornography, is in the domain of sexual expression. Both are intended to arouse sexual pleasure and both raise issues of censorship versus creative freedom of expression.

A series of projects in the feminist art communities of the early eighties contributed to and were in response to these "hot and heavy" debates. The "Sex Issue" of *Heresies* (1981), far more controversial than its earlier and tamer sister, "Lesbian Art and Artists"; *The Second Coming* (1984), an exhibition curated by Carnaval Knowledge at Franklin Furnace in New York that attempted to explore the possibility of a feminist pornography; the 1982 conference "Towards a Politics of Sexuality" at Barnard College, "when anti-S/M activists picketed a speak-out on 'politically incorrect sex,'" along with its subsequent publications, *Pleasure and Danger*, which brought together all the papers and talks from the conference, and *Diary of a Conference on Sexuality*, which discussed the process of the organizers and presenters; and *Caught Looking*, focusing on the sex debates and porn wars, which was compiled by the Seattle Feminist Anti-Censorship Task Force and published in 1986—all of these addressed issues of sexual expression and representation and raised questions:[24]

> How do women get sexual pleasure in patriarchy?
> How do we develop a language to talk about female sexual pleasure?
> Can woman be both subject and object?
> Who possesses the right of looking?
> Is there or can there be a feminist pornography?
> What kind of sexual behaviors are feminist?
> How does this relate to our desires, private fantasies, and actual sexual practice?
> Are there other kinds of sexuality than genital?

In response to the anti-porn movement, which they saw as a potential threat to creative freedom (under anti-porn legislation all sexual imagery can be censored), the women who worked on these projects applauded sexual experimentation and diversity, decried the policing of desire, and saw the necessity to safeguard the circulation of fantasy and creative expression of the erotic imagination. Instead of focusing on patriarchal violence, they opened up potential sexual possibilities for women. A new kind of sex radicalism appeared, which tried to think through the relations of power and sexuality as well as the complexities of butch-femme exchange. Largely in response to being targeted by anti-porn groups, a lesbian S/M community emerged and "a burgeoning sexual literature reasserted the centrality of desire and sexuality in lesbian identity and culture."[25] However, this lesbian presence got lost on the way to the art community, where until the very late '80s sex radicalism as it manifested itself in visual art seemed peculiarly straight. Fighting the battle against art censorship brought out the homophobia not only from the power centers, but from the various nooks and crannies along the margins. In its absence, lesbianism became a subtext.

For instance, a lesbian voice was strangely absent in feminist art dialogues like the 1987 New Museum panel where essentialism was pitted against theory (highly questionable polarities, given the nature of the most interesting feminist art being made at that time). In cool, dry, theoretical language, two feminist critics told us unequivocally that it is only through images of women that female sexuality is constructed, and for women, there is no experience of the body outside of representation. No one referred to actual art, much less to Ana Mendieta's work, which surrounded us and which would have provided an excellent starting point to discuss the problem of an art that attempts to combine essentialism, activism, and theory. I agree with Lucy Lippard, who later wrote in *Heresies* that while we would all agree "that language and the visual representation of women mediates much of our experience," the position being represented by several members of the panel was so narrow that there was no room for dialogue, exploration, supposition, or fantasy. "If for women, 'there is no experience of the body outside of representation,' we are deprived of a center from which to venture forth to change that misrepresentation. . . . Why not concentrate on what the male gaze cannot see?"[26]

Sitting in the audience, I found myself thinking that what was said wasn't entirely true for lesbians, that we had such a small history of visual representation of any kind. And I certainly felt that I had an experience of my body outside of those representations. Not one lesbian on the panel or in the audience, including myself, spoke up and said that perhaps, just perhaps, the lesbian—whose body is least represented and colonized by man—would offer the greatest potential or possibility for creating [or] inventing a "woman" that is not a patriarchal construct, a woman totally free from restrictions or conventional forms and behaviors. While artist Nancy Spero did quote Simone de Beauvoir, no one recalled Wittig's theories of 1978. The lesbian was not in attendance at this panel, and in this case, postmodernism seemed like a particularly heterosexual dead end.

Even within what many are calling the current "renaissance of gay art," lesbians have been in danger of being left out once again. It has taken the activism and strong street visuals of ACT UP and Queer Nation (continued by the Women's Action Coalition [WAC], which is committed to combating "lesbophobia"), along with the development of academic queer theory, to help lesbians burst forth and assert a visual presence. I like the label "queer" and use it often because it is genderless, challenges clear-cut categories of sex and gender, and jumps off the page or out of the sentence. Like I said, these days, one must be horrid, be a goddam dyke, claim and flaunt identities on one's own terms, even while these very identities are constantly changing. Labels like "dyke," "faggot," "queer," originally meant to mark, wound, and scar, can be turned around, claimed, and flaunted (with style, of course) to empower both artist and audience. Actually, to employ these labels visually in one's art, as some artists are doing, let there be no question in anyone's mind as to what this work is about.

I believe in a strong and united queer presence with gay male artists and other fellow "deviants," but I continue to worry about the lagging visibility of and theory around lesbian art. For just as visual art by lesbians has been consistently and conspicuously absent in feminist art dialogues like the one at the New Museum, until very recently it has also been absent from most discussions of gay or queer art. Caught between the straight feminists and the gay male agenda, lesbians, as historian Cassandra Langer puts it, often don't exist at all, or they are "deprived of a political existence by their inclusion as female versions of male homosexuality. Being lesbian is being marginal in an already marginal network."[27]

The fact is that since lesbians don't have the mainstream museum and market-certified counterparts of [Andy] Warhol, [David] Hockney, [Keith] Haring, and [Robert] Mapplethorpe, our work, while it is no longer limited to subculture venues (though thankfully these still exist too), is seen primarily in alternative spaces (some more prestigious or legitimized than others), and rarely in commercial galleries or museums. Those galleries that do make an effort to support gay and lesbian artists are often run by well-meaning gay men who don't have easy access to lesbian networks, and who tend to focus on salable homoerotic work by gay male artists that appeals to wealthy gay male collectors. For example, the exhibition *Queer: Out in Art* at the Wessel O'Connor Gallery in New York in 1990 included work by only nine women compared to fifty-five men.[28] However, this imbalance seems slowly to be changing. Generally speaking, in exhibitions that are cocurated with lesbians, representation is equal. It is in these exhibitions (along with those that are all-lesbian such as *All but the Obvious: Program of Lesbian Art*, curated by Pam Gregg for the Los Angeles Center for Exhibitions [LACE] in 1990) that we get to see the diversity of emerging work that challenges expectations and assumptions about lesbian art. *All but the Obvious* is "not concerned with defining a lesbian aesthetic or sexual identity; rather raising questions about the construction of sexual identity and the intersection of personal and public territory."[29]

Writing about the exhibit in *High Performance*, Terry Wolverton, who was one of the organizers of "GALAS" a decade earlier at the Women's Building [in Los Angeles], discusses the differences between the two exhibits:

> A new generation of lesbian artists came of age between 1980 and 1990. Perhaps at no time in history was it easier to be a queer woman. These young women have inherited the legacies of Stonewall and radical feminism. [. . .]
>
> One unmistakable point is that this generation of lesbians approaches the representation of sexuality much differently than their predecessors.

> Where ten years ago GALAS participant Tee Corinne was arranging multiple prints of women engaged in oral sex into mandalas, equating sex with spirituality, Della Grace makes no attempt to prettify hardcore S/M imagery. Artist Catherine Saalfield, whose collaborative video installation with Jacqueline Woodson [. . .] insists that "the presence of AIDS has necessitated an unromanticized candor about sex." Other artists seem to be reacting against a perceived "anti-sex" bias among '70s feminists (who strove to eliminate images of violence against or sexual exploitation of women). The lesbian artists of the '90s insist on defining their own pleasure in their own terms, demanding access to all images of themselves, including those generated in pornography.[30]

Most of the work was either photography or photo-based and, in its representation of sexuality, asserted a lesbian presence while refusing a monolithic definition of "lesbian."[31] Work ranged from Janet Cooling's painted portraits of dyke couples and Gaye Chan's photographs of women engaged in intimate sexualized activities to Tracy Mostovoy's *Naked Women in Public Places* [1991] and Collier Schorr's mixed-media diptych using text to refer cynically to the betrothal of two women. Woodson and Saafield's video installation *Among Good Christian Peoples* [1991] explored Woodson's experience of growing up lesbian and black in a religious family.[32]

Despite these changes, however, one aspect that outrageously remains the same is the near invisibility of lesbian artists of color. Wolverton points out that in 1980, *GALAS* included two Third World artists of ten. In 1990, *All but the Obvious* included three out of fifteen.[33] "This fact," she continues, "has many causes including the racism and insularity of white lesbians and homophobia in Third World communities, but at a time when segments of the art world are achieving multiculturalism, it is disappointing. Perhaps artists who are already marginalized by virtue of their cultural background feel reluctant to adopt the still more tenuous position of sexual difference."[34]

Why are there so few visual artists of color who make work about being lesbian compared to writers and poets who are "out" in their work? Given the expense of workspace and materials, do fewer women have the privilege or opportunity to make art in the first place? Or is there something inherently different about oral traditions and the written word versus traditional object-making and visual images? Some artists have explained their reluctance to deal with lesbian content or to exhibit in lesbian shows by pointing out that a support community of sorts exists among lesbian writers of color that is virtually absent among artists. For many, just the word "lesbian" signifies a white cultural context that is exclusionary or doesn't adequately describe one's identity. Perhaps as a white woman I can't read lesbian content cross-culturally, but it seems that many artists who are "out" as lesbians, who claim that label, don't make work about identity issues, nor do they choose to focus on race and/or gender over sexuality. Thinking about race and sexuality together is difficult, complex, and scary—an area that needs continued exploration and (re)presentation by lesbians of color and white lesbians. To truly explore identities of difference, we need to expand the dialogues and ask questions such as "How is one's sexuality racialized?" and "How is race sexualized?"[35]

Only a few artists of color come to mind who regularly bring lesbian content into their work—in addition to Woodson, Chan, and Yamaoka. I am thinking of Laura Aguilar and Ester Hernandez, although I am sure there are many others who are not as well known. Carrie Yamaoka has photographed a page of text from Radclyffe Hall's quintessential lesbian novel *The Well of Loneliness* [1928]. The words "Her hair was quite short" stand out in darker typeface from the rest of the text, which seems almost erased, allowing the viewer-reader to focus on the lesbian signifier of short hair and to read between the lines. Ester Hernandez, an ex-farmworker of Yaqui and Mexican ancestry, is well known for her images of "la mujer Chicana." Her silkscreen *La Ofrenda* [1988], reproduced on the cover of *Chicana Lesbians: The Girls Our Mothers Warned Us About*, presents the back of a woman with hairstyle, makeup, and earring signifying Chicana style of "las buenas amigas," and a large tattoo of the Virgen de Guadalupe, who, as the fusion of mysticism and Mexican nationalism, represents a strong female force.[36] The hand of a second woman holds a rose (female genitalia) out as an offering to both the Virgen and the first woman, thus incorporating references of sexuality along with race and gender.

Like the community that produces it, lesbian art is diverse. What is clear is that there is no single fixed lesbian identity and thus no single fixed sensibility, and we lesbians like it that way. By nature we do not want to be domesticated, commodified, or consumed. Even our theory can't entirely embrace our art or vice versa. Perhaps sensibility, like sexuality, is a way of perceiving, of feeling "a space of inarticulation," or simply a space of possibilities. In reaction to the political correctness of the '70s Lesbian Nation, art today asks questions, poses contradictions, explores problematics, and proposes that if indeed we are creating ourselves, then the concept of sexual difference is one of "engaging possibilities."

The multiplicity of work and theoretical discourse is rich in the area of time-based arts (film, video, and performance) and to a much lesser degree in object-making, where photography, because of its movement history, dominates. Perhaps painting and sculpture are too identified with male traditions and institutions, or perhaps it is that the fluid, decentered layered identity of the lesbian refuses to be framed or fixed in the object. Generally speaking, painting and sculpture are just beginning to explore the terrain of gender and sexuality.[37] Because a large body of theoretical work focusing on film, video, and performance already exists, and because I myself am interested in the possibilities and problematics of object-making/constructing, I'm focusing my discussion here on examples of 2-D and 3-D work that contribute to the visual discourse around "lesbian identity."

One way that marginalized artists authenticate themselves is to "paint" themselves into the dominant art historical or popular cultural mainstream. Lesbians, too, are employing this strategy and interrupting the central authoritative narrative by inserting/asserting themselves wherever they wish to be (spaces previously occupied only in the wildest of fantasies), responding to or displacing the existing representations.

In her photomontage series *Dream Girls* [1989–90] Deborah Bright pastes her "constructed butch-girl self-image into conventional heterosexual narrative stills from old Hollywood movies," thus actualizing her adolescent proto-dyke fantasies in the '60s, when (as now) Hollywood offered few desirable images of lesbians. As Bright explains with pleasure, "The lesbian subject roams from still to still, movie to movie, disrupting the narrative and altering it to suit her purposes." The film is lesbianized, for in addition to allowing Bright to light Audrey Hepburn's cigarette, to flirt with Glenda Jackson, or seduce Katharine Hepburn, her montages construct a new lesbian subject. As gender changes or becomes ambiguous, power relationships among characters are subverted and the heterosexist narrative is sabotaged.[38]

In her wall-sized photo-text arrangements, Kaucyila Brooke "considers lesbian relationships within American popular culture" and within lesbian and queer communities.[39] Her pieces demonstrate "the absence of women's desire in classic narratives."[40] Appropriating and subverting popular forms such as cartoons, Westerns, soap operas, and photo-novellas, Brooke manipulates their formal devices and inserts lesbian and queer dialogue:

> "So do you want to sign up for more of this sexual fiction?"
> "We are surrounded by the language. There is no turning back."
> "Let's talk about dominance and submission."
> "Black and white are not the only positions."

The images are staged with actors, photographed, blown up like gigantic film stills, and arranged in various configurations with comic balloons for text to suggest sequential narratives. But Brooke's stories are fragmented: they don't read easily, and, like the identity she proposes, have no climax or closure. As historian and critic Joanna Frueh points out, "Brooke inserts serious content into what is most often used for humor or for stories that can be taken lightly. The small scale of the comic strip is blown up, both made huge and exploded, so that the content itself becomes monumental and disruptive," and the cultural form is critiqued for its role in the construction of stereotyped identities.[41] In *Unknown Deviancies (What a Dish)* [1989], "Badgirl," played by Brooke herself, "following the storyline of Spiderwoman and Batgirl . . . finds herself on the streets of Corporate America uncertain about her future or identity but destined to stage and fight (as all superheroes must do) the battle for women's desire."[42]

Other photographers continue in the portrait tradition, documenting a wide range of lesbian lifestyles: Ann Meredith, Nancy Rosenblum, Laura Aguilar, Danita Simpson, Nan Goldin, Lola Flash, Gaye Chan, Catherine Opie, Terry Rozo, Kathleen Sterck, and Della Grace. Laura Aguilar's *Latina Lesbian* series [1986–90], with text below the informal portraits, allows each photo subject to speak actively about her life, while Nan Goldin's photos include unromanticized portraits of lovers and queer friends as well as images of herself in a halfway house for drug treatment. Lola Flash and Gaye Chan present women engaged in sexual activities. In one of Chan's intimate images, a woman has her head up under another woman's sweater, and in a second image, two women part from a kiss with a thread of saliva still connecting their mouths.

While in the past photographers often felt a need to present only "positive" images of lesbians to the public, they are no longer interested in proving that they are nice girls, but rather in flaunting their bad girl sexual outlaw status. Those territories of contraband dyke culture and activity that used to remain hidden or alienated—bars, softball teams, locker rooms, butch-femme drag, motorcycle gangs, and S/M sex—because they were working class or were disapproved of by straight society or politically correct lesbian feminists, are now common subject matter. While lesbian feminism of the '60s and '70s rejected butch-femme behavior as regressively imitative and patriarchal, there is currently a new and visible interest in cross-dressing and in gender-bashing and bending, all of which reassert the sexuality in lesbianism. Gender, and therefore sexuality, is called into question in Zoe Leonard's photos dealing with the scientific and cultural constructions of "femininity" and "femaleness." Drag is no longer considered to be the exclusive domain of gay men, as [lesbian] photographers such as Catherine Opie [. . .] depict cross-dressers. Both Kathleen Sterck and Terry Rozo photograph biker dykes. In her series on the New York City gang the Sirens, Rozo presents images where role signifiers of dress are scrambled, thus subverting stereotypes or easy readings. Her portrait of one biker clad in helmet, boots, and rhinestone-studded strapless gown is a study in butch-femme mixed metaphors that both biker and artist clearly enjoy.

Both Danita Simpson and Della Grace photograph lesbians within the context of bar culture. Simpson's low-light, seemingly random and spontaneous shots do not feel voyeuristic. In direct contrast to this are the photographs of Della Grace, who is consciously toying with issues of pornography, voyeurism, and the boundaries between pleasure and pain in her explicit lesbian S/M images of rough sex. The photos, which are very self-conscious, seem less about actual S/M sex and the exploration of roles and power for the depicted participants than about a literal positioning and posturing for the camera eye and the photographic frame. For this reason, they do not appear to document lesbian S/M sexual practices, but rather to stage a stylish "look of lesbian S/M." Perhaps they were meant to parody the fashion photographs of Helmut Newton, but if that's the case, they end up dangerously close to the very sensationalized images they are parodying.

Some of these photos are included in Grace's book *Love Bites: Photographs*, along with her images and portraits from punk and leather bar scenes and sex clubs in London and the United States.[43] Because of their contextual and therefore documentative nature, these photographs are interesting not only for presenting alternative sexuality, but because they depict a lesbian sexual subculture. It should be noted that when first published in Britain in 1991, *Love Bites* was seized at the border by US customs officials, who threatened to destroy all copies. Only media outrage and a phone call from *Publishers Weekly* "convinced customs to release *Love Bites* to a lesbian public starved for images of itself. Grace's striking photographs are now familiar currency: they've appeared on the covers of lesbian anthologies, in gay arts journals and on Queer Nation flyers, and have been shown in a number of exhibits both here and in Britain."[44]

However, images of explicit and suggested sexuality are not limited to photographs. Nicole Eisenman's crude, stream-of-consciousness sketches and G. B. Jones's pencil drawings of motorcycle girls, in the style of Tom of Finland, emphasize the cruising eye of the lesbian, while Monica Majoli's tiny meticulous paintings on wood have moved from images of gay male sex in the baths to women with dildoes strapped on, engaged in sexual activities. The work is transgressive in that it visualizes forbidden or taboo sexual fantasies (usually imaged in photography, not painting). A second series of paintings depicts body parts such as a wrist with a tiny scratch or cut, heightening the erotic edge between pain and pleasure. In *Mystery Date* [1990], Catherine Opie combines color photographs with actual objects in a framed assemblage of sexually suggestive items such as dildoes, handcuffs, a leather jacket, lace, studs, whips, and plastic gloves. The piece is either a portrait of a date or the suggestion of fantasy within the frame of S/M role-playing.

Millie Wilson intends to "invade high modernism with a queer discourse" in her installation works that examine gender, sexual stereotyping, and the construction of lesbian identity through the exploration of cross-dressing, roles, and masquerade.[45] "In response to the conspicuous absence of the lesbian in postmodern theory," and paralleling the construction of "the artist" and her "body of work" with the construction of "the lesbian," Wilson utilizes specific art historical references and museum praxis to focus on the role of "presentation" in creating, legitimizing, and authenticating.[46]

In *Fauve Semblant* [1989], Wilson created a retrospective of a fictitious lesbian artist, a young English girl named Peter who worked in Paris at the turn of the century. Using museum conventions such as an entrance wall with large signage and a life-sized black-and-white photograph of the artist (in drag of course), Wilson critiques the grand museum retrospective designed to bestow importance upon an oeuvre by creating a historical narrative fiction that related it to other important modernist art.

Peter is a lesbian who cross-dresses (Wilson "maintains that any woman who undertakes the historically male act of painting is forced to engage in aesthetic cross-dressing"[47]). All that remains of her life are a few artifacts: her smoking jacket, shoes, cane, bow tie, glasses, her last painting palette (a comment on the class privilege of those historical lesbians who could afford to be out?), and a single painting, all represented in the exhibition by life-sized photographs; together they form the documentative basis of the life and work of this artist. Starting with the male clothing as a sign of sexual orientation, the mannish lesbian artist must be constructed. In a sense, Wilson's piece is more about presentation than representation, for how the lesbian artist is presented is crucial to the legitimization of the very male institution that confers authenticity, value, and prestige upon her.

Peter's one surviving painting (presented as a treasured artifact in a plexi-box) hints at exotic lesbian sexuality through symbols of a leopard (bestiality?) and tropical flower (female sexuality) and refers to Les Fauves, thus legitimizing Peter's work by connecting it to male modernism.

Continuing her Duchampian commentary on the museum as the container of the official narrative (a strategy used by other marginalized artists such as Jimmie Durham, James Luna, and Fred Wilson), Millie Wilson critiques medical and pathological stereotypes of lesbian identity in an "anthropological" installation entitled *The Museum of Lesbian Dreams* [1990s], where she pokes fun at the absurdity of psychoanalytic interpretation of lesbian dreams as a way to understand lesbian desire and identity (a theory very popular in psychiatric texts on sexual deviancy from the 1950s and '60s). Parodying minimalism, surrealism, and conceptual art, Wilson isolates Freudian dream symbols of sexuality like the potato and turnip and turns them into serious bronze sculptures on a pedestal. She concretizes them and literally gives them weight. Also among the many artifacts of lesbian desire included in this museum are photo reproductions of a 1761 drawing of periwigs, symbols of authority for men, by Hogarth, which outrageously resembles images of deviant female genitals depicted in a 1948 drawing from *Gynecology of Homosexuality*. Both images are displayed (along with text) on either side of a sculpture of a wig that has been styled to resemble a woman's genitalia. This piece, as well as her genital wig-shaped series *Merkins* [1992] pokes fun at the masquerade of authority and successfully exposes and underscores the absurdity of cultural, sexual, and artistic stereotypes and the institutions that try to create and authenticate them.

The museum as institution is also important to much of Zoe Leonard's work. For years she has photographed supposedly objective, scientific exhibits in medical history museums throughout Europe, thereby calling into question "the male-dominated origin of much that we assume is neutral." While this work dovetailed with her involvement with ACT UP and women's health issues, little of it dealt specifically with lesbianism. However, Leonard states that "being a lesbian has informed my point of view. The work that I do with Fierce Pussy, a lesbian artist collective, is clearly very lesbian work." At Documenta [IX] last summer in Kassel, Germany, Leonard exhibited a series of close-ups of women's genitalia and hung them on the walls between traditional nineteenth-century paintings in the city's fine art museum. She says of this installation:

> I requested a suite of four rooms in an old museum at Documenta because I wanted people to walk through what a museum was, and then see my work in relation to what already exists. I'm installing the photography amidst all these paintings that are ostensibly mythological or historical. But what they really are is naked women. Putting the pussy shots in that setting is cutting to the chase. They're totally erotic images for me, as well as a real mirror, in a sense, of what the viewer's relationship is to female genitals. As far as I know, I'm the only out dyke at Documenta. And this is really gay work. This is me really putting myself out there as a lesbian.[48]

The context is important, or, as Jan Zita Grover has stated, the issue is not just what lies within the frame but the context around the frame.[49] While the photos in and of themselves are not new and continue a body of work begun by earlier lesbian feminists, the context is new and different. The fact that Leonard inserted her pubic portraits into the historical museum system underscores the hypocrisy of "neutral" fine art by men, which depicts women as sexual objects, thereby implying a male subject, and allows Leonard to participate in the contemporary critique of the cultural institutions of authority. These images function as a kind of intervention, an invasion of the female sexual subject, which in turn allows for different readings by viewers of differing sexual persuasions. The context and the theoretical underpinnings of the work minimize possible spectatorship and commodification. The work is a strong statement of female sexual power and the taking of space—a very prestigious space at that, one lesbians in the '70s and '80s didn't have access to. It is to Leonard's credit that she didn't try to be a "good girl" but rather utilized her privileged "inclusion" in the male-dominated Documenta to present her most highly charged and unsafe work to date.

Marcia Salo's color photographs examine the shifting nature of lesbian desire and fantasy. Like Bright, she utilizes the heterosexist narrative of Hollywood films to explore lesbian response to identification and identities in the construction of desire. However, since her images overlap, merge, melt, and dissolve, they suggest a more fluid range of roles and fantasies. In *Vertigo*, installed in the women's bathroom of the Gay and Lesbian Community Center in New York City in 1989 as part of a twenty-five-artist project commemorating the twentieth anniversary of the Stonewall riots, Salo combined image and text to suggest a range of roles and fantasies. [. . .] The following text ran at eye level around the walls of the second-floor bathroom:

> WHEN YOU WATCH THE FILM VERTIGO, ARE YOU SCOTTIE WANTING MADELINE, OR ARE YOU MADELEINE WANTING SCOTTIE TO WANT YOU? OR BOTH? ALTERNATELY OR SIMULTANEOUSLY? IN WHAT PROPORTIONS AND INTENSITIES?
>
> Two photos, one with Scottie, and the other with Madeleine projected onto my face, were printed in multiples and arranged in a variety of configurations on the bathroom walls, and the backs of the stall doors were painted white so people could respond to the question. In addition, a text describing the installation's intent was installed over the sink. Within one month of the opening, three-quarters of the photos were torn off the wall, remarks had spread from the doors to the bathroom walls and the name. Scottie was removed from the running text. The photo-text installation had become a text installation.[50]

Since the piece was installed in the non-art context of the public bathroom at the Community Center, Salo could assume that most of the audience would be lesbians. And because of the "saturated space," which suggested illicit or secret sex, an erotic tone was created not only to explore but to express anonymously one's own intimate fantasies and desires. There was no need to be politically correct here. In its encouragement and incorporation of graffiti, the piece involved the lesbian audience in a dialogue not only about the construction of lesbian identity and the nature of lesbian desire and fantasy, but about art and politics.

Among the graffiti responses to Salo's installation:

I'm usually Madeleine, but sometimes I feel as though I should be Scottie.

I'm me wanting Kim.

We all want Kim, and she wants us.

I don't feel compelled to be either one.

Actually I'm Scarlet wanting Melanie, Melanie wanting Sue Ellen, Sue Ellen wanting Mammy, all simultaneously.

I just want tongue.

I won't answer this question because it's a sexist movie about a man who molds a woman to his wishes, against hers.

Lighten up, *Vertigo*'s a great film.

I'm Liz, wanting dicks out of dykeland.

Lesbian visibility now.

Why is a man's picture in a woman's bathroom?

She's talking about images we get from heterosexist society. Who are we? Who tells us who we are? Do we believe them as sister A. does or hate them as sister B. does, or wonder about them as the artist does?

Madeleine wanting Scottie to want her is classic female submission. I understand this piece was done by a *heterosexual* woman. Why? It shows!

One would think from all this that lesbians were the most narrow-minded individuals on the planet. Go back to your island.

I'd love to.

Why won't anyone answer the woman's question? Me, I'm Scottie wanting Madeleine. I'm a bull dyke and I always identify with the boys in the movies.

Who the hell are you to indicate we're men with movie pictures?

We're lesbians. I'm glad this shit was ripped off our walls. Don't invade our lesbianism.

Are you so fucking insecure that you can't stand to see art that doesn't appeal to the lowest common denominator of dykedom? Can't stand a little bit of ambiguity? A little complexity? The dykes who destroyed this exhibit are an embarrassment. Grow up women.

Put a paintbrush in a dyke's hand and there's a mess.

Whether you like art or not, it's not right to destroy it.

Free speech for all.
Amen.
A women.
Stop censoring art work.
Keep your stupid hands off the walls. Offended dyke.
Censorship = death.
I would *never* put my art on a toilet seat. Then you're obviously not an artist.[51]

Drawing the Line [1988–2015], an interactive photo exhibit by Kiss and Tell (a three-woman collective from Vancouver), is somewhat similar to Salo's *Vertigo* in its focus on roles and the incorporation of viewer participation. But it's more confrontational and controversial because it specifically addresses issues of sexuality and censorship while exploring the borders between pornography and erotica. Is there a difference? Where is the line between the two? Where are you uncomfortable and why?

Drawing the Line consists of one hundred 11 × 14 in. black-and-white photographs of the same two women (from the collective, but not lovers in real life; the third collective member is the photographer). They are engaged in a range of sexual or sexualized activities—from hugging to making love in the bathtub, kissing and cunnilingus to butch/femme role-playing, fist-fucking, S/M, and bondage. The images move from gentle, soft, and tender to hard, stylized, and sado-masochistic as they question lines between pleasure and pain, power and trust.

The viewer is asked to comment on the images by writing on the walls around the photographs. "The comments form part of the piece. Women mark their comments directly on the wall. Men's comments are in a book mounted near the end of the photo series. The book contains prints of the 3 × 5 in. photos in the order they appear on the wall, and room for longer commentary. Men's and women's voices are separate in acknowledgement of our historically different relationship to sexually explicit images. The resultant dialogue—among men, among women, between models—is multileveled."[52]

We are asked to form opinions about sexual imagery and what can go public. Do we draw the line at the sexual practice or at its representation? What is politically correct sex? What is your secret desire? What is a turn on? Are images exploitative only if women were exploited while making them? The comments proved to be far more interesting than the photographs themselves, which are provocative and transgressive simply because we don't usually see public images of explicit lesbian sex. Jan Zita Grover, while applauding the exhibit, has written, "After spending five minutes reading viewer reactions, it's impossible to believe that photographs have any fixed meaning—instead, we see in them what we want or need to see."[53]

Lines were drawn in many different places. What was highly erotic to one woman was boring, threatening, or violent to another. "Woman has sex organs just about everywhere," writes French feminist writer Luce Irigaray. "She experiences pleasure almost everywhere. The geography of her pleasure is much more diversified, more multiple in its differences, more subtle, more complex than is imagined." The diversity of responses in *Drawing the Line* spoke of "choice," and "constructed a female subject as the site of difference, not a fragmentary subject, but one that is whole, with differences intact."[54] However, the representation of two women engaged in sexual or sexualized activity is extremely problematic, for traditionally lesbians have been portrayed as objects for male fantasies of lesbian eroticism. This consuming eye of spectatorship is wonderfully spoofed in Joyce Kozloff's watercolor *Inside the Amber Palace or the Pasha Peeks* [1987] from the *Pornament Is Crime* series where, in the middle of sexual embellishment and ornamentation of the Turkish bath, one woman is going down on another, under the ever-present watchful eye of the Pasha who is getting off on it. Unlike gay men, who have been able to depict differing modes of sexual practice for their own pleasure, lesbians have had difficulty escaping the ever-present male gaze.

To paraphrase Martha Gever, the important issue is how to get past this—how to get free from the male gaze, to reconfigure the terms of lesbian representation to negate the past stereotypes and to create a new erotic self, or, as Lucy Lippard puts it, to "depict what the male gaze cannot see."[55] To date, most erotic art, like pornography, has been rooted in photography and thus in figuration. While *Drawing the Line* with its walls of impassioned text subverted old frameworks of photography, minimizing passive voyeurism and appropriation, the photos could be consumed by any viewer, male or female, straight or gay. To try to get around this problem posed by figuration, lesbian artists have been employing a range of devices and strategies that have been only partially successful: blurring, overlaying, superimposing, fragmenting, abstracting, or symbolizing. For instance, in order "to imply sexuality between women without actually showing it," Tee Corinne has used solarized abstract images of body parts, or sexually symbolic images as stand-ins for women. A photo like *Women Eating Flowers* [1979] is really about women eating women.[56]

This hesitation, shared by many lesbian artists, to depict explicit lesbian sex comes from the fact that often we don't know and can't control who is in the viewing audience. Cindy Patton, who has been exploring a "pornographic vernacular"—gay and lesbian porn films and videos—as vehicles for safe sex education, talked about her ambivalence at showing a lesbian sex tape to accompany a lecture she was giving at Duke University, where the audience was mostly straight white men. Because she wasn't sure what it meant for them to see lesbians "doing it," she censored herself, and stopped short of showing the tape.[57] I, too, frequently find myself in similar situations when I give slide presentations of work by lesbian artists. If the audience is mixed (male-female) I feel very uncomfortable showing images of female genitals or women engaged in sexual or sexualized activities. While I want to claim a public lesbian erotic space in the way that gay men have been able to do, I find that I also want to protect our bodies from spectatorship and consumerism.

This hesitation may also reflect our hesitancy to limit our pleasure, for to rely on boundaries of figuration may restrict the erotic invention. Perhaps it is the invention that turns us on. Lesbian pleasure is multiple and not fixed, and I would suggest that it is precisely in this unfixedness that the lesbian erotic is located. I have long been interested in the potential of erotic abstraction in which the body part or sexual act is not depicted but rather referenced from a combination of abstract form, and the associations and physical manipulations of the materials themselves. For instance, human hair off the body always has sexual overtones, and a material like latex rubber usually suggests skin or body fluids. Since materials can reflect marginalization and minimal forms can evoke emotional states, abstraction offers the possibility of an erotic art that bypasses the problematics of figuration. Instead of focusing on the figure with its fixed contour and impermeable surface of skin, abstraction opens up time and space, allowing us (other women/lesbians) to feel/respond sexually "in the body" (versus "to the figure") to what we see. And since the lesbian gaze is not focused on the "image of orgasm" but rather on how it feels, it can avoid the male gaze and be extended indefinitely.

My own wrapped rag sculptures of the late '70s and early '80s were intended to create a lesbian sensual/sexual presence in the world. They were not about mummifying, binding, or bandaging, but rather about making something out of itself from the inside out, with the insides showing on the outside—a kind of presence as essence made visible. I thought of works such as *Adelphi* [1979], *Durango* [1979], *Grasping Affection* [1981–82], and *Radiant Affection* [1983–84] as lesbian pieces not so much because of the female body parts they referenced, but rather because of the visual qualities and manipulation of materials to convey the interior female body—the muscle, tissue, membrane, fluid body. While related to the work of Eva Hesse and Louise Bourgeois, at the time I made them I was thinking about Wittig. The sculptures, like Wittig's book *The Lesbian Body* [1973], created a raw, passionate, and sometimes violent sexuality, a body (re)membered and whole, taking up a space beyond its physical space. Beautiful and powerful.[58]

In my large-scale mixed-media installation paintings such as *Inappropriate Longings* [1992; see plate 16], old fragments of linoleum are pieced together and combined with paint and latex rubber surfaces as a kind of excavation of memory. The words "goddamn dyke" incised into the rubber skin suggest a narrative of emotional and sexual violence within the domestic site. Gutters and water troughs normally used to collect water become a metaphor for circulatory systems of life fluids which are dysfunctional, empty, or clogged with dried leaves. The crime is not clear. Who or what was violated? By whom? And why? Is the murder real, fiction, or fantasy? Is it self-inflicted? The installation suggests a narrative but does not provide closure.

Because of the metaphoric possibilities a good number of lesbian artists are working in installation, often combining photographic images or elements of text along with a range of painting and sculptural materials. This loosely defined territory which can also include time-based arts (sound, light, film, video, performance) allows for a range of identities and sensibilities and the possibility of not just making work about being lesbian but rather making it from the perspective of being lesbian, and in this way totally reconfiguring lesbian representation. As sites, bodies, interiors, exteriors, danger, and pleasure combine, dissolve, and splinter, bodies of knowledge are constructed, and lesbian experience and identities can be suggested without being fixed or consumed.

Mindy Mills, a young artist and ex-student of mine, incorporates cropped images of women engaged in various sexual activities on fragments of ortho film along with found and weathered materials from the streets, vacant city lots, and construction sites. The photo fragments combine with nails, burnt wood, metal lathe, cement, wire, and light to create a shadowy and dangerous site of destruction, deconstruction, and construction. It is a heightened, intense environment where sexuality can be felt lurking and shifting but, because of the fragmented images, cannot be possessed. While she runs the risk that everyone may not recognize the images as that of two women sexually involved, to most lesbians the space is all too recognizable and familiar. Seemingly about power and survival, her site of desire is a dangerous place to enter in that it speaks of unclear boundaries between pain and pleasure, disintegration and (re)membering. No matter how one identifies sexually, one cannot relax here for a moment—to enter this space is dangerous because there is no sure footing.

Sallie McCorkle's formal bench installations suggest a tension between separation and integration. In a funky little Brooklyn waterfront park, McCorkle turned a bench into a one-person fortress looking out at the Manhattan skyline. The piece emphasizes the overwhelming sense of isolation that a lesbian and/

or artist might have while gazing out at the large city of New York, where "It's all happening." In contrast, *Bench: A Long Seat for Two or More Persons* [1991] is about camaraderie. The piece incorporates a 1920 photo of women workers who are holding hands inside each other's pockets. Not particularly interested in questions of sexual identity, McCorkle speaks of the need for women, lesbians, and gays to bond together "to embrace each other and create stronger voices." By providing diagrams and instructions for building the bench she is "saying that you too can make the bench and we can all sit there, or, we can make the bench together."[59]

Martha Fleming and Lyne Lapointe have worked together on large-scale site-specific works in Montreal since 1983. Renovating old abandoned buildings that are charged with emotional and ideological meanings—such as former warehouses, museums, post offices, and theaters—as sites to combine architecture, objects, text, light, sound, and performance, Fleming and Lapointe have been able to construct fictions that suggest social structures and their effects on the lives of under- or devalued peoples such as women, lesbians, the mentally ill, or criminals.

In an unusual installation at the New Museum in New York City, they "propose a quest for sites of pleasure." *Eat Me/Drink Me/Love Me* was based on "Goblin Market," a highly erotic "allegorical poem of feminine temptation and redemption" by the nineteenth-century poet Christina Rossetti.[60] Fleming and Lapointe created a "haven of sensual delight," a country home with bowls of fruit, baskets of coal, branches of red berries, and secret gardens. Portraits of Rossetti and her contemporary Emily Dickinson were placed in the entry to this domestic space, where "women have traditionally enjoyed each other," thus alluding to passionate bonds for women expressed in Rossetti's and Dickinson's poetry. The lush seductive ambience with its images of bees and flies suggested that "abandonment may lead to liberating possibilities," and a curious buzzing sound heightened the erotic sense, alluding to passionate bonds between women and a lesbian subtext in the form of an "impossible love affair."

Catherine Saalfield and Zoe Leonard's collaborative piece *Outlaws* [1991] takes up "the lesbian as both spoken and speaking," and was created out of a fold-away bed with sheets and pillowcases printed with drafts of proposed antigay legislation. A television next to the bed alternates images of two women making love with ACT UP demonstration footage. "Outlaws suggests both the repressive codes and resistances to them."[61]

As much of this work demonstrates, the field of gender and sexuality is wide open and is occupied by a proliferation of identities. If in a sense "all gender is drag," where men and women impersonate an ideal that no one inhabits, then sexuality, too, is called into question.[62] Lesbian artists are not only challenging the hegemonic, heterosexual regime, but also disrupting and destabilizing many established codes of representation. The art is not stuck on the margins, but free to move about. If, indeed, as Foucault suggests, "our sexuality is *something we make* in our everyday experimentation with sex and pleasure," then the diverse and shifting nature of lesbian identity as it is reflected and constructed in art continues to occupy a space of infinite and pleasurable possibilities.[63] . . .

ED. NOTE

"A Space of Infinite and Pleasurable Possibilities: Lesbian Self-Representation in Visual Art" was first published in *New Feminist Criticism: Art/Identity/Action*, ed. Joanna Frueh, Cassandra Langer, and Arlene Raven (New York: Icon Editions/Harper Collins, 1994), 97–131. The essay is based on an earlier keynote address at the Mid-America College Art Association (MACAA), Tucson, Arizona, 1990. The published version, including the author's endnotes, has been slightly revised for inclusion in this volume.

The numbered endnotes for this essay, below, are by the author.

NOTES

1. I mean more than a superficial acknowledgment, more than merely adding it to what Kobena Mercer has called the "mantra of race, class and gender." Kobena Mercer, "Skin Head Sex Thing: Racial Difference and the Homoerotic Imaginary," in *How Do I Look? Queer Film and Video*, ed. Bad Object-Choices (Seattle: Bay Press, 1991).

2. Martha Gever, "The Names We Give Ourselves," in *Out There: Marginalization and Contemporary Cultures*, ed. Russell Ferguson, Martha Gever, Trinh T. Minh-ha, and Cornel West (Cambridge, MA: MIT Press, 1990), 191.

3. Trinh T. Minh-ha, *Woman, Native, Other: Writing Postcoloniality and Feminism* (Bloomington: Indiana University Press, 1989), 6.

4. Trinh T. Minh-ha, *Framer Framed* (New York: Routledge, 1992), 186.

5. Trinh, *Woman, Native, Other*, 28.

6. This is a variation on Bertha Harris's statement, "The great service of literature is to show us who we are," in "What We Mean to Say: Notes Towards Defining the Nature of Lesbian Literature," *Heresies: A Feminist Publication on Art and Politics*, no. 3 (Fall 1977): 6.

7. Critic Lucy Lippard has repeatedly made this statement in numerous lectures on multiculturalism and the arts.

8. Audre Lorde, "Age, Race, Class, and Sex: Women Redefining Difference," in Ferguson et al., *Out There*, 282.

9. Jeff Weinstein quoted by Edmund White, panel discussion, November 29, 1982, "Extended Sensibilities: The Impact of Homosexual Sensibilities on Contemporary Culture," New York. Sponsored by the New Museum of Contemporary Art in conjunction with their exhibition (October 16–December 30, 1982), *Extended Sensibilities: Homosexual Presence in Contemporary Art*, curated by Daniel Cameron. Panel transcript published

in Russell Ferguson, William Olander, Marcia Tucker, and Karen Fiss, eds., *Discourses: Conversations in Postmodern Art and Culture* (Cambridge, MA: MIT Press, 1990), 92.

10. Kate Millett, panel discussion, "Extended Sensibilities."

11. Stuart Hall quoted by Gever, "The Names We Give Ourselves," 193.

12. Michel Foucault, in Bob Gallagher and Alexander Wilson, "Sex and the Politics of Identity: An Interview with Michel Foucault," in *Gay Spirit: Myth and Meaning*, ed. Mark Thompson (New York: St. Martin's Press, 1987), 29.

13. Gallagher and Wilson, "An Interview with Foucault," 25, 28.

14. Gallagher and Wilson, "An Interview with Foucault," 26.

15. Arlene Stein, "Sisters and Queers: The Decentering of Lesbian Feminism," *Socialist Review* 22, no. 1 (January–March 1992): 33–55.

16. Jill Johnston quoted in Stein, "Sisters and Queers," 34.

17. Jan Zita Grover, "Dykes in Context: Some Problems in Minority Representation," in *The Contest of Meaning: Critical Histories of Photography*, ed. Richard Bolton (Cambridge, MA: MIT Press, 1990).

18. Louise Fishman, personal letter to Harmony Hammond, 1992.

19. Terry Wolverton, "Portraying Sexuality: Young Artists Are Transforming the World of Lesbian Art," *The Advocate* 574 (April 9, 1991): 70–74.

20. Grover, "Dykes in Context," 165.

21. Barbara Asch, "Statements by Lesbian Artists," in *A Lesbian Show*, exh. cat. (New York: 112 Greene Street Workshop, 1978).

22. Monique Wittig, "The Straight Mind." Text [was] first read in New York at the Modern Language Association Convention, 1978. It was later printed in *Monique Wittig: The Straight Mind and Other Essays* (Boston: Beacon Press, 1992). The ideas I've presented are drawn and quoted from Wittig's "The Straight Mind" and "One Is Not Born a Woman," presented at the Second Sex Conference in 1979, [. . .] along with "Paradigm: What Have You Done with Our Desire?," in *Homosexualities and French Literature: Cultural Contexts/Critical Texts*, ed. George Stambolian and Elaine Marks (Ithaca, NY: Cornell University Press, 1979).

23. Stein, "Sisters and Queers," 54. These shifts are also documented in Lillian Faderman, *Odd Girls and Twilight Lovers: A History of Lesbian Life in Twentieth-Century America* (New York: Penguin, 1992).

24. Stein, "Sisters and Queers," 55; Carole Vance, ed., *Pleasure and Danger: Exploring Female Sexuality* (Boston: Routledge and Kegan Paul, 1984), papers presented at the Scholar and the Feminist IX Conference, April 24, 1982, at Barnard College, New York City; Hannah Alderfer, Beth Jaker, and Marybeth Nelson, *Diary of a Conference on Sexuality* (New York: Barnard College, 1982), published in conjunction with the ninth "Scholar and the Feminist" conference, "Towards a Politics of Sexuality," held at Barnard College on April 24, 1982; Feminist Anti-Censorship Task Force, *Caught Looking: Feminism, Pornography and Censorship*, 2nd ed. (Seattle: Real Comet Press, 1988), essays and visuals compiled 1976–86.

25. Stein, "Sisters and Queers," 55.

26. Lucy Lippard, "Both Sides Now (a Reprise)," *Heresies: A Feminist Publication on Art and Politics* 6, no. 24 (1989): 34, 30.

27. Cassandra L. Langer, "The Queer Show," in *Woman Artist News*, Winter 1991.

28. It should be said, however, that the Wessel O'Connor Gallery has primarily and consistently supported and exhibited work by gay men and lesbians that deals with queer identity. Unfortunately, it and the shorter-lived Penine Hart Gallery are temporarily closed as of this writing. Other galleries that regularly exhibit lesbian and gay art include Feature, Trial Balloon (lesbian), Fiction/Nonfiction, PPOW, Paula Cooper, and Mary Boone in New York and New Langston Arts in San Francisco.

29. Press release for *All but the Obvious: A Program of Lesbian Art*, LACE, Los Angeles, 1990.

30. Terry Wolverton, "Generations of Lesbian Art," *High Performance*, Spring 1991, 10.

31. See Pam Gregg, *All but the Obvious*, exh. cat., ed. Catherine Lord (Los Angeles, LACE, 1990), n.p.

32. Gregg, *All but the Obvious.*

33. Wolverton, "Generations of Lesbian Art," 10. While Wolverton states that there are three artists of color in this exhibit, it seems that there might have been four. However, the point of inadequate representation is the same. I [Harmony Hammond] wish to point out here that *A Lesbian Show* in New York in 1978 did not include work by any lesbian artists of color and was rightly criticized for not doing so. I curated that exhibit, and while several artists were invited to participate, they chose not to for various personal reasons. While this was a serious shortcoming of the exhibit, dialogues were started that have continued throughout the years and encouraged artists of color to participate in future lesbian exhibitions and art projects. Betsy Damon, who organized the accompanying performances and readings, was also criticized for not including enough lesbians of color. Since there were many writers and performers eager to participate, the program was opened up and many events by lesbians of color were scheduled every night for the duration of the exhibit. It should be noted that Damon has continuously been committed to encouraging and facilitating the participation of artists of color throughout the feminist art world, and in particular the Women's Caucus for Art of the College Art Association. I mention this because I think that racism is something that we all continue to work on over a period of time, that the ongoing process of self-examination and dialoguing is crucial to activism, and that sometimes the means are more important than the immediate situation and ultimately move toward long-range goals.

34. Wolverton, "Generations of Lesbian Art," 11.

35. Judith Butler raises such questions in "The Body You Want," interview with Liz Kotz, *Art Forum*, November 1992, 85.

36. Carla Trujillo, ed., *Chicana Lesbians: The Girls Our Mothers Warned Us About* (Berkeley, CA: Third Woman Press, 1991).

37. Artists working with lesbian identity in their work include painters (Monica Majoli, Maxine Fine, Marlene McCarty, Nicole Eisenman, Lutz Bacher, Hollis Sigler, Margo Pelletier, Deborah Kass, Fran Winant, Shelley Marlow, and Beverly Rhoades) and sculptors (Carol Hepper, Julia Kunin, and Linda Matalon).

38. Quotes in this paragraph from Deborah Bright, "Dream Girls," in *Stolen Glances: Lesbians Take Photographs*, ed. Tessa Boffin and Jean Fraser (London: Pandora, 1991), 151, 154.

39. Liz Kotz, "Strategics for Lesbian Representation: Kaucyila Brooke's Photography," *Camerawork Quarterly*, Summer 1990.

40. Kaucyila Brooke, artist's statement, n.d.

41. Joanna Frueh, "How Do You Play? The Deviant Narratives of Kaucyila Brooke," *After Image* 17, no. 9 (April 1990): 4.

42. Brooke, artist's statement.

43. See Della Grace, *Love Bites: Photographs* (London: GMP, 1991).

44. Gail Shepherd, "Positive Images," *Women's Review of Books*, no. 5 (February 1992): 11.

45. David Bonetti, "Things Are Not What They Seem," *San Francisco Examiner*, February 28, 1992, 44.

46. Terry Wolverton, "Thoroughly Post Modern Millie," *The Advocate*, November 20, 1990, page unknown.

47. Wolverton, "Thoroughly Post Modern Millie."

48. Zoe Leonard quoted by Faye Hirsch, "A Spy in the Museum," *QW*, May 24, 1992, page unknown.

49. See Grover, "Dykes in Context."

50. Marcia Salo, *Vertigo*, women's bathroom, Gay and Lesbian Community Center, New York City, October 14, 1989.

51. Marcia Salo, graffiti responding to *Vertigo*, women's bathroom, Gay and Lesbian Community Center, New York City, October 14, 1989.

52. Kiss and Tell Collective (Persimmon Blackbridge, Lizard Jones, Susan Stewart), statement for *Drawing the Line*, n.d. Some of the photos and comments are available as a book, *Drawing the Line: Lesbian Sexual Politics on the Wall* (Vancouver: Press Gant, 1991).

53. Jan Zita Grover, "Drawing the Line," *Outlook*, no. 10 (Fall 1990): page unknown.

54. Marusia Bociurkiw, "The Transgressive Camera," *Afterimage*, January 1989, 19. Bociurkiw quotes Irigaray as cited in Rosalind Jones, "Writing the Body," *Feminist Studies* 2 (1981).

55. See Gever, "The Names We Give Ourselves." Lippard, "Both Sides Now (a Reprise)," 29.

56. Jan Zita Grover, "Framing the Questions: Positive Imaging and Scarcity in Lesbian Photographs," in Boffin and Fraser, *Stolen Glances*, 184.

57. See Cindy Patton, "Safe Sex and the Pornographic Vernacular," in *How Do I Look? Queer Film and Video*, ed. Bad Object Choices (Seattle: Bay Press, 1991).

58. See Monique Wittig, *The Lesbian Body* (New York: Avon, 1976).

59. David Hirsch, "Isolation and Sharing," *New York Native*, July 8, 1991, page unknown.

60. Quotes in this paragraph are from Alice Yang, catalogue essay in *Eat Me/Drink Me/Love Me: An Installation by Martha Fleming and Lyne Lapointe* (New York: New Museum for Contemporary Art, 1990).

61. Marcia Salo, "Particles in Motion: Lesbian Thermodynamics," catalogue essay in *Outrageous Desire* (New Brunswick, NJ: Rutgers University, 1991), n.p.

62. See Liz Kotz, "The Body You Want: An Interview with Judith Butler," *Artforum* 31, no. 3 (November 1992).

63. Foucault paraphrased by Gallagher and Wilson, "Sex and the Politics of Identity," 27.

Against Cultural Amnesia

Art Papers (1994)

Cultural amnesia seems to have reached epidemic proportions. Everyone, including lesbians, is acting like the '70s didn't exist. For examples of this (dis) ease, we have only to look as far as the "Bad Girls" exhibitions in New York and Los Angeles, which chose not to acknowledge the groundbreaking generative feminist work of the '70s and to heterosexualize that lesbian work which was included, or the curatorial scope and political economy of the many queer exhibitions of the Gay '90s, including the ten or so group exhibitions in New York independently organized to accompany the twenty-fifth anniversary of the Stonewall rebellion of 1969.[1]

Instead of taking the opportunity to document and celebrate a historical tradition of lesbian, gay, and queer visual art in New York, the curators of these exhibitions (mostly gay men) chose to participate in [the] commodification of queer culture by showing the same few artists—mostly young, newly emerged, and represented by dealers. This is not a criticism aimed at the artists, their gallery representation, or the artworks themselves, but rather a statement about lost opportunity and the privileging of the relationship of curator and dealer over artists and their work to community, thus leaving, once again, lesbian, gay, and queer art dehistoricized—visual fragments floating without context.

I am tired of everyone saying that there was no lesbian art in the '70s when in fact there was. One has only to look as far as the "Lesbian Art and Artists" issue of *Heresies* magazine (1977), *A Lesbian Show* at the old 112 Greene Street Workshop (1979), *The Great American Lesbian Art Show* (GALAS) at the Women's Building in Los Angeles and its fifty sister exhibits across the country (1980), or the exhibition *Extended Sensibilities: The Homosexual Presence in Contemporary Art* at the New Museum (1982) to find work by real live lesbians—and that's not even touching upon shows and projects at numerous small "gay galleries" or feminist and gay conferences, or work produced and circulated in dyke communities outside the art world. These were not obscure exhibitions but rather conscious dyke interventions from the margins in the central whirlpool of the art mainstream. To not acknowledge these exhibitions is, at the very least, sloppy scholarship and irresponsible curating. It is not just that the mainstream art institutions ignore lesbian, gay, and queer creative histories that is so horrifying but the fact that we are doing it to ourselves.

True, lesbians are often caught between straight feminists and a gay male agenda, but lesbian artists are participating in their own commodification and erasure. I have to say that as a lesbian and an artist who, since the early '70s, has continued to sometimes, but not always, make art about the experience of being lesbian, who has remained through the years as one of the few *out* lesbian voices in the art world, I find it offensive and outrageous that not even one lesbian artist (young or old) has recommended my work for *any* lesbian or queer show in the '90s. It's like I don't exist.

What's happened to the girls' network? We used to have one. I've been around long enough to not take it personally, because I know that it has very little to do with me or my work. It's about deprivation. Poverty. Now that there seems to be a piece of the slimy hetero pie set aside for dykes in the art world, politics are out the window and competition is rampant in the girls' ranks. Interestingly, the attention I receive as an art writer is the complete opposite. No one needs another artist to compete with, but everyone wants another critic (to write about their work). The message is old and clear, and the girls are doing it too. When will lesbian artists realize that the artist you don't recommend, don't include, is yourself? Every silence is your own erasure.

Contrary to what popular, fine art, and even queer media would have you believe, lesbian art and artists did not emerge by virgin birth overnight. Many of us have been here making work, wrestling with issues of lesbian subjectivity for a long time. I've never thought of myself as one of the "old girls," but now, somehow as an "older artist" (and I say this ironically as the "other" of the younger), I feel a responsibility to set the record, well not straight, but accurate, or once again I and others will be erased and our work denied an existence.

Because I have been out and around for so long, I am finding that I am a "historical voice." This puts me in a dilemma, for while I believe that the collective historical voice is very important—precisely because we haven't had one—and I feel a responsibility to tell our creative history as I know it, I do not want to invest in nostalgia, to be locked into the past. As an artist and writer, not to mention a lover of women, I am actively and pleasurably engaged in the present moment even as it is shifting. My feminism, like my work, is informed by the '70s, '80s, and '90s and continues to change. In the past, I have frequently functioned as a kind of bridge, insisting on a lesbian consciousness and presence in the primarily straight feminist art world, and bringing an art consciousness into dyke communities, some more receptive to art than others. Now I am seeing myself as some sort of bridge between generations. Bridges, like history, like art, allow for meetings, crossings, mergings. Moving into new time, space, territories.

These days it's easy to be a queer artist. It's in to be out. Whether anyone admits it or not, the new generation of lesbian artists (those who have emerged since 1988) have inherited a lot from radical feminism and the gay liberation movement. Bearing in mind the linguistic and ideologic dangers of constructing oneself in opposition to the so-called normative within binary systems of gender and sexuality (the other of man, the other of heterosexuality), or sounding like I accept the existence of an "I," preformed and separate from cultural and social forces (which I don't), let me just say that "difference" is an old queer discussion but that the strategies of (re)presentation are new.

Because art both reflects and contributes to ever-shifting definitions of lesbian identity, it can be seen to mirror the desexualization of lesbian feminism in the '70s and early '80s, the exploration of lesbian fantasy and desire in the late '80s, and the assertion of sexuality as central to lesbian identity in the '90s. It's not about locating or defining an essential lesbian aesthetic, but rather looking at art by self-identified lesbians, to see what forms it takes, what issues it addresses, what it tells us about individual and collective lesbian lives, and how it interfaces with larger social, political, and cultural fields. To look at and discuss art being made today, we must examine it in relationship to earlier art and our own cultural history.

If, from today's perspective, much of the work from the '70s looks raw, tentative, undeveloped, romantic, or conservative—often not even overtly lesbian—it must be remembered that to be in these early shows, to exhibit as a lesbian, took strength and courage and was a radical gesture not to be underestimated. It made one's personal life public, and artists risked aesthetic stereotyping or dismissal of their work. At least one artist was threatened by her gay male dealer: If she exhibited "as a lesbian," she could say goodbye to the gallery's exhibition and representation of her work. While artists were interested in discovering or defining an essential lesbian sensibility, in the end, exhibits like the one at 112 Greene Street simply presented a diverse range of work by artists willing to be public about their sexual preferences and willing to show in a lesbian context. Thus, these early exhibitions and projects were primarily successful in creating, for the first time ever, a public lesbian presence in visual art, and commencing dialogues on sexuality and art within the artworld and feminist, lesbian, and gay communities.

This is so different from today, when much "lesbian art" is made specifically to be circulated within the art world, where whole careers based on producing lesbian art are made overnight, or where lesbian and/or queer readings of the work are encouraged or manipulated by artists and their dealers, even when the artist is not lesbian-identified. To those of us who have been out there for a long time, to paraphrase Audre Lorde, living and loving in the trenches, this is a very bizarre phenomenon, raising issues of "authenticity," similar but not exactly parallel to new age claims of "being Indian."[2] Obviously both "lesbian" and "artist" remain unstable identities open to change, interpretation, and to a certain degree, self-construction. The question remains: Does sexuality shape subjectification in visual art—and if so, how? This lingering question both assumes and proposes categories of difference. The answer refuses articulation. In fact, it is precisely the unruly, messy, rough edges, which don't or won't fit into clean contours of identity, which go against the grain, that create potential erotic and creative sites—spaces where I would argue the best art is made.

While '70s gender-based definitions of politically correct lesbianism depicted women through abstract landscape symbols or within domestic environments, hinting at fantasies and possible seductions without ever actually depicting sexual or sexualized activities, most of the new '90s work reasserts the right to move back and forth freely between high and low art, and assumes the right to all images, including those generated in art history, popular culture, cartoons and comics, medical texts, fashion, advertising, and pornography. While much of the work is humorous, it is also intensely serious—depending of course on who is doing the looking.

At the same time, some of the iconography of work being made today seems remarkably indebted to earlier feminist and lesbian feminist image-making. A closer look, however, often reveals subtle and interesting differences. Because the artistic, social, political, and economic climate has changed, the work is created, presented, and discussed within a different contextual framework which then, in turn, becomes part of the meaning of the pieces.

For the purpose of this article, I'd like to present two examples of visual art from the '90s that can be discussed in relationship to work by artists from the '70s.[3] This comparison is not meant to say that certain works are better or more authentic than others, but rather to utilize a feminist historical framework to enrich the discourse around lesbian art.

In the 1970s Joan Semmel, a straight-identified feminist, presented close-up views looking down at her own middle-aged, unidealized body which became a kind of sensuous landscape of folds, creases, swellings, wrinkles, and stretch marks filling the pictorial space. What she/we can see is framed by the canvas edge, as if to show us an intimate secret. Semmel was trying to paint the female body from the object's eye, object and subject becoming one.

Patricia Cronin is among a group of emerging lesbian artists who are overtly and subjectively depicting all kinds of lesbian sexual practices in their art—images we have not seen before in the history of Western art. Cronin's watercolors, of a woman with her hand or fist up another's vagina, inserting a dildo, or going down on a second woman, are, like Semmel's paintings, depicted from the subject's point of view (Cronin switches from top to bottom in different paintings), with the subject's field of vision marked by the painting edge, however the visual indication of a second woman's presence lesbianizes the narrative. Thus, one way Cronin's work can be seen and discussed is as a lesbian extension of early feminist concerns to subjectify the female body and female sexuality, in this case lesbianizing it.

In 1974 Tee Corinne started her series of "non-traditional portraits"—close-up photographic images of labia and clits of friends who posed for her. Intimate and beautiful, sometimes printed in sepia tones and framed in oval mats, these photographs were nontraditional because they imaged women's sexual bodies from a lesbian point of view. On another level though, they were about placing lesbian lives and culture within traditions of photography and family portraiture. Combining and subverting histories of lesbian erotic photography (usually done by men) and lesbian portraiture (snapshots by dykes of friends and lovers), her photos were meant for lesbian viewing pleasure and were exhibited or published primarily in woman-only or lesbian contexts. Because the artist publicly identifies herself as lesbian, the work is aimed toward a lesbian audience, and the intended viewer (woman) is also the object of the gaze (a second woman), a viewing dynamic is created that makes the pieces "lesbian." It should be noted that Corinne, over the years, has tried to find ways to avoid male voyeurism and appropriation of images of lesbians, to imply a sexuality without necessarily showing it. In other works, she has used solarized abstract images of body parts or sexually symbolic images such as flowers as stand-ins for women.

For the 1992 *Documenta* [IX], in Kassel, Germany, Zoe Leonard created a series of spread-leg photographs of women friends' genitalia, and casually tacked them up on walls between eighteenth- and nineteenth-century paintings in the [Neue Gallerie, one of the city's fine art] museums. While Leonard's images of cunts are not new to the '90s (there seems to be a resurgence of interest in vaginas) and continues a body of work begun by earlier feminists and lesbian feminists such as Corinne, the context is decidedly different.

In contrast to Corinne's placement of her images in woman-only venues, Leonard inserts hers into what is traditionally male space. The fact that she inserts her "pussy shots" into the historical museum system underscores the hypocrisy of so-called neutral art by men that depicts women as sex objects, thereby implying a male subject, allows Leonard to participate in the contemporary critique of the cultural institutions of authority, and opens a space for the "cruising eye" of the lesbian viewer in those institutions. The piece works best as a "taking of public female space," and a very prestigious one at that—one Corinne and other lesbians in the '70s and '80s didn't have access to. While some people have criticized Leonard's intervention as "queer opportunism," the work is an extension of her early concerns, and I think it is to her credit that she utilized her privileged "inclusion" in the male-dominated *Documenta* to present this highly charged "female work." I say "female" because despite the conceptual underpinnings of the work and her intent to minimize or challenge male spectatorship and allow for possible lesbian readings of the work, Leonard's images, like Corinne's, in and of themselves are still vulnerable and open to appropriation by the male gaze.

Hopefully, these two comparisons suggest ways of looking at lesbian visual art and begin to develop a critical and theoretical discussion that links our work to earlier practices and situates this dialogue firmly within feminist discourse. To date, queer theory has not brought lesbians into the visual field. Lesbian visual discourse has to build on what Laura Cottingham has stated is "perhaps the only genuine mass art movement that has occurred in the United States during this century." Cottingham quotes [a letter to the editor of *The Guardian* by Rosalyn Baxandall, a member of the feminist-activist Red Stockings] saying "The Women's Movement began because we're tired of not being taken seriously."[4] This is still the battle. Obviously, if we wish not to be ignored or erased, and wish to be taken seriously, we lesbians must insist on our history, and develop a generative dialogue around and informed by the work. The Drawing Center panel discussion "Representing Lesbian Subjectivity" and subsequent issue of *Art Papers* are steps in this direction and important specifically because they are happening within the art world context.

But the steps are slippery. In the last year and a half, the heterosexual media have taken it upon themselves to present palatable images of lesbians, so depoliticized and so desexualized (except for those images acceptable to the hetero-imperative of the male gaze), who, as Jodi Kelber has noted, are "too chic to fuck," lesbians who are so mainstreamed that they leave heterosexuality intact—what Deb Schwartz writing in *The Village Voice* has called "lesbian lite" or "radical lite."[5] Placing us in the context of "fashion" ignores and trivializes lesbian lives and experiences, and hides the real histories of survival, resistance, and creative expression around gender and sexual difference.

Now that lesbians have been "discovered," we lesbian artists who have been neglected for so long will have to step carefully to get the attention that is due our work without being co-opted in the process—and it may not be so easy. Exhibits like *Bad Girls*, which reinscribe heterosexuality as normative, and exhibitions such as many of those surrounding the twenty-fifth anniversary of Stonewall, which tried to "out queer" each other, deny our creative histories and feed into the art market and a conservative xenophobic political agenda. I agree with the Fierce Pussy Collective when they say, "Fuck 15 minutes of fame."[6]

I see both current mainstream media attempts to appropriate, commodify, and consume the lesbian as spectacle and recent shifts in the art world that have bestowed momentary visibility on a few lesbian artists (white girls of course) as colonialist strategies to domesticate, silence, and ultimately disempower women, queers, and other minorities. Of course this naming, labeling, representing, authorizing, and commodifying is a violent dynamic that other groups who have been first marginalized and then rediscovered on the basis of their difference have had to negotiate. But it is new to us. Just how much real pussy power will be allowed remains to be "seen."

Self-representation (production and discourse) has the possibility of playing an important role in resisting cultural colonization (and thus erasure) and keeping what Jan Zita Grover has called the "hole" lesbian, in all her fluid, layered, messy, and unruly mutations/manifestations intact—that is sexual, creative, political, and powerful.[7] [. . .]

ED. NOTES

"Against Cultural Amnesia" was originally published in *Art Papers* 18, no. 6 (November/ December 1994): 9–11. The essay, including the author's endnotes, has been slightly abridged and revised for publication in this volume.

The numbered endnotes for this essay, below, are by the author.

NOTES

1. Laura Cottingham, *How Many "Bad" Feminists Does It Take to Change a Lightbulb?* (New York: Sixty Percent Solution, 1994). [Ed.: Reprinted in Laura Cottingham, *Seeing Through the Seventies: Essays on Feminism and Art* (Amsterdam: G+B Arts International, 2000).] A brilliant and passionate critique and analysis of the *Bad Girls* exhibitions and catalogues. Independent exhibitions curated to coincide with the twenty-fifth anniversary of Stonewall included well over a dozen group and solo shows, which ranged in curatorial scope. For me, the most interesting was *Absence, Activism and the Body Politic*, curated by Joseph Wolin, at the Fischbach Gallery. The most questionable was *Stonewall 25: Imaginings of the Gay Past, Celebrating the Gay Future*, curated by Bill Arning at White Columns. In their press, it was never mentioned that the original White Columns was actually the old 112 Greene Street Workshop which was the site of the first lesbian art show in New York City (and possibly the United States) in 1978. Thus this exhibition of "romantic nostalgia" by artists who were all children or not yet born at the time of the riots erases its own history.

No venue took on the task of a historical overview of lesbian, gay, and queer art comparable to the important and moving historical, but more general, exhibit at the New York Public Library, *Becoming Visible: The Legacy of Stonewall.* The only exhibit that included a diverse range of artists from the past or outside of the marketplace was *Pride and Our Diversity*, curated by Ronnie Cohen at the 24 Hours for Life Gallery, which is connected to the Lesbian and Gay Community Services Center.

Also, my criticism does not apply to those official exhibitions surrounding Unity '94 (Gay Games and Cultural Festival), such as those organized or curated by Anne Meredith, which were primarily photographic in nature. Anyone could submit their work to these three shows.

2. Because of decades of discrimination, many Indian peoples, until recently, hid the fact that they were Native American. This strikes me as very similar to the discrimination against homosexuals and the resulting secrecy around their lives. Now, with new age trends, not to mention a potential art market, everyone wants to be "Indian" and "queer." Whether or not they really are doesn't seem to matter as non-Indians and heterosexuals appropriate style and content, and promote Indian and queer readings of their work. While I realize that one is born "Indian" (of a specific tribe) and it is not so clear whether one is born or becomes homosexual, both identities raise moral, legal, political, and creative issues around the right to claim identities.

3. It is important to note that many artists from the '70s continue to make work today and thus are also artists of the '90s. However, for the purpose of discussion in this article, I am using examples of work they created in the '70s.

4. Cottingham, *How Many "Bad" Feminists Does It Take to Change a Lightbulb?*

5. Jodi Kelber, "Too Chic to Fuck: The Fashioning of Lesbianism by TV Talk Shows," unpublished paper presented at "Console-ing Passions: Television, Video, and Feminism Symposium" (Tucson, 1994). See Deb Schwartz, "The Days of Wine and Poses: The Media Presents Homosexual Light," *Village Voice*, June 8, 1993, page unknown.

6. Fierce Pussy Collective, broadsheet, 1994. The full text reads: "Fuck 15 minutes of fame. We demand our civil rights. Now." The broadsheet was reproduced as page art in several publications including Cottingham's *How Many "Bad" Feminists Does It Take to Change a Lightbulb?*

7. See Jan Zita Grover, "Dykes in Context: Some Problems in Minority Representation," in *The Contest of Meaning: Critical Histories of Photography*, ed. Richard Bolton (Cambridge, MA: MIT Press, 1990).

A Lesbian Show

In a Different Light: Visual Culture, Sexual Identity, Queer Practice (1995)

The idea for *A Lesbian Show* grew out of the frustration that I and other members of the editorial collective for the "Lesbian Art and Artists" issue of *Heresies* (1977) felt as we found ourselves not only short of information and documentation on the work and lives of lesbian artists of the past but also on contemporary artists working within the context of the feminist art movement. The hetero-sexualization and erasure of work by lesbian artists in both mainstream and feminist art communities was a reality we were forced to confront. While some artists made the decision never to show in the art world, where women much less lesbians were hardly welcome, others remained closeted out of fear that their work would not be taken seriously. It was hard to convince women who were self-identified as lesbians and as artists to place their work in lesbian art contexts.

In response to this situation, I independently proposed an exhibition of lesbian art to the 112 Greene Street Workshop [in New York City]—in those days a truly informal artist-run alternative space that often functioned as a gallery.

Originally planned as a small exhibition, which was not in any way intended to be definitive, but rather simply a sampling and presenting of art by lesbian artists living in Manhattan, *A Lesbian Show* [January 21–February 11, 1978] grew to include a program of readings, video, film, performances, and discussions on lesbian art and politics coordinated by Betsy Damon. Tina Murch, a young lesbian art student from Skidmore College, received class credit for assisting us and documenting the exhibition, and we received a grant from the Lesbian Lifespace Project to print the poster and announcement [see fig. 1.6]. A xeroxed catalogue, *Book of Statements*, included a curatorial statement by myself and one page for each artist or writer originally part of the project, to do with as they wished [see fig. 1.7].

The "Lesbian Art and Artists" issue of *Heresies* [see fig. 1.4] was the first step in filling the vast silence around lesbian art. *A Lesbian Show*—which developed into a cultural and political site that included, but wasn't limited to the exhibition—became the second, with many steps to follow, leading us right into the '90s. While factors such as the sex debates, censorship, AIDS activism, queer theory, and a declining art market have contributed to this period, the visibility of lesbian art and artists today goes back to these two early projects.

In curating the "show" (noun and verb), I tried to look at as much work as possible without any preconceptions of what "lesbian art" would look like, and to see if some sort of lesbian sensibility or aesthetic emerged. (It didn't.) In the end, eighteen visual artists exhibited, although several additional artists were invited but declined for personal or professional reasons.

My intentions were simple: to provide visibility for, breakdown stereotypes of, and generate discussions around lesbian visual art practice. Although from today's queer perspective, most of the work in *A Lesbian Show* seems raw, hesitant, undeveloped, conservative, and curiously nonsexual, it was reflective of what was being done then. For instance, because lesbianism at that time was gender-based, and lesbians did not want to be solely identified on the basis of their sexual activity, and because artists were leery of the ever-present objectifying male gaze, there was no lesbian erotic art.

However, I think it is important to remember that the times were different, and just to be in this show took tremendous strength and courage, and was a radical and risky gesture not to be underestimated. Some artists found the potential exposure so threatening that they turned down the offer to be included. As one's personal life was made public, artists risked everything from family and community disapproval to job discrimination or artistic stereotyping. One invited artist was threatened by her gay male downtown dealer that if she exhibited "as a lesbian," she could say goodbye to the gallery's exhibition and representation of her work. (She didn't show.) In the '70s, art by lesbians was not considered chic (meaning a commodity to be appropriated and colonized) and galleries did not encourage "lesbian or queer readings" of work like they do today, now that the work is at least temporarily marketable.

Rather than discovering or defining an essential lesbian sensibility, *A Lesbian Show* simply presented a wide range of work by artists willing to be out in this context; and, in doing so, was successful in creating a lesbian presence and stimulating dialogue in the mainstream and feminist art worlds, and in generating an art consciousness in many lesbian communities, some more art receptive than others.

The art itself—mostly paintings, mixed-media constructions, and installations, reflecting diverse visual concerns and aesthetics—dealt with issues of anger, guilt, hiding, secrecy, coming out, personal violence, political trust, self-empowerment, and the struggle to make oneself whole. Only a few pieces even referenced lesbian sexuality, and much of the work did not deal with lesbian identity or experience at all. In contrast to recent exhibitions since the late '80s, which have featured photography and text as tools of lesbian self-construction, *A Lesbian Show* did not include any photography, and text was primarily utilized in a self-confessional diaristic mode.

As Kay Larson wrote in *The Village Voice*, "The show must have been a disappointment for anyone looking for definitions. But something else was at work. . . ."[1] The fact that it happened, she pointed out, is what made the exhibit important, for it prodded one into "considering what an art based on sexual politics might look like." Recognizing that this was new work that needed time and a sympathetic environment in which to develop, Larson, anticipating current language and discourse, went on to discuss the exhibit in terms of marginalization, the representation of difference, and the problematics of self-ghettoization.

As difficult as it had been to find artists willing to exhibit as lesbians, hundreds of women turned out on opening night and packed the gallery space, despite a devastating blizzard that dropped several feet of snow. The collective energy was high. We were in SoHo, trespassing in occupied territory—a territory that had always denied our existence or excluded us. As more and more women wanted to read or perform in this context, the exhibit and its schedule of programs began to take on an importance beyond its initial purpose. In addition to the performances and poetry readings, events included a slideshow on crimes against women, a video documentation on the second music festival in Michigan with a discussion on the responsibility of lesbian media to the women's community, and discussions on lesbians in the work force, the economics of being lesbian artists, classicism and racism among lesbians, and the politics of performing.

Generally speaking, the exhibit was well-received by the art, gay, and women's presses: reviews appeared in *The Village Voice*, *Majority Report*, *Woman Artist News*, *Gay Community News*, and *Screw* (which, in an outrageously misogynist review, gave the show its only "bad press"). Gay men expressed the wish for a comparable focus of art, ideas, and politics as an alternative to their cruising bar scene. And truckers in the neighborhood continually ripped down the exhibition posters even though Amy Sillman's poster did not contain any explicit sexual images. Apparently the words "lesbian show," without any voyeuristic possibilities, were still quite threatening.

The exhibit and accompanying programs, however, proved most controversial in various lesbian communities where (despite the fact that several artists of color declined the invitation to participate) the curators were rightly criticized for not including work by any Third World artists. After a protest and spontaneous meeting, Salsa Soul Sisters, A Third World Gay Women's Organization, and Jemima Writers Collective sponsored an evening celebration of the creativity of Third World lesbian artists. Many women [of color] read and performed, and three visual artists [Amy Scarola, Etana Dreamer, and Yvonne Lindsay] added their work to the gallery walls.

But these were the days when diverse forces battled for political correctness in the visionary Lesbian Nation. There were other criticisms as well, and these too were hotly debated. Some women felt that feminist shows shouldn't be curated at all, much less by one woman, while others felt that they should not take place within what they called "the elitist patriarchal art world" (even though all the participating artists felt marginalized, and the exhibition was taking place in an alternative space).

A Lesbian Show raised issues far more important than simplistic correlations between lesbian sexual activity and artistic styles. Stemming from decades of discrimination, a poverty mentality that afflicts many marginalized populations, and the extreme hunger and desire to see ourselves culturally represented, *A Lesbian Show* raised issues of authenticity and voice. Is there and who comprises *the* authentic lesbian voice? Who comprises the grassroots lesbian community? Who has the privilege of creating? Of participating?

Looking back, it's clear that *A Lesbian Show* was extremely important, not so much for the individual works, but rather as an intervention and occupation of cultural space, to use Judith Butler's concept, a "troubled site," which included the work on the walls, the readings, performances, events, protests, discussions, and reviews. It was indeed "a show." Because of this energy and [the] dialogue it created, and [the show's] total use of the gallery space as a generative site, the

SoHo Weekly News nominated it as the 1978 exhibit with the "Most Challenging or Innovative Concept in Theme or Format."[2]

Artists originally included in the exhibition were: Barbara Asch, Suzanne Bevier, Betsy Damon, Maxine Fine, Louise Fishman, Jessie Falstein, Harmony Hammond, Mary Ann King, Gloria Klein, Kate Millett, Dona Nelson, Flavia Rando, Sandra de Sando, Amy Sillman, Ellen Turner, Janey Washburn, Ann Wilson, and Fran Winant. Amy Scarola, Etana Dreamer, Yvonne Lindsay, and Carol Rutenburg added their work during the course of the exhibition.

ED. NOTES

The essay was first published in the exhibition catalogue *In a Different Light: Visual Culture, Sexual Identity, Queer Practice*, ed. Nayland Blake, Lawrence Rinder, and Amy Scholder (San Francisco: City Lights Books, 1995), 45–49.

In a Different Light, curated by Larry Rinder and Nayland Blake at the University of California Berkeley Art Museum in 1995, seemed radical in 1995. Yet the intervention did not have anywhere near the transgressive impact of Hammond's 1978 *A Lesbian Show*. One measure of the latter's radicality was the backlash and threats participating artists experienced. Participants became visible for the first time as "lesbian artists," a new category. Hammond, in her survey *Lesbian Art in America* (New York: Rizzoli, 2000), discusses *A Lesbian Show* in greater detail, describing artworks exhibited and providing more specific information about the threats to artists considering submitting work and the backlash against exhibiting artists.

1. Kay Larson, "Lesbian Art: The Colonized Self," *Village Voice*, March 6, 1978, 67.
2. "Soho Arts Awards for 1977–1978," *SoHo Weekly News*, May 25–31, 1978, 20.

Desperately Seeking Images

Pre-Stonewall and Pre-Feminist Art

(ca. 1996)

In the pre-Stonewall era, a conspiracy of silence insured that for most women, as the lesbian critic Jill Johnston noted in *Lesbian Nation*, "identity was presumed to be heterosexual unless proven otherwise and you couldn't afford to be so proven and so for all social purposes we were all heterosexual. There was no lesbian identity," she concluded, "There was lesbian activity."[1] I would say, rather, there have always been lesbians, and there have always been lesbian artists—however, we do not have a visual history. Because the social and cultural forces that have worked to silence gender, class, and ethnic difference have also silenced difference based on sexual preference, images of lesbians by lesbians are almost completely absent from the dominant hegemonic history of Western art. Aside from the few documented examples of artists such as Rosa Bonheur, Romaine Brooks, or Gluck, who had the economic privilege to be artists and the freedom to live and paint openly, lesbians have had to read between the biographic lines to discover lesbian artists (or bisexual artists such as Georgia O'Keeffe, Frida

Kahlo, Betty Parsons, and Buffie Johnson who are heterosexualized in most texts) and ask in what manner might their relationships with other women have been reflected in or influenced their artmaking.

Looking at the history of lesbian representation in the United States, it becomes all too apparent that the lesbian subject has been missing. Most images of lesbians that do exist in the canons of fine art (and there are precious few) have been created by men for their own viewing pleasure—objects of the male gaze, spectacle for male fantasies of lesbian sexuality. Few images of lesbians, by lesbians, for lesbians exist prior to 1970. [. . .]

Underlying the quest for representation is the desire to see oneself and one's experience reflected culturally—that is, made real. [. . .]

Generally speaking, pre-Stonewall and pre-feminist lesbian self-representation took two forms—private and public. Private images, usually informal snapshots by women of all class backgrounds, meant for circulation among friends and lovers, were not for public viewing, and were not considered to be "art."

Public images on the other hand, usually created by wealthy lesbian painters and photographers, took the form of portraits which utilized specific signifiers based on the stereotype of the so-called "mannish lesbian," and were meant to be circulated in art galleries and art world publications.[2]

In order to discuss lesbian subjectivity in contemporary American art, it is important and necessary to examine the work of artists who self-identified as lesbian prior to the commencement of the Gay Liberation and Women's Liberation movements, and to ask not only how has sexuality been reflected in their art but what has been the role of self-representation in the creation of lesbian identities (and stereotypes)?

We are all framed by the limitations of the times and places in which we live and work. In *Surpassing the Love of Men: Romantic Friendship and Love Between Women from the Renaissance to the Present* [1981], Lillian Faderman pointed out that, in the nineteenth century, passionate love between women was not considered abnormal or undesirable; however, because Western society sought to deny any possibility of women's autonomous sexuality, few visual or textual examples of erotic exchanges between women existed before the turn of the century.[3] It has been well documented that women had intimate and romantic friendships, in which they held hands, hugged, kissed, slept together, sent valentines, wrote letters and poetry, and gave gifts to each other—all of which were considered quite normal activities, and which may or may not have included genital activity, but whether or not we can call these relationships "lesbian" remains open to debate. However, because documentation of these "romantic friendships" all too frequently heterosexualizes any lesbian possibility, we are left without the history we desire and deserve. I propose we assume that romantic friendships were homosexual-lesbian unless proven heterosexual. We should start claiming these girls' histories for ourselves.

A rare documented example of an acknowledged lesbian "romantic friendship" in a rural environment is that of artist Mary Ann Willson and her lover Miss Brundidge, who are familiar to lesbian readers of the twentieth century as Patience and Sarah, subjects of the fictional biography by Alma Routsong (pen name Isabel Miller).[4]

Apparently, Willson's lifestyle was as striking as her work. In an 1850 letter, found in a portfolio of her watercolors of 1810–1825, "An Admirer of Art," who apparently knew Willson, recounts how she came to Greene County, New York, with a woman named Brundidge, with whom she had a "romantic attachment," and describes a woman farmer and a woman artist supporting themselves independently on the land.[5]

Another contemporary chronicler reports,

> Two old maids [. . .] spent their time in the necessary work about the log-house and garden which was filled with wild flowers and ferns, and in painting watercolor pictures which they sold among the neighboring settlers, for small sums, the highest price being asked was twenty-five cents. These paintings [. . .] are unique in the extreme, showing great originality in conception, drawing and color, as well as in the medium employed for their production. Their subjects were generally selected from the Bible or profane history, in which they seem to have been well versed. The paper used was the wrappings of candles and tea boxes, or something of that sort. The pigments were of home manufacture. They would hunt through the woods and fields for certain flowers, berries and weeds, which they would boil or bruise to obtain the color they desired. These crude materials were sometimes helped out with the addition of brick-dust, and in fact by anything that these primitive artists found suitable for the work in hand.[6]

In an interview with Jonathan Ned Katz appearing in *Gay American History*, Alma Routsong describes her discovery of Willson and Brundidge. The following is an excerpt from their conversation:

> My lover and I were touring New York State and were visiting the folk art museum at Cooperstown. I was wandering through it, not really concentrating on anything, when my lover [. . .] called me back, pointing to this picture of a mermaid by Mary Ann Willson. There was a card beside it that said Miss Willson and her "farmerette" companion lived and worked

> together in Greenville Town, Greene County, New York, circa 1820. Then we went into the next room—a small library—and found a book by Lipman and Winchester, called *Primitive Painters in America*, with a short piece about Mary Ann Willson. It said that she and Miss Brundidge had a "romantic attachment." I was absolutely taken by it. I didn't want to travel any more. I didn't want to see Harriet Tubman's bed. I wanted to go home and research Willson and Brundidge, find out all about them, and write a book about them.[7]

Unlike Willson and Brundidge, who lived in rural isolation, most women artists in the nineteenth century moved to European urban centers of culture where progressive attitudes allowed them to live independently and to take their art studies or careers seriously. Often wearing men's clothes for comfort, style, practicality, power, and fun, and living together in what were widely referred to as "Boston marriages," these women, who were not all necessarily straight, sought to be autonomous from both family and men—no easy task in those days, for popular opinion was that women were not as talented as men and were too delicate to be artists. As Ann Sutherland Harris and Linda Nochlin have stated in the catalogue for "Women Artists 1550–1950," the first major historical museum exhibition of art by women, "Simply being persistent enough to devote a lifetime of effort to being a serious artist was a considerable accomplishment for a nineteenth-century woman, when marriage and its concomitant domestic duties so often meant the end of even the most promising careers."[8]

One of the earliest and best-known examples of this independence and commitment to creative work, was the French artist Rosa Bonheur (1822–1899), who was public about her lesbian identity, although it was only indirectly expressed in her art. Bonheur not only took on the traditions of the male art academy but many male attributes in the way she lived her life—she smoked cigarettes, bobbed her hair, bought her own property, wore male attire (although she didn't think other women should), and settled down to a lifelong relationship with the artist Nathalie Micas, whom she called her wife.[9] Bonheur was able to create a private world for herself in which to live and work with Nathalie in the protected privacy of their chateau in By, on the edge of the Fontainebleau forest, where she was surrounded by a wide variety of animals who were the primary subjects of her art.

The eldest of four children, all artists who specialized in animal painting, Bonheur received her earliest and most definitive training from her father Raymond Bonheur, a landscape painter and drawing master. By the age of seventeen she was selling copies of old masters in the Louvre, and at twenty-seven she superseded her father as the director of a drawing school. The fact that her father was connected with the Saint Simonians, a community that believed in the absolute equality of women as a social and spiritual necessity, also contributed to Bonheur's emancipation from conventional feminine modes of behavior and the complete freedom with which she tackled large-scale heroic paintings.[10]

Not really a member of any artistic school, but working within a romantic tradition of landscape painting based on direct observation of nature, Bonheur was obsessed with technical proficiency and realism. Since the age of ten she had spent many hours sketching animals, studying the particular traits of each species and relating them to human thoughts and feelings. She went to great lengths to achieve anatomical accuracy. She dissected animal parts obtained from a butcher and went regularly to slaughterhouses on the outskirts of Paris during her teens and early twenties. To observe and sketch from life, she attended horse fairs and cattle markets. To avoid the taunts of attendants and observers while she worked, she donned men's clothes, obtaining official authorization for her dress from the prefect of police in 1852. Though her male attire was the subject of much comment, she steadfastly retained working clothes that were practical, comfortable, and masculine.[11] Bonheur—like other women, especially sculptors, who wore men's clothes to move about freely and safely—must have liked the feeling of power that male attire accorded.

Considered a highly successful but conventional animal painter on the heroic scale, Bonheur's challenge to the male-dominated academies of France and England was not due to radical artistic ideas but rather her desire to "achieve equal artistic status with men," to be better and more successful than male artists by their own standards.[12]

"The contrast between [Bonheur's] academically respectable paintings of animals in which every hair and blade of grass was included, and her highly unusual way of life with an unconventional sexual orientation," writes Cooper, "expressed both her determination to succeed as an artist and as a woman, whilst acknowledging Victorian ideas about modesty. If her choice of life partner was another woman, the format of the relationship was that of the conventional and devoted marriage. Of equal importance was her career as an artist. Her artistic and financial success placed her in a strong position to determine the way she organized her life."[13] Arguably the first woman artist to gain recognition as a painter solely on the basis of the work she produced, Bonheur disdained marriage in favor of a career because in her own words, "I well knew that I would lose my independence were I to take on household and wifely duties. [. . .] I preferred to keep my own name. I believe I have been able to give to it some renown."[14] Needless to say, Bonheur was lucky to have Nathalie Micas to handle the details of her life so she was free to devote all her energies to her work. A friend of Bonheur's wrote: "Rosa Bonheur could never have remained the celebrated artist she was without someone beside her, at each instant, to spare her the material cares of the household, daily worries of existence, and to help her also with moral and physical support, as well as with advice in many things related to her art. Nathalie made herself small, ungrudgingly, so that Rosa might become greater."[15] [. . .]

Indifferent to the human figure, Bonheur loved to draw and paint animals, emphasizing their superior strength, depicting them [as] large, beautiful, and indomitable (stand-ins for women who rejected the confines of female roles).[16] Bonheur's painting *Horse Fair* (1853) was the largest animal painting to date, measuring eight by sixteen and a half feet. Cooper observes, "the large horses, proud and untamed, rear and plunge, all but obscuring the men who seek to direct them."[17] With this painting, which captured the raw energy and force of animals in captivity, Bonheur became internationally famous. She was especially well known in England and in the United States where prints made after her paintings were hung on classroom walls, and a popular Rosa Bonheur doll was created in her image dressed in blue painting smock over a finely embroidered peasant blouse. With the rise of the bourgeois class, and a demand for realistic art to decorate homes, Bonheur's anthropomorphic animal paintings enjoyed tremendous popularity with middle-class audiences.

After Nathalie died in 1889, Bonheur fell in love with an American, Anna Klumpke (1856–1942), who was making a name as a painter in France. Klumpke, thirty-four years younger than Bonheur, had been inspired by Bonheur's painting. She wrote to Bonheur asking if she would sit for a portrait. During sittings, their friendship deepened, and Bonheur asked Klumpke to remain with her and write her biography. Klumpke's portrait of Bonheur (1898) is one of her best paintings. While both adamantly believed in the rights of women to be equal to men, neither were overtly political in their lives or in their work. In 1899 Bonheur died in Klumpke's arms and left her the estate. Klumpke, who continued to paint, arranged memorial exhibits and established the Rosa Bonheur memorial museum at the chateau in By. She finally published Bonheur's official biography in 1908.

While the artistic careers of Bonheur, Micas, and Klumpke evolved in the intimacy of domestic life and in a remote private setting, other women artists of the mid-nineteenth century converged in European cities to form supportive communities.

A number of women sculptors, many of whom were lesbian, emigrated to Rome. Harriet Hosmer (1820–1908), the best-known artist of this community, would become one of the most famous women sculptors of the nineteenth century.

As a young woman, Hosmer affected the appearance of "a small, handsome boy, she wore a velvet beret atop her short, curly brown hair, a mannish suit and tie, and sometimes baggy Zouave trousers."[18] Although fine art academies in the United States did not expose women to nude models, Hosmer found an alternative way to study the human body. She enrolled in a medical school in St. Louis, one of the few places that allowed women to acquire knowledge of human anatomy. Unwilling to compromise her independence, Hosmer decided early on never to marry. She was drawn into the artistic circles surrounding Charlotte Cushman, a stage personality, who earned international acclaim for her enactment of Hamlet and other so-called trouser roles.[19] Hosmer followed Cushman to Rome, where many sculptors from around the world (male and female) aspired to establishing careers.

Cushman, whose companion and biographer Emma Stebbins (1815–1882) was a sculptor, believed that women in the arts should have the same opportunities as men, and she fostered a supportive community of women artists that included, among others, Sarah Fisher Ames, Margaret Foley, Florence Freeman, Vinnie Ream Hoxie, Louise Lander, Mary Edmonia Lewis, Blanche Nevin, and Anne Whitney, in addition to Stebbins and Hosmer.[20]

Defying traditions and social conventions of the day, many of these women dressed in men's clothes to minimize their difference from their male counterparts, while maximizing their difference from other women. Referred to as "that strange sisterhood who [...] settled upon the seven hills [of Rome] in a white marmorean flock," they produced large-scale sculptures in their studios and earned international recognition.[21]

Hosmer is most famous for her seven-foot-tall neoclassical marble sculpture, *Zenobia in Chains* (1859), depicting the proud and dignified Queen of Palmyra after she was captured by the forces of Roman emperor Aurelian and forced to march to Rome in chains. Hosmer described her "noble in defeat, walking with stately pride in her captivity."[22] The monumental *Zenobia*, which male critics refused to believe was made by a woman, could be viewed as a metaphor for Woman in the nineteenth century: hailed as queen but captive and deprived of power.

Hosmer received so many commissions, that she could not only support herself handsomely but also preside over one of the largest sculpture studios in Rome and a staff of male stonecutters working under her. Still, as successful as she was, Hosmer suffered ridicule and attack for her clothes and behavior—and for breaking into the all-male enclave of neoclassical sculptors. She was subjected to ridicule by her male colleagues and by critics.[23] However, if her unladylike ways were considered shocking by many, her eccentricities (such as riding horseback astride and unaccompanied) undoubtedly contributed to her charm and popularity with aficionados and patrons of the arts.[24]

Another very successful member of the community working in Rome at this time was Mary Edmonia Lewis (1893–1900), a woman of African-American and Native American heritage. Lewis was raised [in New York and New Jersey] in the Chippewa (Ojibwa) tribal tradition of her mother. Her African-American father was a gentleman's servant in Oberlin, Ohio (a stop-over on the underground railroad, with a large population of free Blacks). As a young woman, Lewis studied art at Oberlin College, the first college in the United States to open its doors to women and the first to admit women of all races.[25] Her years at Oberlin College (during the 1860s, the Civil War years) were marred by racial prejudice, discrimination, and racist attacks. She fled to Boston before graduating and sailed to Rome in 1865. There, she met Hosmer, Cushing, and studied with Hosmer's mentor, the English neoclassical sculptor John Gibson. Lewis, too, adopted his neoclassical style. Known for her superb skill in the technique of direct marble carving, Lewis's ambitious sculptures reflected her dual heritage, expressing the alienation of Blacks and their aspirations for freedom.

Lewis is known for her important sculpture *Forever Free* (1867), which commemorated the passage of the 13th Amendment to the US Constitution abolishing slavery. The sculpture depicts two enslaved Black people, a standing man comforting a kneeling woman, both of whom have broken their chains of bondage and look up to heaven joyfully on the day of the emancipation proclamation.

Her startling *Death of Cleopatra* (1876), exhibited at the Philadelphia Centennial, made her famous in the US. At the exhibition, *Death of Cleopatra* provoked controversy and won an award. It presented the dying Egyptian queen, not idealized but realistically, in the throes of death. Lewis also drew inspiration from the Indigenous side of her family heritage; works such as *Hiawatha* (1868) and *Old Indian Arrow Maker and his Daughter* (1872) were praised for their ethnologic accuracy and detail.

Even though Lewis's life in the United States was marred by gender discrimination and racial violence, she overcame all obstacles in her path to become one of the most successful sculptors of the Rome group.[26] She was almost as well-known as Hosmer. She sold work for equally large sums and her studio, like Hosmer's, became one of the most fashionable places in Rome for tourists to visit. She was the first black American to receive international, as well as national, recognition as a sculptor.

The art historian David C. Driskell has written about the impact of racial prejudice on her work: "A sensitive awareness of her own racial origins and an unending desire to expose the inequities of American society were basic elements in the work of this independent, rather caustic young woman. [. . .] Perhaps it was her work that first expressed the themes of racial injustice that would become the core of black American art in the 1920s and '30s."[27]

Anne Whitney (1821–1915), another member of Hosmer's circle, came from a well-established abolitionist family in Massachusetts. Largely self-taught, she learned anatomy at the Brooklyn Hospital and private studies with a physician. After the Civil War, when she was already past fifty, she went to Rome with the painter Adeline Manning, her lifelong companion.[28] Whitney's sculptures—which include a bust of the militant feminist Harriet Beecher Stowe, a statue representing a freed slave, and a portrait of the Haitian leader François-Dominique Toussaint Louverture—elaborate themes of liberation. In 1875 she won a blind competition for a monumental sculpture depicting the leading abolitionist Charles Sumner. The jury had not realized that the winning artist was a woman, and when it did, they reallocated the commission to a man.[29]

Most of the women sculptors in Hosmer's milieu had a political consciousness and saw similarities between feminist and abolitionist struggles for liberation. While their works remained formally conventional, their subject matter was radical. Using allegorical and classical sculptural conventions, they found ways to inject ideas about their sexual and social roles as women into works whose monumental scale countered received ideas about women's capabilities. Typically, the members of Rome's community of women artists remained unmarried, led independent lives, and had international reputations. Working in the beautiful white Carrara marble, they competed for and won major government commissions for public sculptures and fountains. [. . .]

The migration of women sculptors to Rome is part of a larger pattern formed by the many American-born lesbians who found it easier to express their creativity (and sexuality) away from the confining and defining attitudes of their homes and families. They expatriated to build creative lives in other countries. These communities of like-minded friends provided an important creative base and support network; they created sites where women artists and their work were taken seriously, spaces where ideas and images could develop. [. . .]

In addition to the community in Rome, lesbian expatriate "colonies" flourished in Florence, Capri, London, Berlin, and Paris.[30] [. . .]

Artistic and homosexual subcultures were incubated in the numerous salons that brought together European and American artists and writers in a creative, intellectual environment where unconventional sexualities were quite acceptable or even desirable. In Paris, the sapphic poet Natalie Barney hosted a now-legendary salon that supported lesbian writers and artists. Her lover Romaine

Brooks (1874–1970) created a veritable lesbian pantheon with her portraits figuring this community of "amazons," as the strong, independent, talented trailblazers were known. [. . .]

Chasseresse [hunter] (1920), depicts an Amazon with a goat skin over one shoulder, one bare breast, and a mountain goat at her side. The model for this image, the American artist and designer Eyre de Lanux, was one of Romaine Brooks's lovers. [. . .]

Brooks's portrait of *Una, Lady Troubridge* (1924) presents what is now a lesbian stereotype—a sleek woman wearing a tuxedo, short red hair slicked back, a monocle, and dachshund hounds. For Brooks and her friends, the lesbian art historian Arlene Raven notes, "Cross-dressing [was] a sign of freedom, independence, and unmistakable lesbianism."[31] Raven concludes, "No other lesbian artist contemporary with Brooks made lesbianism a persistent theme in her work nor brought it to her own personal sphere by referring to herself and her colleagues and friends."[32] [. . .]

The year 1925 marked the apex of Brooks's career. She exhibited in Paris, London, and New York, showing mostly portraits of friends, as well as the now iconic self-portrait representing the artist upright in black suit, mouth set in grim determination, and eyes shaded by a top hat. As she grew older, Brooks retreated increasingly from other people, becoming dependent on Natalie to manage the business aspects of her career. She painted little after 1930, turning sporadically to writing her memoir, *No Pleasant Memories*, illustrated by a large number of haunting continuous line drawings, surrealistic evocations of childhood nightmares. Some consider these her most expressive works.

Once considered radical (at least for the subject matter), her figurative paintings, executed in their Whistlerian tones, looked outmoded in the post–World War Two era, when abstraction was ascendant. By the 1940s, Brooks began to feel isolated and neglected as an artist. Reclusive after her long relationship to Barney ended in 1969, Brooks died at the age of ninety-eight in a darkened apartment in Nice, attended primarily by her chauffeur and servants. Her work was largely forgotten by the public until her retrospective at the National Collection of Fine Arts in Washington, DC (where she willed most of her paintings and drawings). The retrospective *Romaine Brooks: Thief of Souls*, curated by Adelyn D. Breeskin at the National Collection of Fine Arts in Washington, DC, in 1971, brought renewed attention to the oeuvre.

As perhaps the most well-known American lesbian artist, and one of the very few lesbian artists before 1970 to overtly depict lesbian lives, Romaine Brooks remains an icon in lesbian culture and continues to inspire lesbian visual artists today. Her persona and her paintings are referenced in works by such contemporary artists as Lili Lakich, who works in neon, and the conceptual artists Millie Wilson, to name just two.

Like Romaine Brooks, the British artist Hannah Gluckstein (1895–1978) was born into a very wealthy family and escaped their oversight as soon as she could. She, too, cropped her hair and wore male clothes. She insisted on being known only as Gluck, dropping her feminine first name. Like Brooks, she dealt with themes of androgyny and lesbian sexuality in her work, which included still lives, androgynous figures, and portraits. In the 1920s, Brooks and Gluck, who were friends, planned to do portraits of each other. Brooks's portrait of Gluck, *Peter (A Young English Girl)* (1923–24), is a sensitive and insightful depiction of Gluck (Peter) with close-cropped hair wearing a fashionable belted jacket, collared shirt, and neck tie. Unfortunately, Gluck's portrait of Brooks was never finished.

Although less social than Brooks, Gluck also painted portraits of friends and lovers from their lesbian circle of friends. After successful exhibits in the '20s and '30s, her works fell out of fashion for many years until they were given serious attention again in the '70s. During the repressive '40s and '50s, Gluck, feeling vulnerable and self-conscious about her work and her way of life, destroyed many of her early self-portraits in men's clothes. Unfortunately, there was no retrospective of her work until after her death. [...]

While, in the nineteenth century and early twentieth century, American women with career ambitions often chose to expatriate to Europe, others like Dorothy Brett, Marie Chabot, Mabel Dodge, Emma Jane Gay, Laura Gilpin, Margaret Lefranc, and Georgia O'Keeffe were drawn to the wide-open spaces of the American West, which provided a freedom from traditional roles. In the West, there was room to do anything, be anyone you wanted to be. To expand. To lead independent lives.[33]

Among the independent women who migrated West were artists, photographers, writers, and anthropologists. Several became close friends with or married Native men. Mabel Dodge married Tony Luhan from the Taos Pueblo; Edith Wharton had a special relationship with Tio from San Juan Pueblo; and Mildred Cox Stevenson, an anthropologist and photographer, lived and worked among the Zuni for many years. Stevenson formed a bond with the famous Zuni berdache WeWah. (Born a biological man, the berdache, who is both artist and shaman, assumes the dress and activities of the opposite sex.)

Emma Jane Gay (1830–1919) became a photojournalist by chance. According to the pioneering grassroots lesbian historian Judith Schwarz:

> In 1888, she [Gay] took a good long look at her friend, the noted ethnologist and Indian rights advocate Alice Fletcher, who had just returned from

an arduous trip out West. Distressed at Fletcher's haggard and exhausted appearance, Emma Jane Gay offered her services to "look after" and cook for her friend on the next trip out in the field. But the Interior Department's budget for Fletcher's project only carried a listing for photographer, one of the few skills Gay had not yet learned. She spent the next few months learning how to handle the chemicals and develop the photographs. Finally in the summer of 1889, she joined Fletcher in Nebraska. For the next three years Gay was the official government photographer for Fletcher's land-allotment work among the Nez-Perce tribe in Idaho; unofficially she did all the cooking and daily camp chores. When Emma Jane Gay learned photography she was fifty-nine years old and she hardly expected to make a career out of it. Photography was merely a means to be with Alice Fletcher.[34]

[. . .] Photographer Laura Gilpin (1891–1979) and her lover Elizabeth Forster (1886–1972) were very open about their relationship which was both romantic and work-based. Gilpin, who was living in Colorado, would visit Forster who, for several years, worked as a nurse on the Navajo Reservation in Red Rock, Arizona. These visits and many subsequent ones over the years established long-lasting friendships between many of the Navajo and Forster and Gilpin (who were seen as a couple). For years Forster and Gilpin planned to publish Forster's Red Rock letters which describe the place, the people, and their lives, the hardships, and beauty of the land at a time when change was coming to the reservation, along with Gilpin's photographs. After many dead ends and delays, this project developed into Gilpin's famous series of photographs presented in the book *The Enduring Navaho* and later a collection of Forster's letters juxtaposed with a selection of Gilpin's portraits of Navajo friends and the landscape around Shiprock.[35]

Dorothy Brett (1883–1977), from a conventional and titled London family, came to Taos in 1924. Like many others who came to Northern New Mexico, she was enchanted by the landscape and cultures and stayed on to become part of the loose circle of women artists, photographers, and writers who participated in the art colonies of Taos and Santa Fe, which also included Margaret Lefranc (who was best friends with Gilpin) and photographer Marie Chabot. Very close to Mabel Dodge and the Lawrences, Brett, as she was called, became known for her expressionist paintings of Taos Indians.[36] [. . .]

The most well-known painter of this milieu, Georgia O'Keeffe (1887–1986), originally came to New Mexico at the invitation of Mabel Dodge and Dorothy Brett in 1917, and then returned in 1929, when she was swept into the circle of people around Dodge. She returned every summer to paint, spending the rest of the year with Alfred Stieglitz on the East Coast. After his death, she moved to New Mexico permanently, purchasing the Ghost Ranch in Abiquiu in 1940, and then the house in the village of Abiquiu in 1945. (At that time, she was the only Anglo in the tiny village of Indian and Spanish heritage.)

O'Keeffe's relationships with men are well documented and familiar history, yet there remains a tremendous hesitancy to talk about the women in her life—as if that would somehow diminish the level or reputation of her work. [. . .]

O'Keeffe responded to Peggy Guggenheim's invitation to participate in Art of This Century's *Exhibition by 31 Women* in 1943 by announcing that she was not a "woman painter"—a phrase she considered pejorative, unnecessary, and inferior to simply "artist."[37] [. . .]

While she denied any consciousness or acknowledgment of it, her images of flowers, which filled the picture frame, figured cavities, folds, depths, and mysterious interiors that stimulated gender- and sexual-based interpretation. And her sensuous landscapes with their "clefts, mounds, openings" combin[ing the] female body with nature or the landscape influenced many contemporary lesbian and feminist painters interested in the same subject matter. Even her more precisionist paintings of buildings have a sensuous edge to them and rely on notions of shelter or contained space and openings of doors and windows (often closed shut, impenetrable, mysterious). The theme of "openings" is central to her oeuvre.

Ann Sutherland Harris and Linda Nochlin write, "The presence of allegedly 'feminine' elements of form or content in the work of art is ambiguous, often, as in the case of Georgia O'Keeffe's flower paintings, hotly affirmed by both admiring and disparaging critics, and as hotly denied by the artist herself."[38] Either way, her works raise the issue of "feminine." Feminists in the '70s who became interested in "central core imagery" built on feminist interpretations of O'Keeffe's work. [. . .]

O'Keeffe's relationship with Stieglitz is legendary. She undoubtedly had deep feelings for him and was also aware that she had him to thank for her connections to the New York art world. She also had affairs and romantic attachments with other men, as well as close intimate and sometimes sexual relationships with women. In addition to coming to New Mexico in the summers to paint, perhaps she also came to be with certain women friends (such as Margaret Lefranc and Marie Chabot). Certainly, in New Mexico, she became part of a circle of women who knew each other and spent time together, some of whom like Chabot assisted O'Keeffe in various ways. [. . .]

What are we lesbians in search of a history to make of women artists who could not or did not identify themselves as lesbian, much less as lesbian artists, but who had important relationships with women? The category "lesbian artist," even as contested as it is today, didn't exist then. And what about loners such as Agnes Martin, Lenore Tawney, Betty Parsons, Louise Nevelson, Buffie Johnson, or Agnes Pelton? Must we read between the biographic lines of even feminist scholarship and criticism to guess if they are one of us? [. . .]

Given the times in which they grew up, came of age as artists, or lived and worked, we must be careful to not force labels or categories on women who lived at different times. As much as we might like to claim them, I think it is important to respect the various life styles these women chose, and not force them into categories. They, like artists today, struggled against being limited, worked hard to not be restricted by labels such as "woman artist." [. . .]

With the rise of conservatism and patriotism in the post–World War Two era, the concept of the emancipated woman found little support. Most women were forced back into roles of housewife and mother. As difficult a period as it was for women artists, it was even worse for lesbians, who were nowhere to be seen in the world of fine art. Ironically, it was during the repressive McCarthy era, with its rampant xenophobia, homophobia, and persecution of homosexuals, that gay and lesbian cultures, forced underground, smoldered and grew in the dark atmospheres of their closets and bars.

Some gay and lesbian artists developed an esthetic based on abstract expressionism, which had the possibility of both denying and veiling subject matter. [. . .]

Betty Parsons (1900–1982), who came from an old wealthy family, and was probably the most open about her sexual relationships with women, remained discreet, with her lesbian "affairs," primarily "out" on Long Island. A rare exception to the continual heterosexualization of the lives and work of women artists prior to the '70s is Lee Hall's biography of Parsons.[39] Hall acknowledges Parsons's lesbian affairs, as well as her fears about being considered "a lesbian," and at the same time, does not dwell on sexuality as a polemic. Named and acknowledged with the "L word," the biographer presents lesbian relationships as just another aspect of Parsons's interesting life.

Parsons, who had more than a dozen solo exhibitions of her colorful abstract paintings, and totem-like driftwood and stone sculptures painted with stripes and dots, was known as the first dealer to represent many of the abstract expressionist artists including a number of women, such as Agnes Martin (to whom Parsons wrote at least one poem), Louise Nevelson, Hedda Sterne, and Lee Krasner, and later Helene Aylon, Sari Dienes, Perle Fine, Anne Ryan, and Sonja Sekula.[40] Aylon, who showed in Parsons's gallery in the '70s, recalled the gallerist as strong and independent, someone not to mess with, a feminist who forged professional and personal connections with and among women. In a 1977 interview with Aylon, Parsons talks about her relationships with the artists she represented and admits: "In those days women didn't really respect each other. I think they do now."[41] Parsons refers to close relationships with women friends which included Emmanuel Boll, Marlena Dietrich, Greta Garbo, and Martha Graham. [. . .]

Parsons also talks about having crushes on her female teachers as a young girl and being scared that someone would find out. "I was brought up in [. . .] New England [. . .] where you never showed to the public what you felt. I remember my mother saying to me, Betty, it doesn't matter much what you do, but never get found out. . . . So, if I had a boyfriend or if I had a girlfriend and I got too close [I] never let the world know it."[42] When Parsons says "Oh, I've had tremendous nourishment from women. Because they like me. Women like me, you know." Aylon, who identifies as bisexual, answers, "You don't play games. You could love a woman and they sense that." And Parsons responds, "Yes, they know it, they know it."[43]

Another artist who has been open about her relationships with women (although she does not identify as a lesbian or lesbian artist) is Buffie Johnson. While married twice to men, Johnson insists that the two major loves of her life (at least so far—she's eighty-four at the time of this writing) were women: an early relationship when she was in boarding school, and later in life, after her marriage ended, a relationship to the young photographer Tracey Boyd. During the early 1970s, Johnson and Boyd lived together and were seen at social events around the art world, smartly dressed in riding jackets, pants, and boots.

In 1988, after many years of research, Johnson published her groundbreaking book on the Great Goddess and her animals.[44] Johnson is known for her simple and (centrally composed) acrylic closeup paintings of plants, seeds, and pods and other organic forms. While her external application of thin paint and closeup images of organic forms is akin to O'Keeffe, Johnson, unlike O'Keeffe, consciously lets her plants reference the Great Goddess and suggest women's genitals.

The openness of Parsons and Johnson about their sexual attraction to women contrasts with the guardedness of Louise Nevelson (1899–1988) about her close relationship with her assistant, Diana MacKown. They lived, worked, and partied together for twenty-five years until Nevelson's death in 1988. According to many accounts, they were always invited to social events as a couple.

MacKown, who acted as Nevelson's buffer with the outside world, ran the household and assisted in the studio, has been described as being fiercely protective of Nevelson and exhibiting behavior consistent with that of a protective and jealous lover who resented anyone else's intrusion into their life. The stage designer William Katz, a close friend, "described Louise's attitude towards Diana as maternal, and their relationship as having the elements of both friendship and romance. But, at [the] age of eighty-two, Nevelson hotly and unhesitatingly denied the inevitable rumors. 'I couldn't live with myself if I was a lesbian.' [. . .] 'I've never had that experience.'"[45] And according [to] Nevelson's biographer, MacKown herself insisted that she and Nevelson "were simply good friends."[46]

Nevelson described herself as a solitary person completely focused on production in the studio. "I just do my work."[47]

Many associate Nevelson with the renaissance of sculpture in the US. She pushed the definitions of sculpture and led [the] move to what today we call installations. Her accumulative assemblages were constructed out of recycled materials: found pieces of wood, stacked crates, broken frames, finials, chair slats, legs, painted one color—black, white, or gold—to divest them of their original associations. She dressed in costumes created similarly out of layered fabrics and jewels from a variety of cultures and civilizations. The exotic persona she performed using costumes and makeup (a kind of drag) positioned her safely beyond the pale of conventional femininity, as an exception to ordinary rules.

She became a strong force, or presence, in the art world but did not find a market for her work until she was in her sixties. Her importance was acknowledged by an invitation to participate in the Venice Biennale in 1962. [. . .]

Lenore Tawney [1907–2007] came to prominence in the '60s as well. Tawney pioneered off-loom weaving in the '50s. Her works were sometimes monumental in scale, reaching up to twenty-seven feet high. In addition to these weavings, she also made delicate poetic drawings, boxes, and collages of handmade and found papers, feathers, bones, shells, pebbles, and text.

She was a member of a loose circle of women that included Betty Parsons. In the mid-'50s she moved to Coenties Slip, along the East River in downtown New York, where a significant number of openly gay and lesbian artists had studios. Chryssa, Robert Indiana, Ellsworth Kelly, Agnes Martin, and Ann Wilson were members of this community. Wilson emphasizes the importance of Tawney's weaving on many of the Coenties Slip group, and indeed it is easy to see the weaving grid in work by Larry Poons, Agnes Martin, and Wilson herself. Tawney has never really gotten her full due in part because of the materials she used. Before feminism, fiber was not respected as fine art material. Tawney's fiber works could be viewed as radical three-dimensional drawing in space.

Tawney was especially close to Agnes Martin, who wrote an essay for the brochure of Tawney's solo show at the Staten Island Museum in 1961 and, in 1963, named several of the pieces presented in Tawney's first New York group show [at the Museum of Contemporary Crafts]. The two took trips together, camped, exchanged ideas, and discussed each other's work. Tawney financially supported Martin for several years when she was having difficulties.

In her 1990 retrospective at the American Craft Museum, Tawney exhibited erotic postcards that she made and sent as mail art to women friends, such as the couple who own the very special Manhattan button store called Tender Buttons. Tawney saw her postcards as "signs thrown to the winds" expressing things that couldn't be said in words.[48] [...]

Ann Wilson [1931–2023] was the youngest member of the group. She has spoken and written extensively about the interactions and mutual influence within the group, and about the impact of Betty Parsons and the artists who showed in her gallery. She recalls, too, that the men of the Coenties Slip group frequently got credit for the ideas of the women, or in some cases, were literally credited for their work.

Wilson, who painted quilts and quilted paintings as far back as the late '50s, shares formal concerns with the artists of this milieu. And, like Tawney and Parsons, she is also known for her many incredible notebooks and letters, which are beautiful personal works of art in and of themselves.

Despite her close relationships with the women artists, and lesbian affairs as a young woman, Wilson did not overtly identify as a lesbian until the feminist movement.[49] And even then, while open about her relationships, [she] remains hesitant about such categories. However, although many of the women artists of this era made no statements that could be understood as evidence of lesbian relationships or identity, they have been claimed as lesbian by their lesbian successors. [...]

In working on this book, I have had many women name "the lesbian painter Agnes Martin" as role model and primary influence on their work. I find this fascinating, for nowhere is there anything in print by Martin or anyone else that gives any indication of sexuality.[50] In fact, Martin, who has lived alone most of her life, denies sexuality and emotion, as well as any political or social content, in her work. Martin's grids, while they can have a feminist reading, do not appear lesbian in any way. On what basis have young lesbian artists claimed her as "one of us"? Apparently young lesbian artists see her as a role model because of her rugged, independent, outsider way of life, her commitment to her work, and presumably the strength of her work.

Lesbian Class Wars

In the '50s and '60s, sexual choices, and therefore lesbian identities, were primarily shaped by class positions. Sexual difference was exhibited and flaunted by privileged upper-class lesbians who were safe from losing jobs, housing, children, etc.; lesbians of differing races and ethnicities, already marginalized; and by working-class lesbians of all races who had little to lose. Middle-class lesbians who had social standing and jobs at risk typically tried to fit in and pass as straight.[51]

Bar subcultures, defined by age and class, were often in conflict with each other, for they had different ideas of what lesbian identity and life could or should be.[52] Functioning as stages to act out roles restricted from the home or workplace, the bars were places to be sexual without fear of social repercussion (other than routine police harassment). There were strict divisions of butch and femme roles, which were not seen as an imitation of heterosexuality but rather as an erotic exchange between [lesbians]. Because, in the eyes of the straight world, the femme wasn't visible, thus didn't exist, the public lesbian stereotype was still the mannish butch.[53]

While wealthy lesbians could travel or expatriate, working-class lesbians didn't have mobility and options to travel or move to other physical or class sites. Thus, most pre-Stonewall lesbian cultures in the United States tended to be urban and working class. But since the working class itself was not considered a site for or subject of serious artmaking (painting and sculpture), and because few working-class women had the time or support systems to make fine art, their creativity frequently took other forms: music, letter or journal writing, needle arts, wood working, and photo snapshots.

The '50s saw the beginning of homosexual organizing. In 1950, the Mattachine Society, which grew out of the Communist Party, began to meet in Los Angeles and Manhattan, although it wasn't until 1960 that the first gay and lesbian action group, the Homophile League, was formed.

Middle-class values and aspirations were exemplified by Daughters of Bilitis [DOB], organized by Del Martin and Phyllis Lyon in 1952, as a much-needed social club for lesbians that promoted "a mode of behavior and dress acceptable to society."[54] Their concern was to minimize or hide difference and adopt whatever conventions were necessary to fit into and be tolerated by the mainstream. Was this doubly true with respect to lesbians of color? Faderman asserts that, "like most middle-class blacks at the start of the civil rights movement in the 1960s, middle-class lesbians [of color] generally aspired to integration" into predominantly white, predominantly heterosexual middle-class society, rather than claiming a status that made them, on two counts, a minority. Lesbians, whether black or white, "felt most comfortable blending in," Faderman concludes.[55]

But even the proper Daughters of Bilitis, and their publication *The Ladder* [1956–72], came under attack, not because of anything outrageous that they did, but simply because of who they were. Anticipating today's right-wing homosexual panic, in the '50s, the very existence of DOB as a public group of lesbians was perceived as a threat to the nuclear family.[56]

In bold contrast to today's lesbian shows which flaunt their difference and badness, the type of information and language utilized in the short biographies printed on the hand-out for the New York Chapter of the Daughters of Bilitis sponsored "Art Show and Sale" reflects not only the times but the class position and desire of the organization to present the ten artists, who were referred to as "Miss," and their work as "respectable." I have been unable to locate additional references or materials on these artists. Without further information it is difficult to know much about any of them except that they appeared to be either painters or photographers, traveled in Europe and Mexico, and had studied art at the High School of Art and Design, Hunter College, The New School for Social Research, Pratt, Hofstra, and CUNY. Only one woman appeared to have teaching experience. For many of the artists, this was the first public showing of their work, although one artist, the handout touts, had "numerous private showings," and another mentioned exhibiting at one "of the fine East Side galleries." An artist listed as Baynar is actually two women, Marie Nares and Linda Bayless, who worked jointly and exhibited together under that name. One artist, a Mr. Daniel Icolari, either used a man's name or was a man—there is no explanation. [. . .]

Looking Out from the Lesbian Gaze

In response to the scarcity of representations that depicted lesbians in a public and positive manner, lesbian writers and artists in the 1960s and 1970s cruised through the territories of literature, fine art, and popular media, appropriating whatever girls and images they found resonant in an attempt "to locate an inherent lesbianism in texts not intended to be read as lesbian."[57]

Early examples of bending heterosexual imagery to meet lesbian needs include Bertha Harris's appropriation of the monster in pre-feminist literature and film as the epitome of difference, the symbol of the lesbian as outsider who threatens the patriarchal structures of heterosexuality, and writings by artist Sarah Whitworth in *The Ladder* and *Amazon Quarterly*, where she interprets paintings by male and female heterosexual artists from [a] lesbian point of view.

In "What We Mean to Say: Notes Towards Defining the Nature of Lesbian Literature," published in the "Lesbian Art and Artists" issue of *Heresies* in 1977, Harris considers the lesbian to be the prototype of the monster, the quintessence of all that is female, the female enraged, who subverts traditional notions of female submissiveness, passivity, and virtue. Monsters, explains Harris, have always been invented to express what ordinary people can't—feeling.[58]

Citing examples of *King Kong* and *Jaws*, she writes that monsters are, among other things, emblems of feeling in patriarchy and that the enemy of the monster is phallic imperialism, which tries to shape chaos around the cock. For example, Jaws is a giant killer shark whose freedom depends on wiping out nuclear families who litter the heterosexual beach. More than phallic flesh or the stake are necessary to kill or tame this monster—great tubes of lethal explosives are necessary.

Beyond identifying this archetypal image of lesbian as monster, Harris claims, indeed flaunts it, for she believes that lesbians have the great potential to be "different," dangerous, outrageous, awesome, and distinguished. Echoing Natalie Clifford Barney who believed in the superiority of lesbians, Harris says, "lesbians can have it all. So why should we try to be like everyone else?" And, anticipating the '90s "discourse of difference," she calls for the development of a lesbian literature based on difference, one that develops outside, through new language, new structures, and new images such as Monique Wittig's *Le Corps Lesbien* (1973).[59] In the meantime, until we have such a literature, sensibility, or aesthetic, which at the time she wrote this article was just beginning to emerge, Harris says that she is on the lookout for books, film, and art that she can pervert to her own queer reality.

Today, some writers—Ellen Moers, among others—are critical of Harris's depiction of the lesbian as monster, believing it feeds into homophobic and sexist stereotypes, ultimately disempowering lesbians. But I think this is a simplification and misreading of her intention—to claim these representations that, in their difference and badness, begin to establish a lesbian tradition of images that interrupt heterosexual assumptions. Harris, who has never been interested in blending in, being good or politically correct, has always taken Southern pleasure in being bad and transgressive—in stealing the woman and making good art. She prompts us to ask, "Isn't this perverse position of difference part of lesbian desire and pleasure?"

Contrasting Moers's belief that the representation of lesbians as monsters is derogatory, to Harris's celebratory approach, Bonnie Zimmerman suggests that "there is an important dialectic between how the lesbian articulates herself and how she is articulated and objectified by others."[60]

In the numerous articles she published in *The Ladder*, Sarah Whitworth was one of the first women to critique male representation of women and lesbians and to challenge a gendered and heterosexual reading of art.[61] Looking at individual works from a lesbian gaze, Whitworth claims the women in the paintings for her own pleasure.

For instance, she discusses Isabel Bishop's paintings, prints, and drawings from the 1930s of female nudes that depict everyday women with all their physical imperfections, and therefore realness, in contrast to the damaging classical "male-chauvinist-nude," and elaborates on Bishop's many images that depict women office workers relaxing together on their lunch hour in Union Square (talking, laughing, touching, and enjoying each other's company to the exclusion of men).[62]

She deconstructs *Conversation* [1930], Henry Schnakenberg's painting of two women lying on a sofa. Examining their body position and gazes, Whitworth fantasizes who the women are, how they got there, and what their relationship might be, concluding that "it is important to note that the women are addressing each other full face and that their bodies are open and not protected. It would be very possible for the woman above to lean down and kiss the young one on the mouth without a second's awkwardness. Such an embrace would not only be very possible but in this viewer's mind, very likely indeed, if the painting were in fact the frame of a film, and the action could continue."[63]

Whitworth's modest writing, published outside of the art world, in lesbian and feminist journals such as *The Ladder*, *Amazon Quarterly*, and the *Feminist Art Journal*, raised issues central to current discourses around the problems and difficulties of lesbian representation. For instance, in discussing the ambiguity of Japanese pornographic prints as discussed in *The Other Face of Love* by Raymond de Becker, Whitworth raises the question of visual inference, and asks, "Where does the meaning of the painting rest?" In the image itself, the intent of the artist, or in the mind of the viewer? She concludes, "Since Lesbianism is not solely a matter of sexuality, it should not be necessary to depict a sexual union in order to depict a Lesbian union. Even if a work of art is not explicit or titled in some way to give the necessary clue, the idea of a complete relationship between two women can be implied."[64]

Whitworth's writing, like her early diagrammatic drawings of organic forms, tried to get inside the outward appearance of things, birthing images and thoughts from the inside out. Today Whitworth is no longer writing about art, but she continues to draw interior life systems from a position of goddess spirituality and ecofeminism.

Lesbianizing existing heterosexual narratives, originally a skill that we developed for survival and pleasure (to combat the poverty of lesbian representation), has become a habit we can't stop, and continues to date, as aesthetic strategy, in the work of many artists. [. . .]

Movements Toward Self-Representation

[. . .] The critic Holland Cotter's pathbreaking 1994 article on "Art After Stonewall" begins with a succinct account of the incident [that] has been attributed with sparking the gay liberation movement: "On the night of June 6, 1969 in

New York's Greenwich Village, the police conducted a routine raid on a gay bar called the Stonewall Inn. It would have been just harassment as usual, except that this time the men ['and women,' Hammond amends] in the bar fought back. Spilling out into the streets, they chased the police off with bottles, rocks and—the crucial ingredients—a united anger."[65] While it is debated who threw the first bottle or stone, it is clear that it was drag queens and working-class dykes who hung out at the village bars, and had the least to lose, that were the initiators of the resistance to police harassment. Within days "gay power" groups were meeting, the American Sociological Association issued a public declaration endorsing the rights of homosexuals and other sexual minorities, the magazines *Time* and *Look* published feature stories on the new visible homosexuality, and the Gay Liberation Front marched with their banner in the anti–Vietnam War march on Washington. Clearly the Stonewall rebellion had mobilized gays and lesbians into a rebellion that signaled the end of years of harassment against passive and fearful homosexuals and triggered the activism [including in the arts] of the next decade.

ED. NOTE

This text was drawn from Hammond's rough draft for an unpublished prologue to *Lesbian Art in America: A Contemporary History*. The research lays the groundwork for contemporary history, effectuating a sweeping corrective to the heterosexualization of art history by (1) retrieving from historical obscurity forgotten women artists (e.g., Mary Ann Willson) who had important same-sex relationships; (2) tracing the connections between and among women that nourished the artistic careers of women artists (e.g., Georgia O'Keeffe) who did leave indelible marks on the art historical record; and (3) foregrounding the vibrancy of women's artistic partnerships and communities. The "missing chapter" traces lineages, including imaginary lineages, for the benefit of contemporary lesbians whose histories have been erased. The essay sets up the discussion of lesbian artists in America of the twenty-first century whose practices engage with repression and erasure.

At the time Hammond drafted this chapter, in the early 1990s, scholarship on many of the artists discussed remained introductory. Since the 1990s, such artists as Rosa Bonheur, Harriet Hosmer, Edmonia Lewis, Romaine Brooks, and Georgia O'Keeffe (among others) have benefited from in-depth scholarly investigation and important monographic exhibitions. Widely accessible digital resources (Wikipedia, for one) have facilitated the discovery of, and popularized, even the most obscure artists figuring in the unpublished chapter.

Working from a heavily marked-up draft of the chapter, the art historian Ashton Cooper interpreted, edited, and considerably abridged "Desperately Seeking Images: Pre-Stonewall and Prefeminist Art" for publication here. I then conducted additional revisions. Ashton and I have, to the best of our ability, provided footnotes based mainly on Hammond's abbreviated parenthetical notations. Keeping faith with the historical time frame in which the chapter was originally drafted, we did not consult contemporary references to update biographical information in the text (with one exception: We added post-1990s death dates). Nor did we reinforce the chapter's arguments by mobilizing evidence that was not available to Hammond in the mid-1990s, when she strategically shifted the focus of her research for the book to privilege contemporary (self-identified) lesbian artists. Our reconstruction of this chapter preserves a record, not of every single one of the predecessors "desperately" sought by Hammond, but of a selection evoking the historical gaps Hammond strove to fill in the 1990s, and her mission to restore a history to lesbians and their art.

Hammond never finalized "Desperately Seeking Images." The word count of Hammond's original draft is twice that of the current version. For the record, and to give contemporary readers a sense of the full scope of Hammond's original undertaking, we list below the names of the artists originally presenced by Hammond but who are not referenced in the abridged version. One hundred and thirty-two women culture makers figure in the original; the abridged version includes discussion of eighty-three.

Dis-inclusion of an artist in the contemporary version does not imply any judgment about the quality of that artist's work or her historical significance. Deletions were based on the sketchiness or illegibility of the draft we had to work with or, in some cases, the unreliability of information (drawn from sources available at the time of Hammond's writing) on certain artists. Artists and culture makers fully or partially edited out of the abridged version range from the lesser known, such as Agnes Pelton, a member of the Transcendental Painters Group, to iconic figures, such as Frida Kahlo. Hammond originally included a few contemporary artists whose work dialogues with historical figures or problematizes the historical erasure of lesbians. Contemporary artists covered in the publication *Lesbian Art in America* (still widely accessible) or referenced in other essays published in this volume have been edited out of the abridged version.

The forty-nine artists (or collectives) left out are as follows: Berenice Abbott, Alice Austen, Djuna Barnes, Lorena Bobbitt, Deborah Bright, Kaucyila Brooke, Dorthey Cardell, Leonora Carrington, Wendy Castor, Colette, Dyke Action Machine, Nicole Eisenman, Jessie Fauset, Perle Fine, Leonore Fini, Janet Flanner, Martha Graham, Dorothy Hepworth and Patricia Preece, Gladys Hines, Anna Hope Hudson, Gwen Johns, Frida Kahlo, Mary Klein, Marie Laurencin, Gypsy Rose Lee, Tamara de Lempicka, Lesbian Avengers, Nina Levitt, Mina Loy, Jeanne Mamman, Mandy Merck, Kate Millett, Rice Pereira, Riot Grrrls, Ida Rubenstein, Anne Ryan, Kay Sage, Ethel Sands, Valerie Solanas, Gertrude Stein and Alice B. Toklas, Dorothea Tanning, Soloka Theota, Renée Vivien, Keri Warnick, Thelma Wood, Aileen Wournos, Carrie Yamaoka.

The numbered endnotes below are by the author and the editor in collaboration with Ashton Cooper.

NOTES

1. Jill Johnston, *Lesbian Nation* (New York: Simon and Schuster, 1973), 58.

2. See Esther Newton, "The Mythic Mannish Lesbian: Radclyffe Hall and the New Woman," *Signs* 9, no. 4 (Summer 1984): 557–75.

3. See Lillian Faderman, *Surpassing the Love of Men: Romantic Friendship and Love Between Women from the Renaissance to the Present* (New York: Quill, 1981).

4. Isabel Miller, *Patience and Sarah* (New York: McGraw-Hill, 1972). Originally published in 1969 as *A Place for Us.*

5. Jean Lipman, "Mary Ann Willson," in *Primitive Painters in America, 1750–1950: An Anthology*, by Jean Lipman and Alice Winchester (New York: Dodd, Mead, 1950), 54. See also Charlotte Streifer Rubinstein, *American Women Artists: From Early Indian Times to the Present* (Ann Arbor: University of Michigan Press, 1982), 33.

6. Richard Lionel Delisser, *Picturesque Catskills: Greene County* (Catskill Mountains, NY: Picturesque Publishing Company, 1894), 134, 136.

7. Jonathan Ned Katz, *Gay American History: Lesbians and Gay Men in the U.S.A.: A Documentary History* (New York: Crowell, 1976), 434. Reprinted in "Lesbian Art and Artists," special issue, *Heresies: A Feminist Publication on Art and Politics* 1, no. 3 (1977).

8. Ann Sutherland Harris and Linda Nochlin, *Women Artists, 1550–1950* (Los Angeles: Los Angeles County Museum of Art, 1976), 57.

9. Emmanuel Cooper, *The Sexual Perspective: Homosexuality and Art in the Last 100 Years in the West* (London: Routledge and Kegan Paul, 1986), 44–54.

10. For Bonheur, see, in addition to Cooper, the chapter devoted to the artist in Harris and Nochlin, *Women Artists*.

11. Harris and Nochlin, *Women Artists*, 223.

12. Cooper, *The Sexual Perspective*, xvii.

13. Cooper, *The Sexual Perspective*, 49.

14. Anna Elizabeth Klumpke, *Memoirs of an Artist* (Boston: Wright and Potter, 1940), 52.

15. Elsa Honig Fine, *Women and Art: A History of Women Painters and Sculptors from the Renaissance to the Twentieth Century* (Montclair, NJ: Allanheld and Schram/Prior, 1978), 60.

16. See James Saslow, "'Disagreeably Hidden': Construction of the Lesbian Body in Rosa Bonheur's *Horse Fair*," in *The Expanding Discourse: Feminism and Art History*, ed. Norma Broude and Mary D. Garrard (New York: Routledge, 1992), 187–205.

17. Cooper, *The Sexual Perspective*, 51.

18. Rubinstein, *American Women Artists*, 76.

19. Rubinstein, *American Women Artists*, 75.

20. Rubinstein, *American Women Artists*, 77–88. Emma Stebbins was primarily known for her Central Park fountain and for publishing the biography of her companion, Cushman. In 1870 Stebbins and Cushman returned to the United States to live together in Newport, Rhode Island, until Cushman's death in 1876.

21. Henry James, *William Wetmore Story and His Friends* (Boston: Harvard University Press, 1903), 257.

22. Fine, *Women and Art*, 109, 111.

23. Rubinstein, *American Women Artists*, 77.

24. Rubinstein, *American Women Artists*, 77.

25. Eleanor Tufts, *American Women Artists, 1830–1930* (Washington, DC: National Museum of Women in the Arts, 1987), unpaginated.

26. Rubinstein, *American Women Artists*, 79.

27. David C. Driskell, *Two Centuries of Black American Art* (Los Angeles: Los Angeles Museum of Art, 1976), 48, quoted by Rubinstein, *American Women Artists*, 79.

28. Rubinstein, *American Women Artists*, 61.

29. Rubinstein, *American Women Artists*, 83.

30. Shari Benstock, *Women of the Left Bank: Paris, 1900–1940* (Austin: University of Texas Press, 1986).

31. Arlene Raven, "The Eye of the Beholder: The Lesbian Vision of Romaine Brooks," *Sinister Wisdom*, no. 16 (Spring 1981): 41.

32. Raven, "The Eye of the Beholder," 40.

33. See Vera Norwood and Janice Monk, eds., *The Desert Is No Lady: Southwestern Landscapes in Women's Writing and Art* (New Haven, CT: Yale University Press, 1987).

34. Judith Schwarz, "Lesbian Photography, a Long Tradition," in *Eye to Eye: Portraits of Lesbians*, photographs by Joan E. Biron (Washington, DC: Glad Hag Books, 1979), 8.

35. Laura Gilpin, *The Enduring Navaho* (Austin: University of Texas Press, 1968).

36. Sharyn Rohlfsen Udall, *Contested Terrain: Myth and Meanings in Southwest Art* (Albuquerque: University of New Mexico Press, 1996), 12–13, 26.

37. This oft-repeated story about O'Keeffe appears, for one, in Jimmy Ernst, *A Not-So-Still-Life: A Memoir* (New York: St. Martin's/Marek, 1984), 236.

38. Harris and Nochlin, *Women Artists*, 59.

39. Lee Hall, *Betty Parsons: Art Dealer, Artist, Collector* (New York: H. N. Abrams, 1990).

40. "May the leaves of yesterday not follow you. / May the birds of the future guide you, / and the voice of the wind inform you / and the rays of the sun embrace you." Betty Parsons's poem to Agnes Martin was written in 1967, as Martin was leaving New York to return to New Mexico. The poem was published along with Helene Aylon's interview with Betty Parsons in *Womanart Magazine*, Fall 1977, 11. The interview was originally supposed to appear in the "Lesbian Art and Artists" issue of *Heresies*, but Parsons balked, and Aylon found another (presumably more acceptable) outlet.

41. Betty Parsons, interview by Helene Aylon, *Womanart Magazine*, Fall 1977, 11.

42. Parsons, interview by Aylon, 13.

43. Parsons, interview by Aylon, 14.

44. Buffie Johnson, *Lady of the Beasts: Ancient Images of the Goddess and Her Sacred Animals* (New York: Harper and Row, 1988), later published under the title *Lady of the Beasts: The Goddess and Her Sacred Animals.*

45. Unattributed quote. [According to Julia Bryan-Wilson, "the direct quote from Nevelson is hearsay." Bryan-Wilson reproduces and problematizes this quote in "Keeping House with Louise Nevelson," *Oxford Art Journal* 40, no. 1 (2017): 120.]

46. Laurie Lisle, *Louise Nevelson: A Passionate Life* (New York: Summit Books, 1990), 251.

47. Nevelson's declaration appears in many contemporary publications, including Roy Bongartz, "Darkness into Light," *New York Times*, January 24, 1971, section SM, 12.

48. Kathleen Mangan, ed., *Lenore Tawney: A Retrospective* (American Craft Museum, New York, 1990), 27.

49. Hammond and Wilson, to cite one verifiable example, shared a lifelong, at times intimate, relationship.

50. Martin's romantic relationships with women were known to members of her close circle, such as Lenore Tawney, Ann Wilson, and Jill Johnson.

51. See Eve Kosofsky Sedgwick, *Epistemology of the Closet* (Berkeley: University of California Press, 1990).

52. Lillian Faderman, *Odd Girls and Twilight Lovers: A History of Lesbian Life in Twentieth-Century America* (New York: Columbia University Press, 1991), 160.

53. Joan Nestle, "Butch-Fem Relationships: Sexual Courage in the 1950s," *Heresies: A Feminist Publication on Art and Politics* 12, no. 3/4 (1981): 21–24.

54. Faderman, quoting *The Ladder*, in *Odd Girls and Twilight Lovers*, 180.

55. Faderman, *Odd Girls and Twilight Lovers*, 180. Audre Lorde's essays, collected in *Sister Outsider: Essays and Speeches* (New York: Crossing Press/Random House, 1984), participate in a far more complex analysis of multiple marginality.

56. Faderman, *Odd Girls and Twilight Lovers*, 149, 191.

57. Bonnie Zimmerman, "What Has Never Been: An Overview of Lesbian Feminist Criticism," in *Making a Difference: Feminist Literary Criticism*, ed. Gayle Green and Coppélia Kahn (London: Routledge, 1988), 195. [Ed: Zimmerman's essay was first published in *Feminist Studies* 7/3 (1981): 451–75.]

58. See Bertha Harris, "What We Mean to Say: Notes Towards Defining the Nature of Lesbian Literature," *Heresies: A Feminist Publication on Art and Politics*, no. 3 (1977): 5–8.

59. The English translation, *The Lesbian Body*, was released in 1975.

60. Zimmerman, "What Has Never Been," 193.

61. For Whitworth's articles, see Barbara Grier and Coletta Reid, eds., *The Lavender Herring: Lesbian Essays from The Ladder* (Baltimore: Diana Press, 1976).

62. Isabel Bishop is discussed in this letter: Jean Louise [aka Sarah Whitworth], "Foundations of the Male-Chauvinist-Nude Part II: Alternatives," *The Ladder* 15, nos. 11–12 (June–July 1971): 30–34.

63. Sarah Whitworth, "Henry Schnakenberg—'The Conversation,'" in Grier and Reid, *The Lavender Herring*, 286–87. See also Jean Louise [Sarah Whitworth], "Journeys in Art: Henry Schnakenberg—'Conversation,'" *The Ladder* 15, nos. 4–5 (February–March 1971): 21.

64. Sarah Whitworth, "The Other Face of Love," in Grier and Reid, *The Lavender Herring*, 339–40.

65. Holland Cotter, "Art After Stonewall," *Art in America*, June 1994, 14.

Painting Allowed

Lesbians Trespass in the Modernist Painting Field

SITE SANTA FE (1997)

> Any woman who undertakes the historically male act of painting is forced to engage in aesthetic cross-dressing.

This statement was made by mixed-media artist Millie Wilson in connection with her 1989 installation *Fauve Semblant*, where she created a museum retrospective for a fictitious lesbian painter, a young English girl named Peter, who worked in Paris at the turn of the century.

In this statement Wilson refers to the noticeable absence of women from museum spaces and art historical canons. It used to be that to be a woman and to be a painter were mutually exclusive and no one even mentioned the messy existence of lesbian artists, who may or may not be "women," depending upon your definition. For a woman painter to be taken seriously she had to paint like a man but remain a woman.

Millie Wilson's installation refers to the artist Romaine Brooks (1874–1970) and her portrait of the British artist Gluck (1895–1978), entitled *Peter (A Young English Girl)* [1924]. Both painters were very wealthy, had the privilege to live and paint openly as lesbians, and were respected artists in their day. However, their work, like that of many women and lesbian artists, has been noticeably absent from art historical and museum spaces. Gluck died a bitter recluse after her work went out of fashion, and there was little interest in Brooks's work until her American retrospective, curated by Adelyn D. Breeskin in 1971 at the National Collection of Fine Arts in Washington, DC, after which it began to receive more serious attention.[1]

Wilson gives her fictional artist Peter the retrospective that neither Gluck nor Brooks had in their lifetime, and in doing so, honors a tradition of lesbian creativity that has gone unnamed and unacknowledged. Paralleling the construction of "the artist" and her "body of work" with the construction of "the lesbian," Wilson utilizes specific art historical references and museum praxis to focus on the role of "presentation" in creating, legitimizing, and authenticating. Using installation conventions such as an entrance wall with large signage, and a life-sized black-and-white photograph of the artist (in drag, of course), Wilson critiques the grand museum retrospective designed to bestow importance upon an oeuvre by creating a historical narrative fiction that relates it to other important modernist art.

Like Brooks and Gluck, Peter is a lesbian who cross-dresses. All that remains of her life and work are a few artifacts: her smoking jacket, shoes, cane, bow tie, glasses, her last palette, and a single painting, all represented in the exhibition by life-sized photographs. Representing that which is absent, together they form the documentary basis of the life and work of this artist. Starting with male clothing as a sign of sexual orientation, the mannish lesbian artist must be constructed. Exploring an alternative history in which Peter symbolizes the "other," Wilson's piece is more about presentation than representation, for how the lesbian artist is presented is crucial to the authority and the legitimization of the very male institutions that confer authenticity, value, and prestige upon her.

Peter's one surviving painting (presented as a treasured artifact in a plexiglass box) hints at exotic lesbian sexuality through symbols of a leopard (bestiality) and an eroticized arrangement of tropical flowers (female sexuality), and refers to the late nineteenth-century group of French painters called Les Fauves (to signify their wild lifestyle and savage or primitive handling of paint and color). This curatorial practice legitimizes Peter's work by connecting it to the male modernism.

It's a complex piece that works on many levels. "Invading high modernism with a queer discourse," Wilson is able to examine and critique gender stereotypes, the construction and representation of the lesbian subject, and art world styles and conventions.[2] The title *Fauve Semblant*, which translates as seeming or appearing to be or looking wild, also refers to the relationship between painting and photography, emphasizing the new role of photography (invented in 1839) and what Roland Barthes calls its "power of authentication" in documenting a sexuality written on the body.[3]

But, now days, cross-dressing is in and lesbians don't really give a damn how categories of creative production or even style itself have been historically gendered. In the '90s, the lesbian artist, queer as she is (performing as herself or in drag), is going where she wants, how she wants, and is taking perverse pleasure in doing so.

Gone is the "good girl," just like everyone else's image of the lesbian—the new painter, just like the dyke she subjects, is a sexual outlaw who, assuming different positionings that may or may not be politically correct, insists that she can move freely back and forth between high and low art, and that she has the right to utilize all images and gazes, including those generated in art history, popular culture, cartoons, and comics, fanzines, medical texts, fashion, advertising, and pornography. While much of this work is humorous, it is also intensely serious, sometimes angry, difficult, or disturbing, and certainly doesn't allow for neat detached readings. Unlike painting from the '70s, it does not come out of the desire for a simple, positive, essential lesbian sensibility or aesthetic (nor assimilation into the modernist mainstream), but rather freely and pleasurably enters in and explores what Judith Butler might describe as "troubled sites," that is spaces where contradictions, layers, tensions, complexities, and possibilities abound and are negotiated.[4]

* * *

Painting does seem like the ultimate bad object.—LIZ KOTZ

The title of my talk this evening, "Painting Allowed," refers to recent lesbian occupation of the masculinist painting field as a site of engagement.[5]

Like photography in the '80s, painting—as an act, an object, and a site—represents many of the issues surrounding lesbian representation in the '90s. Until recently, lesbians have been hesitant to enter traditional male-dominated fields of object-making like painting and sculpture, choosing instead to work in and contribute much to the formation of the less fortified and calcified areas of film, video, and performance. However, the range of aesthetic strategies being used in the '90s indicates a shift from the time-based, performative arts and photography to the modernist painting field, which historically has been dominated by white men. With total disregard for barriers of gender and sexuality constructed around sacred historical sites such as Euro-Western painting—that is, ignoring signs to stay out, violators will be prosecuted—lesbian artists are consciously trespassing, irreverently tramping across the modernist painting field, lesbianizing it as they go.[6]

By "the modernist painting field," I mean not only that two-dimensional space delineated by the perimeter of the canvas or paper, and the painting surface as edge, but rather Western painting as a language and all the institutions it supports and that support it—an immense privileged historical, social, political, economic, and cultural site of representation—an occupied territory that has been especially hostile to women, lesbians, and anyone else outside the "mythical norm," or that which is "white, thin, male, young, heterosexual, christian, and financially secure."[7] Our very presence and the visual tracks we leave on the skin of paint assert multiple subjectivities and specificities that throw into question the assumed gender and sexuality of artist and audience, thereby disrupting and destabilizing the authoritative voice of the whole two-dimensional territory.

But trespassing into enemy territory, as critic Liz Kotz warns, is always risky business.[8] So, why do it? For many of us who consciously choose to work in this problematic, mine-ridden field of historic and contested meanings, underlying these painterly transgressions is a belief in the possibilities of painting—a belief that a critical space can be opened up and a lesbian voice articulated within such a masculinist site, even one that has for centuries excluded the lesbian subject.

Painting is a complex network of not just pigment on canvas or other support but references that allude to painting's historical relationship to photography, drawing, collage, and other visual disciplines. I'd like to suggest that it is here, in these cracks/fissures, these unstable spaces/overlaps, and seams that lesbian artists have entered in.

Difference is an old queer discussion, but today's strategies of representation are new and constantly shifting as are the notions of lesbian identity.

We are now seeing images of lesbian self-representation that we have never before seen in the history of Western art. With painting and drawing, what we are seeing is radical new content in a traditional field. Contemporary painting strategies range from those frequently employed by marginalized groups—revisionist approaches such as appropriation, turning the tables and insertion, often literally painting oneself into the dominant art historical discourse—to those that are gender-, race-, or sexuality-specific. Of course, these approaches overlap and none are limited to painting alone. Lesbian-based content is rendered via a critique of master paintings, the institutions that support them, and their appropriation for lesbian ends.[9] Additionally, it is rendered through the ambiguous relationship of painting and photography; the manipulation and presentation of paint as an embodied material; the decision to work with an "outsider aesthetic"; references to sexual subcultures; playful bad girl fantasies; and by figuring lots of outrageous, confrontive in-your-face genitalia and sexplicit imagery.[10]

Unlike art from the '70s, lesbian art of the '90s does not come out of the desire for a simple, positive, reductive lesbian sensibility or aesthetic. And, unlike work from the '80s that remained cool, disembodied, detached and distanced, art of the '90s delves into "troubled sites." Given its history, the painting field itself could be described as a troubled site, which is precisely why it interests some of us.

Like most recent lesbian and feminist art in general, paintings and drawings of the '90s are often excessive, either raw and messy (Brenda Goodman and Shelley Marlow), compulsively repetitious (Ellen Gallagher), or obsessively tight—a realism informed by both photography and old master painting traditions (Judith Bamber, Monica Majoli, and Riva Lehrer). Elaine Marks has written that "to undomesticate the female body one must dare reinscribe it in excess—as excess."[11] We must make it extreme enough and strong enough to resist appropriation, to resist the male gaze, and, thus, to reconfigure the terms of lesbian subjectivity in visual art. Indeed, [this] [. . .] has been the project of lesbian painting since its inception in the early '70s.

Of course, as Teresa de Lauretis has observed, the difficulty of inscribing lesbian experience visually is that we come up against the limitations of historical forms of representation, in this case the figure, and more specifically the female or lesbian figure as the visual representation of the lesbian body.[12] And the language of painting itself. Certainly not all lesbian art is sexual, nor figurative nor narrative, but given the objectification of the female body in general, and the tradition of lesbian images engaged in sexual or sexualized activities created for or consumed by the male gaze—that is, fantasies of lesbian eroticism by men—it has been particularly problematic for lesbians to create their own sexually explicit or erotic art. The difference from artists who began working twenty to twenty-five years ago is that the new crop of young painters, while aware of this ongoing problem of who is looking at whom, how and from where, do not really give a damn, assume different gazes, and just make their work no matter who else is looking.[13]

Several exhibitions in the early '90s challenged '80s notions "that only the media arts [could] mount social critique, that a painting was simply too precious, too tradition-bound to make a difference."[14] While it was not a gay or queer show, *Post-Boys and Girls: Nine Painters* (1990–1991) at Artists Space in New York, anticipated new "inqueeries" about gender and re-established painting as a field in which to work. "Meant to stimulate people to think about what men and women are supposed to be and what a painting in 1990 could say about that," the exhibition presented work that questioned authority, reintroduced language into painting, and asserted the existence of subjectivities that had mostly been ignored or suppressed.[15] Most of the paintings involved the use photographs or slides as a means to bring social or political content and different points of view into the painting field. In her catalogue essay for the exhibition, Carol Zemmel announced transgressions into the field and notes, "If postmodernism has shown us anything, [. . .] it is that style can be deployed as a fluid critical language with new meaning in its present usages and as such, it can decode and disrupt [. . .] older values and mythologies."[16]

So, in a sense we are talking about painterly revisions. Zemmel called for a "new more inclusive painting practice" with a multiplicity of artist-subject positions and giving the example of Millie Wilson's *The Painter Who Is Not One* [1990] pointed out that "lines between genres are no longer rigidly drawn."[17]

Painting Culture, an exhibition at Fiction/Nonfiction Gallery in New York (1991), also signaled a new interest in painting as a site of social and, in this case, feminist intervention.[18] Based on the premise that "a number of women artists with theoretical roots [. . .] moved into the field of figurative painting, often via the issue of representation as it pertains to hand-painted renditions of mechanically reproduced imagery,"[19] the exhibition prompts us to ask, "Can voices of the colonized be heard in painting, a language that has excluded women and artists of color? Or is painting too overdetermined as a system and site? Can it be radicalized?" As painter Deborah Kass [who cocurated the exhibition] explained:

> We have no alternative but to use the available language of the culture, even though this language, like the culture—its meanings, myths, and history—have been produced by and for men. When a woman makes a painting, she is [. . .] using a language that has denied her and been denied her. [. . .] By making this painting, she is insisting on the viability of her expression, its right to exist on its own terms. She is insisting on her right to use this language to her own end, to describe her position and place in a way that this language has not been used before—to represent herself.[20]

In an interview with Kass, the only lesbian in the exhibition, critic Laura Cottingham stated that she is anti-painting because she believes that painting and feminism are mutually exclusive: Feminism is against patriarchy and painting is for it. Cottingham asks, "Given the ongoing misogyny represented in painting's historical conversation, both before and after modernism, why would feminists want to enter such an obviously one-sided dialogue?"[21] It is a good question. But there are answers.

Kass disagreed with Cottingham, as I do, and answered that "if painting can't escape its status as a sign for modernism, as a sign for bourgeois individualism, then it really is dead. But painting is a cultural language, and like any other cultural language, it doesn't have to rely on its historicized meanings. . . ."[22] A better question might be, "From what and whose perspectives have paintings been made?" Addressing the difficulty of working within existing patriarchal language systems, Kass quoted lesbian poet Adrienne Rich, who struggles with similar issues. Rich writes, "This is the oppressor's language. Yet I need it to talk with you."[23] The issue for lesbians is, How can we make painting speak to our experiences? What are the various ways we can bring lesbian content into the male-dominated painting field?

Kass's personal solution was to employ postmodern strategies of appropriation, fragmentation, recontextualization, and layering to undermine and poke fun at the masculinist site of painting. Other artists have had other solutions. Some have inserted blatant lesbian content or juxtaposed photographs, materials, objects, and text that insist on lesbian readings, and in doing so interrogate and destabilize the painting site.[24] It is not so much about pushing borders as disregarding them—irreverently trespassing and tramping across the modernist field. Kass quips, "Unless [painting] can speak from something other than a Eurocentric male point of view, it deserves to be dead."[25] Either painting accepts multiple voices or it dies.

Kass appropriates Warhol's popular icons and replaces them with her own to construct a presence of difference: Barbra Streisand (the object of her diva worship) and Andy Warhol (whom she calls the first great queer). Kass was an adolescent when Streisand exploded on the Broadway scene and on television in the '60s. She recalls: "Her gorgeousness was not universally embraced, especially by first-generation Jews in suburbia busy trying to assimilate—such as my parents. I thought she was positively divine. Her 'awkwardness,' her 'nose,' her difference thrilled me. She embraced glamour of a particularly American kind, and did it with a vengeance and great aplomb. That a Jewish girl with wit, talent, and brains could be herself and 'make it' spoke volumes to me. And she did it consciously, put it on and wore stardom like the diva she had yet to become. Drag? Absolutely."[26]

Kass uses an image of Streisand in her "Jewish Jackie" series . . . a series that references Warhol's portraits of celebrities. In her *Yentl (My Elvis)* paintings [1992–93], Kass impersonates Streisand cross-dressing as [in the film] *Yentl* [1983].[27]

While '70s gender-based definitions of lesbianism were depicted through abstract landscape symbols, self-confessional text, or images of women within domestic environments, hinting at fantasies and possible seductions while rarely actually depicting sexual or sexualized activities, much of the new painting is figurative, narrative, often photo-based, and overtly reasserts sexuality as central to lesbian identity and desire.

At first glance, some of the materials, iconography, stylizations, and concerns of work being made today seem remarkably indebted to feminist artmaking in the '70s. Indeed, much '90s work can be seen and discussed as an extension of work by feminist and lesbian feminist artists of the 1970s. The strategies of representation are not necessarily the same. Because the artistic, social, political, and economic climate have changed, the work is created, presented, and discussed within a different contextual and theoretical framework that, in turn, becomes part of the meaning of the pieces. I do not mean to imply that certain works are more authentic or more powerful than others. Rather, I intend to mobilize historical feminist and lesbian feminist art to inform and enrich the discussion around specific artworks and lesbian art in general. [. . .]

Earlier feminist paintings with cunt/vulvar (exterior) and vaginal (interior) imagery were usually abstract, symbolic, and generic.[28] Early feminist photography, on the other hand, realistically documented a spectrum of female genitalia, proving that there was no such thing as "*a* cunt." Photographs of cunts (meaning an opening of labia lips to reveal the clitoris and space beyond) were often ironically presented as portraits of specific women or placed in grids, cataloguing different colors, shapes, and sizes to emphasize individual variation.

Because it is theorized differently, recent cunt imagery differs from earlier feminist representations. The following discussion elaborates on work that Mary Patten, Zoe Leonard, Judith Bamber, and Marlene McCarty produced in the '90s. Their work critiques the masculinist history of pornographic images of women in the name of fine art and attempts to reclaim painting, a woman's body, and the gaze for lesbians.

In her installation *My Courbet . . . or, a Beaver's Tale* (1991–92), Mary Patten hung nine framed color photographic portraits of women posed spread-leg in the manner of Courbet's famous 1866 painting the *L'Origine du monde* (The Origin of the World) on walls covered with beaver-patterned wallpaper. Intended as a lesbian commentary on Courbet's painting (in contrast to the Courbet, Patten's portraits are titled with each individual woman's name), Patten's installation raised issues of class distinctions between art and pornography. The art world legitimized the Courbet, originally commissioned for a Turkish ambassador who was a well-known collector of erotica. In reality, his close-up realist painting of female genitalia "crammed into his voyeuristic little frame . . . was simply 'a beaver shot' created in the name of art."[29] Patten's critique was reinforced by a humorous video modeled as a PBS documentary about lesbian representation throughout history.[30] Combining fine art images (including those by Courbet, Tee Corinne, and Judy Chicago) with those from sex magazines and agit prop posters, the documentary focused on how we have been represented and how we are representing ourselves. It consisted of information, critical commentary, and "a few lies or half-truths about the sexual orientation of a number of well-known women artists."[31] As one critic observed, Patten "deftly delineate[d] a historic struggle for power, starting with female sexuality as depicted by straight white male culture, and then how lesbian artists have taken their gender's sexuality back, in a similar way that women have worked to 'take back the night,' from rapists."[32]

For the 1992 *Documenta* IX in Kassel, Germany, Zoe Leonard also referenced Courbet's *L'Origine*.[33] She created a series of small black-and-white close-up photographs of women friends' genitals and casually hung them between the eighteenth-century paintings of women in the Neue Galerie. While Leonard's images of cunts continued a body of work begun by earlier lesbian feminists, the context was decidedly different.[34] As Jan Zita Grover has observed, "The issue is not just what lies within the frame but the context around the frame."[35] In contrast to Corinne's tiny framed pubic portraits from the '70s and the elaborate "framing" of the precious historical paintings in the museum collection, Leonard's rough prints were hung "unframed" behind glass. In this way, she was able to remove the protective frame, situate and (re)frame the work and a lesbian gaze within the history of looking and possessing, while remaining vulnerable and different.

Leonard's installation also differed from Patten's in its siting within an actual museum, thereby literally intervening in the fine art history of veiled beaver shots that Courbet represented and Patten referenced. In contrast to Corinne's placement of her images in primarily woman-only venues or Patten's installation in alternative spaces, Leonard consciously presented her work in what is traditionally a male space. The fact that she inserted her "pussy shots," as she called them, into the historical museum system underscored the hypocrisy of neutral fine art by men that depicts women as sex objects, allowing Leonard to participate in the contemporary critique of authoritative cultural institutions and opening a space for the "cruising eye" of the lesbian viewer in those institutions.

The piece worked best as a taking of public female space, and a very prestigious international one at that—one that other lesbians have not had access to.

It is to Leonard's credit that she did not try to be a "good girl" but rather used her privileged inclusion in the male-dominated *Documenta* to present her most highly charged and unsafe work to date.

In 1994, Judith Bamber completed three untitled paintings based on photographs of cunts of women friends.[36] While Patten's and Leonard's photographs referenced and disrupted the Western masculinist history of painting, Bamber used the photographs as references for her meticulous photorealist paintings, thereby spiraling via the intertextuality between painting and photography, back to Courbet's *L'Origine*.[37] However, unlike the Courbet or countless other paintings by countless other men, the subject is not restricted or forced into the traditional horizontal composition of the reclining female figure as terrain or landscape to be dominated, controlled, and colonized. Bamber's paintings are vertical rectangles making the labia/vulva an upright form, both slit and phallus, that begins to rupture male definitions and positionings of the female or lesbian body, thereby reconceptualizing the painterly representation of the site of female sexuality. They are about the pleasure of showing and looking, and the pleasure of painting, of "creating a skin that itself represents the skin and flesh and hair that sight/site lesbian desire."[38]

As with Corinne's, Patten's, and Leonard's imagery, "whatever erotic impulses Bamber's paintings actually elicit is entirely dependent upon the subjective perceptions and sexual proclivities of the viewer."[39] However, heterosexual pornographic consumption is minimized while the paintings remain available for the viewing pleasure of women, getting close to a feminist or lesbian pornography, the possibility of which has intrigued feminists since the mid-'80s. Like Courbet, Bamber disembodies the vulva. Actually, there is less leg and pubic area in Bamber's paintings (less woman as site of the vagina), than in the Courbet, or for that matter in the Patten and Leonard simulations, where the female body is tipped back and reclining, positioning the viewer looking out and in from a distance. Since Bamber's cunt is tipped up, audaciously and aggressively filling the frame and occupying the picture plane, there is no perspective other than in your face, no space for the viewer to (re)position themselves. This assertiveness minimizes appropriation and consumption. The painting, of course, can be viewed by anyone, but without the rest of the woman to fill out the fantasy, it is unlikely that many men will get off on it. Any woman however, "knows" the/her whole body, and any lesbian would, I assume, take great pleasure in looking.

Marlene McCarty confronts viewers with sexually charged words as well as images. When McCarty first began to work with the activist groups Gran Fury and Women's Health Action Mobilization (WHAM), she was appalled by the ineffective demonstration placards and visual materials they were using and decided to help develop better graphics. This focus on graphics came back into her own art when, in response to attacks on federal funding of artists and institutions, she consciously began to question what constitutes sexually explicit work.

Referencing language-based art coming out of the '60s and postmodern theory of the '80s, especially the work of Jenny Holzer, McCarty works primarily within the parameters of the painting field, but, as critic Laura Cottingham points out, does not respect its traditional boundaries (is it a painting, a sculpture, or graphic design?) or "the attendant line drawn between the varieties of cultural experiences" (is it art, politics, pornography, advertising, or therapy?).[40] She heat transfers texts onto traditional stretched canvases. As the critic Elizabeth Hess has observed, these words and verbalisms circulate in colloquial usage and popular culture. By recontextualizing emotionally charged words and phrases in her artworks, McCarty opens them to resignification.[41]

In most of her work, McCarty uses words that are both nouns and verbs, such as "love," "fuck," "riot," or provocative and at times even difficult or questionable words like "cunt," "beaver," "pussy," "slash," "gash," and misogynist one-liners such as "Your mouth is bleeding like a cunt." McCarty examines the prejudicial and irrational attitudes encoded in language and challenges the intentionality of modernist painting with its individuality, formal purity, and spirituality. Hess sees these words as verbal substitutions for what male painters have rendered visual throughout history. McCarty's words, borrowed from the media and everyday speech, reclaim and reposition the viewer's relationship to the iconography of pornography in art.[42] Is *Pussy, Beaver, Cunt* [1990] a sexually explicit painting? Is it obscene or pornographic? Is this really the kind of work that the radical right is so afraid of?

* * *

Encouraged by the floundering art market, a renewed interest in drawing surfaced in the early '90s. Traditionally considered to be less important and therefore less valued and less expensive than paintings, drawings are not burdened with the responsibility of making major statements. Consequently, anything goes. Anyone can make their mark or draw their lines. Often, drawings charged with political content or erotic fantasy, especially rough sketches or visual journals, provide a way to make personal art with a sense of directness, immediacy and urgency.

In her insightful essay for the exhibition's catalogue for *Part Fantasy: The Sexual Imagination of Seven Lesbian Artists Explored Through the Medium of Drawing* (1992), at Trial Balloon [New York City], Faye Hirsch writes:

> Drawing has traditionally been the medium par excellence of eroticism [...] a quick responsiveness to fleeting fantasies, the versatility and privateness of place in which drawings are made, the intimate horizontality

of the surface—all contribute to drawing's primary place in the expression of erotic themes. [. . .] It is precisely the graphic line's subjecthood, its quality of prompting an action and unfolding, that makes it well-suited to erotic expression. Rarely do we feel the drawing to be "finished," not to mention public, in the manner of a painting—so often does it function as a sketch, a meditation, an ongoing exegesis, and, in some sense, its "object" is never fully realized.[43]

Drawings by lesbians range from academically rendered scenarios of lesbian seduction by Elise Dodeles; quick sketches of women engaged in all sorts of erotic activities by Ellen Cantor; Eliza Jackson's abstract figures of multiple and layered surfaces and orifices, suggesting Luce Irigaray's geography of women's pleasure; and gendered heads with facial hair by Donna Evans, Daphne Fitzpatrick, and Leslie Bostrom; to the apparent naive innocence of Linda Kramer's portraits; Mary King's adolescent girls; Shelley Marlow's messy diaristic rants; or Amanda Pelham's obsessive texts.

For many artists like Nicole Eisenman, drawing figures as the main focus of their work. Extremely prolific, Eisenman moves back and forth in a kind of visual orgy between huge indoor murals; drawings on paper that humorously reference, alter, and subvert historic masterpieces by Cezanne, Picasso and Matisse that turn the historical tables (thereby inserting her within those traditions); and sappy, bad-assed cartoons that drip with Hallmark sentimentality, reflecting a TV talk show mentality or ridicule lesbian politics and lifestyles. A "killer muralist," known for her signature monumental epic scenes of lesbian debauchery, Eisenman is politically incorrect, frenzied, outrageous, and perverse.[44] Nothing is sacred including art history or lesbian lifestyles, both of which she constantly references and parodies.

* * *

A survey of transgressions into the masculinist art historical site of painting by lesbians (who reference, appropriate, and critique specific paintings, specific artists, or the institutions that authorize them) should by rights include many more artists than it's possible for me to bring into focus, or even name, here. But in conclusion I would like to highlight two more interventions—one by Mary Klein and the other by Deborah Bright—that dramatize discursive turns in lesbian art of the 1990s.

Mary Klein examines male representations of women and language to demonstrate how concepts of lesbianism were created by sexual theorists at the turn of the century, and how these theories are inextricably intertwined with attitudes toward women in general. Her ten-foot-long mixed-media piece *Inverted*

Logic [ca. 1993] includes Cibachrome photographs of portraits representing five sexual theorists (Jean-Martin Charcot, Richard von Krafft-Ebing, F. E. Daniel, Havelock Ellis, and Sigmund Freud). Each portrait is split at the man's mouth with the top and bottom parts of the face framed separately. A short bio of each man is sandblasted onto the glass of the mouth section. And running like a visual timeline between the top and bottom sections is a long collage that includes photographic details of historical and contemporary paintings by male painters from Pablo Picasso to Tom Wesselmann that sexually represent/objectify women, along with text taken from each theorist's case histories of lesbians, and writings about women. Klein's intention is to expose the authoritative male voices that continue to shape culture and link the representation of women and lesbians to the medical discourse around sexuality at the turn of the century.

Deborah Bright, with *The Management of Desire (an unmodified radical response)* (1994) reimagines Thomas Eakins's painting *The Agnew Clinic* (1889), which pictures a radical mastectomy in progress. The triptych includes a reproduction of Eakins's painting, a text by Bright responding to the painting, [and] a post-surgical photograph of Bright, posing like a one-breasted odalisque, attended by the nurse she appropriated from Eakins's painting. In this text, Bright says she is reading *The Agnew Clinic* not only through an art historical lens, but also "through the larger frame of the history of the medical regulation of women's bodies and sexuality." Eakins's inclusion of his own portrait (painted, Bright says, by his wife) among the observers in the operating theater solidifies his bond with the other men pictured in *The Agnew Clinic*. The obvious twitchiness of the observing medical students betrays a certain amount of nervous discomfort at watching a breast being amputated. Medical detachment demands that they objectify the body and not see it as belonging to a fully human being. Hence, explains Bright:

> My self-portrait montage emphasizes the subjecthood of the patient with her direct Olympia-like eye contact with the viewer. She refuses to be an object marked and labeled as "diseased"—whether sexually or physiologically (the "blame yourself for you own cancer" idea is a potent one in our culture). The fact that this patient is also a butch lesbian gives the breast's excision another layer of meaning, too, in relation to the tradition among old-school butches of tightly binding their breasts to "get rid of them," so to speak. Now I can have a "boy body" on one side and a "girl body" on the other. While I'm not recommending mastectomies as a way to engage in gender play, it does have that added effect for dykes like me who see themselves as actively inhabiting some ambivalent territory between masculine and feminine.[45]

The critical dialogue with histories of representation, including art history, is one throughline connecting the works we have considered today. Bright, like all the artists I have introduced, asserted the right to represent lesbians, and lesbians' right to occupy the painting field. This said, the creative choices made by lesbians appropriating painting as a cultural form in the 1990s are extremely diverse, as we have seen, and do not support any homogenous notion of lesbian identity, lesbian art, or lesbian representation.

ED. NOTES

Hammond presented "Painting Allowed: Lesbians Trespass in the Modernist Painting Field" orally at SITE SANTA FE in 1997. Her text for the talk has been edited for inclusion here. Hammond gave numerous versions of this talk, including "Lesbian (ART)iculations: Trespassing in the Modernist Painting Field," presented at the Sixth North American Lesbian, Gay, and Bisexual Studies Conference in Iowa City, Iowa, 1994, and "Painting Allowed: Lesbian Transgressions in the Modernist Painting Field," at American University, 2003.

The numbered endnotes for this lecture, below, are by the author.

NOTES

1. Adelyn D. Breeskin, *Romaine Brooks, "Thief of Souls"* (Washington, DC: National Collection of Fine Arts/Smithsonian Institution Press, 1971).
2. Millie Wilson cited by David Bonetti, "Things Are Not What They Seem: Gender Challenging Art Rewards Those Who Do Homework," *San Francisco Examiner*, February 28, 1992, 44.
3. See Roland Barthes, *Camera Lucida: Reflections on Photography*, trans. Richard Howard (New York: Hill and Wang, 1980).
4. See Judith Butler, *Gender Trouble: Feminism and the Subversion of Identity* (New York: Routledge, 1990).
5. The epigraph to this section is from Liz Kotz, "Beyond the Pleasure Principle," cited in *Coming to Power* (New York: David Zwirner Gallery, 1993), 3. ["Beyond the Pleasure Principle" was first published in *Lusitania*, no. 6 (1994): 125–36.]
6. Painters in the '90s include Shirley Bernstein, Lula Mae Blocton, Judith Baca, Janet Cooling, Sandra DeSando, Maxine Fine, Gloria Klein, Louise Fishman, Ada Medina, Edith Isaac Rose, Christina Schlesinger, Hollis Sigler, Joan Snyder, Joan Watts, Fran Winant, and myself, who have continued painting through the '70s and '80s right into the '90s, to Deborah Kass, Sarah Rapson, Patricia Cronin, Nicola Tyson, Nicole Eisenman, Riva Lehrer, Elise Dodeles, Judith Bamber, Monica Majoli, Jennie Schueler, Brenda Goodman, Kim Anno, Vanessa Haney, and Ellen Gallagher, who have emerged in the late '80s and '90s.
7. Audre Lorde, "Age, Race, Class and Sex: Women Redefining Difference," in *Out There: Marginalization and Contemporary Cultures*, ed. Russell Ferguson, Martha Gever, Trinh T. Minh-ha, and Cornel West (Cambridge, MA: MIT Press, 1990), 282.

8. Kotz, "Beyond the Pleasure Principle," 4.

9. Paintings by Courbet, Matisse, Picasso, Marsh, Johns, Warhol, and Salle have all been lesbianized.

10. I use "outsider aesthetic" here to mean the look of an untrained artist and a conscious decision to place oneself outside the Western tradition of male masters. It includes a range of artists from Hollis Sigler, Rhonda Saboff, Mary King, Linda Kramer, and artists who do cartoon-like drawings such as Leslie Bostrom or zine and comics artists G. B. Jones and Sabrina Jones.

11. Elaine Marks, "Lesbian Intertextualities," in *Homosexualities in French Literature*, ed. Elaine Marks and George Stambolian (Ithaca, NY: Cornell University Press, 1970), cited by Teresa de Lauretis, "Sexual Indifference and Lesbian Representation," *Theatre Journal* 40, no. 2 (May 1988): 155–77.

12. De Lauretis, "Sexual Indifference and Lesbian Representation."

13. This is the result of the fact that when many of these artists were students they were fortunate to have the first generation of openly lesbian feminist artists and historians as their teachers and were encouraged to explore aspects of sexuality in their work.

14. Ken Aptekar, introduction to *Post-Boys and Girls: Nine Painters* (New York: Artists Space, 1991), 1.

15. Aptekar, introduction, 1.

16. Carol Zemmel, "Post-Boys and Girls: The Return of the Suppressed," in Aptekar, *Post-Boys and Girls*, 3.

17. Zemmel, "Post-Boys and Girls," 4.

18. *Painting Culture*, curated by the artist Deborah Kass with Jose Freire, director of the fiction/nonfiction gallery in New York City, included work by Sue Williams, Kathy Burkhart, Julie Wachtel, Jane Hammond, Mary Weatherford, and Deborah Kass (the only lesbian among them, and the person who proposed the exhibit to Freire). Work by Marilyn Minter, Susan Silas, and Kay Rosen was added to the exhibition when it traveled to the University of California at Irvine.

19. *Painting Culture* wall text, 1991.

20. Deborah Kass, "In Her Own Voice," *Bomb* 21 (Fall 1987): 48–49.

21. Laura Cottingham, "Interview with Deborah Kass: Feminism and Painting," *Balcón* 7 (1991): 166.

22. Kass in Cottingham, "Interview with Deborah Kass," 166.

23. Kass citing Adrienne Rich, "The Burning of Paper Instead of Children" (1968), in Cottingham, "Interview with Deborah Kass," 166.

24. The use of montage and the introduction of intruder objects into abstract painting strikes a chord with Brechtian strategies of interruption as outlined by Walter Benjamin in his essay "The Author as Producer," strategies that discover situations in freshly defamiliarized material. See Stephen Westfall, "Deborah Kass: Subject Matters," *CONTEMPORANEA* 22 (November 1990): 64–65.

25. Deborah Kass cited by Zan Dubin, "Painting Themselves Out of a Corner: Women's Works at UCI's Fine Arts Gallery Chip Away at Male-Dominated Societies," *Los Angeles Times*, October 10, 1992, Entertainment and Arts.

26. Kass in Patricia Cronin, "A Conversation on Lesbian Subjectivity and Painting (with Deborah Kass)," *M/E/A/N/I/N/G* 14 (November 1993): 9.

27. The film *Yentl*, based on Isaac Bashevis Singer's short story "Yentl, the Yeshiva Boy" (1962), tells the story of an Ashkenazi Jewish woman in turn-of-the-twentieth-century Poland who dresses as a boy to receive an education (denied to women under Talmudic law).

28. An exception was the realistic diagrammatic drawings of cunts in Tee Corinne's *Cunt Coloring Book* of 1975.

29. Mary Patten, Artist's Statement, *My Courbet . . . or, A Beaver's Tale* (1991–92).

30. In 1992, Patten transferred the slide documentary to videotape, a self-sufficient video, *My Courbet*, that can be shown on its own or as part of the installation.

31. Patten, Artist's Statement, *My Courbet . . . or, A Beaver's Tale.*

32. Kevin Lynch, "2 Art Shows at UW Pull No Punches," *Capital Times*, October 21, 1993, 3F.

33. Leonard was consciously referencing the Courbet but apparently was unaware of either Corinne's or Patten's work. In two or three of Leonard's photographs, the woman's fingers part her labia to show and invite our visual investigation and admiration—a notable difference from the Courbet. This "labial posing" is also true of some of Corinne's cunt shots, but not Patten's. Of further interest is the fact that Lacan once owned this Courbet painting.

34. Much of the discussion in the catalogue for the exhibition *Sexual Politics* centers around Chicago's cunt imagery (now called vulvar imagery) and central core imagery—contrasting and relating it to the Courbet, as well as work by other feminist artists. Unfortunately, the catalogue does not deal with lesbian sexuality, even though it discusses work by lesbian artists including Zoe Leonard and Judy Bamber, whose relationships to cunts and therefore cunt imagery would be a bit different than Chicago's (or for that matter, Courbet's). See the catalogue for a more detailed discussion: Amelia Jones, ed., *Sexual Politics: Judy Chicago's Dinner Party in Feminist Art History* (Berkeley: University of California Press, 1996), with essays by Laura Cottingham et al.

35. Jan Zita Grover, "Dykes in Context: Some Problems in Minority Representation," in *The Context of Meaning: Critical Histories of Photography*, ed. Richard Bolton (Cambridge, MA: MIT Press, 1990), 168.

36. Nearly photographic, there are some brush strokes and painterly marks of the artist's hand in the pubic hair, around the anus, and near the edges of the painting.

37. See Jones, *Sexual Politics*, for an extensive comparative discussion of Bamber's photorealist paintings of cunts in relationship to Judy Chicago's more abstract ones made over twenty years earlier.

38. Catherine Lord, "Queering the Deal," in *Pervert* (Irvine: University of California, Irvine, Art Gallery, 1995), 15.

39. Kathy L. Maschke, "Judy Bamber," *Art Papers*, November–December 1994, 36.

40. Laura Cottingham, "Playing Around: Marlene McCarty," exhibition pamphlet (Berlin, Germany: NGBK, 1992), 23.

41. Elizabeth Hess, *Village Voice*. [Hess wrote at least three articles that mention McCarty. Hammond seems to have paraphrased elements of the following texts: Elizabeth Hess, "Dirty Laundry," *Village Voice*, May 12, 1992, 91; Elizabeth Hess, "Gutter Politics," *Village Voice*, July 3, 1990, 91; Elizabeth Hess, "Twisted Sisters," *Village Voice*, March 23, 1993, 86.]

42. Elizabeth Hess, *Village Voice*.

43. Faye Hirsch, "The Body That Sees," in *Part Fantasy: The Sexual Imagination of Seven Lesbian Artists Explored Through the Medium of Drawing* (New York: Trial Balloon Gallery, 1992), 14.

44. Linda Yablonsky, "Drawing Fire," *Out* 3, no. 6 (February 1995): 52.

45. Deborah Bright, undated artist's statement.

Meetings with Agnes Martin

Agnes Martin: Works on Paper (1998)

In 1978, when I was living and working in New York City, I was invited to be a visiting artist at the University of New Mexico in Albuquerque. Friends asked if I would look up Georgia O'Keeffe and Agnes Martin. As much as I wanted to meet them, I felt it would happen if it was supposed to. Our paths would cross. I never did meet Georgia. But I did meet Agnes. This is about our first meeting.

When my good friend Ann Wilson decided to visit me, I dropped Agnes a note and told her that Ann was coming to New Mexico and would like to see her. Ann and Agnes were old friends from the '50s and '60s when they and other artists had pioneered living and working in old sailing lofts on Coenties Slip in Lower Manhattan. Over the years, the two had stayed in touch. Ann had written about Agnes's work and transcribed her parables. The three of us spent the day together, primarily in Agnes's truck. That night, Ann and I, exhausted as we were, decided to write in our journals about the day, with the idea that sometime in the future we would present our entries side by side.

I moved to New Mexico in 1984 and began living in Galisteo in 1989. Going back and rereading my journal, I notice it reveals as much about me as about Agnes and Ann. I obsessively recorded every detail. I was clearly new to Northern New Mexico's land and cultures. And, like many women artists, totally in awe of Agnes. The edited excerpts have been rearranged to give a sense of the day as I remember it.

Tuesday

Agnes called here about eight in the morning to talk to Ann. We were in bed. When could they get together? Ann mentioned Saturday or the following week. Agnes said, "How about today? I'll pick you up in fifteen minutes in front of the church."

At first I was disappointed since I was supposed to teach and couldn't go with them. But Ann said, "There might not be another day. This is the way Agnes does things." I called up the art department, canceled my class, and told them to put a sign on the door that I was spending the day with Agnes Martin.

Ann went into the church—San Felipe de Neri on the old plaza—while I waited outside. Eyes closed, face up to the sun's warmth. I felt a truck pull up. It was Agnes at the wheel of her red truck. She was smiling. Glowing. Beautiful. Light tan, deep wrinkles, short hair. I jumped up, opened the door, shook hands, introduced myself, and told her Ann was in the church. I'd get her.

Soon We Were on the Road

They in front, I in back. It was wonderful for me to see Agnes and Ann together since I always think of them together, even though they are usually apart. First Agnes took us to her studio near Corrales. A cement block building next to a grocery store. Not what I expected. No character. It was painful to think of her working there after years of living and working in what I imagined to be the open spaces of Cuba [New Mexico]—like confining a free spirit. But if Agnes felt that way, it didn't show. The studio had a few basic living things—single bed, toaster oven, etc., and drawings on the wall. The front windows were covered with white paper except for the top foot, so there was a slice of sky, a band of blue, like her paintings.

Agnes showed us some small works on paper. They were rejects, she said, from her show of fifty paintings, explaining that she had made hundreds in order to get fifty good ones. She hurriedly fumbled through them, so we really didn't get a very good look. When I told her that I had liked her show of the small paintings on paper in New York, she looked up and said, "Oh, really? Did you 'see' the show?" She didn't seem to believe anyone actually went to "see" it.

Back to the Truck

Ann bought coffee, apples, and sandwiches at the grocery while Agnes asked me about Ann's opera and my part in it. (I had sent her Ann's libretto.) Agnes drove us all around that day—up through Jemez, Bandelier, Santa Fe, and back to Albuquerque. It took a while before I realized that we weren't going someplace but rather were driving for the day. We talked while Agnes drove, or rather mostly she and Ann talked, or rather mostly Agnes talked. Ann says it's because Agnes lives alone and is isolated for long stretches of time. When she does see people, she doesn't stop talking. It is difficult enough sometimes to get a word in with Ann, but even more difficult with Agnes. Ann herself only said a few things. I sat in the back and strained to catch every word.

Throughout the day, Agnes spoke about many things like absolute trust, Einstein's theory of relativity, intellectual ideas of measure as an "agreed-upon postulate," and the necessity of not seeking security. Speaking of the relation of things, Agnes talked about poetry, the worst kind being descriptive. We talked about degrees of abstraction and the relationship of words to experience. Agnes felt that there was something beyond words, maybe music could do it. She said poetry was the expression of realizations we have had in the past.

Agnes, nearing sixty-seven, was twenty years older than Ann, forty-seven. I was thirty-four. They often referred to the old loft days back on Coenties Slip and to Ann's previous visit to New Mexico with Cindy Lubar. Agnes said that Cindy depressed her. She couldn't stand all that unhappiness. Ann explained what Cindy had been going through then, but Agnes insisted on the need for happiness and the social necessity for joy in art. Art should not be political or critical, for art cannot save the world or relieve suffering. The purpose of art is joy and positive energy. Joy, happiness, innocence, pride, and humility were the themes in her painting. Not what most people in the art world talk about!

Agnes talked about the Shalako kachinas at Zuni, Kabuki theater, and the need for restrained or ritualized expression of emotions, where the actors act out one emotion at a time to the audience rather than to each other. One can truly feel only one emotion at a time. Then she imitated the Kabuki sounds, and the gestures of wailing and grief. She compared Fellini's *La Strada* [1954] with Kurosawa's film *Rashomon* [1950], saying that Fellini missed the mark because he did not immediately and fully define the main character. We don't know how to relate to him. In contrast, the thief in *Rashomon* was clear right away. He reacted to the immediate situation. He was the "unthinking man" and therefore the happiest. She and Ann joked about Bill Wilson, Ann's ex-husband, who had the problem of being a "thinking man."

Agnes said Robert Rauschenberg's theater pieces were good because they were restrained—just one touch. Isamu Noguchi's work for Martha Graham was also good. We laughed about contemporary theater and movies. Speaking of *Star Wars* [1977], Agnes said, "You know something is wrong when a tin can gets the best actor of the year award!"

Explaining that her first film (*Gabriel* [1976]) was about joy, Agnes described how she had no problem carrying the heavy camera equipment but when she began to shoot the wildflowers up close, her hands would begin this terrible shaking, and she couldn't figure out why or what was happening. Finally her voices showed her that she was trembling for joy because of the beautiful flowers.

As I understood it, Agnes's new film in progress represents the ritualized emotions of Kabuki. Something about a fence with a Kabuki dancer on one side and a Native American on the other. To Agnes, it was about sorrow, fear, and acceptance, about love and fences . . . about two individuals on either side of a fence—about how we are all ultimately separate. Our joys and sorrows are separate. All anyone sees is what one needs to see. We cannot claim to have influenced anybody. Conceptualized emotion represented as ritual, as art.

Agnes Pulled Over near the Soda Dam in Jemez

Ann and I jumped out to feel water dripping and seeping through cracks in the porous rock. It was hot, not warm, but hot. The springs were nearby, but you had to climb to them. This was clearly impossible since Agnes's leg was in a cast. Four months ago during the process of building her studio, a viga fell on her leg, breaking it and requiring three pins. This led into a discussion of how Agnes objects to healthcare—with healthcare, she felt that everyone would become a hypochondriac and take advantage of the system. Her simplistic and conservative, if not right-wing, views about feminism, abortion, "the women," "the poor," or "the Indians" were quite shocking and disturbing to me. I tried to question her, but you couldn't really have a conversation. She just held forth, so I pushed my questions and objections aside and stayed with that part of what she was saying that was simple, pure, and insightful. The Zen-like truths, unencumbered by art world dogma.

Contradictions

Her presence is that of a rock, solid and contained, but there is something vulnerable and fragile about Agnes. I wanted to protect her. A handsome face. Glassy eyes looking beyond to somewhere else. She seemed happy.

Agnes drove us to Galisteo where she is building a house and studio on land shared with some man. She will cover the mortgage payments in exchange for the right to lease the land for the rest of her life. When she dies, he gets all her buildings and everything except the work. She had a similar, unusual arrangement for her land in Cuba where she used to live, but a relative of the owner of the land proved that Agnes had built her house across the agreed-upon property line, so she had to leave. She explained that her voices would not let her own land. That it was dangerous to be secure. Just a few chickens. No dogs. Judging from the presence of numerous yellow trucks and horse trailers lying around the property, I gathered that trucks were also okay. She had to do what her voices told her to do, even if it seemed wrong. And sometimes they were wrong. I was told that the trucks and trailers were tax write-offs.

Her site was on the northern edge of the tiny old Hispano village—what appeared to be all of a dozen houses, a half-empty museum of odds and ends in an old hacienda, and lots of ruins with people building on top of, around, or in them. Agnes told us about how she had discovered the village and assumed no one would bother her there because it was out of the way, only to find that it was very chic and that many people who lived behind those adobe walls were rich artists. "But of course," she said, "they aren't real artists."

Her flat scruffy meadow-type land overlooked the Galisteo Creek. Barren and open. It was very windy and dusty. Little green plants tried to hold onto the earth. Golden-leaved trees down in the arroyo. Snowcapped mountains far off in the distance.

Agnes's House Seemed Strange

I couldn't figure out why it felt so odd, and why she didn't take Ann and me over to see it, or go inside it. It was tiny. I want to say seven feet by twenty feet. Then, I noticed how the metal window frames were out of place with the adobe. Suddenly, I got it. Agnes had simply covered over an old trailer with adobe, and rigged a shower up outside. I remember pointing to the house and screaming against the wind, "Agnes! Agnes! There's a trailer in there!" She howled back, "Yep! I fooled them all!" I'll never forget the three of us holding our sides and rolling around in the dust laughing.

In contrast, Agnes was very proud of the adobe studio she was building. Due to her leg injury, work had come to a temporary halt, so it stood unfinished. The studio, too, seemed small—under 500 square feet, I think. The roof was to be slanted and have an arched or vaulted plaster ceiling that would reflect indirect light on the painting wall all day. The south wall had a slit of windows just below the roofline to let in light. The east wall was a grid of window panes overlooking the landscape. Agnes said she made the wood frames. Pink earth walls against sky blue.

Agnes Liked Big Open Spaces

and that meant you had to deal with the wind (but consequently, no flies). Eventually, there will be a row of poplars hiding the buildings from the road that will also act as a windbreak. And she will build a fence. One usually gardens between the house and the fence, she explained. She had already planted fruit trees—apple, cherry, apricot, and pear.

Agnes said that she works daily from eight to three or four. She only exhibits drawings now. The large paintings are for individuals. She hadn't made any large paintings for a while and was anxious to get back to work. Then, no visitors. She does not like distractions and views friendship as a distraction. Similarly, she doesn't like teaching because the students talk too much and get you involved.

Clearly Agnes's Voices Take Care of Her

She says that they keep telling her to cut back. The first thing she learned to get rid of was obsessive thinking. You might as well not be alive as to think the same thought over and over every day. Then she got rid of excessiveness in her life and dropped all those things she did not like about herself. We start out as children, innocent and loving, but we lose this by age three. The point, she says, is to get back to that simple state. To do this, one must risk. Not invest in security.

I was amazed that this woman who has "made it" as an artist, who has the money and freedom to spend all her time on her work, has such a small studio and chooses to live in this funky little place. It was a sparse, clean feeling. Coming from New York, I was impressed with the simplicity of her life and found myself fantasizing something similar.

Driving Again

Agnes talked of wanting to write about the abstract expressionists—Mark Rothko, Barnett Newman, Clyfford Still, and Jackson Pollock. All men. Agnes considers Rothko a master painter and says his painting is about joy. He only committed suicide out of remorse, from having money, fame, and therefore a terrible responsibility. Agnes says that artists' suicides, like Rothko's, are because of remorse.

And, it was remorse, although she didn't know what it was then, that made her leave New York one night years ago. When she left, she sold all her work to a dealer. She doesn't know where most of it is. She stopped at the first Howard Johnson's and slept for two days before going to West Virginia where she had friends. She spoke of having only thirty years left to paint and so much to do.

Speaking of her mother's death, Agnes seemed sad. Once when she asked Betty Parsons about death, Betty said life was like the ride from New York to New Haven. "So short," said Agnes.

Agnes teased Ann about being "religious" and going to church. Agnes does not believe in God. She believes in absolute reality like a stream bubbling and dancing in the morning sun.

Back in Albuquerque

We drove around, seemingly forever, looking for a bar where we could get a drink. Every place was closed until six or so, because it was election day. Earlier Agnes had tried to take Ann and me to the Pink Adobe, her favorite restaurant in Santa Fe. But it too was closed. Finally we ended up here, in the little house I rented on San Felipe Street in Old Town, talking over wine and cheese. Agnes with her leg up on one of my few chairs. Ann showed Agnes photos of her opera *Butler's Lives of the Saints* [1977].

We laughed, drank a little too much, and Agnes told us stories, such as the one about when she was sixteen and was into seeking degradation in speakeasies but she couldn't do it, she couldn't succeed at degradation because "there just aren't enough people in the world who want to prey on innocence."

Agnes recounted the story of a man who approached her and said he needed a house, a wife, a dog, and couldn't she give him some money. She replied, "If you say all that just to get money, you'll make it my boy." Another story. Once a woman threw herself on the ice in front of Agnes and asked Agnes to take her home. Agnes told her, "You are in need. You need food, warmth, love. You need so much you'll pull me down. Your path is to waste and degradation. See those baths over there? Go there. It is full of degradation."

Eventually we went out and looked for a restaurant. Agnes wanted one with tablecloths and liquor. She treated us to dinner at the Sheraton Hotel—raw oysters, coquilles St. Jacques, huge steaks, and fancy liqueur ice cream desserts. She obviously found joy in treating us and lamented more than once how when one finally has money one never gets to use it. I am not sure if she meant that there is no one around to share it with or that her voices wouldn't let her.

Agnes and Ann

Their goodbye was very formal but lingering. A tenderness, a closeness, but careful, so as to not let the emotions slip out through cracks like hot water at the Jemez Springs. Meeting Agnes helped me to see Ann in clearer light. Feelings felt but not expressed in usual ways. The ritual gesture holding things in check as if too easily we would tremble out of control like Agnes's camera hand. Restrained passions.

ED. NOTE

"Meetings with Agnes Martin" was originally published in the exhibition catalogue *Agnes Martin: Works on Paper*, by Aline Chipman Brandauer with Harmony Hammond and Ann Wilson (Santa Fe: New Mexico Museum of Modern Art, 1998), 33–34, 36–37, 39–40.

Ann Wilson's journal entries, also titled "Meetings with Agnes Martin," appear along with Hammond's in the catalogue on pages 19–22, 24–25, 27–28.

Camping Out in the Southwest

Out West exhibition catalogue (1999)

[. . .] There is a long history of lesbian, gay, bisexual, transgendered, and two-spirited (LGBTT) artists born here [in the Southwest], raised here, or moved here. And that's not counting the ones who just pass through. But this pre-Stonewall and pre-feminist gay history and presence in the arts, and the living history of contemporary gay and lesbian art and artists since then, needs to be acknowledged and documented. The social and cultural forces that have worked to silence gender, class, and ethnic difference have also silenced difference based on sexual preference. All too often art by LGBTT peoples has been ignored or erased from art history (even more true for queers of color and lesbians) in what critic Arlene Raven has called an "academic douche," a kind of heterosexual cleansing that continues to this very day.[1]

Out West, an exhibition of contemporary visual art that reflects and examines the diverse experiences of LGBTT artists working in Arizona, New Mexico, and Texas [see fig. 3.3] refuses this silence and historical erasure. As far as I know, it is the first curated exhibition in Santa Fe, and perhaps all of New Mexico, that is more than a general survey of who is queer and who makes art. It is the first exhibition that focuses specifically on object-based visual art that deals with issues of sexual identity, to see what it tells us about the lives, struggles, experiences, and cultural expression of LGBTT peoples living here. It examines stereotypes of LGBTT visual art, and creates and broadens dialogue around issues of the representation of sexual identity, and the freedom of creative expression. In a certain sense, it is about place. Where we came from, where we are now. Occupying space. It may be that since LGBTT peoples don't assume "a place," we are very sensitive to it.

Out West has been made possible by a grant from the National Gay and Lesbian Community Funding Partnership through the Santa Fe Community Foundation, one of sixteen community foundations in different cities across the country invited to participate in a two-year partnership to encourage projects that address the needs of its gay communities. Plan B Evolving Arts (a.k.a. the Center for Contemporary Arts) is an ideal noncommercial site for this kind of exhibition and it has been a pleasure to work with Zane Fischer, Michael Lujan, and their staff.

The curatorial process [for *Out West*] included open calls for slides in gay and art publications, on the internet, and an invitational flyer sent to individuals and gay and art organizations and spaces in the tri-state area. The response was overwhelming. Far beyond even my expectations. Close to one hundred artists of different genders, race, and ethnic backgrounds responded from rural and urban areas in all three states: from Tucson, Phoenix, Tempe, Mesa, and Rough Rock, Arizona; and Dallas, San Antonio, Lubbock, Manor, El Paso, Fort Worth and Granbury, Texas. In New Mexico, I received materials from artists in Santa Fe, Cerrillos, Questa, Coyote, Las Cruces, Albuquerque, Socorro, Vallecitos, Ojo Caliente, Dixon, Edgewood, Cordova, Tres Piedras, Chacon, El Prado, Taos, La Cieneguilla, Abiquiu, and Truth or Consequences.

Initially, I was open to considering almost anything. I wasn't sure what I was going to find, but based on the fact that I already knew of a lot of good work by LGBTT artists, I just assumed that there was more I didn't know about. That turned out to be an understatement. Curating the exhibition was not easy in that much of the work was honestly engaged, innovative, and provocative. The limitation of the physical space at Plan B necessitated a highly selective exhibition. Consequently, many excellent artists who are publicly out but whose work does not deal with issues of sexual identity [. . .] are not represented. Even with this selectivity, *Out West* presents the work of forty-two artists (ten from Arizona, twenty-one from New Mexico, and eleven from Texas).

It needs to be said that the successful response to my call for art, at least in New Mexico, was partially due to the ongoing outreach work by the Human Rights Alliance, Operation Outreach, P.O.C.A.F [People of Color AIDS Foundation], the Coalition for Equality in New Mexico (which organizes the annual LGBTT "Summit"), and the many early grassroots art activities, projects, and exhibitions based in the gay community over the last twenty years. The art is just one thread that weaves in and out of the gay history of Santa Fe and surrounding counties, a history that desperately needs to be written.

In 1981, visual artist Frankie Daley put pink flyers around town for the first gay gathering. Only twelve people showed up, but these spontaneous gatherings continued throughout the '80s. Inspired by the big gay march in Washington, DC, in 1987, Common Knowledge, the first gay social organization in Santa Fe, sponsored a gay gathering on the plaza in 1988. Fifty people turned out. There was no permit, no platform, and no PA system. But the next year, they had a permit, a platform, a sound system, a crowd, and speeches by city councilors. The first official Gay Pride parade, organized by Lyn Shepodd, Bob Guidice, and the Pride Committee was in 1993.

Throughout the '80s, a loose group of activist artists, many of whom were gay, initiated art exhibitions and projects. Often it was the same people, but with each new project, there were a few new faces. For the next six or seven years, there was a series of exhibitions around World AIDS Day and projects in conjunction with A Day Without Art. While these exhibitions weren't entirely queer, they definitely came out of our gay community.

Richard Hooker, an early participant in many of these events, remembers the *N.O. Show* (the "national offensive show") of 1982. *N.O. Show*, an exhibition of political art, sponsored by the Santa Fe Council for the Arts in collaboration with Galeria de la Raza in San Francisco, was installed in Cecil Sherwood's old gas station on Palace and Johnson, next to the Safeway downtown.

For *N.O. Show*, Hooker, well known for his suitcase pieces that allow him to easily and surreptitiously cross boundaries and borders of all kinds, created a memorial for the famous and infamous Senate Lounge, that was closing its doors. The Senate opened on downtown Galisteo Street as a rough topless bar in the late '60s. By 1971, it attracted a "mixed" crowd and by 1974 was considered to be "the gay bar" in town, although (as with its predecessor Claude's Bar on Canyon Road in the '50s and '60s) "everyone," meaning gays and straights, locals and out-of-towners, representing a mix of cultures, hung out, drank, and danced all night. The Senate was forced to close in 1982 because of competition from the short-lived Gold Bar in the newly renovated El Paso Theatre. Hooker taped interviews with people at the Senate and Kitty Leaken took photographs.

The interviews and photos were saved in a suitcase (memories and history that hopefully can be opened and displayed one of these days). Hooker, who now lives in Nevada, considers this his first overtly gay piece.

OUT 90: A New Mexico Celebration of Gay and Lesbian Art, Ideas & Culture was the first specifically gay exhibition in Santa Fe. A grassroots effort, it grew out of the community organizing that started in Albuquerque in the late '80s to introduce a gay rights bill into the legislature. Organized and co-coordinated by Richard Hooker, Ada Medina, and Ernesto Torres, *OUT 90* was a month-long celebration of over one hundred artists at twenty-five sites around town.

Since *OUT 90*, there have been small open, juried, and informal invitational exhibitions in donated spaces and galleries, during most Gay Pride weekends. These exhibitions always generate an enthusiastic response and great energy. Unfortunately, there's not room to present large work and the shows are only up for a few days. *Visibility 97*, a juried exhibition, honored invited artists Herb Lotz and Ada Medina.

In Albuquerque, *Out! Magazine*, and until a few years ago, the "Out and Proud" radio program and the gallery space at Common Bond next to Sisters' and Brothers' Bookstore, regularly featured work by gay and lesbian artists. The annual Wiminfest music concerts at the Kimo Theater, that have continued since their inception in 1985, are usually accompanied by an invitational exhibition of work by lesbian artists, although Ada Medina and I were invited to co-jury the exhibition in 1992.

Out West is not intended to separate LGBTT artists from mainstream, feminist art, or ethnic-based art movements, nor to elide sexuality with gender and race, but rather to acknowledge the existence and range of an extensive body of visual work from diverse queer subject positions within the cultural and geographic landscapes of the Southwest.

What does it mean to be a lesbian, gay, two-spirited, or queer artist? Presumably it means that one makes lesbian, gay, two-spirited or queer art. But, what is lesbian, gay, two-spirited, or queer art? While there is no agreement as to what exactly constitutes let's say, queer art, it is generally thought to reflect queer identity and to contribute to the development of that identity. Just as there is no fixed queer identity, there is no single queer aesthetic or sensibility, and we like it that way.

While we don't all fit neatly under one label, I am going to use the term queer because it reclaims a word that has historically been used against homosexuals, flaunts it with style, of course, and turns it around to empower the very people it was directed against. By nature, queer, a label coined by gay men and lesbians working together in ACT UP in the later half of the '80s, is unruly, uncontrollable, noisy, without boundaries, anti-PC, confrontive, militant, provocative, sexy, defiant, angry, irreverent, oppositional, transgressive, anti-separatist, and anti-assimilationist. It refuses silence and promotes visibility. Queer was immediately embraced by many lesbians and gays, who felt that the labels homosexual, gay, and lesbian were too dated, conservative, desexualized, and depoliticized. It also was contested by others who painfully recalled its past homophobic uses. For some, it still problematically privileges white male experiences and agendas.

I like queer. Even though it is no longer oppositional, it still jumps off the page and in your face. At its best, queer is genderless. Queer demolishes binary constructions and includes bisexuals and transsexuals. While it is not the same thing as two-spirited or berdache traditions, it shares a view of gender and sexuality as a fluid continuum with infinite identity positions versus a set of oppositions. Queer plays with visual signifiers of gender and sexual identity and messes up what Marjorie Garber has called the "crisis of category," the patriarchal insistence on pigeonholing everyone into opposite genders and the social obsession with knowing who is who.[2] Years ago poet Judy Grahn commented that one of the strongest measures of heterosexual culture is how close each of its members comes to being "like a faggot" or "like a dyke." We are essential to them in knowing who they are.[3]

So, is a quality like "queer" embodied in the art object, the sexuality of the artist, the sexuality of the viewer, or the viewing context? This question circulates around all discussions of LGBTT art and refuses easy answers. It can be any or all of the above. It assumes and proposes difference at least in some ways, from art by heterosexually identified men and women. Queer art is not a stylistic movement but rather art that comes out of a consciousness of being LGBTT in a primarily heterosexual (and for most of us, patriarchal) culture. This consciousness may be implicitly or explicitly articulated. It may vary in style, imagery, materials used, concept, or content and can be figurative, symbolic, abstract, or conceptual.

Is queer art any and all art made by self-identified queers regardless of subject matter? Or just that which "looks queer"? Who decides what looks queer? What about work by queer artists that deals with other issues and concerns? What role do stereotypes play as visual signifiers of gender, sexuality, and race? Who maintains these stereotypes? What about coded imagery? Is any art viewed by LGBTT peoples or given a queer read automatically queer? Might queer sensibility be something entirely separate from queer sexual practice? Might it not be characterized by its outlaw status? By a certain dialectic of freedom and imprisonment? Could it be a place of inarticulation, of invention? A space of infinite and pleasurable possibilities? While they have been articulated differently with each decade, these are the messy questions that will not go away. They are raised over and over by the artwork itself.

Personally, I am not interested in defining an essential queer identity, sensibility, or aesthetic, but rather in looking at work by self-identified LGBTT artists working today in the Southwest to see what forms it takes, what issues it addresses, what it tells us about our lives, and how it interlaces with larger social, political, and cultural fields. The very range of work in *Out West* disrupts stereotypes of LGBTT identity and art and reveals a fluid field in which assumptions of gender, sexuality, and representation are continuously called into question. In particular, it emphasizes art that reflects on intersections of gender, race, class, and sexuality. Work by Laura Aguilar, Gay Block, David Zamora Casas, Armando Espinosa, Tom Holmes, Jim Quinnan, Chuck Ramirez, and Hulleah Tsinhnahjinnie negotiates multiple identities, challenging the illusion of what artist David Wojnarowicz called the ONE TRIBE NATION, and what poet Audre Lorde called "the mythical norm" or that which is "white, thin, male, young, heterosexual, Christian, and financially secure."[4] (The real motivation behind censorship attempts is the fundamentalist and radical right's agenda to eradicate all difference.)

Defining, identifying, categorizing, quantifying, labeling, and authenticating "the other" are colonizing practices that serve the needs of the dominant group. The categories heterosexual and homosexual were both invented in 1892. Historian Jonathan [Ned] Katz explains that heterosexuality only gradually became identified with "normal" sexuality, and homosexuality with "contrary sexual feeling" and "inversion."[5] With Freud, the pathologizing of same-sex desire became institutionalized, with penisvagina intercourse, procreative or otherwise, elevated to the status of a religion. Kelly Kievet, Isa Gordon, Tom Jennings, Susan Walsh, Hulleah Tsinhnahjinnie, and other artists, wary of these practices, make work that addresses the importance of self-identification and self-representation.

In the '80s, the deconstructive work of postmodern feminists combined with that of artists of color to examine the representation of difference. Issues of authorship, subject, gaze, and audience were examined, repositioned, gendered, and colored. Because of its supposed authenticating properties, photography is an excellent vehicle for the interrogation of existing pathological or cultural representations of sexual difference and for self-inventing and self-representing new queer identities. Laura Aguilar, Gay Block, Carlotta Boettcher, Adrain Chesser, Elizabeth Dondis, Herb Lotz, Joyan Saunders, Sharon Stewart, and Hulleah Tsinhnahjinnie insert queer subjects into portrait and social documentary traditions. In some cases, text is added as part of the image in order to give voice to the subject, suggest a narrative, give information and commentary, or juxtapose fact and feeling. Portraits of individuals who make a community are collectively read as a documentary portrait of that community—transvestites, transsexuals, leather and s/m crowd, cowboys, dyke writers, or Latina lesbians.

One way that marginalized artists are authenticated is by literally inserting themselves into the dominant art historical canon or appropriating that canon for themselves. Traditional painting by Delmas Howe, Gerard Huber, and Geoff Laurence is subverted by its nontraditional homoerotic content. Queering existing heterosexual narratives to satisfy our hunger for images of ourselves is a survival skill we developed long ago. In *Saints for Boys*, Tom Holmes gazes up to the bulging crotches of public sculptures in Austin. Jim Quinnan, Gerard Huber, and Delmas Howe looked to classical painting and sculpture, while Glenn Halak turns to television and Hollywood.

Chaps, spurs, boots, ropes, whips, brands, leather, bandanas. I am struck by how many signifiers of the West are also signifiers of gayness and gay culture, and how that has been appropriated by the fashion and advertising industries. As I made studio visits, I noted the frequency of butt shots (and in abstract, material-based and conceptual work, an interest in holes and the underside of things). For gay men, the classic gaze seems to be from behind. Delmas Howe's cowboys at the rodeo are all about the cruising eye and looking. Chuck Ramirez uses the well-worn chaps as a mediated stand-in for the men he desires. He writes, "The taboo world of leather intrigues me. I [see] the chaps as representing the hedonistic desire that still burns deep inside queers with HIV. We are still worthy of being touched, loved, cared for as lovers." Lots of lesbian artists are into leather too (especially saddles), but that work is not represented in this exhibition.

Out West contains few images of explicit sex, male or female. Visually representing or presencing the lesbian erotic has always been difficult for lesbians. Unlike gay men, who have been free to depict differing modes of sexual practice for their own pleasure, lesbians have had difficulty escaping the ever-present male gaze. The representation of two women engaged in sexual or sexualized activities remains extremely problematic because traditionally lesbians have been portrayed as objects for male fantasies of lesbian eroticism.

A tightening economy in the '90s has meant the reactionary reinvention of "traditional family values" and the portrayal of homosexuals as a cultural elite asking for "special rights." LGBTT, people of color, immigrants, and other minorities have had to fight powerful organized right-wing assaults on difference and the freedom of expression. When queers challenge constructs of gender, we find ourselves in the middle of that sacred territory the family—a hetero minefield that homosexuals disturb by their very presence. LGBTT artists are scrutinizing family histories displayed above the sofa, on dresser tops, in scrap books, photo albums, or stored in boxes in the closet, examining, representing, and reconstructing the families we came from and the families we make. Hulleah Tsinhnahjinnie, David Zamora Casas, and David Keating work in response to or with old photos of themselves and family members. Gay Block, on the other hand, examines her relationship with her mother and the affluent Jewish society in which she grew up.

Traditionally, family is based on blood connection or socially legitimated commitments like marriage and adoption. However, in lesbian and gay communities, friendship becomes elevated to the level of family. Laura Aguilar, Adrain Chesser, Elizabeth Dondis, and Herb Lotz document those chosen families of "difference." Ironically, the more domestic and assimilationist the images of gay lifestyles are, thus "naturally" extending to representations of same-sex marriages and queer families with or expecting children, the more they challenge and rattle the very heterosexual foundations of that mythic institution, the American family.

Other reoccurring and overlapping themes include: the queer as monster or outsider, anger against organized religion and the government, bondage and its relationship to religion, homophobia, gender slippage, the closet, fantasy, identity, queer codes, communication, relationships, obsessiveness, memorials, the gendered, sexed, and raced body and, of course, because it is so prevalent in our lives, HIV/AIDS. Because few dealers will show their overtly homoerotic art, many artists in *Out West* have several bodies of work. The fact that James Magee actually works as two artistic personae who have different studios and careers (heavy metal sculptor James Magee and symbolist landscape and flower painter Annabelle Livermore), strikes me as quintessentially queer.

By the mid '90s, queer activism and the accompanying queer cultural renaissance were institutionalized and commodified as the media took it upon themselves to market queer culture and desexualized, depoliticized images of queers, made palatable for the mainstream. The twenty-fifth anniversary of Stonewall 1994 with its mile-long rainbow flag and rainbow credit cards, and the accompanying gay games advertised by wholesome bodies unmarked by disease, symbolize the culmination of this commodification. The art media hasn't been far behind. Of course, this colonization is not new. It is a violent dynamic that other groups who have first been marginalized and then rediscovered on the basis of their difference have had to negotiate.

Simultaneously, the '90s have seen drastic cutbacks in the arts. As we approach the year 2000, there are few queer shows for numerous overlapping reasons: partial or complete withdrawal of federal and state funding for the arts resulting in the closure of many noncommercial art spaces; right-wing censorship attacks that affect funding and drain energies of not-for-profit spaces; a reduction in queer funding opportunities (we could not get foundation funding for this catalogue); the general shift away from identity-based politics and exhibitions; the fact that the queer market moment passed as we knew it would (actually the queer moment of the early '90s ricocheted from coast to coast, but never hit the Southwest); and the absorption and assimilation of queer identity to include heterosexuals. The queer field is inclusive but not so open as to have the boundaries disappear, because in fact, they do exist.

One has only to remember that three out of the "NEA four" denied grants in 1989 were gay to get a feeling for those boundaries. One has only to remember that the new round of censorship attacks aimed at the National Endowment for the Arts in 1997 ordered investigations of selected grantees, "specifically searching for subject matter relating to gay, lesbian, and female sexuality." One has only to note the increase in sanctioned gay-bashing and hate crimes. One has only to witness the antihuman rights referendums and organizing against gay rights bills in Colorado, Arizona, and Texas, and the failure right here at home in New Mexico to pass a human rights bill banning discrimination based on one's sexual orientation or a bill outlawing hate crimes (twice vetoed by our governor). How will artists fight these new rounds in old battles?

Exhibitions like *Out West*, at spaces like Plan B, are more important than ever. We cannot afford to be silent or let others decide what kind of art we may or may not make, nor let our creative voices be silenced or ignored. Queer cultural expression has the potential of not only empowering lesbian, gay, bisexual, transgendered, and two-spirited peoples, but playing a major role in the empowering of many marginalized peoples. It is only through an understanding of our connectedness to others, a connectedness that can embrace difference and individual expression, that we will be able to withstand the reactionary forces at work.

ED. NOTE

This curatorial essay has been abridged for publication here. It was originally published in Harmony Hammond, *Out West*, exh. cat. (Santa Fe, NM: Plan B Evolving Arts [CCA, Inc.], 1999), n.p.

The numbered endnotes for this essay, below, are by the author.

NOTES

1. In curating this exhibition and writing this catalogue essay in 1999, I intentionally used "LGBTT," adding an additional "T" (for two-spirit) to the then customary LGBT: Lesbian, Gay, Bisexual, Transgender, and Two-spirit. I had hoped that the formulation would catch on, but it did not. Since then, in the desire to be inclusive, there have been many community additions and variations to how we refer to ourselves. I like "2SLGBTQIA+"

which I became aware of with the exhibition *Fluid Gaze* (September 30–December 30, 2023), at 516 Arts, in Albuquerque, New Mexico, curated by Rachelle B. Pablo (Diné). Putting two-spirit, thus indigenous people, first makes conceptual sense!!!

2. See Marjorie Garber, *Vested Interests: Cross-Dressing and Cultural Anxiety* (New York: Routledge, 1992).

3. See Judy Grahn, *Another Mother Tongue: Gay Words, Gay Worlds* (Boston: Beacon Press, 1984).

4. David Wojnarowicz coined the term "One-Tribe Nation" in *Close to the Knives* (New York: Vintage, 1991). See Audre Lorde, "Age, Race, Class, and Sex: Women Redefining Difference," in *Sister Outsider: Essays and Speeches* (Freedom, CA: Crossing Press, 1984); also published in *Out There: Marginalization in Contemporary Culture*, ed. Russell Ferguson, Martha Gever, Trinh T. Minh-ha, and Cornel West (Cambridge, MA: MIT Press, 1990).

5. See Jonathan Ned Katz, *The Invention of Heterosexuality* (New York: Dutton, 1995).

4

2000s

Editor's Introduction

The release of *Lesbian Art in America: A Contemporary History* in 2000 (fig. 4.1) culminated ten years of research and hundreds of studio visits with self-identified lesbian artists throughout the United States. In addition to ensuring the historical visibility of lesbian art—and grappling with the terminology—*Lesbian Art in America* initiated "a critical and theoretical dialogue around art [. . .] situated within feminist discourse and the history of visual production."[1] The publication sparked events on university campuses and in libraries, bookstores, and queer community centers around the country (fig. 4.2), heightening Hammond's visibility as a historian and critic of contemporary art. A flurry of solicitations ensued, from journalists, curators, teachers, and panel organizers interested in the impact of lesbian feminism on contemporary artistic practice.

During the 2008–9 recession, Hammond's output as an art critic escalated, providing supplementary revenue while facilitating her dialogue with artists and institutions regionally and nationally. She wrote weekly reviews for the

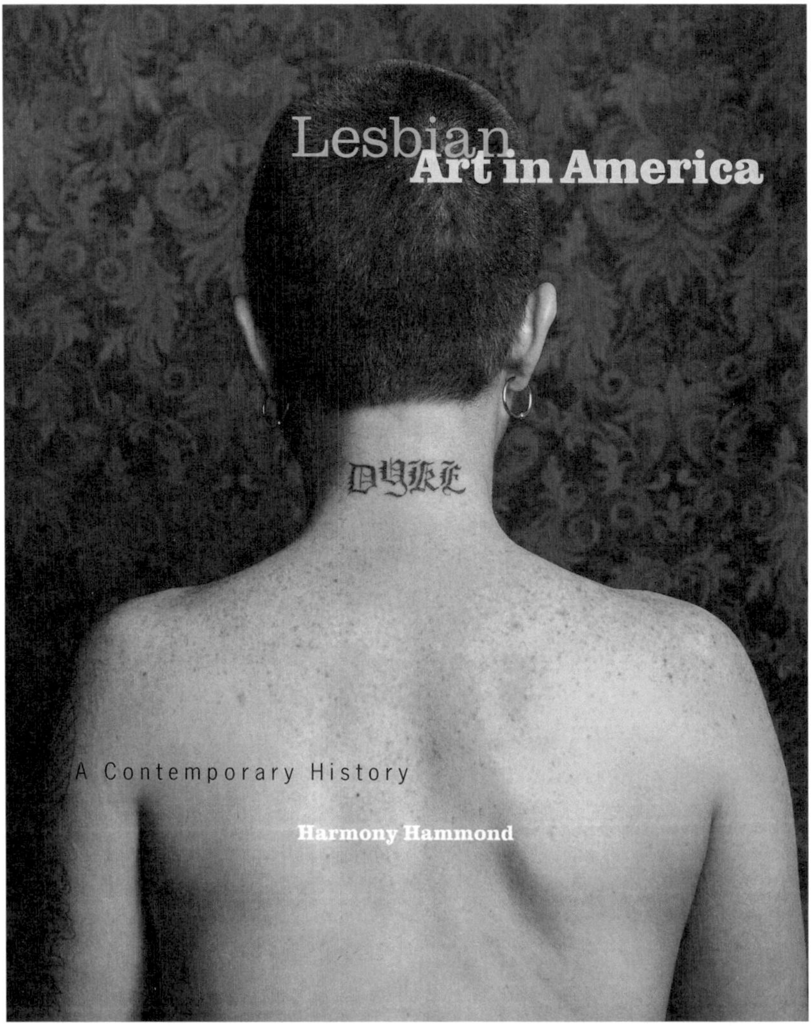

FIGURE 4.1. Harmony Hammond, *Lesbian Art in America: A Contemporary History* (New York: Rizzoli, 2000). Cover image: Catherine Opie, *Dyke*, 1993.

Albuquerque Journal North (Santa Fe Edition) from 2009 to 2011, and she served as the Santa Fe correspondent for *Art in America* from 2009 to 2012.

Throughout the decade, Hammond continued to actively advocate for the historical visibility and cultural agency of women and queers (fig. 4.3). Concurrently, her curatorial work and studio practice vigorously responded to culture war debates, and fought back against each new campaign of silencing and censorship (figs. 4.4 and 4.5). She cocurated iterations of the exhibition *Erasing*

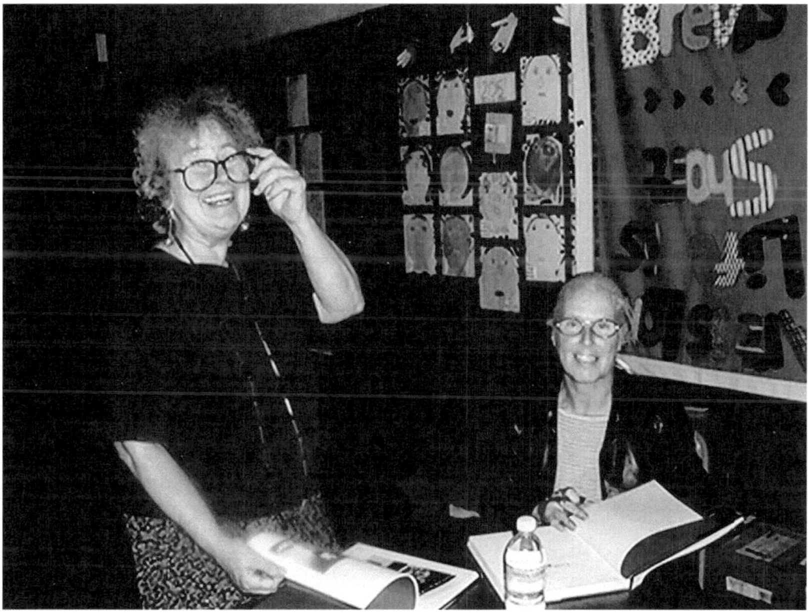

FIGURE 4.2. Art historian Moira Roth with Harmony Hammond at book signing for *Lesbian Art in America*, Harvey Milk Center for the Arts, San Francisco, June 2000. Roth, a longtime friend and supporter of Hammond and her work, attended several events in the San Francisco Bay Area celebrating the release of *Lesbian Art in America* and used the book as a resource for her Modern Art History class at Mills College. Feminist, lesbian, and queer networks ensured the wide circulation of Hammond's book, now a classic. Snapshot: Harmony Hammond personal collection.

Censorship in three different venues across the country, exhibiting works that take the issue head-on with their powerful material presence and accompanying texts.

Her 2007 exhibition *¿Y QUÉ? Queer Art Made in Texas* at Texas Tech University School of Art in Lubbock, Texas, built on the show *Out West* (see fig. 3.3), which she had organized in Santa Fe, New Mexico, in 1999. Both initiatives provided spaces of visibility and dialogue for queer artists living and working in regions lacking the relative security and more abundant opportunities queers found in metropoles like New York, Los Angeles, and San Francisco.

Looking back over decades of queer feminist activism in the arts from the vantage point of a new millennium, Hammond conscientiously fleshed out a body of work (including artworks, curatorial statements, catalogue essays, reviews, letters, interviews, public talks, and personal narratives) committed to recording marginalized or erased histories.

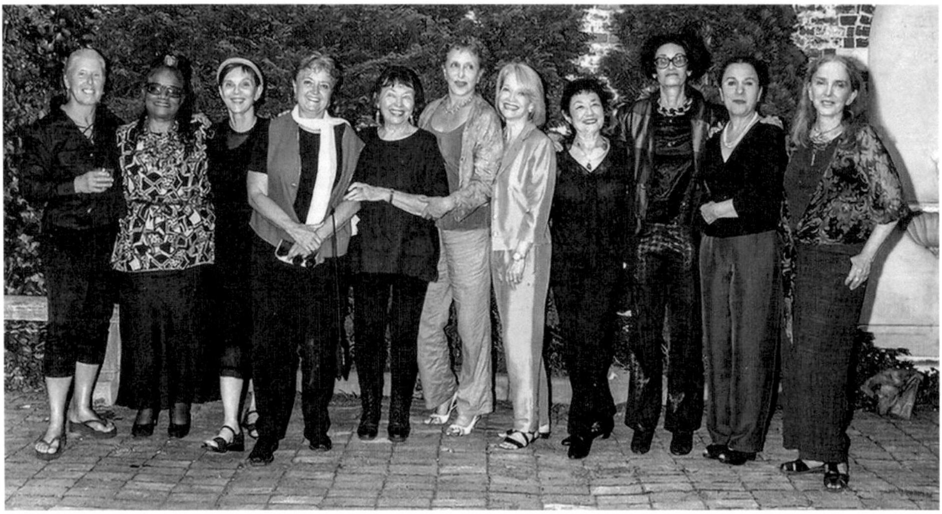

FIGURE 4.3. Participating artists and curator, *The Personal Is Political: The Women's Art Movement 1969–1975*, Guild Hall Museum, East Hampton, Long Island, New York, August 10–October 20, 2002. Curated by Simon Taylor and Nathalie Ng. *L to R:* Harmony Hammond, Faith Ringgold, Mary Beth Edelson, Michelle Stuart, May Stevens, Carolee Schneemann, Ruth Appelhof, Eunice Golden, Judith Bernstein, Mary Grigoriadis, Joan Semmel. Photo: © Walter Weissman.

NOTE

1. Harmony Hammond, introduction to *Lesbian Art in America: A Contemporary History* (New York: Rizzoli, 2000), 7.

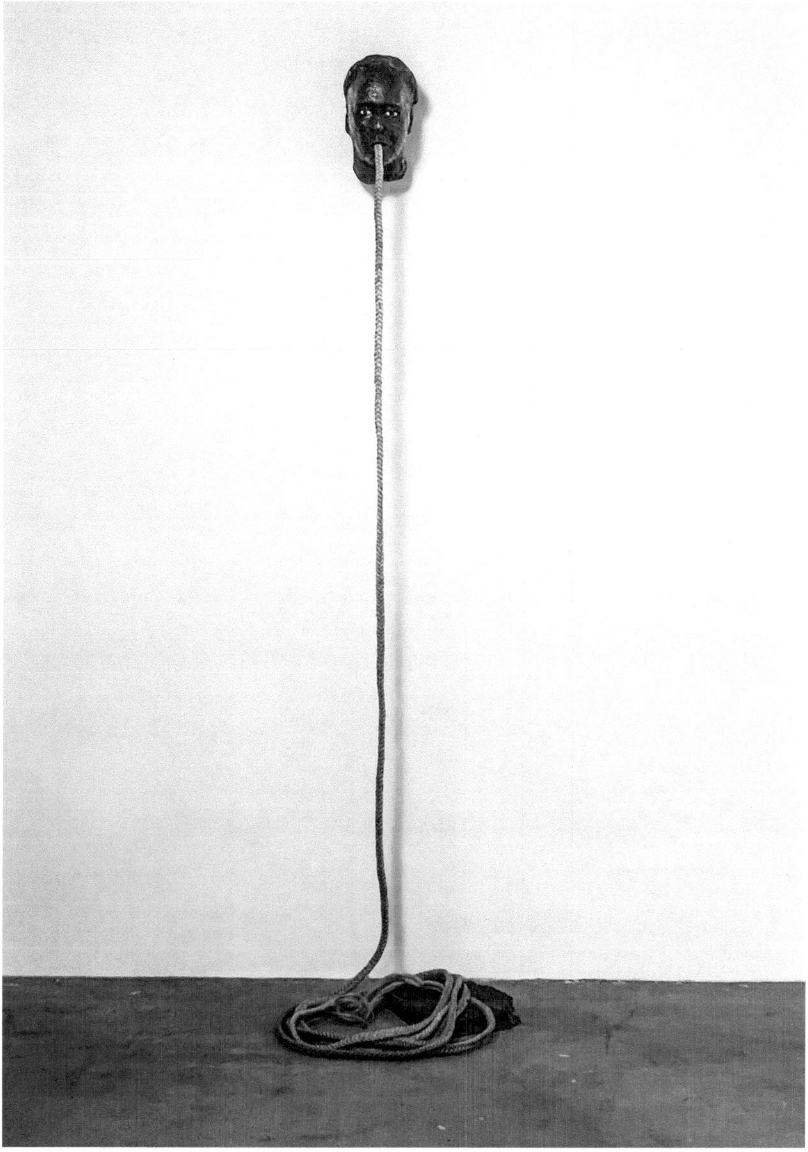

FIGURE 4.4. Harmony Hammond, *Speaking Braids*, 2002. Bronze, hemp, wax, paint. 83 × 72 in. (210.82 × 182.88 cm). Hammond created this sculpture in the wake of writing *Lesbian Art in America: A Contemporary History*. The female face, based on a cast of the artist's own face, has been modified to make it unidentifiable, more all-inclusively generic. The braid represents the intertwining of multiple voices, multiple histories, strengthened by coming together. The metaphor evokes the complexities and ethical imperatives of speaking/writing a visual history about diverse subjects who have been systematically marginalized, effaced, and silenced. Harmony Hammond Core Collection.

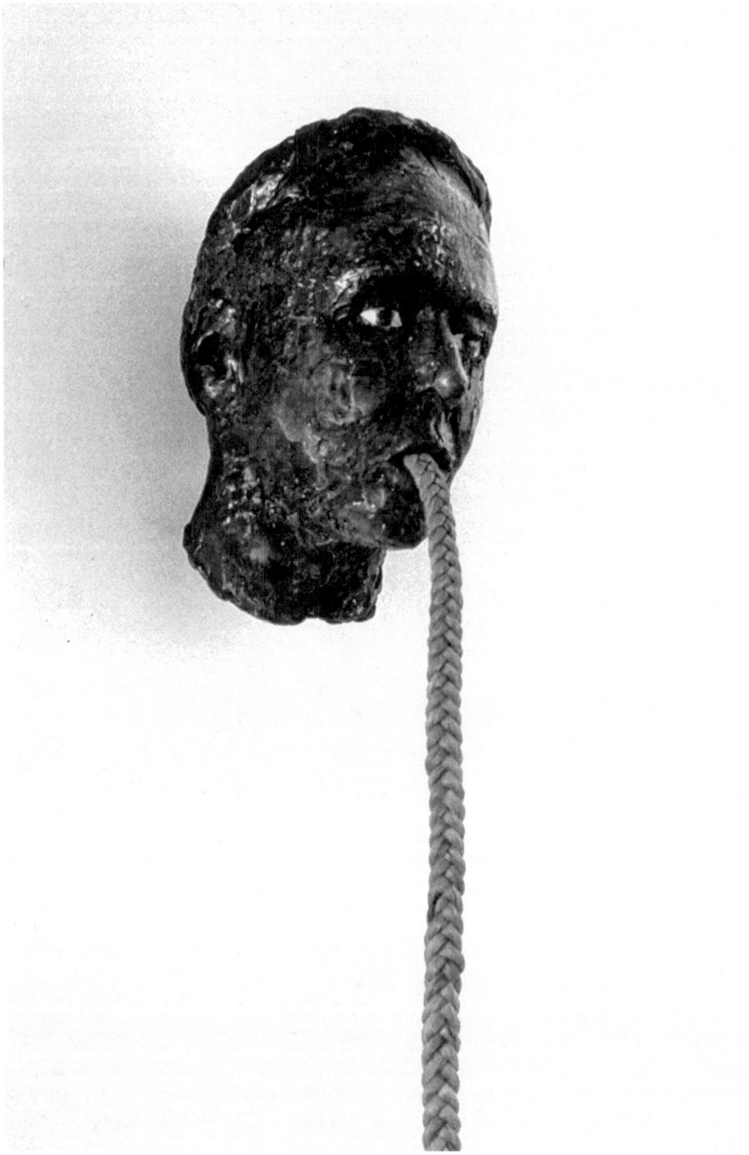

FIGURE 4.5. Harmony Hammond, *Speaking Braids* (detail), 2002. Bronze, hemp, wax, paint. 83 × 72 in. (210.82 × 182.88 cm). Harmony Hammond Core Collection.

Introduction, *Lesbian Art in America: A Contemporary History*

(2000)

There have always been artists who were lesbian, and lesbians who were artists, but the category "lesbian artist" scarcely existed before 1970. In that year, the gay and women's liberation movements—based, respectively, on sexual orientation and gender—introduced the newly formed identity "lesbian feminist" and her cultural counterpart, the lesbian artist, who was assumed to be feminist.

My aim in *Lesbian Art in America* [see fig. 4.1] is to document lesbian visual art since 1970 in the United States, in relationship to gay and women's liberation, lesbian feminism, mainstream art, feminist art, ethnic-based art movements, queer activism and theory, media attempts to commodify and consume the lesbian (and her art) as chic spectacle, and resistance to this appropriation. Besides describing individual works and examining various artistic strategies, I suggest ways of looking at lesbian art and attempt to initiate a critical and theoretical dialogue around the art, a dialogue situated within feminist discourse and the history of visual production.

This is a history of which girls made and showed what, when, and where. Moving back and forth between the mainstream art world with many alternative spaces situated along its borders, popular dyke culture, and feminist art spaces, I discuss exhibitions, projects, conferences, publications, and art by women who identify themselves as lesbian. To be a lesbian, Martha Gever has written, "means engaging in a complex, often treacherous, system of cultural identities, representations and institutions, and a history of sexual regulation."[1]

What is a lesbian artist? It's natural to respond that she is one who makes lesbian art. But there is no agreement as to what constitutes lesbian art, though it is generally thought to reflect lesbian identity and to contribute to the development of that identity. However, just as there is no fixed lesbian identity, there is no single aesthetic sensibility—and we like it that way. Both vary with class, race, age, and geography. Both change with the times. For example, as lesbian identity shifted from a gender-based definition rooted in the radical lesbian feminism of the 1970s to a sexually based definition in the late '80s and '90s, imagery in lesbian art shifted as well, from symbolism and organic abstraction that suggested women's genitalia to in-your-face realistic paintings of cunts or women engaged in explicit lesbian sex. The art moved from a celebration of sameness to a flaunting of difference.

Is the quality "lesbian" embodied in the art object, the sexuality of the artist, or the viewer, or the viewing context? This question circulates around all discussions of lesbian art and refuses easy answers. It can be any or all of the above. It assumes and proposes difference, at least in some ways, from art by men and straight feminists. Lesbian art is not a stylistic movement but rather, in its simplest definition, art that comes out of a feminist consciousness and reflects the experience of having lesbian relationships or being lesbian in patriarchal culture. This consciousness may be implicitly or explicitly articulated. It may be expressed through an array of styles, imagery, materials used, concepts, or content, and may be figurative, symbolic, abstract, or conceptual.

But such a definition leaves a lot of questions unanswered. Is lesbian art any and all art made by lesbians regardless of subject matter? Or just that which "looks" lesbian? Who decides what looks lesbian? What role do stereotypes play as visual signifiers of gender, sexuality, and race? Who maintains these stereotypes? What about coded imagery, whose content is apparent only to lesbians? Is any art viewed by lesbians or given a lesbian reading automatically lesbianized? Is work by lesbian artists "lesbian" when it deals with nonlesbian issues and concerns? If work by a lesbian artist with lesbian subject matter is viewed by a straight man who gets off on it, is it still lesbian? Might lesbian sensibility be something entirely separate from lesbian identity or sexual practice? Might it not be characterized by its outlaw status? By a certain dialectic of freedom and imprisonment? Could it be a place of inarticulation, of invention? A place of infinite possibilities? How do gender and sexuality shape visual images and how do visual images construct gender and sexual identification? While they have been articulated differently with each decade, these are the messy questions that will not go away. They are raised over and over by the artwork itself. [. . .]

Initially I had planned to write about lesbian self-representation in visual art, but the scope of the project shifted to becoming a history of contemporary lesbian art in the United States—the missing history. Self-representation suggesting figuration of some sort is only one part of a much larger queer field that I am calling "lesbian art" and that includes not only representations of lesbians by lesbians but any art created from a lesbian subject position. The field includes artists like myself who "always sometimes" make art about lesbian experience; artists whose work does not overtly reflect lesbian concerns but who are important because of their conscious decision to participate in lesbian and queer exhibitions and be public about their sexuality; and artists who cannot or choose not to be out. If artists and their work are "out there" in the dialogue that circulates around lesbian art, I feel a responsibility to examine how their images, objects, and persons participate in the discourse. [. . .]

I like to think of lesbian art as a braid with three strands—gender, sexuality, and art—though from time to time other strands, such as history or identity, are woven in and out. Each strand touches the others as it weaves back and forth across the center line, giving it dimension, fullness, and presence—a flexible rope of incredible strength and beauty. Each strand is composed of many fibers, and occasionally there are knots and tangles.

ED. NOTE

The version of the introduction we present above is excerpted from Harmony Hammond, introduction to *Lesbian Art in America: A Contemporary History* (New York: Rizzoli, 2000), 7–10.

The numbered endnote below is by the author.

NOTE

1. Martha Gever, "The Names We Give Ourselves," in *Out There: Marginalization and Contemporary Cultures*, ed. Russell Ferguson, Trinh T. Minh-ha, Martha Gever, and Cornel West (New York: Museum of Contemporary Art; Cambridge, MA: MIT Press, 1990), 191.

Harmony Hammond, a Narrative Chronology

Part I, the Years 1944 to 1980

(ca. 2000)

COMPILED FROM INTERVIEWS BY MOIRA ROTH

[. . .] I can thank my high school art teacher, Berta Caul, for introducing me to a new world through art. She had something to do with the extension classes at the School of the Art Institute of Chicago and once a year we would take a field trip downtown to the museum and to the James Goodman Theater. It was all quite exciting.

When I was a junior in high school (around fifteen years old), my portfolio of drawings won a competition sponsored by the arts club. The prize was a class of my choice at the Saturday School of the Art Institute of Chicago. I took dress design and fashion illustration so I could become sophisticated and classy. I recently came across some of these sketches—really strange! Anemic figures with bubble hairdos, big eyes, and long skinny disappearing limbs. They couldn't possibly stand upright. So different from my martial arts presence as an adult.

Probably more than anything else, though, this class—that afforded the opportunity for me to get out of Hometown, have some time to myself, and to see art—cemented my identity as "an artist." Every Saturday, for however long the class went on, my mother would drop me off at the train station and I would take the "L" downtown. The elevated train went through immigrant neighborhoods and a lot of slums and I could literally see into people's houses and backyards. A world very different from Hometown. In those days the school was literally in the basement right under the museum. After my class, I would wander around the hallways, following the smell of paint and rotten still lifes, peeking into classrooms, seeing people all dressed in black who were very different from the people in Hometown. I decided I would be one of them. I hung out in the museum looking at the collections of impressionists, postimpressionists, German expressionists, and abstract expressionists (thinking, "I can do that!"), walked by the lake, and poked into stores on Wabash Avenue in the dark shadows under the "L." I bought my first leotard, jazz albums ([Charlie] Parker, [Gerry] Mulligan, and [Stan] Getz), and Beat Poetry—Jacques Prévert and Jack Kerouac. My favorite book was Kerouac's *On the Road* [1957].

Hometown and Oak Lawn, where I went to grade school and high school, were white Protestant and Catholic. I had one Jewish girlfriend. [. . .] I did not personally know any black people until I went to Girl Scout camp with black campers and counselors. I saved up babysitting money, which my parents matched, so I could go every summer.

1961: Graduates from Oak Lawn Community High School.

Attends Milliken University in Decatur, Illinois. Majors in Studio Art.

Meets Stephen Clover, a studio art major, from St. Paul, Minnesota.

1963: Marries Stephen Clover. Wedding ceremony in Hometown, Illinois. They immediately move to St. Paul, and soon after to Minneapolis to attend the University of Minnesota, living first in "Dinkeytown," then on the "West Bank" of the University, and finally in an apartment on Franklin Avenue, the city's "Indian Ghetto."

My husband and I moved to Minneapolis thinking we would attend the university as a young married couple, but I wasn't considered a resident and therefore wasn't eligible for in-state tuition. So, Steve went to school while I worked full-time in the office at Red Wagon Products, a restaurant supply company, and took classes in night school. Eventually, I became a full-time student, earning a living by working as a slide projectionist and as an artist's model at the university, the School of the Minneapolis Institute of Fine Art, and for various groups of architects and artists who used to get together to draw from the model. That's how I got to know the sculptor Alonzo Hauser, who had been the barker for Gypsy

Rose Lee, and his wife, the dancer Nancy Hauser. Years later, in New York, I modeled for Raphael Soyer, but that's another story. . . .

At the university there was one woman who taught sculpture but I never worked with her. My painting teachers were all men—second generation abstract expressionists—like Peter Busa, who were bitter because they never made it. All they talked about were the good old days when they sat around the Cedar Bar having a beer with Bill [Willem de Kooning] and Jackson [Pollock].

As a woman student I didn't get much attention, but there was a sense of camaraderie among a certain group of undergraduate art students. (I never went to graduate school.) I was the only woman in this group. We thought of ourselves as artists and took ourselves and our work very seriously.

My figurative paintings at that time recalled [Leonard] Baskin, Edvard Munch, Odilon Redon, John Graham, the German expressionists, de Kooning, and California expressionists such as Nathan Oliveira, David Park, and Richard Diebenkorn. Going back and forth between earth and bright colors. Wet into wet. Drippy paint . . . Often a larger-than-life-sized solitary figure or two figures that didn't relate to each other against a field of color, with angst-ridden titles such as *Lover and I* (for a painting with one figure) or *Mother and Daughter on Carnival Day* (but, of course, it wasn't a festive carnival day). I would take a large canvas, lean it against the wall, and cast my shadow on it to paint from. Because the canvas was leaning on an angle, the figure would be distorted and abstracted.

Some of the figures were huge, colorful hermaphrodites, but no one, including myself, talked about my subjects. No one talked about content, only Hans Hofmann's "push and pull" and formal issues. My work was intensely personal, but I had no vocabulary to talk about it other than the painting itself. I was very schooled in formal approaches—you see that in the work I do today, only now the formal abstraction is consciously loaded with content.

Art was our life. Like many young artists then, Steve and I lived on welfare, surplus food (rice, beans, peanut butter, Spam, powdered eggs and milk), and food stamps. I always staked out studio space in our apartments (separate from school), and later claimed a room in an abandoned vacant building on a street known for its prostitution and seedy element. It was a dark multi-floor building where homeless people lived and roamed the halls. There was one other artist—Mike Lynch. I was so broke that I used to paint on brown paper sacks and the butcher paper that our hamburger was wrapped in—it came in pink, brown, and white (the building was so damp that mold grew on all the paper). After that I worked in a storefront under the Franklin Avenue apartment. One place we lived was so cold, that water froze in the toilet.

1963 First solo exhibition, Coffman Memorial Union, University of Minnesota.

1964: Solo exhibition, Bottega Gallery, Minneapolis.

Work is included in the Walker Art Center Biennial (and again in 1966 and 1968).

1966: Worked as Assistant Director of the Sales and Rental Gallery, Walker Art Center, Minneapolis.

During these years, my work became more abstract and I began using collage. It was still very painterly though—influenced by [John] Altoon, [Cy] Twombly, [Robert] Rauschenberg, and [Claes] Oldenburg's early plaster reliefs. Probably Rauschenberg's work was the greatest influence—both the use of paint and the recycling of found materials in his combines. I think it was around then that his bed painting won the prize in São Paulo or Venice Biennale. I liked the physical presence without the figure being there. It's still a favorite painting of mine.

1967: Graduates with a BA *from the University of Minnesota. Travels with Stephen to Europe. They hitchhike around England, France, Belgium, Netherlands, Italy, Spain, Switzerland, and Ibiza. In London, Paris, and Rotterdam, they see collections of African, Oceanic, and Native American art, and are particularly excited by an exhibit of "primitive art" from the collections of artists that is at the Musée de l'Homme in Paris. They purchase a Dogon Kanaga mask, a Baule water buffalo mask, two Dan masks, and a Senufu bird from galleries in Paris.*

While we did protest against segregated housing, Steve and I weren't politically active. We had friends in SDS [Students for a Democratic Society] and other leftist political groups, but mostly we went to see Bergman and French films and hung out in coffee houses and the Triangle Bar to hear Bob Dylan or blues musicians like Lazy Bill Lucas. We were part of the Bohemian counterculture scene in Minneapolis.

Mid-1960s: Hammond switches to acrylic paint and her work becomes more minimal and hard-edged. Large shaped paintings, often diptychs or triptychs reminiscent of Frank Stella's work.

There was a growing consciousness that things were moving in the direction of minimalism, which I was finding out about through art magazines and shows at the Walker. I realized that if I wanted to make it with the big boys, I had to do what they did, so I learned to paint myself "out" of the work. I made huge intricately shaped canvases. Looking back, what's interesting is that my shapes and colors were often very intuitive and loaded with suggested meanings. For instance, I would use pink, a color that no male minimalist would be caught dead using! The surfaces were very fragile and could easily be spoiled if touched. This is what I was doing when we moved to New York in 1969.

1967–69: Works as Assistant Director of Dayton's Gallery 12, Minneapolis.

Dayton's Gallery 12, on the top floor of Dayton's department store, was a very good gallery. We had shows of George Sugarman, Tom Wesselmann, Robert Indiana, Charles Ross, and others. I became the buyer of nineteenth- and twentieth-century works on paper, mostly prints—I've always had this archival side. Through the gallery, I made my first trip to New York.

While I worked at Dayton's Gallery 12 (Steve also worked there briefly), we began to collect prints. It was a time of the rebirth of lithography. Tatyana Grossman's Universal Limited Art Editions (ULAE) had started in Long Island (at the University of Minnesota, and I had learned lithography from Zigmunds Priede, one of her early master printers), and she was working with [Larry] Rivers, [James] Rosenquist, Marisol, [Lee] Bontecou, [Jim] Dine, [Jasper] Johns, and [Robert] Rauschenberg. As a student Steve had purchased [Odilon] Redon and [Käthe] Kollwitz—re-strikes. Now we bought two Johns, a Dine, a Rauschenberg, a Stella, and a Reinhardt. We also bought a Pop portfolio and a whole portfolio of Andy Warhol's Marilyn Monroes. We really had an eye, the two of us. We collected things that we really loved. Luckily they were cheap—many under $100. When we divorced, we split our collection. I chose the African sculpture and two prints. Several years later I had to sell the Johns *Target* [1960s] and the Rauschenberg *Post Rally* [1965] in order to support myself and my daughter.

Steve later died of AIDS, and we don't know what happened to his collection. He probably needed to sell it. I wish I had just one of those Warhol Marilyns today. I could quit teaching, pay off my mortgage, take care of all my debts and my daughter's school loans too!

My husband was dealing with his sexuality as a gay man. He was struggling at a time when there were no frameworks or support systems (these were pre-Stonewall days), and also we weren't in San Francisco or New York. Eventually he told me he was gay but talked about it as if it were a sickness. He went into therapy, where his sexuality was pathologized. He thought he could get over it. And I thought if I could be a better wife, it would work out OK.

I hung out with him and the gay boys (mostly hairstylists and decorators) and a few diesel dykes. I was fascinated with gay culture, and I would go with Steve to the bars and gay parties. I shopped in stores that catered to gay men, and wore faux leather pants and a black T-shirt with the sleeves rolled up like Jimmy Dean. Women were interested in me and figured if he was, she was. And I was, but didn't know it. I was reading [Jean] Genet's *Our Lady of the Flowers* [1943, first US English edition 1963], and identifying with the sense of outlaw, the sexuality of the forbidden—all that was very erotic for me. These were very difficult, intense times for me. I didn't have anyone to talk to, however I learned to trust my work, to know that whatever happened in my life, that my art wouldn't go away. That is what I took from this period.

1969: Travels with Steve to France, Corsica, Tunisia, Algeria, Morocco, and Spain.

Gets dysentery and spends two weeks in a clinic in Tunis. Sees work by the Living Theatre in Paris.

That summer we gave up our apartment, stored our things in Minneapolis, and went to Europe and North Africa. We were trying to find a way to connect through traveling, looking at art, and buying things. When we returned to the States, we moved to New York because we felt we had outgrown Minneapolis, and our good friend the painter Brad Davis had already moved there and was working for George Sugarman.

1969–70: Moves to New York. Works as a sales clerk at Altman's Department Store.

We arrived in New York the August after Stonewall, and rented a sixth-floor walkup on 4th Street, across from the La Mama Theatre in the East Village. Through Brad, we met Joe Schlichter, Trisha Brown, Alex Hay, Steve Paxton, Joan Jonas, and other dancers who were experimenting with non-Western movement and working with non-dancer bodies. We joined a loose group of artists who went to the lofts of Deborah Hay and Yvonne Rainer; there would be a little basket or can by the door—if you had any money, you would throw it in. Basically, we did whatever they told us to do. We would be told, for example, [...] to bend over and touch the floor, or to walk in a straight line until we bumped into someone, and then turn left and continue walking in a straight line until we again bumped into someone. This "minimal choreography" was the beginning of what turned into "contact improvisation."

During this time, I found out I was pregnant. I wanted to have the baby, so I did. Although we were already separated during my pregnancy, Steve helped me get my first loft, which was on the corner of Broadway and Spring Street at the time that SoHo was still an industrial district. That's where I lived—a tiny little loft on the top floor of the building that later housed the Spring Street Bar—when Tanya was born.

In 1970, after Tanya was born, I started studying T'ai-chi Ch'uan with Cheng Man-ch'ing ("the Professor") in Chinatown. Meredith Monk and Ping Chong were among the students in that class. The T'ai-chi form, an accumulation of repetitive body positions and movements, was a big influence on dancers like Yvonne Rainer (*The Mind Is a Muscle* [1968]) and Trisha Brown. [...]

Martial art forms are genderless, so they provided me with a way of acting out feminist principles, of physically and therefore psychologically occupying space, without relying on strength or domination. I did T'ai-chi for about six years but started studying aikido with sensei Yoshimitsu Yamada in 1973, so the two overlapped for a while. After teaching classes to women in my loft, and at a women's martial arts school, I stopped studying T'ai-chi and continued with aikido, which I have done ever since. T'ai-chi and aikido are similar in that both are nonaggressive martial arts, about receiving and redirecting negative energy rather than blocking it. Because they are not based on size or strength, they are ideal for women. The WLM empowered women to "take space." T'ai-chi gave me a physical (and genderless) way to do just that—to fill and occupy space. [...]

ED. NOTE

"Harmony Hammond, a Narrative Chronology: Part I, the Years 1944 to 1980" (unpublished), ca. 2000, Trustees of the Moira Roth Revocable Trust; University of California Board of Regents. The manuscript compiles citations and data from Moira Roth's interviews with Hammond. Roth's undergraduate art history students at Mills College (Oakland, California) braided biographical information with excerpts from these interviews to create a chronological narrative. This collaborative initiative served as the capstone project for Roth's Art of the Modern World undergraduate class. The originally intended "Part II, the Years 1980–Present" never transpired. The inclusion here of excerpts from "Part I" pays tribute to Moira Roth's engagement as a mentor of students and a champion of younger colleagues, while marking her due place among Hammond's interlocutors.

Local Artist Makes Good

El Puente de Galisteo (2002)

Driving into Taos I pass the Sagebrush Inn, its sign proclaiming "Happy Birthday Agnes Martin" in large black letters. On March 22, 2002, the University of New Mexico's Harwood Museum of Art celebrated Agnes Martin's ninetieth birthday with a celebratory dinner, educational symposium, and exhibition.

Everyone was there to honor Agnes, one of the world's most renowned and legendary living painters (who lived in Galisteo from 1978 to 1992). The Friday night birthday dinner was complete with a welcome by Charles Lovell, Director of the Harwood, short comments from her dealer and several friends, a champagne toast, and a proclamation by Frederick Peralta, Mayor of Taos, who declared Agnes Martin Week.

Approximately half of the 400 people at the dinner were local Taoseños honoring Agnes for all that she has given to the town. Talk on the street has it that her generous "anonymous" donations are helping to save the hot springs and to build a youth center and a new community swimming pool for Taos (in her youth, Agnes was a champion swimmer).

On Saturday the Taos Center for the Arts hosted an all-day seminar where five artists and scholars presented papers on Agnes's work—paintings based on delicate penciled lines and thin washes of blue, orange, or gray acrylic paint. While some historians want to claim her as the mother of minimalism, Agnes insists she is an abstract expressionist because her work is about light and emotion. Especially notable were presentations by artist friends Richard Tuttle (who once lived in Galisteo but now lives up near Abiquiu) and Ann Wilson. Both have known Agnes since the late 1950s when they were all part of a small group of artists working on the Coenties Slip in Lower Manhattan.

In the evening, the Harwood Museum opened an exhibition of her new work (ten paintings completed in Taos in 2001, plus one new painting just finished last week). On Sunday, her 1976 film *Gabriel* was screened and the Taos Chamber Music Group dedicated a concert to Agnes.

Galisteans spotted at the weekend festivities included: Mike and Dora Anaya, Ramona Scholder, Priscilla Hoback, Denise Lynch, and former Galistean David McIntosh.

Agnes has a long relationship with the Harwood. Born in 1912 in Saskatchewan, Canada, she moved to the United States in 1931, became a citizen in 1950, and enrolled at the University of New Mexico [UNM] in Albuquerque where she eventually taught art from 1947 to '48. In 1947, she attended the UNM Summer Field School of Art, which was headquartered at the Harwood where her work was included in a student exhibition. Thus it is believed that the Harwood is the first museum to ever show Agnes's work. Later she had a studio next door.

In 1957 art dealer and painter Betty Parsons invited Agnes to show in her New York gallery and encouraged her to move to New York. Her first solo show at the Parsons Gallery was in 1958. In 1967, she abruptly left New York City, wandered the country in her camper, and eventually settled on a mesa in Cuba, New Mexico, where she built her adobe house and studio. In 1978 she built her studio in Galisteo. [. . .]

Soon after moving to Taos in 1992, Agnes became friends with Bob Ellis, then the director of the Harwood. He arranged for an exhibition of her work in 1994. Following the exhibition, she donated seven of the paintings to the museum. These paintings are now on permanent display in the octagonal chapel-like Agnes Martin Gallery.

At ninety years old, Agnes, who attended all the weekend events except the opening (she said she had already seen those paintings), now lives at the Plaza de

Retiro and paints daily a few blocks away at her studio on Camino de la Placita. Happy Birthday, Agnes!

ED. NOTE

"Local Artist Makes Good" was originally published in *El Puente de Galisteo*, May 2002, 2. This version is slightly abridged.

Material Girls

Gender, Process, and Abstract Art Since 1970

Santa Fe Art Institute (2003)

Tonight's lecture has two aims:

1. To loosely trace the work of feminist artists, from the late '60s to the present, who brought a gendered content to postminimal concerns with process and the manipulation of materials—where the physical properties of a material determined form and content.
2. To situate my work within this context and continuum.

The title of my talk refers back to an exhibition I curated in 1997, at Gallery 128 in New York City, called *Material Girls: Gender, Process and Abstract Art Since 1970* [see fig. 3.2].[1] The abstract art in this show tracked an important lineage of feminist art history that has not been given its due, as most contemporary feminist exhibitions and histories focus through the 1980s lens of representation, privileging figuration and photography.

Coming out of the '80s analysis of gender and representation, focusing on photo-text work and figuration, critics writing in the '90s all too often have misread or given limited readings to feminist abstract work. Statements that feminist abstract artists repressed or suppressed content are erroneous. What indeed was so exciting at that time (at least in New York) was our excitement at bringing/seeing content in the very materials, techniques used to manipulate them, and the notion of process itself.

I remember endless excited discussions about the personal and political implications of the grid, repetition, the physical properties and emotional associations of materials. Content was believed to not only come from image or symbol but also from the very choice of the material itself and the techniques/activities used to manipulate it . . . stitching, tearing, stacking, ruffling, pleating, weaving, layering, connecting, etc.

The feminist histories being written have failed to address feminism and abstraction (at most, they offer a limited discussion of pattern and decoration and women's traditional arts). And most considerations of abstraction have avoided the issue of gender.

Abstract Art

Contemporary readings by young well-intended critics, historians, and writers who say that abstract feminist work from the '70s (in New York) suppressed or repressed content have it all wrong.

Abstraction as a visual strategy.

Abstraction can be seen as a site where two subjects meet (artist and viewer).

Abstraction has enabled women to speak of the unfixed nature of human experience, refer to a feminist identity that is not essential but cultural/political, use an artistic voice that speaks in first person without presuming to be universal, that has intentionally multiple rather than universal associations, and presents alternatives to the "unified structures" and "enduring objects" of minimalism.

Women have derived new meanings from minimalist systems (seriality, repetitive units, grids).

They have invested seriality and repetition with humanist content, often looking to cross-cultural models.

Feminist art has begun to develop a language of abstraction that articulates multiple subjectivities.

Feminism's validation of the personal counters the coolness and alleged neutrality of geometric abstraction.

More Than Minimal

In 1996, Susan Stoops curated one of the rare exhibitions investigating a feminist language of abstraction: *More Than Minimal: Feminism and Abstraction in the '70s*, Brandeis University [Rose Art Museum]. The show brought forward a generation of artists whose visual sensibilities were strongly shaped by the abstract aesthetics of minimalism—but whose lives were empowered and informed by feminism.

While not necessarily ideologically driven, all these artists [Lynda Benglis, Jackie Ferrara, Nancy Graves, Eva Hesse, Ana Mendieta, Mary Miss, Ree Morton, Michelle Stuart, Dorothea Rockburne, Hannah Wilke, and Jackie Winsor] began to have a "gendered engagement" with practices and issues of postwar American art.

Their cultural position as women shaped the environments in which they worked and informed material process, technique, and audience reception (other women). [. . .] Feminist interpretations of the grid, a privileged point of reference for artists, included its nonhierarchical restructuring (from quilt-related works, for instance, to Hannah Wilke's erotic chewing gum grids). Minimalist notions of repetition [. . .] were rethought in light of repetitive activities in women's lives (diaries, stitching, needlework, chores . . .). [. . .]

Many visual investigations of the times contributed to a broadening exploration of the ways material and the handling of material carries content—gendered, sexed content—into both figurative and abstract art. [. . .] Lynda Benglis, Hannah Wilke, and Joan Snyder, to name just three examples, started inflecting materials with traces of the gendered body as a necessary component of artistic identity.

Just their presence in the artistic arena disrupted the minimal masculine field and began to decenter subject and audience; their presence as women opened alternatives to minimalism's monolithic male voice. They tended to use handmade or hand-manipulated materials versus austere industrial fabrication. They altered elemental forms; their formal repetition evoked human [rather than mechanical] experience, natural occurrences. Like many postminimal artists of the time, they crossed/eliminated/extended boundaries between sculpture, painting, and drawing. In early works by such artists as Ida Applebroog, Louise Fishman, and Joan Snyder, among others, we see the gradual "feminizing of the material stuff of minimalism."[2] Gradually, they brought personal/political/emotive associations to pure materiality. CONTENT.

Material Girls

The exhibition *More Than Minimal: Feminism and Abstraction in the '70s* evoked "the postmodern abstract practices and conceptual postures [that] unfolded and inevitably overlapped with feminism."[3] The exhibition featured works by women artists who, through feminist consciousness, transformed the abstract aesthetics and visual strategies characterizing minimalism of the 1960s.

In a sense, my exhibition *Material Girls* took over where *More Than Minimal* left off. The intergenerational show presented thirty-one artists—primarily New York City–based. Due to extremely limited space and resources, *Material Girls* was not able to fully examine the thesis that *feminist content not only comes from image or symbol but also from the very choice of the material itself.* However, *Material Girls* introduced the range of work engaging, via material choices, with issues of gender and sexuality coming out of [the] late '60s and early '70s, through the '80s to the present.

As a big subject presented in a small artist-run space, the exhibition *Material Girls* at Gallery 128 was conceived as an introduction and mini-examination of a large subject that manifestly deserves further serious examination in a larger venue (major museum exhibition, catalogue, or book). [. . .]

ED. NOTES

This text is based on Hammond's notes for a guest lecture she gave at Santa Fe Art Institute in July 2003. She concluded the lecture by speaking extemporaneously from talking points while showing works by some of the artists whose practices further elaborate the thesis of the exhibition *Material Girls*: Kiki Smith, Sheila Hicks, Lenore Tawney, Claire Zeisler, Magdelena Abakanowicz, Brenda Miller, Kazuko, Lisa Suzuki, Joan Jonas, Deborah Hay, Trisha Brown, Yvonne Rainer, Carol Hepper, Sarah Rapson, Michelle Stuart, and Haleh Niazmand.

1. *Material Girls*, contributing artists: Diyan Achadi, Kim Anno, Lisa Beck, Lynda Benglis, Sydney Blum, Kate Chura, Sarah Draney, Ana Ferrer, Maxine Fine, Maria Elena Gonzalez, Harmony Hammond, Carol Hepper, Eliza Jackson, Kazuko, Gloria Klein, Julia Kunin, Linda Matalon, Joanne Mattera, Rosemary Mayer, Mary Miss, Patsy Norvell, Howardina Pindell, Sarah Rapson, Andrea Reynosa, Kiki Smith, Joan Snyder, Michelle Stuart, Carla Tardi, Jackie Winsor, Carrie Yamaoka, Nina Yankowitz.

2. Lynn Zelevensky cited by Kate Linker, "A Feminine Subject for Minimalism?," in *More Than Minimal: Feminism and Abstraction in the '70s*, ed. Susan L. Stoops (Waltham, MA: Rose Art Museum, Brandeis University, 1996), 36.

3. Susan L. Stoops, "An Introduction," in *More Than Minimal*, 6. The eleven women artists Stoops featured in the *More Than Minimal* exhibition—Lynda Benglis, Jackie Ferrara, Nancy Graves, Eva Hesse, Ana Mendieta, Mary Miss, Ree Morton, Michelle Stuart, Dorothea Rockburne, Hannah Wilke, and Jackie Winsor—brought feminist consciousness to practices "referred to in the critical literature of the late '60s and early '70s as 'process' (Robert Morris), 'anti-form' (Lucy Lippard), and 'post-minimal' (Robert Pincus Witten)" [Stoops, "An Introduction," 6].

The Front Line, the Big Picture, the Long Haul

An Essay in Two Parts: Theory and Practice

From Our Voices: Art Educators and Artists Speak Out About Lesbian, Gay, Bisexual, and Transgendered Issues (2003)

Part One: M(art)ial Engagements

I am a lunatic with lethal martial skills.
—XENA, Warrior Princess

The path of the warrior is a lot more daring:
you are cultivating a fearless heart,
a heart that doesn't close down in any circumstances;
it is always open, so that you could be touched by anything.
—PEMA CHÖDRÖN

I look for moments of engagement in art and life.[1] Art makes connections. It is a tool. It is a weapon. It makes the strange familiar and the familiar strange. I am writing as a visual artist and art educator who has also studied and taught martial arts for twenty-eight years. The visual and martial arts are not separate practices in my life nor are they separate from life. Rather, they are connected creative activities that manifest themselves differently over time and in relationship to each other. Both are about occupying and negotiating space, moving through it, with an awareness of how you affect the world around you, moving with intent and ethical responsibility. They are parts of my shifting whole.

I have been an artist as long as I can remember. I grew up in a postwar lower middle-class housing project on the South Side of Chicago. I went to two years of college in Decatur, Illinois, got married at age nineteen to an artist, a gay man, moved to Minneapolis, where we lived for seven years, got my undergraduate degree in art, had my first exhibition in 1964 and arrived in New York City in 1969, the August after the Stonewall rebellion in June that marked the beginning of the gay liberation movement. We got divorced. I had our child and continued to make art. I was lucky to be in the right place at the right time. It was a period of civil rights and anti-war activism in the art world. It was the beginning of the women's liberation movement and the birth of the feminist art movement. I was influenced by and contributed to early feminist and lesbian feminist art projects. Feminist artists, including myself, brought a "gendered engagement" or content to minimal and postminimal concerns with process and the physical manipulation of different materials.

It was also a period when visual artists and performers were interrogating the definitions of different art forms and collapsing the boundaries between object-based and performative arts. As part of this interdisciplinary atmosphere, many visual artists participated in movement workshops and dance performances with avant-garde choreographers Yvonne Rainer, Deborah Hay, Steve Paxton, Trisha Brown, and Meredith Monk. Using the body as simply another postminimal material, they worked with untrained dancers of different body types and sizes and explored the natural non-narrative movement implicit in everyday activities. They also studied non-Western movement and philosophies found in the theater, dance, and martial arts of Eastern cultures. It was in this circle of artists, choreographers, and dancers that I first heard about and then began studying the ancient Chinese martial art T'ai-chi Ch'uan. In T'ai-chi, which I studied for six years, I met people who introduced me to the modern Japanese martial art aikido that I have done ever since [see fig. 2.1]. That was twenty-five years ago.

Aikido is a nonaggressive, nonviolent martial art that was developed early in the century by Morihei Ueshiba (1883–1969). His experience fighting in the Russo-Japanese war of 1905–6, as well as subsequent experience in two World Wars, forged his opposition to the use of martial arts for destructive purposes. Aikido reflects Ueshiba's belief that at their deepest level, martial arts are a path of spiritual realization, based on an underlying reverence for life. (Any serious martial artist knows that fighting is the last resort.) The word aikido means "way of harmony: moving with the force and principles of nature."

Based on Kenjitsu, or sword, techniques, aikido utilizes large circular movements to implement principles of nonresistance and blending. However, this does not mean being passive or without energy (ki). An attack is neutralized by redirecting the energy, rather than confronting or rejecting it. Or, to put it another way, one's opponent or attacker is not blocked but rather the force and energy of his or her intent is redirected back without escalating the conflict. Muscular strength is irrelevant because there is always someone bigger or stronger. One tries to stay in the present moment, blending, with no resistance but no anticipation. As such, it is said, the bamboo or the willow are free to bend and withstand the force of the gale while remaining strongly rooted.

There is no competition in aikido. Because there is no winning or losing, all people, with different body types, physical abilities, personalities, life experiences, or energies, train at their own speed and level, focusing on their own improvement and growth through daily practice. The training and discipline consist of three levels: physical, psychological, and spiritual. On the physical level, mastery of form is the crux of training. The teacher demonstrates the form, the student observes carefully and repeats it countless times until she/he has completely internalized the form. We train by doing the same techniques over and over again. Having a partner attack us, performing a technique, then reversing the positions. Taking turns throwing and being thrown. Repetition. There is little talking. Explanations are not given: the burden of learning is on the student. Eventually, with the ultimate mastery of form, the student is released from adherence to the form.

Communication is established through the body and transcends barriers of lifestyle, language, and culture. Aikido, like art, has no gender, race, class, or sexuality. People do. Through repeated physical contact, we learn to observe, listen to, and respect others, to know their limits and ours. Of course, these movements or techniques that we do are not really aikido. But rather the physical manifestation of aikido principles. Through the repeated practice of movements embodying these principles, we extend beyond our self-perceived boundaries or limitations. We take aikido out of the *dojo* (training hall) and into the world.

Much can be said about aikido's relationship to art and teaching. In addition to the notions of listening, process, and discipline described above, I wish to focus here on its concepts of engagement and encounter as a means to communication, connection, interaction, and creativity. Because aikido is dynamic and fast, it requires an intense focus and clarity of intent and movement so you don't get hurt or hurt anyone else. In traditional swordsmanship, it is believed that each sword cut must be made as purely and fully as if it were life's last. Ideally one would train and live one's life with that same commitment to the moment.

Commitment (in this case, an attack) is essential to establish a true meeting of energies or an encounter with others. This meeting or encounter, in turn, is necessary to enable a blending or harmonizing. And this harmonizing is necessary if we are to have any sort of exchange, expression, or communication. It is necessary if we are to find ways of working with others to make change, build, or create. As students and teachers of aikido, we create openings for encounters and responses (to practice techniques and make an exchange of energies possible).

Now, this is powerful stuff. If you take these principles out of the martial arts context, you can see that we are talking about a profound life philosophy. We are talking about how we interact with the rest of the world as part of that world. I see art as a kind of opening. Discussed within the context of recent theoretical dialogues that circulate around contemporary art practices, this concept of blending energies does not mean a loss of individuation or difference, of self or culture. Nor does it necessarily mean assimilation, conflation, appropriation, erasure, displacement, or exile from one's own body or culture. It means taking space and moving out from self, from center with the self as subject. It also implicitly means taking responsibility for one's actions and the way they affect others.

I am interested in an art of engagement, whatever its style or concerns. Simply the act of making art is not enough; the art has to say something more, give something more. Risk touching, being touched. Art that refuses engagement simply takes up space. It does not contribute to the world. A lot of art today is strangely mute—there is no engagement or encounter in the martial arts sense, and therefore no possibility for communication or interaction. In its conscious refusal to participate, this art born of boredom and apathy and the artists who make it reinforces isolation, passivity, pessimism, defense, and defeat, a position that I find extremely disturbing. I believe that as artists and teachers, we have a social responsibility to create openings and invite response. My actions as student, teacher, and artist must be as clear, committed, and responsible as that of the swordsman or swordswoman.[2]

Part Two: Daily Terrors

[In] November 2000, I was informed by the head of the School of Art at the University of Arizona, where I have taught since 1988, that he received a letter from an ex-student of mine who had been in my Spring 2000 Graduate Painting class, claiming that I "snuck" gay content into the class, that she was sexually harassed by sexually explicit images and language, that the class was made up of my "gay groupies," and that she was discriminated against and received a grade of C instead of A because she was straight. The same letter was also sent to the dean of the College of Fine Arts, the provost and the Office of Affirmative Action, which handles student complaints against professors.

In her eight-page letter, this student, who had been completely silent throughout the semester, quoted me and students both incorrectly and out of context, citing examples of how, according to her, I encouraged students to do work that "turned [me] on" and "shocked [me] into arousal." These included:

- a discussion of how meanings associated with a particular material change over time, for example how latex rubber shifts from abstract references to the body and skin in the postminimal pre-AIDS sculptures of artists like Eva Hesse, Bruce Nauman, Hannah Wilke, and myself, to a sexually saturated material carrying associations of body fluids and safe sex in the late 1980s and 1990s in work by Robert Gober, Linda Matalon, Anna Ferrer, Gregory Sale, and others;
- a discussion as to whether or not a woman who was exploring patriarchal notions of feminine beauty, eating disorders, and her own body image should wear a leotard or perform nude;
- a discussion following *State of the Art: Art of the State?*, an excellent video about censorship and First Amendment rights produced by the National Campaign for Freedom of Expression, in response to the 1989 controversy surrounding the NEA.[3] It includes interviews by anthropologist Carol Vance, author Michelle Wallace, artists Rachel Rosenthal, David Wojnarowicz, Hans Haacke, Andres Serrano, Guillermo Gomez-Pena, and Karen Finley, as well as several art historians and lawyers interwoven with visual art, video art, and performance works.

Apparently, almost every discussion I initiated or encouraged, and the class eagerly engaged in, was to this woman's mind "trash talk," inappropriate, unprofessional, and on some level extremely threatening. Ironically, she wanted to censor a video on censorship.

Only three of the class's eight students identified themselves as queer. Of these, one man painted portraits that scrambled notions of masculinity; one woman occasionally dealt with lesbian identity, but most often with gender, culturally received and rejected notions of beauty, and body image issues; and another made paintings that didn't overtly deal with lesbian identification at all. None of their work was sexually explicit. One of the five women in the class was African-American, one of the three men, Choctaw. No matter how you cut it, in this class, as straight and white, this woman was in the majority.

While the content and format are left up to the instructor, graduate classes generally meet one evening a week to critique student work. I almost always begin each class meeting with a one half-hour to one-hour slide presentation and discussion of contemporary work relevant to that being produced by class members or report on what's happening in the art world. Sometimes the work is difficult to look at, intellectually provocative, or controversial. Although sexuality and sexual difference were discussed a lot, there was very little *sexplicit* work shown in class (hetero or homo). Most of the semester's discussions centered around the following issues: which artists and what kind of images and art are not represented in the Western art historical canon and why; representation and the politics of difference; labeling/defining/authentication/assimilation/commodification/colonization, etc.; intersections of race, ethnicity, class, gender, sexuality, etc.; negotiating multiple identities; concepts of place and displacement; the body as social/political/cultural site; and censorship and First Amendment rights (this was during the time of Mayor Rudy Giuliani's censorship of the *Sensations* exhibition at the Brooklyn Museum).

Discussions were lively, but this student was completely inarticulate. She didn't participate and only spoke when we looked at her work or if I asked her a direct question. All she could say is that she wanted to make "paintings of clowns and circuses in happy colors." I and the other students went out of our way to be supportive and to provide gentle constructive criticism, to suggest that there might be layers of content with "clowns and circuses" that she could explore, and that she might think about notions of "clowning," masquerade, performance and performativity, as well as exoticism and the sensationalizing of "otherness," or being a transient "family" on the road. We recommended she look at the work of Pablo Picasso, Georges Rouault, John Graham, Walt Kuhn, and Claude Cahun, and contemporary artists such as Bruce Nauman, A. P. Gorney, Phyllis Bramson, Maureen Mullarkey, Patrick Webb, and Beverly McIver, most of whom she had never heard of, and didn't bother to look up.

Her appeal and complaint raised many unanswered questions. If the class only dealt with "gay issues" as she charged, and was so offensive, why did she stay in it? Why didn't she drop the class? It wasn't required. Why didn't she talk to me and say that she was having difficulty with some of the images, subject matter, and language? If she had a problem with the grade I gave her, why did she wait until November to appeal it? How is it that a person who doesn't talk all semester suddenly writes an eight-page letter? Was there someone telling her to do this, someone helping her write the letter? Was there an outside influence and agenda? Was she acting as an isolated individual, or possibly as a plant of a right-wing campus organization that targets openly gay teachers? What was I really dealing with?

The whole event was highly disruptive and consumed a lot of my time and energy. It was hard to stay in the present, remain focused, and continue teaching.

I had to respond to her grade appeal and meet with the head of the School of Art. I couldn't talk with the other students but was able to get support from a few colleagues. Because I didn't know where this woman was coming from, I had to strike a delicate balance between responding as if she was merely appealing her grade, and preparing myself in case there was a larger, strategized agenda. That meant that I had to start researching groups such as Young Americans for Freedom, a national right-wing group with a deceptive name, that often focuses on bringing "morality" and a conservative agenda to college campuses, begin networking with queer organizations such as the Queer Caucus of the College Art Association, the Lesbian, Gay, Bisexual, Transgendered Issues Caucus of the National Art Education Association, the Human Rights Alliance, the National Gay and Lesbian Task Force, Feminists for Freedom of Expression, and the Arts Advocacy Project of the National Coalition Against Censorship, and lining up a First Amendment lawyer.[4] If this woman planned litigation, I planned to go bigger than she ever imagined, making it a nationally profiled case for academic freedom.

While the then-head of the School of Art supported me, this woman's grade appeal was denied by the Dean's Office on the technicality that more than six months had passed since she had received her grade. She still had the option of filing a formal complaint of sexual harassment and discrimination (her original letters were just that, letters, not a formal complaint to the Office of Affirmative Action). The fact that she didn't suggests that she was acting on her own and not as part of an organized group, and that her charge of harassment and discrimination was primarily an attempt to manipulate culturally entrenched homophobia to get a better grade. It was easy to do, and she had nothing to lose. Fortunately for me, it didn't work this time. I was relieved, as litigation was not on my calendar and I did not relish having to rev up for it. But what about the next time?

The Office of Affirmative Action reports that litigation is becoming commonplace (they even cite an increase in student and parent complaints about nude models) and recommends that faculty include warnings in their class syllabi if they will be presenting material that might be offensive or controversial. The increasing use of litigation as a punishing retaliation against any perceived slight by a teacher is frightening. Like any form of censorship, it can have a chilling effect. I now include this warning in my syllabi and I talk about it at the first class meeting. However, I have not changed what or how I teach.

All this was happening at a time when my partner was being harassed at her workplace, and my car was being vandalized in the working-class neighborhood where she lived in Santa Fe, by a neighbor who apparently didn't like where I legally parked my 1973 Volkswagen Beetle on the street. Instead of talking to us about it, she, or her kids, repeatedly vandalized my car with eggs, hot dogs, condoms, and eventually tampered with the tire so that I had a blowout. Like the woman in my class, my partner's neighbor just assumed, if you've got a problem, it's okay to harass and scapegoat queers. It was hard not to overreact or jump to conclusions, but I was pretty sure that these "daily terrors" were separate incidents, reflective of a conservative political climate and heteronormative culture.[5] More disturbing to me was the fact that I was being targeted implied that I was already being seen as a "target." I've always been out since coming out in 1973, have been very visible as an artist who is a lesbian, have lectured extensively for years on gender, sexuality and the representation of difference, and was hired at the University of Arizona for my feminist politics as much as my art credentials. However, with the publication of my book *Lesbian Art in America: A Contemporary History* in the summer of 2000, I was visible (and vulnerable) to a wider public than ever before.[6] This book had been discussed in my class.

I regard this whole situation, the grade appeal and complaint, as a reality check, a wake-up call, a warning of shifting winds and change in the political climate. One thing was clear: If this was happening to me, it was most likely happening to others, or soon would be. The 1990s had become so queer-friendly, especially for white artists and academics (since the 1980s, most artists teach when they leave graduate school), that it was easy to take our space for granted. In the martial arts sense, I'd let my guard down and lost sight of the larger picture outside the frame of academia and the various art worlds I inhabit. Despite the fluid nature of the queer field, all too real boundaries do, as I found out, still exist. A year and a half later, when I taught a graduate seminar listed as "Lesbian Art in America," there were no problems. Presumably, everyone knew what they signed up for. It's when we move outside of our allotted "special focus" space into general classes not sexually designated, but assumed therefore to be heterosexual, when we bring "difference" into the mainstream or the modernist field, that there are problems. Of course, this is precisely the reason to trespass. While none of us wants to be reduced to sexual identity alone, it is essential to continue being out there as queer artists and teachers so that sexuality and sexual identity can be part of the discussion when it is relevant and appropriate.

I'm worried about our universities and their art departments. Academic terrorism may seem like nothing compared to the daily violence enacted by all parties in the Middle East, however one creates a climate for the other. While our nation focuses on terrorism from outside its borders, there are "daily terrors" within our national boundaries—in our homes, workplaces, and schools—sites where discrimination, hate crimes, and the violence bred out of ignorance and a conservative political agenda seep through the cracks.

Ironically, it is the rights and values of the First Amendment that have come under attack in the United States. The Bush administration's "war on terrorism" threatens our right to privacy and freedom of expression. Historically, the university is a place of open dialogue, debate, informed opinion, disagreement, dissent, and protest for professors and students. It's crucial that universities protect this space of academic freedom, and in doing so, protect the rights of free speech and creative expression guaranteed by the First Amendment. We must be vigilant. I continue, I create openings and invite responses, even though they are not always what I anticipate or desire. As an artist, a teacher, and a m(art)ial artist, you'll find me here, engaged in the classroom, on the front line.

ED. NOTES

"The Front Line, the Big Picture, the Long Haul: An Essay in Two Parts: Theory and Practice" was published in *From Our Voices: Art Educators and Artists Speak Out About Lesbian, Gay, Bisexual, and Transgendered Issues*, ed. Laurel Lampela and Ed Check (Dubuque, IA: Kendall/Hunt, 2003).

The numbered endnotes for this essay, below, are by the author.

NOTES

1. The concepts in "M(art)ial Engagements" were first presented as a paper in 1997 on a panel at A Teacher's Institute, in conjunction with the international biennial exhibition TRUCE: *Echoes of Art in an Age of Endless Conclusions* (curated by Francesco Bonami) at SITE SANTA FE. Subsequently, they were developed and rewritten as "M(art)tial Engagements" for "TEACH ART," a special issue of *New Observations*, guest edited by Lucio Pozzi and Bradley Rubenstein (Spring 1998, pp. 8–10). Resources include Kisshomaru Ueshiba, *The Spirit of Aikido* (New York: Kodansha International, 1984); video of the Aikido Celebration, 1984, Hunter College, New York City, produced by the United States Aikido Federation; and video of the Los Alamos Aikido Dojo Demonstration at the Los Alamos YMCA, June 1996.

2. "In Japanese history we find a tradition of fighting arts (bugei), originally devised to inflict injury and death on the battlefield, transformed into the Way of martial arts (budo), dedicated to perfecting the human self by integrating mind, body and spirit. Starting in the early seventeenth century, the Way of the sword transformed the sword that kills into the sword that protects life. . . ." Taitetsu Unno, foreword to *The Spirit of Aikido* by Kisshomaru Ueshiba (New York: Kodansha International, 1984), 7.

3. *State of the Art: Art of the State?*, video produced by the National Campaign for Freedom of Expression, 1991. From the Deep Dish TV Series: *Behind Censorship: The Assault on Civil Liberties.*

4. Professional organizations such as these need to take an activist position supporting academic freedom and the rights of gay professors and teachers to be out and to teach queer subject matter by writing letters on organization letterhead letting colleges, art schools, universities, and other institutions know that they are being watched and held accountable.

5. Refers to *Daily Terrors*, an exhibition of works that explore the everyday terrors experienced by nearly everyone: social terrorism, religious terrorism, political terrorism, cultural terrorism, corporate terrorism, and domestic terrorism. Organized by Diane Karp at the Santa Fe Art Institute, opening September 2002. In this essay I am adding academic terrorism to this list.

6. Harmony Hammond, *Lesbian Art in America: A Contemporary History* (New York: Rizzoli, 2000).

Letter to Christian Rattemeyer, Curator

(2004)

Dear Christian,

I am disappointed to learn that Artists Space has decided against presenting *Living Legacy: Queer Art Now*, an exhibition of "neo-queer" work by queer artists that would have been cocurated by Ernesto Pujol and myself, or any of the other variations of the exhibition that I proposed in response to time limitations and budgetary constraints. These proposals laid out various curatorial approaches intended to go beyond '80s–'90s identity-based models of thinking and creating, to focus on the complexities of current queer artistic production.

"Neo-queer" might variously be translated to mean work by a new generation of queer-identified artists under the age of thirty, or any work created by queer artists since 2000 (artists of all ages and generations). In either case, we did not presume that the work of queer artists would necessarily "look" or even "be" queer. Our proposal was intentionally open and our list of possible artists purposefully diverse. Indeed, Ernesto and I are examples of artists whose main body of work is not overtly queer but who "always sometimes" make queer work in response to certain events, situations, or experiences. I would say that our queerness (among other factors) informs all our work, even that which is not queer. My guess is that many artists fall in this category and that perhaps this is a reflection of the times.

With all due respect for your curatorial perspective, your explanation of your decision presupposes a "post-queer," "postfeminist," "postcolonial" society. It ignores the very real margins which do unfortunately still exist and posits queer identity as static and queer art as a commodity, thereby feeding the market imperative to move beyond the visual articulation of identity politics in a way that erases very real social inequities and their cultural representation. I take issue with your premise because my lived experience tells me something very different. Being an out artist and writer out West, whatever form the work takes, is still a territory I negotiate daily.

Ironically, your response came as I have just completed a piece for *Reversing Vandalism*, an exhibition this month at the Jewett Gallery at the San Francisco Public Library. At the beginning of 2001, the SFPL staff began finding books carved with a sharp instrument hidden under shelving units. Over six hundred books relating to issues of gay, lesbian, bisexual, and transgender individuals, as well as AIDS and women's health issues were vandalized. Eventually the vandal was caught, and charged with and convicted of a hate crime. The damaged books have been given to artists to create works of art, thereby transforming the destructive acts into visual statements on homophobia and censorship.

Censorship, be it in the crude slashing of books in the stacks, or trendy "cutting-edge" rhetoric of post-identity politics (calling up the Reagan era of "postfeminist" fiction that the art world glammed onto in the early '80s), always feels violent on my body. While differently performed, these acts of censorship demonstrate that we still live in a culture that is anything but "post-sexist," "post-homophobic," "post-racist," or "postcolonial" (the battles mounted by the religious right against a woman's right to abortion, gay marriage, and basic human rights guaranteed by the First Amendment of the US Constitution are a few additional examples).

I, too, want work by queer artists to be included in "mainstream" exhibitions, and hope for a critical discussion of work beyond its relation to sexual practice or choice, but not to the exclusion of exhibitions and publications based solely on gender, race, ethnicity, nationality, or various geographies of time and place. I don't share the belief that they merely reinforce a colonial center and colonized margins. Indeed, it is precisely their position outside the "mainstream" (as it is usually defined) that suggests multiple centers, and their interface with that "mainstream" that offers a fluid, rich and powerful site for cultural productions reflective of the complexity of people's lives as lived. Until there is lasting radical social change and true integration, I stand firmly behind such projects.

Sincerely,
Harmony Hammond

ED. NOTE

Hammond sent this letter on January 10, 2004, to Christian Rattemeyer, curator of Artists Space, New York.

Interview with Lester Strong

Survivor Aesthetic

A & U: America's AIDS Magazine (2004)

Art by Harmony Hammond has been called "monumental," "embattled terrains where conflicting cultural aspirations bump up against each other," "landscapes of gendered and sexualized bodies," "the debris of the modern erotic unconscious, with its connection to the fear of death."

Powerful words about art by a woman who herself describes her work as embodying a "survivor aesthetic." That aesthetic played a role in her emergence on the contemporary art scene in the '70s as a "first-generation" feminist artist. It played a role in her writing the groundbreaking *Lesbian Art in America: A Contemporary History* [see fig. 4.1], published in 2000 by Rizzoli, which surveys a field of art denied a historical context until only recently through its all but complete erasure from mainstream accounts of art history. And it certainly was a factor in her life and art during the '80s when she ran up against the illness and death from AIDS of her ex-husband. Interviewed at her home and studio located in the rural Northern New Mexico village of Galisteo, Hammond responded to some questions about how AIDS has influenced her life and art.

* * *

LESTER STRONG: How has AIDS affected your life?

HARMONY HAMMOND: As we all know, AIDS has had a devastating impact on the art world. We've lost so many creative minds. By the mid-'80s I knew dozens of gay men, most of them artists, who were sick and dying. We didn't know what was happening, and it seemed so out of control. The government wasn't helping. It was scary. At that time, I didn't know any women who had AIDS.

I've been most immediately affected by AIDS through the death of my ex-husband Stephen Clover, the father of my daughter Tanya. Stephen was diagnosed in the mid-'80s and died in 1987. While Steve's death was devastating for me, it was hardest on Tanya. Steve and I had been divorced and leading our separate lives for many years when he became sick. I don't presume to speak for Tanya, but I know it wasn't easy. She had two gay parents and was growing up in a society where many people don't think gay parenting is acceptable. Then, as a teenager, she loses her father to AIDS. The lack of education and social stigma surrounding gays and lesbians, and people living with and dying of AIDS, attached itself to her. Some guys assumed that if both her parents were queer, she was queer. Others didn't want to date or have sex with her, fearing that they would get AIDS. Fortunately, Tanya is an artist, a healing person, and a survivor. She made art about her dad and about her feelings toward him—love, pride, anger—the whole range of feelings, and presented it to the public.

STRONG: How has AIDS influenced your art?

HAMMOND: It's social attitudes, issues, and concerns that surround labor, sex, sexuality, and the body that inform my art. Since the early '70s, my work has had to do with what I call survivor aesthetic—notions of layering and piecing things together, building "wholes" out of bits and pieces and fragments. That started with the women's movement, which had a profound effect on me personally and professionally. I belonged to a consciousness-raising group of women artists, and we talked a great deal about how fragmented women's lives were and how women's work (in the workplace, domestic environment, and art world) was unacknowledged, underrepresented, neglected, or devalued. I started making sculptures out of acrylic paint and rags torn from discarded sheets, curtains, and clothing that women friends gave me—literally putting my life in my art. The resulting sculptures looked old and weathered, as if they had been through a lot.

Much of my work is abstract, but it's concerned with the gendered body and sexed body as a social and political site acted upon by forces outside itself, such as the government or medical establishment. Works like *Rupture* [2001–2, see plate 18] and *Suture* [2002, see plate 17] are examples. I often use wounds as metaphors. Is that from seeing Kaposi's sores? Maybe. I'm not sure, but the wounds in paintings like *Sieve* [1999] visually announce a violence, pain, and bleeding. As a place of passage, wounds suggest both the physical survival of the damaged body and emotional healing.

The materials used always bring associations to works of art. I am interested in how certain materials, for example, blood, hair, and latex rubber, which have been used by artists since the '60s if not before, take on different meanings and resonate in the time of AIDS. Like numerous artists, I've used human hair and blood (in my case, menstrual blood) in my work. It can be beautiful while simultaneously having an edge of danger or violence. Latex rubber suggests bodily fluids, safe sex, or certain sexual practices.

I've made a few latex rubber paintings that specifically relate to AIDS. *Acts Performed* [1992], for example, combines the light and dark hair of two different people in the skin-like latex rubber covering the canvas, suggesting the mixing of bodily fluids. In *Untitled* [1995], a torso shape of poured latex appears to be held to the linen by the kiss of a crude latex head impaled on a metal gutter and leaning against the painting as if it were trying to hold onto the physical body and keep it from leaving this world. You can't look at either piece without thinking of the body and AIDS.

STRONG: Much of what you're describing relates to violence. And since AIDS is a form of violence committed against the body, it also resonates that way in a time of AIDS.

HAMMOND: Yes. There's a lot of violence in the world—violence done to us, violence we do to others, violence we do to ourselves. While my work looks minimal and formal, there's an edge of violence and loss that asserts itself and disrupts the formal presentation. It's always lurking nearby. It can be suggested by materials such as burnt wood, battered and rusty metal, or a crusty dark red paint surface that reminds one of dried blood. It can also be suggested by process. The act of nailing through or incising into the paint surface violates the modernist painting tradition, the skin of paint, and the body it represents.

STRONG: You've talked about your art in relation to surviving, to the body, to violence, and to AIDS. Do you think it carries a message that people living with HIV and AIDS need to know?

HAMMOND: I want my art to engage people. I want a physical response from the viewer. I think my work is very much about occupying space, taking space, demanding that you pay attention to it. It's not passive. Much of it is about the violence and devastations we see in the world around us—war, atrocities, illness. But it does not illustrate them. It's not about being victimized. It's about the things we do to the environment and each other. About realizing we're all complicit in what happens, about taking responsibility and demanding that attention be paid to our needs, be it as women, as queers, or as people living with HIV and AIDS.

ED. NOTE

The interview, titled "Survivor Aesthetic," appeared in *A & U: America's AIDS Magazine*, no. 111 (January 2004): 20–21. Lester Strong was special projects editor for *A & U (Art and Understanding).*

Statement, *Paint on Metal* Exhibition

Tucson Museum of Art (2005)

Paint on Metal

Monotypes

Since 1980, I have been painting with oil paint or inks on metal in order to make monotypes. Monotypes are made by painting directly on a plate and then running the plate and paper through the press in order to obtain a unique imprint on the paper. I have preferred the surface and color of metal (be it aluminum, copper, or steel) to that of plexiglass. I consider the press to be my collaborator in these images. Because I apply the paint/ink thicker than most people using this process, the pressure from the press creates wonderful accidents, pushing the limits of the technique. Working in a state of what I call peripheral control (in the postminimal sense of process and materials), I welcome these accidents. While the scale varies, many are quite large (up to five-by-ten feet!). I am interested in doing monotypes on a painting scale. The monster prints (the five-by-ten footers) were exhibited unframed in a solo exhibition at SITE SANTA FE in winter 2002.

Tin

During the late '70s and early '80s, when I lived and worked in New York City, I collected old frames from the streets, Goodwill, and the Salvation Army (taking out the pictures of Jesus or other reproductions), and from a framer who, when she reframed work for customers, gave me the old frames rather than just throwing them out. I painted and recycled these "found frames" into my work, where they became more than "just frames" for presentation. They became part of the art object. So, when I moved to New Mexico in 1984, I had this history of using old frames, recycling them and using them in my own art practice. I found myself drawn to the old Mexican and New Mexican decorative tin frames frequently used for presenting retablos (traditional painting on tin) or religious prints. I began to collect, recycle, and paint on old tin frames just as I used wood frames in the past.

In a sense, the processes of painting on metal plates for monotypes and recycling old frames merged. At that time there were a lot of empty old frames around, and they didn't cost much money. And since most of the tin frames actually have a backing that is a sheet of tin, it wasn't long before I began to paint directly on that instead of inserting a painting or drawing on a piece of paper. It was familiar to me. The color, surface, and "feeling" was like painting on metal plates for the monotypes, only this time the painting wasn't run through the press or imprinted onto another surface. I often paired and juxtaposed one of my small paintings on tin with one of my large oil paintings on canvas (an example of this is in the permanent collection of the Phoenix Art Museum).

While I was interested in retablos, I was more interested in decorative (stamped) tin work, eventually researching and writing an article "Historias: Women Tinsmiths of New Mexico" for the twelve-year anniversary issue of *Heresies: A Feminist Publication on Art and Politics* (vol. 6, no. 4, issue 24, 1989). My paintings on recycled tin frames referred to, but did not copy, the rich tradition of retablo painting in New Mexico. However, because I feared what I was doing could be read as "cultural appropriation," and because many of the recycled frames I was using were in and of themselves works of art, I became uncomfortable with this practice and ceased painting on the frames by 1987.

Mixed-Media Paintings

I have always responded to "place" (like using the rags from the streets of SoHo in the early '70s). Around 1988, when I first began coming to Tucson to teach at the University of Arizona, I began to incorporate long panels of rusty roofing tin into my large-scale installational paintings, such as *Farm Ghosts* [1990, see plate 12]. At times the metal was affixed to the surface of the painting, but more often than not, I preferred to create what I called uneasy juxtapositions of the recycled metal panels (used "as is" with histories and narratives suggested by the worn and weathered surfaces) with Euro-Western painting and the modernist painting field. The works referenced both body and land, and therefore social landscapes. I would paint on the metal, using the paint as a material to suggest blood, wounds, healing—not to depict things—or I would write words. I wanted the paint and the materials such as tin, burnt wood, straw, leaves, or linoleum, or objects such as buckets, water troughs, or old gutters, to be used equally (what I call, an "aesthetic of survival"—much like [Robert] Rauschenberg's early work but with a greater consciousness of the meaning of the materials).

At this time, I was living in the Barrio Viejo, where I first found the discarded corrugated metal. It had been used for roofs, sheds, chicken coops, and fences, and now was being used to board up vacant houses or was piled up in the alleys and empty lots. I let the paint ooze out between the panels of metal, suggesting something (social bodies?) refusing to be hidden. In a sense the pieces were about gentrification. Eventually, I also began to gather the corrugated tin from abandoned farms that I came across as I drove back and forth between Arizona and New Mexico. The materials of paint on metal suggested narratives of place (peopled space, though the people were now absent except through these material traces). Many of these works were included in my exhibition at the Tucson Art Museum in 1993 (with catalogue essay by Lucy Lippard).

Recent Paintings on Metal

By the mid-'90s I began using less corrugated roofing tin and began to incorporate more metal gutters and troughs into my paintings. The gutters became metaphors of circulatory systems. But there was no water or life fluid. Only a trace of flesh (latex rubber) or trickle of blood (paint). Everything was dried up. Since then, the work has become more minimal, more condensed and reductive, as I try to embody content into the paint itself (or other selective materials, including metal).

In the summer of 2001, I was able to make a series of five-by-ten-feet "monster monotypes" on one of the largest noncommercial presses in the country. As usual I worked on metal plates, however because the plates were so large and unwieldy, I never moved them off the press bed or cleaned them for the two weeks I was printing. This process contributed to the velvety rich, almost iridescent, surface of the monotypes. When I did finally clean the plates, traces of the inks and paints remained, "evidence" of the process, creating their own painting on the metal. Since then, I have made several other paintings on metal in the same way. Sometimes I paint back into the surface. As with the early monotypes, and the paintings on/in tin frames, I am still interested in the color of the bare metal juxtaposed with the paint and inks. Most of my paintings on canvas are comprised of thick layers of oil paint. And my monotypes use thicker than usual oils and inks. What I like about these new paintings on metal is the "thinness" of the painting surface—a film or trace of pigment on the thin sheet of metal (in the sense that Robert Ryman explores "thinness" of paint and paintings). These works are in progress. I am not yet sure whether I will attach them to a wooden support or affix them directly to the wall.

ED. NOTE

The exhibition *Paint on Metal*, Tucson Museum of Art, 2005, was curated by Julie Sasse.

Statement, *How American Women Artists Invented Post-Modernism* Exhibition

Mason Gross School of Art Galleries, Rutgers University (2005–2006)

[. . .] In Minneapolis [where I was living in the 1960s], I made large geometric hard-edged acrylic paintings that frequently consisted of shaped and/or multiple canvases. I knew from the art journals that if you wanted to be taken seriously as an artist you did what the big boys in New York did. So I did them bigger and better. The hand of the artist was not visible. In fact, you couldn't touch these paintings without damaging the matte surfaces—very different than the pieced-together, weathered, patched surfaces of works I made [in the 1970s] after my arrival in New York City.

I began to work with the grid and notions of "marking" to create repetitive pattern paintings—mostly on paper. I was looking at the art of non-Western cultures and began to question the relationship of my work to my life, and the function of art in general. Feminism brought a new understanding of how the experiences of "being a woman" in patriarchal culture might be articulated in the work. I and other feminist artists began to investigate and resuscitate creative work that had been ignored, dismissed, or relegated to the margins of the Euro-Western modernist painting field, including but not limited to women's traditional arts such as needlework (stitches composed a woman's visual language), art of other cultures, and work that relied heavily on pattern, decoration, and ornamentation. Slowly I began to experiment with various devalued materials and practices. [. . .]

ED. NOTE

The exhibition *How American Women Artists Invented Post-Modernism* was curated by Judith Brodsky and Ferris Olin at the Mason Gross School of Art Galleries, Rutgers University, December 2005–January 2006. The text above is an excerpt from Hammond's unpublished statement.

Statement, *High Times, Hard Times: New York Painting* Exhibition

(2006)

The postmodern focus on representation, and therefore figuration, has contributed to an inaccurate reading of the creative climate in New York during the late 1960s and '70s, a period of postminimal interdisciplinary experimentation that resulted in work both conceptual and abstract. Artists moved between the disciplines, ignoring, crossing, and dissolving boundaries. Abstract painting, especially that coming out of postminimal concerns of materials and process, was central to this experimentation period.

Painters interrogated the components of traditional painting—support, ground, pigment, shape, pictorial space, as well as placement and relationship to architecture and viewer. Paint was a material to be manipulated like any other, such as felt, wax, fiberglass, dirt, steel, or old wood. Likewise, nontraditional materials—such as latex rubber, polyurethane, lacquer, tar, blood—could be used as pigment. Paintings were shaped, unstretched, draped, woven, pleated, flocked, stitched, bejeweled, and grommeted. Slowly, painting was subjected to the force of gravity, taken out of the rectangle and off the wall, relaxed, collaged, and reconfigured, frequently occupying a three-dimensional space that could be called sculpture. And while there wasn't a theoretical framework articulated, feminism brought a gendered content to this way of working.

I moved from Minneapolis to New York's Lower East Side, and then to the corner of Spring Street and West Broadway in the fall of 1969. It was a period of civil rights and anti-war activism, the gay liberation movement, the second wave of the feminist movement, and the birth of feminist art. I was influenced by and contributed to early feminist art projects. My work referenced women's traditional arts, such as weaving and needlework, by using recycled hand-me-downs—rags given to me by women friends, literally putting my life in my art. I began to paint with acrylic on worn-out blankets, curtains, sheets, and bedspreads. Rag strips were dripped in paint and fixed to the painting surface, so they hung down like three-dimensional brushworks. In these *Blanket Paintings* (1971), the weight of the rags and paint altered the painting rectangle. Eventually the rags took over and activated the painting field. *Girdle* (1971) consisted of a soft crocheted grid altered by the weight of the painted rags. This led to the series *Bags* (1971), which were hung on the wall, and the slightly larger-than-life-size *Presences* (1972) [see plate 2], which hung out in space. These pieces could be touched, retouched, repaired, and, like women's lives, reconfigured.

In 1973, I created six floor paintings out of knit fabric my daughter and I picked from dumpsters.[1] Strips of fabric were braided according to traditional braided rug techniques but slightly larger and thicker in scale, coiled, stitched to a heavy cloth backing, and partially painted with acrylic paint—the "braided rug" literally and metaphorically becoming the support for the painting. *Floorpieces* [see plate 4] negotiated a space between painting (off the wall) and sculpture (nearly flat), although, because of my background, I thought of them as paintings. They were placed on the floor, thereby questioning assumptions about the "place" of painting.

ED. NOTES

Hammond wrote this statement in 2005 for the exhibition *High Times, Hard Times: New York Painting*, organized by the curator Katy Siegel as an Independent Curators International project. The show opened at the Weatherspoon Art Museum, Greensboro, North Carolina, in August 2006 and then traveled to five additional venues in the United States and abroad, closing at ZKM Center for Art and Media, Karlsruhe, in June 2008. The statement was reproduced in the exhibition catalogue, Katy Siegel, ed., *High Times, Hard Times: New York Painting 1967–1975* (New York: Independent Curators International and D.A.P., 2006), 121.

1. Hammond later discovered a seventh *Floorpiece*, forgotten in storage. *Floorpiece* title numbers do not reflect the chronological order of making. Five of the *Floorpieces* now travel and are exhibited together as a single installation (as per the installation for the exhibition organized by the Aldrich Contemporary Art Museum, *Harmony Hammond: Material Witness, Five Decades of Art* in 2019). The other two (less colorful) *Floorpieces* have never been exhibited. In the future they could be exhibited separately or together, but not with the other five.

In Her Own Words

The Meeting of Passion and Intellect

For the National Museum of Women in the Arts (2007, 2023)

I moved from Minneapolis to New York City in 1969. I was lucky to be in the right place at the right time. It was a period of civil rights and anti-war activism. It was the beginning of second-wave feminism and the birth of the feminist art movement. I was influenced by and contributed to early feminist art projects.

My earliest feminist works (the *Blankets*, the *Bags*, and the *Presences*) consciously recalled women's traditional arts. They incorporated rags given to me by women friends, literally putting my life into my art. Constructed of discarded, recycled cloth that I painted with acrylic, these pieces were about layering, connecting, building wholes out of fragments, calling forth a narrative on women's creativity, and placing my work within that narrative.

By 1973 I was also using fabric found on the streets, a practice I continued until 1984. This work must be considered in relation to the Lower Manhattan Garment District being colonized by artists such as myself. Lofts in SoHo still housed sweatshops where poorly paid immigrant women turned out garments

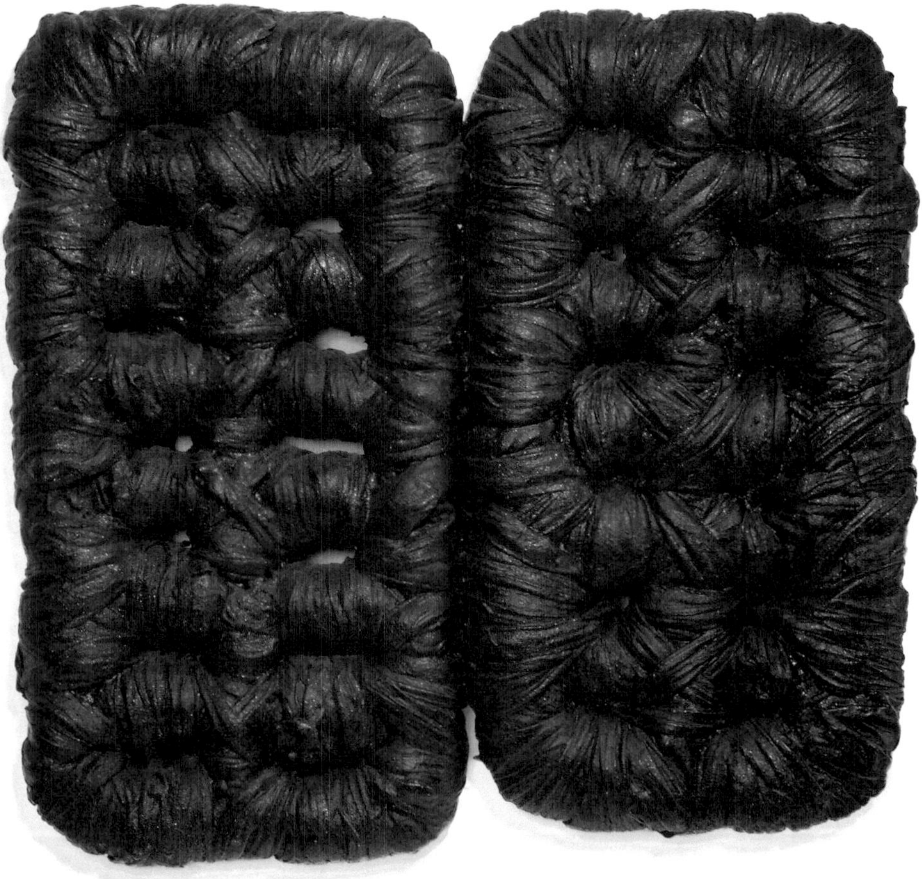

FIGURE 4.6. Harmony Hammond, *The Meeting of Passion and Intellect*, 1981. Mixed media. 33 × 36.5 × 5 in. (83.82 × 92.71 × 12.70 cm). Photo by Lee Stalsworth. National Museum of Women in the Arts, Washington, DC. Gift of Lily Tomlin and the artist. [1998.108]

for the fashion industry. Every night the end cuts of bolts of knit fabric were thrown out in dumpsters to be carted away as waste. Using this discarded fabric, I was able to reference the women working in the sweatshops and myself—a woman and an artist in a capitalist patriarchal culture with what I called an "aesthetic of survival."

In the "wrapped sculptures" that I made from 1976 to 1984, the cloth was wrapped around a wooden armature that functioned as a skeleton. The fabric was like muscle, and the acrylic paint or latex rubber painted on the surface became skin. The forms were not about mummifying, binding, bandaging, or bondage, but rather about making something out of itself, with the inside showing on the outside—a kind of presence as essence made visible.

The first of the wrapped sculptures were forms to hold the body: cradles, rafts, and ladders. They called up the body without being figurative. Gradually they became stand-ins for the female body and therefore bodies. While these pieces were related to the postminimal work of Eva Hesse, at the time I made them I was thinking about Monique Wittig's novels. The sculptures, like her "*corps lesbien*," created a raw, passionate, and sometimes violent sexuality; a body reconstructed and (re)membered whole, occupying a space larger than its physical size.

The Meeting of Passion and Intellect [1981; fig. 4.6] is a double-grid form wrapped with layers of fabric from the streets. Suggesting two torsos or possibly two heads, it is covered with additional layers of gesso, acrylic paint, glitter suspended in Rhoplex, and powdered charcoal mixed into wax, all of which create a rich black surface.

I often work with pairs, two forms that are similar but different. It is about relationships (be it people or ideas), about the meeting of equals without one dominating the other. Instead of being in opposition or representing a dichotomy, *The Meeting of Passion and Intellect* implies a merging of two into one while remaining discrete and two. In this case, passion—the feeling body, activism, sensuality, even sexuality—and intellect—the world of ideas and theory—go together, like twins joined at the hip.

ED. NOTE

The wrapped sculpture *The Meeting of Passion and Intellect* (1981) was acquired by the National Museum of Women in the Arts in 2006. Hammond's statement about the piece was first published in the museum's journal, *Women in the Arts* 25, no. 4 (Winter/Spring 2007): 20–21. A slightly revised version, reproduced here, appears in *National Museum of Women in the Arts: Collection Highlights*, with foreword and acknowledgments by Susan Fisher Sterling, director NMWA (Munich: Hirmer, 2023), 182.

Curatorial Essay, *¿Y QUÉ? Queer Art Made in Texas* Exhibition

(2007)

In early 2006 when Tricia Earl, adjunct instructor in art at Texas Tech University, invited me to curate an exhibition of work by Texas-based queer artists for Landmark Arts, the School of Art gallery, my answer was a fast "yes." Frustrated about the lack of queer presence in and around Lubbock, Tricia decided to do something, and began by talking with her colleague Ed Check, associate professor of visual studies. Together, they approached Joe Arredondo at Landmark Arts who helped them write a proposal to the Exhibitions and Visiting Artists Committee of the School of Art. Once the proposal for the exhibition was approved, Tricia contacted me.

In 1999 I had curated the highly successful exhibition *Out West* [see fig. 3.3], at Plan B Evolving Arts in Santa Fe (now the Center for Contemporary Arts), a regional exhibition of work by queer-identified artists from Arizona, New Mexico, and Texas. Ed was one of the artists in that show. More people turned out for the opening of *Out West* than any other opening in Plan B's history. More importantly, the exhibition provided an opportunity for the artists to meet each other, and rendered queer lives, work, and culture visible to the larger Santa Fe community. People still talk about it.

Around the time Tricia called, I was also invited to consider curating exhibitions in San Francisco and New York. Three shows at one time is too much, so based on my experience of not living in a large urban environment (Santa Fe, despite its self-promotion as the second or third largest art center in the United States, depending on who's doing the promoting, remains quite provincial), I decided that Lubbock was most important of the three, and bowed out of San Francisco and New York for the time being.

Tricia and Ed have elaborated on the category "queer" in their foreword ["What Is Queer"]. [. . .] While there is no agreement as to what exactly constitutes queer art, it is generally thought to reflect queer identity and to contribute to the development of that identity. Just as there is no fixed queer identity, there is no single queer aesthetic or sensibility, and we like it that way. [. . .]

Personally, I am not interested in defining an essential queer identity, sensibility, or aesthetic, but rather interested in looking at art by self-identified queers at different times and locations, to see what forms it currently takes, what issues it addresses, and how it relates to larger social, political, and cultural concerns of the moment. Given the proliferation of queer shows during the queer renaissance of the 1990s, one might ask, aren't we beyond all this? An ongoing discussion in queer art and academic circles in recent years has been: Why queer exhibitions? Aren't they an idea whose time has come and gone? Don't they just ghettoize queer art and artists, thereby perpetuating marginalization?

In 2005, the Queer Caucus for Art sponsored a panel on the subject at the College Art Association [annual conference]. Short presentations by panelists led into a lively and instructive audience discussion. Art historian James Saslow [and Jenni Sorkin, cochairs of the Queer Caucus for Art] reported on this discussion in the May 2005 issue of the *Queer Caucus for Art Newsletter*:

> The topic had been framed as an opposition between two models of queer art production, the Stonewall identity politics idea of group solidarity and community institutions versus a "post-queer" position, that such identities are too unstable and irrelevant to constitute a valid category of cultural discourse or exhibition. But what emerged, encouragingly, was the realization that such a dichotomy is false and misleading: We continue to need both sorts of production but for different purposes and audiences. As a community, we should continue to nurture work that might otherwise not be seen or properly understood. At the same time, we need

> to acknowledge that the mainstream commercial art world has as Jenni [Sorkin, cochair of the Queer Caucus] put it, "gone global": the decline of interest in queer arts coincided with widening commercialization and globalization of the 1990s, in the wake of which many mega-media have aimed their sights away from minority "niche markets" and toward a broad, if shallow, common denominator. Attracting the attention of the queer community and the international art world are both valuable goals but aren't the same enterprise.[1]

Despite queer inroads in academia or urban centers, or the inclusiveness of "queer" itself, my experiences in the trenches (I seem to hang out there as much as anywhere) confirm the panel discussion. While it may not be momentarily trendy, commercially viable, or considered the cutting-edge of radicality on the global biennial trade routes, contrary to the belief that we are "postqueer" or "postfeminist," there continues to be a need for and value to identity-based exhibitions (remember, on the simplest level, an exhibition is "a show"!). This is especially true outside of major urban areas with large queer populations, but even there, I would argue, queer-based exhibitions, historical or contemporary, give us an opportunity to study certain aspects of our creative work that often get diminished or erased when the work is contextualized within the mainstream. With democratic presidential hopefuls bumbling about gay marriage and partner benefits ("the country just isn't ready"), the increase in sanctioned gay-bashing and hate crimes, the high suicide rate among queer youth, and continued right-wing organizing against gay rights bills, queer exhibitions in spaces like Landmark Arts, and cities like Lubbock, are more important than ever. Queer cultural expression has the potential not only of empowering LGBTT peoples, but also of playing a major role in the empowering of many marginalized peoples. It is through an understanding of our connectedness to others, a connectedness that can embrace difference and individual expression, that we will be able to withstand the reactionary forces at work today. If we need a term to rally under, then let's claim "neo-queer" (itself the title of a queer caucus-sponsored exhibition in 2004 at the Center of Contemporary Art in Seattle), or "neo-feminism" to acknowledge a tradition of creative practice and simultaneously allow for change and fluidity.

¿Y QUÉ? Queer Art Made in Texas expresses defiance and attitude. "¿Y QUÉ?" has a double meaning. On the one hand it implies, ". . . yeah, I'm queer, so what? What's it to you?" But it also implies a continuation ". . . and what else? Okay, so you're queer but what else are you?" Texan, Chicano/a, African-American, Anglo, Indio, Asian, urban, country, Mestizo, Norteño, Barrio, East, West Side,

disco, punk, hippie, yuppie, Gen X, Gen Y, teddy bear, Radical Faerie, academic, bulldagger, cowboy, drag queen/king, cross dresser, transexual, bisexual, sadomasochist, feminist, artist, performer, top, bottom, activist, law breaking, law-abiding, *la buena amiga*, butch, femme, collaborator, street-smart, fatty, skinny, person living with HIV/AIDS? "Made in Texas" resonates with *hecho en Mexico*, acknowledging ties with our geographic and cultural neighbors south of the border as well as the histories and cultures of many Tejanos. [. . .]

I did not have any curatorial agenda at the onset, other than knowing that I wanted to avoid stereotypes of Texas and "the West" unless there was a rigorous examination of those stereotypes as tropes of the cultural landscape. At the same time, I desired to acknowledge the specificity of place (which I define as peopled space). While an exhibition of fewer artists would have allowed artists to show more work, I opted for a more inclusive approach. There are twenty-six artists in *¿Y QUÉ?*, two of whom collaborate. They range in age from mid-twenties to age sixty and seventy-five, with most born in the 1960s and 1970s, that period of social and political unrest and activism that gave birth to the civil rights and gay and women's liberation movements. [. . .]

¿Y QUÉ? is an intergenerational assemblage of artworks by well-known Texas artists who have exhibited extensively and others who are just starting to show.[2] The diverse work in the exhibition employs a wide range of visual strategies to address issues such as sexuality, race, and ethnicity. Some of the work deals with overtly queer content. In others, it is more subtle and nuanced, or perhaps engages with other issues, both in and out of the mainstream. One of the main points of the visual diversity is to break down the stereotypes of what looks like or constitutes queer art. At the same time, the art in *¿Y QUÉ?* is not intended to be separate LGBTT art from the mainstream (we need a queer presence in nonqueer spaces) or other identity art movements. Nor does it mean to elide sexuality with gender, class, or race, but rather to acknowledge the existence and range of an extensive body of visual work from diverse queer subject positions within the geographic and cultural landscape of Texas. The range of work disrupts stereotypes and reveals a fluid field in which assumptions about gender, sexuality, race, class, and representation are continuously called into question.

Interestingly, I saw very little sexually explicit work. Nor did I find the work falling into one or two overarching categories of subject, concept, or formal concerns. Instead, I discovered a network of reoccurring themes including: empowerment; gender identity crisis; messing with binary sites of gender; the creation or occupation of third or queer spaces, art historical interventions and revisionings; gendered materials and techniques that reference the body; the raced body; absence and loss; longing and belonging; waiting; nostalgia; popular culture (comics and the internet); performativity; sketchbooks and notebooks as an art form; subversive uses of "illustration"; embroidery and other kinds of stitching; class and taste; display; timing and pacing as content; and site-specific and activist interventions in public spaces.

[. . .] The subjects are the same as queer work created elsewhere but done Texas style. As queer artists living and working in Texas represent, reflect upon, and negotiate their specific multiple identities and positionings in the world, they contribute to a national discourse on the visual articulation of queer culture and, indirectly, global "intersections," making what does or doesn't happen in Dallas/Fort Worth, Houston, El Paso, Austin, San Antonio, and places like Lubbock, San Marcos, and Elgin, Texas, part of the big picture.

ED. NOTES

The curatorial essay, titled "¿Y QUÉ?," was published in the exhibition catalogue *¿Y QUÉ? Queer Art Made in Texas* (Lubbock: Landmark Arts/Texas Tech University School of Art, 2007), n.p. Reprinted with permission from *¿Y QUÉ? Queer Art Made in Texas*, © Landmark Arts, Texas Tech University School of Art (2007), Lubbock.

1. "Letter from the Co-Chairs," signed Jenni Sorkin and James Saslow, in *Queer Caucus for Art Newsletter*, May 2005.

2. The exhibition catalogue includes short texts about each of the exhibiting artists and their work: Lora Alaniz and Jennifer Beth Guerin, Phillip Avila, Sarah H. Booth, David Zamora Casas, Ed Check, Celesta Danger, Tricia Earl, Ali Fitzgerald, Heyd Fontenot, Wesley Harvey, Mike Krone, Michael Marinez and René Saenz, Shanti Matulewski, Horace Mayfield, Wura-Natasha Ogunji, Kristy Perez, Angela E. Piehl, Jim Quinnan, Amber Rademacher, Chuck Ramirez, Chris Sauter, Silky Shoemaker, Annie Simpson, Jeanne Stern, and Deborah Kuetzpalin Vasquez.

Memories of the Feminist Art Institute

(2008)

By the mid-'70s, the feminist art movement, like the feminist movement in general, was divided along reform versus radical lines, and many feminist artists had settled into a comfortable state of apathy. With some, albeit minimal, presence in university art departments and art world visibility for their work, they were fearful of rocking the boat, and activism fell by the wayside. Others were restless. In New York (I believe it was early winter, 1976), a group of women from the art world began to meet and discuss the state of feminist art and artists. There emerged a desire for "a voice" and "a space" separate from men. "The voice" became *Heresies: A Feminist Publication on Art and Politics*, which began publication in 1977 and "the space" developed into a feminist art program/school that went through changes over the years, eventually becoming the Feminist Art Institute that offered classes and workshops and sponsored events. (I met with both groups for a while during the brainstorming and early planning stages, but eventually dropped out of the meetings for the school because *Heresies* was moving along quickly and demanding so much of my time. I couldn't do both.) I believe the institute finally opened its doors in 1979.

I taught Painting and American Women Artists of the Twentieth Century (a wildly successful art history class that I had previous taught once at the University of North Carolina in 1983 and once at Hunter College in 1984).

The classes I taught met at night. I remember taking the subway, and then walking over to that big empty building above the bus station. The New York Feminist Art Institute office and studio space was upstairs. It wasn't big but it was a space. The studio facilities weren't great to say the least but it was a supportive educational environment outside of university or art school structures, where women artists of varying ages and degrees of experience, or women who wanted to be artists, could meet and take classes from feminists who were practicing professional artists.

Painting

In the painting classes I taught, the emphasis was on identifying, developing, and articulating personal content (often based on women's history and experiences) in abstract painting, something many of the students were interested in.

The physical logistics were difficult as there really weren't enough walls, tables, floor space, or storage racks to spread out and work large or store works in progress. While they could come in and work in the studio off-hours, most of the students chose to lug wet paintings back and forth each week on the subway. . . . However, this spirit of roughing it contributed to a camaraderie among the women and an empowering sense of making art "despite" all the restrictions and limitations that conspired against it.

Many of the students took more than one class and/or continued to repeat the same class, allowing them to develop their work over a period of time. They became good painters! In particular, I remember Darla Bjork, Eleanor Pironti, Priscilla Green, and Helen [Stockton].

American Women Artists of the Twentieth Century

Many of the women in painting also took this class. We met at my loft on West 22nd St., where we could project slides, and I could share catalogues and books from my library.

I remember when we decided to offer this class, we did not know if anyone would even be interested much less willing to meet on Friday evenings! But, every week, eight to twelve women came (often bringing friends) for what basically amounted to a slide lecture about American women artists (both in and outside the mainstream) and their work from the late 1890s to the present.

ED. NOTE

"Memories of the Feminist Art Institute," New York Feminist Art Institute Archives, MC 892, Special Collections and University Archives, Rutgers University, 2008.

This unpublished reminiscence was written in response to a request by Nancy Azara, director of the Feminist Art Institute, who was compiling personal histories concerning the New York Feminist Art Institute for preservation in the New York Feminist Art Institute Archives housed at Rutgers University Library.

Letter to Ferris Olin and Judith K. Brodsky Regarding "The Group"

(2008)

Dear Ferris and Judy,

I am writing you in regard to the exhibition *A Group of One's Own: Women's Visual Art Organizations in the United States*, scheduled to open September 2009 at the Zimmerli Art Museum at Rutgers.[1] I gather that you have been advisors to the curatorial process and will be cowriting about the history of such groups from 1960 to the present for the exhibition catalogue.

I don't know if you are familiar with the feminist art group of which I was a member. The group consisting of Sarah Draney, Louise Fishman, Patsy Norvell, Jenny Snider, and myself, all primarily abstract artists, and Elizabeth Weatherford, a feminist anthropologist who also wrote about art, met almost weekly from 1970 to 1974. We thought of ourselves as a "consciousness-raising [CR] art support group."

We exemplified a kind of women's group, the small CR group, that was central to the feminist art movement of the '70s. However, unlike similar groups formed through feminist art programs or the Woman's Building in Los Angeles, based on student-teacher relationships and discovery of oneself as an artist through consciousness-raising, we were peers and all already identified as practicing professionals. We used the CR format and process to critique our work and to focus on issues related to being women artists. Each week we met at the loft of a different group member and focused on her work. We simply referred to ourselves as "The Group."

At a time when to be a woman and an artist was still considered a contradiction of terms or identities, we took ourselves and our work very seriously. While we worked individually in our studios (versus making art collectively), The Group was crucial to identifying and validating gendered content, to our artistic development of this content (mostly through abstract means versus iconography), and to locating ourselves in a lineage of women's creativity.

In the winter of 1974, we exhibited together as "A Women's Group" at the Nancy Hoffman Gallery. I believe that this was the first exhibition of a preexisting women's group in a commercial New York gallery. The response ranged from people being perplexed as to why we would choose to show as "a group" to those who were blown away by the work and understood that the exhibition was a statement about artistic interaction and how we had influenced each other within the context of the larger feminist art movement. This was antithetical to the still prevalent view of artist as unique isolated genius.

We were not an activist organization, although individual members of The Group participated in most of the feminist art actions, organizations and exhibitions of the early '70s. Works by Louise and Jenny were included in early Whitney Annuals that responded to pressure by the Ad Hoc Women Artists' Committee to represent more women artists in their exhibitions and permanent collection.[2] Patsy and Harmony were founding members of the A.I.R. Gallery [Artists in Residence] in 1972. Sarah joined later. Harmony went on to cofound *Heresies: A Feminist Publication of Art and Politics* with twenty other women and worked editorially on three issues of the journal including the groundbreaking "Lesbian Art and Artists" issue [see figs. 1.4 and 1.5]. Louise was not a member of the mother collective but also worked editorially on the "Lesbian Art and Artists" issue. Elizabeth, also a cofounder of *Heresies*, was coeditor for several issues including "Women's Traditional Arts: The Politics of Aesthetics" and "Patterns of Communication and Space Among Women."

Thanks to The Group, and of course the larger feminist revolution, we have all continued to work, exhibit, and publish. This would not have been true a generation earlier. We write, curate, teach, and organize. Patsy completed numerous site-specific public commissions. Sarah has integrated sculpture into her internationally renowned garden in upstate New York. Elizabeth is Founder and Director Emerita of the Film and Video Center of the Smithsonian's National Museum of the American Indian.

We pioneered loft living in SoHo, Chinatown, Tribeca, and the Bowery. Our history as individuals and as The Group is not only part of the history of feminist art in the United States, but is intertwined with that of the experimental downtown art scene of Manhattan in the late '60s and '70s.

The Group is a history waiting to be written. Most of the feminist artists who made a name for themselves in the '70s are artists of the twenty-first century. It is my hope that someday there will be an exhibition, in the spirit of the Nancy Hoffman Gallery exhibition [of 1974], that revisits, documents, and re-presents work by members of The Group, including Elizabeth, tracing its development from that time period to the present.

I hope that the Zimmerli exhibition and catalogue, especially your essay, will include a discussion of this kind of group, which has been so basic and important to the fabric of the early feminist art movement.

I am attaching a list of contact information for members of The Group, should you be interested in talking with us or would like us to send you visual materials. Everyone is still based in New York, except myself. Let me know if I can be of any help.

I'd like to take this opportunity to thank you both for your Work (yes, that's Work with a capital "W") and ongoing contributions to feminist art, artists, and art history.

Warmly,
Harmony

ED. NOTES

Harmony Hammond, letter to Ferris Olin and Judith K. Brodsky about "The Group," January 30, 2008.

1. Ultimately, the exhibition imagined by the feminist art historians and curators Ferris Olin and Judith Brodsky, *A Group of One's Own: Women's Visual Art Organizations in the United States*, did not come to fruition.

2. Hammond's work was exhibited in a Whitney Biennial for the first time in 2024. Works by Louise Fishman, Patsy Norvell, Jenny Snider, and Harmony Hammond are conserved in the Whitney Museum's permanent collections.

Interview with Julia Bryan-Wilson

Archives of American Art, Smithsonian Oral History Program (September 14, 2008)

[Writing]

HARMONY HAMMOND: My writing started as assignments at Sagaris. I began writing nonfiction, some horrible poetry, and letters to editors of art magazines. I think I wrote something in response to Donald Kuspit or someone like that. I can't remember who. Afterwards *Heresies* [*Heresies: A Feminist Publication on Art and Politics*, founded in 1977; see figs. 1.3–1.5 and 2.4] provided a place for me, and [. . .] I began to write as an artist, in other words, to find a voice, which is pretty remarkable considering that fifteen years before that, I couldn't speak. I didn't think I had anything to say—now try to shut me up!

So now I'm writing, and I'm thinking, "People should damn well read what I write!" (Laughs.) But I had been lecturing a lot before then. I need to say that one of the things that came out of A.I.R. [Artists in Residence] was visibility [see figs. 1.1 and 1.2]. I mean, A.I.R. made feminist work visible. You didn't find it in commercial galleries at the time. Because it was good, once it was visible, I and some of the other women got invited to lecture—I'm backtracking a little bit, because A.I.R. was crucial that way, in that it set a certain standard and opened up possibilities of lecturing, teaching, and exhibiting.

I began to lecture around the country. There was a beginning consciousness that women were underrepresented not only in museum exhibitions and collections but as faculty in art departments. We began pushing art colleges and art departments to hire more women. In response, they started to bring people like Lucy [Lippard], myself, and others in as visiting artists and lecturers, but we were just a notch in their belt. When called on their sexism, the men in the art departments would say, "Well, we had two women here last semester." But, of course, they weren't hiring us as permanent faculty, they were just bringing us in and out.

Typically, the art department would pay to bring me in, but I would connect with other departments such as Women's Studies and groups of women in the local community who might be starting a feminist art organization or gallery. I would meet with them for free. So I already was talking and getting my ideas out there. I would talk about my work at the university, but whether they wanted it or not, they also got my slide presentation on lesbian artists, and another presentation on work by feminist artists using fabric and referencing women's traditional arts, or in the late '70s, my lecture about WAVAW [Women Against Violence Against Women], examining the visual representation of violence against women in fashion magazines, advertisements, billboards, and record album covers, etc.

But the writing, I began to do that seriously in *Heresies*, and to write about feminist art in and from the voice of an artist activist. I tried to write about what I knew. It usually wasn't historical. My first article was in the inaugural issue of *Heresies*. It was about content in feminist abstract art, an aspect of feminist art that until recently few historians or curators have addressed. I was also one of the editors of that issue.

In 1984, Time and Space Limited [TSL] published my first book, *Wrappings: Essays on Feminism, Art, and the Martial Arts* [see fig. 2.2]—not the MARITAL arts, as it often gets said when men are introducing me before a lecture! TSL was a small press run by Linda Mussman and her partner, Claudia Bruce, that was an offshoot of their TSL theater. Linda and Claudia were close friends of mine who also lived and worked on West 22nd Street between Sixth and Seventh Avenues. [HH lived at 129 W. 22nd St. for about seven years before moving to New Mexico.] Linda was doing very interesting off-off-Broadway theater, language-based restagings of Gertrude Stein and Virginia Woolf, Japanese and German translations in collaboration with other artists, and her own plays. Claudia was the main actor.

So TSL published *Wrappings*, which was a collection of my writings, including those published in *Heresies*. By then I had written a number of additional articles: "Class Notes" for the "Lesbian Issue," and "A Sense of Touch" and "Horseblinders" for later issues.

Wrappings is a little embarrassing to me now when I go back and look at it—quintessential '70s feminist art. A kind of recap. It's a compilation of the articles that I wrote for *Heresies* and other journals, presentations, and introductions that were like catalogue essays.

JULIA BRYAN-WILSON: There's artist statements.

HAMMOND: Yes, artist statements, and also a talk that I gave at one of the annual Barnard Women's Conferences [Barnard College, New York, NY]. We put the texts together with reproductions of my work and other women's works—the whole point was to weave it together conceptually and contextually—feminist artwork and the other focus in my life, the martial arts.

[*Lesbian Art in America: A Contemporary History*]

Lesbian Art in America: A Contemporary History [Rizzoli, 2000; see fig. 4.1] was originally intended to be a book about lesbian self-representation in art. However, as I began to write, I realized that there was a book missing, and the book that was missing was the history. The few other books being written about lesbian art at this time, in the '90s, had a lot of stuff wrong. They were missing the history. They didn't know the history because it wasn't written down anywhere.

I realized I was one of maybe a handful of people who could write it. So then the book switched from being a book about lesbian self-representation to being a contemporary history. That's a real shift. A weight and responsibility come with writing a history of a marginalized group. Even though we know all histories are fiction and subjective, there's a burden of representation. So how to navigate that, how to negotiate that, weighed heavily on my shoulders.

Since no other similar history existed, *Lesbian Art in America* became the only book and, actually, to date, still is. That was the weight, the burden of representation. [. . .]

BRYAN-WILSON: Well, I want to draw more out from you about [...] the writing and publishing and great acclaim surrounding *Lesbian Art in America*. You've stated that there was this gaping hole of knowledge, and the book has served an incredibly important critical role in filling that hole. I'd love to hear you talk a little bit more about how you gathered the information that appears in the book, how you went about finding this history that has been so erased, including the questionnaires that you sent out and the contacts you made with other artists.

HAMMOND: Well, writing the book took a decade. That needs to be said. Initially, the book was to be on lesbian self-representation. I spoke to an agent in New York who I knew, and who was an agent for many feminist writers. I said, "I think maybe there's a book here, and maybe I could write it. I don't know." She said, "Well, yes. Here's how you write a book proposal." Then she told me the name of this paperback to go buy. So I bought the book and wrote my proposal, which, like I said, was not a history to start with.

At a certain point in my writing, I realized that there was a need for a history of lesbian art and that I could write it. This was around 1990 or 1991. I wrote the history because no one else had. I could write it because I've lived most of that history. It's both contemporary and alternative. Also, I sit on incredible archives, materials that document the history. Many of those projects I was involved with personally, and if not, if I didn't have the materials, I knew who does have them or where to get them.

Research for the book was not done in libraries because, for the most part, the material was not in libraries. It was primary research—artist statements, correspondence, essays in exhibition catalogues, reviews and articles in alternative journals, and movement papers of different kinds, most of which were not catalogued material.

That's why I was writing the book. It was really more about contacting artists, visiting studios, collecting visual and written materials from them, and utilizing my archives. This was pre-internet, so I wasn't using email or Google. It was all done by snail-mail correspondence.

BRYAN-WILSON: And you drew from the gay press as well as the art press?

HAMMOND: Sure. I have an incredible network from all those years of traveling to lecture and teach. I've been on the road since 1972, I think. Or '73. Early '73 was my first visiting artist gig, at the Art Institute of Chicago. I was a stand-in for Vito Acconci, who couldn't make it. (They laugh.) Go figure that one.

BRYAN-WILSON: That was quite a substitution.

HAMMOND: Every place I would go, I would do more than what was expected of me, in terms of my duties as a visiting lecturer. Like I said before, I would meet with small groups of women artists who were just starting to organize. In addition to seeing their work and sharing work by feminist artists I knew, I would tell them about A.I.R. or *Heresies*, and other women artists who were initiating and organizing their own exhibitions, galleries, journals, and art organizations. We were all doing that, those of us who traveled—Lucy [Lippard], Mimi [Miriam Schapiro], May [Stevens], Joyce [Kozloff], and I. We were networking, spreading the word, and inspiring other women to take action on their own behalf.

BRYAN-WILSON: Well, you were self-historicizing as you were presenting.

HAMMOND: I was, but I didn't know it. I wouldn't have said it that way; I thought of it more in terms of a kind of activism. I was saying, if we're forming A.I.R. in New York City, you can organize your own women's gallery here in Minneapolis or Chicago, and they did. A.I.R. inspired other women's cooperative art galleries, like WARM [Women's Art Resource of Minneapolis, Minneapolis/St. Paul, 1973], ARC [Gallery, Chicago, 1973], and Artemisia [Gallery, Chicago, 1973–2003], among others. So it was that kind of thing. I know a lot of artists, both within the art world and in lesbian communities outside the art world. I was privileged in that I could move back and forth between those worlds, in addition to traveling across country. And at a certain point, I moved here to New Mexico.

Even with those networks in place, and my archives, writing the book still took ten years. I didn't do a lot of questionnaire stuff because my approach as a writer or curator usually is to start with the work. While I want to talk to the artist, I'm more interested in the ideas and concepts as articulated in the work. The discussion, the conversation, the narrative, comes out of the art versus having a predetermined discussion and then finding work to fit it.

So that's how I begin. Unlike some other writers who start with the concept first, I start with the artwork and take it from there. When I began what eventually became *Lesbian Art in America*, I didn't have a clear outline in mind. Initially, the book intended to encompass pre-liberation lesbian artists, which, of course, was very messy and tricky. We've talked about a few of those women today off-tape. Agnes Martin and Georgia O'Keeffe had intimate and most likely sexual relationships with women but did not identify as lesbian, and certainly would not have wanted to be in my book. And there are others—others from that period who even acknowledge their relationships with women. But they were pre-liberation, and so the idea of claiming the word "lesbian" or "lesbian artist," or the political consciousness of what it means to put those two words together, was very different for those women than it is for women like myself.

Initially, the first chapter attempted to address these issues in relationship to time and place. I could do a feminist, lesbian, or queer read on their work even if they didn't identify as such—for example, doing a lesbian read of the grid, now that's really exciting! (Laughs.) As you well know, there's limited space in all books, so you have to edit, hone, and refine. Eventually, that initial chapter needed to go because there was so much work by women who did self-identify as lesbian and who put the terms "lesbian" and "artist" together, albeit in different ways. The book needed to focus on them.

But there's one thing I do want to mention. Very early on, I asked artists if there was a woman artist who had really influenced them, who was a role model in some way, and if so, to please name her.

It was amazing how many artists named "the lesbian artist Agnes Martin." Not Agnes Martin, or the painter Agnes Martin, but "the lesbian artist Agnes Martin." At this point, there was no writing out there anywhere, no way, no how, about any of Agnes's lesbian affairs, involvements, or relationships. There's still not a lot out there, but back then, there was nothing. As someone who does know a little bit about Agnes's life, I knew that these women who were stating that "the lesbian artist Agnes Martin" influenced them didn't know anything specific about her personal or sexual life other than the absence of the usual heterosexual narrative.

What was so fascinating to me was that they sensed this with such surety. When pushed, what they were really talking about was a strong identification with Agnes. Now some of it, of course, was that they liked her work, or that she's a serious artist, and why not claim the best? But what they really were identifying with was this kind of outsiderness, you know, being a loner, an outsider, not fitting in—one could even say being a little crazy perhaps. That's another role women who didn't fit in chose to play, right?

BRYAN-WILSON: Sure. The hysteric, madwoman.

HAMMOND: Agnes has this genderless "spiritual" myth around her that she herself has helped to construct. Lesbian artists relate to this woman who dressed in overalls, went west, did it her way, on her terms, and never had a man standing nearby. You know, physically, Agnes was strong and handsome-looking, although in later years there was this innocence and frailness in her eyes. Lesbian artists just claimed her as one of their own. It was a felt connection. But done with such surety—that's what was amazing to me, as if they had read Agnes's personal diaries, but no such diaries exist. So it was extremely fascinating to me that quite a number of the artists named "the lesbian painter Agnes Martin," without knowing anything.

BRYAN-WILSON: That's astonishing.

HAMMOND: It was to me. You know, and it's not like you can—I mean, it's not even like Georgia O'Keeffe, when you're looking at the imagery in her work and doing a read on it and coming away with a sexual interpretation of the work. You can't do that easily with Agnes.

BRYAN-WILSON: Absolutely astonishing. But let's keep talking about the reception of the *Lesbian Art in America*, because it won a prestigious prize, the Lambda award, in 2000.

HAMMOND: It did. You know, I'm very proud of the book. It sure was a hell of a lot of work, and like I said, it took a decade to write and publish. I don't imagine I'll ever do one again. The next book on lesbian art should be written by someone else.

The reception was interesting: There were people who loved it and people who were critical of it. Those who were critical wanted it to be more theoretical. But I'm not a theoretician, even though it was written during a period when there was a lot of queer theory around. *Lesbian Art in America* is written by an artist who is interested in theory, but it was important that it be written in nonacademic English, and at the same time participate in current discourses. I had to give history and facts, but I also had to speak within the queer theoretical discourse happening throughout the '90s, since the late '80s really, and have it contribute to that discourse, but not have it be in an exclusionary language. I also had the problem of how to write about myself and my work in the book. Normally, the author wouldn't write about herself, but if I am not in the book, it would not be a true history.

Those were probably my two biggest challenges. Some feared that the book would be essentialist and were quite pleased to find that it wasn't. I think most people felt that it gave a ton of information and, at the same time, contributed a lot to discourse. Because the book was published by Rizzoli, a few people tried to dismiss it as a coffee table art book. My response to that was, "Well, if it's a coffee table book, I've sure got a hell of a lot of information in it that isn't anywhere else."

I was honored that the book received the Lambda Literary Award. It's still the primary text. There is nothing else that has taken its place to date, but of course, the publishing world has had a hard time, and art books and things lesbian are no longer commercially viable.

BRYAN-WILSON: Were you aware of any instances of censorship around the book?

HAMMOND: Not really. I had no issues of censorship with Rizzoli. It's interesting, because at one point early on, when I showed slides of some of the art to Christopher Lyons, who later became my fabulous editor, Chris said something to the effect of, "Well, you know, all this work isn't of equal quality." Gulp. I thought, "Oh, this is a flag about censorship. They're not going to want certain images." I got very defensive and talked to a few friends of mine who write and publish a lot, and they basically said, "Calm down, Harmony. You've got to keep up the conversation. What they really want to see is that you can work with them."

I heard my friends, but to myself I thought, "This is just the old quality issue used as a smokescreen for censorship." But I began a conversation. I was incredibly nervous about it, but I said: "You're right. The work is not all of the same quality. It's not. However, if this is to be a history of lesbian art, it did not all happen in the art world. This is not where the history happened. If I write it that way, then we cannot call it a history, because I will be called on it by people, and rightly so. Given that fact, I will review any image you want me to review and reconsider it if you have a problem with it. However, since I am the authority on the subject, I make the final decision." Then I was so scared (laughs) that I had gone across some line or something. But that was really the clarity that I got. I will revisit; I will consider anything. But I know the history. I'm the authority here, and I will make the final choice, because if it's going to be a history, then it's going to be the history as I know it and I see it, and that's the best that I could do.

In the end, it really never became a problem. The publisher was never an issue. We negotiated about word count, number of pages, and number of reproductions, as I was always trying to get more artists in the book. But there never was an issue about a specific work. Interestingly, the issues that arose came from those artists who censored themselves. Certain artists—a very small number, but there were a few—did not want to be in the book. But they were only a handful.

I'm proud that there are artists who initially did not want to be in the book but eventually agreed to be included. Since the book took me so long to write, I didn't give up. I just kept talking with them. Artists like Judith Baca, who was out as a lesbian but had never positioned herself or let her work be contextualized that way. Also Joan Snyder and Hulleah Tsinhnahjinnie, they trusted me, maybe because I'm also an artist. Or maybe it had to do with our conversations. I don't really know.

That these women are brought into this historical discussion makes the book a valuable resource. That said, there were a handful of women who did not wish to be in the book, and they, of course, will have to remain unnamed. They are some of the most homophobic people I know. You have to remember, the book was being written in the '90s, during the gay renaissance when there was a brief commercial market for those works that looked queer. Certain artists benefited from this market, but when the market moment moved on, they no longer wanted to be identified as lesbian or queer. Or they benefited from a "feeling" that the work is lesbian without naming it—hence no politics.

One woman in particular, who had been on the cover of *The Advocate*, got hysterical when I asked to include her work. I responded that I really didn't need her and her work for my book, so she could just rest easy if she was having a problem, which she obviously was. I said, "I really don't need you. It's okay. I won't put your work in the book." But she was so homophobic that she didn't believe me and served legal papers on the press [HH: At that time Bay Press, and later Rizzoli] and on me. There were a few other artists as well, who, for various reasons, some more understandable than others, did not want to be mentioned—but she was the only one that was really hostile.

I made the *Small Erasure* series [1999] in response to this self-censorship. Some of their reasons were more acceptable to me than others. I mean, if you're an African-American woman, and you live in the South, and black churches around you are being burned, there's a reality that's very different than somebody who's worrying about selling her work. But in the end, whatever the reasons, they all contribute to the problem—self-erasure contributes to cultural erasure. I took their letters, photocopied them, erased their names and any geographical references, and then covered them with a skin of latex rubber—the first one was covered with a dental dam.

So what you have are these letters from artists of varying ages seen through the skin or the body, telling me why they can't be in the book or don't want to be in the book. Like I said, some of their reasons were more understandable than others. Most wished me luck. One of the *Erasures* is actually a compilation of two letters by the same woman, written about ten years apart. In the first letter she's telling me how tough it is to be black and lesbian in the South. No, she can't write about it. She'll have to talk to me in person. By the time I'm writing the book, and I write back to her, she says, "I'm not a lesbian anything. I'm a God-fearing black woman, and I would not say anything that would jeopardize the people around me." It's the same person.

BRYAN-WILSON: Heartbreaking.

HAMMOND: I thought it would be great to have these *Erasure* drawings on the inside of the book jacket for *Lesbian Art in America*, presencing these lesbian artists in their absence, but that didn't happen. Still, it's a series of pieces that I'm rather fond of. (Laughs.)

BRYAN-WILSON: Well, it goes directly to Richard Meyer's point about censorship, which is that it often generates other works and even more discourse.

HAMMOND: Yes.

BRYAN-WILSON: What was meant to be a form of silencing often bubbles forth in other ways.

HAMMOND: Those really did. I mean, they really did.

[Teaching]

BRYAN-WILSON: Can we talk about your teaching and pedagogy? That's something that you have done partially to support yourself, I'm imagining, but also partially because it has its own psychic rewards.

HAMMOND: Well, you know, I was never on the track to teach. The idea of coming out of an MFA program and then immediately beginning to teach started in the '80s. When I went to the University of Minnesota, it was just undergraduate school. I've never taken a graduate course in my life. I have a BA, so don't have MFA credentials and wasn't steered towards teaching. But once I started exhibiting, and the work was visible, then was reviewed and written about in art journals, becoming visible to an even larger audience, then I was invited to lecture and teach.

Amazingly, my first exhibition in New York, at A.I.R. in January 1973 [see fig. 1.2], was written about in almost every art journal—which says something about A.I.R. and maybe even my work at the time because we weren't taking out big ads or anything. There was no reason for A.I.R. exhibitions to be reviewed, but they were. People at the Art Institute of Chicago, or in Colorado or California and other places, saw and read about my work, were interested, and invited me to lecture.

My teaching grew out of lecturing. Often you're doing what I call a one-night-stand lecture and then critiques the next day. I'm very good at doing critiques. I like doing them, and I think I'm helpful. Teaching's a different thing, but I began doing a lot of summer workshops, short-term teaching, or substituting for professors who were on sabbatical. Eventually, I taught at the University of Arizona in Tucson for seventeen years, where I was a tenured, full professor.

I came into that accidentally, through the back door. They had a teaching position advertised, and I applied. But I only wanted to teach one semester and have the rest of the year to do my work. At that point in time, they weren't interested.

But then a year or so later, when Bailey Doogan, who had taught painting for many years, wanted to go half-time because her career was starting to take off, the university remembered me, and brought me in for one semester as a visiting artist. Because of the enthusiastic student response to my classes, they invited me to stay on.

Moira Geoffrion, the chairperson of the department at that time, hired established, practicing professional artists like myself, Luis Jiménez, and Robert Colescott. All of us were target-of-opportunity hires. We all cut different deals to teach part-time so we could continue with our own work—that just wouldn't happen today!

My deal was that I worked my butt off one semester each year. I was tenure-track, but only there every fall. So there was a regularity, a rhythm to my presence. The students knew when I would be there and when I wouldn't. If they wanted to work with me, they had to sign up for my classes now, as I wouldn't be there next semester. Also I sat on a lot of thesis committees. I forget which came first, but the first year I was hired, I was given tenure, and the next year made full professor, or vice versa.

I never went through the agonizing process of going up for promotion and tenure that most tenure-track faculty do—mostly because I didn't understand the tenure process, and nobody ever explained it to me because they just assumed that everybody who teaches knew how the system worked. But I didn't. Consequently, I never worried. I remember at one point somebody said, "We need some recommendations, some references." I went, "Well, here's a few names, but don't bother them. They're very busy." I liked teaching. I knew I was a good teacher. I knew that from the students. In my mind I thought, "Okay, if I don't get tenure, big deal. I mean, what do you get out of it anyway?" I didn't understand that if you don't get tenure, you're out the door. Nobody told me. I never knew it, so I never got worried. And I got tenure. It's the funniest thing.

I'm sort of the accidental professor, in a way. My value as a teacher is as a practicing artist who brought critical thinking to the classes that I taught—primarily, all levels of painting and interdisciplinary graduate seminars. Of course, that was my favorite thing—working with the graduate students.

That's sort of it. At a certain point it was time to leave, because of departmental politics. I'm too political and too outspoken. I would not be hired today. The university system, and especially University of Arizona, became unbearable as the place became more and more corporatized. You have a classic worker situation of fewer workers, less faculty in the painting area—teaching more overenrolled classes, advising more students, and everybody's in denial of it because they are afraid they will lose their job. Also certain deans, department heads, and co-faculty made it very difficult for women, especially women who had what they viewed as successful careers. It was competitive. They were jealous. At a certain point I felt that it was time to leave, so I did, and I've never regretted it. I view my teaching years at the University of Arizona as a very long artist residency.

Now I am what my friend Jan Brooks calls a "recovering academic." She's one too!

BRYAN-WILSON: What year did you stop?

HAMMOND: I stopped in December 2005. So fall 2005 was my last semester teaching, but I was officially retired spring 2006. Now I go around and do gigs—lecturing, mentoring, and short-term teaching. It's good.

BRYAN-WILSON: You just had a gig in Skowhegan, for example.

HAMMOND: Yes, and that was great, because the students were primarily emerging artists just out of the Whitney [Independent Studies] program or CalArts [California Institute of the Arts, Valencia, California] or perhaps were going into those programs in the fall. Most were in their late 20s and early 30s, but there was a range of age. The main thing is that they were serious about being artists, and their work was interesting. Generally speaking, the level of critical thinking and the level of studio practice was much higher than other places. I enjoyed it thoroughly.

When you're teaching full-time, you need to stay up on what's happening and pay attention not just to what you're doing, but what everyone else is doing, as well. What's the current discourse? When you are not teaching, it's easy to fall out of the conversation. So, Skowhegan was good for me. Since I hadn't been teaching for several years, I had to pull that engagement forth again.

ED. NOTE

Oral history interview with Harmony Hammond, September 14, 2008, Archives of American Art, Smithsonian Institution. The Smithsonian oral history interview took place at Hammond's studio in Galisteo, New Mexico, and was conducted by Julia Bryan-Wilson for the Archives of American Art. The full sixty-five-page transcript, from which the excerpts above were culled, is available on the Smithsonian Archives of American Art website, https://www.aaa.si.edu/collections/interviews/oral-history-interview-harmony-hammond-15635.

Taking Space

A.I.R. Gallery: The Formative Years

(2008)

When A.I.R. Gallery [see fig. 1.1] opened on September 16, 1972, at 97 Wooster Street, it signaled to the New York art world, and by extension the rest of the country, that art by women could be as good as art by men and sometimes better. Empowered by the women's liberation movement [WLM], women in the art world had already begun to publicly protest the lack of work by women artists in museum exhibitions and permanent collections, but still did not have access to the commercial gallery system.[1] This perpetuated the fiction that somehow art by women wasn't "as good" as art by men and that curators and collectors weren't interested in it. Without anyone's permission, support, or promises of funding, A.I.R. was founded because women could not get gallery representation (the main showcase for emerging art) and decided to take things into their own hands.

In 1971, Susan Williams and Barbara Zucker, frustrated by their unsuccessful attempts to interest galleries in their work, decided to start their own cooperative.[2] Initially they considered including men but eventually determined to make it women only. Toward the end of that year, they met with Dotty Attie, Maude Boltz, Mary Grigoriadis, and Nancy Spero. Out of that nucleus of six, a committee of four was formed to look at work by women artists that they might invite to join the co-op.[3]

The committee contacted Lucy Lippard (the first art critic looking at work by women) for suggestions of artists they should consider and she turned them on to the Women's Slide Registry founded by the Ad Hoc Women Artists' Committee in 1970. They combed the registry, which already contained slides of work by over six hundred women artists, then visited fifty-five studios, always bringing slides of their own work to share with the artists they were considering (so the selective process was mutual). There was no curatorial agenda. The committee was not looking for a particular kind of work, or even work that was overtly feminist, but rather for what they considered to be "really, really good."[4] Artists were selected on the basis of quality. Unfortunately, several who were invited to join declined, fearful that their work would be ghettoized or diminished as "women's work," but most were very enthusiastic.

The first meeting of all the members was on March 17, 1972. Everyone brought slides and talked about their work and what it meant to form a co-op that only showed work by women artists. Three artists dropped out, and three more quickly replaced them. The twenty founding members were a disparate group—ranging in age from twenty-eight to forty-six, with most in their thirties—and like the early WLM, mostly middle class and white.[5] All had been working and exhibiting professionally for a number of years. Several had been included in recent Whitney Annuals but few had had solo exhibitions, and even fewer had gallery representation.[6] For most, A.I.R. was their first New York City gallery representation (Agnes Denes, who left her uptown gallery to join A.I.R., was an exception). Everyone knew someone. No one knew everyone.

Artists joined for individual reasons: some were interested in A.I.R. as a separatist, artist-run space, others saw it as a stepping stone to a commercial gallery. The common denominator was getting one's work out and seen. By April, the membership was finalized, and the name of the gallery was unanimously decided upon. The name A.I.R., an acronym for Artists in Residence, was first proposed by Howardena Pindell with a nod to Jane Eyre [pronounced AIR], but members also liked the reference to the required "A.I.R." street-level signage identifying floors where city-certified artists lived legally in commercial loft buildings.[7]

While the gallery stridently announced that women artists and their art were taking and occupying space in SoHo, then the heart of the art world avant-garde, the founding members did not choose to identify as a feminist gallery but rather as "the first women's co-operative art gallery in New York."[8] In fact the word "feminist" was not used even once in the gallery brochure published on the occasion of its opening. Truthfully, most of the women were in the process of becoming feminists at that time, and feminism meant different things to different women: for some it meant equality of representation and opportunity, for others, a sexual revolution that would change patriarchal culture, and by extension, the foundations of the art world. While the formation of A.I.R. was a radical political gesture, members disagreed as to how overtly political the gallery should be, and ultimately chose to "tone it down" and not use that noisy "F" word.[9]

Over the course of the next four to five months, the gallery's exhibition schedule and structure were decided upon, committees formed, not-for-profit status and grants applied for, and a former machine shop in SoHo was renovated by members into a professional gallery space.[10] Costs and labor were shared equally.[11] Each founding member agreed to a fee of $150 and fifty hours of labor to start plus "gallery sitting," and dues of $21 per month thereafter, although it wasn't long before the gallery hired a part-time nonmember coordinator to act as a liaison and help out with day-to-day operations.[12]

In order to provide the opportunity for solo exhibitions, and assure each founding member a time slot during the first season, it was decided to schedule two solo exhibitions simultaneously, one in each room of the gallery (versus a single two-person exhibition).[13] After the first season, each artist had the entire gallery for her solo show. Publicity was limited and most announcements were simple postcards with black-and-white reproductions.

From the beginning, A.I.R. was a huge public and critical success. At the inaugural opening, people packed the gallery and overflowed into the street, blocking traffic. Gallery goers were excited by the seeming explosion of new art that no one had seen before because there had been no place to show it.[14] The exhibition of work by ten members presented a wide range of work that reflected the multiple artistic concerns of all the gallery artists, work that was experimental, professional, ambitious, and engaged with current aesthetic discourses; at the same time, it introduced feminist subject matter.[15] Because it was serious and good, the work could not be dismissed or diminished as second-rate just because it was done by women.

The opening exhibition received glowing reviews.[16] Almost every show that first year received critical attention from the *Village Voice*, *SoHo Weekly News*, and the major art journals—remarkable considering that neither the gallery nor individual artists had money for advertising (then as now, taking out an ad was considered a necessity if you hoped to be reviewed). A.I.R. quickly became a cutting-edge player in the downtown art scene, as work by A.I.R. artists participated in, contributed to, and shaped current critical dialogues.

A.I.R. artists did not share a common aesthetic philosophy or style of work. At the time of the gallery's inception, about half of the members consciously made feminist work as a political statement. Most of the work was conceptual and/or abstract. Those artists who did work representationally were not figurative in the traditional sense but rather subverted or re-visioned historical representations of gender.[17]

While only a few were painters, several artists used drawing as their main creative arena.[18] Interestingly, there was no "straight" photography (and little photo-based work), video, or performance art, although this changed as artists expanded their practice, and as new members were added to the gallery (the performative photography of Mary Beth Edelson and Ana Mendieta), or work by nonmembers was presented in supplemental exhibitions and programming.[19] Time-based work was represented by Rachel bas-Cohain's minimal sculptures formed by processes such as condensation or freezing and the use of sound in some of Nancy Kitchel's installations.

Over half of the founding members worked three-dimensionally with mixed-media sculpture or installations incorporating materials such as latex rubber, human hair, plastic, celastic, hydrocal, tape, fabric, yarn, embroidery thread, branches, brown wrapping paper, and kitchen shelving paper, along with more traditional materials such as paint, charcoal, pencil, canvas, paper, wood, metal, and rope.[20] Reflecting visual strategies and ideas in the air at the time such as "repetition" (of marks, forms, or units), "the grid," or the "gap" between painting and sculpture, the focus was on postminimal concerns with materials and process (often from a gendered perspective); the dismantling of gendered hierarchies of art, craft, and decoration; and what historian Julia Bryan-Wilson recently referred to as "a kind of femo-primitivism that linked women's art cross-culturally and transhistorically with Indigenous or traditional craft practices."[21] Anticipating postmodern concerns of the '80s, text, the body (versus the figure), and issues of representation were present but not yet theorized.

Work by A.I.R. artists, like New York feminist art in general, didn't fit neatly into a package. It was pluralistic, anarchistic, and messy. It was not dominated by one or two artists, aesthetics, or didactic definitions of feminism, much less feminist art, but rather employed diverse aesthetic strategies to reflect a range of feminist politics. While noting the frequency of ovoid forms in art by women, A.I.R. artists resisted the idea of an essential female aesthetic based on the biological female body, such as central core imagery put forth by Judy Chicago and Miriam Schapiro in Southern California around the same time. The physical female body was embraced but understood as a social, economic, political site. We were interested in opening a space for gendered content through the use of materials, techniques, processes, and histories that referenced women's bodies, lives, and experiences.

A.I.R.'s first season was ambitious: ten sets of two solo exhibitions that opened simultaneously, two group exhibitions of gallery members, two invitational exhibitions of work by nonmember artists, and an exhibition of feminist artists from Washington, DC. It also began the Monday Night Programs, a well-attended free and open-to-the-public educational series of panels, speakers, performances, screenings, and workshops. A.I.R.'s impact and influence extended far beyond its SoHo address. It quickly became an activist model for feminist cooperative galleries that sprung up around the country such as ARC and Artemesia in Chicago, WARM in Minneapolis, Muse in Philadelphia, Hera in Wakefield, Rhode Island, and Central Hall in Long Island, as well as SoHo 20 and Ceres in New York. While each of these galleries shared A.I.R.'s mission to exhibit work by women artists, provide programming of relevance to women artists, and contribute to a national network of feminist art, artists, and art organizations and their local and regional art scenes, they should not be conflated, as differences of structure and programming were specific to their geographical locations and the constituency of their membership.

That said, A.I.R. was considered by many to be the best and most prestigious of the feminist cooperatives—possibly because it was first, possibly because of its New York City location, or possibly because of the work it presented. Certainly New York had something to do with it, but SoHo 20 and Ceres who followed A.I.R.'s model (and, like A.I.R., still exist today) never enjoyed the same critical attention—partially because of timing and partially due to the work they showed. SoHo 20, for example, initially emphasized representational/figurative work, which was not considered cutting-edge at that time (by men or women). When opportunity arose for A.I.R. to take on new members as others left, Sari Dienes, Sylvia Sleigh, and Nancy Azara moved from SoHo 20 to A.I.R.[22]

Over the years, A.I.R. has had to adjust to a changing art world and political climate, changes in feminism, and therefore the changing needs of women artists. With the feminist backlash of the Reagan era, feminism became a dirty word. A.I.R. lost its cutting-edge status in the art world but quietly continued to exhibit work by women artists, both members and nonmembers; sponsor the Current Issue series (replacing the Monday Night Programs) that included timely debates between cultural and postmodern feminist artists, historians, and critics; and expand its outreach programming to include internships and apprenticeships for credit, an artist-in-residence fellowship, and a mentoring program to help emerging artists navigate the art world.[23] Originally an alternative to "the system," A.I.R. was now additionally positioned to help women artists secure positions within "the system." Women around the country who had been hired in tenure-track positions at universities (as a result of '70s feminist activism) could join A.I.R. as affiliate members (now called national members) and be guaranteed a solo exhibition in New York, thereby fulfilling the research requirement for promotion and tenure.

Through different addresses, loss of funding, financial crises, and restructuring, as well as an expanding and ever more commercial art world, A.I.R. has continued to demonstrate resiliency.[24] For thirty-six years, A.I.R. has continued to provide professional space where women artists can exhibit their work without pressure, limitations, or censorship, and sponsored programming that supports women artists and their work. Additionally, it has facilitated an international and intergenerational dialogue between emerging and midcareer women artists.

While inequities still exist between male and female artists, virtually all gallery members benefited from the visibility A.I.R. gave their work. In the '70s, curators regularly visited 112 Greene Street, Artists Space, 55 Mercer Street, and A.I.R. because artist-run, not-for-profit spaces were where cutting-edge work was being exhibited. Getting one's work out and seen led to inclusion in important group shows such as the Whitney Biennial, Documenta, *Sexual Politics* at UCLA's Armand Hammer Museum, *WACK! Art and the Feminist Revolution* at the Museum of Contemporary Art in Los Angeles, and other museum exhibitions here and abroad; solo, survey, and retrospective exhibitions; and in many cases to commercial gallery representation, although it should be noted that this was not the goal or choice of all A.I.R. artists.[25] I know that having three solo exhibitions at A.I.R. encouraged critical writing on my work, and that in turn led to exhibitions, grants, residencies, and invitations to lecture and teach.[26] Certainly the careers of Dotty Attie, Mary Beth Edelson, Ana Mendieta, Howardena Pindell, Elaine Reichek, and Nancy Spero, among others, were jumpstarted at A.I.R.

New York Times critic Holland Cotter has written, "Most of the interesting American artists of the last thirty years are as interesting as they are in part because of the feminist art movement of the early '70s. It changed everything. [. . .] What art in the next thirty years will look like I don't know, but feminist influences will be at its source."[27] Feminist art, which has been called the only genuine mass art movement that has occurred in America in this century, radicalized the art world.[28] A.I.R. played a central role in that movement.

Stimulated by *WACK! Art and the Feminist Revolution*, the first and long overdue survey of feminist art from the '70s, as well as a more general renewed interest in the '70s, A.I.R. has begun to focus on documenting its own history.[29] Recent projects include *A.I.R. Gallery Retrospective: 1972–1979* at the Werkstätte Gallery, and *A.I.R. Gallery: The History Show*, a two-part exhibition of work by A.I.R. artists from 1972 to the present at A.I.R. Gallery, accompanied by an exhibition of documentary materials from the A.I.R. Archives at New York University's Fales Library.[30] A member-authored book is in the works. However, A.I.R.'s full significance and contribution to the art world and to the women's movement has not yet been fully addressed in historical writings and exhibitions and remains an area for future research and analysis.

ED. NOTE

Hammond wrote "Taking Space: A.I.R. Gallery: The Formative Years" in 2008 as a catalogue essay for the unrealized exhibition *A Group of One's Own: Women's Visual Art Organizations in the United States*, conceived by Ferris Olin and Judith Brodsky, codirectors, Institute for Women and Art, Rutgers University. The essay has never before appeared in publication.

The numbered endnotes for this essay, below, are by the author.

NOTES

1. Most famously, the 1970 actions organized by the Ad Hoc Women Artists' Committee at the Whitney Museum of American Art protesting the inclusion of less than 4 percent women artists in their Annual, and an equally low percentage of work by women artists in the museum's permanent collection.

2. They originally planned to model it after the co-op 55 Mercer Gallery, founded in 1969.

3. Dotty Attie, Mary Grigoriadis, Susan Williams, and Barbara Zucker, *In Residence: A History of A.I.R. Gallery*, dir. Meredith Drum, exec. prod. Kat Griefen, A.I.R. Gallery Archives, Fales Library and Special Collections, at the Elmer Holmes Bobst Library, New York University, 2008.

4. Attie et al., *In Residence*.

5. The founding members were Dotty Attie, Rachel bas-Cohain, Judith Bernstein, Blythe Bohnen, Maude Boltz, Agnes Denes, Daria Dorosh, Loretta Dunkelman, Mary Grigoriadis, Harmony Hammond, Anne Healy, Laurace James, Nancy Kitchel, Louise Kramer, Rosemary Mayer, Patsy Norvell, Howardena Pindell, Nancy Spero, Susan Williams, and Barbara Zucker.

6. Laurace James had work in the 1970 Whitney Sculpture Annual, and Blythe Bohnen was included in the 1971 Whitney Painting Annual.

7. The gallery's name is pronounced by saying each letter, A, I, R, separately.

8. An early women's liberation movement phrase was "taking space." In fact, although A.I.R., founded in 1972, was the first major women's cooperative gallery in New York City (and possibly the United States or even the world) during the era of second-wave feminism, it was preceded by Gallery 15, founded in 1958, which operated briefly at 59 W. 54th St., New York City. An even earlier initiative, Argent Gallery, was founded by the National Women's Association of Painters and Sculptors in 1889 and had an active

exhibition agenda up until the 1940s. Although these, and perhaps other, earlier galleries devoted to art by women had paved the way, A.I.R. was the first feminist gallery, even if its members opted not to present the gallery in this way in in its early days.

9. While the politics of individuals continued to vary, the membership eventually recognized that the gallery's goals were decidedly feminist.

10. The nonhierarchical gallery structure reflected the collective spirit and idealism of feminism. Business meetings (with a rotating chair) utilized the consciousness-raising format of going around the circle, letting each woman speak uninterrupted, hopefully moving toward consensus, although decisions were made by a two-thirds majority vote of those present.

11. Information regarding current membership requirements, costs, and application can be found on the gallery's website (https://www.airgallery.org/).

12. This position later grew into a full-time paid director hired by and accountable to the gallery membership.

13. This was an important consideration because we didn't know if the gallery would last more than a single season! Straws were drawn to choose the exhibition schedule. The two artists could decide to mix their work throughout the whole gallery space and share an announcement, but since solo shows were considered more prestigious than two-person shows, most didn't. Over the years, artists have tended to list these first exhibitions differently in various texts—some as solo shows and some as two-person shows. See, for example, bios of A.I.R. artists in Barbara J. Love, ed., *Feminists Who Changed America 1963–1975* (Champaign: University of Illinois Press, 2006).

14. A.I.R. Gallery brochure, 1972: "Because women artists have always met with such difficulty in showing their work there was strong pressure to produce work which conforms to already long accepted norms, if they want their work to be shown at all. Thus the work of women artists is made to seem less innovative than that of male artists, as only the more conservative work is ever made public."

15. Ten members whose shows were scheduled in the second half of the first gallery season had a piece in the inaugural group exhibition (Rachel bas-Cohain, Judith Bernstein, Maude Boltz, Daria Dorosh, Loretta Dunkelman, Nancy Kitchel, Laurace James, Rosemary Mayer, Patsy Norvell, Nancy Spero). Those with solo shows during the first half of the season had work in an end-of-season group exhibition in the spring (Dotty Attie, Blythe Bohnen, Agnes Denes, Mary Grigoriadis, Harmony Hammond, Anne Healy, Louise Kramer, Howardena Pindell, Susan Williams, Barbara Zucker).

16. Including the *New York Times* and *Ms.* magazine.

17. Dotty Attie, Judith Bernstein, and Nancy Spero. Sylvia Sleigh was the first traditional figurative artist to join the gallery in 1974, but her work too reversed historical representations of gender.

18. Originally, [those painting were] Blythe Bohnen, Daria Dorosh, Loretta Dunkelman, Mary Grigoriadis, Howardena Pindell, and Nancy Spero, and later in the '70s, Pat Lasch, Sylvia Sleigh, and Clover Vail. [Those drawing were] Dotty Attie, Judith Bernstein, and Agnes Denes.

19. Although she was not a member of A.I.R., Hermine Freed's documentary videos of gallery members and her other video work were shown at the gallery.

20. Rachel bas-Cohain, Maude Boltz, Harmony Hammond, Anne Healy, Laurace James, Nancy Kitchel, Louise Kramer, Rosemary Mayer, Patsy Norvell, Susan Williams, Barbara Zucker. Donna Byars, Sari Dienes, Sarah Draney, Mary Beth Edelson, Ana Mendieta, Kazuko, and Elaine Reichek, who joined later, also made material-based work. Some of this work was site-specific and/or public art.

21. Julia Bryan-Wilson, "Queerly Made: The Lesbian Handiwork of Harmony Hammond's *Floorpieces*," paper presented at "Craft at the Limits," symposium, Getty Research Institute, June 1, 2007.

22. In 1973–74, Susan Williams and Barbara Zucker left the gallery. Nancy Kitchel and I dropped out later in 1974. We were quickly replaced by Sari Dienes (1973), Pat Lasch (1973), and Sylvia Sleigh (1974). In 1975, Mary Beth Edelson, Kazuko, and Clover Vail joined the gallery. Donna Byars joined in 1977 and Ana Mendieta in 1979. Elaine Reichek and Sarah Draney joined in 1981. Rachel bas-Cohain died in 1982 and Sari Dienes, who joined the gallery at age seventy-four, died in 1992. As of this writing, two original members, Daria Dorosh and Louise Kramer, are still members of the gallery.

23. A.I.R. is one of the few North American feminist spaces that, over the years, has consistently presented curated exhibitions of feminist art from other countries, including France, Japan, Sweden, and Israel.

24. From 97 Wooster Street (1972–81), the gallery moved to 63 Crosby Street (1981–94), then 40 Wooster Street (1994–2002), then 511 W. 25th Street (2002–8). In fall 2008 it moved to DUMBO, first to 111 Front Street, Brooklyn, and then to its current location, 155 Plymouth Street, Brooklyn, NY.

25. A significant number of A.I.R. artists have or have had gallery representation since their early shows at A.I.R.: Dotty Attie, Judith Bernstein, Agnes Denes, Harmony Hammond, Pat Lasch, Ana Mendieta, Howardena Pindell, Elaine Reichek, Nancy Spero, and Barbara Zucker, among others.

26. If a member was not ready to show during the time designated for her exhibition, she could sell her time slot to a nonmember artist. This artist must be approved by the gallery members. I had one exhibition as a member (1973) and two exhibitions as a nonmember (1982 and 1984). By the mid-'80s quite a few nonmembers were having solo exhibitions.

27. Holland Cotter, "Art Review: Two Nods to Feminism, Long Snubbed by Curators," *New York Times*, October 11, 2002, section E, 35.

28. Laura Cottingham, for one, has made this case.

29. *WACK! Art and the Feminist Revolution*, curated by Cornelia Butler, originated at the Museum of Contemporary Art in Los Angeles and traveled to the National Museum of Women in the Arts, Washington, DC; P.S. 1 Contemporary Art Center, Long Island City, New York; and the Vancouver Art Gallery (March 2007–January 2009).

30. *A.I.R. Gallery Retrospective: 1972–1979*, curated by Patsy Norvell, Werkstätte Gallery, New York City, May 2–June 14, 2008. *A.I.R. Gallery: The History Show*, work by A.I.R. artists from 1972 to the present, curated by Carey Lovelace and Kat Griefen. An exhibition in two parts at A.I.R. Gallery, October 2–November 1 and November 6–29, 2008. Exhibition of A.I.R. archival materials, curated by Kat Griefen and Dena Muller at the Tracey/Barry Gallery, Bobst Library, New York University, September 16–December 12, 2008.

Interview with Courtney Dailey

(2009)

Harmony Hammond is an artist, art writer, and independent curator who lives and works in Galisteo, New Mexico. Considered a pioneer of the feminist art movement, she lectures, writes, and publishes extensively on feminist art, lesbian art, and the cultural representation of difference. I spoke with Hammond over the phone, and what was initially scheduled to be a twenty- to thirty-minute interview turned into an hour-and-a-half-long conversation. When speaking with Hammond, I got the sense that there were hours upon hours of stories to share: from her days in New York in the 1970s, to her work in New Mexico and Texas, to her own art practice as an abstract painter over the past forty years. I was particularly interested in two of her latest curatorial projects, *¿Y QUÉ? Queer Art Made in Texas* (Lubbock, Texas, 2007) and *Out West* (Santa Fe, New Mexico, 1999) [see fig. 3.3]. Both exhibitions were curated from open calls that led to studio visits and finally to exhibitions after several years of work; their scope was regional, and Hammond talks about the advantages of those boundaries, about disciplinary boundaries, and about the multiple ways we can perceive them.

* * *

COURTNEY DAILEY: In an essay in *Feminism-Art-Theory*, edited by Hilary Robinson, you talk about the fact that there was lesbian and gay art in the 1970s but that people didn't recognize it historically. You said, "These exhibitions were happening. . . . They were not obscure exhibitions but rather conscious dyke interventions from the margins in the central whirlpool of the art mainstream."[1] That was in 1994; what do you think about margins and the mainstream now?

HARMONY HAMMOND: What I meant by "obscure" is that those exhibitions didn't take place in separatist communities (though they were happening there as well). The early exhibitions that I was referring to, and my writing in the '90s, were conscious archival interventions. My comments were intended to hold queer artists, curators, historians, and critics accountable for knowing their own gay art history and not erasing it because they are uninformed and haven't done their homework. The task is ongoing. Yes, we've had the Gay '90s and yes, there's more queer presence in the art world than in the '70s, but there's still a need to constantly resist erasure of queer art and artists in the larger art historical narrative.

DAILEY: What kinds of strategies are people using to do that?

HAMMOND: We do it by constantly asserting a queer presence in exhibitions, curation, and writing. And we do it on all levels: local, regional, and national. We do it in queer spaces, in not-for-profit spaces, galleries, museums, classrooms, and publications. Not just having exhibitions of queer art but insisting where appropriate that the sexual identification of the artist is important to any discussion of the art. Art historian Jonathan D. Katz is a good example. He frequently curates historical exhibitions of work by, and writes about, preliberation gay artists such as Jasper Johns, Robert Rauschenberg, or Agnes Martin, and insists that any discussion of their work take into account their sexual preference.

He constantly runs into resistance from the commercial mechanisms that surround artists and their work—museums, galleries, estates, and even sometimes the artists themselves who want to avoid the subject because they fear "it will take away from" serious consideration of the work or affect its market value, an attitude that continually reinscribes homophobia.

Sometimes an artist's sexuality is very crucial to the work, sometimes it's just another one of many things that can be talked about that adds to an understanding or discussion of the work, but in its absence, becomes more important than it might really be if it were discussed. Like Jonathan, I feel like we can never let up; we have to be ever vigilant. That's just the way that it is. Unless we continue to do battle, in whatever ways it is that we best do battle, the social and historical forces at work will heterosexualize queer art and artists, and therefore erase the experience of what it means to live queerly.

There are all kinds of interventions. Take for example the painter Louise Fishman. Most of her work is not overtly queer, but it's hugely important that she is out there as a queer artist and willing to put her work in queer exhibitions.

DAILEY: Do you think about these strategies in your paintings?

HAMMOND: In my art practice? Rarely. These days, I just make my work. Sometimes, in response to a particular event, I decide to make a political piece or create a piece especially for a queer exhibition or audience, but mostly no. In my curating and writing, however, I do intentionally think and write about things queer, or curate and write queerly, with this consciousness of archival intervention. And by that I don't just mean me, Harmony Hammond, but: I, a woman artist; I, a feminist artist; I, a lesbian artist; I, a queer artist, refuse to be erased. And so the curating and the writing are tools to keep erasure from happening.

DAILEY: Both *¿Y QUÉ?* and *Out West* are close to where you live. Is there an importance that you see in that local context about presence?

HAMMOND: I was interested in curating both exhibitions precisely because they were regional. They did not take place in major urban environments like New York, Los Angeles, or San Francisco. *Out West*, at Plan B Evolving Arts in Santa Fe (1999) [see fig. 3.3], included work by artists from Arizona, New Mexico, and Texas. *¿Y QUÉ?*, at Texas Tech University in Lubbock (2007), only included work by artists who live and work in Texas.

Some people think that we are postqueer, that we don't need feminist, lesbian, or queer shows anymore, and that those kinds of shows don't have agency. To some degree, that may be true in New York, or San Francisco—urban environments with large queer populations and histories of gay activism—but it's a totally different story in most communities across the United States. Anyone who thinks we are postfeminist or postqueer, who thinks discrimination no longer exists, needs to get real.

Take Santa Fe, for example, the town where I live. It has a sizeable queer population, but the LGBTQ people who live there are, for the most part, apolitical. They are not closeted, but they also are not public about their queerness or the politics of being queer—despite the fact that the West does have its history of same-sex couples—it's just not named. In not naming, there's no political presence or power.

So, the point of organizing *Out West* in Santa Fe was to remind people that we dykes and faggots are part of the "general population," we are *la raza*, we are the voters in this town. It's about queer presence interrupting heteronormative assumptions. Another function was to give something back to the queer community, to see ourselves reflected in the art. It was also about giving something to the artists, many of whom feel isolated or fear censorship. Despite the visibility and marketing of queer culture in the '90s, the problems that queer artists confront making their work and getting it out there have not gone away. It's still a struggle.

Curating, for me, is a way of checking in, a way of checking outside of my own studio, my own head, my own world. In the case of these two exhibitions, I had some loose curatorial parameters but not a narrow definition of what's queer or what's art or anything like that. . . . I was interested in looking at anything that was presented to me as art by anyone who self-identified as queer. I did want the work in some way to reflect the experience of being queer, but I was very open as to what that might be or how it would visually articulate itself. . . . I'm always interested in seeing what's out there; of course, I can only see as far as I can cast my nets, or networks, and look at what comes back to me. What's reflected in the art: Are there any themes? Threads? What does it mean to be queer in the year 1996? How is it different in 2007? Or to be queer in Austin, San Antonio, El Paso, or Lubbock, Texas? How is that different than Tucson or Santa Fe? Or Los Angeles or Brooklyn?

With both shows, there were artists who initially did not want to have their work presented in a queer exhibition because they thought it was a limited context that would encourage misreadings of their work. Through ongoing discussions and conversations, they eventually came around and agreed to have their work in the exhibition. So, curation is an educational and political process as much as it is about producing spectacle.

I ran into the same thing when I was writing *Lesbian Art in America: A Contemporary History* (Rizzoli, 2000) [see fig. 4.1]—this internalization that somehow the identification lesbian or queer, and therefore art that was lesbian or queer or presented in a lesbian or queer context, was limiting. It was through dialogue with the hesitant artists—sometimes over the course of several years; in one artist's case, ten years—about work, identity, and politics, that a sense of trust was established, and they agreed to let me include their work. Again, process was crucial to the final product, in this case, a book.

When it comes to curating, I am always learning from the process. Often I don't fully understand the impact of an exhibition until long after the show is down. It's in hindsight that I understand the dynamics of that particular show . . . and it is with this hindsight that I am talking about *Out West* and *¿Y QUÉ?*.

DAILEY: From doing those two shows, could you come to any theories?

HAMMOND: If you mean repeated themes or formal strategies that would include all the work, the short answer is no. In both instances, however, there were lots of shared mini-themes, between two or three artists. Generally speaking, I saw less sexually explicit and overtly queer work while curating *¿Y QUÉ?* than I did eight years earlier when curating *Out West*, but I don't think that has anything to do with geographic location. It's more a sign of the times. Probably more than anything, the type of venue affected the nature of each exhibition: a large, alternative warehouse space in Santa Fe [for *Out West*] versus a small university gallery [for *¿Y QUÉ?*].

DAILEY: So you don't plan out a thematic kind of exhibition, where you set out with an idea and find the work to support your claim?

HAMMOND: I'm not against thematic exhibitions—in fact I like them. I'm just saying that the way I've worked on *Out West* and *¿Y QUÉ?* was to put out a call, see what was out there, follow through on leads, go after people, etc. . . . The goals are different, but both curatorial approaches are equally valid.

DAILEY: Did your installation strategies or the way you structured the exhibitions change based on those contexts?

HAMMOND: Absolutely. The gallery space influenced both exhibitions. The small size of the university gallery limited the kind of work that could be included in *¿Y QUÉ?*. I am by nature very materials and process oriented and interested in installation and intermedia, but there wasn't room for that kind of work, unless I gave the whole gallery to one artist, and that would have defeated the purpose of the exhibition. This was unfortunate because a number artists made large installations as part of their regular art practice. I simply was not able to accommodate that work. I was however, able to use an adjoining room to continually project videos.

In contrast, the Plan B warehouse space was fabulous for installations. *Out West* included groups of work by a single artist, presented as mini-installations, several small installations, two large-scale tableaux, one of which had a video component, and two outdoor installations. The whole space, including the outside of the building, was activated. Additionally, there were two evenings of video programming.

Work grows out of work. Unlike "gay" art in the '70s that often seemed hesitant at best, the work in *Out West* and *¿Y QUÉ?*, having developed out of approximately thirty years of earlier work, was strong. That's another reason we need the historical narrative—we need that history. Our work grows out of that history and its documentation. If we don't have that history, we have nothing, and we are always starting over rather than building on or responding to what came before.

DAILEY: It seems like you are saying that you have a political agenda: a reflection back to a queer community of their production, along with a projection out. . . .

HAMMOND: Absolutely. That's a good way of putting it; it is both. And I definitely have my political agenda.

DAILEY: Don't we all?! (Laughs.)

HAMMOND: Every person should have a political agenda! (Laughs.) Right now, I am very interested in archival issues because I have a collection of close to seven thousand slides of work by other artists that needs to be placed where it will be catalogued and accessible to the public for research. The majority of these slides constitute what is probably the largest collection of photo documentation of work by contemporary lesbian artists in the United States. It is politically important to me that these slides to go into a major archive of American art, thereby inserting lesbian art and artists into the mainstream narrative.

DAILEY: Do you know where that might be? Do you have dreams of where they might live?

HAMMOND: Oh, I'm further along than that, honey! (Laughs.) I'm in conversation with libraries now but can't really say yet where the collection will end up. Quite a few people are interested. Oftentimes, the focus and scope of an archive has to do with the interests of the archive's curator. So if you have a curator who's interested in the Lower Manhattan art scene of the '70s, feminist art, and LGBTQ art . . . that's me! That's what I represent. Of course, I've continued to keep working in many different ways, on many different fronts since the '70s. I've moved through time, but I've also moved from East to West Coast. So, I am of interest to scholars and curators for many reasons! Not I, Harmony Hammond, but what I represent, in terms of time, place, and movement. That's why people are interested in my archive, because I represent these other things. I am a walking archive!

DAILEY: Why do you think that there's a resurgent interest in the art of the 1970s?

HAMMOND: Well, it's about time! The late 1960s and early '70s were an exciting time in the New York art world, which of course was much smaller than it is now. There was a lot of experimentation and a lot of breaking down of genres and categories. Artists did more than one thing: You could paint, you could sculpt, you could do video, you could do performance, you could do dance, and you could do something in between, in the cracks between those genres. People were doing everything, and they didn't care what the fuck you called it. Much of the work was conceptual or abstract. Most artists, even if they weren't consciously making "political" art, were politicized. It was a period of political consciousness and activism in terms of civil rights, gay liberation, the women's liberation movement, and [protests against the] American-Vietnam War. It was a very energizing and exciting time, but not much has been written about it until recently.

DAILEY: It seems like contemporary artists and writers have been taking a newly critical look, though.

HAMMOND: There's been interest in conceptualism and in Fluxus art, but art coming out of postminimalism in the early '70s, much of which is feminist art or art influenced by feminism, has been overlooked because most writers, historians, and curators have been looking at the '70s through a postmodern lens of representation. And while that lens can be very helpful, if you look through that lens, you totally miss the creative experimentation that was happening in the '70s in Lower Manhattan. . . .

It was not about representation, nor was it about the figure. There were figurative artists, obviously, but nobody was interested in that work at that time. The cutting-edge excitement had to do with postminimal experimentation with materials and process, and in the case of feminism, bringing a gendered consciousness to that exploration of materials and process. There was interest in the body but not the figure.

WACK! Art and the Feminist Revolution, the first (and long overdue) museum exhibition to revisit '70s feminist art, is a move in that direction. Another exhibition that revisited the '70s was *High Times, Hard Times: New York Painting from 1967 to 1975*. It examined that postminimal work that I just described through an abstract painting lens. One could take that same work and look at it through a sculpture, video, dance, or performance lens, but this show looked at it through the lens of expanded painting. Interestingly, the exhibition included work by many women and African American artists.

DAILEY: Understanding the "lens," as you are saying, as being so essential to how you're viewing, I wonder if you think that there could be multiple lenses at play, at once.

HAMMOND: Sure, why not? (Laughs.) I can conceive of that easily with shows like *WACK!* and *High Times, Hard Times*—as long as you are clear that there are multiple lenses and you know which lens you're looking through at any given moment is not the only one. Multiple lenses make sense because most work participates in multiple narratives.

DAILEY: Do you think then that the idea of margins and mainstream is outdated? Maybe it's overlapping circles, lenses, that might more adequately convey the sense of relationships.

HAMMOND: I don't know if it's outdated, but it isn't that useful anymore. I mean what's on the margins one day can be in the mainstream the next and vice versa. Margins and mainstream aren't fixed. Overlapping narratives seem more accurate and offer the possibility of correspondences and relationships. Often what happens is that an artist's work only gets discussed within one particular narrative, and that is misleading. I'm interested in how my work, and how other artists' work, engages with multiple discourses. And since we're talking about things queer here, I think we do queer art and artists a disservice if we only talk about the work in terms of a queer discourse. If we want to treat the work seriously and fully, we need to talk about it within multiple discourses. This is what I want out of new queer criticism, out of new feminist criticism: I want a more layered, in-depth, complex, contradictory kind of discourse or conversation.

DAILEY: What kinds of limited narratives do you see applied, either contemporarily or historically?

HAMMOND: I know that with a lot of my early work incorporating fabric the conversation even today begins and ends with a feminist discussion of women's traditional arts such as needlework. That reference is there, say in my braided and painted *Floorpieces* [1973, see plate 4], but those works can also be discussed in terms of abstract painting, painting off the wall, very flat sculpture, targets, mandalas, the circle, recycled materials, martial arts, meditation, vulnerability, or even queerness. I did not think of these pieces as queer when I made them, but Julia Bryan-Wilson has written a very perceptive and speculative article about their queerness.[2] She's informed, knows her history, and quotes earlier writing but doesn't just repeat what's been said before. This is the kind of new critical thinking and writing that I am talking about.

DAILEY: Do you think that it's inevitable? Since the context for viewing that work has changed, the lens that you bring to that work has changed through time, isn't it likely that interpretation of the work will also change?

HAMMOND: One would hope so, but unfortunately a lot of writers are lazy, and they just repeat the same old stuff. New thinking and writing is not automatic or inevitable. We have to encourage it, invite it, make it happen . . . do it!

DAILEY: It seems like we would like to have both of these things: points of view from older and younger folks.

HAMMOND: Sure! And, thank goodness, our views aren't fixed! Your view (as a younger person) is not static, and my viewpoint isn't locked in the '70s.

I think about location as a kind of time-space continuum, as a historical positioning. I never used to think about things like this, but when you've worked long enough, you become very aware of historical positionings, accidental and chosen, and the narratives that get constructed around them. What are the places and locations we choose and how do we take responsibility for them?

DAILEY: Or that we're able to choose. . . .

HAMMOND: Right. For me, the notion of place is a "peopled space." So I go back to thinking about time and space as fluid, as a continuum, and the various locations within that that I might inhabit or that I might visit, or that I might engage with. I go back to this sense of multiplicity, and then we're back to these multiple lenses or narratives.

DAILEY: When I think about what the struggle for visibility might mean, it's just that. About demanding visibility in a real way, not in a tokenistic way.

HAMMOND: That involves spending time with something, what my friend Rebecca Solnit would call "thinking long thoughts." In the same spirit as curating and writing as interventions, my recent work trespasses in the modernist painting field, a site that my near-monochrome paintings engage and resist. The question could be asked: What's a nice feminist like you doing in the modernist painting field? It's not an easy read.

DAILEY: After the identity politics of the '90s, this seems more and more apparent: that it can't just be a gestural, topical engagement. . . .

HAMMOND: Well, painting is a language and, despite its sexist history, it's the language that I use to speak to you. However, unlike that kind of modernist painting that is a hierarchy of purification that refers only to itself, my painting is all about content. I invite the world outside to come into the painting field; so it's in opposition to the modernist painting field at the same time that it formally engages with it. There's a funny kind of tension that comes from that. I'm interested in that tension, that difference. . . . This would be one lens for discussion. The paintings could also be discussed as an extension of postminimal concerns with materials and process. Or performance. Or we could talk about them in relation to queer space. Different lens, different narratives . . . I want—no, I insist—on them all!

ED. NOTES

This interview has not been published previously. It was conducted by Courtney Dailey, transcribed, edited, and submitted, with the title "Reflecting Back, Projecting Out: An Interview with Harmony Hammond," in partial fulfillment of a course requirement at California College of the Arts, San Francisco, where Dailey was a curatorial studies graduate student.

1. Harmony Hammond, "Against Cultural Amnesia" (1994), excerpt published in *Feminism-Art-Theory: An Anthology 1968–2000*, ed. Hilary Robinson (Oxford: Blackwell, 2001), 555–61.

2. Julia Bryan-Wilson, "Queerly Made: Harmony Hammond's Floorpieces," *Journal of Modern Craft* 2, no. 1 (March 2009): 59–80.

5

2010s

Editor's Introduction

With the fifth decade of her career as an artist and activist underway, Hammond continues to vigorously protest the silencing and censoring of feminist and queer artists, and redress their historical erasure. Not because, by now, protestation and contestation have become habitual, and their artistic expression formulaic, but because a pressing need remains. Hammond's creative strategies, ever evolving, remain constant in at least one way—they are informed by lesbian feminist critical thinking (and lesbian feminist critical doing).

Hammond's artwork figures prominently in major exhibitions that look back over decades of lesbian feminist and queer activism.[1] Her words circulate in these contexts as well as wall text, podcast script, catalogue essays, and interviews. The mounting critical interest in Hammond's work intensifies an already heavy demand for her participation in symposia, roundtables, and panels. These conversations—published, broadcast, or recorded live—cover a broad time span and array of topics. They offer Hammond opportunities to reflect on over fifty

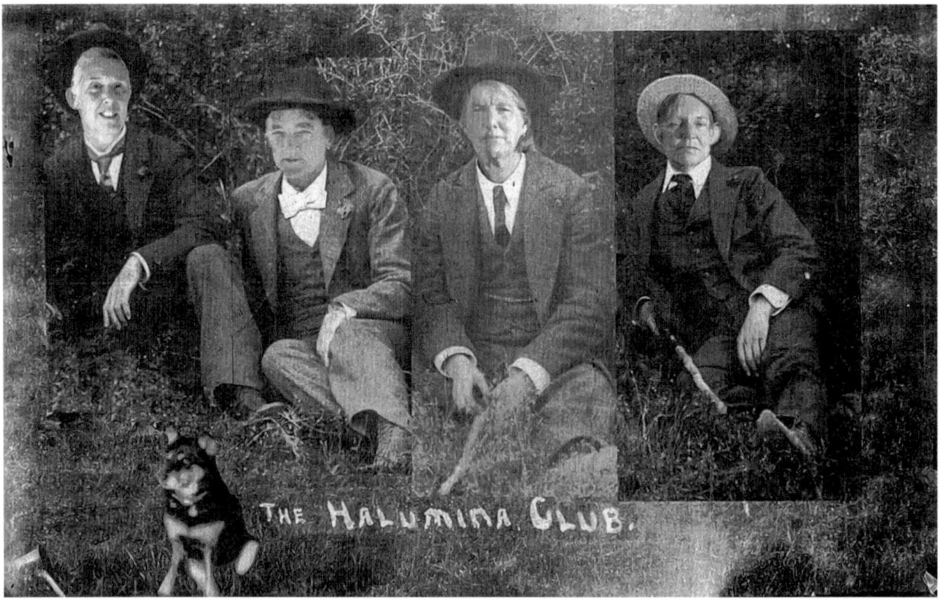

FIGURE 5.1. Michelle Goodman, *The Halumina Club*, ca. 2011. Goodman digitally transformed a vintage photograph of miners decked out in their Sunday best, kicking back in a natural setting. The artist replaced the four men's heads with those of (*L to R*) Harmony Hammond, Lucy Lippard, Michelle Goodman, and Nancy Holt. (Goodman also added Jack, her dog, to the foreground.) The composite group portrait commemorates an epic hike from Los Cerrillos to Galisteo along the Galisteo Creek by the members of the informal hiking group, the Halumina Club (HArmony LUcy MIchelle NAncy). Collection: Harmony Hammond.

years of "life in art"; to presence her collaborations, communities, and queer creative networks (figs. 5.1 and 5.2); to recall such historical turning points as the launch of *Heresies* and the Stonewall rebellion; to ponder anew visual and textual vocabularies of queer feminist artistic practice (fig. 5.3); and to reaffirm the potential of material to express sexual and gendered content.[2] Her writings for *Material Engagements* (2013) and *Harmony Hammond: Material Witness, Five Decades of Art* (2019), shared here, carry this line of thinking about material-as-meaning forward.[3]

A new priority emerges during this decade as well: the archive (fig. 5.4). Lesbians, feminists, queers, women, and others who have struggled for cultural equity and visibility, must, Hammond exhorts, "not only make and present our work, but . . . document it, . . . preserve the work, and rewrite existing histories—or we too will be erased, and I refuse to let that happen."[4]

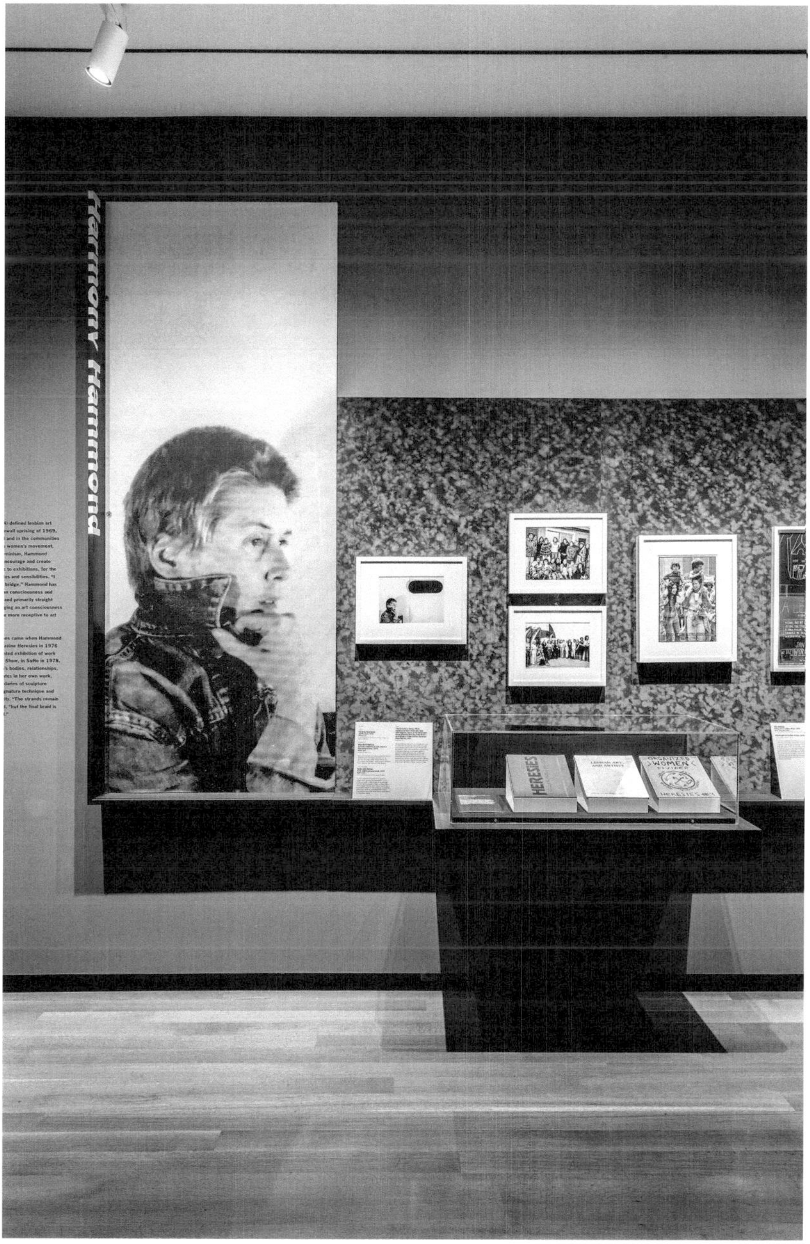

FIGURE 5.2. Harmony Hammond, *Gay Gotham: Art and Underground Culture in New York*, 2017, exhibition installation, Museum of the City of New York, October 5, 2016–March 30, 2017. Curators: Donald Albrecht and Stephen Vider. Photo: Courtesy Museum of the City of New York.

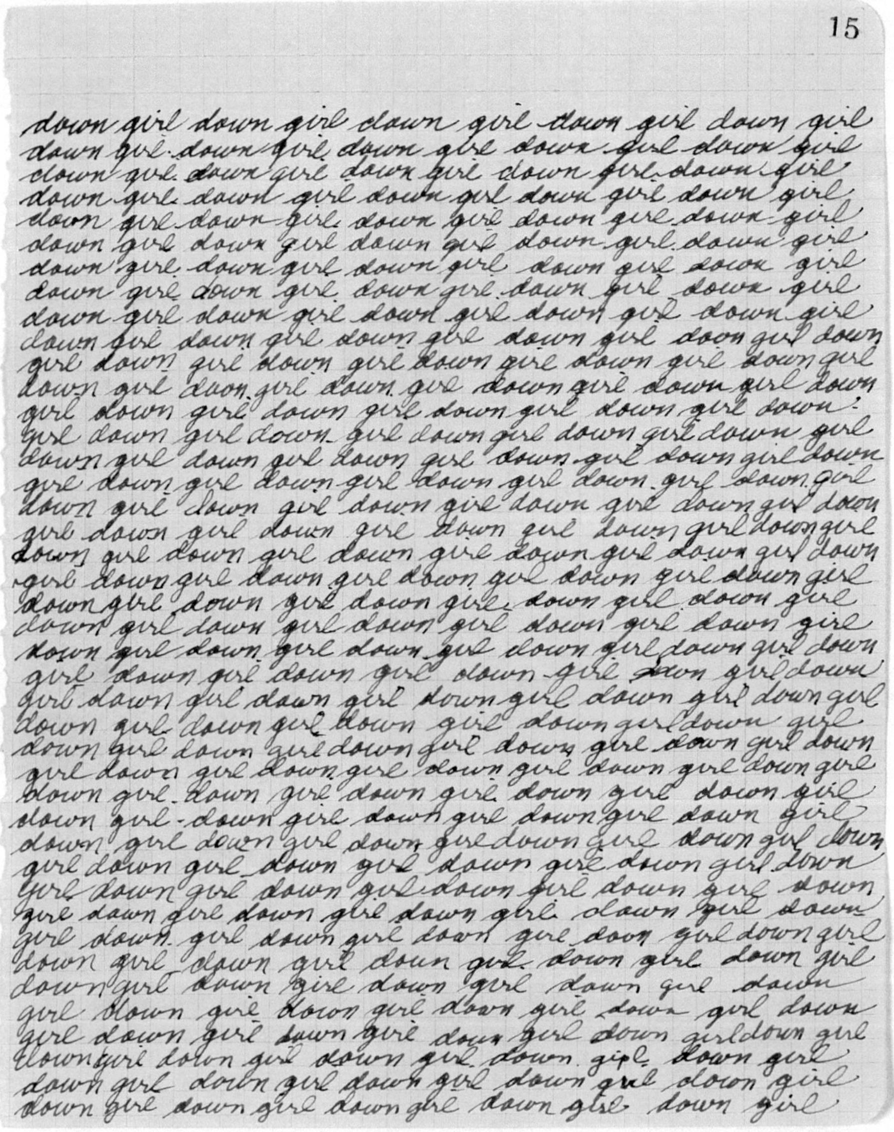

FIGURE 5.3. Harmony Hammond, *Down Girl, Ledger Drawings Suite A, 5*, 2015. Ink on paper. From series in five parts, each page measuring 11.625 × 9.5 in. (29.84 × 24.13 cm). Tia Collection.

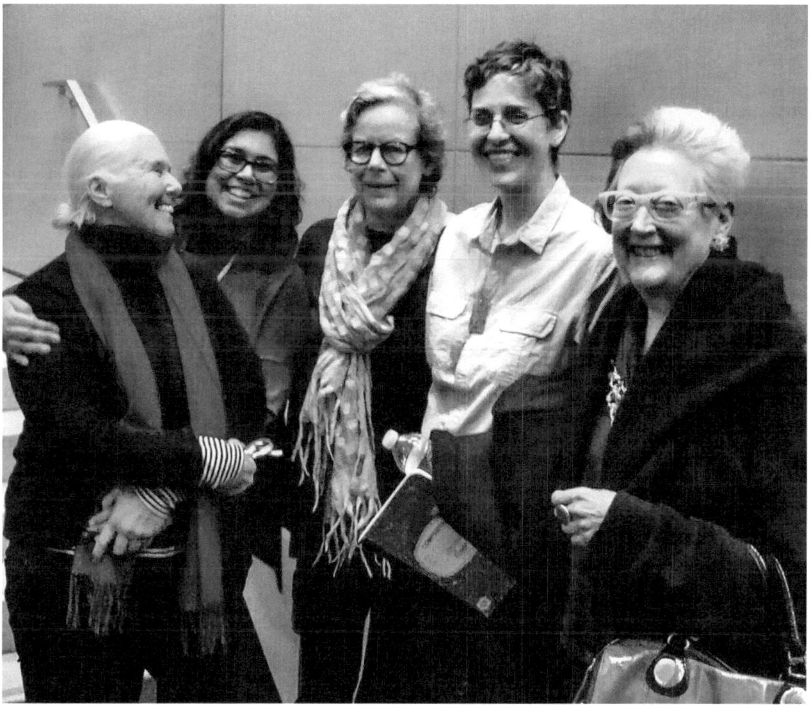

FIGURE 5.4. Participants, "The Artist as Archivist," TFAP@CAA: The Feminist Art Project Day of Panels, Brooklyn Museum, February 15, 2013. *L to R:* Harmony Hammond, Aruna D'Souza (panel moderator), Catherine Lord, Ulrike Müller, Martha Wilson. TFAP@CAA (the Feminist Art Project at College Art Association) brings together artists, art historians, curators, and critics for a free and open-to-the-public day of dialogue during the annual College Art Association (CAA) conference time frame. This panel, moderated by Aruna D'Souza at the Brooklyn Museum, addressed questions about how artists' archives operate—as both physical and conceptual spaces of feminist resistance—in relation to art institutions, to individual and collective artistic practices, and to historical narratives. Snapshot: Harmony Hammond personal collection.

NOTES

1. *Art After Stonewall: 1969–1989*, organized by Columbus Museum of Art and curated by Jonathan Weinberg (2019), is just one example. The exhibition generated a scholarly catalogue and circulated to several venues: Leslie Lohman Museum of Art and NYU's Grey Gallery in New York; and Patricia and Phillip Frost Art Museum, Miami, Florida.

2. On Hammond's "life in art," see Holland Cotter's interview with Hammond in a program titled "My Life in Art: Harmony Hammond and Holland Cotter" at SITE SANTA FE, August 24, 2019.

3. *Material Engagements*, RedLine Contemporary Art Center, Denver, Colorado, 2013; *Harmony Hammond: Material Witness, Five Decades of Art*, The Aldrich Contemporary Art Museum, Ridgefield, Connecticut, 2019.

4. See "On Harmony's Archive" at the Western States Artist-Endowed Foundations annual meeting, Museum of Contemporary Art (MOCA), Los Angeles, March 5, 2019.

A Manifesto (Personal) of Monochrome (Sort Of)

(2010)

Painting, like any cultural language, doesn't have to rely on its historicized meanings. I don't accept that painting is an overdetermined site, a privileged domain of the authoritative masculine voice, or that monochrome painting is necessarily a dead end—the inevitable conclusion of a history of art as a hierarchy of purifications.

I make large, thickly painted near-monochrome paintings. While these paintings engage with (and I like to think, interrupt and resist) the history of modernist painting—more specifically, narratives of abstraction and monochrome—they come out of postminimal and feminist concerns with materials and process rather than modernist reduction.

They are formal, frontal, reductive, condensed. They resist pictorial space and assert the painting object. But they also invite content. My work is NOT pure, isolated, authoritative, universal, self-referential, self-sufficient, or removed from social function. I invoke references and associations. I welcome the world outside the painting edge into the painting field.

Because monochrome painting is typically one surface and nonhierarchical in composition, the focus is on nuance of sameness and difference within and between paintings. I disagree with readings of monochrome based on absence, emptiness, or blankness because they define monochrome as the "other" in relation to image and signification. These readings do not take into account the materiality of paint as a carrier of meaning.

The paintings are layered and built out of themselves—from the inside out. Paint is applied with a brush but it's not about the stroke or mark in the abstract expressionist sense. The blotchy encrusted surface, both matte and gloss, simultaneously elegant, raw, crude—definitely handmade—functions as indexical sign of maker and making—and yet we aren't sure how it is made.

Despite the thickness of the paint—surface, color, and space are indeterminate, unstable, fugitive. You can't quite locate them. They resist definitive articulation. Unlike a lot of monochromes, the paintings refuse to settle down. The painting surface references other materials and substances at the same time it stubbornly remains itself—paint. Color freed from representation retains referentiality. Dried blood and other body fluids; wounds, scabs, scar tissue, scraped hides; burnt, weathered, and patinated surfaces; topographical locations. The body is always near.

Monochrome refuses disembodiment. It allows one to escape figuration but presences the body. All painting is about the skin of paint. The skin of paint calls up the body and therefore the painting body. At their best, the paintings transmute the painting field into the body.

If monochrome is a sign of painting's materiality, then near-monochrome, what I do—the not quite monochrome, the becoming or unbecoming monochrome, the disruption of monochrome—is one place that content enters in. Up-close underlayers of color are visible through surface cracks and crevices. It's about what's hidden, what's revealed, buried, muffled, pushing up from underneath . . . a surface under stress. Might the painting surface as edge between art and life be a site of negotiation?

In their refusal to be any one thing, at the same time they are themselves; the paintings can be seen to occupy some sort of fugitive or queer space, and in doing so remain oppositional. Both in their refusal to participate fully in the received narrative of modernist painting and, at the same time, their refusal to "look" queer (though we might say that the paintings perform queerly).

ED. NOTE

The original manifesto, reproduced here, dates from 2010. A revised version appeared in *Harmony Hammond*, exh. cat. (New York: Alexander Gray Associates, 2013), 3; it was then reproduced in *Vector*, no. 3 (February 8, 2014): 69–71. The third published version appeared in *Harmony Hammond: Becoming/UnBecoming Monochrome*, exh. cat. (Denver: RedLine Contemporary Art Center, 2014), 2–4.

Censorship

College Art Association (2011)

The institutionalized silence around the relationship between homosexuality and art is a form of censorship, and like all censorship, it is about the regulation of difference—in this case same-sex desire. Whatever is unspoken becomes unspeakable, unthinkable, ceases to exist. I am going to briefly talk about [several] protests I was involved with that began to address and redress this institutionalized silence. I will be moving back and forth, speaking as coeditor, curator, writer, and visual artist. Three of these projects were groundbreaking: the first journal devoted to lesbian art, the first exhibition of lesbian art in New York City and the country, and the first contemporary history of lesbian art.

What I want to emphasize about these projects is that they didn't just "happen," as if by immaculate conception. They were born out of debate and argument, passionate disagreement, controversy, and differing strategies, differing goals. In other words, they were contested, limited, imperfect, and, as such, incomplete. To be the "first" anything (book, exhibition, project), to redress the erasure of work by any marginalized group, carries a tremendous weight or burden of representation—it can't be everything for everyone. It alone can't make up for a century of erasure. I speak from experience. How to balance the shortcomings of these projects (limitations due to time, space, money, context) with thoughtful constructive criticism was, is, and has been the challenge.

First, the "Lesbian Issue" of *Heresies: A Feminist Publication on Art and Politics*, the journal I helped cofound with nineteen other feminists in New York City in 1976 [see fig. 1.3]. Initiated as a quarterly, each issue of *Heresies* had a different content-oriented theme and was edited and designed by a different collective of women. With two lesbians in the founding collective to insist from the beginning on the importance of lesbianism to feminist art and politics, it was collectively decided that the third issue of the magazine would be on lesbian art and artists. Editorial work began in 1976. The resulting issue, "Lesbian Art and Artists," was published in 1977 [see figs. 1.4 and 1.5].

If safe and conservative by today's standards, the "Lesbian Issue," as it was informally called, reflected the state of lesbian feminism and lesbian art in the United States from 1975 to 1980. It was edited by a group of eleven white, primarily middle-class, college-educated women privileged or crazy enough to be out in the art world when others could not or would not be out. Age, politics, professional experience, years out, and years making art differed radically within the editorial group. Being older did not necessarily mean being out longer. Nor did radicality of politics necessarily coincide with youth. It was clear that there was not one lesbian vision, much less one definition of lesbian art among us.

While the cover, an aquamarine map of the Isle of Lesbos, connected us to a previous site of lesbian community and culture, we found that we were not only short of information on the lives and work of lesbian artists of the past but also artists working within the context of the feminist art movement. Other than a few early articles on Rosa Bonheur, Romaine Brooks, Gluck, and Berenice Abbott (by James Saslow, Arlene Raven, and Cassandra Langer), and writing by Sarah Whitworth in *Amazon Quarterly*, scholarship that considered homosexuality in relationship to works of art was nearly nonexistent.

It was difficult to get lesbian artists, historians, and critics to contribute material, for fear it would jeopardize their careers. The pressure of being the first publication to focus exclusively on lesbian creative work, primarily visual art, was huge. We could only work with what we could get. We did not receive sexually explicit material for editorial consideration. So, strangely, this special issue on sexual difference did not contain overtly sexualized images.

The "Lesbian Issue" included writings on Natalie Barney, Gertrude Stein, Alice B. Toklas, Renée Vivien, Alice Austen, Mary Ann Wilson, and Elsa Gidlow;

work by Barbara Hammer, Kate Millett, Louise Fishman, Dona Nelson, Bettye Lane, Betsy Damon, Su Friedrich, Leora Stewart, Ann Wilson, Amy Sillman, Nancy Fried, Ulrike Ottinger, myself, and others; plus reprints of important essays by Adrienne Rich, Charlotte Bunch, Bertha Harris, and more. . . .

A collaboratively designed poster announcing publication of the issue was based on an image we used to illustrate Bertha Harris's brilliant essay on the lesbian as monster in literature.

If the "Lesbian Issue" of *Heresies* was the first step in filling the vast silence around lesbian art, *A Lesbian Show* was the second [see fig. 1.6]. In response to the frustration I felt regarding the lack of visibility surrounding lesbian art and artists, I independently organized and curated an exhibition of lesbian art at the 112 Greene Street Workshop, an avant-garde, artist-run not-for-profit space in SoHo.

The exhibition was simply intended to present a sampling of work by lesbian artists living in Manhattan, but again, it was difficult finding artists who would exhibit in this context. There were no historical models. What I encountered was an incredible feeling of isolation and lack of support not only from mainstream and feminist art worlds but within dyke communities. The poverty mentality and level of struggle was overwhelming. Many of the women had nearly stopped working or had little to show. There were as many closet artists as closet lesbians. Reasons artists hesitated or declined the invitation to participate (perhaps some of these sound familiar):

- Art was a bourgeois activity that didn't really address the oppression of women.
- Feminist and lesbian exhibitions should not take place within "the elitist patriarchal art world"—only in woman-only spaces.
- Artmaking was a private world—"coming out" in public meant giving up that one safe space.
- Placing your work in all-lesbian shows contributed to the ghettoization of an already marginalized group of artists. The work would not be treated seriously.
- Those who operated in the art world or on its margins, who were semicloseted—out but didn't flaunt it—feared professional repercussions. In fact, one artist was told flat out by her dealer that if she participated in the exhibition he would no longer represent her work . . . (she didn't show).

In the end, eighteen artists exhibited; others were invited but declined for personal or professional reasons. From today's perspective, most of the work in the exhibition seems raw, hesitant, undeveloped, conservative, and curiously nonsexual; however, it reflected what was being done then in New York City and to a large degree across the country.

A Lesbian Show was important, not so much for the individual works but as an occupation of a cultural space. We were in SoHo, the art world, trespassing in a territory that had always denied our existence and excluded us.

While Amy Sillman's poster for the exhibition [see fig. 1.6] was continuously torn down—even though it did not contain any sexual images—the exhibition received favorable press (including in the *Village Voice* and *SoHo Weekly News* as well as various feminist and gay publications), thereby initiating a conversation as to what an art based on sexual politics might look like.

Fran Winant's 1975 painting of her beloved dog Cindy was emblematic of the exhibition. Cindy is surrounded by the secret language Winant had invented as a child for writing journals and poems full of inexpressible love about persons of the "wrong" (same) gender. Referencing the work of earlier lesbian painters Bonheur and Brooks, who used animals as symbolic stand-ins, Winant painted a different sexuality, a forbidden or unnatural love without being sexually explicit. [. . .]

Following ACT UP, AIDS activism, and the culture wars of the late '80s, the '90s saw a proliferation of queer art practice, exhibitions, scholarship, publications, and activism. In this context, I began writing a book on lesbian self-representation, but as I started writing, I realized that there was a book missing—the history of lesbian art in the United States—and that I was one of a handful of people who could write this history. *Lesbian Art in America: A Contemporary History* was published in 2000 [see fig. 4.1]. Writing a history of any group that has been marginalized carries a huge burden of representation, a huge responsibility. We must not shirk that responsibility, even knowing that the absences and elisions can never be fully redressed.

ED. NOTE

Hammond drafted "Censorship" for presentation at the College Art Association annual conference, February 9, 2011, Centennial Session, "Against Acknowledgement: Sexuality and the Instrumentalization of Knowledge," chaired by Jonathan D. Katz. This unpublished conference paper has been edited and abridged for publication here.

Interview with Carlos Motta

For *We Who Feel Differently* (2011)

[. . .]

CARLOS MOTTA: When did you move to New York?

HARMONY HAMMOND: I moved in fall of 1969. The Stonewall rebellion was in June 1969 so it was a time of political activism: Civil rights, anti-war protests, as well as the gay and feminist liberation movements. It was also a time when the downtown art world was very experimental.

I came out through the feminist movement. I joined an art CR [consciousness-raising] group with other women who took their work and themselves very seriously. I was around all these fantastic dynamite women who were discovering and validating women's lives and histories, including their own. It was quite natural to extend our relationships sexually. You know the WLM [women's liberation movement] saying, "Feminism is the theory, lesbianism the practice"? That's kind of the way it was. I am one of many women who came out in the context of the feminist movement. I never went through the pain, say, that a teenager who thought she might be a lesbian did, before the liberation movements. For me coming out and claiming a lesbian identity was quite pleasurable.

MOTTA: What was your entry into the feminist movement or the art scene?

HAMMOND: My friend Brad Davis had already moved [to New York City] from Minneapolis [where I lived before]. Through Brad, I met other artists and dancers. Indirectly through him, I met a couple of women artists who had decided to put together a CR group. We did not have a name; it was not a political action group, but we would participate in feminist art events or political actions. Our group, consisting of Louise Fishman, Patsy Norvell, Sarah Draney, Jenny Snider, Elizabeth Weatherford, and myself, was interested in consciousness-raising. The CR process was about literally going around in a circle and everybody was allotted the same amount of time to speak to whatever topic had been decided upon without being interrupted regardless of what you said. When you were speaking, what you said was taken to be true. We also used the CR process to critique our art. We would go to a different woman's studio each week and focus on that woman's work. The way we talked about the art was very different than, say, in art school, where content, much less content based on women's experiences, was rarely addressed. In our group, we talked about content in a way that was beyond and not limited to symbolism or iconography.

Most of us worked abstractly, coming out of postminimal concerns with materials and process and brought a gender consciousness to that way of working. I have always been very interested in how you bring content into the world of abstraction. I do not think that was unique but it was very much part of that experimental period in Lower Manhattan. People were experimenting with materials and they did not care what you called it; nobody cared if it was performance, video, dance, painting, or sculpture, you were just doing your thing and could call it *this* one day and *that* another day.

MOTTA: Was your group of artists already in conversation with women in other fields also forming the movement?

HAMMOND: Sure, we definitely knew feminist writers and activists and one member of our group, Elizabeth Weatherford, was an anthropologist. The art world was small and the feminist art world even smaller. There were very few out lesbians in the art world. I'm thinking of Kate Millett, a sculptor who was outed publicly in the broo-ha-ha around the publication of her groundbreaking book *Sexual Politics* [1970] and of *Village Voice* dance critic Jill Johnston. They are the women who went first and paid a heavy price. The group initially included

Esther Newton, who wrote *Mother Camp: Female Impersonators in America* [1972], the groundbreaking book on transvestites, and her friend Shirley Walton, a writer and hockey announcer. Esther and Shirley self-published *Womenfriends: A Soap Opera* [1976], a joint journal they kept from 1970 to 1972, at the height of the Women's Liberation Movement. As the focus began to shift from all kinds of "creative work" to visual art, Esther and Shirley left the group. The remaining members were Sarah Draney, Louise Fishman, Patsy Norvell, Jenny Snider, Elizabeth Weatherford and myself. In 1974 we exhibited as *A Woman's Group* at the Nancy Hoffman Gallery, New York City.

I read feminist newspapers from all across the country like *Country Women*, *The Lesbian Connection*, *Ain't I a Woman*, and *Big Mama Rag*. You had to have an opinion about every feminist issue: feminist credit unions, FBI infiltration, or whether or not to allow male children, or later M to F [male to female] transsexuals, at women's music festivals. Not only were these huge issues, they really mattered.

MOTTA: What was the relationship between the feminist and the lesbian feminist? Was there a break at some point within the feminist movement and how did this manifest politically?

HAMMOND: Well, very early on there were splits in the feminist movement as lesbians demanded recognition. I'm thinking of Betty Friedan famously referring to lesbians as the "lavender menace" or Jill Johnston's famous lesbian disruption of the Town Hall meeting between Norman Mailer, Jill, and several other famous feminists. In the art world it was different. Of course there were others, but Jill was the only publicly out lesbian that most people knew of. I myself functioned as a sort of bridge—moving back and forth between groups. I brought an art consciousness to lesbian separatist, socialist feminist, or Marxist cadres on the Lower East Side, many of whom were anti-art because they considered artmaking a bourgeois art world activity, and I brought a political consciousness and a consciousness of sexuality into the art world.

MOTTA: Did you think of yourself as a political person at the time?

HAMMOND: Sure.

MOTTA: Or was it just something natural?

HAMMOND: I did it naturally but I had full political awareness of what I was doing, absolutely. You don't take on editing a lesbian issue of a magazine or organizing a lesbian exhibition unless you have full awareness of the political implications of your actions.

MOTTA: Can you talk to me about some of the strategies that were used both by the feminist movement and the lesbian feminist movement in terms of generating zines, magazines, newspapers, and radical lesbian theories?

HAMMOND: Acknowledging and giving value to women's experiences, lives, labor, and cultures were at the very heart of feminist and lesbian organizing. And making our histories visible. Collectivity and "the means" being as, if not more, important than "the end" in terms of organizing. These strategies spilled over into publications. Early position papers and publications such as *The SCUM Manifesto*, *Red Stockings*, *Women Identified Women*, and *Our Bodies Ourselves* were mimeographed or xeroxed. Distribution happened at events, readings, and meetings. You had to be present to get a copy or get a Xerox copy from a friend who had been at the event. There were no women's bookstores. Once there were women's bookstores, it all changed. Supporting women's businesses, say by buying women-authored books at women-owned bookstores, became the political gesture, gradually replacing a more engaged political activism. [. . .]

ED. NOTE

The exchange above is an excerpt from an interview with Hammond that took place on March 6, 2011. The interview was produced for artist Carlos Motta's multiplatform project *We Who Feel Differently* (2012), originally presented at the New Museum, New York, and archived at *We Who Feel Differently*, https://wewhofeeldifferently.info/interview7b1d.html?interview=109.

Inroads and Outposts
Curating Queer Exhibitions in the Southwest

Pennsylvania State University (2011)

This afternoon, I am going to talk about two regional queer exhibitions that I've curated.

In 1999, *Out West* [see fig. 3.3] presented work by forty-two artists from Arizona, New Mexico, and Texas. The show was hosted by Plan B Evolving Arts, a large not-for-profit alternative art space in Santa Fe. The city, a geographical and cultural site rich with histories of gender and sexual difference, nevertheless, for the most part, maintains a "don't ask, don't tell" policy.

In 2007, *¿Y QUÉ? Queer Art Made in Texas* featured work by twenty-six artists living and working in Texas. Landmark Arts, a tiny gallery at Texas Tech University in Lubbock, was the venue. Lubbock is a small university town, ranked by some as the second most conservative city in the US, a town with three churches on every four corners, over two hundred churches in all; it's a town off all gaydar maps and charts.

I'd like to briefly address how different geographical locations, venues, and times affected the curation of and responses to each exhibition . . . and share some of the art that was in both shows.

One of the purposes of local and regional queer exhibitions is to insert a queer presence in the local public consciousness, hopefully educating folks about queer experiences, lifestyles, and culture. Of course, another purpose is to give visibility to the art and artists in a context that generates dialogue about the politics of representation.

What constitutes queerness and queer experience and how might it be visually articulated? Is sexual content an obligation or an intervention? Must the work "look queer" or read queerly in order to have a queer impact? Who creates stereotypes and what is the function of these stereotypes? Are stereotypes regional or time based? Can we reinvest them with new meanings? If the art engages with mainstream discourses of art and visual culture, is it still queer? These and similar questions continue to circulate around queer art practices. They circulated around *Out West* and *¿Y QUÉ?*, and they continue to circulate around queer art practices today.

In recent years there's been an ongoing conversation about the relevance of queer-based exhibitions, books, panels, and conferences such as this one. In 2005, the Queer Caucus for Art sponsored a panel on this subject at the College Art Association where the topic was framed as an opposition between two models of queer art production: the Stonewall identity politics idea of group solidarity and community versus a "postqueer" position that such identities are too unstable, and therefore, irrelevant, to constitute a valid category of cultural discourse or exhibition, which translated means identity politics and art based on them are outdated in the global art market. What emerged in the ensuing discussion was the realization that such a dichotomy is false and misleading: We continue to need both sorts of production but for different purposes and audiences, and that this might relate to regionalism.

Despite queer inroads in urban centers, the art world, and academia, or the inclusiveness of "queer" itself, my experiences in the trenches confirm the panel's conclusion. Queer exhibitions have a different role outside of major urban environments. They (along with interventionist art practices) occupy physical space and presence LGBTTIQ [lesbian, gay, bisexual, transgender, two-spirited, intersex, and queer] in the local community in a way that virtual exhibitions can't. While it may not be momentarily trendy, commercially viable, or considered the cutting edge of radicality on the global biennial trade routes, contrary to the belief that we are "postqueer" or "postfeminist," there continues to be a need for and value to identity-based exhibitions. If we need a name to rally under then, let's claim the term "neoqueer" (itself the title of a queer caucus–sponsored exhibition in 2004 at the Center on Contemporary Art in Seattle). Let's claim the term "neoqueer" to acknowledge a tradition of creative practice and simultaneously allow for change and fluidity.

I didn't have a curatorial agenda at the onset of either *Out West* or *¿Y QUÉ?*, other than focusing on visual art that dealt with issues of same-sex desire or non-heteronormative sexual identity in some way. I was interested to see how LGBTTIQ identity interfaced with age, gender, class, race, ethnicity, and geography, how that intersection was visually articulated, and what those articulations might tell us about the lives and experiences of being queer in the Southwest.

Out West

"Out West." The very words suggest an imaginary of being "out there," beyond social boundaries, a vast space with plenty of room for outlaws and those who don't fit in elsewhere. There's room to be who you want to be or who you think you are.

The two-year curatorial process for *Out West* included open calls on the internet, an invitational flyer sent to individuals as well as art and gay/queer publications and organizations in the tri-state area, email, and of course word of mouth, networking.

Over one hundred artists from rural and urban areas in all three states responded. If their work interested me, I tried to make a studio visit to select specific pieces for the exhibition. In the end, there were ten artists from Arizona, twenty-one from New Mexico, and eleven from Texas, ranging in age from twenty-four to sixty-seven.

Out West was made possible by a $10,000 grant from the National Gay and Lesbian Community Funding Partnership through the Santa Fe Community Foundation, one of sixteen foundations in different cities across the country invited to participate in a two-year partnership to encourage projects that address the needs of its gay communities.

Out West was a huge success. More people turned out for the opening than any other in Plan B's three-year history, rendering queer lives, work, culture, and politics visible to the larger Santa Fe community. And high attendance continued throughout the month and a half the exhibition was up. People still talk about it.

Most everyone, but especially young queers, loved the show; some but not all older "gays" (they still use that word in Santa Fe) thought there was too much sex, too much leather, and too much text. In reality, *Out West* contained very few sexually explicit images, little leather, and little text. While some of the work engaged signifiers of the Southwest, the exhibition included a wide range of work employing diverse visual strategies to represent various queer subject positions.

Some of the work occupied queer messy spaces such as Tom Holmes's snapshot for the series *Fags with Guns*. Holmes writes:

> I was raised a Southern Baptist on a ranch in rural West Texas. Full of the fervor of Christian fundamentalism, I had every intention of becoming a preacher until I figured out that I liked boys. It was an easy transition from evangelical to militant queer.
>
> Four or five years ago I became involved with the Texas hate crimes bill, intended to provide protection for gays and lesbians—it failed miserably. At the same time a law passed making it legal to carry a concealed handgun. The message from the Texas government seemed clear: "Faggot, if you want to stay safe, pack an iron."
>
> So I have been photographing queers who own guns. This group with seemingly contradictory politics is a good example of the kind of queer spaces I'm interested in. I see myself outside the myth of the queer that moves from the small town to the big city and becomes a dancer. I want to be the queer that stays and dances in the small town.

The *Fags with Guns* project started with self-identified fags who responded to Holmes's classified ads in gay papers, but he soon found it more interesting to open up the term "fag" and use it as an oppositional term like "queer" before it was institutionalized by academia.

We are not sure who we are seeing (a man or a woman) or how we are to respond. Are we seeing a strange blend of politics at home with each other, or are we seeing a member of a queer militant group that fights back?

Then there is Sharon Stewart's photograph of a man and woman in bed together, seemingly a common heterosexual image, but in the context of *Out West*, the photo of Roy Oakes dying from AIDS lying next to his former wife and caregiver, one from a series of photographs requested by Roy, takes on a different and poignant meaning. . . .

The work stimulated a lot of public dialogue, interestingly not so much about queerness itself but rather how sexual identity interfaced with other identities. [. . .]

The most controversial work was Geoff Laurence's painting titled *Tefillin* [1999], (which means "prayer" in Hebrew), depicting a nude woman's body wrapped around with the leather strap of a phylactery [a small leather box containing Hebrew texts worn by Jewish men at morning prayer as a reminder to keep the law]. The strap encircled her arms three times, connecting the self-imposed nature of bondage to the idea of metaphorically binding oneself to spirit or God. A letter to the editor of the local paper did not take issue with the fact that women are not allowed to wear a phylactery but rather with the associations of sex play and prayer.

Despite Hulleah Tsinhnahjinnie's catalogue statement and Carrie House's documentary video *I Am What I Choose to Be*, exploring lives of gay Native Americans, the most-asked question around the exhibition was "What is two-spirited?," an identification that includes both a sexual and a Native racial and cultural identity that is acknowledged and valued within tribal cultures, an identification many but not all Native Americans prefer, feeling that it is more accurate than gay, lesbian, homosexual, or queer, labels they feel reflect a white heritage. This was a surprising question, given the fact that the exhibition was taking place in Santa Fe, which has a large population of First Nations peoples and artists.

In a spirit of criticism and self-criticism, I have to admit that I too was educated. Despite the fact that I had consciously searched for and used an image of a brown-skinned cowboy, Hulleah, the one full-blood Native artist in the exhibition, protested the announcement, explaining that for Indigenous peoples, "the cowboy is always white." Additionally, she felt that the performativity of the image and the postcard context called up the history of "Wild West" shows in Europe and the merchandising of an exotic West romanticized to encourage tourism. She pointed out the privilege of playing with signifiers of the West if you haven't been identified with and colonized by them! She asked, where was she in this imagery?

Out West received a lot of positive local press; however, censorship reared its ugly head, as it so often does with queer exhibitions. On the day of the opening, *Pasatiempo*, Santa Fe's weekly arts and entertainment magazine, was to publish a two-page cover article on the exhibition. At their request, we had submitted images of every work in the show to be considered for the cover, only to find on the morning of publication that SURPRISE! an innocuous image of clouds graced the cover instead of any work from the exhibition. Apparently, all the work in the show was too sexual, or rather too homosexual, or too abstract and conceptual and not sexy enough, not recognizably gay to a straight audience—the patronizing assumption being that the paper's readers were straight and wouldn't get it or couldn't handle it.

Also, the article was strangely titled "Rendering Gender," versus, say, "rendering sexuality," a subtle censorial shift from what was perceived as the controversial subject of sexuality to the safer subject of gender.

Of course, writers and art editors have the right to their own opinions, cover images, and titles, but the canceling of an *Out West* cover image and choice of the article's title functioned as the kind of insidious censorship that happens all too often, sometimes going unnoticed by all parties, including an unsuspecting public.

I don't know if the arts editor (like so many in Santa Fe—not closeted but not really out either) even saw the exhibition, but on the morning of the opening festivities, unbeknownst to me, she took it upon herself to call members of the Santa Fe Community Foundation board, the organization that had funded the exhibition, to complain about the [quality and character of the] show, demanding to know why they were using their money to fund the exhibition.

The board members, who knew little about art but who had trusted me, went to the opening, prepared to see the worst but instead encountered the huge multicommunity crowd that had turned out. The buzz of excitement and positive energy in the air was undeniable. I did not have to say anything to defend the exhibition.

¿Y QUÉ?

¿Y QUÉ? Queer Art Made in Texas, eight years later, was a different story. Based on the success of *Out West*, I was invited by two queer artists on the faculty at Texas Tech and the director of the Landmark Arts, the university gallery, to curate an exhibition of queer art for the gallery. Even though I didn't live or work in Lubbock, I was interested precisely because it was in a small university town. [. . .]

While quite a few musicians grew up in Lubbock, it did not have the queer history or art history of Santa Fe, or even of Austin, San Antonio, or Houston, cities where alternative art spaces had mounted queer exhibitions in recent years. Obviously both queers and artists lived in Lubbock, and many taught at or attended the university . . . but what was missing, according to organizers, was a queer art presence or at least a rupture in the assumed heteronormativity—on campus and around town. [. . .]

A two-year curatorial process started with my visit to Lubbock to lecture, see the gallery space, meet faculty, artists, and others in the community who would be supportive of a queer exhibition, and to generate the interest of and get backing from the university administration. Other than that, the curatorial process and parameters were similar to *Out West*, except that I was only looking at work by Texas artists and video would be part of the exhibition instead of a separate program.

Also, I had help. Angie Piehl, my assistant curator, had grown up in San Antonio, and at the time lived in Austin. A painter and graduate of the MFA program at the University of Arizona, Tucson, where I taught for seventeen years, Angie proved to be an invaluable link to younger artists who had heard about the exhibition but might not have submitted work, except that they were personally encouraged by her to send me their materials. When I traveled to Austin and San Antonio, she coordinated a marathon schedule of what turned into twenty-two studio visits with artists in two and a half days. Also, being from Texas, she could fill in the cultural context I sometimes needed, outsider that I was.

We still ran into curatorial difficulties. A few of the *Out West* artists from Texas had moved, so I lost track of them. Some excellent artists were not making work at the moment, had no work available, or their current work didn't deal with queer issues in any way whatsoever.

Also, a number of well-known artists, who had been and were out, who eagerly participated in queer shows in the '90s, during the postmodern heyday of the queer renaissance when it was cool (and profitable) to be queer, now did not wish to place their work in this context.

Again, as with *Out West*, the work I looked at, considered, and ultimately chose did not fall into one or two overarching categories of subject, concept, or formal concerns, and interestingly, I saw even less sexually explicit work, and for that matter, less work playing with stereotypical representations of queerness (or the West). Much of the work in *¿Y QUÉ?* did not scream *queer*, to the disappointment of the queer organizers who had invited me to curate. It wasn't in your face, provocative, or controversial (like queer art made in the '90s).

Probably the edgiest work in the show didn't represent anything sexual at all, but rather photographs of children—always a hot button for right-wing, knee-jerk reactions, raising issues of censorship and freedom of creative expression.

Thankfully, the children depicted in Celesta Danger's photos, jumping on the bed, oblivious to the triangular merkins of synthetic fur sewn to their underpants, did not stir up any major censorship controversy. Rather viewers, in conversation, differed as to how they felt about using children in photographs, using children in photographs with sexual overtones, or using children in any photos sexual or not, presented and therefore positioned within a queer exhibition.

In the end, *¿Y QUÉ?* was an intergenerational assemblage of artworks, with artists ranging in age from their mid-twenties to age sixty and seventy-five, three of them being from Lubbock. Some of the artists had a long history of exhibiting and others were just emerging and starting to show, whatever their age. Some taught in or recently graduated from MFA programs. Others were loners or worked totally outside of any academic framework. Some had exhibited extensively in queer exhibitions; for others this was new.

Unfortunately, geography impacted reception of the show. Because of the location, no one in the art or gay press, and even many of the artists, thought that the exhibition was important or merited attention. Only a handful of artists attended the opening. Those who had gone out of their way to attend the opening of *Out West* in Santa Fe eight years earlier didn't bother to attend this opening—after all, it was only Lubbock.

The academic context proved to be important to both the limitations and success of *¿Y QUÉ?*. Like many university galleries, the space was small (virtually eliminating inclusion of installation work). The university context and brick architecture on campus restricted work placed in public spaces outside of the gallery. We received and were grateful for university funding. Viewing the exhibition as a pedagogical opportunity, we had no desire for illegal guerilla art interventions that might undermine this support (as much as we might encourage them in other situations!).

While *¿Y QUÉ?*, the work in the exhibition, and the context in which it was presented did open dialogues and publicly de-heterosexualize the halls of academia, it certainly didn't shake its foundations—nor that of the three churches on the four corners. In fact, strangely there was little public dialogue. This was partially due to the fact that one of the professors who had invited me to curate this exhibition organized a second show that piggy-backed on *¿Y QUÉ?*.

That exhibition, *Out in the Mainstream: Queer Social Landscape*, a one-night-stand exhibition of work opening the same night as *¿Y QUÉ?* [and] featuring work "about queer issues by artists of all sexual identities," most of them straight students, was problematic in that it allowed everyone to perform queerness, or rather their idea of queerness, for a night. This meant that the work had to "look queer."

Most of the art in this second show, based on stereotypes of gender and sexuality without any examination of those stereotypes, was simplistic, embarrassing, and at times downright offensive. To many eyes, work by real queers in *¿Y QUÉ?* didn't look queer enough but work by heterosexuals did, and it was this work that was featured in the local town newspaper.

Theoretically, a spin-off exhibition with a differing queer position or in a postqueer spirit could have been interesting, had there been some sort of engaged dialogue between the two shows . . . but that's not what happened. Without getting caught up in the nuances of performing queerness versus queer performance, we might ask, "How did performing queerness for a night give any understanding of non-heteronormative lives, experiences, or cultural production?" If queerness has become so open that anyone can be king, queen, or queer for a night, it means nothing.

Contextualized in a month of interdepartmental queer events on campus intended to educate the university administrators about the importance of addressing and including queer-based curriculum and programming, in hindsight

¿Y QUÉ? is probably best viewed, and most successful, as part of an ongoing academic conversation—an extension of contemporary queer discourse through the exhibition of visual art rather than scholarly papers. [. . .]

ED. NOTE

This is an abridged version of the keynote address, "Inroads and Outposts: Curating Queer Exhibitions in the Southwest," that Hammond presented at the "Outlandish! Life, Love, and Sex in the US, from the Viewpoint of Queer Regionalism" symposium at Pennsylvania State University, March 18, 2011.

During this lecture, Hammond showed slides of works exhibited in *Out West* and *¿Y QUÉ? Queer Art Made in Texas* by the following artists, in addition to her own works: Laura Aguilar, Lora Alaniz and Jennifer Beth Guerin, Philip Avila, Ed Check, Adrain Chesser, Armando Espinosa, Heyd Fontenot, Isa Gordon, Keith Gossiaux, Wesley Harvey, Caroline Hinkley, Tom Holmes, Delmas Howe, Tom Jennings, Kelly Kievit, Mike Krone, Patti Levy, Scott Lifshutz, Annabel Livermore, Herb Lotz, Shanti Mataluski, Horace Mayfield, James Magee, Angie Piehl, Amber Rademacher, Chuck Ramirez, Camille Ross, Gregory Sale, Joyan Saunders, Chris Sauter, Greg Stadler, Deborah Vasquez, and Barbara Zusman.

Wall Text, *Erasing Censorship* Exhibition

Left Coast Books, Goleta, California (2011)

Harmony Hammond—Artist's Statement

While I am primarily an abstract painter, I also make more overtly political work. Over the last decade, this work has dealt with issues of voice, intolerance, and censorship. The work exhibited was made in response to obstacles encountered while writing *Lesbian Art in America: A Contemporary History* (Rizzoli, 2000) [see fig. 4.1] and in response to the vandalism of LGBT books at the San Francisco Public Library in 2001.

Speaking Braids and *Untitled (Head)*

Speaking Braids (2000–2002) [see figs. 4.4 and 4.5] is about voice: It was made in direct response to writing *Lesbian Art in America: A Contemporary History* (Rizzoli, 2000), and the burden/responsibility of writing a visual history of a marginalized group. The bronze head is made from a life cast of myself but has been carved afterwards so that it no longer looks like me—it is only important that it was made from me. The hemp braid, a weave of three equal strands, represents voice. The voice comes through me and cascades down to the floor, landing on a chunk of brown wax representing the book. It is not carved or cast into a book form but rather represents a history still being written. *Untitled (Head)* (2001–2) is a reality check, lest we forget the radicality and risk of speaking out. Whether metaphorical or real, blood is always shed.

Small Erasures

These drawings also relate to the writing of *Lesbian Art in America*. There were a handful of lesbian artists who did not wish to have their work included in the book. While some of their reasons are more understandable than others, in the end, they all are part of the problem. Through their chosen self-erasure they contribute to the ongoing cultural erasure of lesbian art and artists. I have photocopied their letters (and in one case, legal papers) addressed to me, and covered over names, places, and other information that might reveal their identities. The letters can be seen through skin-like latex. The point is not to guess who the letters are from but to underscore the chilling effects of self-erasure, and to presence these artists in their absence.

Represent Women: A Primer, *A Queer Reader*, and *Portraits*

At the beginning of 2001, the San Francisco Public Library staff began finding books carved with a sharp instrument hidden under shelving units. Over six hundred books relating to issues of lesbian, gay, bisexual and transgender individuals as well as AIDS and women's health issues were vandalized. Eventually the vandal was caught, charged with, and convicted of a hate crime. The damaged books, now out of circulation, were given to artists to create works of art, thereby rendering visible but transforming the destructive acts.

Represent Women: A Primer (2003) [figs. 5.5 and 5.6] responds to the damaged copy of Linda Nochlin's book *Representing Women* (1999), a Marxist analysis of the representation of women in nineteenth-century French painting. The back half of the book was missing—sliced off at the spine after page 160. It felt so violent. I felt I needed to reconstitute the book whole, to (re)present women and women's bodies whole again. I made a new cover out of flesh-like latex rubber pages stained with red ochre/blood and the word "erasure" carved into the surface. *Represent Women: A Primer* was exhibited in the *Reversing Vandalism*

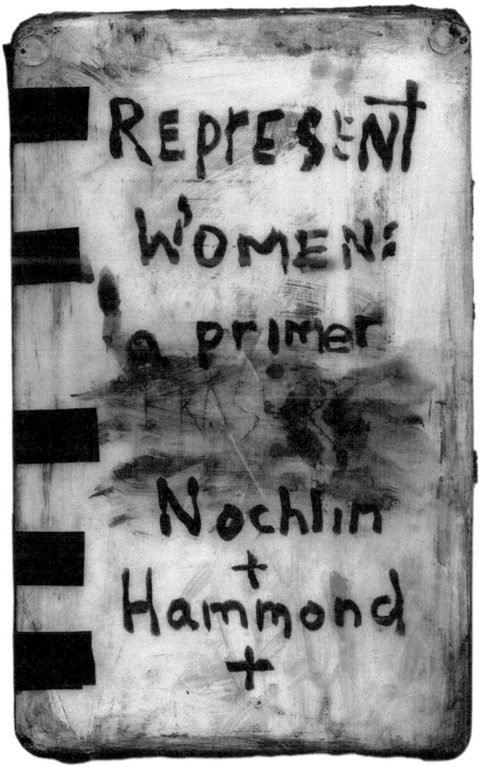

FIGURE 5.5. Harmony Hammond, *Represent Women: A Primer*, 2003. Latex rubber, acrylic, and vandalized Linda Nochlin book *Representing Women* (1999). Cover of closed book. 10.25 × 6.25 in. (26.04 × 15.88 cm). Collection Richard Meyer.

FIGURE 5.6. Harmony Hammond, *Represent Women: A Primer*, 2003. Latex rubber, acrylic, and vandalized Linda Nochlin book *Representing Women* (1999). Open book. 10.25 × 13 in. (26.04 × 33.02 cm). Collection Richard Meyer.

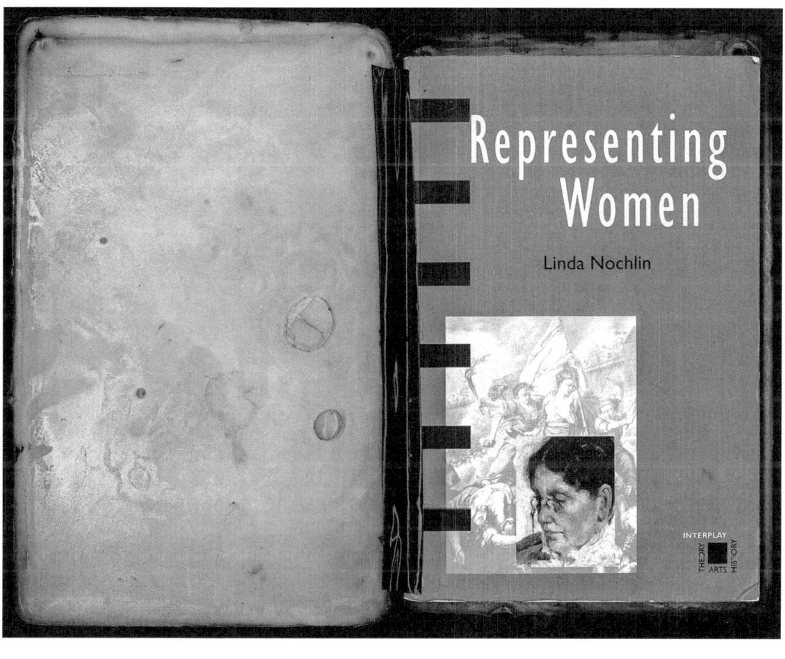

FIG. 5.7. Harmony Hammond, *A Queer Reader*, 2003. Digital print on archival paper. 66.75 × 44 in. (169.55 × 443 cm).

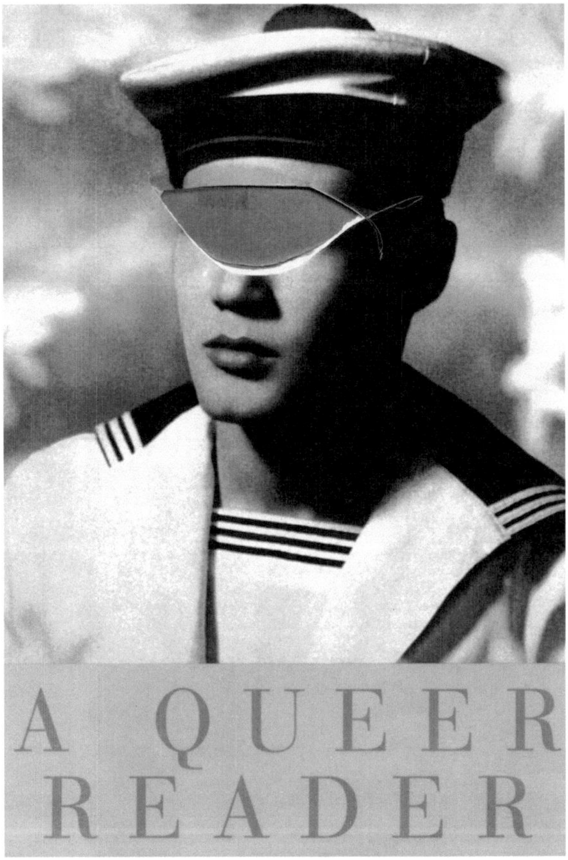

exhibition at the James C. Hormel Gay and Lesbian Center at the San Francisco Public Library (January–May 2004). Proceeds from sales of the artworks were used to replace the vandalized books.

A Queer Reader (2003) [fig. 5.7] and the series of seven smaller digital prints titled *Portraits* (2004) [see fig. 5.8] were in response to the damaged anthology *A Queer Reader: 2500 Years of Male Homosexuality*, edited by Patrick Higgins (1993). They were first exhibited in the "spin-off" exhibition *Insight Out: Reversing Vandalism*, at the Center for Contemporary Arts, Santa Fe (June 4–July 5, 2004).

In 2003, I scanned the vandalized book jacket that already incorporated the photograph *Le Marin (Philippe Gaillon)* (1985) by Pierre and Gilles, two

FIGURE 5.8. Harmony Hammond, *Portrait: Jean Genet*, 2004. Digital print on archival paper. 19 × 12 in. (48.26 × 30.48 cm).

ements gave him a full awa
ve. He said, almost sobbingl
and at the same time impaled
tered in, and Riton's behind
them was great . . . Riton mu
you more than before.' Eri
been expressed, for as their
feel its natural effects. O
d each oth

French photographers who work as a team and are well known for their highly stylized and heavily retouched performative portraits of gay male archetypes. I then eliminated the subtitle and name of the editor, thereby shifting the word "reader" from the book to the sailor or possibly the viewer or one who reads, and enlarged the resulting image to poster proportions.

Is the sailor a queer who reads or does he read queerly? With his eyes cut out, he is not allowed to see or read at all—much less queerly. Why this fear of queer eyes? The violence of the vandalism suggests mythological themes of blinding and self-blinding. Pierre and Gilles's idealized sailor is all lipstick, rosy, and sanitized in contrast to queer realities of AIDS, gay bashing, anti–human rights initiatives, and cultural censorship. *A Queer Reader* forces the icon and the image to address homophobia and censorship. The vandal cut the same eye-shaped hole on the pages inside the book. The suite of *Portraits* repositions suggestive texts by gay male authors included in the anthology, the earliest being Oscar Wilde, and the most recent Allen Ginsberg, so that they are partially seen through the orifice [fig. 5.8].

ED. NOTE

Various artworks by Hammond referenced in these short texts appeared in the group exhibitions *Dialogues and Meditations*, Museum of Contemporary Art, Tucson, Arizona, 2002; *Reversing Vandalism*, James C. Hormel Gay and Lesbian Center, San Francisco Public Library, 2004; and *Insight Out: Reversing Vandalism*, Center of Contemporary Arts, Santa Fe, New Mexico, 2004. Hammond later brought together works addressing censorship in the solo exhibition *Erasing Censorship*, which she reconfigured with the collaboration of three different cocurators for three different venues between 2007 and 2018. She cocurated the first iteration with Christopher Reed at Lake Forest College, Lake Forest, Illinois (2007); the second with Simon Taylor at Left Coast Books, Goleta, California (2011); and the third with Eve Fowler at Artist Curated Projects, Los Angeles (2018). Each version of the exhibition presented a slightly different combination of artworks chosen in relation to the size and configuration of the exhibition space. Hammond wrote the statement reprinted here for the 2011 exhibition at Left Coast Books.

Sexuality and the Museum

Brooklyn Museum (2012)

Thank you for the invitation to participate in this "Sexuality and the Museum" conversation. You know, this is an important topic. I'd like to make a few observations and raise a number of issues.

While art and homosexuality have always been intertwined in the public imagination, the historical and conceptual links between the two are missing. The art world, indeed, most art museums, operating in "don't ask, don't tell" mode, have failed to acknowledge same-sex desire as a meaningful constituent of art production, history, and criticism. There's a kind of HETERONORMATIVITY underlying most queer exhibitions, publications, projects, indeed discussions like this symposium. Even scholarly exhibitions such as *Hide/Seek: Difference and Desire in American Portraiture* [National Portrait Gallery, Washington, DC, October 30, 2010–February 13, 2011; Brooklyn Museum, November 18, 2011–February 12, 2012] or *Gertrude Stein: Five Stories*, currently at the National

Portrait Gallery, exhibitions intending to do the opposite, are read against a backdrop of assumed heteronormativity.

How to change this? Remain vigilant, chip away—shifts happen little by little. Shifts. For example, my book *Lesbian Art in America: A Contemporary History* [see fig. 4.1] could be/was written to be used as [a] definitive text on American feminist art from 1970 to 2000, with other texts brought in to examine heterosexuality in feminist art.

All art participates in multiple narratives—just as to overemphasize one narrative (say feminist or queer) is reductive and simplistic, to eliminate (gender or sexual) identity-based narratives (under an art world and museum policy of "don't ask, don't tell"), leaving the work without a social context, creates a huge gap leading to misreading, misinterpreting, and misunderstanding. Ultimately censoring difference. The conversations are multiple, nuanced, and complex.

Speaking as an artist, one can easily do a queer read of my recent wrapped and grommeted near-monochrome paintings. Genre-bending paintings such as *Muffle* (2009) [see plate 19] or *Rib* (2021) [see plate 21] do indeed perform queerly, however they can and should also be discussed in relation to narratives of postminimalism (concerns of material and process), feminism, modernist abstract painting, monochrome, the body, etc. [. . .]

The subject of sexuality should not always be ghettoized. Museums afford the opportunity to examine certain aspects of queer lives, experience, and culture IN DEPTH, but works also need to be contextualized in terms of other narratives as well. Art's relation to sexuality is just one narrative. Institutionalized silence around the relationship of homosexuality and art is a form of censorship/erasure and is about the regulation or policing of DIFFERENCE—in this case same-sex desire. [. . .] Museums construct and reinforce certain narratives—therefore have a responsibility.

Why is homosexuality [among other forms of difference] still an issue? Because hate, bigotry, sexism, racism, homophobia, and xenophobia still exist.

With a new round of controversy around these exhibitions [exploring art and sexual difference] are we doomed to repeat the culture wars over and over again? WE MUST BE EVER-VIGILANT—AND CONTINUE TO CHIP AWAY—MY EXPERIENCE IS, IT DOES MAKE A DIFFERENCE!

There is much discussion within queer art communities: Do we still need identity-based exhibitions? Aren't we postfeminist and postqueer? I use the terms "neofeminist" or "neoqueer" to acknowledge a history, at the same time [to] suggest moving forward. I believe in the need for these exhibitions for several reasons. For one, because exhibitions physically take up time and space.

[. . .] It is important for this work to be viewed and housed in MAINSTREAM ART INSTITUTIONS (exhibitions/permanent collection[s]/archives). Even where work and archives are placed makes a statement. I want my extensive archives on me and my work (but also on other artists, primarily contemporary feminist and queer) to go into a highly respected mainstream archive. It's a political decision about the importance of being part of, central to, contemporary culture.

Museums also need to COLLECT queer work—it is when work is collected that it becomes "collectable," valued, given importance—saved, taken care of, hopefully exhibited and written about from time to time. It becomes part of the art historical narrative. The importance of "homo" difference within narratives of continuity (art history) cannot be overstated.

The National Portrait Gallery and Brooklyn Museum are to be commended for chipping away at this long-standing institutional and historical silence (which constitutes a kind of censorship) by presenting controversial exhibitions organized around gender/sexuality. As Adrienne Rich [. . .] and others have pointed out, whatever is unspoken becomes unspeakable, whatever is unspeakable becomes unthinkable, and whatever is unthinkable . . . ceases to exist.[1]

ED. NOTES

Hammond wrote text for this oral presentation during the "Sexuality and the Museum" roundtable organized by Johnathan D. Katz at the Brooklyn Museum, January 21, 2012; the text has been abridged for publication here.

1. Hammond alludes to Adrienne Rich's oft-quoted and paraphrased statement, "Whatever is unnamed, undepicted in images, whatever is omitted from biography, censored in collections of letters, whatever is misnamed as something else, made difficult-to-come-by, whatever is buried in the memory by the collapse of meaning under an inadequate or lying language—this will become, not merely unspoken, but *unspeakable*." Adrienne Rich, "'It Is the Lesbian in Us . . . ,'" in *On Lies, Secrets and Silence: Selected Prose 1966–1978* (London: Norton, 1980), 199–202 at 199; italics in original. Rich's essay was written in 1976 and first published in *Sinister Wisdom* 1, no. 3 (Spring 1977): 6–9.

Artist's Talk

Brooklyn Museum (2012)

I'd like to thank Catherine Morris and the Sackler Center for Feminist Art for inviting me to talk about my work in the context of their current exhibition, *Materializing "Six Years": Lucy R. Lippard and the Emergence of Conceptual Art.* Lucy and I go back to the early '70s. Many of you know this story, but I wish to tell it again, as it reflects the radical social and political change taking place at that time thanks to the women's liberation movement. . . .

Word was out that this critic Lucy Lippard was making studio visits to look at work by women artists for an exhibition she was guest curating. I called—too late to be considered—but she came to my studio on the corner of Spring and West Broadway anyway, her son Ethan (then six or seven years old) in tow. My daughter Tanya, less than a year old, lay asleep in her crib. I showed Lucy my work—sculptures of *Bags* made of rags recycled from women friends and neighborhood sweatshops. We talked about the work, its meaning, and its relationship to women's lives. We were women, mothers, AND art professionals. One identity did not rule out another. In other words, we did not have to hide the fact that we were mothers in order to be professional as we would have a decade earlier. To my surprise, Lucy bought one of my pieces, *Bag IX*. My first sale in New York. Since then, Lucy and I have worked together in New York and New Mexico, both in and outside of various art worlds.

We were both members of the collective of twenty women who founded the quarterly *Heresies: A Feminist Publication on Art and Politics* in 1976 [see fig. 1.3], and we worked together as editors for the inaugural issue published in 1977 and Issue 9, "Women Organized/Women Divided: Power Propaganda and Backlash," published in 1980 [see fig. 2.4].

In 1984, I moved to Santa Fe for one year, stayed on, and, in 1989, bought a place in Galisteo, a traditional Hispano village of approximately three hundred people, half-gentrified with Anglos like myself. It's twenty to thirty minutes outside of Santa Fe. Lucy would come visit and eventually she too bought land in Galisteo, where she has become an invaluable member of the community—most notably, as editor of *El Puente de Galisteo*, our monthly community newsletter. Since then, we have hiked the high desert, fought against oil and gas drilling, and trespassed in many places where we were not welcome.

These days, Lucy is mostly interested in notions of "place," or peopled space—the intersection of land, environment, and culture . . . but she also continues to write about art and to curate exhibitions (all, I might add, from a feminist perspective). Over the years, I have been lucky to have her write about my work in relation to the diverse sites I inhabit.

Basically, I do two kinds of art: Abstract work that consists of large near-monochrome paintings, and related works on paper that participate in the narrative of modernist painting at the same time they insist on an oppositional discourse of feminist and queer content, and more overtly political work dealing with issues of intolerance, censorship, and self-censorship.

This afternoon I am going to talk primarily about painting, about abstract painting.

My intent is twofold: TO MAKE THE POINT THAT ALL ART PARTICIPATES IN MULTIPLE NARRATIVES AND to counter simplistic and stereotyped notions of feminist and queer art.

In early fall 1969, I moved from Minneapolis (where I had been making large geometric hard-edged-shaped paintings) to Lower Manhattan. It was a period of civil rights and anti–American War in Vietnam activism, the beginning of the gay liberation movement, the second wave of the feminist movement, and the birth of the feminist art movement. I was influenced by and contributed to early feminist art projects. It was also a period of postminimal interdisciplinary experimentation with materials and process, resulting in work that was both conceptual and abstract. Artists moved back and forth between what might be called painting, sculpture, video, and performance, calling it one thing one day and another thing the next. Feminists brought a gendered content to this way of working.

By 1970 my work had changed radically. I and many other feminist artists abandoned the male-dominated site of painting, consciously using materials, techniques, and formal strategies associated with women's traditional arts precisely because of their marginalized histories and associations. Underlying this practice was the belief that materials (in my case fabric) and the ways they are manipulated (weaving, stitching, wrapping, braiding, etc.) contribute to content as much as form, sign, or symbol.

My earliest feminist work made reference to women's traditional arts such as weaving and needlework by using recycled "hand-me-downs," rags given to me by women friends, literally putting my life in my art. Partly for financial reasons, and partly because I wanted to move away from the masculinist tradition of painting, I began to paint with acrylic on worn-out blankets, curtains, sheets, and bedspreads. I liked the old weathered, leathery effect of the paint saturating the unprimed, unstretched cloth. Ripped strips of cloth were dipped in paint and attached to the painting surface so they hung down like three-dimensional brush strokes. The weight of the rags and paint began to alter the painting rectangle. Gradually, the rags took over, activating the painting field.

This led to the series of *Bags* (1971), like the one Lucy purchased, which were hung on the wall, and the slightly larger-than-life-sized *Presences* (1972) [see plate 2], which hung out in space. These were featured in my first solo exhibition in New York City, at A.I.R. Gallery in January 1972. [The poster for this exhibition featured one of the *Bags*; see fig. 1.2]. The *Bags* and *Presences* were about layering, connecting, and building whole presences out of accumulated fragments of found materials, initiating a "survivor aesthetic" that continues to inform my work to this day. In contrast to my [earlier, minimalist] work in Minneapolis, these new pieces, given their physicality, could be touched, retouched, repaired, and, like women's lives, reconfigured.

In 1973, I created a series of six floor paintings made out of knit fabric my daughter and I picked from dumpsters in the garment districts of Lower Manhattan. Strips of the fabric were braided according to traditional braided rug techniques but slightly larger and thicker in scale, coiled, stitched to a heavy cloth backing, and partially painted with acrylic paint, the "braided rug" literally and conceptually becoming "the support" for the painting. Referencing rag rugs, but nonfunctional as such, the *Floorpieces* [see plate 4] occupied and negotiated a space between painting (off the wall) and sculpture (nearly flat), although, because of my painting background, I thought of them primarily as paintings.

Approximately one inch high and five and a half feet in diameter, the *Floorpieces* were to be placed directly on the floor and shown as a group without anything on the walls, thereby calling into question assumptions about the "place" of painting. These two *Floorpieces* were included in the exhibition *High Times, Hard Times: New York Painting 1967–1975*, an important and long overdue exhibition, curated by Katy Siegel and David Reed, that revisited a time and place and reviewed the work being made then and there, through a painting lens. (The traveling exhibition opened at Weatherspoon Art Museum in 2006.)

Later work with fabric included a series of *Wrapped Sculptures* [1970s and early 1980s], which I approached as a painter (they are primarily additive). They were not stuffed fabric forms but rather fabric wrapped around wooden armatures—made out of themselves from the inside out—consciously presencing bodies more than figures, although the wood armatures functioned as skeleton, the fabric as muscle and tissue, and the paint and latex rubber painted on the surface functioned as skin.

In *Hunkertime* (1979–80) [see plate 11], ladder forms stand in for gendered bodies, both hard and soft, referencing the collectivity of feminist movements. The ladders hunker down, hang out, lean on, and touch each other, as if waiting for their moment of collective action. Perverse pleasure . . . minimal yet ruffles and dots are flirtatious. They were recently included in the also long-overdue exhibition *WACK! Art and the Feminist Revolution*, curated by Connie Butler at the Museum of Contemporary Art, Los Angeles, and traveling here to New York, at PS1 [Museum of Modern Art] in 2007 until 2009.

One other example is *Radiant Affection*, the last wrapped sculpture I made in 1984 before moving to New Mexico (now in the collection of the Metropolitan Museum of Art).

In the mid-'70s I created a series of small oil and wax paintings (1973–77) that looked as if they were woven out of paint. The surface was slowly built up with successive layers of oil paint mixed with Dorland's Wax. Weave patterns (at first, grids with marks; later, braid patterns) were obsessively incised into the paint. The surface was irregular, lumpy, and bumpy, emphasizing the painting surface as skin and indirectly the body. For me, the painting skin, that edge where art and life literally meet, always relates to the body as site. To layer strokes of paint is to accumulate, to build on the body. To caress. To incise into the painting surface is to cut into the body. Looking beautiful and woven from a distance, almost monochrome, up close, the underlayers of color were exposed, and little points protruded from the surface of the painting. These points were at once menacing and fragile.

Sometimes, I tucked scraps of fabric and wads of newspaper in between the stretcher bar and the back of the canvas—creating a slight rounding or swelling around the edge of the painting—much more subtle than the early shaped paintings I had made in Minneapolis.

By 1976, many of the paintings became lozenge shaped, the curved ends mirroring swellings in the painting surface. That year, these paintings were exhibited at the Lamagna Gallery, here in New York City, along with *Collection of Fragments* [see figs. I.1 and I.2; plates 7 and 8], an ethnographic display case and vitrine featuring fabricated clay shards imprinted with basket weaves that set up an abstract dialogue with the paintings. The accompanying labels identified the artist, me, as the maker of the shards and included text I wrote [see fig. I.3] based on a foundational reference by the Navajo School of Indian Basketry: "Baskets are the Indian Woman's poems, the shaping of them her sculpture. They wove into them the story of their life and love."

By employing conceits of museum display, I was able to bridge and engage ethnographic, craft, and fine art disciplines, anticipating the '90s discourse of the museum's role of collecting, labeling, and displaying artifacts in the creation and authentication of a historical narrative. *Collection of Fragments* functioned to create a narrative of women's creative practices and place my work within that narrative. By referencing baskets and exhibiting clay shards along with the paintings, I was able to take the feminist project of creating a historical narrative of women's creativity back into the painting field, merging traditional and fine arts in the skin of paint.

Abstract Painting

I've always been interested in the possibilities of content in abstraction, especially what Kobena Mercer calls "discrepant abstraction," or all that does not fit neatly into the institutional narrative of abstract art as a monolithic quest for purity.[1] For years I worked with found and recycled materials and objects as one way to introduce content into the world of abstraction. Found materials and objects have their own associations and histories that they bring with them. I utilized *materials* such as fabric, rusted corrugated roofing tin, linoleum, latex rubber, straw, leather, and burnt wood; *objects* such as water troughs, gutters, buckets, screens, and dead birds; along with *oil paint* to create mixed-media installational paintings suggesting narratives of loss, violence, and survival. These tableau-like paintings often sat on the floor and leaned against the wall with objects placed on or in front of the painting surface—occupying a place between painting and sculpture—or what we might call expanded painting.

Over time, these mixed-media paintings got simpler and simpler, as I tried to get "meaning" into the paint itself and its application. For the last twelve years or so, I have made large, thickly painted near-monochrome paintings. When I am asked, "What's a nice feminist like you doing in the modernist painting field—a territory that has notoriously excluded women and lesbians?" I answer, "Painting, like any cultural language, doesn't have to rely on its historicized meanings. I don't accept that painting is an overdetermined site, a privileged domain of the authoritative masculine voice, or that monochrome painting is necessarily a dead end—the inevitable conclusion of a history of art as a hierarchy of purifications." [. . .]

If monochrome is a sign of painting's materiality, then near-monochrome, what I do—the not-quite monochrome, the becoming or unbecoming monochrome, the disruption of monochrome—is one place that content enters in. Up-close underlayers of color are visible through surface cracks and crevices. It's about what's hidden, what's revealed, buried, pushing up from underneath . . . the painting surface under stress. Might the painting surface as edge between art and life be a site of negotiation?

In their refusal to be any one thing at the same time, they are themselves. The paintings can be seen to occupy some sort of fugitive or queer space, and in doing so, remain oppositional . . . both in their refusal to participate fully in the received narrative of modernist painting and, at the same time, their refusal to "look" queer (though we might say that the paintings perform queerly).[2]

Take *Muffle* (2009) [see plate 19], which marks a transition to my current work. (Is it black? Dark blue?) The near-monochrome surface, and at times metallic color, are difficult to locate, thus incarnating the concept of "fugitive." The painting is wrapped with straps of grommeted canvas. Grommeted cotton canvas speaks of tarps, tents, drop cloths, and awnings; it's tough and functional; it has a job to do. It suggests the possibility of connecting, securing, restraining. Grommets are found along the edges of the material, in hems, reinforcements.

For me there are additional associations. Many of these paintings are on recycled canvas that was used to cover the woven tatami mats used in aikido, the Japanese martial art I studied for thirty-six years. Long, six- to eight-foot-wide strips of canvas are sewn together to form a rectangular cover for the tatami mats that in turn cover the dojo floor. These mat covers wear out over time and need to be replaced. The old covers were given to me and I have used them as the painting support. Thus, they are charged with repeated body contact, including my body.

I have included the seams of the canvas in some of the paintings. Seams or sutures, the traces and evidence of the two edges meeting, piecing, connecting—a sign of indexical intention. *Flap* (2008–11) utilizes the "under" or "other" side of the aikido mat cover, revealing not only the sewn seam but the "flap" caused by two pieces of canvas joined together. At first glance, there's not much there except surface and color. The FLAP, and the hidden space it alludes to, seemingly BISECTS the painting into upper and lower halves; however, "the flap" functions as an active and equal third zone or space, resisting binaries. The flap casts a shadow on the painting surface, indicating a hidden and possibly gendered space beneath.

Grommets in the four corners tweak or torque the space/surface—the feeling is that you can peel off the painting—emphasizing the painting's surface or skin or something that might be peeled or pulled off, and revealing something behind or under the painting . . . AND, asking the question: Where is the painting located?

A gendered association is reinforced by the painting's peachy color. It's a pretty outrageous painting in its color and simplicity. A minimalist painting, peach-colored?! The painting, which is almost too big for itself, has a kind of GLOW that makes it weightless despite its obvious thick paint. The play on the word *flap*—which asks, "What's all the flap about?"—contributes to the painting's insolence.

My newest work (2010–12) includes straps, staples, grommets, and pushpins suggesting binding, bandaging, bondage, restraint, and constraint—possibilities of connecting, tying down, securing, reinforcing, embracing, muffling, and covering up. There's a sense of immediacy and provisionality. Countering digital seamlessness, these paintings reveal the facture of their making, thereby providing the opportunity to examine materiality and the indexical as a means to assert content and investigate the agency of materials and process in visual production. The surfaces have more ruptures, more seams than the earlier monochromes. Paint collects along edges of the straps like scar tissue—builds up around the pushpins or fills in the grommet holes. Some straps cast shadows, suggesting that we could pull them off. . . . The shift to a lighter palette [in certain paintings] allows for surface manipulation, holes, shadows, connecting strategies, to be seen and therefore play an active conceptual role. Restraint and constraint . . . suggesting a body or bodies negotiating for freedom of movement. Titles like *Cinch* and *Lace* evoke corsets, breast plates, but the laces around the paintings are not pulled tight; there is not constraint other than the possibility of constraint. The straps are intentionally wrapped around the painting as object and body (appearing at first glance to embrace/restrict/hold the painting together). However, the straps are never that tight, they do not cinch or constrict. The straps (or for that matter, the pushpins and staples) do not hold the painting together. The paint (and therefore the act of painting) does. The paint holds the painting together just as the act of painting holds the painter together. [. . .]

The grommets have many references. Originally, the hemmed and reinforced grommeted edges of the aikido mat. Additionally, grommets have a painting history—they were used extensively in the late '60s and early '70s by artists painting on unstretched canvas as a way to hang or informally present painting. But I use them on stretched canvas, in a manner more visual/conceptual than functional—semiburied or filled in—opening up the surface—orifices to the painting body. . . .

In their layering, these wrapped "monochromes" reference both my "weave" paintings of the mid-'70s (what's hidden and what's revealed) and my wrapped and painted sculptures of the late '70s and early '80s (that also emphasized the additive process of constructing something out of itself and where the physical manipulation of the material activates the surface).

More broadly, they also reference Gee's Bend quilts. I'm thinking of the early Gee's Bend quilts, handcrafted from worn-out pieces of denim, recycled from worn-out jeans and overalls, then used in denim quilted blankets for years, retaining the subtle body imprint. While the paintings are in conversation with a wide range of works, as one critic visiting my studio put it, they are totally self-sufficient—in the sense that they demand you accept them on their own terms.

As I was working on *Red Bed* (2011) [see plate 20], a favorite of mine, I became aware of its reference to Rauschenberg's series of red paintings and his famous *Bed* painting of 1955, a huge influence on me when I was an art student—not only because of its color but because of its single bed size, and the manner in which it insists upon the upright flatbed picture plane . . . and so *Red Bed* became an homage. [. . .]

Most writing on these recent paintings focuses on the straps. I am more interested in the grommet holes.

For my most recent monotypes, with grommeted holes all the way through, Lucy Lippard coined the term *grommetypes*. These are works of/on paper, but at a glance they could pass for some other material (animal hide? painted metal?).[3] Genre trouble.

I think I'll stop here, take comments, and try to answer any questions. . . .

ED. NOTES

This invited lecture anchored the exhibition programming for *Materializing "Six Years," Lucy R. Lippard and the Emergence of Conceptual Art*, Sackler Center for Feminist Art, Brooklyn Museum, 2012. While the script for this presentation includes fully fleshed-out passages, it is primarily composed of notes for oral extemporization, as is typical of Hammond's lectures. The script was somewhat recomposed, reorganized, and abridged for inclusion here.

1. See Kobena Mercer, ed., *Discrepant Abstraction* (Boston: MIT Press, 2006).

2. This paragraph repeats/cites the closing of "A Manifesto (Personal) of Monochrome (Sort Of)" (2010), the first text in this chapter.

3. These grommetypes were made in collaboration with Marina Ancona, 10 Grand Press.

The Collective Archive as Feminist Art Narrative

The Feminist Art Project Day of Panels, Brooklyn Museum (2013)

This is a practical presentation. I wish to address two things: artists taking responsibility for organizing and archiving their papers, files, and images in order to create a feminist art narrative that is both collective and diverse, and along the way, address the state of photographic documentation of visual art in library and archival collections.

Like many of you in this room, I am an activist who has cofounded, organized, or participated in many feminist art projects, exhibitions, and organizations.

I . . . have . . . archives. By artist's archives, I do not mean the works of art which constitute my estate but rather papers—including, but not limited to correspondence, bios, bibliographies, flyers, exhibition announcements, press releases, posters, installation photographs, source materials, reviews, articles, catalogues, periodicals, anthologies, books, artist statements, published and unpublished writing and interviews, lectures, videos, notes and minutes from meetings, photographs of the women who have created and participated in various feminist art projects, organizations, and exhibitions, ephemera such as awards, T-shirts, buttons, bumper stickers, snapshots, and most importantly, extensive visual documentation of the work itself, hopefully in digital format.

At the risk of being self-indulgent, I am going to use myself as an example. Because I have had the opportunity to teach, lecture, write, and curate, I have a good sense of what is out there and what is not out there. I know what valuable material I sit on. . . . I know what valuable material you sit on. . . .

We all have archives, or rather we have materials that could constitute archives if we could just get them organized and vetted. Yes, it can be daunting—overwhelming—but if we don't do it, who will? This is a political question.

Those of us who have been missing or marginalized in cultural histories have to insist on our historical positionings even as they constantly change. If we don't wish to replace the patriarchal canon with a new feminist canon based on one or even several publications and exhibitions, but rather desire to collectively author a feminist art history that is inclusive, then we artists need to take responsibility and get our papers and images in order and place them in some sort of library or archival collection where they will be available to students, curators, historians, and others doing research and writing—which, in turn, also become part of the archive.

I see my job as getting my house, or rather my office and studio, in order—providing information to resist erasure, fill in the empty spaces, get the facts right, connect the dots, and contribute to multiple historical narratives and conversations.

As the author of the first contemporary history of lesbian art and artists in the United States, I can tell you firsthand about the problems confronting "research" on a marginalized group of artists: the near lack of archives, and the poor cataloguing and physical handling of visual documentation of art and artists in those archives and libraries that do exist—be they big, small, private, government funded, institutional, or "renegade"—due to insufficient staff, space, and financial resources, but also due to priorities. Most libraries value printed material over images and quite frankly don't know how to—nor have the resources to—store, care for, transcribe, catalogue, and circulate visual documentation of works of art (which now spans black-and-white prints and 35 mm slides to digital images).

Researching *Lesbian Art in America* [published in 2020; see fig. 4.1] transformed my professional practices as an artist.

To make my archives manageable, I have divided them into two sections (which somewhat overlap).

Section One

Everything about Harmony Hammond and her work (all the catalogues and things listed above), including:

1. High-resolution digital photographic documentation of individual works of art and installations from the mid-1960s to the present. I've spent years professionally translating and color correcting 35 mm slides, four-by-five-inch color transparencies, black-and-white prints, negatives to digital images. Work since 2006 has been documented with high-resolution digital photographs. These images form the basis of my archival website.
2. Complete inventory of my work entered into a database that is cross-referenced with the digital files. This inventory will include, title, date, medium, dimensions, materials, process and conservation notes, shipping and installation directions, exhibition history, collections, bibliographic references and reproductions, current location, and minimally, a thumbnail image.

Section Two

Everything about other artists and their work that I have gathered over the years, especially the decade it took me to write *Lesbian Art in America* (in addition to the same types of exhibition and written materials, I add the following):

1. I have an extensive collection of over six thousand 35 mm slides of work by other artists—primarily contemporary American lesbian and feminist artists (from the '70s to the present), some men (mostly queer), and some historical women. These are filed alphabetically by artist or exhibition in slide boxes. Also included is an expanding collection of work documented on disc, sent to me by artists or their galleries. This important collection comprises the largest visual documentation of work by contemporary lesbian artists in the United States.
2. I also have correspondence with, and files on, over eight hundred contemporary lesbian artists. While I am not actively developing these files, I continue to update them as I receive materials.
3. Additionally, I have files on exhibitions that I've curated or cocurated which are cross-referenced with my collection of slides and digital images.

Thirteen years after the publication of *Lesbian Art in America*, I am still using the slide collection I amassed in its writing. When I need an image for research or lecture purposes I simply go to my alphabetized file, scan the slide, and use it as a digital image—it's that easy. In most cases, I have more and better-quality images than what you can Google and download, or what is available through Artstor.

So what I'm saying is: If I can organize the images, a library should be able to do the same thing. It's no big deal to file and then digitize a slide, or photograph flat art as it is requested, and have an agreement form saying that the image is to be used for educational purposes only. For any other use, permission must be obtained from the artist, their gallery, or copyright agent.

Unfortunately, I am the only person using this collection of slides and files. I am not a librarian, nor do I have an assistant to handle requests for images and information. At this point, my main concern, and I would say my political responsibility, is to get these archives permanently placed and housed in the very best context where they can be made easily available to the public for research.

It's not just about acquisition, who wants or will take the archive, but about an institutional or organizational commitment. I've made the political decision to place my papers in a major art archive, and in doing so, I am able to insert a lesbian presence into the larger art historical narrative.

So, what I am saying is that our collective feminist art history is dependent on all of our archives. I urge everyone here to get your house/studio/office in order. Thank you.

ED. NOTE

"The Collective Archive as Feminist Art Narrative" was written for oral presentation at TFAP@CAA: The Feminist Art Project Day of Panels: "Feminism and Institutions," "The Artist as Archivist" panel chaired by Aruna D'Souza, Brooklyn Museum, February 16, 2013. The Getty Research Institute, Los Angeles, acquired Hammond's archives in 2015.

Curatorial Essay, *Material Engagements* Exhibition

RedLine Contemporary Art Center, Denver (2013)

I am an artist, but I also write about art and curate exhibitions—activities that give me the opportunity to think about creative practices other than my own. Over the years, I've worked with many not-for-profit art spaces and projects across the country. My experience in the trenches suggests that not-for-profit and artist-run spaces are where we see interesting, experimental art, unmediated by the market—where we see what artists in any given locale are really up to.

So, when I was invited to curate an exhibition of work by RedLine artists based on a theme or concept of my choice, I jumped at the opportunity. Thinking about the current renewed interest in postminimal concerns with materials and process and the "hand-crafted," as well as discourses of "new materialism," I decided upon the curatorial concept of "material engagements."[1]

As the curator of the 1997 exhibition *Material Girls: Gender, Process and Abstract Art Since 1970*, at Gallery 128 in New York City [see fig. 3.2], and as an artist who has always engaged deeply with material as a bearer of content, I am a "material girl" in more ways than one. I welcomed the occasion to linger in this expansive territory, to "think long thoughts," as my writer friend Rebecca Solnit would say, and see how artists would interpret the conceptual theme of the exhibition.

"Material engagements"—two words intended to counter digital seamlessness. Two words that presume materials and their manner of manipulation and presentation not only function as carriers of meaning as much as image, sign, and symbol, but also imply an intentional use of materials for that purpose.

RedLine artists (resident artists with studios in the RedLine space) were encouraged to respond to this concept however they wished. I assumed that some would already be consciously working with materials as carriers of meaning or with notions of materialism and materiality—and that others would take the opportunity to make new work in response to the exhibition's concept. While I didn't intend the exhibition to reflect on or redefine the construction of "the West," I assumed that geography would inform some, but not all, of the work. What would RedLine artists come up with? I really didn't know.

Several months after the initial call to submit art, I made studio visits (twenty-seven in three days!) to talk with artists and see work they wanted me to consider for the exhibition. *Material Engagements* is the result.

The work engages a wide range of materials—natural, industrial, new, rescued, reclaimed, repurposed, and reperformed—utilized precisely because of their physical properties, histories, and associations: cloth, vinyl, bone, plaster, mattress covers, faux fur, clay, foam, flocking, money, eggs, oil paint, charcoal, graphite, found text, canvas, digital prints, blogs, discarded and recycled materials and objects (including old paintings and photographs), as well as thrift store and garage sale detritus reflecting on the waste of material culture and environmental concerns such as pollution and contamination.

The ways in which materials were manipulated also took on meaning: cutting, printing, casting, up/downloading, stacking, slashing, piecing, repeating, projecting, enlarging, performing, collecting, layering, padding, balancing, painting, stitching, arranging, ordering, lighting, draping, mangling, ironing, and staining.

Perhaps it was the theme, but surprisingly little media- or technology-based work was submitted, although many if not most artists used digital technologies as part of their artistic process. The same was true with totally conceptual, site-specific, or community-based creative projects. While RedLine artists may or may not be working in these areas (I really don't know), the work they submitted reflected studio-based practices. In that sense, the exhibition *Material Engagements* is reflective of RedLine more than Denver per se.

All art participates in multiple narratives. For this reason, I did not divide the exhibition into subthemes. The installation and my writing here are intended to create multiple "sightlines" and encourage a loose but dense web of conceptual threads and shared visual strategies, which emerged from the art itself. Individual pieces could just as easily have been repositioned with other works, resulting in different connections and conversations.

Material Engagements problematizes the notion of matter, questioning what constitutes material reality—normally considered to be "those objects and living organisms which physically occupy space and populate our environment." But what about light, shadow, language, consciousness, culture, memory, dreams, imagination, relationships, horizons—surely they exist, but where are they located? The blurred boundaries of matter and fugitive images of objects, bodies, landscapes, texts, and histories interrogate notions of reality and representation. [. . .]

Material Engagements both celebrates and critiques material wealth, acquisition, accumulation, collection, economies of exchange and consumption—the dream, the longing, the reward, the illusion, the material presence as proof of one's own existence. It asks, "What are the ways we produce, reproduce, and consume our material environment?" [. . .]

Material Engagements examines materiality and the indexical as articulations of agency. If we believe that matter is not inert, passive, static, or "subject to predictable causal forces," but rather lively and vibrant, and we believe in the interconnectedness and interdependency of all matter (whatever form it takes), then all things, including art and artists, have the possibility of equal agency, questioning the matter of nature, "the nature of matter, and the place of embodied humans within a material world."[2]

ED. NOTES

This curatorial essay for the *Material Engagements* exhibition, RedLine Contemporary Art Center, Denver, Colorado (2013), appears here for the first time in publication. It has been abridged for inclusion in this volume. The original version includes commentary on works by all twenty-seven contributing artists: Justin Beard, Terry Campbell, Beau Carey, Katie Caron, Jaime Carrejo, Serena Chopra, Theresa Clowes, Amber Cobb, Kevin Curry, Lanny DeVuono, Heather Doyle-Maier, Donald Fodness, Alvin P. Gregorio, Conor King, Bryan Leister, Laura Merage, Nikki Pike, Zach Reini, Gretchen Schaeffer, Dylan Scholinski, Sarah Wallace Scott, Laura Shill, Joel Swanson, Rebecca Vaughn, Derrick Velasquez, Chinn Wang, and Katie Watson.

1. See Dianna Coole and Samantha Frost, eds., *New Materialisms: Ontology, Agency, and Politics* (Durham, NC: Duke University Press, 2010); and Jane Bennett, *Vibrant Matter: A Political Ecology of Things* (Durham, NC: Duke University Press, 2010). Ideas, paraphrasing, and quotes are from these two volumes.

2. Coole and Frost, *New Materialisms*, 9.

Letter to Carey Lovelace, "Random Thoughts in Response to Your Questions"

(2014)

Was there a direct interrelationship between my *Bags*, Louise [Fishman] cutting up her canvases, and Patsy [Norvell] buying a sewing machine?

No, not direct relationship, but yes, indirect. The general climate of feminism, feminist art, and the conversations within our group were communal, collaborative, shared. We all talked about everything, tried everything—openly influenced each other! This was different than the prevailing male art world mode of "individualism," "ownership," or who did what first! It was exciting. The group's later decision to exhibit "as a group," versus as individual artists, at Nancy Hoffman Gallery in 1974, was to underscore the importance of feminist group process to the development of our work. Even though we primarily worked individually in our studios, it was not about individualism. (There were a few collaborations—I know Patsy and I had a short-lived one.)

Let me talk about the sewing machine first—as it is indicative of the times. . . .

Sewing Machine

I owned a sewing machine and could sew and tailor when I moved from Minneapolis to New York City [in] early fall 1969. However, feminism/feminist consciousness allowed me and other artists to bring these skills and tools into our art practice, to foreground and highlight them—to make them part of the content. Feminism said that women's experiences were important enough that they could be the subject of fine art.

At the time (late '60s and early '70s) women artists were acutely aware that they had to "look professional." The criteria for who was considered a serious artist were vastly different if you were a man or a woman. Women artists who had children or who made their art at home (in New York City this meant in an apartment) were immediately dismissed no matter what their art was like. Work that referenced the domestic environment, or women's creative traditions, or for that matter nonwhite male Euro-Western traditions was diminished, dismissed, or erased.

The fact is, there is a certain amount of preparing the studio when an artist (male or female) has a dealer, curator, art writer, or even another artist over for a studio visit. It depends on who is coming and what you want from the studio visit. How dirty, messy, or clean should the studio be? What do you leave out? Which tools? What source material? Unfinished and finished work? Old and new work? What is prominently displayed? How much process do you show? All artists do this [staging] either consciously or unconsciously. It's part of professional process and constructing a narrative.

Armed with feminist consciousness and analysis, feminist artists were more likely to not only use or buy a sewing machine but more importantly to defiantly leave it out where visitors could see it.

Influences on My Early Fabric Work—Specifically the *Bags*

My work with fabric initially grew out of my interest in the art, architecture, and artifacts of non-Western cultures, and was later informed by a feminist analysis that questioned white Western male definitions of art and art history.

Like many painters in the mid and late '60s, I had been making large, geometric hard-edged shaped acrylic canvases when I moved from Minneapolis to New York City in early fall 1969.

The summers before moving (in 1967 and 1969), I had traveled to Europe and North Africa, where I was introduced to the so-called primitive art of Africa, Oceania, and the Americas, as well as the decorative ornamentation of Islamic cultures in Spain and North Africa (seen in museums, galleries, markets, bazaars, books, and in-situ). [. . .]

The patterns I saw in beautifully crafted and decorated textiles were a huge influence—flat woven Caucasian rugs, Navajo blankets, Amish quilts, embroidery, beaded, feather, and quill work. Other influences: masks and fetishes from Africa, Mexico, etc., and tantric paintings. . . .

Looking at what people in other cultures made and how they made it opened up the idea of using/recycling/repurposing inexpensive found materials—human hair, mussel shells, raffia, straw, pine needles, rags, scraps of fabric, etc., in place of or in addition to fine art materials. Making something out of nothing, out of scraps and snippets . . . leftovers and hand-me-downs—materials and objects with previous histories of use (and sometimes function).

Once settled into my first studio loft at the corner of Spring and West Broadway, I began to make what we now would call pattern paintings. Often grid-based, or repetitive marks within the grid, occasionally pattern motifs appropriated/lifted from my sources of inspiration, isolated, combined differently, or shifted in scale, usually acrylic on paper—some varnished so they became tile-like.

I tried to translate these pattern paintings on paper to stretched canvases as if they were sketches for larger paintings—the scale I used to work on in Minneapolis—but they weren't as interesting. Something was lost. Decisions had to be made—one can't simply blow pattern units up in scale and assume they will be visually engaging. For example, I found that sometimes it was more interesting to keep the pattern unit the original small size and repeat it over and over to fill much larger space. [. . .] At the time, I didn't know of anyone else working with cross-culturally derived pattern, although in retrospect other artists were. I was simply working with "pattern and decoration" visually—not conceptually or politically as some "P&D artists" [Pattern and Decoration movement artists] did later on. It wasn't theorized.

I didn't continue to develop these pattern paintings and become part of the P&D movement, although some of my work hovered around the edges. Instead, pattern, weaving, and textiles, combined with a new understanding of sexual politics, led me to postmodern concerns with materials and process.

Feminist critique of art and art history to include non-Western creative practices and materials that had been marginalized by gender, race, class, culture, or nation . . . opened things up for me, and things were never the same. . . .

It was clear that materials and process are carriers of meaning as much as sign or symbol. This realization was major and continues to inform my art practice to this day, as well as how I look at other artists' work.

I began to question the presumed painting field with all its historical baggage and limitations. While a lot of artists at that time were experimenting with unstretched canvases, often hung informally with grommets, I began to paint on unstretched fabric versus canvas (most often curtains sewn together). These were simply tacked in the upper corners to the wall. I called these paintings "blanket paintings" because visually they reminded me of decorative "blankets" from other cultures, which functioned two-dimensionally like paintings. . . .

Gradually I began to attach torn strips of cloth (rags really) that had been dipped into acrylic [paint] (or occasionally dyed) to the flat surfaces. They hung down and functioned like three-dimensional brushstrokes, eventually taking over/covering the support. . . . The weight of these attached strips began to alter the painting rectangle—a prime example of materials and their properties along with process determining the artwork. At this time, I was gathering cloth from my women friends, so it became a way of literally including my life in my art, and of course I was aware of the associations to fabric/weaving and women's traditional arts. I was bringing gender to postminimal concerns with materials and process.

I moved off and out of the painting rectangle, which feminists considered a masculinist site. Louise [Fishman] cutting up her old canvases and attempting to reassemble them/tie them together on her gendered terms, to reinvent herself through her work . . . was an attempt to do the same, as were her later paintings on irregularly shaped scraps of wood and masonite (even circles!). We were all looking to intervene or abandon these art histories that historically had excluded us.

Eventually I used these acrylic-saturated strips of cloth to cover over old, no longer usable purses or bags (and once or twice even sewed a fabric bag with the intent of covering it over), the "bag" physically and conceptually becoming the ground. I was aware of many gendered associations: The bag is a container/vessel, a private place for women, as at that time not many men carried bags. Bag ladies we all fear we will become. Women are called old bags. Also, visually the *Bags* [1971; see fig. 1.2] called up bodies—depending upon their shape—shoulders, hips, torsos, faces. . . . It was more about referencing bags (or later rugs) rather than being bags or rugs. All these associations of materials, process, and in the case of the *Bags*, the bag itself as sign and symbol, circulated around the artworks, but it was never about "central core imagery."

In New York City we were all interested in gendered associations and readings of shapes—curves versus angles, circles being nonhierarchical (the proverbial feminist circle, etc.) but it was never theorized nor dogmatic like it was for Judy [Chicago] and many women working in Southern California—that was too simplistic. We were anarchistic, unruly, and all over the place. Also, unlike many of the California artists who were coming out as feminists and artists at the same time, most of [the] women in NYC already identified as artists and were now just discovering feminism. So there was a different kind of intellectual and creative base already in place.

In due course, the *Bags* came off the wall into space—became the usually larger-than-life-sized *Presences* [see plate 2]. It was important that they occupied, indeed took a space larger than the physical space they occupied. They were built up out of many layers of rags dipped in acrylic, attached to a clothes hangar that functioned as the armature—the piece itself was in the round but primarily two-sided like the body or garments; they hung from the ceiling with a visible rope. It was important that the bottom rags touched the ground. They were about "connecting," about building from the inside out, making a whole out of fragments, and a kind of power that comes from accumulation.

At some point, I began to use the end cuts of bolts of fabric (mostly knit) that I found in Lower Manhattan garment districts. My daughter and I would go dumpster diving for the fabric. These strips of industrial fabric were used to braid my *Floorpieces* [1973; see plate 4]. [. . .]

My use of human hair was part of a still-ongoing exploration of using body materials like hair and blood (always charged) versus materials such as paint, ink, straw, and thread that reference body materials. I used human hair early on, referencing the tradition of Victorian hair jewelry. Sometimes it mattered whose hair it was and how I got it—like in my tiny *Hair Bags* [1972–73; see plate 1], one for each woman in the group, displayed in my first A.I.R. exhibition along with baskets and sandals I wove—and sometimes it didn't. Sometimes hair was just used visually/formally—for example in *The Gift* [1992–93], recently exhibited [at] Alexander Gray Associates. I think my earliest use of hair was around 1971–72. A hair dress which I destroyed. I do still have a *Hair Blanket* [1971] from around that time—paint on a baby blanket with a fringe of human hair. Patsy began to work with human hair around this time as well, or perhaps a little bit later.

Other Group Activities

As you know, we were very protective of "our group"—we did not have a name. We defined ourselves as a CR [consciousness-raising] work/art group; we implemented the CR process of going around the room as a technique of critiquing our work. . . .

After original members Esther [Newton] and Shirley [Walton] left the group, we never took in new members. . . . Elizabeth [Weatherford], the one member who didn't have a visual art practice, was very engaged in the world of visual culture—both as a feminist anthropologist and writer setting up the earliest Native film festivals, etc., and lived downtown with her husband painter, Murray

Reich. She not only fit right in with the rest of us but brought a slightly different perspective. Other group activities included:

- While we shared information about exhibitions, groups, meetings, and political actions, some of us attended those actions or meetings as individuals.
- Patsy [Norvell], Louise [Fishman], and I collaboratively taught a class for women artists; we used this CR/critique from our group in our meetings with women students. . . . Each week we met in one of our lofts and talked about student work, suggested readings, etc., basically gave other women a new language by which to look at, talk about, and critique work. [. . .]
- In addition to the big Nancy Hoffman Gallery show, which you know about, we did exhibit once or twice as a group in small shows in college galleries or were on panels together in such contexts . . . Sarah Lawrence? Vassar?
- The group wrote a reference letter for me when I was applying for one of those Radcliffe residency fellowships (I didn't get it).
- Just for fun (and somewhat in anger, as to how overqualified we were), we once compiled a group bio or CV, listing all those years of education, lessons, therapies, exhibitions, etc.
- Patsy and Sarah [Draney] often got a summer place upstate; we would all go visit during the summer.
- I taught T'ai-chi Ch'uan women's classes in my loft on the Bowery (about the time I made a videotape on women in the martial arts with Jean Mundy). I also cotaught a women's aikido class with Sybille Hahn. We trained in different lofts (I think there was a women's martial arts space in Tribeca we used a few times). Everyone in the group signed up began to take the aikido classes at the same time. . . . Unfortunately, it didn't last for long.

Carrie, I am sure this is far more than you ever wanted to know, but there is so much detailed history; unfortunately everyone just repeats the same old same old simplistic feminist history (a new litany) when there are MANY nuanced, layered histories, many feminist arts as there are many feminisms. . . . I hope this is helpful . . . as you write YOUR HISTORY.

ED. NOTE

This is a slightly edited and abridged version of Hammond's letter in response to a research request by Carey Lovelace, 2014.

Letter to Sue Heinemann, "Some Thoughts on the Heresies Collective"

(2014)

The most radical aspect of *Heresies: A Feminist Publication on Art and Politics* was its unique collective structure. The founding collective (self-selected over half a dozen meetings or so from an initial call to feminists to counter mid-'70s apathy in the art world, which resulted in identifying the needs for a "voice," which became *Heresies*, and an educational "space," which eventually evolved into the New York Feminist Art Institute) became the "mother collective" [see fig. 1.3]. We collectively determined the journal's name, focus, mission or initial statement, policy, structure, and basic format; chose issue themes; and handled the distribution, fundraising, promotion, and ongoing business aspects of publishing a journal. The women who attended [the] first meetings had a range of needs and agendas, and the profiles of the members of the self-selected "mother collective" [were] diverse in terms of vocation, politics/political experience, age, class, and sexuality. What we shared was a basic commitment to devote time and energy to the collective process necessary to produce and distribute the journal.

Because this required physical meetings (pre-internet), the founding/mother collective was New York City based.

Through a process of discussion and debate, the "mother collective" determined themes for individual issues (for the most part, the early issues came from our personal interests—for example, an issue on lesbian art and artists would never have been Issue #3 if Marty [Pottenger] and I hadn't been part of the mother collective), and the order in which they would be published. Each theme-based issue then had its own editorial board composed of at least two members of the *Heresies* mother collective (to be a link between the mother and issue collectives and so the "how to do it" wheel wasn't constantly being reinvented—though it often seemed like it was) and anyone else who wanted to work on that issue.

Once a thematic issue was determined, a call went out—mostly via personal feminist art networks or flyers to appropriate groups and organizations, inviting women who were interested in working on a particular issue to come to the first editorial meeting. This also became the first call for material that might be included in that issue. (All pre-internet.) These were passionate times, when everything mattered and we strongly believed we could affect change (if not revolution). Bonding through work. It was blood, sweat, and tears, as well as the joy of working together toward a common goal (publication of that issue). As an issue developed, there were frequent disagreements/arguments/splits between the issue collective and the mother collective, or within the issue collective itself. The important role of EDITORIAL STATEMENTS cannot be overemphasized.

Herein [lay] the radicality of *Heresies*, as the politics, views, or opinions of the issue editors (who themselves did not necessarily agree or align) might and often DID DIFFER from those already politically and aesthetically diverse members of the mother collective. This raised a critical concern: IF INDEED *HERESIES* WAS A FORUM FOR DISCUSSION AND DEBATE AROUND FEMINISM(S), ART(S), AND POLITIC(S), WERE WE WILLING TO PUBLISH (DEVOTE TIME, MONEY, SPACE, AND NAME/FORUM) A WHOLE JOURNAL ISSUE ON IDEAS THAT WE DISAGREED WITH, OR EVEN THOUGHT WERE POLITICALLY DANGEROUS? THE SAME WAS TRUE WITH THE CONTENT OF INDIVIDUAL ARTICLES/INTERVIEWS/VISUAL IMAGES that we individually may not have liked or may even have found offensive, politically incorrect, or dangerous . . . (Sex Issue, Goddess Issue, and Lesbian Issue . . .). Given the power of publication, how far were we willing to go in the name of discourse—to walk the talk of diversity, discussion, debate, disagreement? Was there a line, and, if so, where was it?

Any self-identified feminist (woman) could participate in *Heresies*. It was open to everyone. Women could participate in multiple ways (requiring different time and energy commitments): mother collective, individual issue collectives, submitting preexisting material for consideration, making/doing work for [a] specific issue such as interview gathering of statements and images, etc., for an article, graphic design and production, fundraising.

I myself was a founding member; worked on the editorial collectives for Issues #1, #3, and #9; contributed articles and images to many more issues; and was the first office manager at the Spring and Lafayette bank building office, and hired Sandy de Sando and Alesia Kunz to assist (they eventually took over the admin jobs).

This "open structure" and dedication to "diversity" of thought/feminist politics/aesthetics is what made *Heresies* so rich and exciting—however, it also left us wide open to possibilities of "infiltration" (not impossible given the journal's strong leftist leanings and the political background of some of its members) or the occasional dysfunctional person.

Unlike *Chrysalis* (our West Coast sister publication), *Heresies* did not have a consistent design, or, for that matter, a head graphic designer. Instead, the design varied with each issue, to reflect the theme of that issue. It was conceived by a combination of women working on the specific thematic issue, in collaboration with members of the mother collective who had graphic skills (or not, many of us learned!), or sometimes with women who volunteered to work on the design and production aspects of the journal (Cindy Carr, Sue Heinemann, Amy Sillman, Su Friedrich, Janet Froelich, among others).

It was assumed (and encouraged) that each issue's cover would reflect the theme for that issue. The one design decision that was made by the mother collective was consistent formatting/size so that, down the line, issues could be collected and easily bound in libraries (unlike, say, *LTTR*, also a collective journal, and some would say heir to *Heresies*—where each issue had an entirely new and creative format).

The founding collective made a commitment that visual and textual material would be equal. While there were portfolio pages, early page artwork such as that by May Stevens, and cover and interior graphic design varied from issue to issue, we were not entirely successful in this endeavor as text remained privileged with visual images primarily illustrating articles. Look at the role text played on the covers! The mother collective bent over backward to NOT feature/market work by individual artists or writers (and certainly not of the collective), so issue covers tended to be text based or use historical images; however, individual aesthetics still asserted themselves—usually unintentionally (such as Pat Steir's beautiful script on the cover of Issue #2). I still have a visual shock/body response when I look at the cover of Issue #9, "Women Organized/Women Divided," as it is "my hand" that made the lettering and drew the cover diagram [see fig. 2.4].

The founding *Heresies* collective was determinedly anti-individual/antimarketing.

There would be no advertising (unlike *Chrysalis*, which advertised cultural feminist products, organizations, events, etc.). The only ads were "exchange ads" with simpatico presses and publications.

ED. NOTE

Hammond shared with Sue Heinemann "Some Thoughts on the Heresies Collective" in a letter dated September 20, 2014, in response to a research request. This is a lightly edited version of the letter.

Conversation with Ulrike Müller

Pink Labor on Golden Streets (2015)

ULRIKE MÜLLER: I've been thinking about how to approach this conversation about "queer abstraction," and I would like to keep it close to home: I am most interested in questions regarding the work that we make as painters and then, in extension, how the paintings exist in the world, how they are looked at and talked about. The studio part seems both simple and complicated, concerning ideas, processes, and decisions that are direct and others that are at odds with language. I'm proposing to have this conversation from an artist's perspective. What do you think?

HARMONY HAMMOND: I like your idea of staying close to our work and visual practices. I think this current interest in what is being called "queer abstraction" is part of the renewed engagement with abstraction in general (because there isn't the political urgency that there was in the late 1980s and 1990s as we all struggled with AIDS and censorship issues) but must be read against the postmodern emphasis on representation and identity-based politics.

In the late 1980s and 1990s, it was widely assumed that content addressing issues of identity was based in representation, and that representation was about depiction/picturing/the gaze (the dynamics of who is looking at who and from where)—the focus was based on the "figure" as a "representation" of the queer body and therefore the narrative of marginalized bodies. While the postmodern lens of representation is surely a helpful lens, it did not address abstract work or even that work positioned along a continuum between representation and abstraction. Work conceptually presencing gendered and sexed bodies through materials and process was missed or dismissed.

As an artist who works out of an awareness that my chosen materials (including but not limited to oil on canvas, metal, fabric, rubber latex, straw, blood, hair) and the way I physically engage with them carries meaning (that is, they have agency), I find this position limited and "lacking." In fact, the very heightened indeterminacy of abstract painting can be thought of as a queer space. I am interested in "the body" versus "the figure" that is defined by its contour. Abstraction allows me to engage "the body" as a social political site as well as the "painting body" (both the physical painting and the artist who makes the painting). To borrow from Foucault, abstraction like queerness offers a space of infinite and pleasurable possibilities.[1]

MÜLLER: I'm afraid I don't share this positive outlook. I have become increasingly irritated by how an idea of "abstraction" as soon as it is qualified as "queer" seems to fall back into iconography, and by the readings this produces in relation to my work. I would hate it if my work became "about" any one thing and that thing could be spelled out in language. For example, there are many round shapes in my paintings, and they are used in different, and I believe, specific ways. The circles have to do with familiarity—with the scale of things we handle in our everyday lives. I make decisions based on formal relationships, not with the intent to illustrate or depict. I work with and against symmetry, with and against such limitations as format, verticality, a central splitting, and the confines of the support. Somehow an idea of sexualized round body parts has been projected onto these circles. I actually remember the first instance this happened; I cringed but told myself that it was fine as long as it was clear this was one reading of several. Now, when my work is viewed through the lens of queerness and abstraction this gets reiterated to the point that I actually feel like I want to put my foot down, and say NO!! This tits-and-balls reading of my work is neither very sexy, nor helping the work or me as I try to make it. I want so much more than this—a better sexiness—but also to think harder, feel deeper, and see differently. I can see how the desire for intensity that I'm voicing here is indebted to affect theory and queer studies, and I appreciate the work of the writers and thinkers that cross over, reach out, and contribute to the project of bringing language to modes of making art and working with form that have a tenuous relation to words. But sometimes a circle is just a circle.

Of course I'm being polemic, but maybe what it boils down to is that art is a place where identity labels ultimately are not helpful. I know that the term queer once held the promise of being a political category not defined by any one identity, but I must say I lost my trust in that. Labels like "woman artist" or "queer artist" seem to belittle and reassert marginality. I think that we've come far enough as feminists and as artists to consider statements by artists, who also were women, and who reject gender as the basis for their studio work and therefore might have been considered antifeminist at the time. Artists, who consciously strive to separate themselves from their femininity (Anne Truitt), work from a hermaphroditic place (Bridget Riley), or bluntly claim that "art exists sans gender, race, religion" (Jo Baer). I'm with Baer when she claims that this is "in fact, one of the best reasons for making art."[2] I've said before that the person at work in my studio is not a "woman artist," that in my experience in moments of creative absorption the pressures of gender and other social norms are temporarily suspended. This is a space that I want to protect, and that I'm ready to defend if need be.

HAMMOND: I too do not wish to be confined by labels, however, I find they can be useful at times, albeit minimally (providing some sort of historic/political/aesthetic orientation), as long as I continue to redefine and articulate those labels on my own terms in various locations of time and space—in other words, they are only a box if you let them be so. (I've probably paid a price for this.) Given the historical erasure, the issue is how to not avoid, erase, disregard, or minimize the experiences of women and queers, yet at the same time not overemphasize or make these experiences into more than what they are—especially in relationship to the art we make.

With rare exceptions (that work made in response to a particular event), I do not think about making feminist, lesbian, or queer art when I go into the studio. Nor, for that matter, do I think about abstraction, although I've always been interested in the various ways content can be engaged in abstraction. For better or worse, I am a "material girl." My job is to listen and tease meaning out of the materials—their histories, manipulation, combination, and presentation. It's actually a very open sensuous space that I rather enjoy.

But to go back to the issue of labels, clustering works under any rubric such as "painting," "abstract," "monochrome," "modernist," "formalist, "feminist," "queer," etc., allows us to examine sameness and difference without eliminating either. Like I've said many times, all art participates in multiple narratives. Certainly mine does. It can be discussed in relation to any and all of these categories in terms of how it responds to, participates in, interrupts, and/or resists those narratives. Hopefully, this is what makes the work layered and rich.

MÜLLER: In a continued attempt to sort out my terms I have been more interested in form than in abstraction, and more drawn to thinking about figuration than about bodies. Over the past few years it has been productive—and fun!—to try and rethink both form and figuration in dynamic, relational ways. It helps me in calibrating a place for my work where exactitude and openness coexist.

HAMMOND: Can you be a bit more precise?

MÜLLER: In *The Life of Forms in Art* [1989], a book that's pretty old by now and that I have been dragging around for a couple of years, Henri Focillon defines form as not primarily line and color, but rather the "dynamic organization that brings into play the concrete texture of the world as the sum of the body's reactions to that which surrounds it."[3] And the art historian Kerstin Stakemeier suggested after a recent studio visit that the movement in my work isn't as much an abstraction from something concrete (e.g., Mondrian's cow), but might have to be thought of rather as moving "toward." This sounds right to me, and I think that in those movements toward something not yet defined the concrete textures of the world, the sum of the body's reactions, as well as the specific constellations of objects and people, are crucially important.

HAMMOND: How are the forms in your enamel paintings determined? How do you make them? How do they perform?

MÜLLER: For me it seems really important to be able to surprise myself, to look at something that I made and realize that it isn't something that I could consciously construct. In a way I'm trying to push beyond myself, and maybe that is another reason why I resist the label queer for my work—it makes it too much about myself, or about myself in the wrong way.

Since we're talking about the round shapes already, it might be helpful to say that I do not use a compass but rather trace all these circles from round objects. It started with rolls of tape, my water glass, things that I had on my studio table, and now I have a small collection of round things in the studio. It seems to make a difference for those shapes to quite literally be the shadows or footprints of objects.

HAMMOND: I think my favorites are what I am going to call the "scallop paintings." They are both decorative and toothy-edged. Flirtatious. They present positive and negative spaces as equals.

MÜLLER: Funny, I also call those shapes scallops. The larger ones are traced from yogurt cups, the small ones from coins such as pennies or quarters.

HAMMOND: Well, I bring my gendered body to the reading of your work! In many of your enameled paintings the forms initially feel like familiar body parts but refuse to read as such, which is why I like what arts writer Aruna D'Souza says about these paintings—that "the body is everywhere and nowhere."[4] I don't know what you think about her observation, but it rings true for me. At the same time, however, I am semiconsciously noting how your forms relate to each other and the edges of the painting: Do they touch or not, and what is the tension of almost touching? I am interested in how your forms often appear to be flipped, one side the mirror image of the other, except there are calculated differences (sameness and difference again—surely we might consider that lesbian or queer!), and how your forms translate across materials—oil paint on linen, enameled metal, quilts, woven textiles—to expand the painting field, calling up formalist painting but also cloisonné jewelry, craft kits, signage, fashion, home craft decor items—high art and objects that might be sold in a women's bookstore.

MÜLLER: Yes, I guess I can get behind the idea of one's body being "everywhere and nowhere" at the same time. But I also think that around the work I made for my first gallery show in New York about a year and a half ago I started to trust that because of decisions having to do with scale and material and specific formal ideas, body-ness would just be there anyway. I realized I didn't need to worry about it. That actually freed me up a lot and moved me deeper into an actual painting space, which is where I want to be.

I had this realization sometime last year that really I'm a non-antipainter, which means I am moving toward painting in a particular roundabout way that feels a lot like math, when two negatives make a positive. And I look to you as someone who inhabits that space that I circle, someone who has a deeply painterly, material practice.

Reading your manifesto on the "near-monochrome,"[5] I was struck by how you stack up adjectives to describe your paintings and their surfaces. They appear in groups and accumulate in a very particular way across your text. For the sake of argument, I'm going to list only the positively descriptive terms (and leave out the instances where you distinguish your paintings by saying what they are not). Here we go, in order of appearance: large, thickly painted, near-monochrome; formal, frontal, condensed; layered, built from the inside out; blotchy, encrusted, both matte and gloss, simultaneously elegant, raw, crude—definitely handmade; burnt, weathered, patinated; hidden, revealed, buried, muffled, pushing up from underneath.

HAMMOND: Hmmm. Your observation is interesting. I use adjectives to physically describe the paintings, to say what they are and what they aren't, to acknowledge the ways in which they participate in the narrative of the modernist painting field at the same time listing specific qualities that interrupt, resist, or refuse that territory, to say how they materially and conceptually occupy space, to stake out a claim on my terms.

The manifesto was initially written as an attempt to describe what was going on in my paintings—especially the dark blue almost black paintings from 2004 to 2009, where despite the thick paint, color and surface are elusive, or to use my word "fugitive" (in all its outlaw meanings). While the paintings don't "look queer"—whatever that means—we could say they perform queerly. From a distance they appear to be monochrome but up close one sees that other colors show through. Accumulation and layering are extremely important—what is buried, hidden, or muffled—pushing up and asserting itself from inside or underneath—the painting surface under stress. The paintings are "near-monochrome," almost but not quite monochrome, becoming or unbecoming monochrome.

I first used these words "becoming" and "unbecoming" in my manifesto to describe the unfixed state of my paintings as material objects. Art historian Tirza True Latimer then situated my words in relation to Deleuze and Guattari's concepts of becoming and unbecoming, where, to quote Latimer, "becoming something different always requires unbecoming that which came before. Deleuze and Guattari use the term 'becoming' to describe an evolutionary dynamic where unbecoming is an integral part of becoming."[6] As Latimer points out, "Unbecoming resists continuity, unity, coherence. [. . .] Becoming reassembles, resignifies. Because of this give and take, becoming can never be absolutely definitive; it engages perpetually in its own reconception."[7] While I wasn't aware of Deleuze and Guattari's concepts when I began these paintings, they feel totally on the mark. The art came first—the theory after.

MÜLLER: I can see that layering is crucial to what you do. My work is slow also, but the process tends to disappear along the way. The enamel paintings are based on to-scale drawings that are premised on a searching movement and repetition. Sometimes I will get an image right quickly, but often I redo a drawing several times until it reaches the place where I want it to be. Working from these drawings as templates, I think of enamel, weaving, and printing as fixing techniques. They move the work away from my hand, without however removing the notion of hand or of touch. And they freeze the form—the drawing would smudge if you touched it, the enamel painting, rug, or lithograph won't—which together with the distancing of the reproductive technique seems to more firmly establish the kind of interior instability/uncertainty and movement that I am looking for in my images.

HAMMOND: My work is the opposite. Despite the materiality of thick textured paint, many of my paintings have this unfixed fugitive quality due to the dark colors I use, how paint is applied, and the way light hits the surface of the brush-strokes. It's not that the surface dematerializes, but it looks almost metallic—you can't quite locate what is happening. Indexicality is important. Lumps, bumps, patches, scars, seams, and connecting strategies are intentionally left visible.

MÜLLER: Would it be fair to say that the organizing principle for you is accumulation, and for me it is editing? Maybe this is why I have had to start this conversation by saying no so vehemently! But, seriously, I have been thinking about negation, as a way of not simply rejecting an idea or concept but rather saying "not like this." In his short essay on "Negation,"[8] Freud says that our sense of judgment has to make two principal determinations: one is whether to grant reality to an idea or imagined thing, the other is to acknowledge or disallow a quality in a thing. We decide what to ingest or what to spit out, and by doing so delimit where inner and outer realities touch. This then could mean that for a woman-identified artist to say that her work is not about gender would be deeply critical of the qualities commonly identified with femininity, which I would argue is a feminist stance.

HAMMOND: This sounds somewhat similar to Deleuze and Guattari's concept of becoming and unbecoming.

MÜLLER: I think I know what you mean. I also wanted to ask how you think about bodies in relation to your work? One thing that I've noticed is the verticality of the support and the horizontality of the straps. Is your painting body always a bound body? A held body? What holds bodies in their place socially, emotionally, economically?

HAMMOND: I prefer the orientation of vertical rectangles because they indirectly reference the body. But people focus too much on the straps. While they certainly circulate around the paintings, I get annoyed by readings that reduce the work to binding/bondage/bandage associations. The meaning is much more complex and nuanced than that.

The restrictions aren't there as much as we perceive them to be. The grommeted straps simply provide the illusion of constriction or tying down. They really aren't all that tight. Despite being affixed to the surface, they are fairly loose—somewhat temporal or provisional. They provide possibilities of connection. If you look carefully, it is not the straps but the paint and the act of painting that hold the painting object and, therefore, the "painting body" together.

Currently, I am more interested in the grommeted holes in and of themselves rather than the straps. They literally open up the painting space, alluding to what is underneath the surface, at the same time they reference body orifices. No longer found only on the straps, the reinforced holes seem to take on a new and different visual and conceptual function that I am still trying to figure out. Frankly, I am not sure if these new paintings perform queerly—it's just not what I think about while working.

MÜLLER: Ha! Now you're resisting the iconographic pin-down! I can't say I don't like that.

ED. NOTE

The original publication bears the title "Editors and Fugitives: Harmony Hammond in Conversation with Ulrike Müller." It was published in *Pink Labor on Golden Streets*, ed. Christiane Erharter, Dietmar Schwärzler, Ruby Sircar, and Hans Scheirl Publication Series of the Academy of Fine Arts, Vienna, vol. 17 (Vienna: Academy of Fine Arts; London: Sternberg Press, 2015), 150–61. Reprint courtesy of Academy of Fine Arts, Vienna, Sternberg Press, London, and Ulrike Müller.

The numbered endnotes for this essay, below, are by Harmony Hammond and Ulrike Müller.

NOTES

1. [See] Bob Gallagher and Alexander Wilson in conversation with Michel Foucault, "Sex, Power, and the Politics of Identity." This essay first appeared in *The Advocate* 400 (August 7, 1984): 26–30, 58. It has been reprinted in several anthologies, including *Gay Spirit: Myth and Meaning*, ed. Mark Thompson (New York: St. Martin's, 1987), 25–35, https://archive.org/details/gayspiritmythmeathom.

2. Jo Baer, "Unused Statement: American Woman Artist, 1971," in *Broadsides and Belles Lettres: Selected Writings and Interviews 1965–2010*, ed. Roel Arkesteijn (Amsterdam: Roma, 2010), 70.

3. Henri Focillon cited in Jean Molino, introduction to *The Life of Forms in Art* by Henri Focillon, trans. George Kubler (New York: Zone Books, 1989), 17. The original edition, *Vie des Formes*, was released in 1934.

4. Aruna D'Souza, "Ulrike Müller's Feminist Forms," in *Franza, Fever 103, and Quilts*, ed. Achim Hochdörfer and Barbara Schröder (New York: Dancing Fox Press, 2012), 41.

5. Harmony Hammond, "A Manifesto (Personal) of Monochrome (Sort Of)," in *Harmony Hammond: Becoming/UnBecoming Monochrome* (Denver: RedLine Contemporary Art Center, 2014), 3–4.

6. Tirza True Latimer, "Harmony Hammond: Becoming/UnBecoming Monochrome," in *Harmony Hammond: Becoming/UnBecoming Monochrome*, 26. As referred to Gilles Deleuze and Félix Guattari, *A Thousand Plateaus* (1980), trans. Brian Massumi (Minneapolis: University of Minnesota Press, 1987).

7. Latimer, "Harmony Hammond," 26.

8. Sigmund Freud, "Die Verneinung" (1925), in *Psychologie des Unbewußten 2, Studienausgabe*, ed. Alexander Mitscherlich, Angela Richards, and James Strachey (Frankfurt am Main: Fischer Taschenbuch Verlag, 2000), 371–77.

Interview with Clarity Haynes

Hyperallergic (2016)

CLARITY HAYNES: In your 2010 pronouncement, "A Manifesto (Personal) of Monochrome (Sort Of)," reprinted in the Alexander Gray Associates 2016 exhibition catalogue, you explicitly declare that your paintings "perform queerly." I'm intrigued. How exactly do they do this?

HARMONY HAMMOND: I was referring to the fugitive aspect of the dark blue/black paintings from 2009 to 2013, the indeterminacy. Despite the materiality of thick paint, you can't quite locate color, surface, or space. Is it blue? Black? Metallic? Color shifts, at times appearing burnished or iridescent. In their refusal to be any one color, the paintings can be seen to occupy some sort of fugitive or outlaw space that rejects the narrative of monochrome painting at the same time it refuses to look stereotypically queer. Thus we can say the paintings perform queerly.

HAYNES: Can you tell us something about your working process?

HAMMOND: It is not clear how the paintings are made, but there are no tricks. They are simply painted. I apply brushstrokes in multiple directions, so that light hitting the ridges or marks made by the brush in the paint, causes some areas to read matte and some glossy. Patchy. These intentional irregularities—activating, agitating, or upsetting the surface—mirror the imperfections and experiences writ upon our bodies. With the new paintings, content continues to emerge from the paint application. The surface texture of each painting is different, but there is a focus on how under-colors are revealed or push up from beneath and through the grommeted holes, disrupting what at first glance appears to be a minimalist monochrome grid painting.

HAYNES: That makes sense. The active surface is very apparent in the works in your upcoming show. In *Things Various* [2015], the surface is brushy, choppy, agitated. I love this piece. It feels less contained than other works, almost as if it is coming apart.

HAMMOND: I don't think it is less contained, but it is more open than previous wrapped paintings. The surface is similar to earlier works, but there are fewer straps. The straps and ropes hang open; they are not tied up tight or blocking the viewer's visual entrance into the painting space. The tracks of previous straps no longer needed are left like scars in the skin of paint; the painting holds itself together. The materiality of the paint has agency. It is the paint, not the straps, that holds the painting body together.

The only painting in the exhibition that slightly suggests the possibility of coming apart is *Bandaged Grid #1* [2015; see plate 23]. Its fraying strips of leftover canvas applied like bandages to the grid of grommeted holes—suggesting bodily wounds but also an interruption of the narrative of the grid in modernist painting, and therefore an interruption of utopian egalitarian order. A precarity. The strips and the paint functioning as poultice also suggest possibilities of holding together, of healing.

HAYNES: You draw such attention to the paintings as objects, yet there seem to be fewer openly sculptural elements in this show, compared to your last show. Could you say a few words about your relationship with painting, sculpture, and hybrids of the two?

HAMMOND: While their objectness and physical presence are emphasized (they occupy a space larger than their physical space), the paintings in this show are not sculptures. They engage with the history of painting, not the history of sculpture.

Most of my work over the years, at least going back to the fabric pieces of the early 1970s, occupies and negotiates a space between traditional painting and traditional sculpture. A third space. Think of my *Floorpieces* [1973; see plate 4], which question assumptions about the "place of painting," or the installational mixed-media paintings of the late '80s and early '90s that sit on the floor and lean against the wall with objects attached or sitting in front as part of the painting. While it is not predetermined, it seems that this is what I do, this is where I hang out. Since I am trained as a painter, I think of this work as "expanded painting" (painting being "additive" by nature) rather than "painterly sculpture." Even the grommeted holes in the recent grid paintings are partially made by layering or building up canvas and surface versus, say, the slash or puncture of [Lucio] Fontana. In this way they are more connected to the material buildup of [Lee] Bontecou or [Alberto] Burri.

It is true that there are less sculptural elements in many of the paintings in this exhibition than in my previous show. Or put it this way, the sculptural elements changed as my conceptual interest shifted from surface, to the underside, the space not usually seen (unless it asserts itself or is exposed). Sculptural or relief elements such as straps, flaps, and pushpins that extend the painting surface out into the world are in conversation with the holes or orifices and the secret, buried, or muffled spaces below. In this way, the painting surface is physically and conceptually extended in both directions.

HAYNES: You've been such an influential force in the art world. Who has influenced you? Who would you describe as your main influences? Are there any names that we would find surprising?

HAMMOND: In their engagement with quotidian materials, physicality, seams showing (what Robert Storr calls "painting roughed-up"), the paintings are in conversation with a wide range of works. They occupy a space somewhere in between the early quilts of Gee's Bend and the work of [Eva] Hesse, [Robert] Rauschenberg, [Lee] Bontecou, [Alberto] Burri, [Salvatore] Scarpitta, [Piero] Manzoni, even perhaps, [Robert] Ryman, [Brice] Marden, and [Milton] Resnick. They share more with these artists than "monochrome" painters such as [Kazimir] Malevitch, [Ellsworth] Kelly, [John] McCracken, [Marcia] Hafif, [Ad] Reinhardt, etc. That said, I rarely think about other artists and their work while I am painting—nor do I think about feminism, queer abstraction, or even abstraction for that matter. I simply engage with materials. My job is to pull meaning out of the materials.

There are a few exceptions, however. Sometimes a painting I am working on reminds me of the work of another artist, or even my own earlier work. An example would be the painting *Red Bed* [2011; see plate 20], which was in my 2013 exhibition at Alexander Gray Associates. As I was working on the painting in

2011, I became aware of its reference to Rauschenberg's series of red paintings, and, because of its single bed size and the manner in which it insists upon the upright flatbed picture plane, his famous *Bed* painting of 1955, which was a huge influence on me when I was an art student in the '60s. On one level, my painting became an homage to early Rauschenberg. At the same time, it was strangely familiar in a different way. It took a while before I realized that I was, with *Red Bed*, repeating many of the visual strategies from my own *Red Blanket* paintings of 1971: near-monochrome, pieced and patched with seams showing, strings hanging down, occupying a space between painting and sculpture (only now the canvas is stretched).

HAYNES: It seems like each body of work pushes you toward something slightly new and different, while also echoing or circling back to previous work at times. Would you agree?

HAMMOND: While I don't consciously try to reference my earlier work, it does happen occasionally. I find that, like most artists, I tend to repeat certain formal strategies, especially in relation to the body. There is a kind of larger flow or cycle to my visual practice. With each "new body" of work, I gradually condense it down in terms of form and content. It becomes more minimal and refined but still with an edge of content not usually associated with monochrome painting. Then, at some point, unconsciously I begin to "rough it up," letting the paintings be more physical or muscular—even crude, awkward, adolescent. Looser. Less controlled. *Bandaged Grid #1* [see plate 23], the most recent painting in the show, is going in this latter direction. Work grows out of work. It is process-based; I don't make sketches. I have learned how to listen, and I have developed a criticality, and therefore intentionality. After all these years of painting, I trust where the process takes me.

ED. NOTE

This interview with Clarity Haynes appeared with the title "Queering Abstract Art with Wrapped, Grommeted, and 'Roughed-Up' Paintings," in *Hyperallergic*, May 12, 2016, https://hyperallergic.com/298095/queering-abstract-art-with-wrapped-grommeted-and-roughed-up-paintings/.

Interview with Phillip Griffith

Brooklyn Rail (2016)

PHILLIP GRIFFITH: Your paintings from the new exhibition [at Alexander Gray Associates, May 19–June 25, 2016] seem appreciably different than the wrapped paintings included in your 2013 show with Alexander Gray.

HARMONY HAMMOND: Well, *Things Various* (2015), the earliest painting in the current exhibition, segues from the 2013 work. The visual vocabulary of grommeted straps—sometimes tied together, sometimes not—attached to the thick paint surface with pigment-covered pushpins, is the same. Only in *Things Various*, most of the straps hang open, untied, suggesting only the potential of connection or restraint.

The new paintings continue to emphasize the material engagement of paint, but differ from the earlier work through the use of the grommeted grid as a disruptive visual strategy and the shift to what is going on beneath/below/under what we perceive as the painting surface. They ask, where is the painting located?

GRIFFITH: Can you tell me where your materials and process came from?

HAMMOND: I provided a text for the exhibition catalogue that repeats part of "A Manifesto (Personal) of Monochrome (Sort Of)," written in 2010, in order to situate the new work in relation to my ongoing concerns with the body and the painting body (meaning both the person who makes the painting and the painting object itself). The catalogue text, however, goes on to discuss the work in expanded terms. For example, many of my near-monochrome paintings include or are painted on repurposed canvas that was originally used to cover the woven tatami mats used in aikido, the Japanese martial art I studied for thirty-six years. Long, six- to eight-foot-wide strips of canvas are sewn together to form a rectangular cover for the tatami mats that in turn cover the dojo floor. Over time, these mat covers wear out and need to be replaced. The old covers, charged with repeated body contact—including my body—were given to me; I have used them as the support in some of the earlier paintings, such as *Muffle* (2009) [see plate 19] and *Flap* (2008–11), as well as in *Witness* (2014), *Naples Grid* (2015), and *Bandaged Grid #1* (2015) [see plate 23], all paintings included in this show.

Connecting strategies such as seams, patches, straps, and flaps, created on the back when two pieces of canvas are stitched together, are left showing. The grommets were initially found in the hems of the canvas mat covers. I had cut the hems off, eventually using them as straps, but soon ran out and started sewing my own straps and grommeting them. In my most recent work, the grommets have jumped off the straps and appear as a gridded field with underlayers of paint asserting themselves up through the holes, suggesting agency and voice—a rupture from underneath, from what has been muffled, covered up or over.

GRIFFITH: I love the casual, almost vernacular, "sort of" in the title of your manifesto for your near-monochrome style. It leaves an offhanded but decisive crack in the self-certainty of the manifesto form.

HAMMOND: Yes, the title is a "crack," an opening. The crack assumes an audience.

GRIFFITH: Your account of the canvas from the tatami mats, as well as your manifesto, describe the relationship of the painter's body to the body of the artwork. It seems to me there is another body present before the painting: the viewer's. Can the viewer have a painting body, too, through the act of looking at the work?

HAMMOND: [. . .] The cracks in the painting surface under stress are one way the viewer enters in, as are the grommeted holes, which act as body orifices. That said, your suggestion regarding the possibility of the viewer also having a painting body is something I have to give thought to. The viewer does exist, is there, but I don't usually focus on their presence. An exception would be my digital print *A Queer Reader* (2003) [see fig. 5.7], which, through the cut/opening/gap, intentionally includes the viewer as reader. At the same time, I believe that if the work is "honest"—a loaded word, I know—the viewer will get it, at least on some level. I have always been interested in what I call "felt content," in other words, content that is felt on and in the viewer's body before it is conceptually translated. The paint treated as a material like any other has agency, the potential to engage through the body. [. . .]

GRIFFITH: Cracks on the surface contribute great pleasure to the experience of looking at your paintings and grommetypes. Your earlier wrapped works, like *Hunkertime* (1979–80) [see plate 11], evoke care and protection, but these near-monochromes privilege cracks, tears, and fissures in the painting's "skin," as you put it. How do you think about violence and force in tandem with care and protection?

HAMMOND: Cracks are not always violent. Cracks can give pleasure. That said, there is a discussion to be had about a subtext of violence in my work. I myself am aware of it, but have not pursued thinking about it in depth. The rupture of the bullet holes in the horse skull of *Meditation* (2001–2) or the grid of metal buckets previously used for target practice in *Untitled (buckets)* (1995) [see plate 13], come to mind, as does the large mixed-media installation painting *Inappropriate Longings* (1992) [see plate 16], which has the words "goddamn dyke" incised into the skin-like latex rubber, interrupting the presumed heteronormativity of both rural America and the modernist painting field. I could go on, and of course, this subtext is present in many of the near-monochromes when seen up close.

I agree that the wrapped paintings are different than the wrapped sculptures. The discussion of the straps intentionally wrapped around the sides of most of the near-monochrome paintings is usually focused on notions of restraint and constraint—of bandaging, binding, and bondage. Those ideas and references do circulate around the paintings, however the straps can also be thought to embrace the painting body, to protect rather than restrict it. In the most recent grid paintings, there are fewer, if any, straps, be they for connection, containment, or protection.

In a certain way, these paintings feel naked and vulnerable to me, perhaps because they let the viewer in more, as does *Bandaged Grid #1* [see plate 23]. With the current paintings, it is not so much about "violence to" (which is passive) as it is "rupture" (which is active).

GRIFFITH: The distinction between a passive "violence to" and an active "rupture" brings us back to the relationship between the two painting bodies.

HAMMOND: Your comments have me free-associating all over the place, in a complex skein of references to and metaphors of violence, disturbance, rupture, resistance, transgression, and agency.

For me, work grows out of work. Generally speaking, there's a kind of cycle my visual practice goes through. Each "new body" of work becomes more "minimal" and "refined," but still with an edge of content. For example, the paintings in this exhibition might at first glance appear to be minimal monochrome grid paintings. A close examination however, reveals not a violence as in earlier work like *Meditation*, *Untitled (buckets)* [see plate 13], or *Inappropriate Longings* [see plate 16], but rather a disturbance or rupture, something unsettled, as the underlying layers of color are visible and push up through surface cracks, crevices, and holes, interrupting both surface and grid.

At some point, I unconsciously begin to "rough it up," to let the paintings become more muscular and physical—looser and less controlled. *Bandaged Grid #1* [see plate 23], the most recent painting in the exhibition, is going in this direction.

I don't think of the content in these new paintings as particularly "feminist" or "queer." Rather, it's the suggestion of content at all in what are, on one level, rather formal paintings that disrupts the usual received narrative.

GRIFFITH: To me, this recalls what you said earlier about "felt content" in your work.

HAMMOND: Found and recycled materials and objects are one way to bring content into the world of abstraction, as they all have histories that accompany them wherever they go. Weathered, patinated, showing signs of previous time, place, function, or use, they suggest a survivor aesthetic. My early *Presences* (1972) [see plate 2] and *Bags* (1971) are obvious examples, as are the mixed-media *Farm Ghosts* (1990) [see plate 12] paintings, but I think this carries forward in the work I do today.

This "roughing up" is not necessarily violent. But let me free associate a bit about violence. Initially, the mixed-media paintings incorporated found corrugated roofing tin from the Barrio Viejo of Tucson, the neighborhood I lived in while teaching at the University of Arizona. The neighborhood was being gentrified by people like me moving in. Paintings made with an uneasy juxtaposition of materials scavenged in that neighborhood became about the violence of gentrification, a process in which we artists participate (willingly or not). Juxtaposition and edges become sites of tension and negotiation.

Later, I gathered old corrugated roofing as I drove between Tucson and Santa Fe. Mixed-media installation paintings, such as the *Farm Ghosts* [see plate 12] series and *Inappropriate Longings* [see plate 16], speak of their own violence—small family farms abandoned. There's no water. There's no one there. The paintings incorporating materials from those sites (roofing tin, gutters, troughs, buckets, linoleum, etc.) are abstract narratives about hard times, drought, and capitalism in rural America, about the violence done to and by the farmer. They are not nostalgic. As much as we try to read the sites through the materials and objects left behind, we don't really know what went on there.

I am often interested in the other side, the back or the underside, of materials—such as the back of the aikido mat cover or the underside of linoleum fragments in *Inappropriate Longings* [see plate 16] suggesting hidden or buried secrets. It's as if the materials know and bear witness to what went on in that kitchen, bedroom, bathroom, attic, basement, or shed.

GRIFFITH: [. . .] You've also mentioned another earlier work, *Meditation*. That mixed-media painting includes a horse's skull with a bullet hole in the center of its forehead, which I read as a definite marker of violence. Your new works make use of the punctured hole of the grommet, a type of penetration. So, they're also violent but perhaps more ambiguously so—or at least in a way that is less overly determined than the bullet hole.

HAMMOND: *Meditation* follows the *Farm Ghosts* [see plate 12] and other mixed-media paintings. I had been working with old water troughs and gutters as metaphors for circulatory systems, for life-giving fluids like water and blood. I knew that I wanted to attach the feed trough, which had been knocking around my studio for some time, directly to the painting and that the painting surface, which looks like dried blood or scabs, was visually powerful enough to hold this protruding object. I was interested in literally attaching objects in the way that we attach meaning to paintings, not integrating them into the painting surface as we are taught in art school, but just attaching them.

It took me a long time, however, to figure out what was to go in the shrine-like trough. I tried many things. Everything seemed like not enough or too much. One day, out of desperation, I just hung this horse skull with a bullet hole through the head in the trough. I had found the skull upstate when I lived and worked in New York. I took it west with me to New Mexico, where it gathered dust for several decades before finding its place in this painting.

GRIFFITH: The skull is an icon resonant of the West, though.

HAMMOND: To my surprise, I liked the skull, but didn't know why. It also scared the shit out of me because it was such a "no-no" to put a skull in a work of art, such a risky act, something a serious woman artist living and working in New

Mexico—the landscape of O'Keeffe and O'Keeffe clones—should not do. At the same time, the fact that it felt so transgressive interested me. And so the horse skull stayed, functioning as a warning sign, like a skull one might find at a toxic waterhole. But maybe some sort of warning, too, in terms of painting and modernism. In hindsight, the painting seems unintentionally in dialogue with O'Keeffe's *Cow's Skull: Red, White, and Blue* (1931).

The bullet hole in bone is certainly a definite sign or marker of violence, but it is more complicated than you might think at first. What initially reads as violent, may not be entirely so. My friend Herb, who has a horse and rides, informed me that when a horse is seriously injured out on the range—say it breaks a leg—it is often shot in the head to humanely relieve it of its pain and misery. It is the responsibility of every rider to know how to do this. He gave me a text and diagram from a book that describes exactly what to do. When I exhibited *Meditation*, I also exhibited a digital scan of the book text and diagram.

To my mind, bullet holes and grommet holes function differently on a conceptual level. Bullet holes read violent but may or may not be so. Holes made in the canvas as part of the grommeting process don't read or feel violent to me (the way the punctures and slashes of Burri or Fontana might). Nor are the holes voids. Maybe it's because the metal of the grommet protects the hole from stretching or ripping, and the bullet hole is ragged, not perfectly round and smooth. Grommeting is more about creating a space for passage that functions like a bodily orifice. And yet, I intentionally do not do a good grommeting job. I smash the grommets so their perfect circles become irregular, perhaps misshapen—animated, alive.

ED. NOTE

The interview, originally titled "Harmony Hammond with Phillip Griffith," appeared in the "Art in Conversation" section, *Brooklyn Rail*, July/August 2016, 68–69. The text has been lightly edited and abridged for inclusion here.

On Harmony's Archive

Western States Artist-Endowed Foundations (2019)

Until the 1970s, women and lesbian artists had no history. Without a history, you don't exist. We are missing from the art historical narrative. If we don't find ways to not only make and present our work but to document it, to preserve the work, and rewrite existing histories, we too will be erased, and I refuse to let that happen. That is why I wrote *Lesbian Art in America: A Contemporary History*, published by Rizzoli in 2000 [see fig. 4.1]. Someone had to do it.

By that time, I had accumulated between five thousand and six thousand slides of work by other artists: mostly lesbian feminists, but also straight-identified feminist artists, historical work by women artists, and a few slides by male artists (mostly gay or queer identified) to supplement slide libraries at universities and art colleges and art books (all representing a white male heteronormative history of Western art).

Acutely aware that I sat on the largest visual documentation of contemporary lesbian artists in the United States (in the majority of cases, that documentation, primarily 35 mm slides given to me by the artists themselves, was more extensive and of better quality than what you can access online). I felt a responsibility to place these images, and related correspondence, exhibition announcements, posters, catalogues, and additional archival materials where they would be freely available to others for research.

I sent an introductory letter to archival collections across country to see if they might be interested in acquiring my papers. I explained that because I am a writer, independent curator, educator, and activist, in addition to being a visual artist, my archives consist of two separate but overlapping areas: everything about me and my work, and everything about other artists and their work. Were they interested in one or the other of these areas? Both? None? All but one library responded that they were very interested in both.

I made a political decision. While I support small special-focus libraries and archives, given the nature of my papers, I felt it was important to place them within a major archive of American art, thereby inserting feminist/lesbian/queer artists into the larger history and narrative of American art. In 2015, the Getty Research Institute (GRI) acquired my papers, where they joined the collections of modern and contemporary artists' papers including those of the Guerrilla Girls, Suzanne Lacy, Faith Wilding, Carolee Schneemann, Yvonne Rainer, Barbara T. Smith, Mary Kelly, Robert Mapplethorpe, and other feminist and queer artists.

Eighty-nine inventoried boxes of materials devoted to my artistic career including source material, exhibition announcements and reviews, writing by and about me, catalogues, brochures, artist statements, and photo documentation, along with boxes of primary correspondence with other artists, slides of their work, and four portfolios of posters and editioned prints were sent to the GRI. While not yet fully catalogued, the GRI reports that the papers and images in my archive are already being viewed and utilized by many art historians, curators, teachers, and other artists. A huge "burden of representation" off my shoulders. Mission accomplished.

ED. NOTE

Hammond delivered the oral presentation "On Harmony's Archive" at the Western States Artist-Endowed Foundations annual meeting, Museum of Contemporary Art (MOCA), Los Angeles, March 5, 2019.

Statement, *Chicken Lady*

Harmony Hammond: Material Witness Exhibition, The Aldrich Contemporary Art Museum (2019)

Fan Lady, Cactus Lady, Chicken Lady, and Ruffled Waters are personages that inhabited my visual work in the late '70s and early '80s. Inspired by petroglyphs and pictographs I saw when I visited New Mexico in 1978, they came and went as they wanted, met each other, strutted their stuff, flirted, and joined forces like characters in abstract fiction.

In 1984, as I was moving from Manhattan to Santa Fe with my partner and daughter, I received a letter from Marian Doherty, a former intern at A.I.R. Gallery where I had recently exhibited. Her letter told of an actual woman called Chicken Lady who lived in discarded cars and mobile homes, surrounded by cats, dogs, and of course chickens, on the marshy land along the water in Milford, Connecticut, as a stand against the state who wanted to use the land for a state park. She considered it her land and refused to move. Weathered from living by the ocean, she did not like to be seen. Marian wondered if this Chicken Lady had any of the qualities of my Chicken Lady.

While I had never heard of the Chicken Lady who lived by the ocean in Milford, the two do seem to share certain characteristics: tough outsiders, doing what they damn well want, caring little about society and its gender roles, government regulations, and the opinions of others. Both are survivors, making wholes out of the conditions and fragments of their lives, as best they can.

For the collaged painting *Chicken Lady* (1989) [see plate 15], I stretched an old quilt my good friend Ann Wilson abandoned at the end of a camping trip over a stretched canvas and framed it with panels of rusted corrugated tin roofing, found in the Barrio Viejo where I lived while teaching in Tucson. The text is taken from Marian's letter. Ann, an outsider of sorts herself, has painted on quilts since the 1950s. The Whitney Museum of American Art owns one of her quilt paintings, and the Emily Harvey Foundation in New York City recently presented a small retrospective of her work. Ann, myself, and many women artists, are "chicken ladies."

I'm interested in why certain materials are considered disposable by a culture, a class, or a group of people, while others save, use, and reuse the same materials for their survival, or for decorative purposes. The work refers to the complexities of gender and social class—the homeless, the misfit, the alien, the artist—who can't integrate themselves into society or who choose not to.

ED. NOTE

Hammond's unpublished statement accompanying *Chicken Lady* appeared in the fifty-year survey exhibition *Harmony Hammond: Material Witness, Five Decades of Art* at the Aldrich Contemporary Art Museum, Ridgefield, Connecticut, March 3–September 15, 2019.

Studio Visit with Jenn Shapland

THE Magazine (2019)

Harmony Hammond is lying on the floor beneath one of her paintings, craning her neck within inches of the canvas. "I'm doing edges," she tells me. I first heard of Hammond when I came across the catalogue for *Out West,* a 1999 show she curated at Plan B Evolving Arts in Santa Fe [see fig. 3.3] that brought together forty-one lesbian, gay, bisexual, transgender, and two-spirit artists from the Southwest.

I was living in Texas at the time, but soon enough I had moved to Santa Fe and was working for Hammond as an ersatz archivist, cataloguing and tracking her works in a database from the office connected to her massive Galisteo studio. I did my best not to interrupt her while she was in the studio, wincing as I heard the bangs, booms, and scrapings from the next room—sounds of her highly physical painting process.

It was apparent to me immediately, and became even more so over the time I worked for her, that Hammond's life and work are utterly continuous with one another. For several months, her series *Presences* [1971–72; see plate 2], over six-foot-high sculptures made of acrylic, dye, cloth, rope, metal, and wood, hung in her living room, some beneath sheets. She called them "the girls." They were "hanging out" and needed space to resume their full embodiments. Originally from Hometown, Illinois, a land of "duplexes, nothingness, and bland sameness," in high school Hammond took the L train to the Saturday School of the Art Institute of Chicago in the bowels of the museum, classes full of "beatniks, nude models, and rotten still lifes—I loved it. Very different than Hometown." She studied dress design and fashion illustration, and after class could walk the museum for free and look at the collections. This was her first real encounter with the art world and the beginning of a lifelong artistic practice that today encompasses her home, studio, and small orchard in Galisteo.

Clayton Porter [photographer] and I visited Hammond in her studio on the eve of a major survey show of her work at the Aldrich Contemporary Art Museum, *Harmony Hammond: Material Witness, Five Decades of Art*, which is on view from March 3 to September 15, 2019, in Ridgefield, Connecticut. A solo exhibition of her work at White Cube in London opens September 5. This year her work will also be included at a number of exhibitions which mark the fiftieth anniversary of the Stonewall rebellion. Hammond moved to New York just after Stonewall, where she cofounded two foundational second-wave feminist institutions: in the A.I.R. Gallery, the first major women's cooperative gallery of its era [see figs. 1.1 and 1.2], and *Heresies: A Feminist Publication of Art and Politics* [see figs. 1.3–1.5 and 2.4]. An activist, curator, and teacher, Hammond went on to write *Lesbian Art in America: A Contemporary History* (Rizzoli, 2000) [see fig. 4.1], and is known for her use of materials that mingle content with abstraction.

* * *

JENN SHAPLAND: How do you choose your materials?

HARMONY HAMMOND: I think materials and how they're used, how they're manipulated, is one way of bringing content into abstract work. I don't have an idea and then go seek the materials.

I respond to a material for its formal properties, for what the material is like physically, and then I begin to work with it, manipulate it to see what I can do with it. As I work with the material, I begin to think about what I'm getting. But in the beginning, I try to just be open. As I'm working with the materials, I begin to think about what's going on here, and how does the history of that material—be it traditional or not—and what I'm doing with it, how does it suggest meaning in the artwork. In these paintings from the 1990s, latex rubber calls up skin and body. It would be pretty hard to use this material without body associations. They were done at the time when the AIDS epidemic was devastating the New York art world. In this painting, *Codes of Meaning* [1992] the body reference is further emphasized, because I'm bringing the hair of two people together in the latex which suggests body fluids: it's both sensuous and dangerous, very charged. This is blonde hair; this is dark hair. For this painting called *Endangered* [1999], I used a zebra skin that a friend gave me. I just could not put it on my floor, so I placed it, a real animal skin, in a field of latex rubber suggesting or simulating human skin.

SHAPLAND: Can I backtrack for one second and ask whose hair is in this piece?

HAMMOND: I don't remember.

SHAPLAND: Someone you knew?

HAMMOND: Probably, yes. I used hair on and off for years, and when I first did it in the '70s I got some hair from a hair salon—that was not my thing. I usually use hair of people I know; I ask for their hair. Or I use my own hair, or my daughter's hair.

SHAPLAND: And where does the metal piece come from in this work, *Untitled* [1991]?

HAMMOND: Oh, who knows? It's from 1991. These latex pieces with three-dimensional elements came out of the earlier *Farm Ghosts* series [1990s; see plate 12] where I scavenged old rusty corrugated roofing tin and metal gutters from abandoned farms between here and Tucson, where I was teaching. I think of gutters as circulatory systems: they're supposed to be moving life fluids like water, but in my paintings, there are no life fluids. There may be a little dribble of flesh or blood, but no water. Usually, I use materials as I find them. I don't alter them much. I found the gutter this way, bent, pieced, and repaired. Somebody mended it. Also, I like ladders; I like tools, they all have histories; I like gutters; I like water troughs, things that have a purpose.

SHAPLAND: Useful things.

HAMMOND: But people have also altered them. Or personalized them. Going back to materials, especially found, repurposed, or recycled materials, they always bring their history, their stories, their narratives into the work with them. And in this case, one could even say they bring in other bodies, other peoples. We don't know who, but somebody repaired this gutter. Occasionally, I use natural materials. Hopefully, by juxtaposing materials such as hair, straw, metal, or fabric with materials such as latex rubber or paint, I initiate new feelings, thoughts, or conversations. That's why I recycle materials. To bring content into the work.

SHAPLAND: Talk about New Mexico and how living here has changed your work.

HAMMOND: Well, I've always worked with found materials. When I lived in New York, my work was made out of the rags that women friends gave me—thereby literally putting my life in my work—or fabric I found on the streets. My daughter and I would pick rags. We would go to the garment district and collect the end cuts of bolts of knit fabrics that were discarded in dumpsters or left at the curb in big plastic bags. Here, it's different. There's not much thrown out in Santa Fe. But I do find different things in different places, both urban and rural. And these things reflect place. Not landscape but place, which I define as a peopled space. It either is peopled now or it was peopled in the past, but now there's no one there, like on those abandoned family farms—where is everybody? What happened to them? So, it is the materials from the farmsteads, fabric from the garment district, or an old quilt left by a friend, that engage narratives of place.

I think I'm here because I like the big, open space. I can't say that it changed my work, but the very fabrics and textures around me have changed and those have found their way into my work. Rusted roofing tin and straw pieces used in adobe are examples. I paint with oil on canvas (of course canvas is a material, too, as is paint—and they each have their histories). [. . .]

In the most recent paintings, I'm using burlap from recycled coffee sacks, which I get here in town. I cut them up, and collage them onto canvas in order to build a textured surface. In the *Chenille* paintings [2016–present; see plate 27], like the one hanging over there, the texture and warm white color suggest the comfy softness of tufted chenille bedspreads, but with an edge as underlayers of color push up through splits and tears in the burlap, ooze out of grommet holes, or seep into the white paint making it a little brownish gold. It's a question of what is hidden, what's buried underneath and how does it assert itself? I try to give agency to what's hidden or buried underneath the comfy white cover.

When I say something's bleeding through and asserting itself through the whiteness, I mean that metaphorically and not just formally. That's how I work. The physical functions metaphorically to provide content. That's why all the seams: the frayed edges are important to me. It's intentional that the seams show, that we see things are pieced together. I don't like digital seamlessness. Piecing, patching, fraying, layering, suturing are loaded with meaning.

SHAPLAND: Do you feel you're part of a legacy of artists, specifically women artists, working in New Mexico? What about a legacy of queer artists or lesbian artists? Or a queer or lesbian community?

HAMMOND: There's a long tradition of artists coming to New Mexico. I'm one of those artists, and I'm one who didn't just come and go but who came and stayed. I see myself in multiple artistic traditions such as abstract painting, expanded painting, feminist art, or queer art, just like I think any artwork participates in multiple narratives. The art and artist can be addressed within any of those narratives. In terms of New Mexico, I am very aware of being part of a tradition of women artists, photographers, anthropologists, and writers, many of whom identified as lesbian or bisexual, who came West because of the wide, open space. It's outlaw territory. You're free to be who you think you are or want to be. For women who couldn't fit in where they grew up on the East Coast, or who didn't want to be what the social mores of the time expected of a young woman, what she should be, or who just wanted to do something else, but didn't have money to go and carve white marble in Italy—they went west. I love that legacy as well as the history of strong creative women who have always lived here.

SHAPLAND: What made you choose Galisteo?

HAMMOND: Once I had made the decision to permanently settle in New Mexico, I walked around all the places that I liked, and it just had to feel right. I looked at empty land; I looked at existing structures. I liked old buildings, but a lot of them were fixed up and expensive. You paid a lot of money for someone else's taste, which I usually hated. I would walk the land in different weather, different times of day. I liked many villages up north, but I realized that I wasn't really welcome there. This was in the '80s. As much as I wanted to think that people would see me working on the property—working does count for a lot—and I would fit in and be accepted, I slowly realized that I shouldn't be living there. Here, in Galisteo, it felt very good. The land felt good. The mix of people felt good. I had seen this old stone structure, the *lanera* or wool barn, from the highway, but I had never walked back here to check it out because it was on somebody's property. For the most part it had not been lived in, so it was pretty rough going at first. Many people rolled their eyes when I bought it.

Everyone except Lucy [Lippard]. Like me, she had lived in raw industrial lofts in New York, so could imagine how the rough interior space might be fixed up for living.

SHAPLAND: As an artist, do you feel like you have to be selfish, to protect your time or insulate yourself from the world?

HAMMOND: Selfish isn't the word that I would use. Of course I protect my time. I'm very structured about my time, or I wouldn't get anything done. I learned to do that early on as a single mom. Because I was the only one in my group of women artist friends in New York who had a child, I used time very differently than they did. As a single parent, I learned to use little bits of time productively. You can't wait to have long uninterrupted stretches to work on your art, because that time never comes. I could do certain kinds of work when my daughter Tanya was around, but for other stuff, I had to wait until she went to bed. Then I could focus. I also chose to have a half-time job (and half a salary) in order to have regular time in the studio.

SHAPLAND: I remember being here working at the computer and seeing you outside dragging a huge piece of metal across the yard. You are so active. And your work really involves your body. It's really physical. Can you talk about that a little? About how you use your body in your work?

HAMMOND: I am very physical. Manipulating materials is what I do. It's obviously very important to me and I get pleasure from it. . . . Oh, I know what I was going to say about your word, "selfishness." I think what I'm more aware of in relation to time (other than there is never enough of it), is "privilege." I have an awareness of privilege. To be able to work, even as a single mom, or when I was commuting and teaching, to somehow be able to do my work, to be able to do what my passion is, and be recognized for it, is a real privilege. Yes, I have to set boundaries; yes, I have priorities, and the work is the major part of my life, for sure, but other things, like teaching or the martial arts that I did for so many years, they're part of the work too. I don't separate what I'm doing outside and what I'm doing inside, or what I do in the house from what I do in the studio. For me, they just kind of flow together and feed each other. And normally it feels pretty good, unless I get too anxious about something. The multitasking can get out of hand.

SHAPLAND: And so you feel like your garden space, your house, is all continuous with your practice?

HAMMOND: It's all "the work."

ED. NOTE

This interview with Jenn Shapland was first published under the title “Harmony Hammond, the Studio Visit” in *THE Magazine*, April 2019, 21–25. The original text has been slightly abridged for inclusion here.

Interview with Tara Burk

Art After Stonewall: 1969–1989 (2019)

TARA BURK: Which had a greater effect on your life, gay liberation, or women's liberation?

HARMONY HAMMOND: Definitely women's liberation. Gay liberation created a space for lesbian relationships, but many gay men were sexist. The women's liberation movement (WLM), with its political analysis of patriarchy and privilege, had a profound influence on my life and my art practice.

BURK: How did the WLM impact your art?

HAMMOND: Feminist artists protested the historical Western bias against women artists, woman-based subject matter, and the unequal treatment of women and artists of color in the art world. It was a demand for visibility and equality. Tired of waiting around to be recognized by the male-dominated art establishment, we created our own groups, organizations, exhibitions, publications, and networks. [...]

BURK: Did you attend the first Gay Pride parade in 1970?

HAMMOND: I came out in 1973 and participated in my first Gay Pride March in 1974. In the spirit of the Stonewall rebellion they were called "marches" then, not "parades."

BURK: What was it like to be an out lesbian in the art world of 1970s New York?

HAMMOND: The New York art world was full of gays and lesbians who did not wish to be confined by labels. Artists moved back and forth between creative disciplines calling their art practice one thing one day and another thing the next. They were also experimenting sexually, but didn't name it (their same-sex orientation or bisexuality), and in not naming it, their sexual preferences weren't politicized. Because of their power and impact, I chose to claim the labels "feminist" and "lesbian" but redefine them on my own terms. I am sure I was discriminated against but that's not what I focused on, nor is it important.

The downtown art scene was small, interdisciplinary, but strangely straight-identified. The feminist art scene was even smaller and also straight-identified. Jill Johnston, columnist for *The Village Voice* and author of *Lesbian Nation* (1973) was [one of] the only lesbians who was publicly out. While many writers and poets openly identified as lesbian in their lives and work, visual artists who had sexual relationships with other women tended to not identify as lesbian for fear of professional discrimination. [...]

As I wrote years later in *Lesbian Art in America* [2000; see fig. 4.1], there have always been artists who were lesbian and lesbians who were artists, however, putting the words "lesbian" and "artist" together was too risky for most. [...]

BURK: You are an artist, why did you feel you had to be a historian, writer, and curator as well?

HAMMOND: Because lesbian art and artists had next to no history. It was missing. Without a history, you don't exist. I was acutely aware of the historical moment in which I was living and working, and it was clear that if we didn't find ways to not only make and present our work but to document it, to preserve the work and rewrite the histories, we too would be erased, and I refuse to let that happen.

ED. NOTE

The exchange was originally published with the title "Harmony Hammond interviewed by Tara Burk," in *Art After Stonewall: 1969–1989*, ed. Jonathan Weinberg (New York: Rizzoli Electa; Columbus, OH: Columbus Museum of Art, 2019), 106–9. The interview has been abridged for inclusion in this volume.

Interview with Tyler Green

The Modern Art Notes Podcast (2019)

TYLER GREEN: You've talked a lot about Eva Hesse over the years. A number of the *Flesh Journal* works from the early 1990s are built from latex rubber, which is, of course, a material closely associated with Hesse. I imagine you must have been delighted for people to make this the association between the *Flesh Journal* pieces and Hesse's work. Was making that link evident important to you?

HARMONY HAMMOND: The latex rubber I start[ed] using in the '80s, basically with the wrapped sculptures. Some of the wrapped sculptures are covered with liquid latex rubber, which you can buy in different strengths. The more you layer it, the darker it gets. As we all know, it is not stable and it darkens with time. In many cases disintegrates. The fact that it's not stable, it's not an archival material, it's very much like our bodies. It disintegrates. It not only looks like the body, like skin, but it acts like it. It becomes in and of itself a very loaded material to use.

I think, in her work, Hesse used it in a very strong way with all those associations. When I started using it in the wrapped sculptures of the '80s, I was using it in that same way again to help presence bodies. Some of the wrapped sculptures were literally painted with a skin of acrylic paint. Some of them were painted with the latex rubber. What I liked about the latex rubber was, not only that it exaggerated the body reference, which it does, but I could see through the latex. I could see how one piece of fabric overlapped another. I could see colors bled through from underneath.

[...] Working in my state of peripheral control, I knew that red would bleed through in a certain way, or a dark blue might bleed through in a certain way, thereby giving this feeling of showing the inside of the body. In the sense of Monique Wittig's lesbian body, the sensuality of the raw interior body.

The *Journals* came out of a period where I was teaching in Tucson. I didn't have much time. I was on a zillion academic committees, and so forth, commuting back and forth. I had a teeny-tiny studio workspace. I was [...] pouring latex rubber [...] in old broiler pans that I would get from the Salvation Army or the Goodwill store, letting it dry, and then I would rip it out of the pans. I would get these pages of latex rubber. They looked like tablets or pages to me. Then, I beg[a]n to paint on, or often incise into the rubber. That's how these *Flesh Journals* [1993] came to be. At the time, like many of us, I was reading different French feminists.

The writing that I liked so much was often both very political but very poetic. I would take phrases, sometimes my own, but very often lifted from these writers. They would be scratched into the rubber, the skin, the body. By doing all that, I began to think about what I call "the painting body."

GREEN: Speaking of pages [and writing] ... your *Ledger Drawings* [2015; see fig. 5.3] document the insults women have faced during their careers, especially late in their careers.

It's probably the work of yours, or the series of yours—whatever the relevant word would be there—that is most rooted in "traditional conceptual practice," words, writing, wall-mounted. You'd think [of] Adrian Piper, for example.

First, was it an intentional, pointed engagement with conceptualism and forty years of conceptualist practice? If it was, were there reasons why that practice became important to you in the mid-2010s?

HAMMOND: I was aware of it. I'm aware of using words. I'm aware of work over the years that repeats words. I'm aware that to use words, the way I have used words ... You're right. This is a very different way of using words than I had in previous work. Words are used often to label or identify, but who's to say it's accurate or true?

It might be poetic phrasing, an association of words and images. There's a piece in the Aldrich Contemporary Art Museum show [*Harmony Hammond: Material Witness, Five Decades of Art*, 2019] called *Chicken Lady* [1989; see plate 15]. There's a lot of text on two metal panels; it tells an actual story. There are a few pieces like that. Interestingly enough, they tend to be about homeless people, which I realized after the fact. It is their stories. I don't use that much text unless there is a story to be told. *Chicken Lady* is one example of that.

With the *Ledger Drawings* [see fig. 5.3], I was thinking about reinscribing words. What does it mean when you take a word and write it over and over and over and over and over? Does it lose meaning? Does the meaning become intensified or even more important? It was really about reinscription.

Then, of course, we have to ask, what are the words I've chosen? Which, as you've indicated, were words that I find people often use with me as a mid-career woman artist, older woman artist, whatever. Sometimes they think they're being very polite, but they don't say old woman artist. They say, "An artist of your generation." The words "your generation" stand out there in space, like blinking neon. It's so weird to me. These words are used to discriminate, even if people aren't intentionally doing it. I began to just note down different words like that, like "your generation," for instance, or "down girl." Things like that, that I think had a reference to being an artist of my age, longevity of career, stature, whatever.

I decided to repeat them over and over and over. I have, over the years, drawn and painted over found ledger books back from the days when I lived on the Bowery in New York. The loft I rented was full of old ledger books from a business that was there, those are just pages, I can paint over those.

I have a thing about ledger books, anyway, and journals and diaries. I don't keep visual journals, like many artists do. I don't usually like them because I don't like the way they're attached by the spine. I like loose pieces of paper. The *Ledger Drawings* are on loose pieces of paper, pages torn out of a ledger, where I write over and over a word or very short phrase that refers to mid-career women artists, or that I've had directed to me or at me. I just repeat them over and over and over, to eliminate meaning but also to claim it and change it in some way.

ED. NOTE

This is an excerpt from the transcript of Tyler Green's interview with Hammond for *The Modern Art Notes Podcast*, no. 398, June 20, 2019. Courtesy of Tyler Green, *The Modern Art Notes Podcast*.

Conversation with Holland Cotter

SITE SANTA FE (2019)

[. . .] HOLLAND COTTER: I wonder if you have anything to say about the element of violence in your work.

HARMONY HAMMOND: Do you see it?

COTTER: I do see it. The idea of flesh being under assault, scars. [. . .] I once looked at some of your paintings and what flashed through my mind was the torso of the Christ in the *Isenheim Altarpiece* [Nikolaus of Haguenau and Matthias Grünewald, 1512–16]—scourged, cut, and bleeding. If I took a close-up of that, and placed it next to one of your paintings, I would feel there would be some comparative material there.

HAMMOND: Totally. I do feel there's an edge of violence. Sometimes it is about that. There's often an edge there in the work. It is because the materials I use have a bodily presence and an indexicality about them. We read the marks as cuts on the body. You're seeing it on a painting or a sculpture, but I'm hoping that they're really being read on the body. Since a lot of the work becomes torso-like, what you say makes sense to me entirely. I'm not Catholic, but there are quite a few artworks of mine that might seem to have those references, cross forms, for instance. I'm not trying to work with a Catholic iconography or anything like that. But I am interested in the notion of wounds and scars and the markings on the body, not just the physical body but bodies in the larger sense as well. They mark time, wounds being places of passage, of things moving through those wounds, and moving out. It could be purging in a very positive way or it could be a very negative, violent, hurtful way. I can see that in wounds.

I'm hesitant to discuss my work in relation to crucifixes and altarpieces, though, because I don't know that much about Catholicism, to be real truthful. Yet there is an almost sense of martyrdom, in a certain way, about some of the work. I know that it's over there, but I just leave it over there. I don't think I've really explored that association, except in roundabout ways.

Like I've said before—whether we're talking about collective process or just how we move through the world—that being a writer, curating a show, being an artist making work and putting it out there, there's always some bloodshed. There's always a little friction with somebody, somehow. The notion that there's always a little bloodshed is connected with the notion of the bodily presence. That's in all of my work because of the way I use materials. [. . .]

COTTER: The bodies in your work are damaged, they are hurt, but they're always intact, too, which is, I think, an important thing.

HAMMOND: I don't think they're always damaged or they're always hurt. I think sometimes. . . .

COTTER: Frequently.

HAMMOND: It's interesting because there are pieces where really that's very true, but I don't actually think of them that way most of the time. In terms of the materiality, it's about being, constructing, or presencing bodies. There's the painting body, which is the object, the canvas, with the skin of paint on it, and there's the painting body of the artist who's painting that. I don't think of those bodies as damaged or hurt, but in a much more positive way, usually.

COTTER: I meant to be positive, actually. (Laughter.) [. . .] I want to go back to something that came up when we were talking earlier. You mentioned that you taught for sixteen years at the University of Arizona. I wonder, having learned so much just hearing you talk here informally, as an educator, did you feel that you were adding value to the students taking your classes when you were teaching those years?

HAMMOND: I always encourage students. Part of it was about giving students a space. There was always a space for people to express themselves. When we would do critiques, for one example, there were openings. People could deal with things very personally in the class or not, or very politically or not. That was up to them. There was a space very clearly to do that in a painting class, or a mixed-media class, or whatever. When we would do critiques, they would go for it, or not. For many students, it would take time to be able to deal, if they wanted to, say, deal with a touchy subject like their sexuality or something like that.

The best way that we can be supportive is through constructive criticism, which is really helpful if you're the student. Constructive criticism helps you say what you want to say in the best possible way. Not saying what I want your work to be, or what it should look like. Not just talking about the formal and technical issues, but rather asking if the visual strategies are contributing to the content of the work. Or if they are getting in the way of what it is you are trying to say. Not criticizing you for what you're saying, but asking if what you are trying to say is coming across as you want. I also feel I was very lucky to always be able to be myself while I was teaching. I like to think that that was a good model for other artists.

COTTER: Absolutely. [. . .]

HAMMOND: Before we open this conversation up to include members of the audience, there's something I want us to talk about. One question I get a lot—you probably get it, too, Holland—is, "Why do we need these 'queer shows' or 'women shows'? Shows about people who have been marginalized?" My response is, "As long as there are still gay bashings, as long as people can't be out, we need these shows." We don't have equal rights, with what the Trump regime is trying to do. People can still lose their jobs for being gay in the military. . . .

Now with social media, artists don't have to be isolated. They can connect with one another. Women artists or queer artists, you don't have to be isolated. You can show your work to others and you can share it in these online exhibits . . . but there's something about physical shows, about physically occupying space. An exhibition is a presence to people outside and inside the community, seeing the work in person. It's a presence, and it says, "This is a presence. There are a lot of queer people, queer-friendly people, queer artists in this town, right here. We take this physical space. Experience this space with us and this work with us." People respond differently than they do to an online exhibition or a conversation group online. I'm still interested in those physical shows. I support them, and I participate in them.

A really good example would be—one that we both are familiar with, Holland—the queer-based exhibitions this year around the fiftieth anniversary of the Stonewall rebellion. Some of the exhibitions are celebrations, some historical, some more theme based, and some feature work by young artists. I'm thinking of the Brooklyn Museum show. Did you see that show?

COTTER: Sure.

HAMMOND: Talk to us about it.

COTTER: I wrote about the show, actually. It [*Nobody Promised You Tomorrow: Art 50 Years After Stonewall*] was a group show that Brooklyn put together of artists born after 1969. It was an epic show—really, really good. Some of these people have not been in museum shows before. This is an opportunity for them. Twenty-eight artists in total in the show and well worth seeing. [...] Artists who wanted to be, who were, out there, and want to be identified as who and what they are.

HAMMOND: Many of them would probably identify as genderqueer or nonnormative. (Pause.)

AUDIENCE MEMBER: I have a question. Within the queer community today, a lot of times the younger generation, say, objects to the language we older people use to talk about our experiences. How do you approach those political disagreements within your own community?

HAMMOND: I don't have an answer. Those are some of the struggles. Some of the struggles are with "like kind," amongst ourselves, as well as against Trump, and others who are hostile. All I know from my experiences, when I think back over my lifetime, is that those moments where I was in situations like what you're describing . . . they were hard. They were hard. I don't think there's one way you get through them unless you work to get through them. It involves a lot of listening and maybe change. You also find yourself by asking where you stand on these things. Where are your boundaries? Where do you disagree? Where can your politics shift? I don't know. I don't think it's ever easy, that's all. I don't think it's easy. As I've said, blood is always shed, but you have to keep talking.

COTTER: We're all on the same side, basically.

HAMMOND: Yeah, we can't give up. As I say to myself, I have to be ever vigilant. Unfortunately, we must be vigilant.

ED. NOTE

This text is based on a recording of a live exchange between Harmony Hammond and Holland Cotter during the program "My Life in Art: Harmony Hammond and Holland Cotter" at SITE SANTA FE, August 24, 2019. The transcript has been edited and abridged.

6

2020–2023

Editor's Introduction

This volume closes shy of mid-decade, in 2023; it is not, by a long stretch, the last chapter of Hammond's career, but simply where she was, where we were, when, in the interests of putting her texts into wider circulation, we concluded the process of compiling content from her writings to date. A series of major exhibitions at the onset of the 2020s provide the material for this section of the book.[1] The shows prompted exchanges that reexamine the political and cultural work of feminist art in relation to its materiality. Textile and fiber art—which feminist artists (including Hammond) have long embraced—held the spotlight in shows at major museums across the United States and abroad.[2] In the forefront, *Woven Histories: Textiles and Modern Abstraction*, organized by the National Gallery of Art, elevated genres historically waved aside as "women's work" to new heights. While scholars and curators have productively studied the patterns, decorative qualities, and social histories of textiles, Lynne Cooke, the curator of *Woven Histories*, made an important intervention into this discourse by focusing on the structural properties of textiles and fiber art. Cooke invited several participating artists to write about the work of another artist in the show. Hammond chose to focus on a small painting (twelve inches square) by Agnes Martin, one of her artistic ancestors. The text—the last entry in this volume—picks up two threads running through the entire book, textiles and abstraction. It also gives us an intimate view of how Hammond looks at a painting. Closely. Respectfully. Not forcing her ideas into the foreground. Taking time. Letting the artwork lead the way.

ED. NOTES

1. For example, the fifty-year survey *Harmony Hammond: Material Witness, Five Decades of Art*, The Aldrich Contemporary Art Museum, Ridgefield, Connecticut, curated by Amy Smith-Steward (2019–20); the solo show *Crossings* at Alexander Gray Associates Gallery, New York (during the COVID-19 pandemic in 2020); the group show *Women in Abstraction: Another History of Abstraction in the 20th Century*, Centre Pompidou, Paris, curated by Christine Macel (2021); the solo exhibition *Accumulations* at Alexander Gray Associates Gallery, New York (2023); and *Woven Histories: Textiles and Modern Abstraction*, curated by Lynne Cooke for the National Gallery of Art, opened at Los Angeles County Museum of Art in 2023 before appearing at the NGA in 2024 and traveling to MoMA, New York, in 2025. *Unravel: The Power and Politics of Textiles in Art*, a major exhibition opening at the Barbican Art Gallery, London, in February 2024, and traveling to the Stedelijk Museum in Amsterdam, where it closed in January 2025, both supplemented and complemented *Woven Histories*. A handful of artists, including Hammond, participated in both exhibitions.

2. A raft of feminist and queer publications preceded and provided resources for *Woven Histories*. This scholarship includes Elissa Auther, *String Felt Thread: The Hierarchy of Art and Craft in American Art* (Minneapolis: University of Minnesota Press, 2010); John Chaich and Todd Oldham, *Queer Threads: Crafting Identity and Community* (Los Angeles: Ammo Books, 2017) (this book accompanied an exhibition organized by Leslie-Lohman Museum of Art in 2014); Julia Bryan-Wilson, *Fray: Art and Textile Politics* (Chicago: University of Chicago Press, 2017).

Audio Tour, *Crossings* Exhibition

Alexander Gray Associates Gallery, New York (2020)

While all art participates in multiple narratives, I like to think of my work as participating in the narrative of modern abstraction at the same time it interrupts and subverts that narrative. Mostly I do this through what I call "material engagement," or the agency of materials and the way they are manipulated, to bring social and political content into formal abstraction.

I often use materials "at hand" to bring the outside world into the painting rectangle, thereby upsetting abstraction's canonical rhetoric of purity and universality.

Chenille #7 [2018]

In the series of *Chenille* paintings [see plate 27 for *Chenille #7*], fraying pieces of coarse burlap cut from coffee sacks, leftover scraps of canvas and other fabrics, and grommets are layered intermittently with thick paint mixed with Dorland's Wax.

Appearing monochrome at first, up close, underlayers of color are visible through cracks and crevices and peek out from flaps in the painting's surface, which is slowly built up over time, drawing attention to both the physical labor of painting and process of its own making. Stitched seams are left showing.

Patterns created by the raised grommets recall the soft cozy texture and domestic warmth of white tufted chenille bedspreads—but with an edge, as browns, reds, and golds assert themselves from underneath the surface, pushing up through splits and tears in the burlap, seeping out of the grommet holes, and staining their surroundings to draw attention to what has been muffled, obscured, covered up or over.

Suggesting bodily wounds, as well as social unrest and political upheaval, the paintings allude to voices of resistance that refuse to be silenced. A rupture from underneath discoloring and disrupting the warm white coverlet. A surface under stress. . . .

Bandaged Grid #9 [2020]

The *Bandaged Grid* paintings also explore concepts of "material engagement and agency" by connecting paint to the body and presencing the body as a social/political site. Strips of canvas and burlap are affixed like bandages over a grid of grommeted holes, which puncture the surface, drawing attention to what is obscured. Once again, underlayers of paint assert themselves from underneath. Paint suggesting body fluids leaks from the holes, refuting the nonobjective nature of the modernist grid by interjecting a corporeal narrative and violent edge into its strict formalism.

Recalling the flap in *Chenille #7* [see plate 27], two blood-red stained pieces of cloth, one of which is identifiable as a domestic linen, have been tacked to the painting's surface, where they hang as both evidence and warning of violent actions outside the picture frame.

Unlike earlier *Bandaged Grids* (like, say, *Bandaged Grid #1* [2015; see plate 23]), where the bandaged strips stanched the paint leaking from the grommeted holes, this painting, *Bandaged Grid #9*, presents the bandages and bloodied cloths as if injury and wounds are matter of fact and routine. Calm and controlled, everything is in its place; a visual text underscored in red but kept "in line" . . . that is what is so disturbing. . . .

A bandage always implies a wound. A bandaged grid suggests a disruption of utopian egalitarian order—but also the possibility of holding together, of healing.

Bandaged Quilts [2018–2020]

The series of *Bandaged Quilt* paintings [see plate 22] continue to use paint and other materials as a metaphor for the body and therefore bodies.

Featuring lengths of burlap and canvas arranged in a basic pieced-quilt pattern, the *Bandaged Quilts* subvert the (male) legacy of minimalist monochromatic painting, reclaiming these abstract compositions through the vernacular of (female) craft traditions, specifically quilting.

Quilters, like chenille tufters, share an undervalued history of needlework and similar techniques of puncturing fabric from the backside. Here, as with the *Chenilles*, quilting is performed with paint rather than needle and thread. This is similar to my early *Bags* [1971] and the *Floorpieces* [1973; see plate 4] performing purses and braided rag rugs without being functional as such.

Double Bandaged Quilt #1 (Horizontal) [2019]

In *Double Bandaged Quilt #1 (Horizontal)* [see plate 22], open sores at the heart of the concentric quilt pattern remind us that the origins of quilts and quilting are gendered, and that, like the female body, they have been violated and exploited.

Double Bandaged Quilt #3 (Vertical) [2020]

In contrast, the wounded centers in *Double Bandaged Quilt #3 (Vertical)* are muffled or covered over. The painting hangs tall, knowing, and silent . . . its secret contained behind the lightly stained bandages.

Fringe [2020]

In *Fringe*, the swollen centers are once again visible behind toothy-edged burlap bandages, which look torn and do not quite cover the wounds. The paint, however, acts as a preservative, protecting the delicate fraying edges. Quilts have always been made out of different types of fabrics. These quilts, now composed of bandages and paint, now bandaged, reclaim their rightful place in the history of abstraction.

Crosses [2019–2020]

The *Cross* paintings [see plates 24 and 25] feature overlapping and intersecting swaths of rough burlap laid over stained-white grommeted fields, like giant cross-shaped bandages. They are crosses and not crosses. While these paintings resonate today in this time of radical social change, I actually began them back in the summer of 2019. What reads as crosses weren't initially meant as crosses, but rather as Xs marking the spot, as plus signs and intersections, as stand-ins for the figure. And yet, I have to admit, they are, indeed, crosses.

There are many kinds of crosses and many kinds of crossings. Cross, crossed, crossing, crossroads, cross-culture, cross-reference, crossover, cross-dress, cross-stitch, crosswind, cross-examine, crossing my fingers, crossing my heart, Red Cross . . . to name a few.

In the *Cross* paintings, as with other paintings in this exhibition, materials have a physical and metaphoric weight that links painting to the body, frequently alluding to trauma of some sort and recovery.

That said, despite the scale and muscular materiality of these paintings, as a sign, the cross is indeterminate: Its form references diverse cultural associations including religious iconography, emblems of medical and humanitarian aid, and the modernist art historical canon. Historically, plagues have been represented by black-and-red crosses.

I think of these as recuperative paintings for this moment—embodying vulnerability and violence, but also intersectionality, the additive, the plural, agency, defiance, and strength . . . using paint as a poultice for survival and healing.

ED. NOTE

Hammond composed this audio tour for *Crossings*, the fourth solo exhibition of her work at Alexander Gray Associates, New York, November 12, 2020–January 30, 2021. A version of this audio tour script appears in the catalogue *Crossings + Accumulations* (Santa Fe, NM: Radius Books, 2023). *Crossings* took place during the COVID pandemic; the audio tour and other forms of online outreach brought the work on display to audiences whose ability to visit the gallery in person was limited. No catalogue accompanied the exhibition. The Radius Books catalogue brings together documentation from *Crossings* and the later exhibition *Accumulations* (Alexander Gray Associates, April 27–June 24, 2023). Both exhibitions presented large-scale, heavily textured canvases that extend the artist's "material engagement" to expand and subvert narratives of modernist abstraction. The audio tour is reproduced courtesy of Alexander Gray Associates, New York.

Interview with Jarrett Earnest

National Academy of Design (2021)

JARRETT EARNEST: Harmony, after weeks and months of correspondence, finally it's the day. I wanted to say thank you for bearing with me, and I'm really looking forward to getting as deep as we can into the thinking and material reality of your most recent paintings, which were recently on view [in the solo exhibition *Crossings*] at Alexander Gray Associates in New York. I happily got to spend a lot of time there.

As a way of diving into them, I want to know, when you start making one of those paintings, how is it that you begin the process? Do you have an image, do you have a material, before it becomes a work in the studio?

HARMONY HAMMOND: Well, first of all, I wanted to say thanks, Jarrett, for spending as much time as you did with the physical work. As with most works of art, the physical effect of the work on the body, I feel, is as important as the more intellectual conceptual concerns. That said, I think it's even more true of my work than many other works of art. I'm glad that you spent physical time with the works. That's, of course, how they're meant to be experienced.

Anyway, to answer your question . . . for me, work grows out of work. I'm not an artist who does sketches in advance, rough or detailed. I just don't do sketches. I don't really like to use sketchbooks. People give me beautiful sketchbooks with handmade paper. I love them. I love handmade paper and sketchbooks, but I don't work well in them because they're bound. The paper's bound. I'm confined already on the left-hand margin.

I don't do sketches planning for future paintings or make notes for future paintings. I have stacks of empty, beautiful notebooks sitting around. Nor do I do research. Artists work in different ways. Some artists either have an idea in relation to what's happening, the contemporary issues of the time, or maybe they're doing research, but I don't tend to do that per se. They do research, then they choose their materials or they get a vision and work with compositions and materials to carry out that vision because it might be different materials that they need for each idea.

I tend to start with the materials, the physical handling of materials. I have a lot of materials that I'm currently working with lying around the studio. I just start working with them. For me, work always grows out of work. Work grows out of my previous work. There's this thread. For a long time, the thread is semicontinuous in the sense of similar ideas, variations, things I obsess about, or maybe different, that probably you or another viewer wouldn't even notice, but it's something that's crucial to me. Sometimes it can be a radical change, but usually it's not.

Usually, I'm not thinking about what I want the piece to be about. I'm not thinking about other artists' work. I'm not thinking about abstraction. I'm not thinking about feminism. I'm not thinking about queer abstraction. All that always sits in my brain, it is just back there, but it's just not where I go while I'm in the studio. [. . .]

My approach is still the same as it was in the '70s, or what I learned in the '70s. Understanding that materials and the way that they're manipulated bring social and political content into the work. I refer to this as "material engagement" or the agency of materials to do this. That's certainly true of the work that was up at Alexander Gray [in *Crossings*]. There are only seven paintings in that show. The *Chenille* paintings [2016–present; see plate 27], the *Bandaged Grids* [2015–present; see plate 23], and the *Cross* paintings [2019–present; see plates 24 and 25].

Let's take a *Chenille* painting, like *Chenille #7* [2018; see plate 27], which is the long horizontal that's in the show. It's kind of unusual because the *Chenille* paintings tend to be vertical, which indirectly call up the body. They're usually larger than my size, but that verticality in relationship to the figure is there. The *Chenille* painting in the show at Alexander Gray is one of three large horizontals. The reason for the three horizontals is that I often work with what's at hand, materials at hand, in this case old stretcher bars. I recycle everything. Even though I now buy new, beautiful aluminum stretcher bars, I'm recycling old wooden ones as well.

The way I would have begun any of the *Chenille* paintings, including *Chenille #7* [see plate 27], is I start with a stretched canvas. That's important to me.

I always laugh at myself. I think, "Harmony, why a stretched canvas, girlfriend? You would do such thick painting. Why not paint on wood or metal panels?" My paintings are really fucking heavy. The few I painted on plywood were much heavier. I paint on stretched canvas, one, because that's how I learned to paint. I'm very comfortable there. But also, I paint on the stretched canvas because I like the way it refers to a history of modernist painting and dealing with flatness and pictorial issues.

I also like that hard-edge objectness of it, and how we make assumptions that the front picture plane is at right angles to the side of the painting, that then goes back to the wall. I sometimes mess around with that angle intentionally. Anything I put on the surface or that I extend off the side edges is very, very intentional.

What I do is about layering and edges. I think of the painting surface as edge and of the perimeter of the canvas as edge as well. Edge, therefore, being the mediation between the work of art and life out here, that's just a given. I don't even think about that. That's what I do. There are certain things I just do, for better or worse.

I've got a stretched canvas—it's down on the floor flat—I cover it with three layers of gesso. Then I start building the surface. In this case, the *Chenille* paintings [see plate 27], the surface is collaged with pieces of burlap that I've cut from recycled coffee sacks. Like I said, I use materials that are at hand, that come to me some way. Why coffee sacks? You can buy burlap, but I get crude burlap coffee sacks from an ex-assistant I had, a student, then assistant, who now manages a coffee shop. I began using it because it gave me another woven texture. The sacks tend to be similar in size, but not exactly. Actually, they have different textures because the sacks come from different countries. I like all of that material variation.

The earliest monochrome paintings [the "wrapped paintings" before the *Bandaged Grids* and *Chenilles*] were already about surface and brushstrokes, building this physical presence of surface, which is, of course, so important to monochrome painting or near-monochrome painting. I had already been piecing and patching pieces of canvas and other fabrics onto the surface. The addition of burlap gave me a rougher texture that I liked, more of a physical presence.

At this point in my career of painting and making art for so long, I just trust my instincts. I try to do what I want to do. "I don't have to show it to anybody. Just do it. Try it. See what it looks like. Come back tomorrow, look at it."

The burlap sacks have a certain human proportion—with one, two, or three seams on the sides. When I cut them open, they retain those body proportions because they are one side or another of a two-sided coffee sack, which was once lifted and carried by a strong person.

Why would I want to even mention that? It's just that if you look at the compositions in the *Chenille* paintings, you can begin to see there's repeated scale of pieces and shapes, and where seams fall. That's because it's coming from the materials themselves. It's just what I work with. It's the same thing I did when I was working with recycled roofing tin in paintings from the late '80s and '90s. You can pick up roofing tin from abandoned farms and bend it, alter it, and cut it. But for some reason I don't do that. I can't explain why, other than that I like working with things as I find them. I could alter them. I could cut the metal. I could cut up the burlap into any shapes, but for the most part, I tend not to do that. I tend to work with "what is," which means making those shapes and sizes and proportions work on whatever arbitrary canvas I happen to have on hand. I will tend, therefore, to, instead of cutting burlap, I overlap it. You can see the overlap. I leave the seams showing. I've always liked the seams. Seams have always been not only visually interesting but conceptually important to me as they show evidence of connecting, of joining, of making wholes out of pieces or fragments. When I do cut, usually along the seams, I cut arbitrarily. It's not planned. It's not measured, nothing is measured. The cuts are irregular and the burlap starts fraying. I like all that. I like loose threads and fraying edges.

All of that comes into the painting surface from the materials, from the handling of the materials. I let it happen. The loose threads and the fraying edges. I would even say more than letting it happen, I encourage it to happen. I trust it. Does that make sense?

EARNEST: As you were describing it, it made me wonder if the extent to which you leave legible the arbitrary foundness of the things that you bring into the work has something to do with creating the sense of you inhabiting or collaborating with the found or inhabited world. That there's some dynamic between the thing that you're bringing to it and the world as it is coming to you.

HAMMOND: That's definitely what it's about. It's an afterthought for me, but I think what you just said is entirely true. That's the way it is. It's like, how do you deal with your life? That's what you're really talking about. How do you move through the world? My work in this studio, as isolated as it is, is where I learn how I move through the world. Sounds weird, I know, but it's true.

Anyway, I've got the canvas down there flat on the floor. I freely place large pieces of burlap from the sides of the sacks, plus some odds and ends of loose small pieces of burlap or other fabrics. Usually, at this point, they're not grommeted, but sometimes they are. Then the pieces have to be archivally glued down to the surface of the canvas and painted with three more coats of gesso, because, of course, the burlap absorbs paint like crazy.

What begins happening before I even put any oil paint on the surface is all those coats of gesso begin to fill in the porousness of the burlap. In doing that, they begin to catch on the nobs, and the little fuzzy parts, and the knots, and threads. The paint begins to build up around those seams as well. In general, I know that's what's going to happen, but I don't know exactly what's going to happen and catch and build up nor where. I don't worry about it in detail. I just know that it's a larger process that's going to happen and that I'm wanting to have happen. If there's something I really don't like I can just pull it off or change it. The way that I work, which is basically very additive, is very forgiving. I can change anything, pretty much.

If there are any grommets on there, which there would be, in the case of the early *Chenilles* [see plate 27], the holes go down in through the fabric itself. Later, I also started attaching and fixing the grommets to the burlap or canvas so they actually protrude. So the grommets work two ways. One, to open up the surface by being grommeted into the fabric or burlap. In others, where they're on the surface, they protrude into space. Like the layering of the pieces of the fabric, this is important to me because it opens up pictorial space, even though that's not what you think about when you're looking at the canvas. I don't think someone looks at the canvases and says, "Oh, look, isn't that interesting how she opened pictorial space?"

EARNEST: (Laughs.)

HAMMOND: That's not really what they're about, but it is what it does. (Laughs.) Once I'm done gessoing the burlap, the painting is tipped up and leans against the wall. Which means, in most cases, even if it's a big painting, I can stand on a crate or I have a moving platform. The paintings lean against the wall until a certain point when I have to hang them on the wall to really finish, to clearly see the bottom edge. But most of the painting takes place while they are leaning against the wall. That's the point when I start applying oil paint. I try to work in a way that is pretty physical and crude, in the sense of not obsessing, not making beautiful passages of color. I have done things underneath where I felt like, oh,

I should be blending the paint the way I used to, wet into wet, Euro-Western painting, blending the colors versus layering the colors.

But if I do these beautiful passages, I have to cover them up. I try to use paint as a material like any other material, knowing, of course, that I can't entirely do that. But that's where I try to linger. To not be precious with the paint, just apply the stuff, the material of the paint, the material of the pigment, onto this surface, going over all the knots and the seams, and so forth. Sometimes there are panels of burlap that are not completely affixed, so they hang off the surface like flaps, suggesting a hidden space underneath.

A lot of this is a slow process, even though I'm working with oil paint mixed with Dorland's Wax as a medium. The Dorland's Wax isn't there to give me a thick surface quickly. It's really about slowly building layers of paint through time. I'm not in a rush. It just takes what it takes. It catches the paint. The material stuff of the paint catches around the edges of the burlap, catches on the seams, globs around the grommets and pushpins, so you almost don't even know what's there. At times the grommet holes get clogged, or they might have paint spilling out onto the painting surface, staining it. Other times they just look like deep dark holes.

Even though you're looking at these flat pieces of burlap where you can see the edges, you're reading it on one level as a flat piece of burlap on a piece of canvas, the darkness of the grommeted hole contradicts the flatness, making it feel deeper, like it goes through to the wall and behind the canvas.

Those grommeted holes open up pictorial space, but then they also become like body orifices. Since I'm using paint to presence the physical body and therefore bodies, the suggestion of orifices in the painting body comes from those grommeted holes. A lot of it is just layers built up and built up and built up.

I can do anything because it's going to get covered up. I can use odds and ends of leftover paint from other canvases. I use colors I would never use, I'm not interested in, knowing that it's going to all be covered up. However, I also know that odd things are going to happen because I let odd things happen where colors are going to show through in unexpected ways or peek through here and there.

In most cases, I'm not planning where a color shows through. It just asserts itself for one reason or another. This is what I call working in a state of peripheral control, which is the ideal place I like to linger—which is kind of knowing what you're doing but not knowing too much because if you know too much, the work goes dead.

EARNEST: It's beautifully evocative. . . .

HAMMOND: Does that make sense?

EARNEST: Yes, peripheral control. When you're adding the layers of oil paint once the canvas has been tipped up vertically, is it the feeling that you've added enough paint? That the canvas becomes a unified surface? You experience it palpably as joined by the paint, but also there's the integrity and recognition of the many parts underneath that are disparate. How do you balance those two things vis-à-vis the paint?

HAMMOND: I do that, but it's not particularly conscious. I pretty much just try to work intuitively, or we would say extemporaneously, and not think too much. Then—often it's at the end of the day before I leave the studio, but certainly when I think a work is getting close to what might be finished, or it's becoming something, it's finding itself—I sit back and, with a critical eye, and look at what's going on, and ask, What does it mean? What could it mean? Do I want to emphasize this, or do I not like that?

That's when I sit there and make those decisions. I don't make them while I'm working but in that process of looking. People ask me, How many layers of paint? I don't know. For the most part though, I can tell you I tend to cover the whole canvas with a layer of paint. I don't tend to build up areas of paint, unless it's about glopping it around pushpins or staples or grommets. It tends to be pretty uniform—one somewhat varied color over the whole canvas, what I call near-monochrome—but like I said, maybe not in the beginning, maybe not even later on if I'm using up other paint.

As I move along, I begin to choose what those colors are that I am painting with—using a really cheap paintbrush, by the way, a house paintbrush, across the whole painting. One color or a variation of that color, working in that state of peripheral control I'm comfortable with because I have made (laughs) a lot of paintings.

Right now, I've been making *Chenille* paintings [see plate 27] for years, that's how I know certain colors that I want to bleed through from underneath. I tend to work with different dark browns or umbers, burnt siennas, gold ochres, yellow ochres, and cadmium reds, what I think are going to be the underlying layers of paint. It's what I think, based on what my body knows from before, but that's always risky because so often I'm wrong and so often it takes many more layers. Sometimes I just have to go back, and even though I like the color of the top layer, the surface, the physical presence might not be there yet. If that's true when I sit back with that critical eye and I go, like, "Girlfriend, you've got the color. It's working, but the paint itself isn't speaking, doesn't have the presence. I don't care how much it costs, you have to go back and repaint those last three layers. Even if it's cadmium red and very expensive, you have to do that."

There's a point where I know I'm honing in. I'm getting there. I'm getting there in terms of surface and color coming together. What I've been using in the last year or two, but not exclusively, is a very warm off-white color. I like the way that the dark umbers and ochres or reds show through in seams, cracks, and crevices in the warm white surface and around the grommet holes or splits in the burlap. Color asserts itself from underneath, either through the grommet holes or at the seams. Sometimes it just blends into the white paint on the surface, subtly staining and bleeding into it.

It was after making one or two of these paintings that the patterns of the raised grommets covered with thick paint reminded me of the tufted patterns of chenille bedspreads, and I began to think of the paintings more conceptually.

Before I talk more about that, I want to go back a little, if you don't mind, to just say that when I started working with the burlap versus other pieces of canvas or other fabrics, and fixing it archivally to the surfaces of the gessoed canvases, and then I had four canvases leaning up vertically against the walls . . . I always lean canvases around the studio, move them around in relationship to each other because I'm looking for what I call "uneasy juxtapositions" of things. It's not necessarily about joining them together—it could be—but I work through juxtaposition more than integration. I'm interested if there's a tension, and if so, just what is that tension where edges meet?

Well, I had four paintings covered with burlap leaning against the wall. The burlap was so beautiful. Those paintings, those burlap-covered canvases sat there in my studio . . . I don't know, I want to say close to a year, but maybe it wasn't that long. I didn't know what to do with them because I was so enamored with the burlap itself. That sometimes happens. It can happen with the material, where I have to sit with it, come to terms with it, to make it my own. I went through a very long process before applying paint. . . . I didn't just put paint on them automatically like I thought I was going to, like I had done with other fabrics. Burlap was an ubiquitous material, a common material that I was responding to in the way you might pick up a beautiful piece of patinated metal, or a beautiful stone, or a rock with lichen on it. That was my initial gesture of being drawn to it for its physical properties.

I had to go through these layers of visual analysis, like the politics of where the coffee sacks came from, because those are the kinds of questions I always ask, and I would ask about anybody else's work. I had to realize, no, Harmony, that's not what these are about. This is not what you're doing. That freed me up to paint over the burlap sacks. I just covered over a common material. Likewise, the holes. Other artists have used holes in their canvases. How do my holes function?

I let my painting speak to me. What was going on here with the layers of burlap, and the textures, and the edges, and the fraying threads, and so forth.

The holes open up the surface, but also protrude out into your space. What's going on here? Once I got to that point, I was on a roll. I "got it," but it wasn't easy getting there. Then, like I said, the paintings themselves, their surfaces, get built up very slowly.

Now to go back to the idea of chenille. Again, it's not anything I researched. I looked it up a little bit later but not ahead of time. I didn't start out to make paintings that look like chenille bedspreads or reference them. I was looking at the paintings that I was doing, which were a near-monochrome warm white color and had these protrusions that reminded me of the patterns of tufted threads on chenille bedspreads and what was going on. I liked that reference. I grew up with those bedspreads. It's a warm, cozy feeling. We know them. Chenille's not always white, but a lot of the bedspreads were white. Then I noticed, though, there was an edge to the paintings as well [. . .] coming from these protrusions and the splits, as colors assert themselves from under the cozy white cover. That's the territory I tend to work in. That might explain how I get there. After the fact, I thought, "Well, this is interesting, Harmony." Chenille to me referred to both yarns but also certain fabrics, and then bedspreads, and bathrobes, and things like that.

I looked chenille up, but way after the fact, because I'm interested in textiles. I've had a history of interest in textiles and also an interest in the domestic environment and creative traditions. Those are some of the threads throughout my work. Indeed, chenille does refer to both a yarn and a fabric made out of yarns, which are chopped off and you get this pile, or these threads, these tops of fibers that stick up at a right angle to the background of the fabric. It apparently was started with rug makers and people like that, way back in the nineteenth century, but there have been periods, like in the 1950s, when making chenille became mechanized and industrialized, say, for the lettering on high school athletic jackets. That's chenille on those varsity letters, but that's not what I was thinking of. (Laughs.) I was thinking of the bedspreads and so forth.

When you go back historically, there were people—they were called tufters—who actually were hired to make the tufts on patterns that they were given. A lot of it was done in the South. Apparently, there was a town in Georgia where people made a lot of money as tufters. Patterns were dropped off, they did the stitching and cutting that would make these tufts. They got paid. The tufted fabric was hauled off and made into bedspreads or whatever. It interested me because it turned out there was a handicraft to it. The tufters, like quilters, have not been fully recognized or given their due. It also interested me, after the fact, that tufters, like quilters, do the stitching with needles and the puncture of the material is from behind or the underside of the fabric. [. . .]

EARNEST: On this point about the *Chenille* paintings and your strategy of juxtaposition, my experience of the burlap is as a material that performs its wovenness. It's coarsely woven, and even under those dense layers, it makes you aware of its condition as a woven textile. It's also material that I think of as very rough and not often coming into proximity of the body. It's like you don't have clothes made out of burlap, you don't have blankets made out of burlap. However, when you introduced this language to those paintings made out of burlap as the *Chenille* paintings, you then introduce this juxtaposition with a fabric which is very soft, and that you always think of in proximity to the body. I'm wondering how you think of the language itself as a material that you are using in these very formal material paintings to cultivate those kinds of juxtapositions you talked about?

HAMMOND: I like that you made that observation a lot because I always thought that the burlap is crude, it's rough. I almost think of it as a rough hair shirt or something, almost with a sense of martyrdom about it or something like that. That's the tension of interest about these paintings. They perform chenille tufting with paint, so they look warm and cozy, but given their materials, they're pretty rough and coarse. I like that. [. . .]

I think a lot of my work is about performing, just as the chenille painting we were talking about—it isn't chenille. It performs chenille with paint. It performs needle and thread with paint and fabric. The same way the *Floorpieces* [1973; see plate 4] are not rugs. They perform rugs but are not functional as such. The *Bags* hang on the wall. They perform bags, but they are not bags. They are not functional.

A lot of the references in my work I think of in an almost performative way, like the *Chenilles* are certainly that way. They're not chenille fabric. They perform chenille, and that's important. They perform. They're active. [. . .]

ED. NOTE

 The text above is an edited, abridged transcript of an oral interview by Jarrett Earnest titled "RE: Harmony Hammond," produced by the National Academy of Design, New York, released August 3, 2021. "RE:" is a series of video conversations with leading members of the National Academy of Design, created and hosted by Jarrett Earnest. Hammond was elected to the National Academy of Design in 2017. A video of the full interview is archived on the NAD website: https://nationalacademy.org/perspectives/harmonyhammond_2021.

Interview with Elvan Zabunyan

"Women in Abstraction: Another History of Abstraction in the 20th Century," Centre Pompidou, Paris (2021)

ELVAN ZABUNYAN: I would like to start our conversation by going back over your artistic career and, taking your *Floorpieces* [1973; see plate 4] in the *Women in Abstraction* exhibition as a pretext, ask you to describe the development of these works since the 1970s. I am particularly interested to see how this installation prefigured your contribution to the history of abstraction over the last five decades.

HARMONY HAMMOND: Let me briefly go back to that moment in the early 1970s, when I and many feminist artists in the United States abandoned the male-dominated site of painting and consciously began to use materials, techniques, and formal strategies associated with women's traditional arts and the creative practices of non-Western cultures, precisely because of their marginalized histories and associations. Underlying this practice was the belief that materials and the way they are manipulated bring meaning into works of art. We consciously brought gendered content to postminimal concerns with materials and process. In 1973, I created a series of five floor paintings, three of which are included in the Pompidou exhibition. My daughter and I would go to the garment district in Lower Manhattan and collect the end cuts of bolts of knit fabrics, industrial waste that was discarded in dumpsters or left curbside in big plastic bags. Strips of the knit fabric were braided according to traditional braided rug techniques, but slightly larger and thicker in scale, coiled, stitched to a heavy cloth backing and partially painted with acrylic paint—the braided rug physically and conceptually becoming "the support of the painting." Referencing braided rugs, but nonfunctional as such, the *Floorpieces* negotiate a space between painting off the wall and nearly flat sculpture. Placed directly on the floor as a group without anything on the walls, they call into question assumptions about the "place of painting."

ZABUNYAN: Although I thought it was important to start with the *Floorpieces*, we agreed to focus on your most recent work. However, I think it is important to briefly consider an intermediate period that, to my mind, enables us to understand your current production. I am thinking in particular of all your wrapped sculptures.

HAMMOND: The wrapped sculptures, from the late 1970s and early 1980s, were influenced by Eva Hesse. Her work had a profound influence on many feminist artists, including myself, and in fact remains a huge influence to this day. Recycled fabric was wrapped around a wooden armature, which functioned as a skeleton. The wrapped fabric became muscle or tissue, with the surface literally a skin of acrylic paint or latex rubber. So, the resulting forms were not stuffed. Nor were they about binding and bandaging. They were about building something out of itself from the inside out—a metaphor for that early women's liberation movement phrase: "the personal is political." Moving from the personal out into the world, occupying space. The wrapping process, which is a three-dimensional spiraling process, is additive, I would even say painterly, in that it is the wrapping process that activates the surface.

While the title *Radiant Affection* [1983–84] comes from Annie Besant's book *Thought-Forms*, at the time I made these sculptures, I was thinking about Monique Wittig's very important writing *The Lesbian Body*, where she describes the raw, passionate interior of the gendered body.[1] The colors of the fabrics bleed through the gesso and subsequent layers of skin-like latex rubber, suggesting the interior of the physical body. The forms themselves are stand-ins for the body or body parts. *Radiant Affection*, for example, suggests both female body openings and eyes. I'm very interested in all body orifices as places of passage.

ZABUNYAN: These elements that create a physical connection between the body and the making of the sculptures have a very strong spatiality. It is the human scale that guides the format of the works, and there is a powerful interaction between an interior and an exterior; as you just mentioned, the sculpture tells a story about the body in its multiplicity. How does the materiality of painting allow us to connect with these mixed physical and sculptural narrative forms?

HAMMOND: Eventually, I returned to the painting field, but on my own terms with gendered content. I did a series of small weave paintings [see plates 5 and 6] that look like they're physically woven out of the paint. The weave paintings share some of the same visual strategies I still utilize in my work. From a distance, the paintings look monochrome, but up close, underlayers of differing colors are revealed.

For the last decade or so, I've made large, thickly painted, near-monochrome paintings on stretched canvas. [. . .] The paintings, which include frayed pieces and patches of canvas and rough burlap, straps, laces, and grommets, along with layers of thick paint, engage formal strategies and material metaphors, suggesting connection, restraint, agency, and voice—what some call social abstraction. [. . .]

Like the wrapped sculptures, these paintings are built from the inside out. They are layered. It's very much a back-and-forth process—painting, wrapping, then painting, then wrapping, etc. Once again, the physical manipulation of the materials activates the surface. There's no prior sketch, no prior research or anything that is considered preliminary. The work grows out of the process of making.

ZABUNYAN: I would like to pick up on this last sentence, which seems to me to be very characteristic of your work but also of many of the practices that flourished during the 1970s. Making and creating are linked to this process of becoming that you mention. The materials you use are also materials that can be unrolled and rolled up, which give the visual and physical sensation of a spatiality linked to a temporality. This created space evokes the idea of protection, but at the same time also of injury and being cared for. The canvas and the body are once again treated as correlated, interdependent forms.

HAMMOND: For many people the straps [in paintings such as *Cinch VI*, 2012–13] suggest binding, bandaging, bondage, and restraint. A body suggesting negotiation for freedom of movement. I have intentionally wrapped the straps around the stretched canvas, around the painting object as body. At first glance, the straps look restrictive, like they're holding the painting together. But if you look closer, it's quite clear the straps are not that tight. They do not restrict or constrict. The straps, which in fact are often pieced, or for that matter, even the laces or pushpins that were originally used to position the straps in place, do not hold the painting together. It's the paint, and therefore the act of painting that holds the painting body together.

Cinch VI is torso-sized. The parallel straps call up ribs but possibly also a corset. While the laces threaded through the grommeted holes suggest the possibility of drawing tight, pulling in, and compressing, they hang down untied. This presents a tension. It speaks of potential. We could pull the laces and tighten the straps, or perhaps we could undo them, which would make the painting body more vulnerable. The same is true in *Rib* (2013), a much larger painting; however, the ends are just tied off. There's no lacing that zigzags back and forth between the rib-like straps. Instead, we have a long rope and a long cord, which provocatively hang there suggesting possible actions.

I would like to talk about the role of color in relation to light, shadow, and meaning. The relief surfaces of the light-colored paintings like *Blanco* (2013), *Buffer* (2011), and *Cinch VI* catch highlights and cast shadows, emphasizing the sculptural aspect of the painting, thereby expanding the flat picture plane. The shadows are as important as the paint itself. In the darker paintings, like *Muffle* (2009) [see plate 19] or *Rib* [2013; see plate 21], you can't quite locate color and surface. Despite the thick paint, depending on the angle of light and your position in relation to the painting, color and surface change. . . . They are indeterminate, unstable, fugitive. I like the "outlaw" association with fugitive. In their refusal to be any one thing, at the same time they are themselves, the paintings can be seen to occupy some sort of fugitive or queer space, and in doing so remain oppositional, both in their refusal to participate fully in the received narrative of modernist painting and at the same time their refusal to look queer, though we might say the paintings perform queerly. [. . .]

ZABUNYAN: In this conversation, you have emphasized the need to consider details of the paintings. Detail enables us to see texture in a different way and allows unprecedented visual immersion in the material. The art historian Daniel Arasse proposed a "close-up history of art" and said that, "The function of detail is to call out to us, to stand aside, to provide anomaly."[2] When I reread this sentence, it reminds me of the term "queer," whose etymology from the German word *quer* links it to the idea of "crossing," i.e., of not moving linearly but of moving across. [. . .]

In one of your most recent series, your *Cross* paintings [2019–present], exhibited in New York [at Alexander Gray Associates, in *Crossings*, 2020–21], suggest both the Red Cross and, visually, [. . .] a dialogue, a back-and-forth, between the *Cross* paintings exhibited. This dialogue is a *crossing* that echoes the cross visible on each wall.

HAMMOND: Yes, this is how you would see the work entering the gallery as you came up the stairs. The exhibition featured [works from 2018 to 2020] *Cross* paintings [see plates 24 and 25], *Bandaged Quilts* [see plate 22], a *Chenille* painting [see plate 27], and a *Bandaged Grid* [see plate 23]. I did not start out to make paintings about crosses. They grew out of the *Chenille* paintings with big panels of coarse burlap from recycled coffee sacks placed over stained-white chenille fields like giant arms or cross-shaped bandages. Initially, I didn't even think of the shape as a cross, but rather as X marks the spot, an intersection, a plus sign, and even an abstract stand-in for the figure because the burlap sacks are a size that human bodies can lift and carry. For the most part, I cut the sacks along the seams, so they retained that body proportion. Initially, I tried to disregard the resulting cross form but it continued to assert itself. It was just so visible. After thinking to myself, I don't do crosses, which in hindsight turns out not to be entirely true, I found enough courage to deal with them not only as a flat shape but as a signifying form. Interestingly, despite the muscular scale and thick paint, as a sign, the cross is indeterminate. It references diverse cultural associations, including emblems of medical and humanitarian aid, religious iconography, martyrdom, plagues, and like the grid, the modernist historical canon. I really like what you said, Elvan, about the conversation going back and forth among canvases, across the gallery space. The white painting in between the two crosses is *Double Bandaged Quilt #3* [2020] with its central red gash bandaged over.

The *Cross* paintings, started in the early summer of 2019, intensified in meaning over time given the stressful environment we find ourselves in today. You can see how the arms of the cross overlap in a kind of embrace, similar to the straps in the earlier paintings which embraced the painting body. You can also see my interest in edges as sites of negotiation and boundaries between the painting body and life. Ultimately, the *Cross* paintings, with their crossings placed over agitated white fields, speak of social injustices, BIPOC assertion, intersections, sacrifice, medical and humanitarian aid, and possibly healing and recuperation. . . .

ZABUNYAN: To end with, I'd like to talk to you about the question of scale. In your work, this is very closely linked to body proportions. You say that the body occupies space and it seems to me that there is a common thread that has run through all your work since the 1970s. We started the conversation with the *Floorpieces* and continued to your most recent works. Even when presented in a white cube, your production resonates with the bodies of those looking at and experiencing it. There is an exchange that I would say is body to body.

HAMMOND: The relationship of the work to my body, and therefore bodies . . . that's just the way I work. It's not predetermined or conscious. It's just what I do. When I was working on the *Floorpieces*, I would literally sit in the center, coiling or spiraling the braids outwards to approximately five and a half feet. They're all a little different in size, but it was pretty much my arm width, my body space. They were made at the same time I was doing a lot of aikido. I would literally sit in the middle of a *Floorpiece* as I worked on it—stitching the braided fabric, from the center out, onto a circular cloth backing. Then I'd take a break and go to aikido class, where we would move in circles and roll around. After class, I'd come back and work on the pieces some more. It was all part of the work.

ZABUNYAN: A last point. You refer to the notion of crossing as an intersection. Could intersection also suggest intersectionality, in the contemporary definition of the term? I would love to hear your final words on this subject!

HAMMOND : Regarding the intersection and intersectionality: It is very clear to me. All art, including mine, participates in multiple narratives. So there are many intersections and many points of entry. That's what keeps the art alive and relevant.

ED. NOTES

First published in French as Harmony Hammond and Elvan Zabunyan, "Conversation," *Les Cahiers du Musée national d'art moderne*, no. 159 (2022): 134–43, by Éditions du Centre Pompidou, Paris. This text is an edited transcript of an interview that took place on the occasion of the symposium "Women in Abstraction: Another History of Abstraction in the 20th Century," organized by the Centre Pompidou, Paris, on May 21, 2021, partnering with AWARE: Archives of Women Artists, Research, and Exhibitions and the Laboratory for Gender and Sexuality Studies (LEGS—Paris 8 Vincennes Saint-Denis/Paris Nanterre), in conjunction with the exhibition *Women in Abstraction (Elles font l'abstraction, une autre histoire de l'abstraction au 20e siècle)* organized by the Centre Pompidou, Paris, May 19–August 23, 2021. Reproduction of this edited version of the English-language transcript is courtesy of the Centre Pompidou and Elvan Zabunyan. Elvan Zabunyan, contemporary art historian, is a professor at Paris 1 Panthéon-Sorbonne University and an art critic. The full English-language transcript, which has been abridged for inclusion here, is archived at "Conversation: Harmony Hammond and Elvan Zabunyan," Centre Pompidou, https://www.centrepompidou.fr/fileadmin/user_upload/symposium_women-in-abstraction_harmony-hammond.pdf.

1. The first edition of Annie Besant and C. W. Leadbeater's *Thought-Forms* was released by the Theosophical Publishing Society, London and Benares, in 1905. Monique Wittig's novel *The Lesbian Body* was originally published in French as *Le Corps Lesbien* in 1973. The first English translation was published in 1975.

2. The reference is to Daniel Arasse, *Le Détail: Pour une histoire rapprochée de la peinture* (Paris: Flammarion, 2008).

Agnes Martin. *UNTITLED*, 1960. Oil on linen. 12 × 12″

Woven Histories: Textiles and Modern Abstraction (2023)

Black and white lines, irregular in width and weight, painted on unprimed rough linen. There is no ground, no "grounding." The linen is exposed. It's more of a drawing. A weave on a weave. Only twelve by twelve inches.

Agnes Martin is feeling it out, finding her way. Visual decisions made as she works across the painting field, placement considered but not measured. The indexical dominates the formal. A sense of immediacy and process. The artist's hand.

Dark lines, placed lengthwise and roughly equidistant from each other evoke the large-scale open warp work of Lenore Tawney, Martin's intimate friend and sometimes lover—but more importantly, the creative exchange between two artists and their work. Comparable equivalents.

Between, five to six lines are applied with a lighter touch. And in between those, glowing white lines, all stroked from the top or bottom in toward the central horizontal, first white, then black. A line not to be crossed.

Occasionally however, a vertical is re-emphasized, darker, heavier, more insistent, and stepping out of line, crosses over the horizontal boundary, opening up both physical and visual space.

The lines of either color are not all painted at once, in one pass—there is a back-and-forth layering. An open weave. Between the painting surface and the textured linen, there is a shallow space. This is where Martin lingers.

Bordered on four sides as an afterthought. The top and bottom are laid over and distinctly different than the sides, consisting of crosshatched lines over the verticals. Like textile selvage, the side borders prevent fraying or unraveling. In the wider and more emphatic top and bottom borders, weft-like lines run horizontally, intersecting and interlacing with the vertical warp lines, and diagonals of one direction. They hold each other in place and keep artist and viewer from "going over the edge."

Lying parallel to each other in the central body of the painting, the dark verticals give way at the top and bottom to prominent white slits or gaps between what looks like six densely woven sections where the ends of vertical strokes, like warp yarns extending out from a woven textile, are turned over and inward, creating a soft curved fringe of irregular strokes within the painting format, which is all squares and rectangles. Fringed. A flirtatious border on top and bottom, with an inviting dip in the middle of the top. A point of entry. A stage. A curtained window. A mirror of sameness and difference.

The pictorial framing of the repetitive field is important to this early painting as Martin tussles with her relation to space before letting go of the edges. She eventually eliminates the borders, but here in this transitional painting, they play a major role as boundary, eliminating any thought of possible continuum. Containment. Protection. Even cover-up.

To stroke. To loom. To warp. To interlace. To weave. To border. To fringe. The painting surface as edge between art and life.

ED. NOTE

Hammond's catalogue entry "Agnes Martin. *UNTITLED*, 1960. Oil on linen. 12 × 12″" appears in Lynne Cooke, ed., *Woven Histories: Textiles and Modern Abstraction* (Chicago: University of Chicago Press with National Gallery of Art, Washington, DC, 2023), 57–58.

Acknowledgments

Our gratitude to the kindred spirits and allies who have contributed to this volume's contents (from the interviewers whose conversations we share here to the photographers and rights holders who granted us permission to reproduce images and texts). We equally acknowledge those who have nurtured the book's development. Although such lists can never be truly comprehensive, we would like to name a few key members of communities where ideas take form and circulate:

Donald Albrecht, Nicole Archer, Taylor Bluestone, Claudia Bruce, Bay Area Writers Group (Kim Anno, Paula Birnbaum, Jeanne Finley, Amy Lyford, and Jennifer Shaw), Julia Bryan-Wilson, Lynne Cooke, Le Club, Ashton Cooper, Alla Efimova, Armando Espinosa Prieto, Françoise Flamant (encore et encore), Alexander Gray and his associates, Marilyn Hacker, Harmony Hammond Revocable Trust Board (Elizabeth Hess, Carolyn Kastner, Tirza Latimer, Louise Martorano, Merry Scully, T. T. Takemoto), Sue Heinemann, Faye Hirsch, Peter Jemison, Katharine Kagel, Jonathan David Katz, Jonathan Ned Katz, Karen Levine, Helen Molesworth, Linda Mussman, Steven Nelson, Fernanda Perrone, Jaune Quick-to-See Smith, Jordana Saggese, Nick Serpe, Kathleen Shields, Simon Taylor, Lauren Tresp, Hrag Vartanian, Stephen Vider, and our valiant project manager Nancy Zastudil.

At Duke University Press (sine qua non), our editor Kenneth Wissoker adroitly accompanied the project from start to finish; Kate Mullen, Liz Smith, Courtney Richardson, and the entire DUP team transformed the manuscript into the handsome book you hold in your hands as you read these words of thanks. To our anonymous external readers, who conducted two time-consuming rounds of review, please know that we took your thoughtful feedback and your solidarity very much to heart. We are grateful to the Wyeth Foundation for American Art for the Publication Grant (administered by the College Art Association) that enabled us to double the number of images included and ensure the quality of the reproductions. Shout-out to our indexer, Kitty Chibnik, for enhancing access to the content of this volume.

Many thanks to all those unnamed, but not forgotten, who have shown support for the transmission of these "still dangerous" texts and the models of artistic practice, activism, and collective engagement that they and the accompanying images body forth.

—Harmony Hammond and Tirza True Latimer

Index

Credits

TEXTS

ENDNOTES

When the endnotes are by the author, as they appear in the original publication, the attribution is clearly indicated by a statement to that effect at the end of the editor's note(s) for the text. The author's notes have sometimes been edited for clarity, continuity, citation completion, and/or accuracy. If not otherwise indicated, notes are by the editor in consultation with the author.

PHOTOGRAPHY

 All images of Harmony Hammond's art are courtesy of the artist and Alexander Gray Associates, New York, unless indicated otherwise. The photographers of the artwork include Harmony Hammond, John Kasparian, Herbert Lotz, Eric Swanson, Brad Trone, John Vokoun, and Alexander Gray Associates, New York. Color correction by Armando Espinosa Prieto. Archival documents and images are courtesy Harmony Hammond unless otherwise acknowledged in captions. Every effort has been made to contact potential rights holders of images reproduced in the book for appropriate credit.